Japanese
Graphic Design

日本の
グラフィックデザイン

Style Evolution and
Contemporary Expressions

スタイル
の進化と現代表現

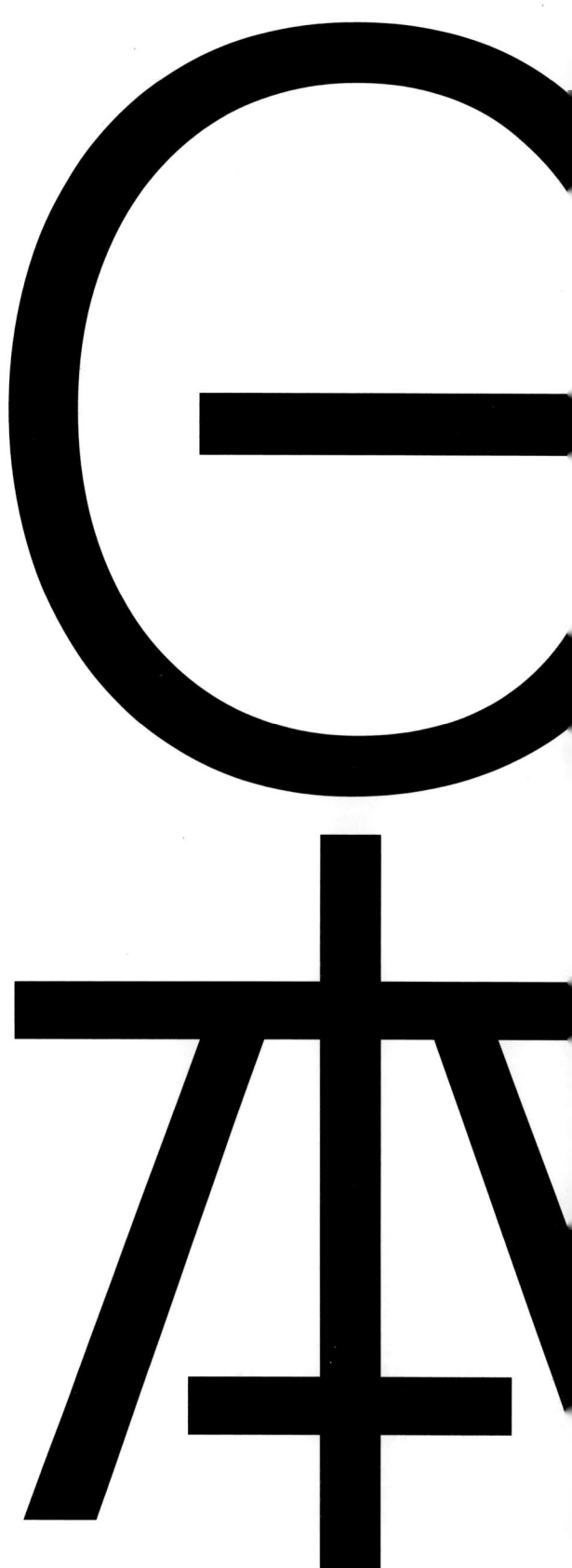

Japanese Graphic Design
Style Evolution and Contemporary Expressions

日本のグラフィックデザイン
スタイルの進化と現代表現

First Published in the USA in 2023 by

GINGKO PRESS

Gingko Press Inc.
217 W Richmond Ave, Suite B
Richmond, CA 94801
Tel: (510) 898 1195
Fax: (510) 898 1196
Email: books@gingkopress.com
www.gingkopress.com

ISBN 978-1-58423-782-2

By arrangement with
Sandu Publishing Co., Ltd.

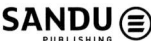

Edited and produced by Sandu Publishing Co., Ltd.
Contributing Author: Huang Qifan (Author of "The Professional Development
of Japanese Graphic Design")
Executive Editor: Liz Yao
Copy Editor: Kim Curtis
Typesetting: Wu Yanting

Book Design: Makkaihang Design

info@sandupublishing.com
sales@sandupublishing.com
www.sandupublishing.com

Printed and bound in China

Contents

カタログ

To Those Who Create the Future

Preface

Keiko Hirano
Communication Design Laboratory

In recent years, an unprecedented epidemic raged around the world, mercilessly taking away many precious lives. In Japan, the Olympic Games Tokyo 2020 was held without sufficient strategies against Covid-19 and the majority of Japanese citizens opposed holding the games. Historical architecture, such as the National Stadium and the Tsukiji Market, was demolished. It seemed like a chain of terrible events. Living in a time when individuals' voices are often drowned out and elitism is widespread, living in a time when reality invokes fear and grief, and living in an era in which the evaluation of good and evil has been challenged and even reversed, a soul could feel uncertainty for the future. While I cannot return to the old state of mind in which I single-mindedly sought ideal design and immersed myself in design so innocently without any hesitation, I have been questioning what I can do as a designer and as a person who lives in the time when life should be treated with more respect.

Tracing back 60 years in time, during the post-World War II reconstruction period of Japan, the Olympic Games Tokyo 1964 was held. Masaru Katsumi became a design producer for it and young enthusiastic graphic designers who gathered around him made full use of their expertise. Visual images pointed to a direction for the future and succeeded in visualizing the image of the reconstruction of Japan. Further, during the period of high economic growth, graphic designers contributed to Japan's development, using their design specialties to support the flourishing of the nation's peaceful growth and prosperity.

In 2004, I curated the exhibition, "Icons of the Times: 50 Years of Graphic Design in Japan," to record the ideals and accomplishments of graphic designers who wanted to improve people's lives through their design expertise. At that time, I planned the show motivated by concerns about the lack of design evaluation criteria or design reviews. Based on the selection criteria of "designs that possess universality, symbolize the era, foreshadow the future, point to the direction the future should take, and satisfy the conscience of design," I summarized 50 years of Japanese graphic design history. It was the story of a time for design to lift people's spirits.

As the 2000s progressed, social conditions changed drastically. With the expansion of PCs and social media, the environment provided equal opportunity for anyone to distribute visual images and information volume increased drastically, while its quality declined, and creative and critical thinking has shrunk. Essentially, design can bring order to a disorderly world, promote a transition from a chaotic universe to an orderly one, and provide convenience, safety, and beauty. I believe that a designer holds a socially responsible position because images derived from the designs can raise or lower the fortune of an organization and influence its destiny. However, in an era when information could be deceptive, it became arduous to reach the heart of many topics. What kind of world will be created if people cannot escape the notion of "how best to present his/her existence?" Because we live in such a time, I think I must, as a design professional, strive for human maturity and establish a measure of good and bad, even before gaining skills and knowledge.

When I was asked by the editorial team what character strengths are required for professional designers to deliver the best solution and fulfill their given responsibility, I think they are the following: "Do not lie. Self-discipline is not dictated by greed. Have a critical spirit. Objectivity is not influenced by self-centeredness. Insightfulness perceives truth without being misled by surface appearances. Use thought that desires better results. Sensitivity brings one close to others' sadness. Be free." I believe these are the traits of a qualified designer.

And it goes without saying that today's designers need to have an attitude of improving themselves by humbly acquiring skills with flexible thinking and without resting on past achievements. With the proliferation of new infrastructures and communication tools, the possibilities for expression are significantly expanded and it would be such a waste not to master them. A universe expands along with acquired skills.

In Japan, graphic design reviews are rare and it is difficult to examine Japanese graphic design as one country, as a single unit. Therefore, I am deeply moved by the fact that Sandu Publishing has recorded and examined the state of Japanese graphic design from an unbiased position. With this publication, I hope there will be more people who design with a flexible approach and a broad perspective suitable for contemporary times, freed from the fixed concept of graphic design in Japan.

序文

Design with "Newness"

Preface

Taku Sasaki
Art Director and Product Designer

I always want to design something "new," "new" design for me and "new" design for society. But what is "new?" It could be new ideas, new expressions, new processes, new methods or new ways of communicating. My interests differ from time to time, but I have been thinking about what is "new."

My grandfather was an elementary school teacher and his expertise was Japanese history. When I was little, whenever I was alone with my grandfather, he always told me stories about history. Unlike what I had learned in history lessons in school, he told me interesting stories about who had done such amazing things and under what circumstances.

In college, I studied product design. I loved being exposed to the work and thoughts of different designers as much as designing by myself. More than the beauty of form, I was interested in how they came up with that form and how it was shaped in a way that did not exist in my preconception of the value of beauty. After several years of designing furniture for a company, I became interested not only in designing products, but also in how to present and communicate my designs and my work gradually expanded from product design to graphic design. As I became more involved with graphic designers, I met people who continued to create strong expressions that could not be explained within product design and my view of design changed.

I am always attracted to things that are wonderful even if I don't know what they are, rather than things that are easy to understand and clear. I became absorbed in design because of the joy of encountering "new" wisdom and ingenuity, things I had never known before, things that do not extend from my thinking and things that shook my sense of values.

And I always try to create new options that are never-before-seen when I am designing. In Japan, we often use the words "pine, bamboo, and plum" to describe differences in price and quality. I do not want to create a plum tree in a world that already has pine and bamboo. I want to create something completely different from the previous axis, something like a peach. And if there is a peach, there could be an apple, as well. The existence of the peach indicates more options. A good design expands creation even further from the design itself.

For me, design is also a point of contact with contemporary society. In today's world where things and information overflow, the required design rarely foresees and solves a problem. We need to find and bring to light problems and objectives that have been lost in the flood of things and information. When I am working on a logo or a product, I am always asking myself why such a design is necessary. Finding the object of design is essential. Given that so many things in society have been designed, it is exciting to find something that is natural and unprocessed and to create a new design. Even if something has already been designed, we can still find room for the design.

In an age when design should exist with a reason, the newness that I always consider in design is not just anything new, but if it is new, it should be more correct than before and it should give a sense of hope for the future. This explains why we still make things and why new designs are still needed today. The need to think across disciplines, from product design to graphic design, is not only to explore new expressions, but also to arrive at the right design. This is an opportunity to review societal frameworks and preconceived notions.

I have lived almost all of my life facing design. It is an activity to maintain hope in today's society. Even before I began studying design, I loved learning about the wisdom and ingenuity of others. Newness is not something that is created from inside one person, but when a person takes a great idea from others and develops it, various things are renewed.

In this age of renewal, I would like to be a part of it, as a designer, if I can improve society as much as possible by drawing on my wisdom. To this end, I need to keep being influenced by designers and many other people involved in the creative process. I want to have many relationships in which we learn about, admire, envy or even reject each other's ideas. I need to expand the field of design, so that I can encounter diverse ideas. I want to keep learning, so that I can keep stepping into new areas, from product design to graphic design, motion design, and spatial design.

Attractive design is full of madness. It may be more particular than anyone else's, and no one may understand it, but the desire to give it shape anyway and the pursuit to have it somehow understood, is beautiful. I hope that design in the world will always be uncompromising and full of beautiful madness.

DA	Design Agency
CD	Creative Direction
AD	Art Direction
D	Design
ID	Interior Design
PD	Product Design
AR	Architecture
IL	Illustration
CA	Confectionary Art
CW	Copywriting
PH	Photography
PR	Produce
CL	Client

The Professional Development of Japanese Graphic Design

日本のグラフィックデザインの専門化発展

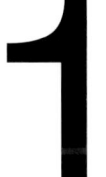

The Professional Development of Japanese Graphic Design

Incubation: The Germination of Graphic Design Thinking in Painting from the 17th Century to Meiji Restoration / In a broader sense, the idea of Japanese graphic design was already reflected in the paintings of the Azuchi-Momoyama period (16th century), the Ukiyo-e and the Rinpa School (a school of plastic arts) of the Edo period (17th-19th centuries).

In the 16th century, the representative painter of the Kanō School, Kanō Eitoku, created the screen painting *Cypress Trees*, in which the artist simplified the background by applying gold leaf to a large area of clouds and created a strong visual contrast with the cypress trees in the foreground.

In the 18th century, the famous painter Tōshūsai Sharaku created a series of ukiyo-e busts of kabuki actors with extremely bold compositions. The main figures bleed off the page and the flattening of shapes and colors give the images a strong flat decorative quality.

Similarly, in the masterpiece *Red and White Plum Blossoms* by Ogata Korin, a representative painter of the Rinpa School, the artist represents the winding river through large areas of flat color and abstract textures with little perspective, thus the picture is of flat composition. These unique expressions, hidden in traditional paintings, had a profound influence on later Japanese graphic design.

Independence: The Rise of Modern Advertising and the Emergence of Professional Designers from Meiji Restoration to World War II / Since the Meiji Restoration in 1868, Japan has actively learned from the West and started the process of modernization. Japan's economy and social culture have developed rapidly and the modern advertising industry has gradually emerged. At the end of the 19th century, Japan introduced the concept of graphic design from Europe and, in 1896, the Department of Graphic Design was established at the Tokyo Fine Arts School (now the Tokyo University of the Arts) and professional graphic design education and professional designers began to appear.

Hisui Sugiura (1876-1965) was a pioneer of modern design in Japan. He graduated from the Tokyo Fine Arts School and, in 1908, was commissioned by the Mitsukoshi Kimono Store as the first head of the graphic design department. He designed posters and magazine covers for 27 years until he left the company in 1934. He also designed posters and cigarette packages for other companies and these works are said to be the origin of today's graphic designs. His representative work in 1927, *Tokyo Underground Railway (present Tokyo Metro Ginza Line Ueno-Asakusa section) opening advertisement poster*, uses the focal perspective of Western painting and the thinking of modern typography, while preserving traditional painted scenes.

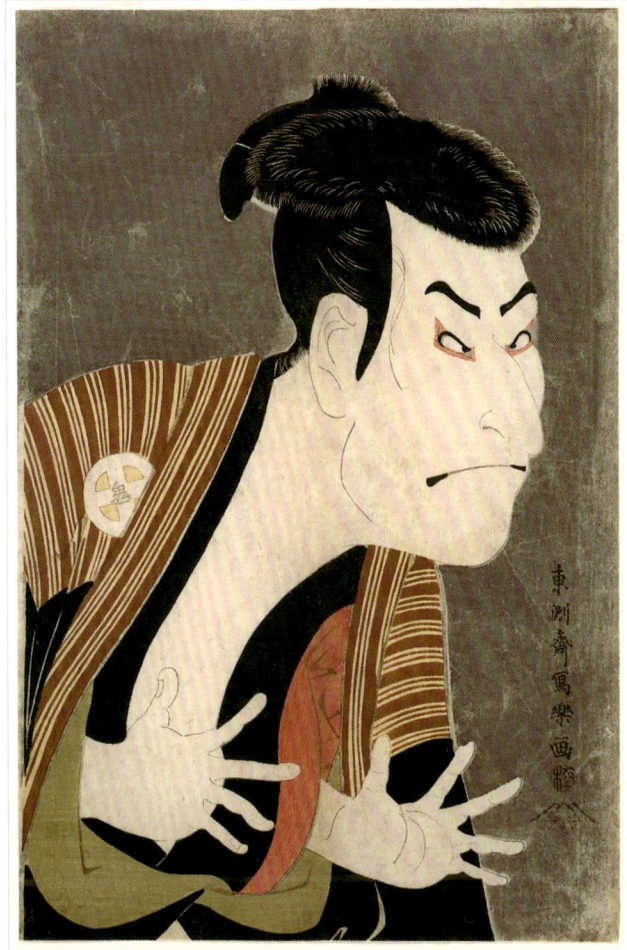

日本のグラフィックデザインの専門化発展

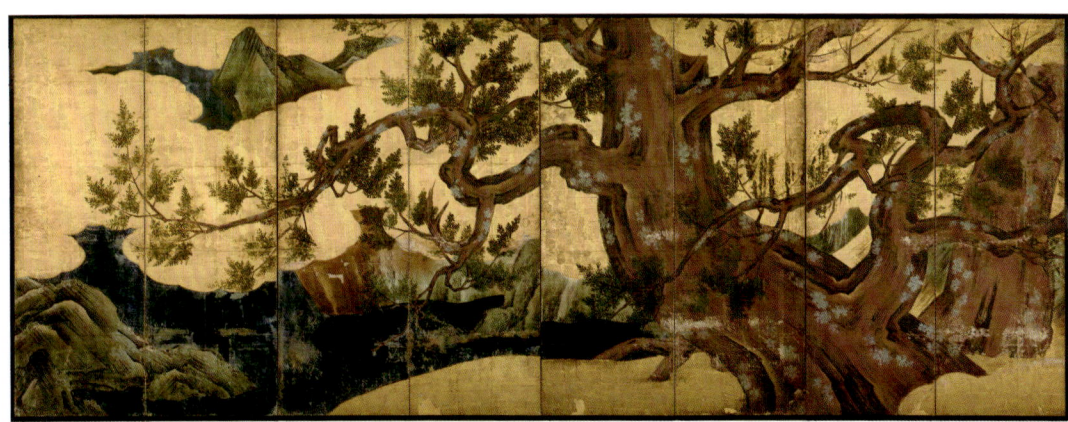

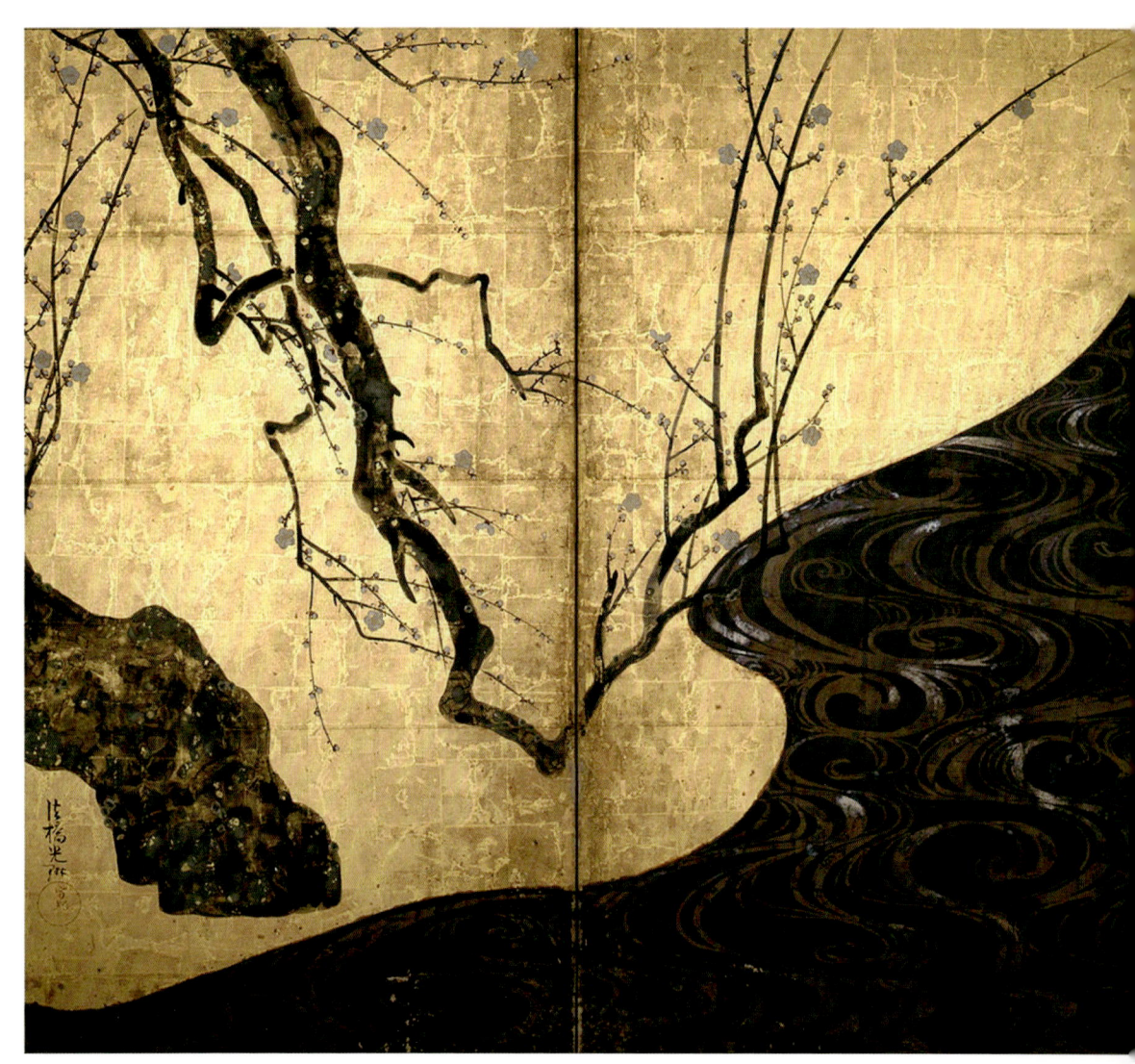

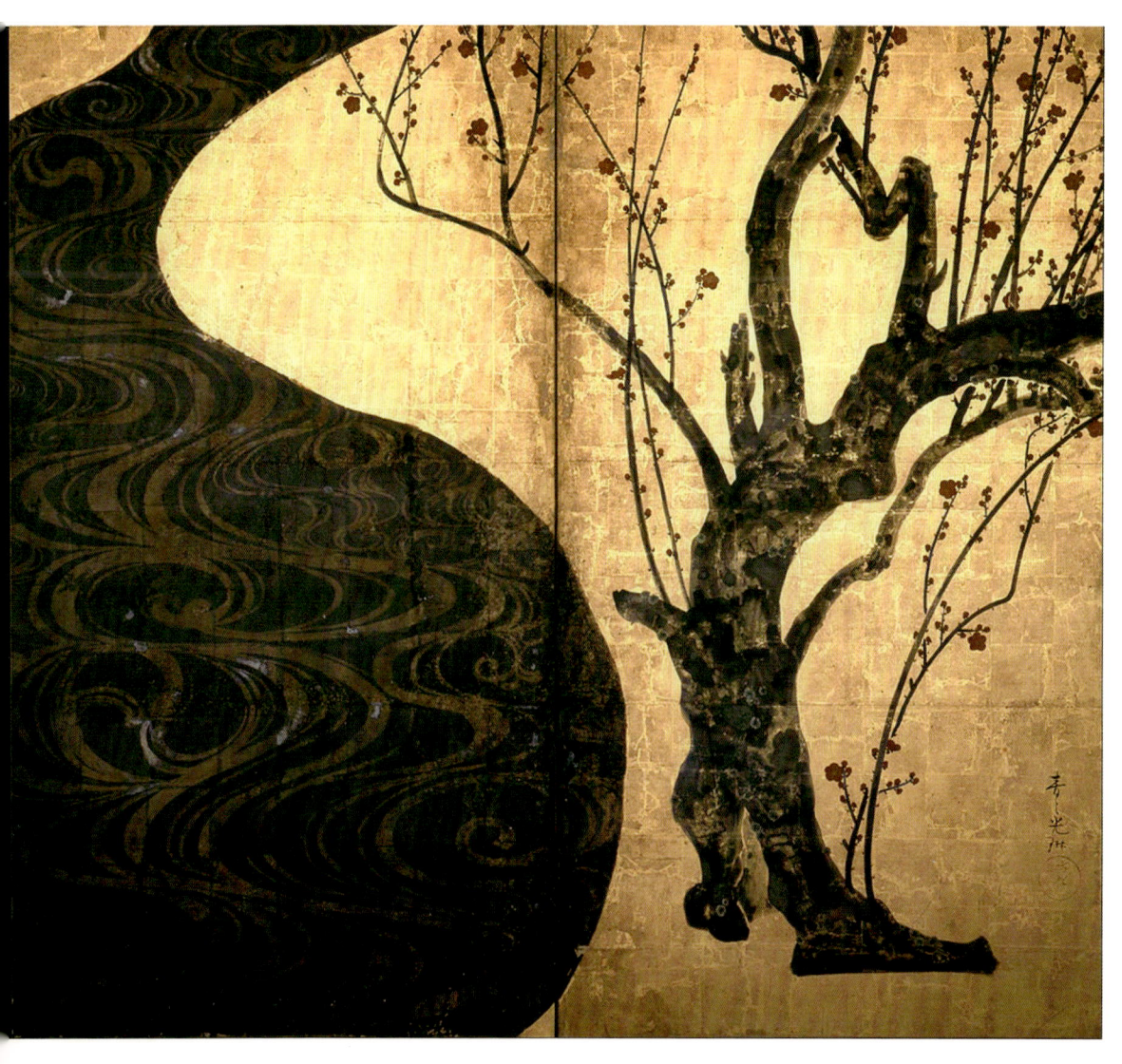

Red and White Plum Blossoms
by Ogata Korin

In 1921, Hiromu Hara (1903-1986) began teaching in the printing department of the Tokyo Metropolitan Kogei High School. At the same time, he actively introduced the modernist graphic design theories of Europe and was the first designer to introduce Western typography theory to Japan with his translation of *Die neue Typografie* by Jan Tschichold in 1932.

Takashi Kono (1906-1999) was a pioneer of commercial design in Japan. After graduating from the Tokyo Fine Arts School in 1929, he joined the advertising department of the Shochiku film company and worked on a wide variety of designs, such as posters, stage art, costumes, packaging, displays, and outdoor signs. Those posters broke away from the traditional poster design of painted scenes and combined traditional Japanese cultural imagery with Western design expressions, which was an important transformation in modern Japanese poster design from complexity to simplicity.

In 1931, Hideshige Oota, advertising director of the Nagase Chamber of Commerce, together with Tomiro Nagase, sales manager of Kao soap and photographer Shigene Kanamaru, produced a print advertisement for Kao soap, *Purity 99.4%*. The creation received much attention in the field of advertising and showed that photography in Japan had been taken out of the realm of art and started to commercialize in the 1920s and 1930s. Subsequently, Hideshige Oota founded Japan's first advertising agency, Kyodo PR. The company's name reflected Oota's philosophy of advertising production and emphasized that advertising was not the independent creation of a painter alone, but rather the joint production of designers, photographers, copywriters, media people, and salespeople.

From a professional point of view, graphic design education, theory, and practice all began to take off during this period and Japanese graphic design gradually dissociated from the influence of painting and began to professionalize. However, to the general public, the professionalization of graphic design was still not well understood and, at the time, people thought that design was the side job of painters and graphic design was still a branch of painting.

Restriction: Disruption of Advertising Design, Rise of War Propaganda During World War II / At the end of the 1930s, war clouds loomed large. The National Mobilization Law was introduced in November 1938 and corporate activities were in an era of extreme hardship because no goods could be sold and ad-

vertising became non-essential, so corporate propaganda departments were abolished one after another.

On the other hand, in response to the national policy, the Cabinet Intelligence Bureau intensified its foreign propaganda activities and many designers commissioned national war reports and began producing war advertisements.

In 1941, Takashi Kono was drafted into a propaganda squad with a group of writers, journalists, poets, cartoonists, and other cultural figures, and was sent to Indonesia to produce war propaganda materials, material packaging, and camouflage paint for military bases. He almost died as a result. When the propaganda team was torpedoed while landing on a boat, they fell into the sea and survived by grabbing pieces of wood covered with heavy oil. After Japan's defeat, Takashi Kono became a prisoner in Indonesia, and was arrested and detained.

Within Japan, design education lost its meaning as commercial design shrank. During the Pacific War, Hiromu Hara resigned from his teaching job at the Tokyo Metropolitan Kogei High School and became the art director of Touhou Press' *FRONT*, which produced foreign political propaganda publications. In March 1945, when Tokyo was attacked by air raids, the premises of Touhou Press were bombed and eventually disbanded and *FRONT* and other war propaganda was thrown into the furnace and burned.

As the war spread, Shiseido stopped producing cosmetics and the Shiseido gallery, which was originally used to showcase female beauty, was decorated with pictures of military-style horns. Ayao Yamana, who was originally in charge of Shiseido's propaganda design, became the chairman of the Reporting Technology Research Council of the Cabinet Intelligence Ministry. He put aside the patterns of gorgeous maidens and scroll, which he was good at, and created war propaganda materials.

Morinaga stopped making cakes and sweets and Shinichiro Arai, head of the propaganda division, became a permanent member of the Reporting Technology Research Council, and instead of appealing to the playfulness of children, he urged the nation to support the war. During the Tokyo air raid, the office of the research council was also moved several times and, with the defeat of Japan, eventually disbanded.

From the beginning of World War II until Japan's defeat in 1945, the free exploration and social development of Japanese graphic design were interrupted as it became a tool of war propaganda. Many design materials were destroyed

日本のグラフィックデザインの専門化発展

or banned after the war and they sank into the river of history. This particular period of history was a major blow to the fledgling art of Japanese graphic design.

Survival: Graphic Design Relaunched in the 1950s / In the 1950s, as the clouds of World War II gradually dissipated and Japan's post-war reconstruction began to bear fruit, manufacturing industries developed rapidly and the advertising industry and graphic design got the opportunity to develop. However, graphic designers did not gain as much attention from society as painters. Therefore, some pioneering designers started to realize the importance of establishing the status and value of graphic designers as soon as possible.

In 1950, the Japan Advertising Artists Club (JAAC) was established with Yusaku Kamekura at its center. It aimed to define the existence of the design profession, protect the right to work, and promote awareness of publicity art. 1951 saw the first JAAC exhibition, which treated the work of designers like painters, as works of art to be appreciated. The exhibition venue was moved from a gallery to a department store to affirm the social and living nature of design.

In the early days of JAAC, only insiders knew about it and its influence was limited. But then it began to openly solicit works and actively explore new designers and it gained worldwide recognition bit by bit. By its third exhibition, the venue had become crowded with visitors, creating an unprecedented scene in Japanese advertising art. In its sixth exhibition, the poster *Peacefully Use Atomic Energy* designed by Yusaku Kamekura won the JAAC membership award and was selected for *The Year Book of Japanese Art* the same year. It was the first graphic design work to be included in the art yearbook.

In 1955, the Takashimaya department store held the Graphic '55 exhibition, which was intended to be a comprehensive display of the exploration and thinking of professional designers in advertising design and to show the strength of Japanese commercial design. The exhibitors included Takashi Kono,Yusaku Kamekura, Hiromu Hara, Yoshio Hayakawa, Kenji Ito, Ryuichi Yamashi-ro, Tadashi Ohashi, and the special guest American designer Paul Rand, all of whom were designers active at the frontline. The creations they exhibited were printed, demonstrating the close connection between graphic design and society and causing a sensation at the time.

Yusaku Kamekura exhibited many posters in this exhibition, including one

he designed for Nikon cameras, which established a publicity department in 1954 and invited Yusaku Kamekura to produce advertisements. Through his simple and precise design, Yusaku Kamekura succeeded in conveying the high quality of Nikon cameras and the Nikon brand instantly gained recognition among the populace.

However, behind the heated social response of the JAAC and Graphic '55, the future of the graphic design industry was still grim. In 1955, of the 300 members of JAAC, only 50 were able to make a living from graphic design. The professional advertising designs presented in Graphic '55, the exhibition, was still not free from the role of "corporate appendage," and designers were still treated as craftsmen for capitalists.

Despite the successful cooperation between Yusaku Kamekura and Nikon, the company had a very limited advertising budget and the matter of charging design fees became a subject of negativity. Companies even had to reduce costs by limiting the number of prints to save printing expenses. In the decade after the war, the road to economic recovery in Japan gradually opened up, but the Japanese graphic design industry was still not completely on its feet.

The Rise of Graphic Design in the 1960s / After the end of World War II, the entity that controlled Japan's finances was dismantled and it became increasingly difficult for a single company to fight against powerful overseas capital. Entering the 1960s, Japanese companies began to form united teams. Yusaku Kamekura, Hiromu Hara, and Ryuichi Yamashiro, the preeminent creatives in Japanese advertising, joined forces with eight companies, Asahi Breweries, Asahi Kasei Corporation, Nippon Steel Corporation, Toshiba, Toyota Motor Corporation, Nikon, NKK, and Nomura Securities Co., Ltd., and contributed equal amounts of money to establish the Nippon Design Center, Inc. Under this new model, designers could communicate with entrepreneurs on a reciprocal basis, operate together, and gradually get rid of their subordinate status.

In May 1960, the World Design Conference, the first international design conference in the history of Japanese design, was held in Tokyo. This conference was attended by 84 people from 26 countries along with 143 people from Japan, including 40 designers from the graphic design industry. The fact that such a large-scale design conference was held showed the importance of design at the time. The World Design Congress discussed many important issues, one of which was how design could benefit humanity, a concept that was put

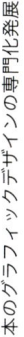

日本のグラフィックデザインの専門化発展

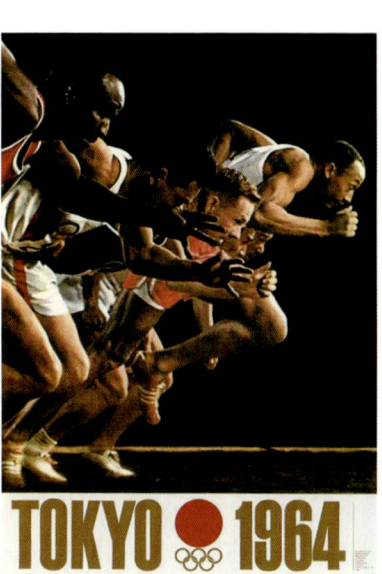

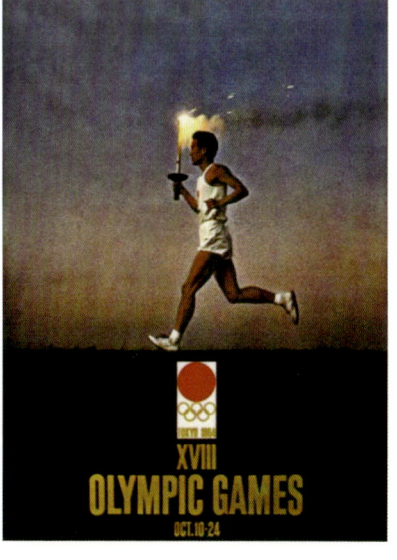

into practice at the Olympic Games Tokyo 1964, Expo '70, Sapporo 1972, and Expo '75.

At the General Assembly of the International Olympic Committee held in 1959, Tokyo was selected as the venue for the 18th Olympic Games in 1964. To host the Olympic Games, the Japanese government established a special design committee with design critic Masaru Katsumi as its top leader.

Masaru Katsumi gathered Yusaku Kamekura, Hiromu Hara, Takashi Kono, Ikko Tanaka, Tadanori Yokoo, and Mitsuo Katsui to work specifically on designs related to the Olympics. The Olympic logo and Olympic posters designed by Yusaku Kamekura and the Olympic icons produced by a team of a dozen designers, including Yoshiro Yamashita, Hiromu Hara, and Ikko Tanaka under the direction of Masaru Katsumi received high international acclaim.

In addition, there was a whirlwind of young designers growing and in 1965, an exhibition called "PERSONA" was held in the department store Matsuya Ginza and featured the works of 11 young designers from JAAC, Kiyoshi Awazu, Shigeo Fukuda, Gan Hosoya, Toshihiro Katayama, Mitsuo Katsui, Tsunehisa Kimura, Kazumasa Nagai, Ikko Tanaka, Aquirax Uno, Makoto Wada, and Tadanori Yokoo.

The exhibition showed new images, concepts, and ideas of graphic design through a variety of new design techniques such as pop art, optical illusion art, decorative art, lyrical illustration, and spectral visualization. In just one week, 35,000 people visited the exhibition, and the individuality and diversity of designers began to receive social attention, promoting niche culture and subculture in the late 1960s.

Also in the late 1960s, industrialization deepened, rationalism, the orientation towards efficiency, order, and norms became the dominant culture, giving the public feelings of indifference and rigidity. Among young people, subcultures began to appear and underground dramas and movie screenings, which were mainly held at the small theaters in the Shinjuku neighborhood, flourished and developed into a larger social movement.

Influenced by the PERSONA exhibition, poster design activity for underground theater was active and designers and performers worked together to create new and unconventional visual expressions. For example, Tadanori Yokoo's Koshimaki-Osen, Aquirax Uno's La Marie Dison, Masamichi Oikawa's The Crime of Dr. Caligari, and Koga Hirano and Katsuhito Oyobe's The Dance of Angels Who are Burning Their Wings created a tense, grotesque, and psy-

chedelic world and served as a stylistic exploration of the history of Japanese graphic design.

Development: Design and Management as One in the 1970s and 1980s / In the 1960s, Japan experienced speedy industrialization and an unprecedented boom in the sales market, leading to a production-oriented society. In the 1970s, consumer goods became popular, people began to pursue product differentiation, and a consumer-oriented society was formed. Companies started to pay attention to the construction of corporate culture, corporate image, as well as their communication with consumers.

In 1971, Motoo Nakanishi's book DECOMAS: Design Coordination as a Management Strategy was published. In the book, he introduced the American concept of corporate identity (CI) to Japan for the first time and explained the value of CI and design as a business strategy. This had a significant impact on both business operation and graphic design. The era of building brands based on designers' intuition and spontaneous ideas alone came to an end, and many companies began to reorganize their operations and develop markets through new design theories. Design and management became inseparable.

In 1978, the century-old Matsuya department store was pressured to develop a new CI system and reorganize its management by inviting Motoo Nakanishi's company, PAOS. Motoo Nakanishi hired designer Masayoshi Nakajo to conduct a detailed study of Matsuya's management philosophy, social image, and industry trends, and changed the corporate image from a century-old store of the heavy industrial era to an urban department store with a sense of modernity. They completely changed the visual design of the store, including the logo, signage, packaging, shopping bags, decorations, and publicity, to create a unified image.

After the reorganization, Matsuya was revived from the dead and its turnover increased year after year.

In the 1970s, the young PARCO department store proposed an advertising strategy that shifted from promoting products to promoting phenomena, severing the link between advertising and products and making the promotion of phenomena, the core of advertising. This created a new era of advertising design.

The 1970s were a time when Japanese women were moving away from tradition and pursuing freedom. Designer Eiko Ishioka captured this sensation well by creating a series of posters for PARCO, which showed the bold and resolute side of women and conveyed the theme of the times when women were awakening from older social norms. On the surface, these poster designs had little to do with the products of PARCO but, in essence, they were part of PARCO's unique business strategy to create an overall corporate image. The posters contributed greatly to PARCO's establishment of influence among young people.

Entering the 1970s, people were aware that only by organizing experts in different fields such as planning, copywriting, and design, could they produce excellent advertisements and achieve better publicity effects, thus a new profession—art director—was born.

The most iconic art director of this period was Katsumi Asaba, who was responsible for Suntory's advertising in 1978. Suntory is a well-established company whose main business is the production and sale of alcoholic beverages. Most of its products are derived from the bounty of nature and the idea of reverence for nature has always been its brand philosophy. In 1979, Katsumi Asaba and photographer Katsuji Takasaki used documentary photography to portray the beauty of nature in an ad for Suntory Old Whiskey. The commercial was shot in China and showed a lone boat being paddled across a calm lake with the tagline "Indulge in the stillness of China," written by Takeo Nagasawa. This perfectly expresses Suntory's brand concept. In the noisy 1980s, this poster evoked the serenity people longed for in their hearts and was a huge success.

Starting in the 1970s, Seibu Department Stores initiated a cultural strategy to make them centers of life and culture for Japanese society. In 1982, Katsumi Asaba, photographer Eiichiro Sakata, copywriter Shigesato Itoi, and famous American filmmaker Woody Allen created a commercial for Seibu Department Stores called *Delicious Life*. The commercial showed a sophisticated Japanese lifestyle scene with Woody Allen dressed in a traditional Japanese costume, carrying a Japanese banner with words written by Shigesato Itoi. It created a Japanese lifestyle culture that reflected the business philosophy of Seibu Department Stores.

Cross of Disciplines: Design and Development as One from the 1990s to Early 21st Century / In the 1990s, after the frenzy of the bubble era, the Japanese economy fell into a long silence and corporate activities and lifestyle con-

sumption became increasingly inactive. People began to think about what was real and Japanese design returned to the everyday. Designers found problems in everyday life, formed new common sense, and extended this all the way to design development. As a result, the boundaries of traditional graphic design were breached and the design perspective became broader, gradually forming a communicative design that crossed industries and organizations.

Kenya Hara, a representative figure in Japanese contemporary design, began working across industries and organizations in the 1990s. He curated various exhibitions with a unique perspective that attracted public attention. He graduated from Musashino Art University with a master's degree in 1983, then joined the Nippon Design Center, Inc. to work on graphic design.

In 1995, the Japan Institute of Architects commissioned Kenya Hara to plan an exhibition to showcase the design skills of architects. Inspired by a common ingredient in food, macaroni, Kenya Hara invited 20 architects and designers to design macaroni, a seemingly simple task that tested the architects' professionalism and creativity, requiring them to consider issues such as ease of production, uniformity of heat, the beauty of shape, and comfort of taste. The design process was rigorous. And the exhibition was named Architects' Macaroni Exhibition.

In 2000, to commemorate the 100th anniversary of the founding of Takeo paper company, Kenya Hara curated the RE_DESIGN—Daily Products of the 21st Century exhibition. He invited 32 designers from various fields, including graphics, architecture, products, and lighting, to rethink and redesign everyday objects. Both exhibitions produced surprising design results through cross-border communication, showing the power and resources of design in everyday life.

As the Japanese economy rebounded in the 2000s, business activities became active again, and new projects and products were developed. It became less unusual for graphic designers to engage in design development activities across industries and organizations and their involvement in the entire process from planning to production changed the status of Japanese graphic design.

Japanese graphic designer Taku Satoh has worked in a wide range of fields, from commercial branding to TV production and regional industrial regeneration. Taku Satoh worked as an art director for the Japanese National Broadcasting Corporation's children's design education program, Design Ah!, which was first broadcast in 2011. From the program's name and content to the offline exhibi-

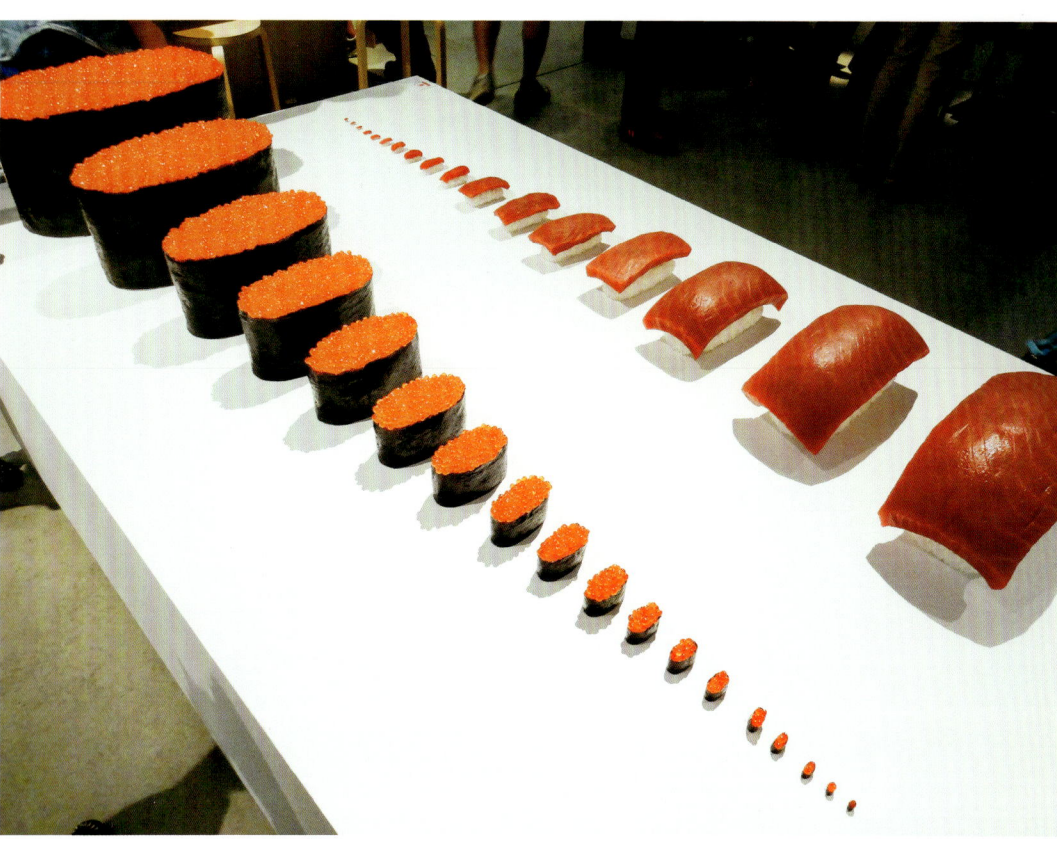

tion, Taku Satoh has been involved in all aspects of the program and made it a popular show.

In 2007, Taku Satoh went to Hitachinaka in Ibaraki Prefecture to develop the Hoshiimo-gakko (dried sweet potato school) project with the local people. To promote the regeneration of the traditional local industry, Taku Satoh participated in the research, co-created with local producers, and designed brand packaging and planning events like the sweet potato festival and tasting.

From the TV program Design Ah! to the regional development project Hoshiimo-gakko, Japanese graphic design improved greatly and has played an important role in industrial development activities.

Kashiwa Sato is a well-known figure in the Japanese graphic design industry and he works in the fields of advertising design, product design, space design, and television production.

In 2005, Kashiwa Sato designed the concept of Fuji Kindergarten in Tachikawa, Tokyo. He proposed the idea of kindergarten as a medium for fostering children's creativity and incorporated his ideas into the logo design, typeface design, and architectural design. He turned the kindergarten into a huge playground and won high acclaim internationally. In 2007, Kashiwa Sato designed the brand strategy for Uniqlo's shirt brand UT to be a future T-shirt convenience store, a new way of shopping where T-shirts are displayed in bottles on a shelf that looks like a vending machine. The design was well received by the public.

From Fuji Kindergarten to the shirt brand UT, Kashiwa Sato investigated the environment in the store as well as user behavior, and decided on the branding strategy. This broke the stereotype that graphic design is equal to visual communication.

Co-creation: Design and Technology as One from the 2010s to Now / Entering the second decade of the 21st century, new developments emerged in the world of science and technology, and technologies and concepts such as artificial intelligence, virtual reality, and the metaverse have become social hotspots.

In 2016, Google's artificial intelligence system, AlphaGo, defeated the world Go champion, Lee Sedol, causing a worldwide sensation and redefining the relationship between humans and machines. Tools became partners that can communicate and collaborate. Meanwhile, Japanese designers have also started to think about new models and possibilities of co-creation between design and technology.

Kota Iguchi attended Musashino Art University where he studied graphic design. With the rise of digital media applications in graphic design, Kota Iguchi turned to research motion graphics and completed a series of high-quality motion design projects including the design of the motion icons for the Olympic Games Tokyo 2020.

In 2021, Iguchi and Intel's Shooting Star drone team designed a drone show for the Olympic Games Tokyo 2020's opening ceremony and it became a classic image. More than 1,800 drones in the stage canopy formed a emblem in three dimensions. The emblem then rotated and became a blue earth. The scene was full of futuristic elements. In 2022, Kota Iguchi and Nike Tokyo produced the Nike naked eye 3D advertisement—Air Max Day, in which a huge version of the Air Max shoe broke through the screen and made a strong visual impact. The brand marketing campaign was successful and became widely disseminated.

Whether it's the drone show at the Olympic Games Tokyo 2020 or Nike's naked-eye 3D ads, designers needed to perform skillfully. Those results cannot be accomplished by the designers alone but by the co-creation of designers and machines.

The Expo 2025 will be held again in Osaka and the planning organization has released the Expo 2025 design system to unify the interface design of promotional messages and provide a complete and coherent brand experience

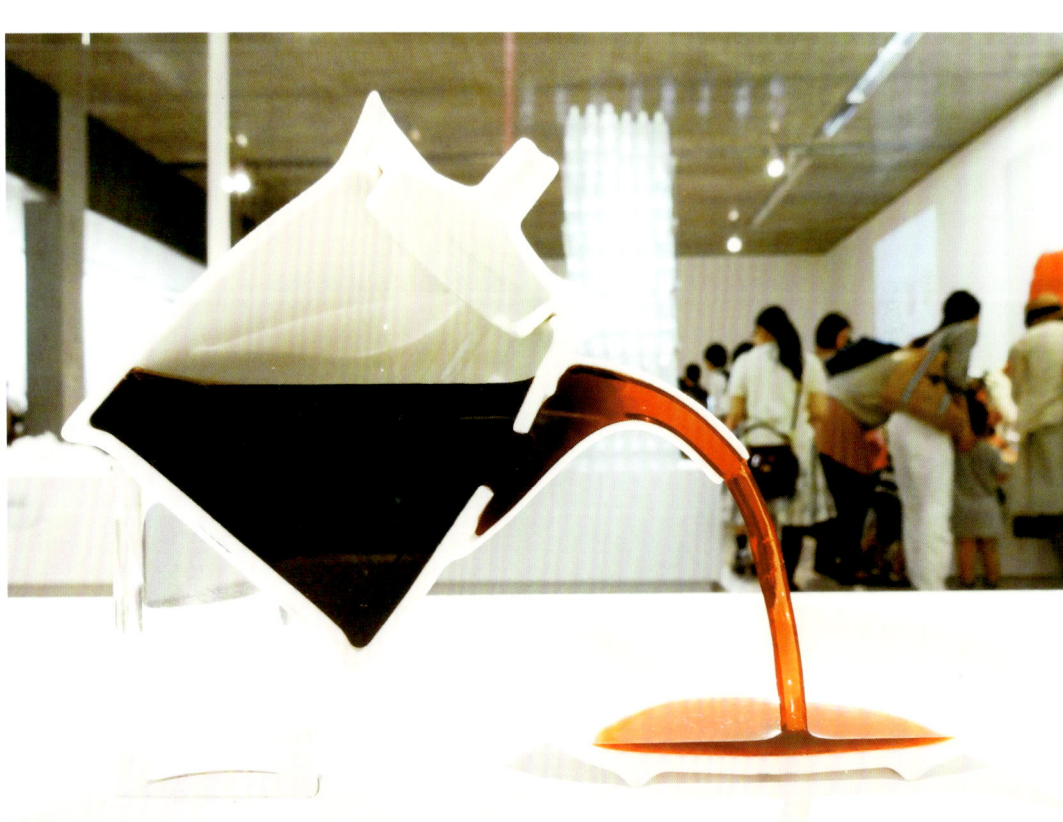

日本のグラフィックデザインの専門化発展

for the exhibition.

The system will be co-created by humans and machines with the computer generating the designs through algorithms and the human designer selecting and adjusting the generated designs to reflect human ideology. Through repeated communication and collaboration between humans and machines, the system will be like a living organism that is constantly updated and evolving.

Summary / For more than 100 years, the professional development of graphic design in Japan began with Japan's modernization, stalled by the war propaganda of World War II, emerged from the post-war economic development, changed with the burst of the bubble economy, and integrated with the technological innovation of the 21st century. The way going forward is full of twists and turns.

In the second half of the 19th century, as Japan modernized, the contemporary advertising industry gradually emerged, graphic design education and professional designers began to appear, and Japanese graphic design gradually broke away from the influence of painting and stepped on the road to professionalism.

At the end of the 1930s, World War II broke out and the development of Japanese companies entered an extremely difficult era. The commercial market shrank and advertising design withered. Many designers committed themselves to serving the country's war propaganda machine, and the free exploration and social development of Japanese graphic design were interrupted.

In the 1950s, as Japan's post-war reconstruction began to bear fruit and economic activity gradually recovered, graphic design was given a rare opportunity to prosper. Designers began to form associations and organizations to clarify the way design existed as a profession, and the right to work and to promote public awareness through exhibitions.

The 1960s saw the rise of Japanese graphic design. The establishment of the Nippon Design Center, Inc. allowed designers to communicate with entrepreneurs on a reciprocal basis and operate together, freeing them from a subordinate position. The World Design Congress and the Olympic Games Tokyo 1964 gave Japanese graphic design an international showcase and high recognition.

In the 1970s and 1980s, Japan's accelerated economic development and the formation of a consumer-led society directed many companies' attention to the construction of corporate culture. Design and management became inseparable.

Entering the 1990s, the economic bubble burst and the Japanese economy fell into a long silence. Designers began to return to the everyday, finding problems in life and extending them all the way to design development. As a result, the boundaries of traditional graphic design were breached and the design perspective became broader, gradually forming a communicative design that crossed industries and organizations.

In the second decade of the 21st century, science and technology developed at breakneck speed and technological innovation has become the theme of the times. Japanese designers began to explore a new model of human-machine collaboration, opening up a new era of design and technology integration and co-creation.

Reference / Makato, Baba. *The Memory of Vermilion: Yusaku Kamekura and the Design of the Showa Era*. Translated by Qingwen Cai, Shanxi Education Press, 2021.

Uchida, Shigeru. *Sixty Years of Japanese Design: 1950–2010*. Translated by Yu Zhang, CITIC Press, 2019.

Meet the Japanese Designers

日本のデザイナー
との対談

2

Human beings are just one of the many creatures of nature that were born on earth. We must humbly accept this, listen to nature, touch it, absorb it with our five senses, and then construct and design it with a certain purpose.

Kazumasa Nagai

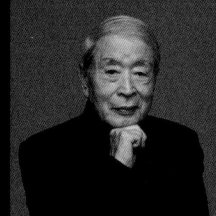

Kazumasa Nagai was born in Osaka in 1929. He participated in the founding of the Nippon Design Center Inc. in 1960, and currently serves as senior executive advisor of the center. He became a member of the Tokyo Art Directors Club (Tokyo ADC) in 1965 and a member of Alliance Graphique Internationale (AGI) in 1966. He is also the special advisor to the Japan Graphic Designers Association (JAGDA). His numerous major awards include the Japan Advertising Artists Club Award, the Asahi Advertising Award Grand Prix, the Yusaku Kamekura Design Award, the Masaru Katsumi Award, the Japan Advertising Award Yamana Prize, the Tokyo ADC Grand Prix, the Medal with the Purple Ribbon, the Order of the Rising Sun and many more.

Q You have been working as a designer for more than 70 years. How has your understanding of design changed?

A In the beginning, I was obsessed with creating designs. Gradually, I became aware of design as a form of visual communication. It enriches people's lives both spiritually and practically, making it more rewarding.

Q You have been working on the LIFE series for many years. What message do you want to convey through this project?

A Technological advances and inventions have been encouraging humankind to create a more and more self-centered environment. This leads to the destruction of nature and the overhunting of animals and other species. The survival of all life forms is now in jeopardy. This is why we need symbiosis, the symbiosis of all life on earth, including plants. Life is threatened in many ways nowadays. We have been trying to emphasize the importance of "life" with our LIFE poster series, using animals as examples.

Q The latest piece of work you created for the LIFE series shows a new style, with blue as the main color. What is this design concept and how did you create it?

A This time, I chose the beautiful blue of the ocean as the base color to highlight sea creatures. I chose three common images among sea life, whale sharks, octopuses, and starfish, to emphasize the meaning of life in a series of three works. The blurred surroundings depict the gradual disappearance of the creatures as they dive into the sea.

Q You express your ideas through LIFE. How does this series bring you feedback and reflections?

A People see this series and realize the importance of life and symbiosis.

永井一正

Q Your style is constantly changing and refreshing. What motivates you to seek breakthroughs?

A About 35 years after I started designing, I looked back and found that I had been creating abstract designs until then. Though later I combined them with live-action photographs to create a cosmic world, my design style was still abstract. One day, I realized that I would fall into a rut if I continued, so I decided to try something I had never done before, which was to make living creatures appear on the screen. I started to leave myself the task of drawing by hand instead of using a ruler and compass, which I had been doing for a long time. Moreover, I changed my expression every year. There are ways to carry on my style, but I always want to try new things and stay fresh.

Q In your opinion, what elements are needed to make a good piece of work?

A Any design that inspires people to take action and enrich their minds and lives.

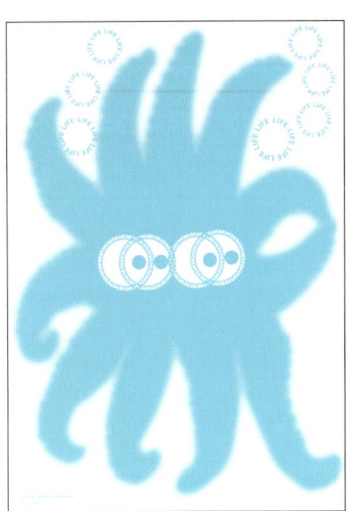
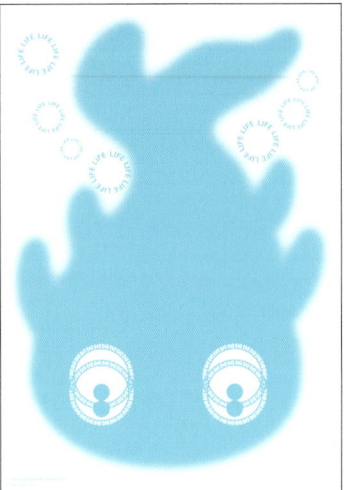
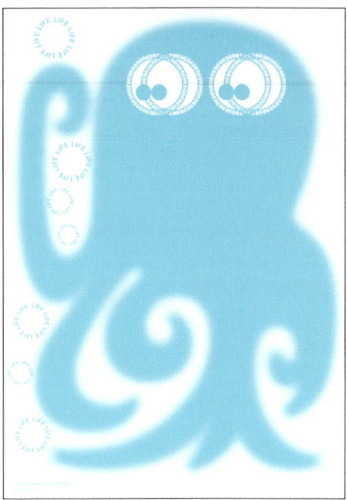

Q You have said that people's personalities are reflected in how their senses respond to stimuli. What does this mean for designers?

A I believe that everything that people feel with their five senses can be found in nature. Human beings are just one of the many creatures of nature that were born on earth. We must humbly accept this, listen to nature, touch it, absorb it with our five senses, and then construct and design it with a certain purpose. This is where the common foundation of mankind is created, and the designer's individuality is added to this foundation to create a unique design.

Q In addition to the LIFE series, you have also helped companies design logos, many of which have become classics and are still in use today. How do you think designers can play a role in business?

A It is said that images and perceptions are the strongest for humans through the eyes. Corporate graphic design provides visual collaboration for corporate activities. They are also important for companies to make business sense.

Q After the 1950s, the concept of graphic design spread and the design industry flourished. What do you think are the key points and major events in the development of Japanese graphic design?

A In 1951, an organization called the Japan Advertising Artists' Club was formed, bringing together all the major designers in Japan. In 1953, an open call for entries began, attracting young designers from all over the country. I became a member in that same year. And in 1960, more than 4,000 works were submitted. These were held in department stores in the heart of the city and graphic design became popular among young people.

It was at the World Design Conference in 1960 that Japanese design changed dramatically. The world's leading designers in the fields of architecture, product design, graphic design, interior design, and textile design gathered in Japan to discuss how design could be useful to mankind. This was put into practice at the Olympic Games Tokyo 1964, the Expo '70 held in Osaka, the Winter Olympics Sapporo 1972, and the Expo '75 held in Okinawa in which Japanese designers participated with all their might. I also designed the emblems for the Sapporo Winter Olympics and Expo '75.

Q What do you think is the common aesthetic sense underlying Japanese design that is unique and highly recognized?

A Japanese art, such as wall paintings, the Rinpa school, Ukiyo-e, etc., which are highly regarded around the world, is the origin of the design. In Japan, the four seasons change and people can enjoy beautiful nature in each season. The climate has given birth to paintings and designs unique to Japan. The main figures and landscapes depicted in ukiyo-e and other works are often flat, and the backgrounds are often solid, without perspective. I believe these elements have been utilized in Japanese graphic design.

Q Graphic design in Japan has undergone digitalization since the 1980s and digital design is now a worldwide trend. How do you see the relationship between technology and design?

A Changes in technology have had a profound impact on graphic design. A computer is now an indispensable tool for graphic designers. While the design has changed, hand-drawn, simple illustrations and other forms of design that explore the origins of human beings also exist.

Q How do you see the future of Japanese graphic design?

A Japanese design will continue to carry on the Japanese tradition. However, it is also the fate of design that the old is transformed into the new. We need to deconstruct tradition and assemble it with new modern sensibilities. However, if we don't keep in mind that design is for the benefit of the people, we will see many new designs that are just empty expressions. I would be happy if young people would also expand digital expressions with a firm focus on their origin.

NOTES:
Kazumasa Nagai has been working on the LIFE series since the 1980s. These are his creations dating from 2010 to 2020, revealing his thinking about life, environment, and symbiosis.

永井一正

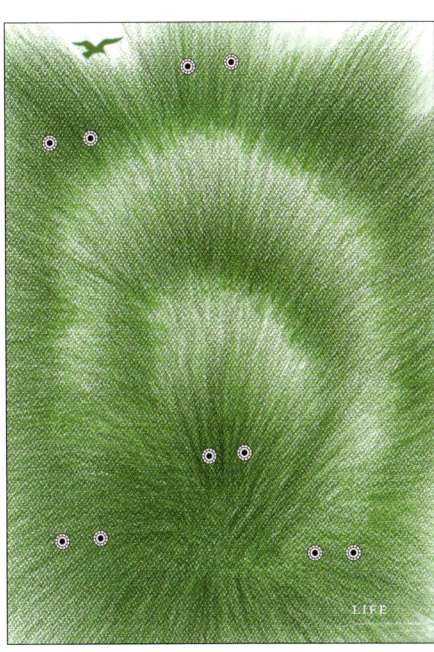

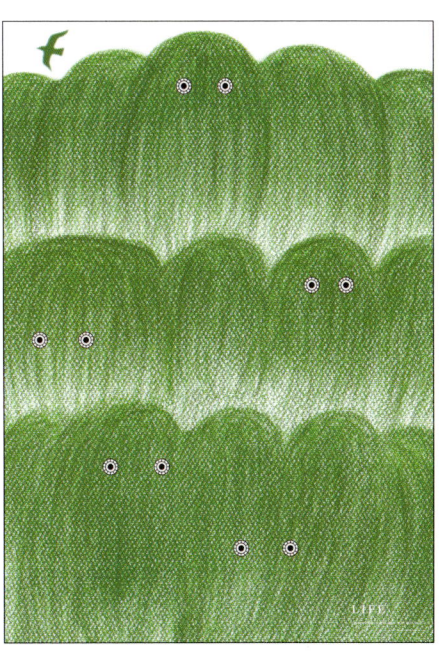

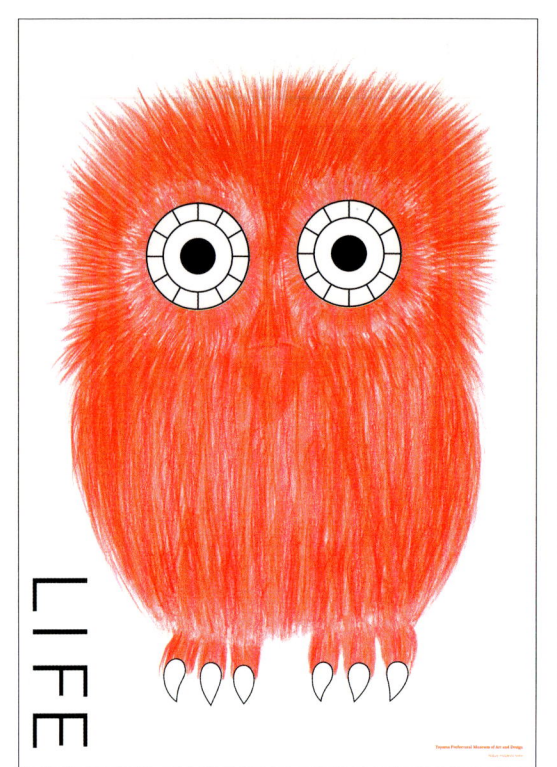

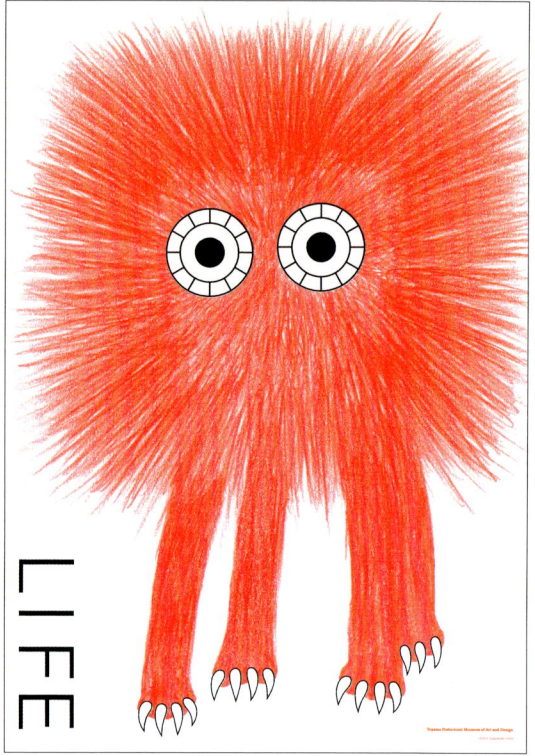

LIFE

LIFE

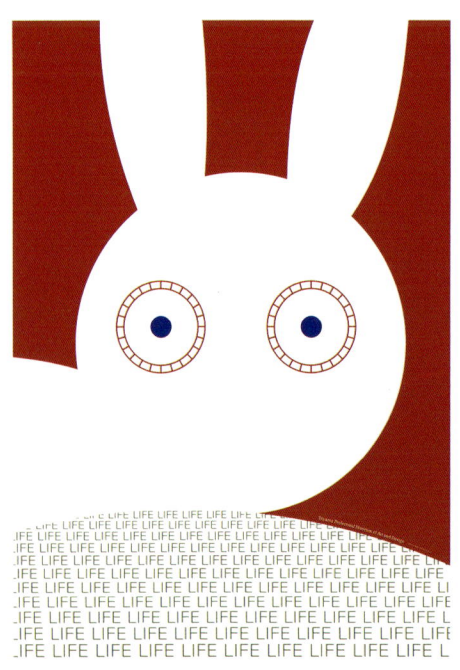

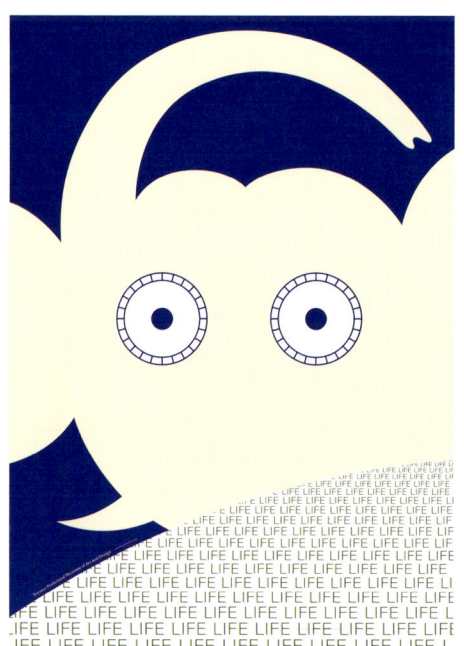

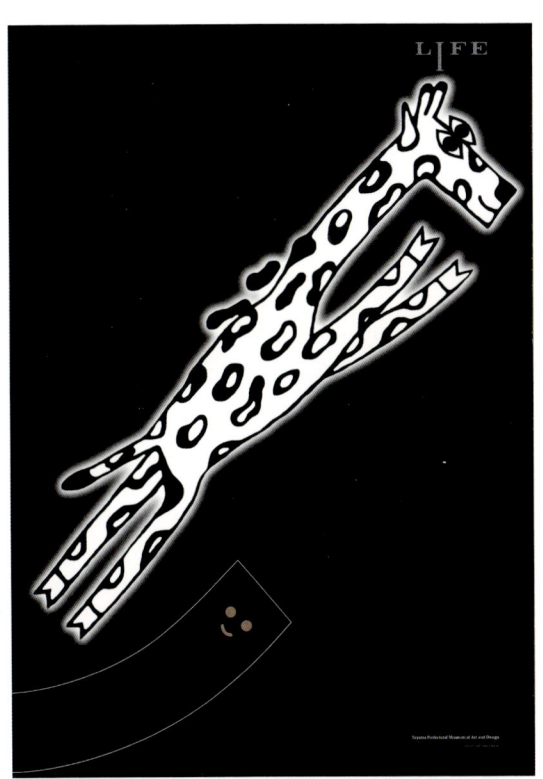

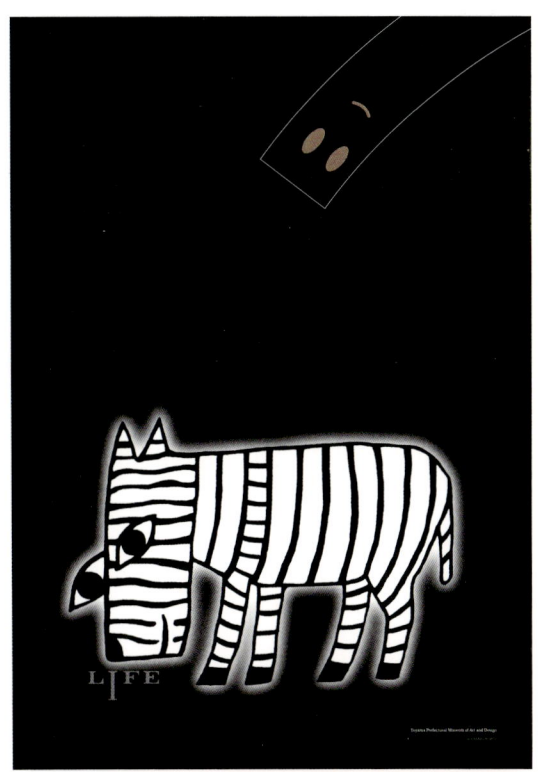

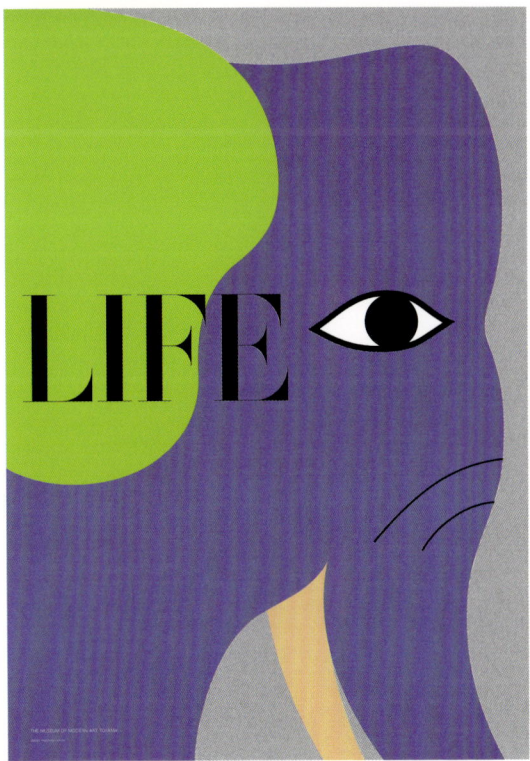

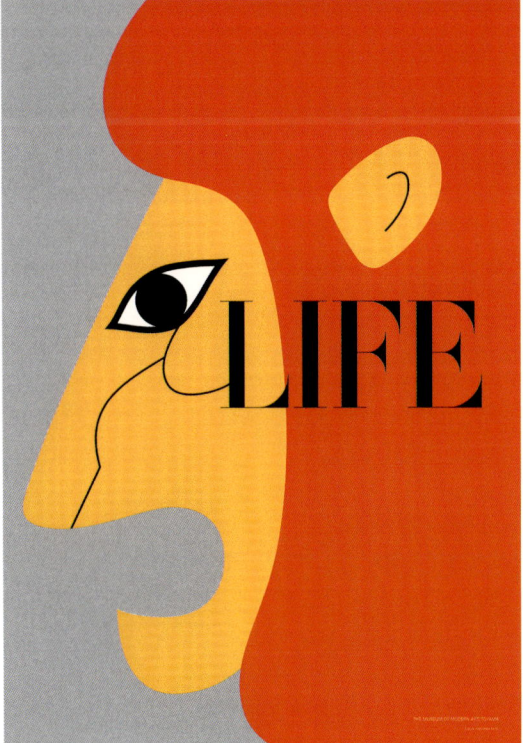

永井一正

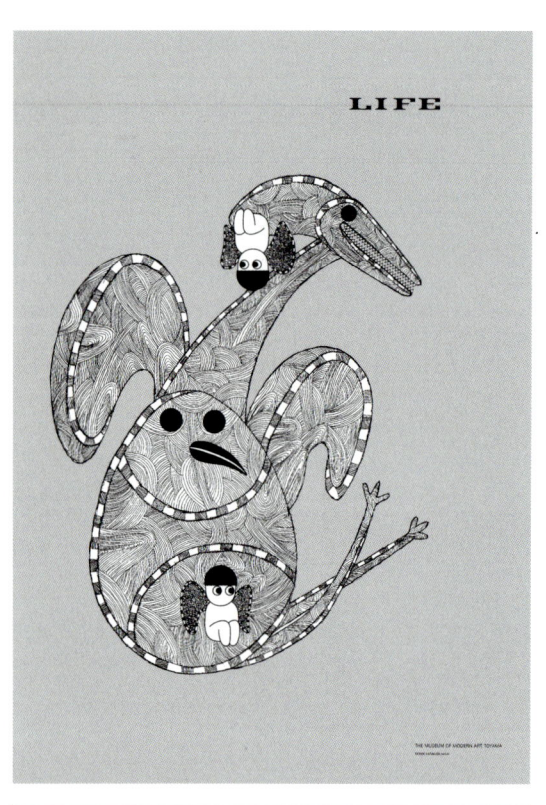

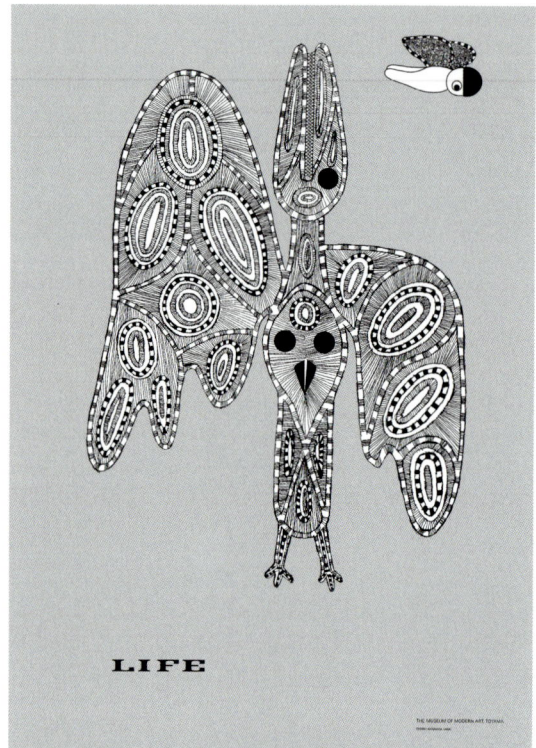

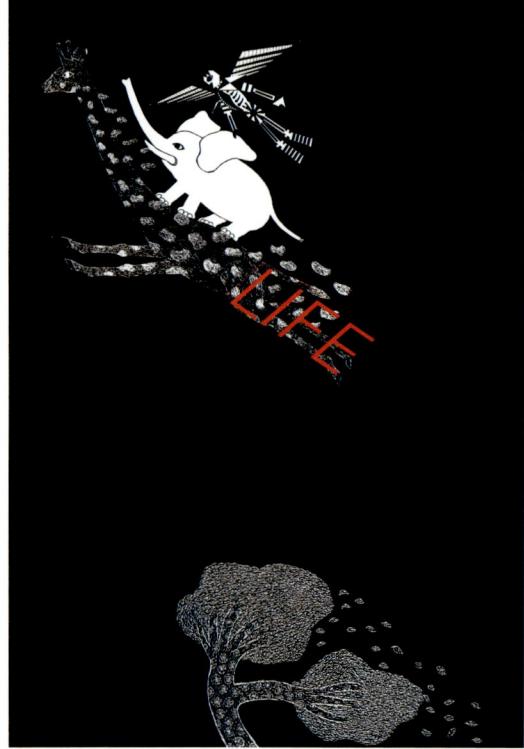

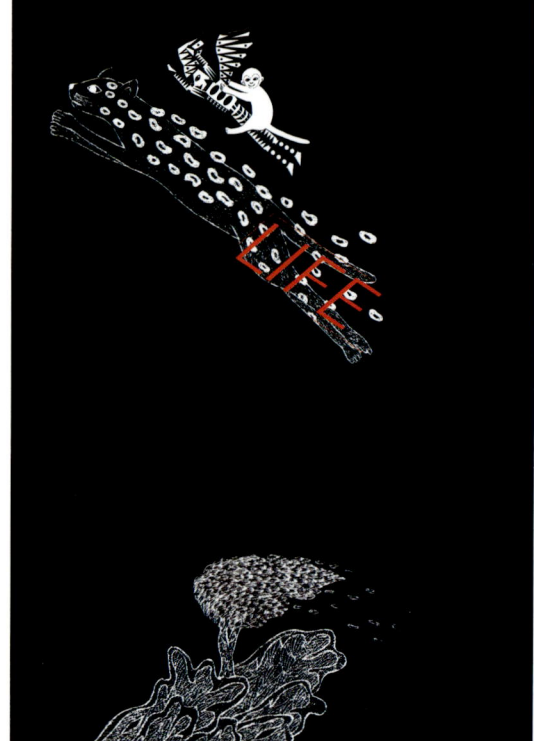

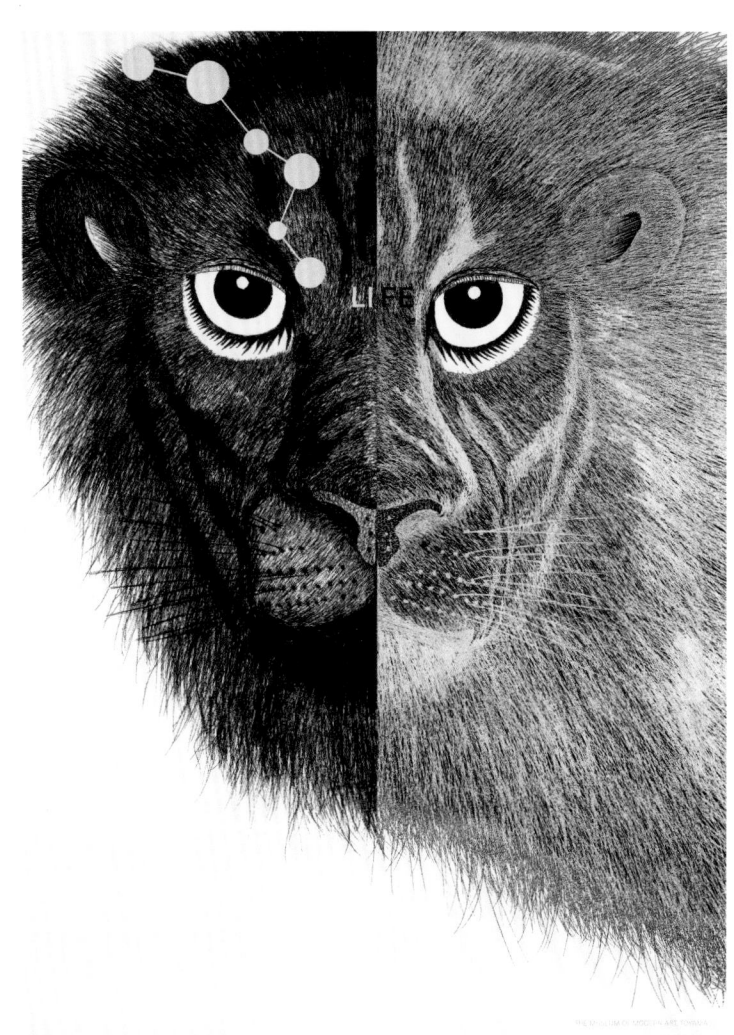

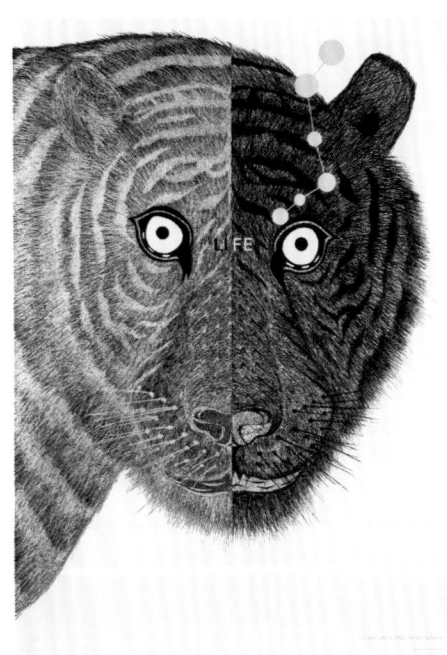

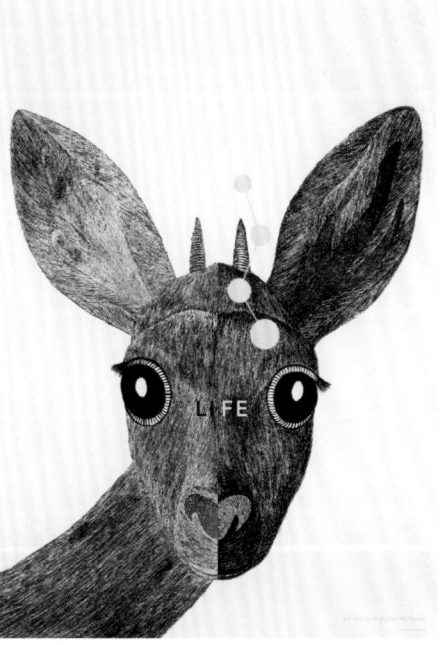

A principle that I always follow is not to allow a lie, deceit, or impurity at any stage of my creative process. Once an impurity is mixed in the process, no matter how minor it might be, ideal beauty cannot be achieved.

Keiko Hirano

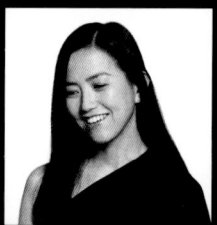

Keiko Hirano, a designer and visionary, is the executive director of Communication Design Laboratory, an award-winning multidisciplinary design lab. Her clients include IPSA, The National Museum of Modern Art, Tokyo, and Kajima Corporation. Hirano has curated design exhibitions, authored/designed books on graphic design, and won prestigious awards such as the NY ADC Gold Award, and the Yusaku Kamekura Design Award. She was a member of the first selection committee for the 2020 Tokyo Olympic Emblem and is a member of AGI.

Q Could you share a piece of work that left the deepest impression on you? What is its design concept?

A The symbol mark and visual identity (VI) planning for the National Museum of Modern Art, Tokyo left a deep impression on me. Its design concept was for the logo to be transparent, not dominant while promoting awareness and functioning as a logo. It was a model case for identifying an ideal symbol and visual identity for a museum as a public institution, a design that could endure for a long time.

I believe that endurance is one of the most important elements of a design concept. Given the trust, cooperation, and mutual respect with the museum, I continue to design for them now, 20 years after I designed the logo. Today, I designed business cards for their new employees based on my original design.

Q You mentioned that you wanted to eliminate decorative language and instead use language to reveal the essence of design. When designing, do you tend to use restrained visual language? Are there any design principles you have always followed?

A Up until 2007, I advocated the importance of language. And my stance on eliminating decorative language has not changed even now. The reason is that I think excessive explanations using words are ostentatious and deviate from the essence of design.

In terms of the visual language for my design activities around the year 2000, many expressions were considered minimalistic in style, but they were only a fraction of the activity that was seen on the surface. If you examine my current creative activities, you understand that they cannot be defined as restrained visual language, but as organic, glamorous expressions.

A principle that I always follow is not to allow a lie, deceit, or impurity at any stage of my creative process. Once an impurity is mixed in the process, no matter how minor it might be, ideal beauty cannot be achieved.

Q You have a project called DESIGNPiece and one of the works is a desktop calendar called "wave motion." What was the reason for starting this project?

A I received a request in 2005 from Shoichi Kajima, the owner of Kajima construction company, for a desktop calendar design, which I did for him. Expressing the client's corporate conscience, the design aims to form a shape that does not affect the beauty of the environment and to create a product that can be used perpetually, minimizing waste, as the main acrylic part can be used continuously and only the date sheet refills are replaced.

Kajima highly praised the final design and said, "wouldn't it be better not only for Kajima to use them, but for your company to sell them so more people can use them?" With this advice, Communication Design Laboratory decided in 2007 to sell them along with the ones Kajima distributes.

I thought an ideal design could not be discussed only from a designer's perspective, but there must be a world that was not revealed unless the designer also became a merchant. I started DESIGNPiece with this belief as a motivation.

中野敏子

Q What mindset should designers consciously develop?

A Do not lie. Self-discipline is not dictated by greed. Critical spirit. Objectivity is not influenced by self-centeredness. Insightfulness perceives truth without being misled by surface appearances. Thought that desires better results. To learn true guidelines from sages from the past such as *The Analects of Confucius*, and to possess a measure for correctness. To do everything to deliver the best answers and fulfill the responsibilities assigned to him/her. Sensitivity that brings one close to others' sadness. To be free.

Q Could you share your overall impression of Japanese graphic design?

A People recognize and understand the past through mythology. In the history of Japanese design, in 1964, a monumental work was achieved as a historical fact. It was the Tokyo Olympics logo and poster series designed by Yusaku Kamekura and a signage design by a design team of young Japanese graphic designers led by Masaru Katsumi as a total producer.

I think, up until 2000, a few leaders of the graphic design category and editors of the trade media could control information and they were successful in building the image of the design of Japan. We could say that the centralized power structure functioned and succeeded in making a mythology. With the spread of the Internet, however, a creator who had worked at an advertising agency and was well versed in information control, began designing propaganda that can be interpreted as self-promotion. Though I think advertising and design have different specialties and are different occupations, in the graphic design industry, advertising art directors actively ran image campaigns that positioned advertising in the center of the graphic design.

After 2000, with the spread of PCs and graphic software, the age when anyone can call him/herself a designer arrived. The line between professional designers

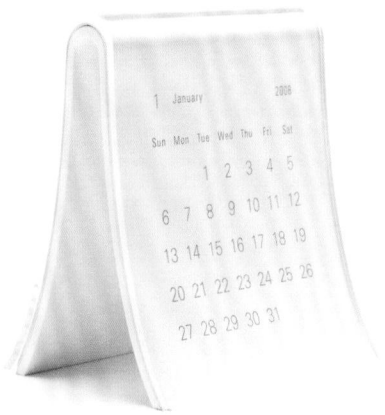

DESK CALENDAR "WAVE MOTION"

In this three-layered construction, the calendar pages are sandwiched between two gently curved acrylic sheets. The notion of time, invisible to the eye, is likened to a water flow, an entire year flowing in unbroken continuity with the acrylic wave designed to blend unobtrusively into its ambient setting. To perpetuate the concept of continuity, the calendar uses a minimum of parts destined for eventual discarding as the acrylic form is reusable over multiple years and the calendar can be updated annually with page refills. In this way, the product generates minimal waste.

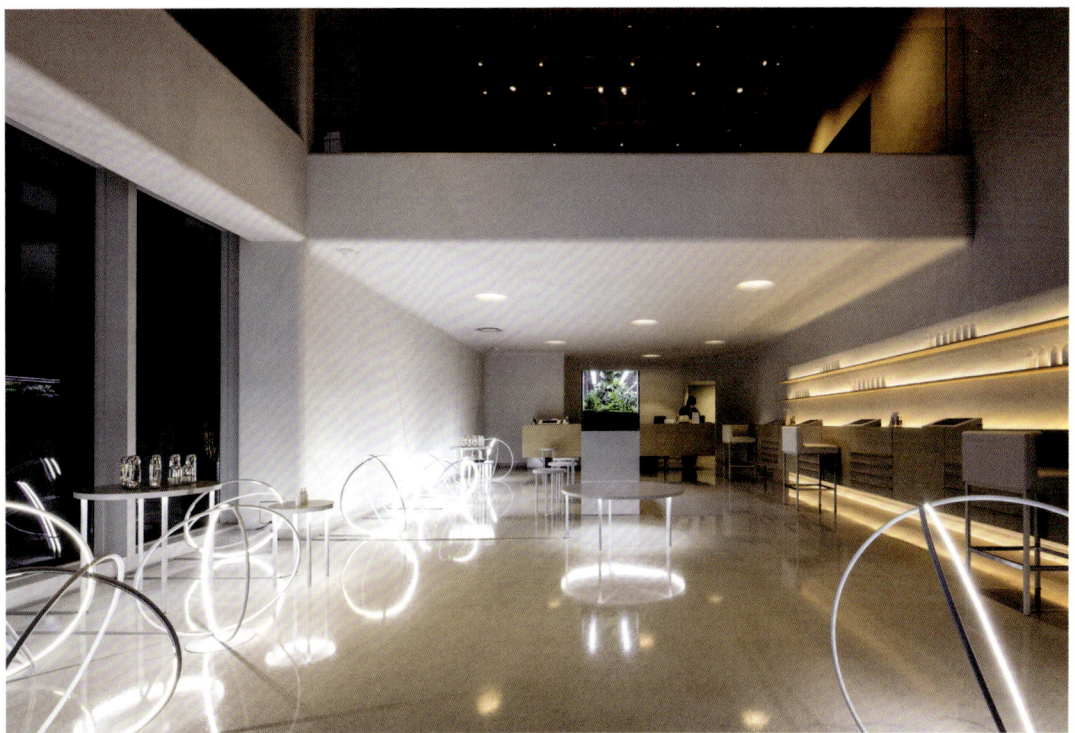

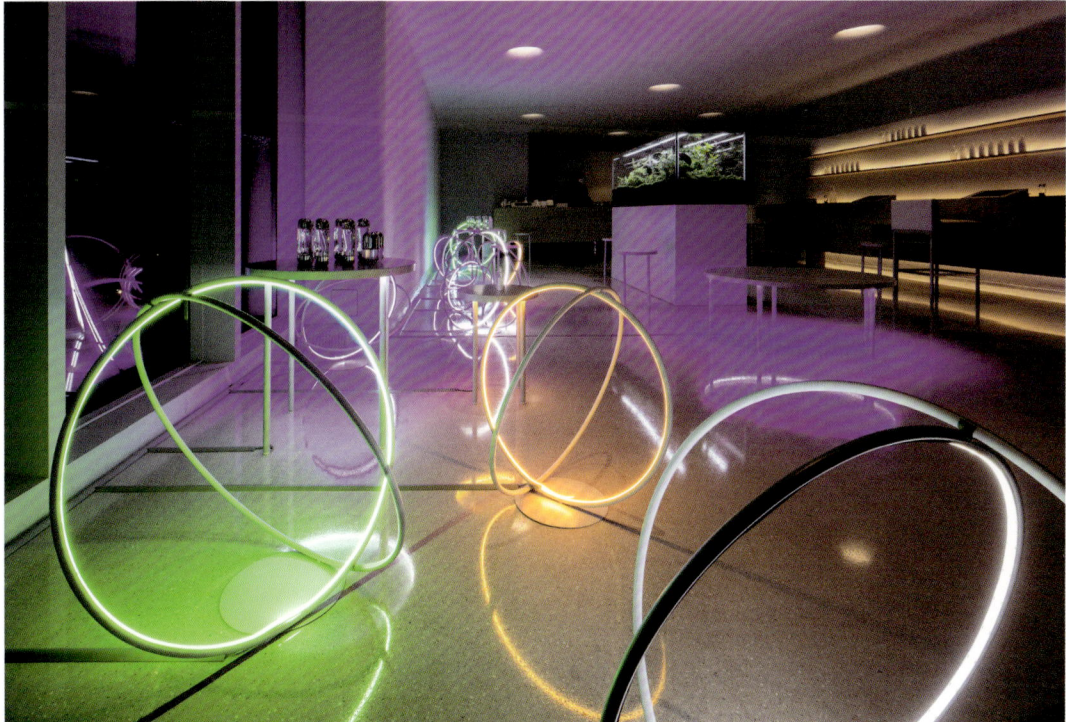

平野敬子

IPSA AOYAMA SPACE DESIGN

In 2019, IPSA AOYAMA opened in central Tokyo as the flagship store of the IPSA brand. Keiko Hirano was tasked with the store's spatial design and seasonal installations. From autumn 2021 through summer 2022, she decorated the interior with illuminated interlocking circular objects. In autumn and winter, multi-colored LEDs—blue, green, and yellow—created a lively atmosphere. In spring and summer, LED strip lights were substituted to evoke an air of quiet tranquility. This experimental approach, using wholly recyclable objects adaptable for seasonal mood changes, was her response in opposition to scrap-and-build.

and amateurs blurred, a confusing chaotic situation quickly developed and we entered an illusional era when people could become professional graphic designers without having job experience.

I have not researched the contemporary graphic design industry enough to discuss its current situation in Japan. That is because I feel there is a large gap between design works that prevail in the graphic design industry and functioning designs in the real world. Many works that are highly regarded in design annuals are designed for design's sake and not for reality.

Q   What do you think of the influence of the Japanese aesthetic heritage, social culture, and graphic design education? How do they work into your design philosophy and practice?

A   I have been greatly influenced by the art form of haiku, which reveals a spectacular universal view with only 17 letters, a composition of 5-7-5 phonetic units. I particularly like haiku by the poet Matsuo Basho. I think I have been practicing deciphering truths that reside deep within highly abstract expressions.

I was influenced by Basho's *The Narrow Road to the Deep North* for my style of design expression up until 2007, which was a minimalist expression with abstract composition based on white.

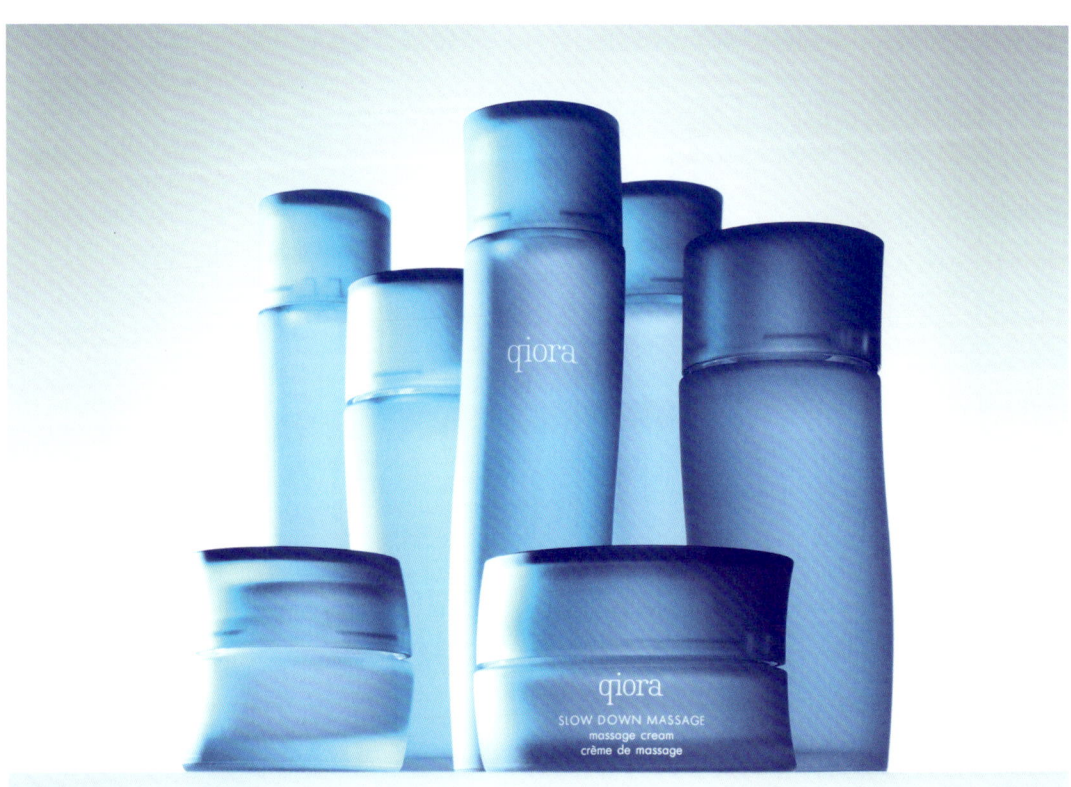

QIORA BRANDING

qiora is a Shiseido brand of cosmetics that took more than a decade to develop. Shunning repetitive use of a single symbolic feature, Keiko Hirano focused on the organic and curvaceous shape of its blue bottle and adapted the product design to create the gradation-based visual identity for the brand's shop space, display units, product photos, etc. By combining diverse stimulating factors—the tactile appeal of paper, spatial experience, visual language, and connections to all five senses—she sought to convey the spirit behind qiora's creation, taking inspiration from several shared concepts of light, blue, and organic qualities.

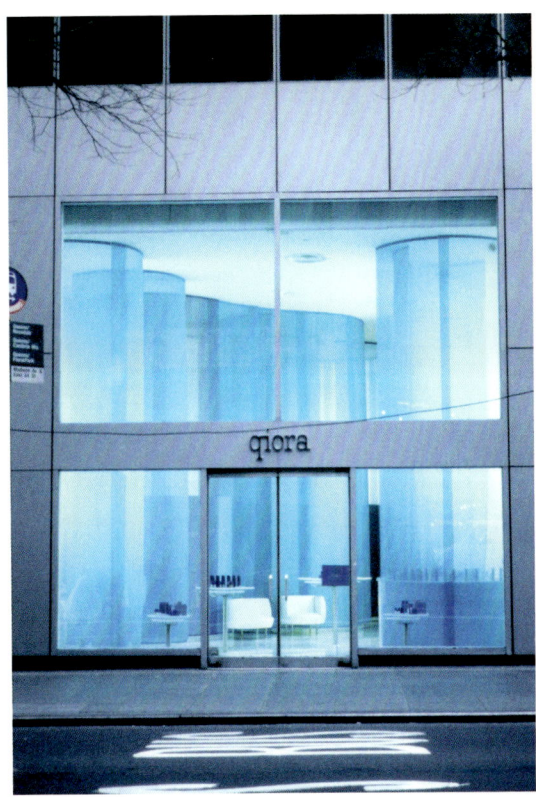
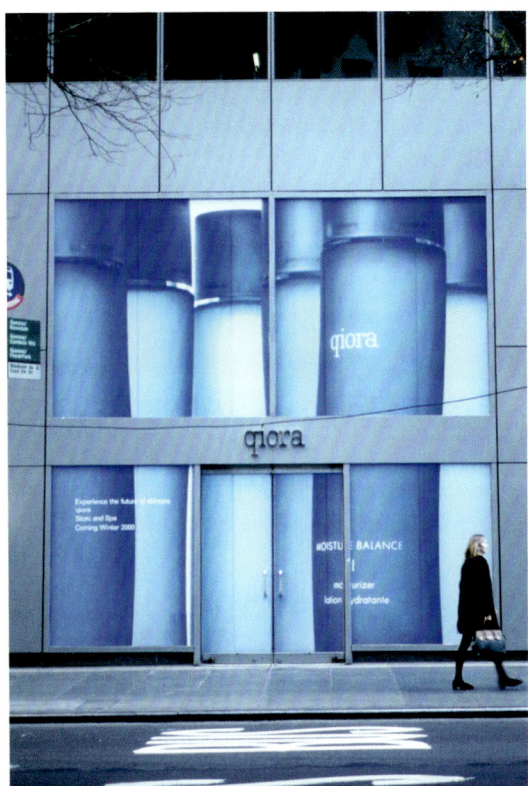

平野敬子

Q   In recent years, many creations
from Japan are presented through
new media or forms. How do you look
at contemporary graphic design in
Japan and what is your expectation?

A   I analyzed and summarized 50 years of graphic design
in Japan for the "Icons of the Times" exhibition, which
I planned in 2004. As I have not examined Japanese
graphic design as a single theme since then, and do not
have knowledge or information, I cannot comment on
that.

I founded the Communication Design Laboratory with
Aoshi Kudo in 2005. The scope of communication design
that I handle has cut across many categories, such as
product, space, and online media designs, and not limited
to graphic design. My habit or sensitivity of perceiving the
world through the particular lens of graphic design has
been fading. As a result, I cannot discuss contemporary
graphic design in Japan.

With the development of social media, we have an
environment in which anyone can distribute information.
I hope there will be more people who design with a
flexible approach and a broad perspective suitable
for contemporary times, being freed from the curse of
recognizing the world through graphic design in Japan.

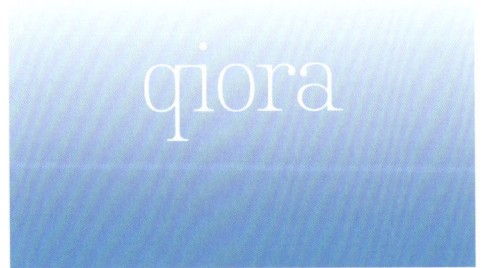

The National Museum of Modern Art, Tokyo or MOMAT, originally opened in 1952 as Japan's first museum dedicated to modern art. Keiko Hirano was initially commissioned to create a new logo and VI to mark MOMAT's semicentennial renewal in 2002. Given the museum's location directly across from the Imperial Palace in Tokyo, she aimed for a design that would be readily recognizable and also mesh beautifully and harmoniously with its surroundings. Ten years later, in 2012, she was asked to design a logo commemorating the museum's 60th anniversary. Now, another decade later, in 2022 she continues to manage design at MOMAT. She believes management and maintenance are elements integral to the ideal functioning of the museum's logos.

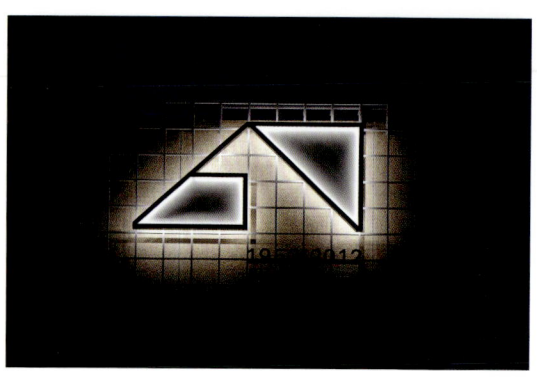

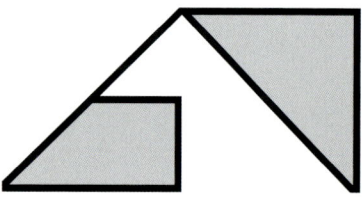

1952-2012
60th Anniversary

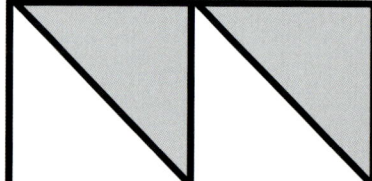

1952-2052
100th Anniversary

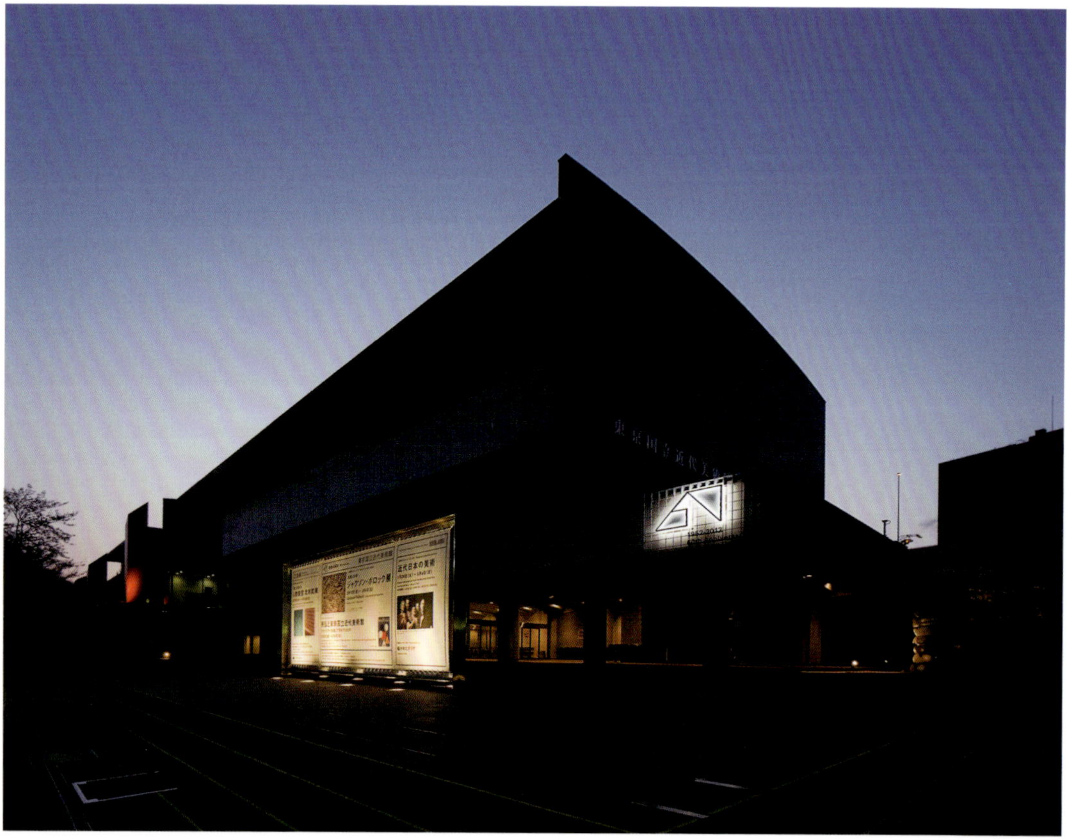

Keiko Hirano

40

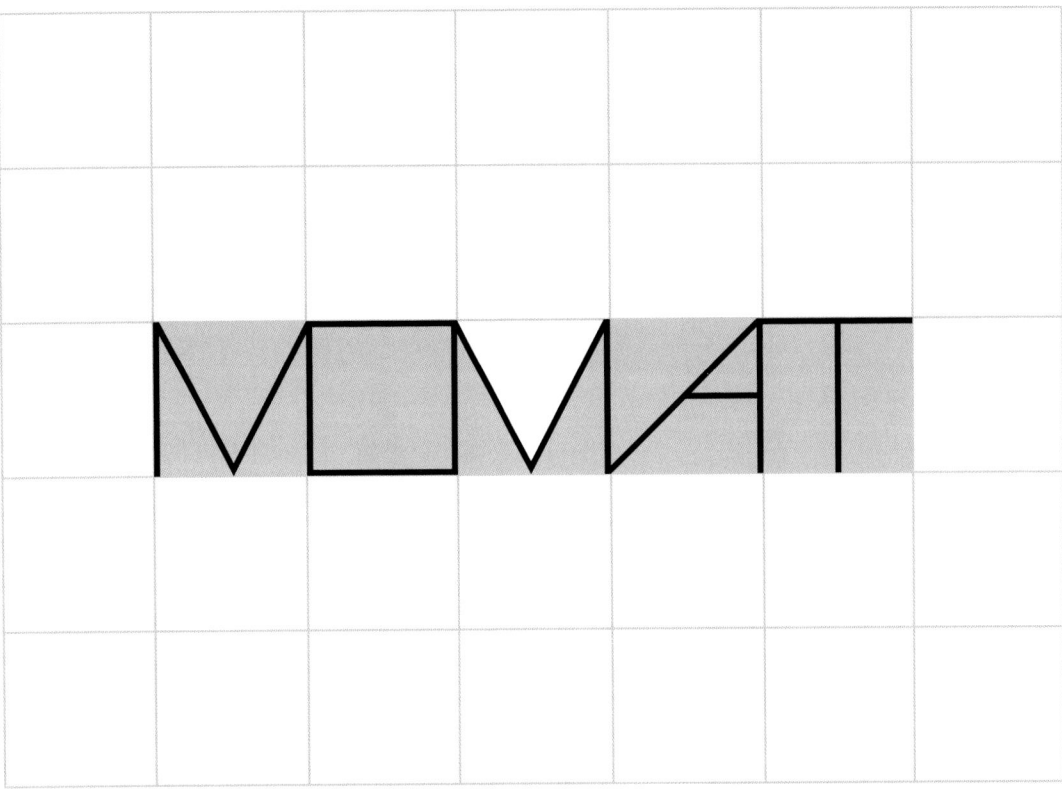

Seiji KOYAMATSU
Manager
Exhibition Support
Department of General Affairs

Independent Administrative Institution National Museum of Art
The National Museum of Modern Art, Tokyo

3-1, Kitanomaru-Koen, Chiyoda-ku, Tokyo 102-8322, Japan
Tel. +81 3 3214 25✱✱ Tel. +81 3 3214 25✱✱
Fax. +81 3 3214 25✱✱
e-mail: ✱✱✱✱✱✱✱@momat.go.jp

MOMAT
独立行政法人国立美術館
東京国立近代美術館

尾崎 正明
副館長

〒102-8322
東京都千代田区北の丸公園3-1
Tel. 03 3214 25✱✱
Fax. 03 3214 25✱✱
e-mail: ✱✱✱@momat.go.jp

Masaaki OZAKI
Deputy Director

Independent Administrative Institution National Museum of Art
The National Museum of Modern Art, Tokyo

3-1, Kitanomaru-Koen, Chiyoda-ku, Tokyo 102-8322, Japan
Tel. +81 3 3214 25✱✱
Fax. +81 3 3214 25✱✱
e-mail: ✱✱✱✱@momat.go.jp

Reiko NAKAMURA
Assistant Curator
Department of Fine Arts (Painting and Sculpture)

Independent Administrative Institution National Museum of Art
The National Museum of Modern Art, Tokyo

3-1, Kitanomaru-Koen, Chiyoda-ku, Tokyo 102-8322, Japan
Tel. +81 3 3214 25✱✱ Tel. +81 3 3214 25✱✱
Fax. +81 3 3214 25✱✱
e-mail: ✱✱✱✱✱✱@momat.go.jp

Eriko SHIRAHAMA
Assistant Researcher
Education Section
Department of Programs Development

Independent Administrative Institution National Museum of Art
The National Museum of Modern Art, Tokyo

3-1, Kitanomaru-Koen, Chiyoda-ku, Tokyo 102-8322, Japan
Tel. +81 3 3214 25✱✱ Tel. +81 3 3214 26✱✱
Fax. +81 3 3214 25✱✱
e-mail: ✱✱✱✱✱@momat.go.jp

Akiko ICHIJO
Curator
Education Section
Department of Programs Development

Independent Administrative Institution National Museum of Art
The National Museum of Modern Art, Tokyo

3-1, Kitanomaru-Koen, Chiyoda-ku, Tokyo 102-8322, Japan
Tel. +81 3 3214 25✱✱ Tel. +81 3 3214 25✱✱
Fax. +81 3 3214 25✱✱
e-mail: ✱✱✱✱@momat.go.jp

Tohru MATSUMOTO
Chief Curator
Department of Programs Development

Independent Administrative Institution National Museum of Art
The National Museum of Modern Art, Tokyo

3-1, Kitanomaru-Koen, Chiyoda-ku, Tokyo 102-8322, Japan
Tel. +81 3 3214 25✱✱ Tel. +81 3 3214 25✱✱
Fax. +81 3 3214 25✱✱
e-mail: ✱✱✱✱✱✱✱@momat.go.jp

MOMAT
独立行政法人国立美術館
東京国立近代美術館

松本 透
企画課長

〒102-8322
東京都千代田区北の丸公園3-1
Tel. 03 3214 25✱✱
Fax. 03 3214 25✱✱
e-mail: ✱✱✱✱✱✱✱@momat.go.jp

Rei MASUDA
Curator of Photography
Department of Fine Arts

Independent Administrative Institution National Museum of Art
The National Museum of Modern Art, Tokyo

3-1, Kitanomaru-Koen, Chiyoda-ku, Tokyo 102-8322, Japan
Tel. +81 3 3214 25✱✱
Fax. +81 3 3214 25✱✱
e-mail: ✱✱@momat.go.jp

Wako KOYAMA
Exhibition Support
Department of General Affairs

Independent Administrative Institution National Museum of Art
The National Museum of Modern Art, Tokyo

3-1, Kitanomaru-Koen, Chiyoda-ku, Tokyo 102-8322, Japan
Tel. +81 3 3214 25✱✱ Tel. +81 3 3214 25✱✱
Fax. +81 3 3214 25✱✱
e-mail: ✱✱✱✱✱@momat.go.jp

Mika KURAYA
Curator
Department of Programs Development

Independent Administrative Institution National Museum of Art
The National Museum of Modern Art, Tokyo

3-1, Kitanomaru-Koen, Chiyoda-ku, Tokyo 102-8322, Japan
Tel. +81 3 3214 25✱✱ Tel. +81 3 3214 25✱✱
Fax. +81 3 3214 25✱✱
e-mail: ✱✱✱✱✱✱@momat.go.jp

Eriko SHIRAHAMA
Assistant Researcher
Education Section
Department of Programs Development

Independent Administrative Institution National Museum of Art
The National Museum of Modern Art, Tokyo

3-1, Kitanomaru-Koen, Chiyoda-ku, Tokyo 102-8322, Japan
Tel. +81 3 3214 25✱✱ Tel. +81 3 3214 26✱✱
Fax. +81 3 3214 25✱✱
e-mail: ✱✱✱✱✱@momat.go.jp

Reiko NAKAMURA
Assistant Curator
Department of Fine Arts (Painting and Sculpture)

Independent Administrative Institution National Museum of Art
The National Museum of Modern Art, Tokyo

3-1, Kitanomaru-Koen, Chiyoda-ku, Tokyo 102-8322, Japan
Tel. +81 3 3214 25✱✱ Tel. +81 3 3214 25✱✱
Fax. +81 3 3214 25✱✱
e-mail: ✱✱✱✱✱✱@momat.go.jp

Tohru MATSUMOTO
Chief Curator
Department of Programs Development

Independent Administrative Institution National Museum of Art
The National Museum of Modern Art, Tokyo

3-1, Kitanomaru-Koen, Chiyoda-ku, Tokyo 102-8322, Japan
Tel. +81 3 3214 25✱✱ Tel. +81 3 3214 25✱✱
Fax. +81 3 3214 25✱✱
e-mail: ✱✱✱✱✱✱✱@momat.go.jp

MOMAT
独立行政法人国立美術館
東京国立近代美術館

増田 玲
主任研究員
美術課 写真係長

〒102-8322
東京都千代田区北の丸公園3-1
Tel. 03 3214 25✱✱(代表)
Tel. 03 3214 25✱✱(直通)
Fax. 03 3214 25✱✱
e-mail: ✱✱✱✱✱@momat.go.jp

Rei MASUDA
Curator of Photography
Department of Fine Arts

Independent Administrative Institution National Museum of Art
The National Museum of Modern Art, Tokyo

3-1, Kitanomaru-Koen, Chiyoda-ku, Tokyo 102-8322, Japan
Tel. +81 3 3214 25✱✱ Tel. +81 3 3214 25✱✱
Fax. +81 3 3214 25✱✱
e-mail: ✱✱@momat.go.jp

MOMAT
独立行政法人国立美術館
東京国立近代美術館

保坂 健二朗
研究員
企画課 企画渉外係

〒102-8322
東京都千代田区北の丸公園3-1
Tel. 03 3214 25✱✱(代表)
Tel. 03 3214 25✱✱(直通)
Fax. 03 3214 25✱✱
e-mail: ✱✱✱✱✱@momat.go.jp

Kenjiro HOSAKA
Assistant Curator
Department of Programs Development

Independent Administrative Institution National Museum of Art
The National Museum of Modern Art, Tokyo

3-1, Kitanomaru-Koen, Chiyoda-ku, Tokyo 102-8322, Japan
Tel. +81 3 3214 25✱✱ Tel. +81 3 3214 25✱✱
Fax. +81 3 3214 25✱✱
e-mail: ✱✱✱✱@momat.go.jp

Akiko ICHIJO
Curator
Education Section
Department of Programs Development

Independent Administrative Institution National Museum of Art
The National Museum of Modern Art, Tokyo

3-1, Kitanomaru-Koen, Chiyoda-ku, Tokyo 102-8322, Japan
Tel. +81 3 3214 25✱✱ Tel. +81 3 3214 26✱✱
Fax. +81 3 3214 25✱✱
e-mail: ✱✱✱✱@momat.go.jp

Seiji KOYAMATSU
Manager
Exhibition Support
Department of General Affairs

Independent Administrative Institution National Museum of Art
The National Museum of Modern Art, Tokyo

3-1, Kitanomaru-Koen, Chiyoda-ku, Tokyo 102-8322, Japan
Tel. +81 3 3214 25✱✱ Tel. +81 3 3214 25✱✱
Fax. +81 3 3214 25✱✱
e-mail: ✱✱✱✱✱✱✱@momat.go.jp

平野敬子

OPAM/OITA PREFECTURAL ART MUSEUM

Keiko Hirano began the design for this new museum by creating a nickname—the acronym OPAM—that would be easily recognized and remembered. She then had a large monument of the logo "OPAM," more than 2 meters high, installed outside the museum entrance. The monument provides an ideal photo spot for visitors and is an installation that would be an effective means of publicizing OPAM on social media. For the sign system, she opted to use color-coordinated fixtures and mobile signs covered in original textiles. This enables intuitive recognition of different functions within the overall white, ambient space.

Keiko Hirano

OpAm

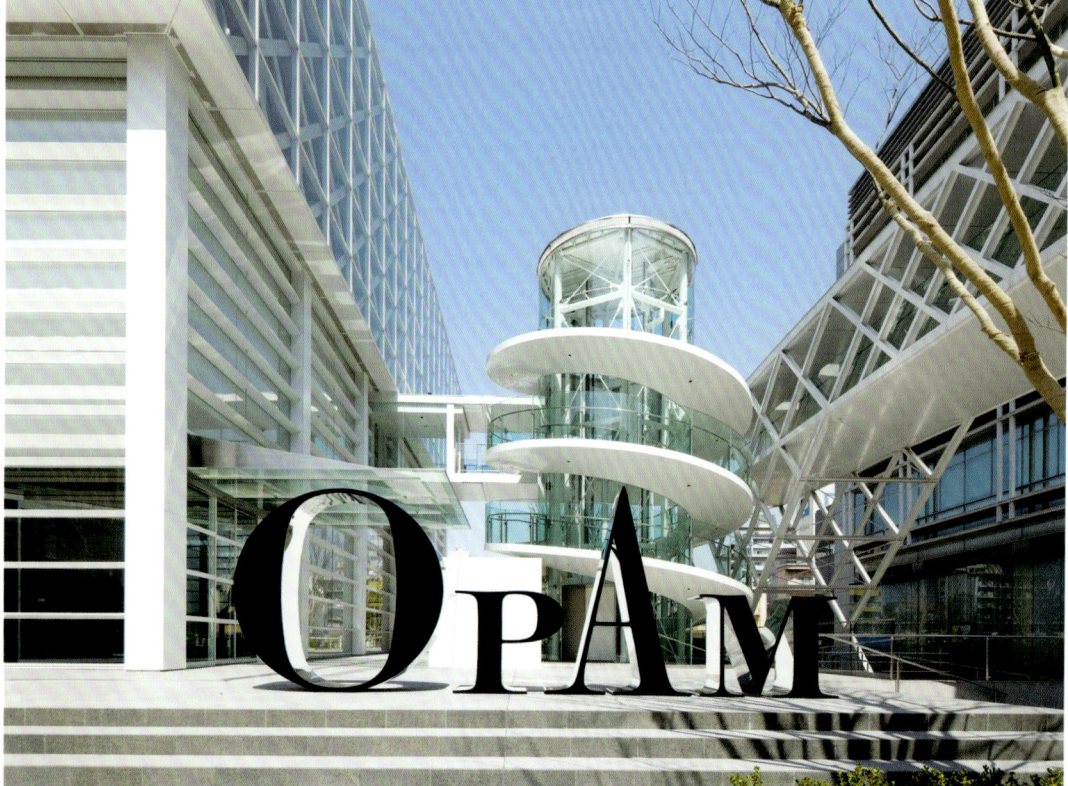

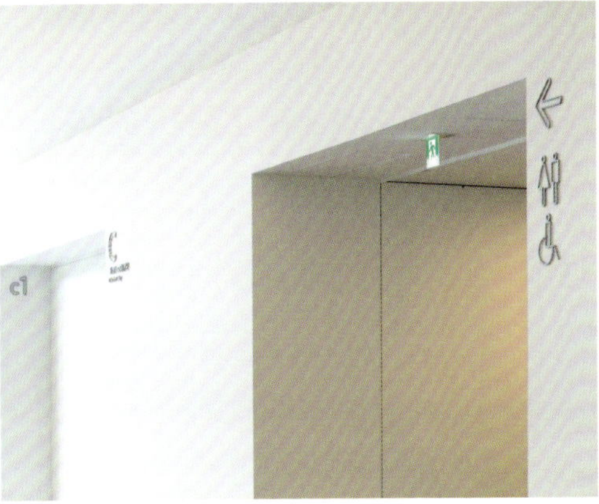

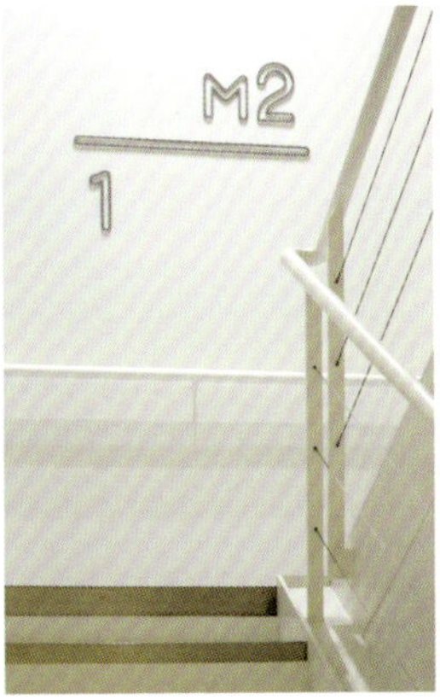

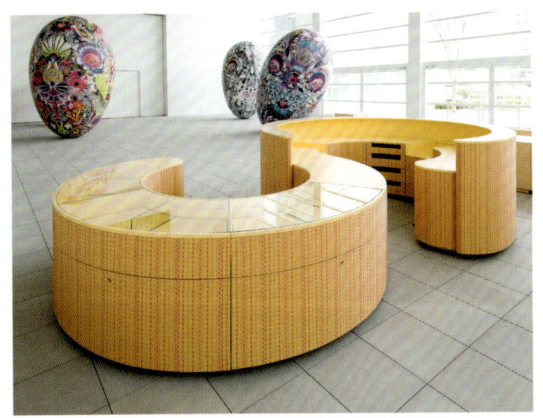

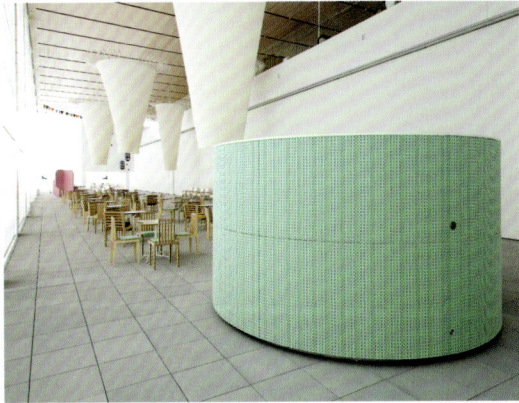

平野敬子

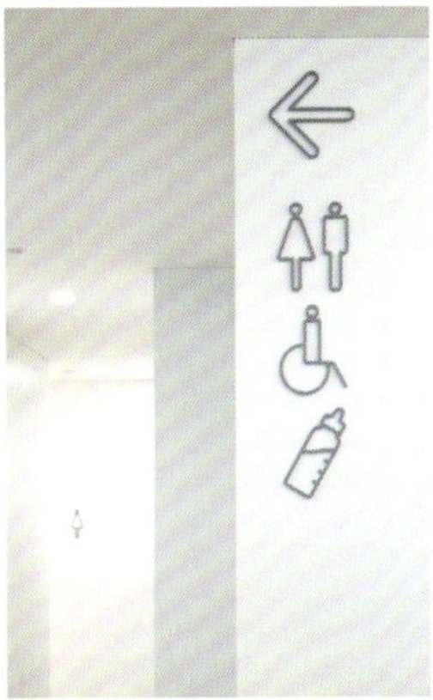

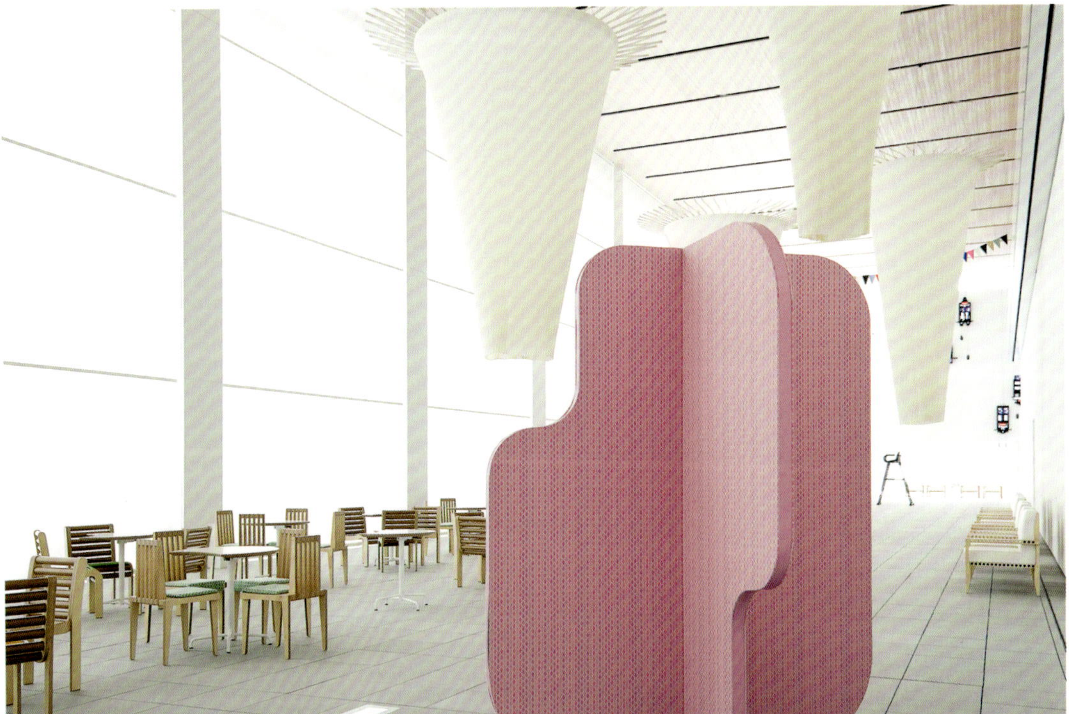

I always try to create
an easy-to-understand
design. That means, the
design is easy to see
and understand, even for
children and the elderly.

Norito Shinmura

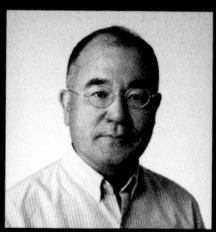

Norito Shinmura was born in 1960. He once worked
at Shin Matsunaga Design and established Shinmura
Design Office in 1995. In 2021, the office's name was
changed to Garden Inc. He is a member of JAGDA and
Tokyo ADC. He has won the JAGDA New Designer
Award, the New York ADC Silver Award, the Gold Prize
granted by the International Biennial of Graphic Design in
Brno, and so on.

Q Could you share your overall impression of Japanese graphic design?

A I think the same is true in China. The number of designers with a wonderful artistic sense is increasing. The development of digital technology has made it possible to express oneself in many ways, and the completeness of design and the sense of color is improving rapidly. However, what I am concerned about is that more and more designs are similar to each other, and the number of original works is decreasing.

Q What do you think of the influence of the Japanese aesthetic heritage, social culture, and graphic design education? How do they work into your design philosophy and practice?

A I am a technical college graduate, so I did not receive an academic education. However, I believe there are some designs that only I can express. And this is because my knowledge is limited.

Q What are the principles you have always followed when doing design?

A I always try to create an easy-to-understand design. That means the design is easy to see and understand, even for children and the elderly.

Q The poster series you created for the MUJI Campground illustrates the theme of nature in different ways. How do you decide on the point of view and approach to present the theme?

A My ideas come from the things I played with in childhood, things I found while taking a walk in nature or the inspiration I get from seeing an exhibition. I mix them in my head to come up with an idea. Once I have one, I further research how to express it and how it should look when I create the poster. At the same time, I try to improve the quality of design with advice from experts.

新村則人

Q The poster for MUJI Campground "Water and Branches" includes the elements of land, silhouette, and branches. What's your design idea?

A When you were a child, you may have seen tree branches as animal horns or tails. You may have also used water to draw pictures. I made a poster of such childhood memories. First, I used water to draw a silhouette of animals. On top of the silhouette, I placed tree branches collected at the MUJI campsite to make it look more like an animal. I believe this can express the fun and wonder of nature.

Q Your creations are straightforward, yet ingenious. How do you ensure the readability of the form and content, and produce an intriguing work?

A When I create visuals, I use the expression that is easy for children to understand. Perhaps that is why my visuals look simple. However, simplicity alone is not attractive, so to enhance the completeness of my visuals, I collaborate with artists. And I research methods of expression because this might help improve the completeness of design.

Q Authentic scenes and elements from reality are appealing. How can a work created with computer software achieve the same effect? Take Shinmura Fisheries' "Fish Basket" as an example. What's your opinion?

A Shinmura Fisheries' "Fish Basket" is one of the few works that was completed with computer software. To create a true-to-life feel, I had the actual basket sent to me from my hometown and I created the work while looking at it. Although the octopus was digitized, it is possible to create a sense of reality by making the viewer aware that the object exists, as in the case of the basket.

Q Nowadays, designing with software has become a necessity. How can traditional means and modern techniques balance each other and contribute to creating outstanding works?

A When it comes to finalizing the product, it is now 100% computerized. Therefore, computer technology is indispensable. However, if we only use computers, we will end up with similar expressions, so I include manual work in the process. When we create by hand, we have a fluctuation that gives the viewer a sense of security and spiritual richness. And this cannot be achieved digitally. The craft became our ancestors' treasure and has been treated as a traditional way of creating.

Norito Shinmura

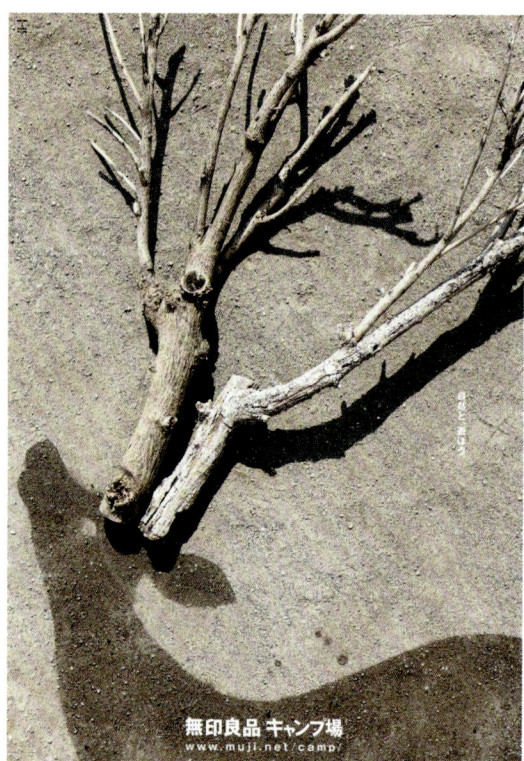

MUJI CAMPGROUND "WATER AND BRANCHES"
People have probably painted on the earth using water. And the idea of this poster was inspired by that. Norito Shinmura used acrylic plates and sprays to draw and added tree branches to make the image of a deer or a fox. He also mixed a little ink in the water to draw a clear picture.

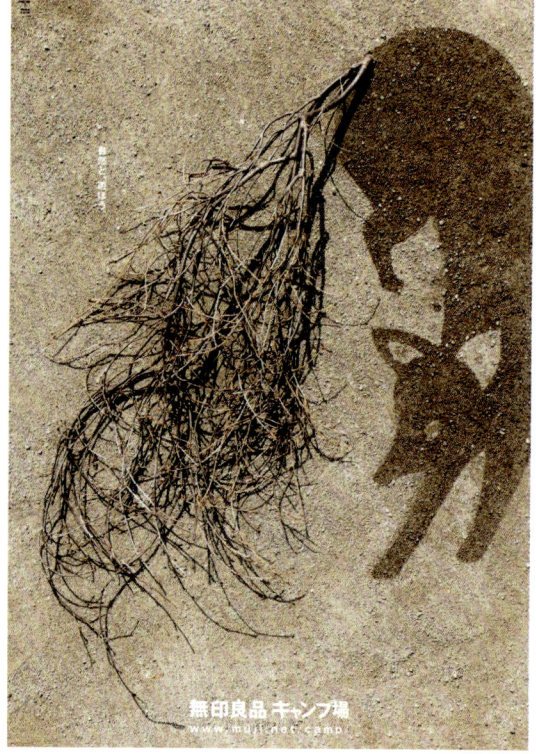

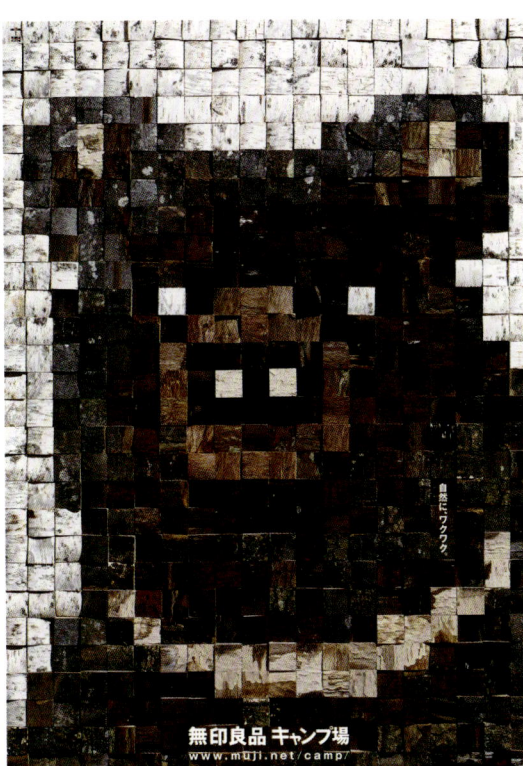

MUJI CAMPGROUND "WOOD CHIP BLOCK"

This project was conceived from the idea to reuse wood that would otherwise be thrown away. The designers of Garden Inc., Hirosuke Niwano and Kosuke Mizoguchi, asked wood carving artist Masatake Shimizu to create a total of 3,000 blocks. The process took about two months. The bark has different expressions even in the same color, and it is impressive and fun just to look at each block. The piece of wood used for the frog in particular also had moss growing on it. The creation conveys the workings and beauty of nature.

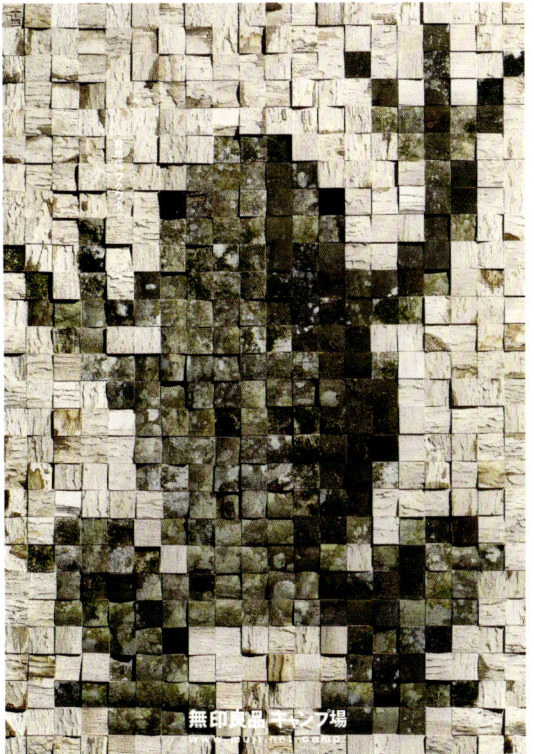

新村則人

Q　How do you observe and record people, objects, and events in your daily life, then turn them into inspiration for your creations?

A　I often get ideas when I am walking. When I take a walk in nature, I am impressed by the colors of new shoots and flowers. When I take a walk in the city, I look at the words on signs and the fashions of people walking by. I get a lot of inspiration from those things. I have such a weak memory, so when an idea comes to me, I immediately record it in my MUJI notepad.

Q　In your opinion, what elements are needed to make a good piece of work?

A　The ability to discover is necessary for good work. When I am walking in nature, I discover something unusual or when I am listening to a client, I discover what is important. If we develop this ability, we can decide what visuals to use and what to communicate. To acquire the power to discover, we need to experience many things and absorb them with an open mind.

Q Many of your creations have projected your thinking upon society and the environment. In what way do you think design can influence society?

A I feel the helplessness of a solo designer. No matter how good a poster is, it is meaningless if it does not spread. Nowadays, although a piece of work can spread widely through social networks, there is a limit on the form of posters. However, design can have an impact on society if we research media and methods of communication, so we need to do more research and improve our design skills.

Q In recent years, many creations from Japan were presented through new media or forms. How do you look at contemporary graphic design in Japan and what is your expectation?

A This is the most difficult question for those who are not educated in academia. So, I honestly don't know what the future holds for graphic design. But the scope of graphic design activities is changing. On top of this, I would like to think about designs that move people's hearts and minds.

Norito Shinmura

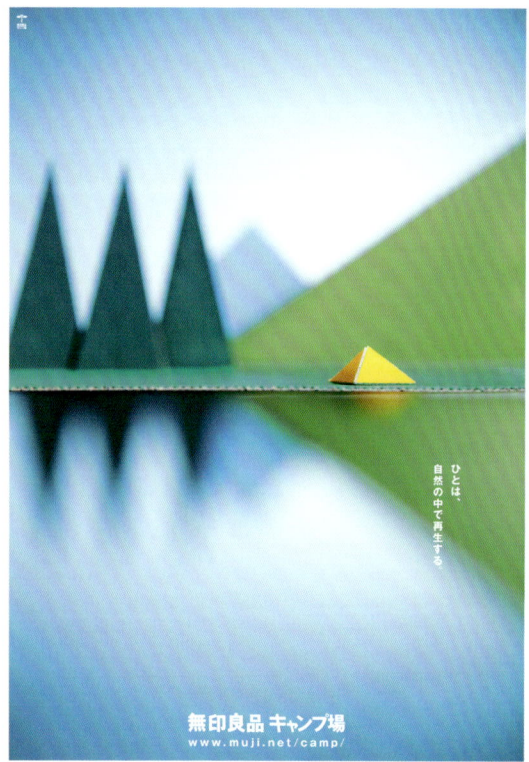

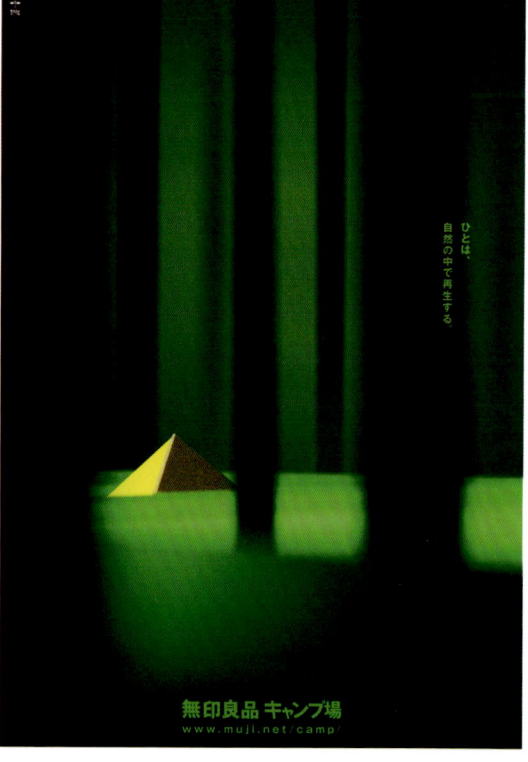

MUJI CAMPGROUND "CARDBOARD"
The visuals for the 2019 MUJI Campground were created using cardboard. As the catchphrase says, "People regenerate in nature." The designers collected discarded cardboard boxes and reused them to create tents and mountains in the illustration. What they wanted to create was very simple photography, even simple enough to make people feel like "This is what you get from this photoshoot spot?"

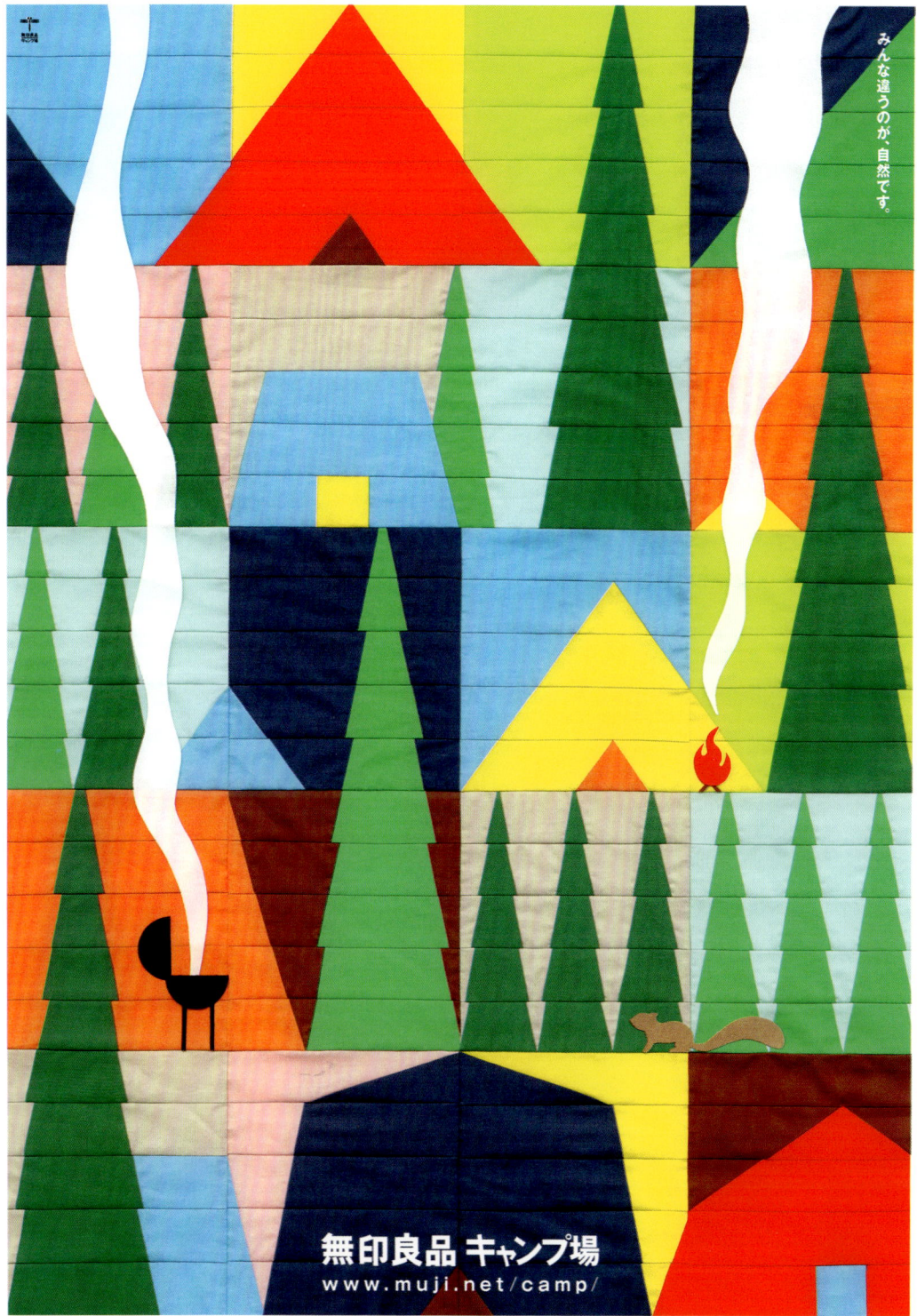

みんな違うのが、自然です。

無印良品 キャンプ場
www.muji.net/camp/

MUJI CAMPGROUND "QUILT"

These illustrations were created by a designer from Garden Inc., Kosuke Niwano. The illustrations had a bright and gentle color composition, but to add a little more nuance, Norito Shinmura thought about covering the entire surface with a quilt. When he saw Kumiko Fujita and Kazue Nakajima's *Style of Modern Art Quilts*, his team immediately contacted the artists and commissioned them. Most art quilts have a homey image, but their work is graphical and perfect for the theme in this work. The artists completed three large pieces in the end, each of which took over a month to make.

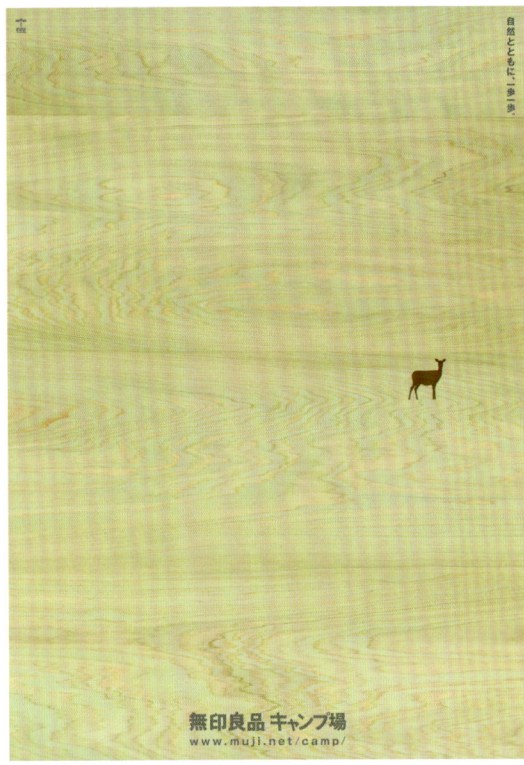

Norito Shinmura

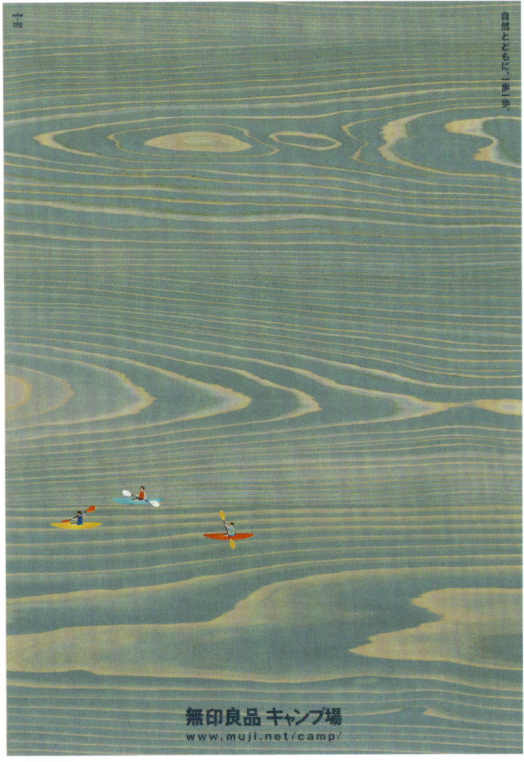

MUJI CAMPGROUND "GRAIN"

The designers of Garden Inc. wanted to use the grain of the wood to display the campground. Troubled by how to color the actual board, they tried coloring the boards with acrylic paint and woodworking paints, but failed. After learning that Masatake Shimizu was a board dyeing artist, Norito Shinmura immediately asked him to help create the work. In the end, the blue lake was dyed with indigo on a cedar board, the green meadow with nanten on a cypress board, and the sunset meadow with lac dye on a zelkova board. This technique colors the beautiful gradation while preserving the grain of the wood.

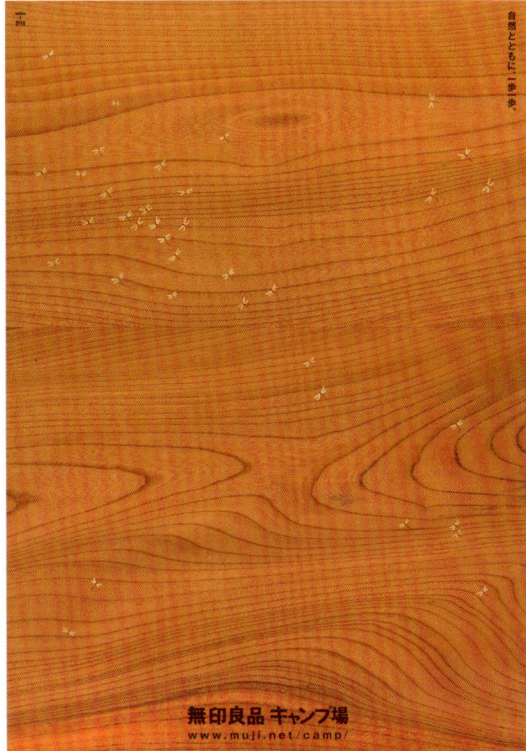

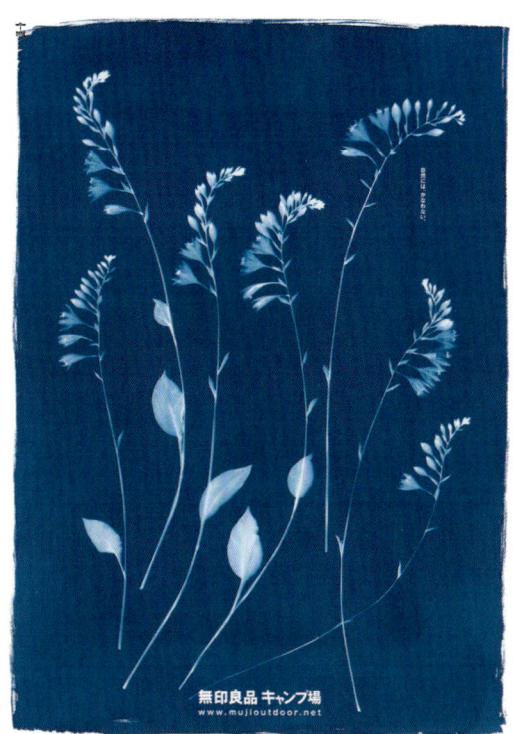
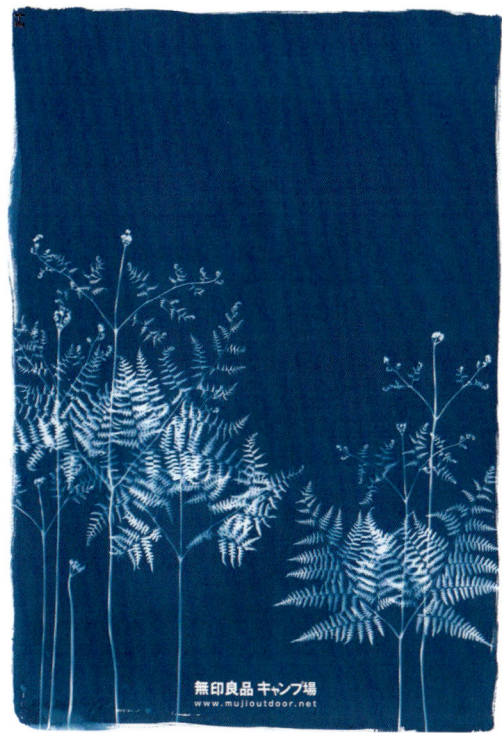
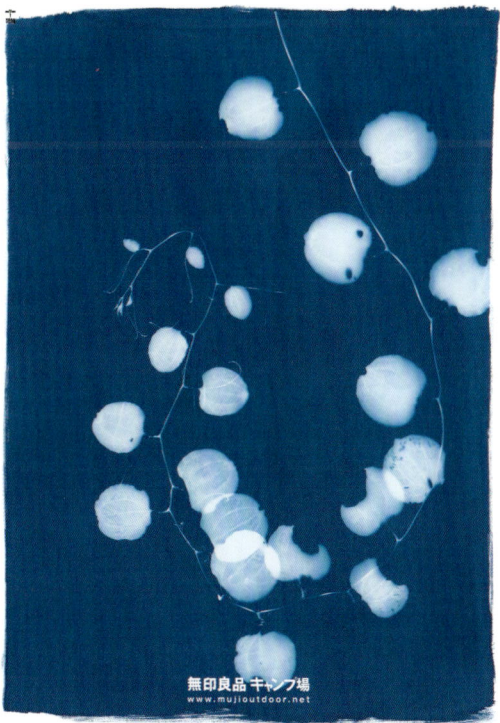
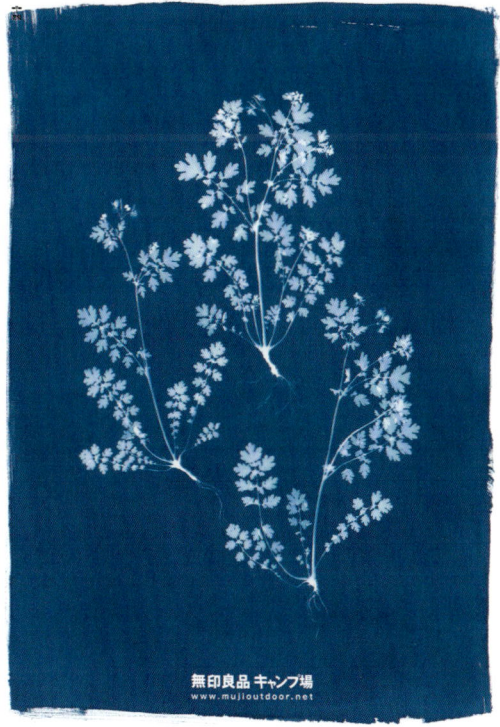

無印良品 キャンプ場
www.mujioutdoor.net

新村則人

MUJI CAMPGROUND "BLUE PRINT"

About 15 years ago, Norito Shinmura received a book on plants from New York. Printing negative images of plants in blue instead of black and white got him interested in the style. When he saw that photographer Michael Feather used this style, he wanted to collaborate with him. In the process, the pressed flowers emerge vividly against a deep blue background, showing the wonders of the fusion of nature and science. A limited-edition collection of blueprint originals produced by the bookbinder Tachiko Ohira, was then released.

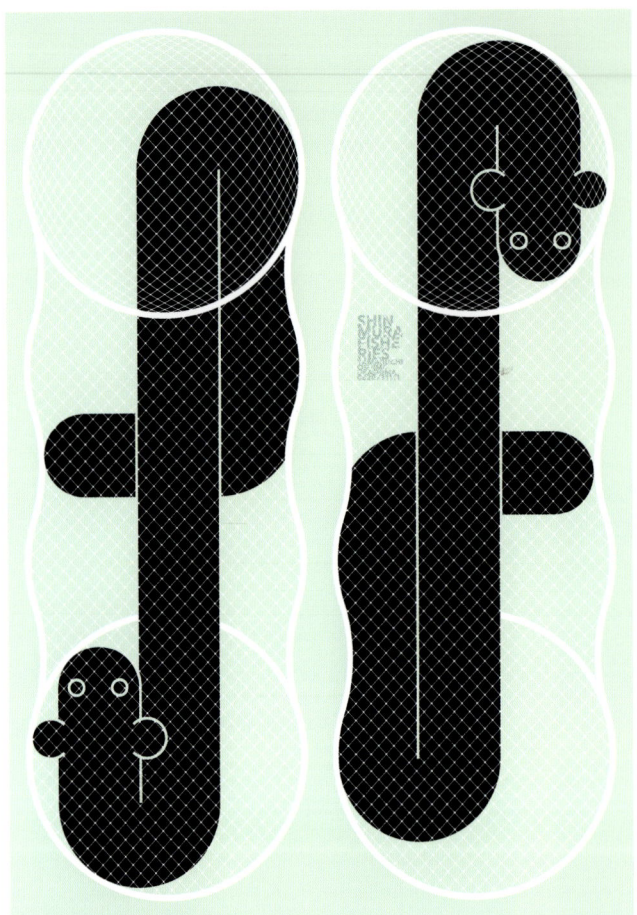

SHINMURA FISHERIES "FISH BASKET"

In the Seto Inland Sea, where the waves are calm, people sink fish baskets into the sea for fishing. Inspired by this, Shinmura decided to put fish and baskets on the poster. The staff member Kosuke Mizoguchi illustrated the baskets. The fish, which is deformed, makes the illustration more interesting and attractive.

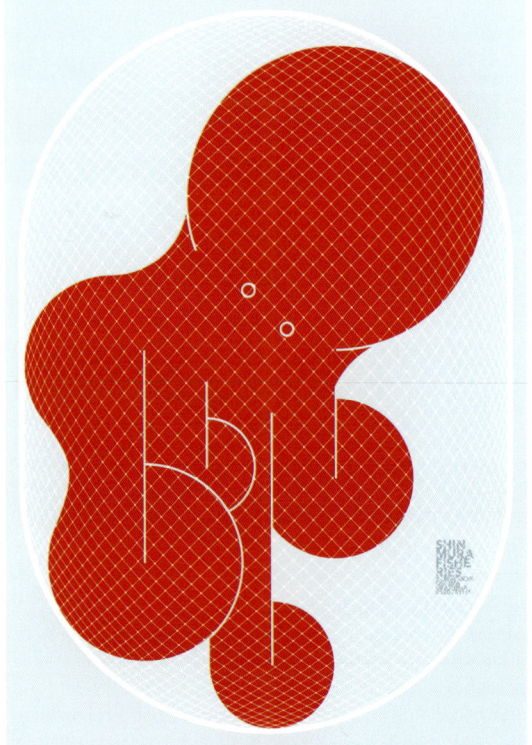

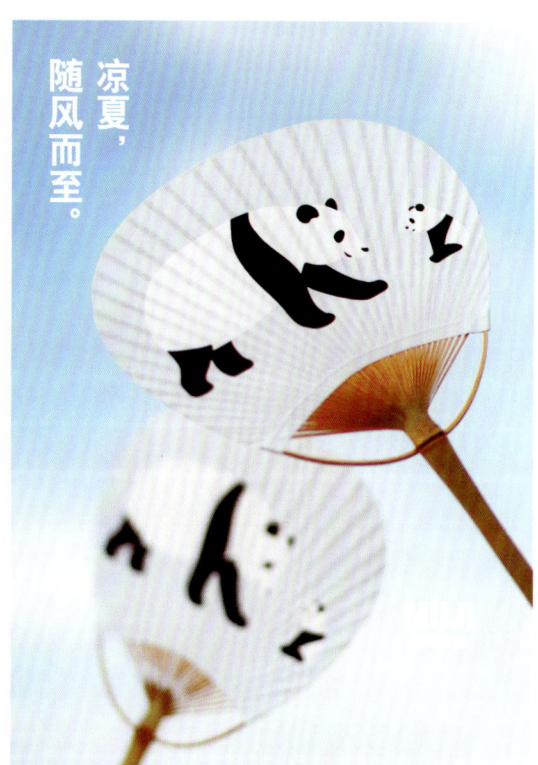

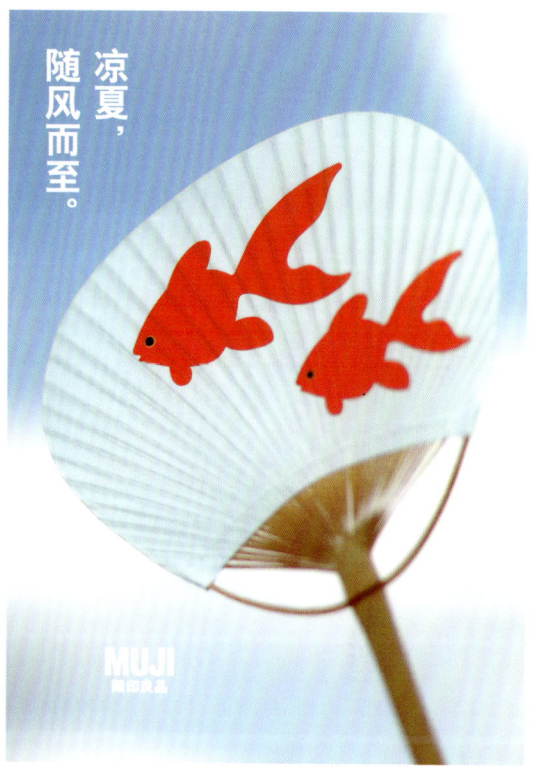

MUJI SHANGHAI

These mugs and bags are sold at MUJI China. The illustrations created by the designer Niwano are popular with customers.

新村則人

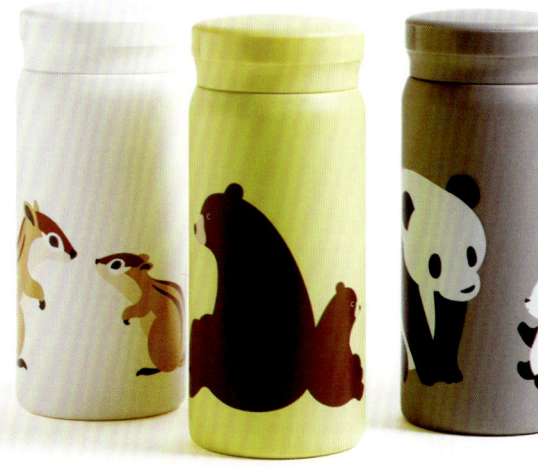

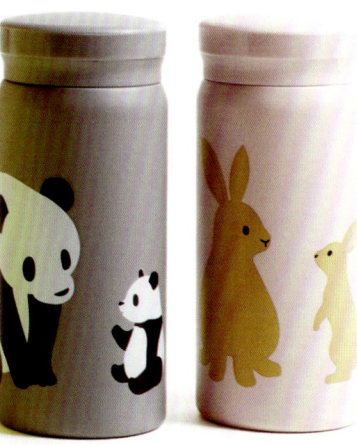

From a graphic designer's point of view, a piece of work should be beautiful in form and novel in visual communication, even if the media is different. From a social perspective, graphic design needs to contribute more to society. My goal is to achieve both of these at a high level as this equals good work and good products.

Yoshiaki Irobe

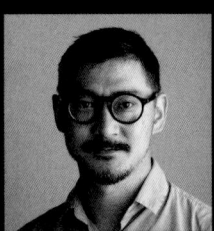

Yoshiaki Irobe was born in Chiba. He completed a master's course at the Tokyo University of the Arts. Being the head of Irobe Design Institute, he works as a graphic designer and art director. He has won numerous domestic and international design awards, including the Yusaku Kamekura Award, the ADC Award, the Japan Sign Design Award (SDA Award), the JAGDA New Designer Award, and the One Show Design Gold Pencil. He is also a member of AGI, the Japan Design Committee, Tokyo ADC, and JAGDA.

Q Could you share your overall impression of Japanese graphic design?

A Looking back, there is a tendency to focus on flatness, as in the flat expression represented by the Rinpa school. The design language of Japan is unique and it was developed along with the rise of the domestic economy and I think it has evolved in a unique way that differs from the international styles of Europe and the United States.

Q What do you think of the influence of the Japanese aesthetic heritage, social culture, and graphic design education? How do they work into your design philosophy and practice?

A Japan's traditional aesthetics and cultural atmosphere have developed by incorporating various cultures through trade with the continent and re-editing them. I believe that the skillful incorporation of different cultures and the art of re-editing are unique to Japan.

Regarding the education system, it is different these days. The Japanese design education I received was not as well developed as it is now. Meeting talented creators of my age was a great experience for me and I believe it influenced me.

Q What is your focus when you are turning a design proposal into actual work?

A We value the entire process from beginning to end. Design is always a series of unique encounters with new clients, issues, and regional characteristics. We believe this is the fun of design and we always want to carry out the process of research, conception and proposal following the unique characteristics of the client, then execute the proposal accordingly.

Q In the visual identity for Ichigaya Letterpress Factory, the use of movable type and book silhouette fits the theme well. Could you share your design concept with us?
Were there any difficulties when doing the project?

A We wanted to create a flexible visual identity with a background of silhouettes of type and books drawn isometrically and characters that could be freely reconfigured so that the VI could match the various topics of the exhibition. We wanted the VI to not only function as a symbol, but also to immerse itself into the space of the exhibition, creating a fusion between the VI and the pavilion. We put great effort into reproducing the type's texture for the signage system.

Q We feel the uniqueness of Sony Park through the visuals of the exhibition. What was the overall design concept? Did you try to build connections among these exhibitions or distinguish them from each other?

A Ginza Sony Park is a free and open space that has a street-like atmosphere with rough materials like exposed concrete and the grout between the tiles. We used a variety of rough expression techniques, such as stickers with pop colors, free directional typography ignorant of the horizontal axis, and sprayed graphics for street art. Though there were some restrictions, we were able to create an experimental expression that could only be done with the creative background of Sony.

色部義昭

Q   You value the bonding between people and their surroundings. When designing signage systems for spaces of different functions, how do you observe, research, and come up with solutions that suit their users?

A   The first step is to analyze the environment by researching the materials used, their shapes, and their differences from the surroundings. Meanwhile, we analyze the priority of the sign's legibility. For example, the priority of sign legibility differs with transportation facilities, which embrace quick movement and cultural facilities or lodging facilities, where emotions are valued. The number of people using the sign and the size of the space matter, too. We always try to provide the best solution for the environment.

Q   You have done many projects that combine branding identity with a signage system. Materials used to make signs are usually thick and heavy, in contrast to thin and light materials for branding products. Take TokyoYard as an example. What is the key to maintaining consistency between these two components?

A   TokyoYard is characterized by its originally developed brand-specific typeface. The typeface is designed to symbolize the city's policy, to be playable. We incorporated the texture of a steel frame to echo the manufacturing features of the street. The key color is a rust-proof reddish-brown that comes from the rust-proof covering of the bare steel frame. The use of this distinctive lettering and key color allows for a natural fusion and textural harmony between paper and steel.

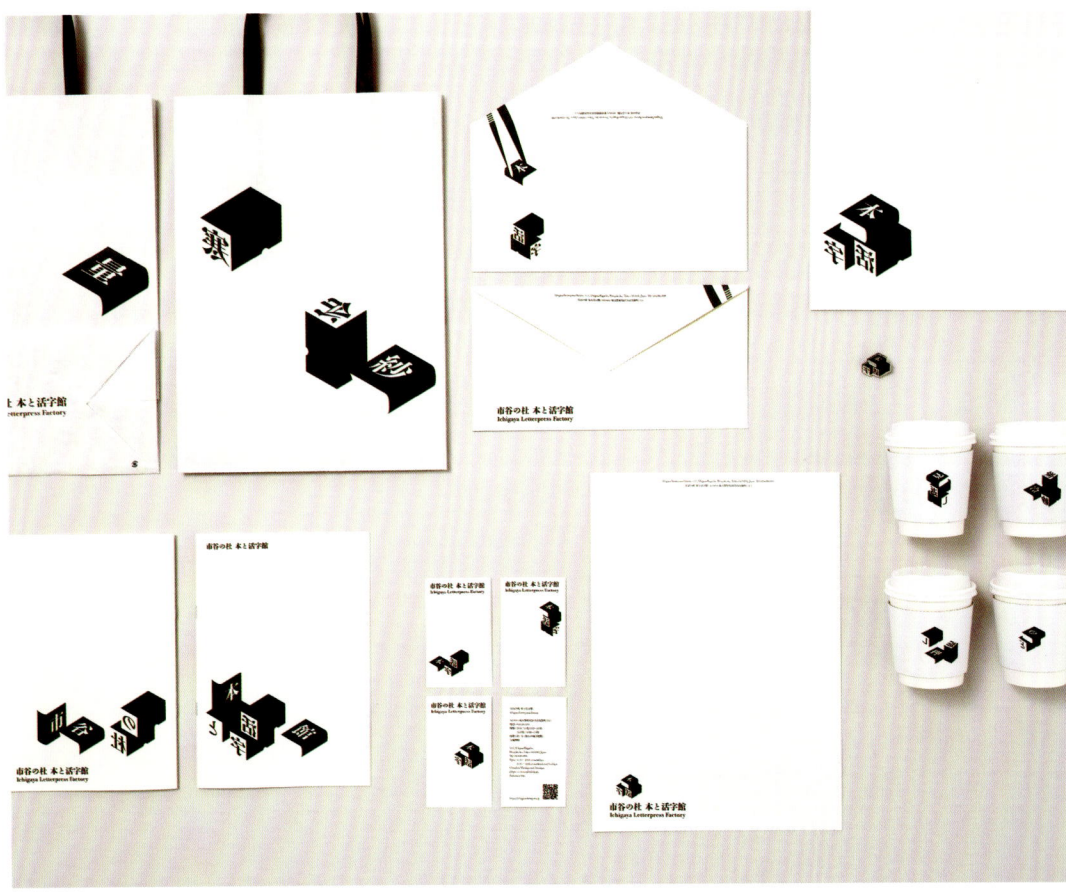

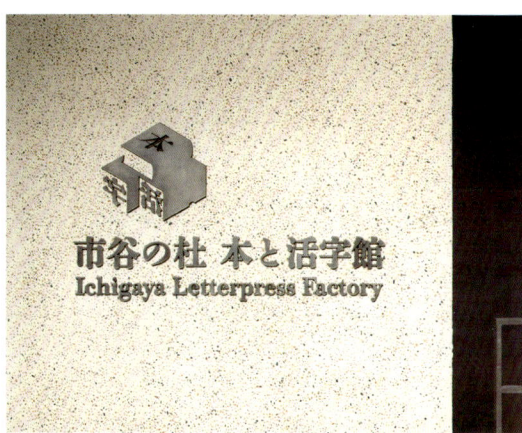

ICHIGAYA LETTERPRESS FACTORY

The Ichigaya no Mori Book and Type Museum is a partial reproduction of a letterpress printing factory, which is the origin of Dai Nippon Printing Co., Ltd.'s business. The museum exhibits and introduces the processes from letter design and type casting to printing and bookbinding. The VI system is dynamic. The silhouettes of the type and books, drawn isometrically, express the physical properties and weight of the books and give a sense of the individuality of the facility. Inside the restored Taisho era-building, the designers created a sign with elaborate reproduction of metal type.

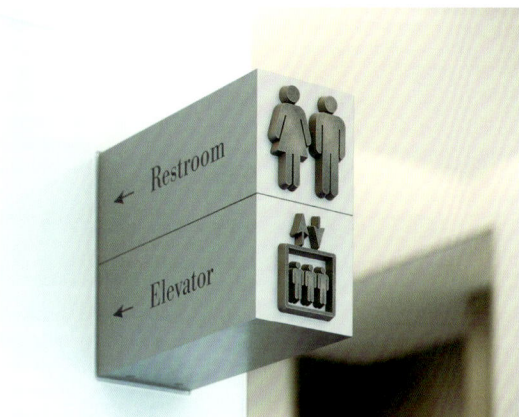

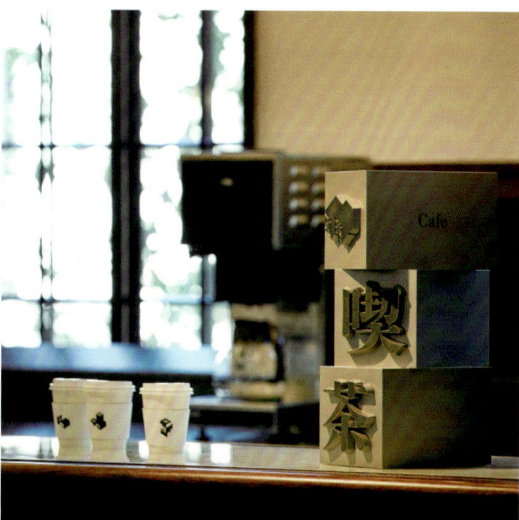

色部義昭

Q You used motion graphics in the rebranding project for the Chinese fashion brand LESS. Compared with graphic design that is normally static, is there anything you need to consider when presenting the concept with motion graphics?

A Motion graphics have become a more effective communication tool than ever before because of signage and social networking. Graphic design, which conveys the voice of the brand, also seems to be more important as the daily contact points between the brand and brand users are increasing. Nowadays, brand logos and graphic design renewal are the channels for brands to update information to their users and I believe one of the best ways is through motion graphics. When we create motion graphics we try not to be descriptive, but to emphasize the emotional aspects such as the rhythm and quality of movements.

Q The branding identity you designed for the Spanish furniture brand kettal is also used on social media. Are there any adjustments to make in the design strategy when there are multiple platforms to present the brand?

A The rebranding of kettal began by redefining its brand strategy. We began by taking kettal's core values, including creative, premium, timeless, and human, then inspected and reported on whether they were being expressed in the catalog, web, packaging, social media, and uniforms. From there, we created a massive guide of more than 100 pages.

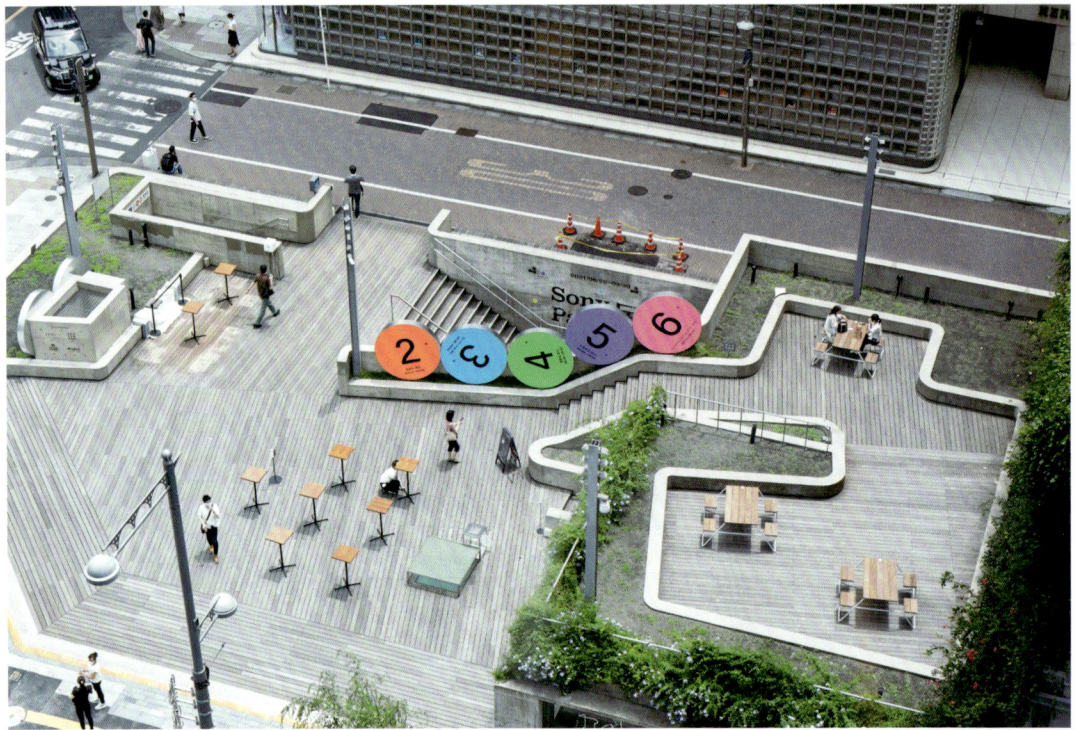

Yoshiaki Irobe

Q The design techniques, context, and scenarios have changed drastically along with the development of technology and the internet. What do you think graphic designers should do to face the changes?

A Graphic design as a way of visual communication through colors and shapes has developed along with human sensation, so I believe that it remains universal as long as the way human sense does not change significantly. On the other hand, new media are like a canvas on which new expressions are created. Graphic designers should view changes in means, context, and scenarios as an opportunity to propose new ideas and should respond proactively to sensory information shared by everyone.

Q What makes good work has been redefined as graphic design continues to develop. In your opinion, what is an excellent piece of work?

A I think we can see the problem from both a graphic designer's perspective and a social perspective. From a graphic designer's point of view, a piece of work should be beautiful in form and novel in visual communication, even if the media is different.

From a social perspective, graphic design needs to contribute more to society. My goal is to achieve both of these at a high level, and this equals good work and good products.

Q In recent years, many creations from Japan have been presented through new media or forms. How do you look at contemporary graphic design in Japan and what is your expectation?

A There should be a precondition that the spread of the Internet seems to be erasing regional disparities and local characteristics in media expression. I believe that visualization for local authenticities, such as regions and products, is the only field for unique evolution to take place in the future. Also, if we eliminate the regional characteristics of Japan, there will be many opportunities for us to play an active role in the intersection with new technologies and services.

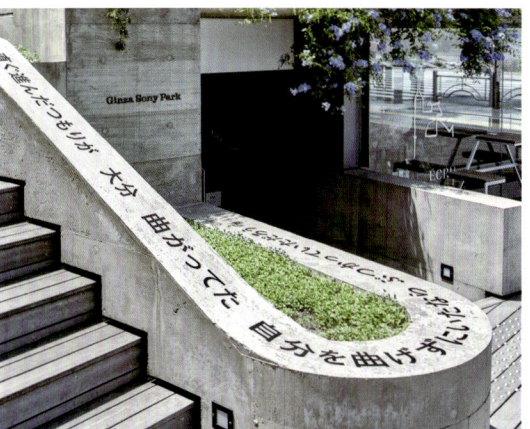

SONY PARK

These are the main graphics, signage, and exhibition graphics for Sony Park Exhibition, the last exhibition at Ginza Sony Park before it was temporarily closed. The exhibition logo, based on the Ginza Sony Park logo, is combined with the colorful numbers one to six to represent the six exhibitions that change every two weeks. The six colored number signs resemble coins rolling down the slope in the park. The design was intended to give a playful and unique street feeling to Ginza Sony Park.

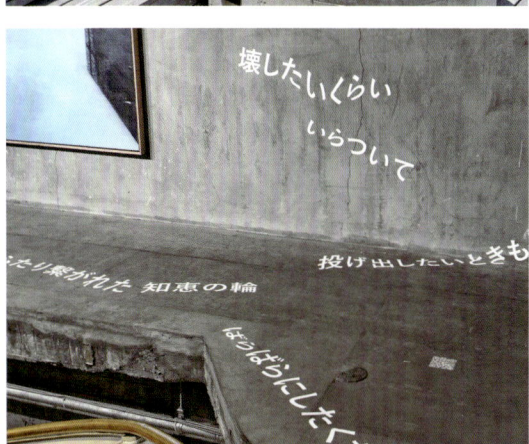

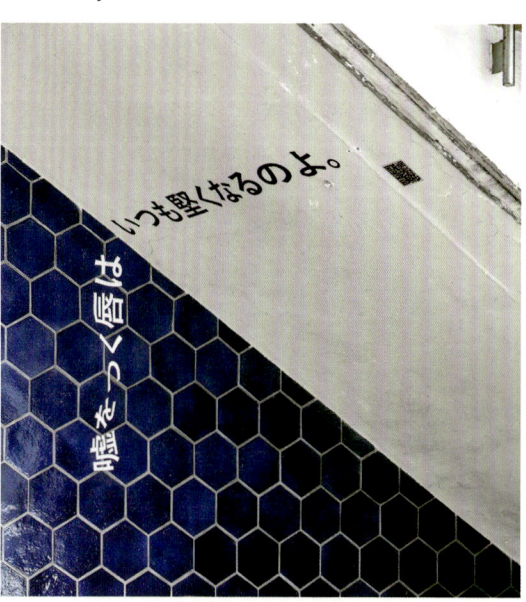

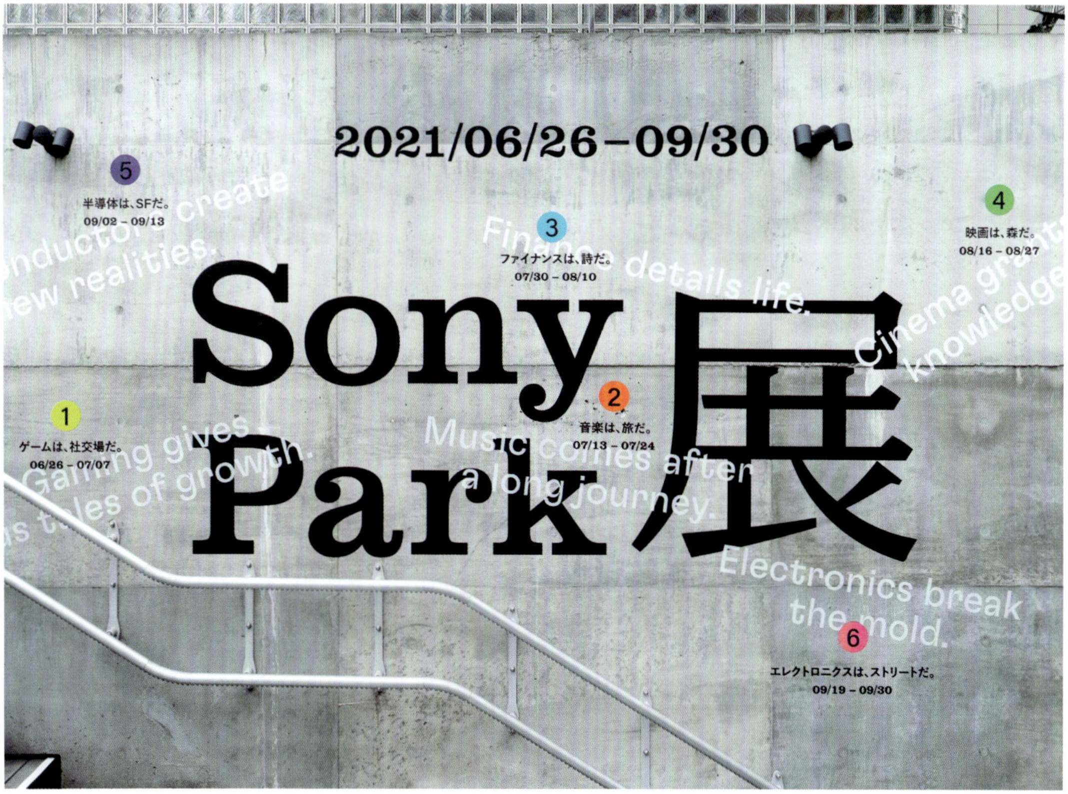

色部義昭

2021/06/26 – 09/30

5 半導体は、SFだ。
09/02 – 09/13

3 ファイナンスは、詩だ。
07/30 – 08/10

4 映画は、森だ。
08/16 – 08/27

1 ゲームは、社交場だ。
06/26 – 07/07

2 音楽は、旅だ。
07/13 – 07/24

Semiconductors create new realities.

Finance details life.

Cinema grows the knowledge.

Gaming gives us tales of growth.

Music comes after a long journey.

Electronics break the mold.

Sony Park 展

6 エレクトロニクスは、ストリートだ。
09/19 – 09/30

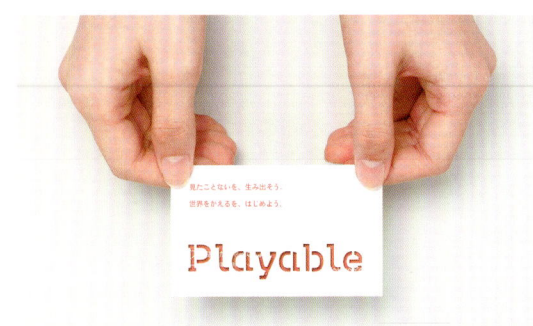

TOKYOYARD

This was a branding project for the area around Takanawa Gateway Station on the JR Yamanote line. Based on the history of the station as a rail depot, the designers designed the "T" and "Y" in the shape of a warehouse. They created a slab serif typeface with hard elements like braces and bouncy curves for a playful vibe. The concept of the area as a "playable" place for creativity and the background as a rail depot both contribute to spreading the image of the area. In this project, even letters, which display the most minute information, are used to introduce the place to every corner of the city.

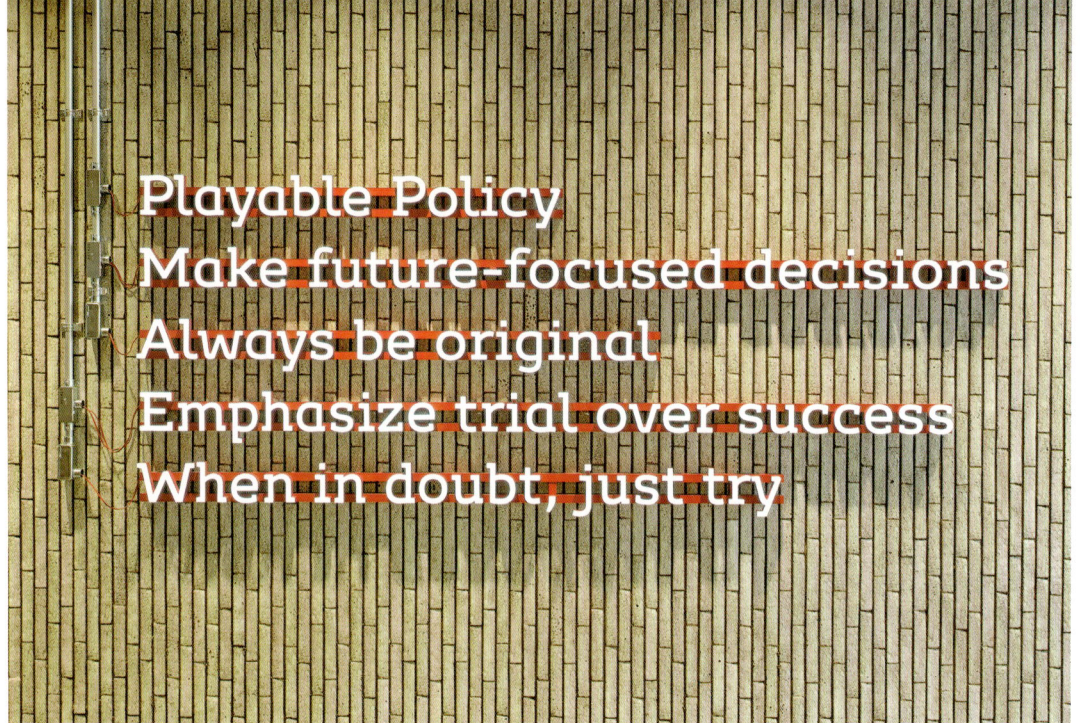

Yoshiaki Irobe

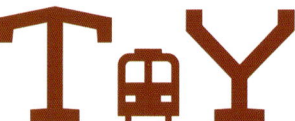

Here we come!
TokyoYard Regular
& *Italic* ☑

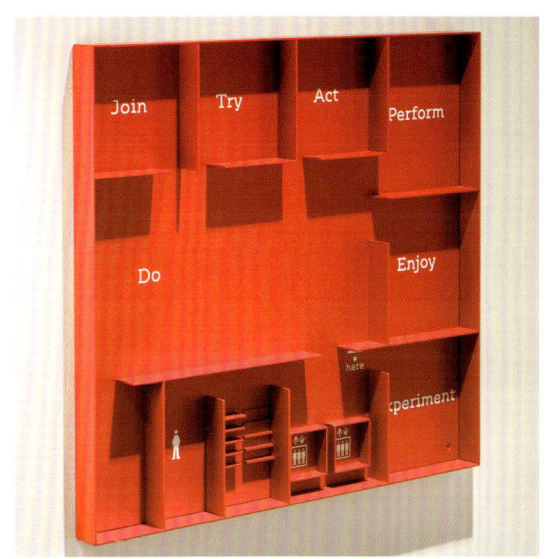

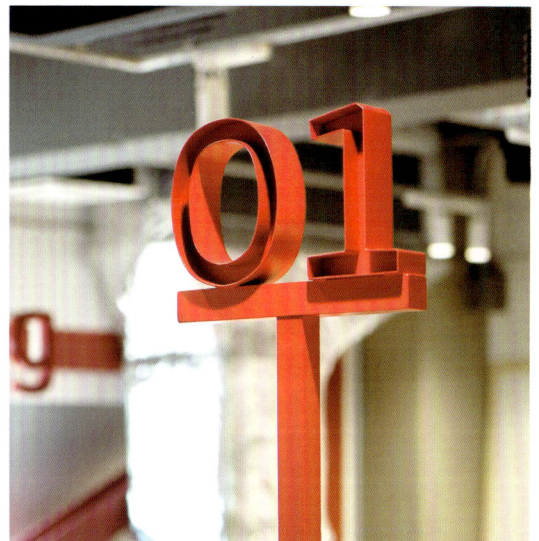

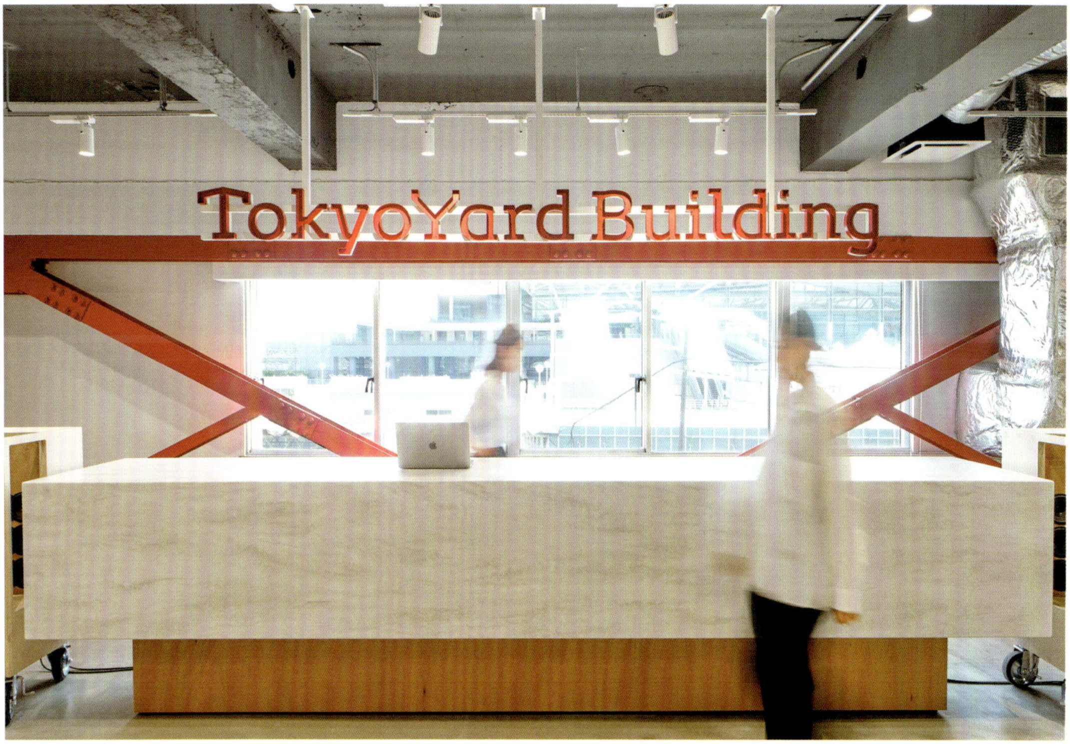

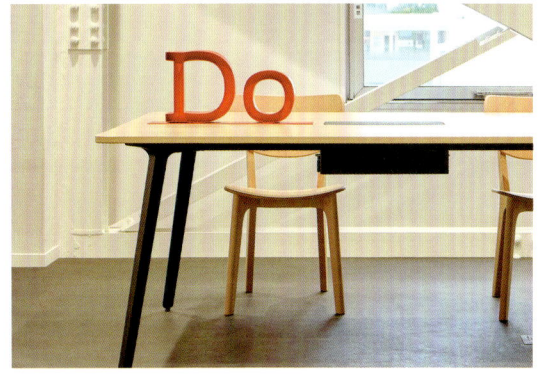

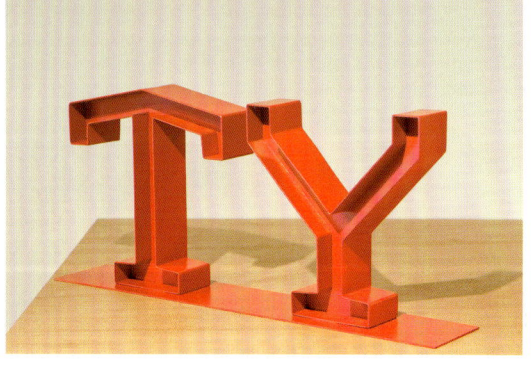

LESS

LESS Bold

SS

BB CC DD EE FF GG
MM OO PP RR SS TT ZZ
bb cc dd ee ff gg oo
pp rr ss tt zz
00 11 22 33 55 66 99

Yoshiaki Irobe

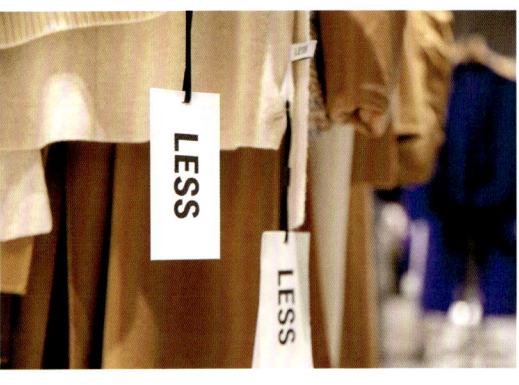

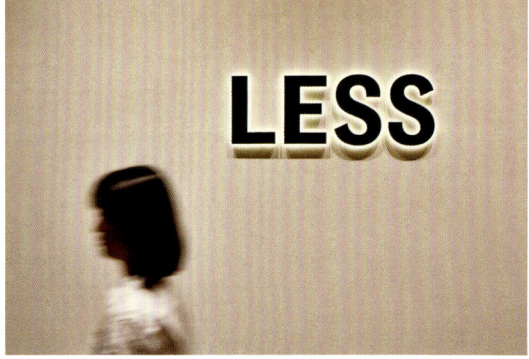

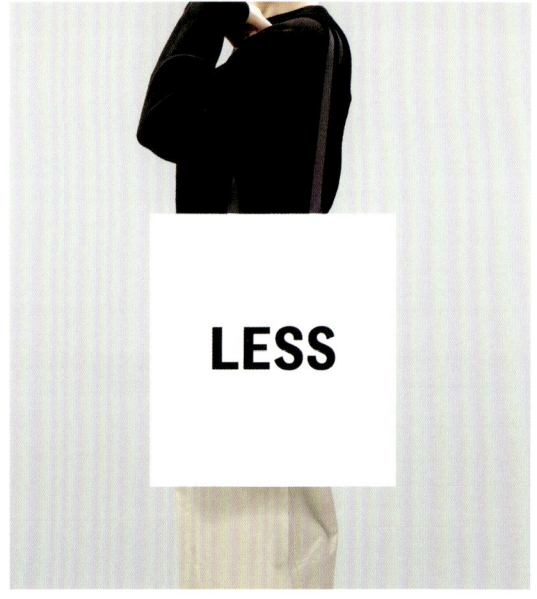

LESS

This was the rebranding of LESS, a women's fashion brand from the Chinese apparel company Jiangnan Clothing Group. The brand name is derived from the phrase "Less is more." The new logo and special typeface express the strength of LESS, which combines universal and individual elements for independent women living in the modern age, while maintaining the precision and elegance of LESS from the past. To align with the brand's neutral impression, the shape of the two consecutive S's were changed to look like a natural object, each of which has a different shape and exists powerfully. The designer extended this idea to the typeface, creating one with many variants.

KETTAL

This is a rebranding project for kettal, a furniture manufacturer in Spain that has been around since the 1960s. From the hard uppercase "KETTAL" to the lowercase "kettal," the designers designed a more mature and humanistic shape for the name and made it look like a piece of furniture on the ground. In addition to the print media, the guidelines for all visual elements such as typography, layout, color system, drawing, and photo direction for digital media, including social media and video, were meticulously designed to create an innovative and clear brand.

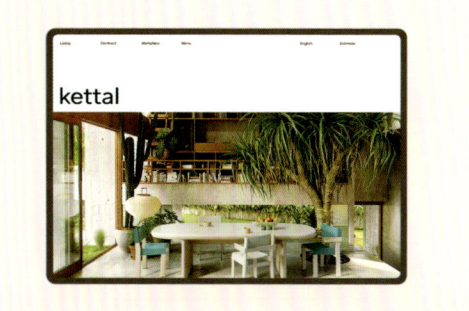

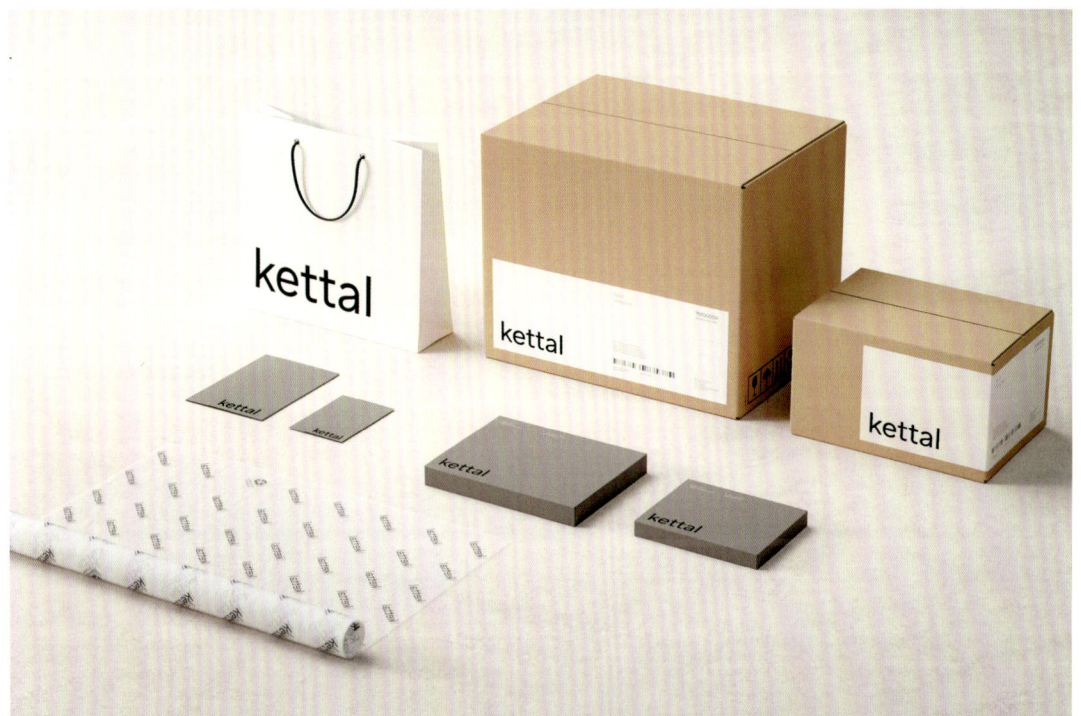

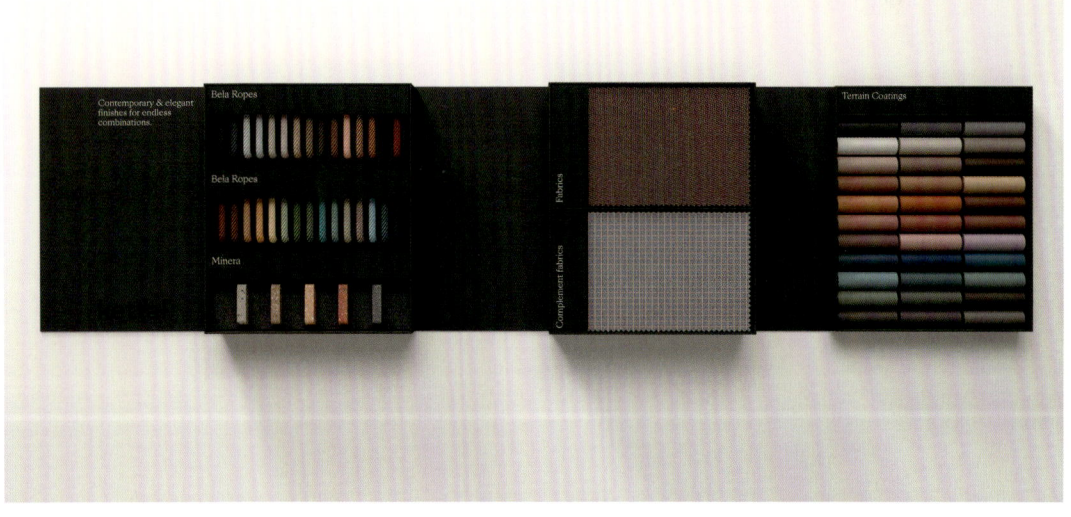

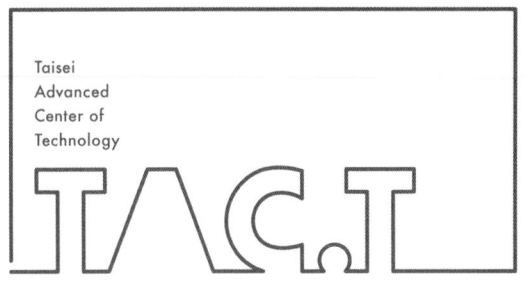

Taisei
Advanced
Center of
Technology

T.A.C.T

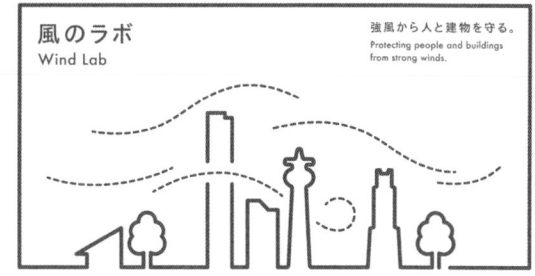

風のラボ
Wind Lab

強風から人と建物を守る。
Protecting people and buildings
from strong winds.

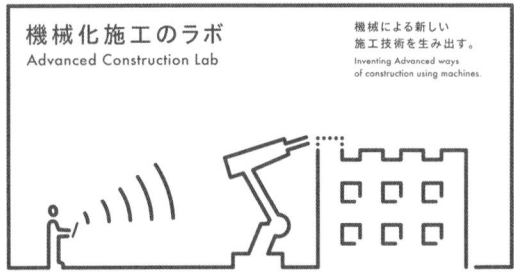

機械化施工のラボ
Advanced Construction Lab

機械による新しい
施工技術を生み出す。
Inventing Advanced ways
of construction using machines.

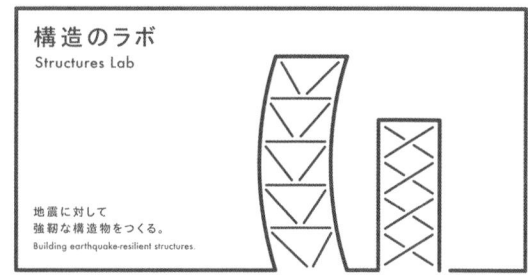

構造のラボ
Structures Lab

地震に対して
強靭な構造物をつくる。
Building earthquake-resilient structures.

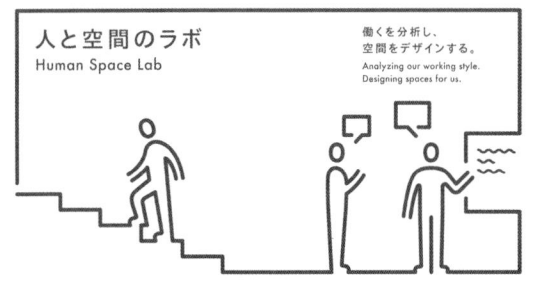

人と空間のラボ
Human Space Lab

働くを分析し、
空間をデザインする。
Analyzing our working style.
Designing spaces for us.

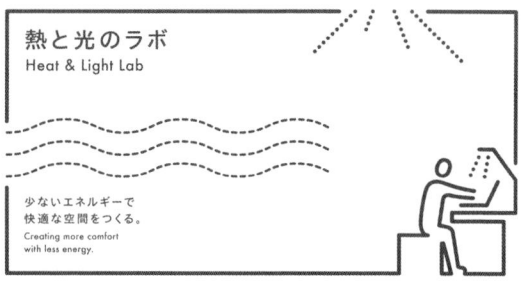

熱と光のラボ
Heat & Light Lab

少ないエネルギーで
快適な空間をつくる。
Creating more comfort
with less energy.

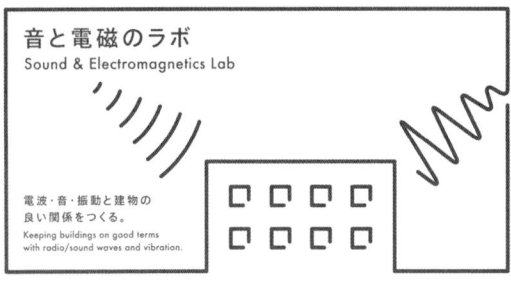

音と電磁のラボ
Sound & Electromagnetics Lab

電波・音・振動と建物の
良い関係をつくる。
Keeping buildings on good terms
with radio/sound waves and vibration.

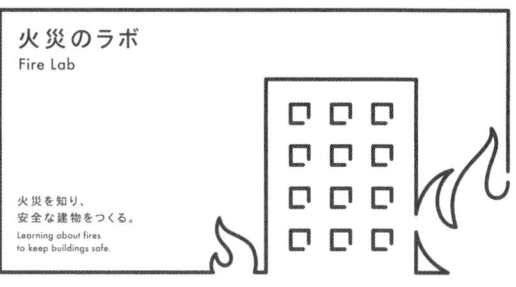

火災のラボ
Fire Lab

火災を知り、
安全な建物をつくる。
Learning about fires
to keep buildings safe.

Yoshiaki Irobe

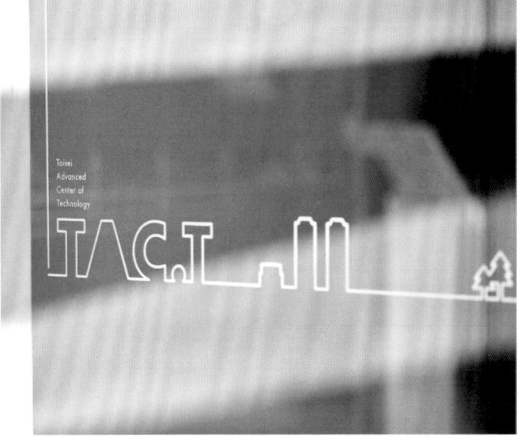

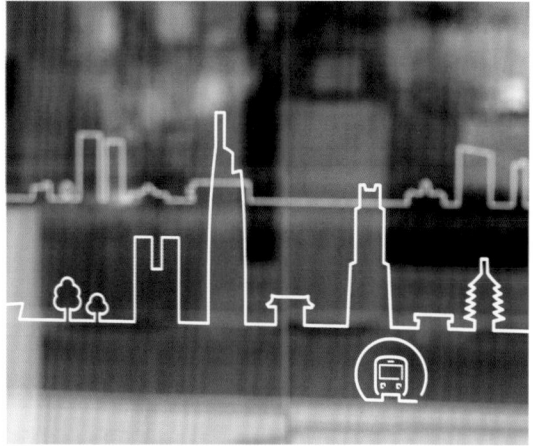

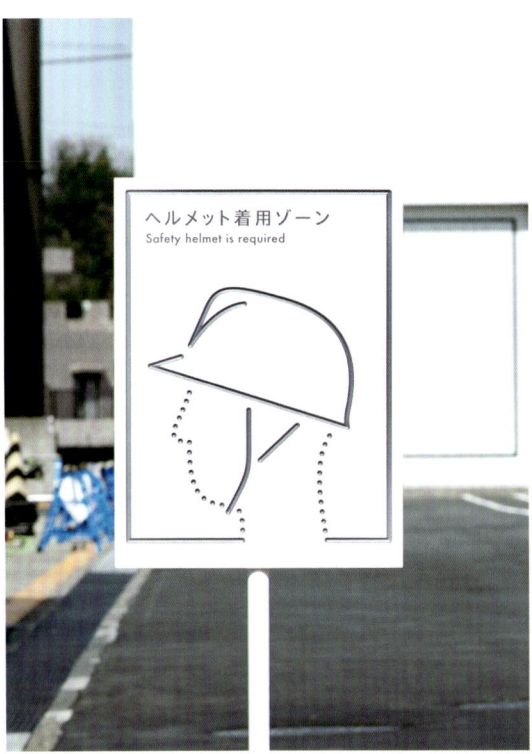

TAC.T

This is a branding project for TAISEI's research and development (R&D) department. A logo "TAC.T (Taisei Advanced Center of Technology)" was developed based on the concept of stimulating the future. Sixty years of R&D pride and potential were connected by a single line in a VI system that depicts continuity. The signage was developed with bright expressions for a fresh and exciting look. The designers created a brand movie and space to present the functions and missions of the 13 laboratories. This aimed to create a common space under the theme of stimulating the future.

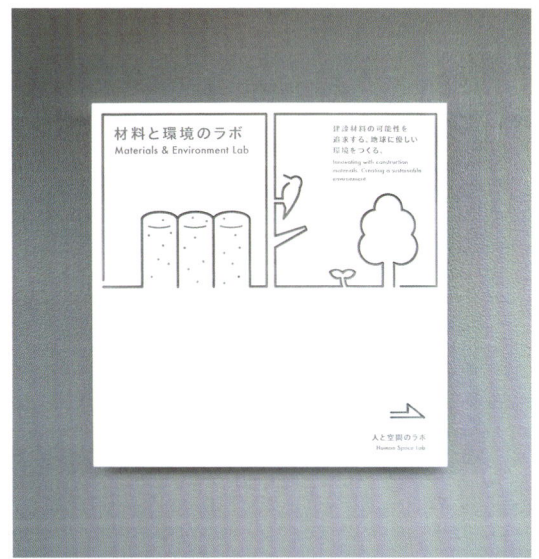

色部義昭

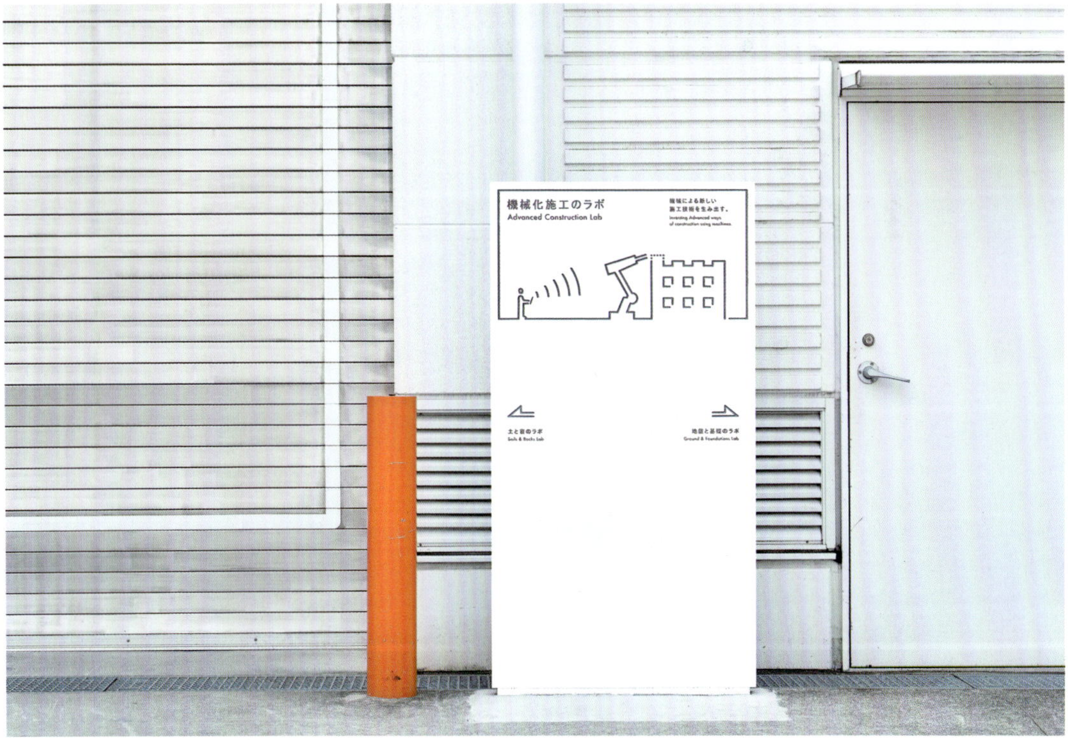

I would like my design
to convey difficult things
in a simple way, simple
things in a deeper way, and
profound things in an easy-
to-understand way.

Daigo Daikoku

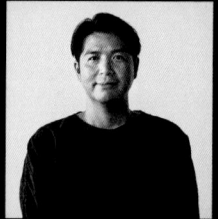

Daigo Daikoku entered the Nippon Design Center, Inc.
after graduating from the Kanazawa College of Art in
2003 and started Daikoku Design Institute in 2011. He
moved to Los Angeles in 2018. His interests are art,
lifestyle, and technology and he works closely in the
above fields to create new value. His major awards
include the D&AD, the NY ADC, the Clio Award, One
Show Design, the FRAME Award, the Tokyo ADC Hiromu
Hara Award, the JAGDA New Designer Award, the
JAGDA Award, the SDA Award, and many more.

Q Could you share your overall impression of Japanese graphic design?

A My impression is that many designers show excellence in formative ability and sophisticated expression. Graphic design in Japan is diverse and idiosyncratic. Although the works are not flashy, their details, shapes, compositions, and color schemes are condensed with intended information, attractive, and unique, showing the quality of Japanese design.

Q What do you think of the influence of the Japanese aesthetic heritage, social culture, and graphic design education? How do they work into your design philosophy and practice?

A Japanese design has a well-established tradition and has a great influence on us. Traditional patterns include various motifs from the four seasons, plants, animals, and natural phenomena such as wind, water, and fire. The aesthetic sense fostered by the Japanese culture nurtured my ability to grasp the essence of things.

Q Daikoku Design Institute aspires to create values through simple, clear, and bold design. How do you come up with this working philosophy and vision in your career as a designer?

A Through visual communication, my goal is to move people, to inspire them. Simplicity does not mean less information. To find out the unique feature of an object, I extract the essence and visualize it. By doing so, we can imprint the subject easily on people's minds. The impression extends and flows as an artery does.

Whenever I look at the stones and rivers that have been chipped away over the years, the leaves in different forms, as well as flowers and trees, I am greatly influenced by the naturally occurring shapes and lines that I intuitively find pleasing. This inspires how I think.

Q The HIDA exhibition at Japan House Los Angeles was a project that presented Japanese woodwork traditions. How do you make sure that the information is delivered to the audience from all over the world, while preserving the aesthetics that are unique to Japan?

A If people want to understand Japanese culture, they need to understand its history. However, people with more or less knowledge of Japan understand the context to different extents. For this reason, the exhibition focuses on four keywords—forest, people, time, and technique—to express the regional character of Hida, which boasts the highest percentage of forests in Japan and its woodworking culture.

To stimulate intellectual curiosity, features such as the climate, natural scenes, customs, culture, and the history of Hida are introduced with an emphasis on numbers. And signs are simple and strong, such as those directly imprinted on plywood, to give as much of a forest feel as possible. Many Americans are also interested in woodworking and they viewed the exhibition with great interest. They were surprised by the curved wood, compression techniques, and the completion of high-dimension woodworking without nails or glue.

大黒大悟

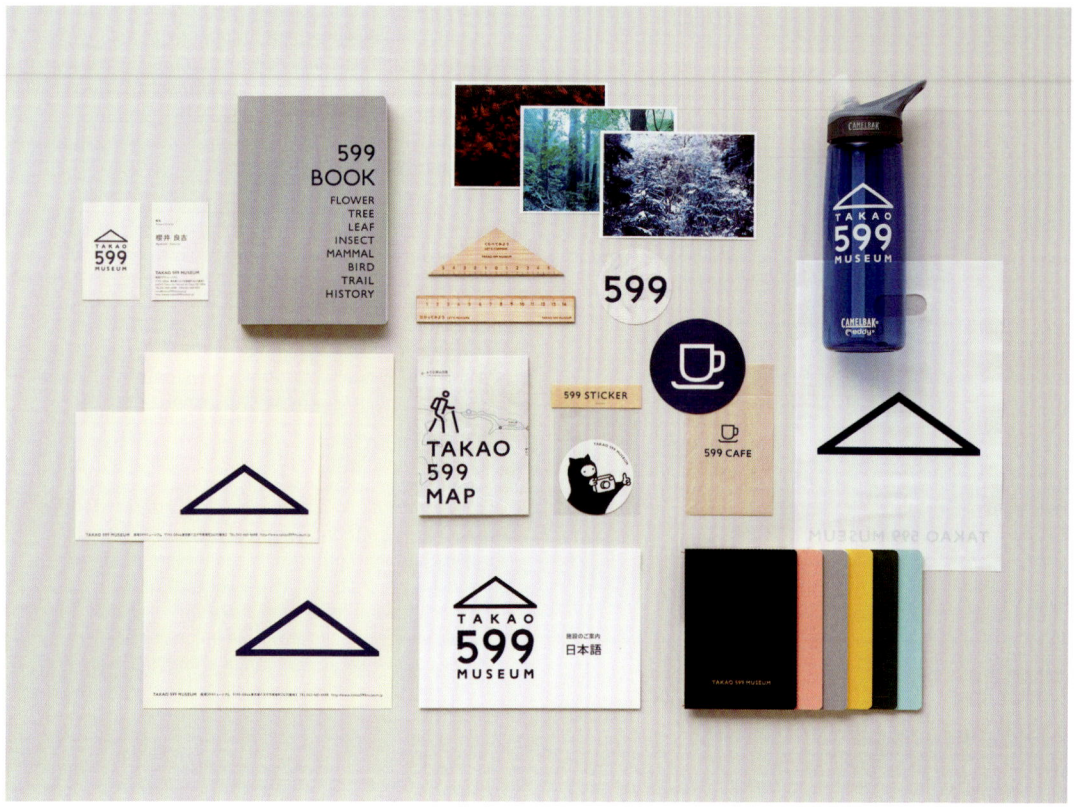

Q *The Art of Bloom* explores the relationship between humans and nature. Could you share the thought process behind putting the idea into practice?

A *The Art of Bloom* is an exhibition about the symbiosis between nature and man. By creating installations that appeal to multiple senses—with the help of sound, light, smell, and touch—people can experience their relationship with nature in a completely different way. With an ongoing focus on art, lifestyle, and technology, the Daikoku Design Institute does not confine itself to one creative area.

When we are designing, we are delivering our perspectives on the world. At the same time, we find out what we can contribute to society. *The Art of Bloom* is a collaboration with Los Angeles-based design firm Intertrend Communications, and we are actively thinking about the value we can bring through this partnership.

Q Design is the combination of graphic design, product design, media, etc. Coordination is not an easy task for a design proposal to be implemented. What are your thoughts on project coordination?

A We believe that a designer is someone who can visualize the way things should be, and the way they should work, rather than simply creating shapes. Consistency is very important to us because the moment when people's hearts are moved is the moment when the dots are connected. We don't want to create something that doesn't have meaning so, in every project, we value the vision and make every effort to consider the people involved.

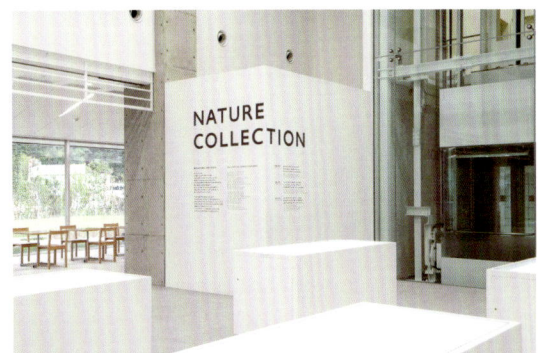

TAKAO 599 MUSEUM

In the Hachioji district at the edge of Tokyo, at an altitude of 599 meters resides Takao Mountain, said to be one of the mountains closest to a city. At its foot stands the Takao 599 Museum, for which Daigo Daikoku is the creative and planning director. With 3 million climbers per year, Takao Mountain is the world's most visited mountain. To best present its allure, the designer sought a system of communication that sparked the viewers' curiosity, creating a unified concept for the space and its architecture, exhibition graphics, and exhibited works. Takao 599 Museum provides a fresh point of view on the bountiful nature of Takao Mountain.

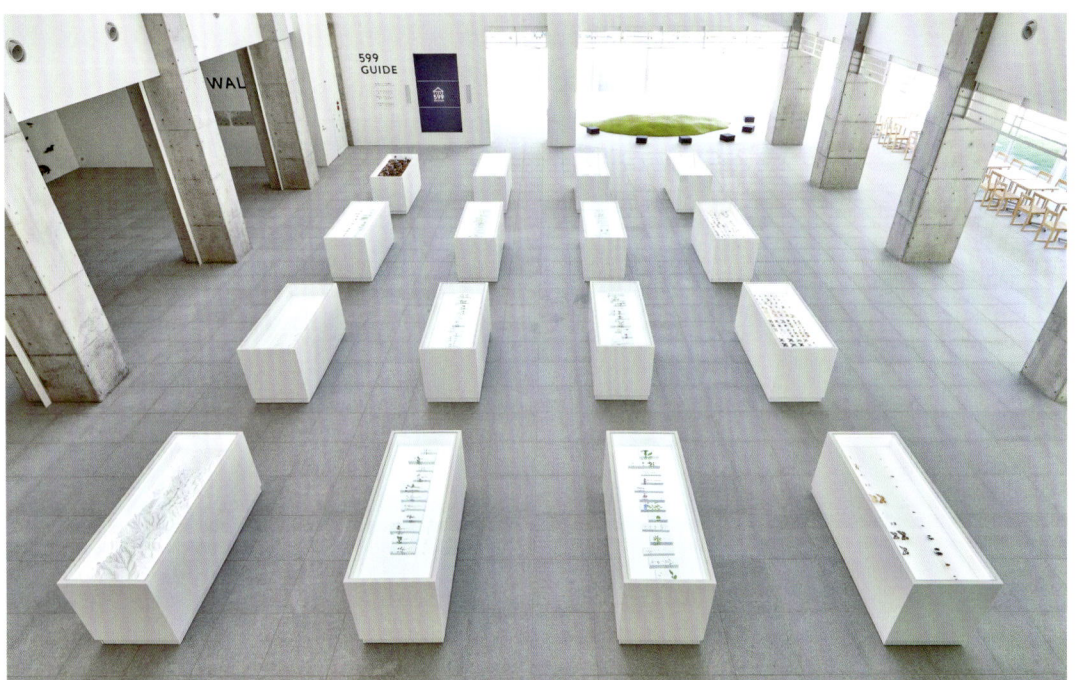

大黒大悟

Pictogram for Mt. Takao

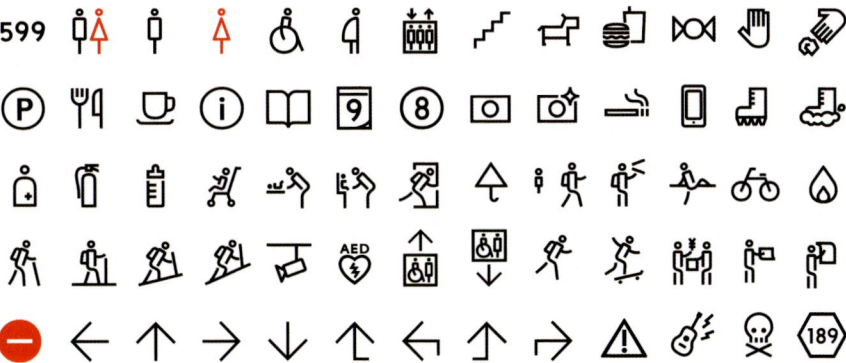

Q We've learned so much about Japanese culture and lifestyle through the project Experience Japan Pictograms. During the design process, how did you decide what elements would represent the Japanese lifestyle?

A Experience Japan Pictograms aims to support the Japanese tourism experience through design. With the theme "the second encounter with Japan," the project aims to convey the attractions of Japan in a more in-depth way. To achieve this, we have thoroughly examined the typical things to do and see in Japan in seven categories, including food, vehicles, history, experiences, landmarks, and so on. As there are 47 prefectures in Japan, we are still updating the pictograms, taking care not to bias visitors towards any particular region.

Q In your opinion, what is the responsibility of a designer?

A Our focus is on contributing to a better society. The era of mass production is over. From now on, we need to understand diversity and start thinking about the global future as if it were our own. I think of myself as a kind of translator. I would like my design to convey difficult things in a simple way, simple things in a deeper way, and profound things in an easy-to-understand way.

Q As a Japanese designer based in Los Angeles, you also take commissions globally. In your opinion, what is the difference between projects from Japan and projects from other countries and regions?

A The objectives of both the Japanese and global projects are the same, but the way they are communicated may differ slightly.

I feel that in the US, people are more straightforward than in Japan. Japan tends to be more subtle and weave in more details. This is reflected in the design, as communication must be as to the point as possible to convey what you want to say. Telling people with diverse cultural backgrounds a story that only a limited number of people can relate to can lead to misunderstandings.

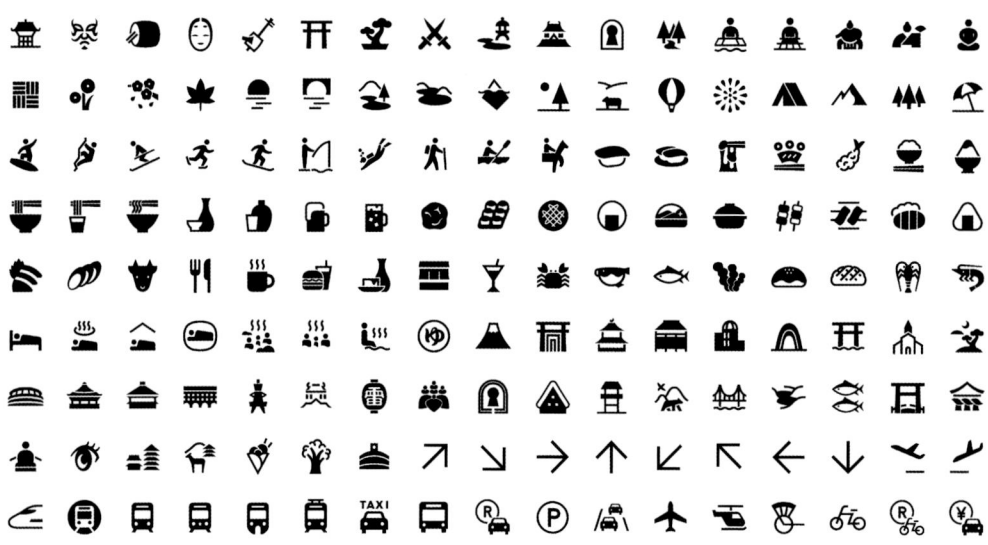

EXPERIENCE JAPAN PICTOGRAMS

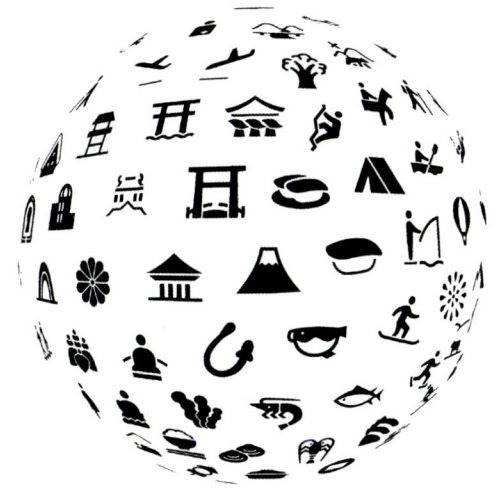

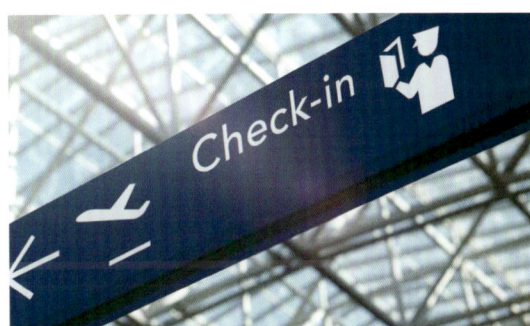

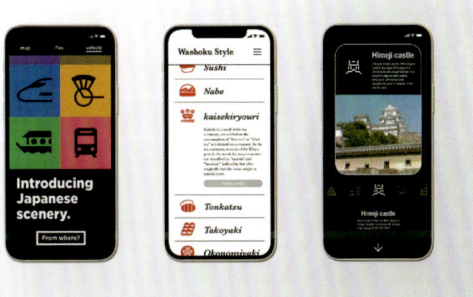

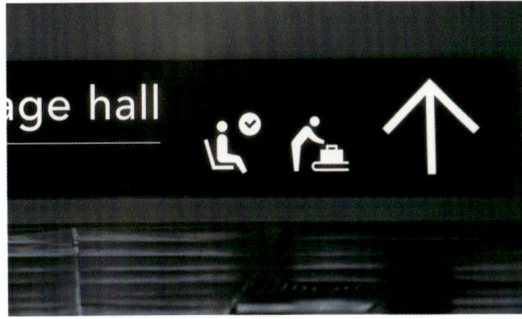

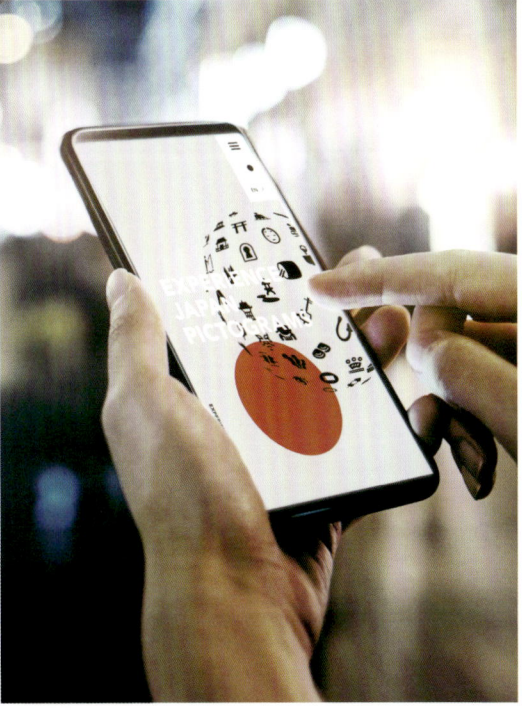

大黒大悟

EXPERIENCE JAPAN PICTOGRAMS

Experience Japan Pictograms are a novel set of visual symbols developed for people of all cultures and ages to enhance their tourism experience in Japan. These uniquely simple and easy-to-understand pictograms are designed under the theme of "the second encounter with Japan" to invite visitors to explore and enjoy Japan a little deeper than before. The pictograms are available for free download from the official website: *https://experience-japan.info/en*

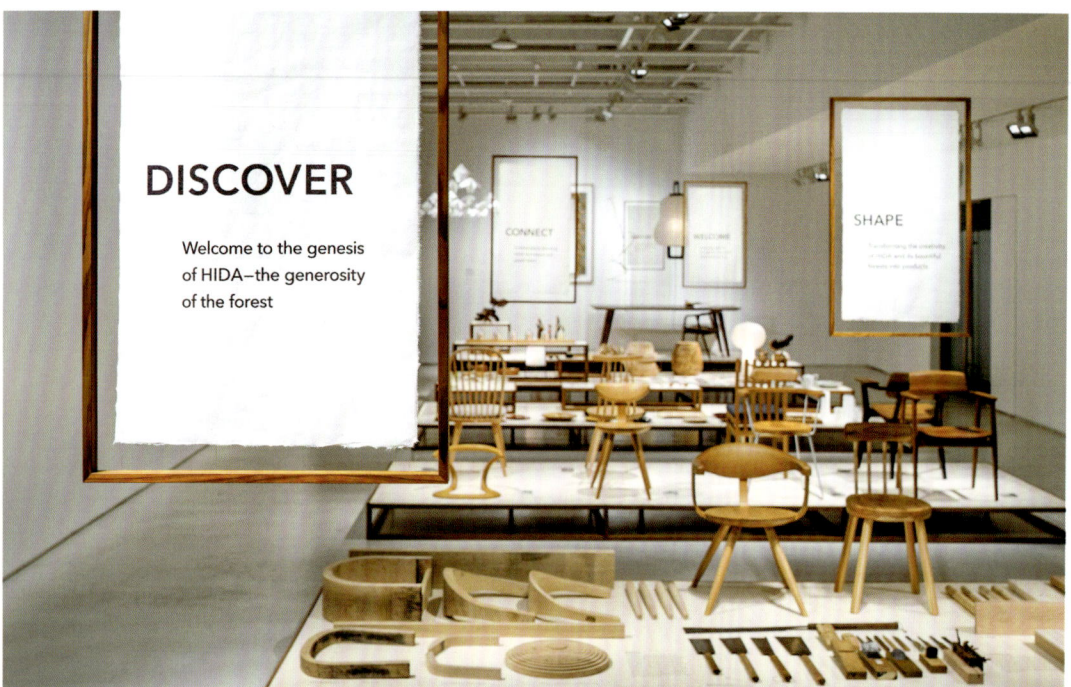

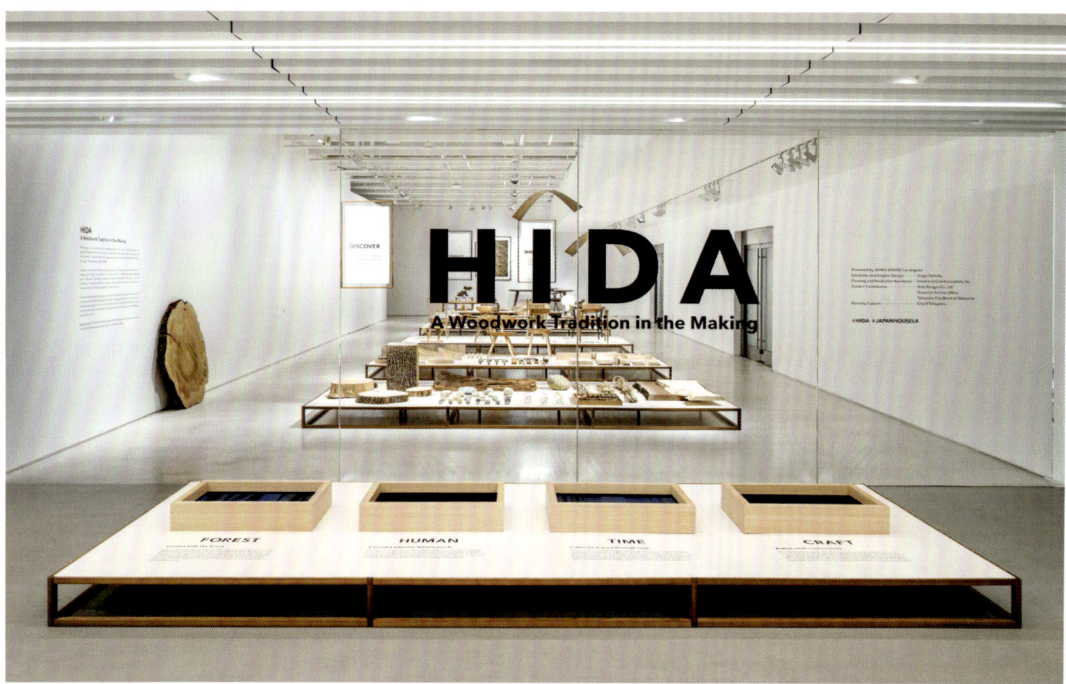

Daigo Daikoku

HIDA

In the Hida Takayama region of the Gifu prefecture, Japan, a woodworking tradition dating back more than 1,300 years has been passed on and continually refined, thriving to the current age. *HIDA: A Woodwork Tradition in the Making* explores the core of Japanese aesthetics and craftsmanship through the woodworking tradition of Hida. This exhibition explores the interaction of forest, humans, time, and craft through the products of Hida Sangyo Co., Ltd., one of the oldest furniture manufacturers in Japan. *https://www.japanhousela.com/*

Q Your creations often involve a combination of technology and design. How do you look at the relationship between these two?

A Culture has always progressed through art and science. My design constantly explores the possibilities of communication with the changing and diversifying times. While I understand the appeal of physical objects, I also believe in the power of technology to make a quantum leap forward in the communication of ideas and values. Design and technology may seem to be opposites, but I believe they interact to create the future.

Q Is there anything you want to try or explore in the field of design?

A My design focus is on art, lifestyle, and technology. I am particularly interested in projects that propose sustainable lifestyles, such as projects on environmental issues, diversity, and health. I want to think about how to deal with social issues and contribute to a better society.

Q In recent years, many creations from Japan have been presented through new media or forms. How do you look at contemporary graphic design in Japan and what is your expectation?

A Japanese graphic design is seen worldwide as highly accomplished and sophisticated. The ability to find the uniqueness of an object and give it shape, as well as the composition that places importance on pauses, are aesthetics nurtured by Japanese culture. As the next generation of designers seek new forms of expression within Japan's hybrid culture, mixing both traditional and cutting-edge aspects, we will see an expansion of creative possibilities never seen before.

大黒大悟

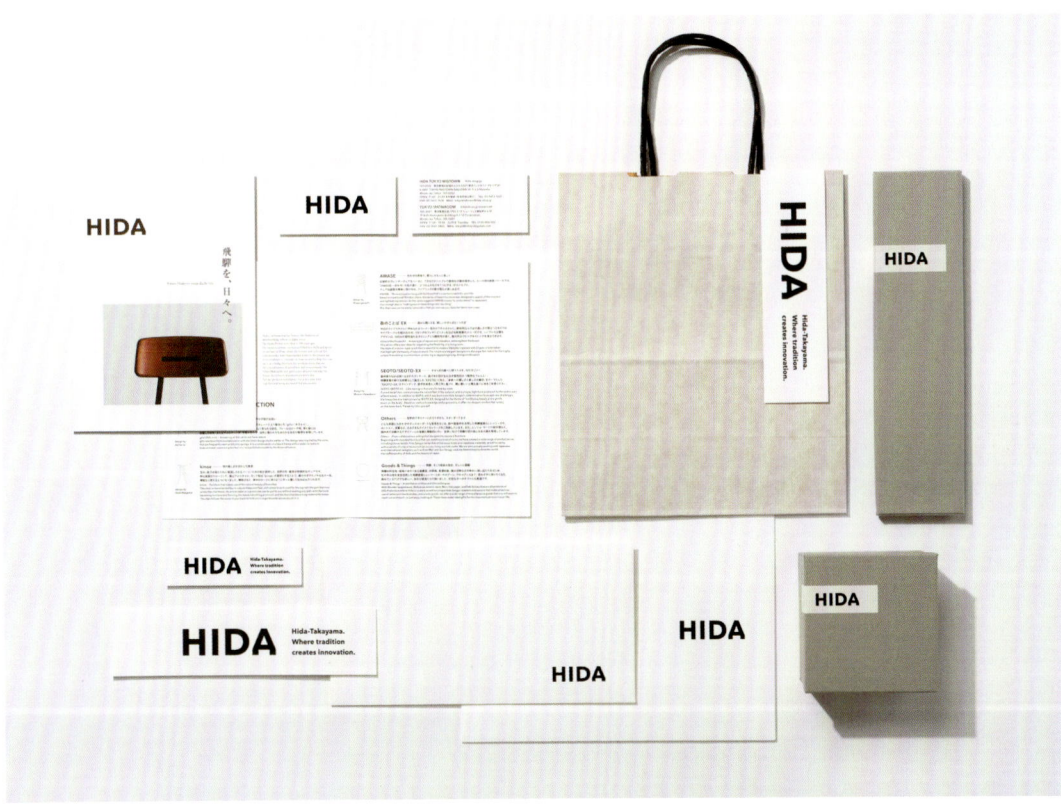

KOSHINO KANBAI

Daigo Daikoku designed the branding and art direction for Ishimoto Shuzo, a sake brewery in Kameda-go, Niigata prefecture. Koshino Kanbai, the brewery's signature sake series, is one of the most famous and prestigious sakes in Japan. To communicate the brand's quintessential value, the logo, statement, packaging, and naming were developed carefully under a unified concept.

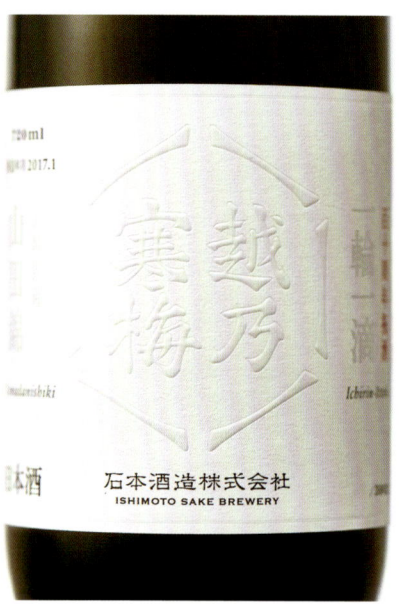

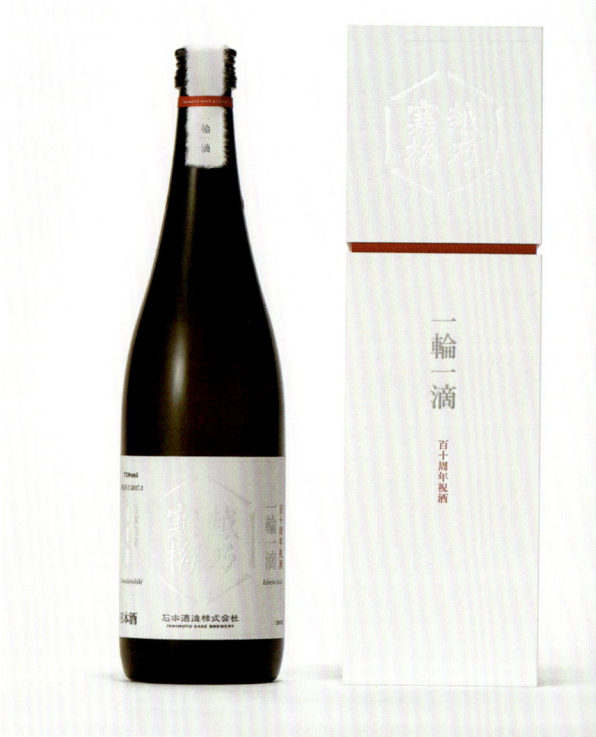

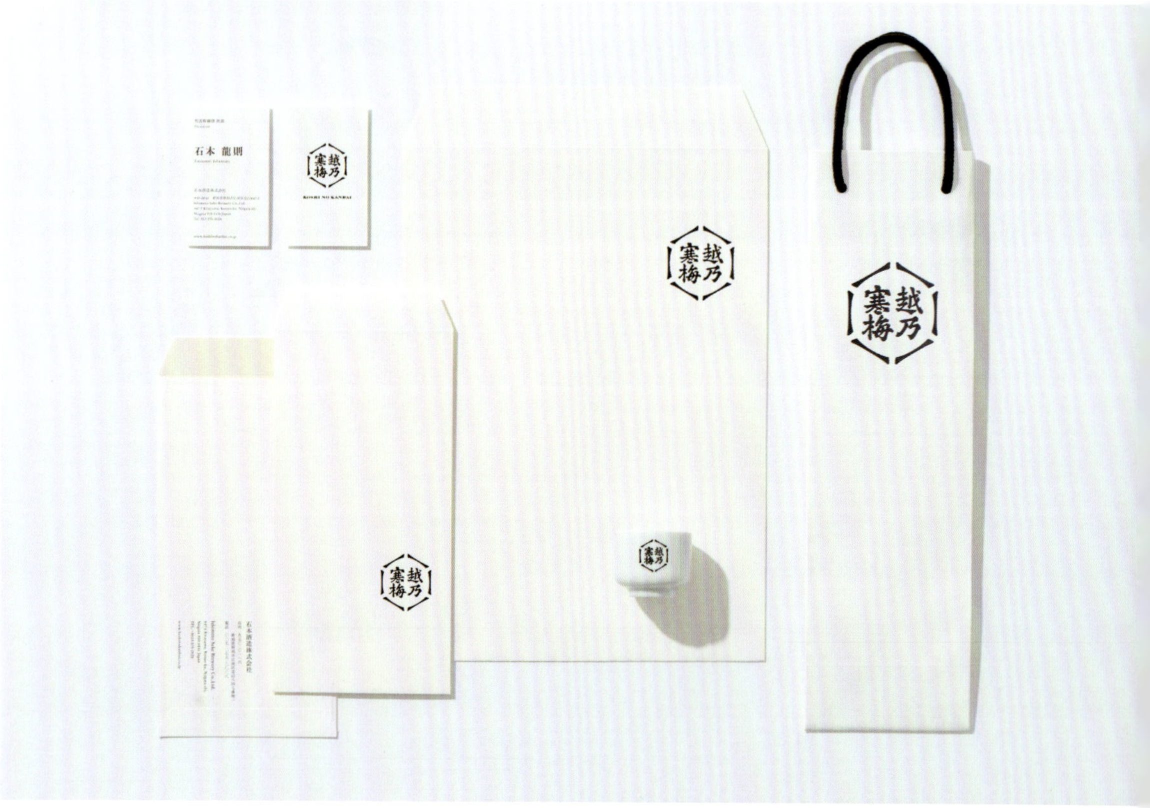

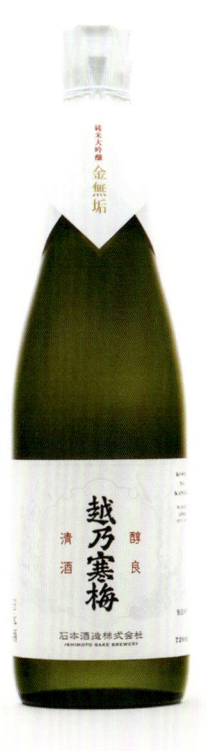

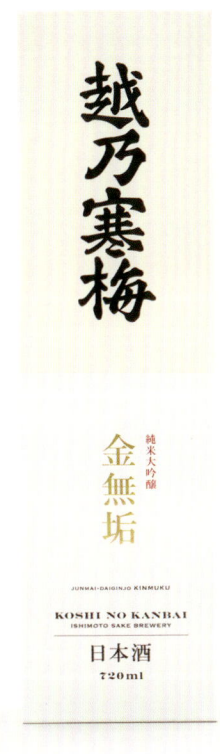

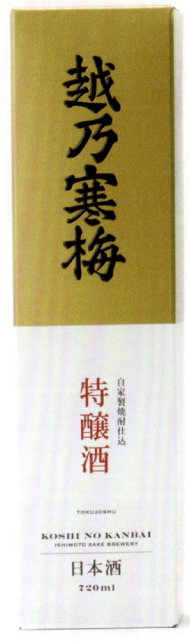

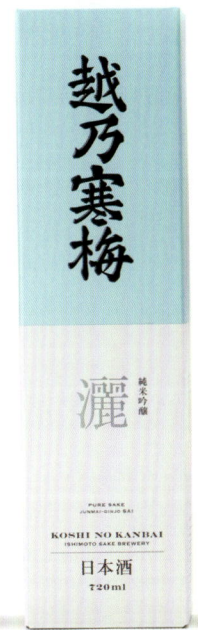

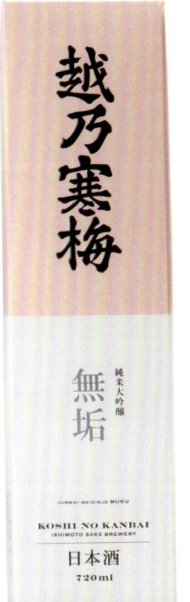

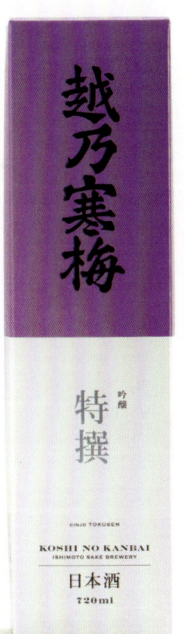

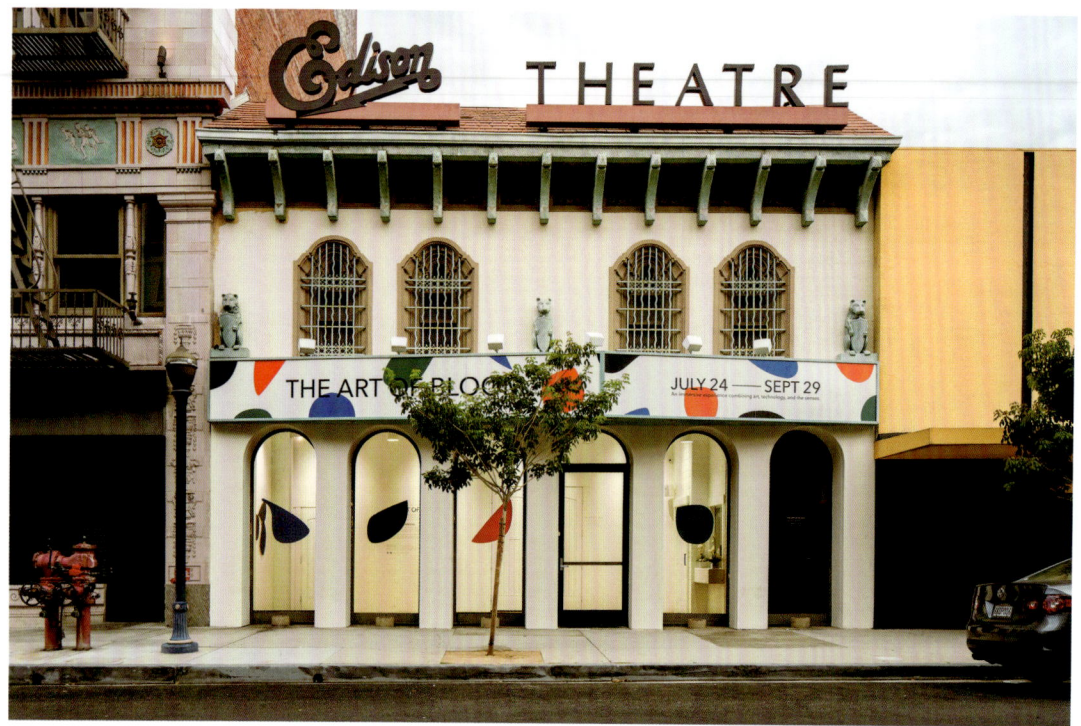

Daigo Daikoku

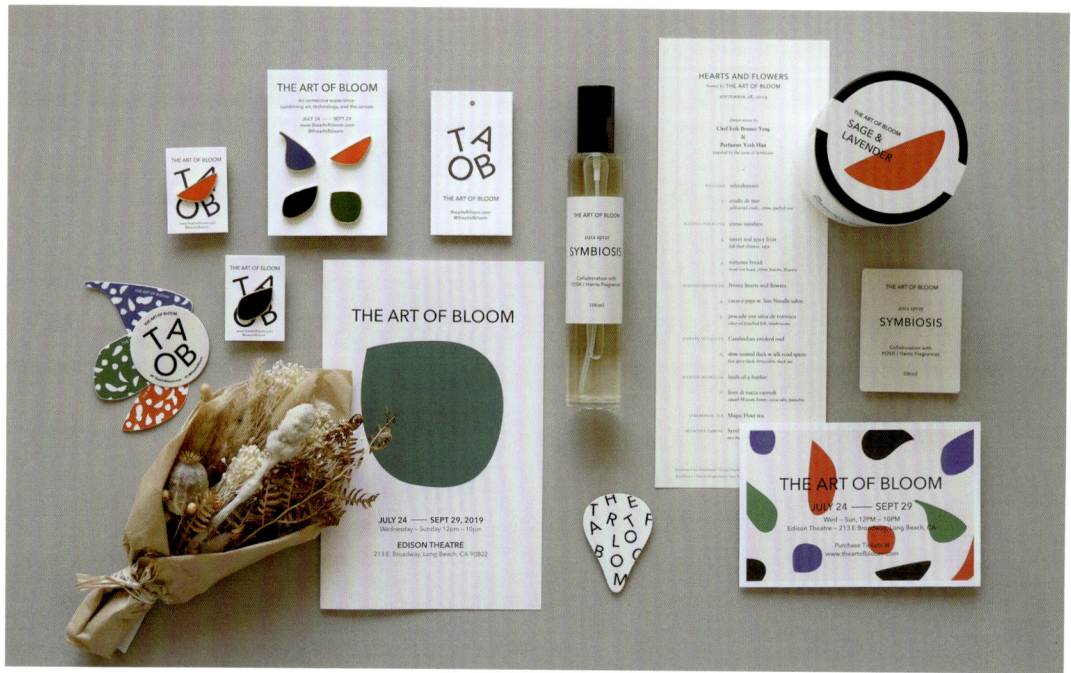

THE ART OF BLOOM

The Art of Bloom is a multi-sensory exhibition that focuses on the symbiotic relationship between humans and nature. Throughout history, people have seen flowers as vessels to project a variety of meanings and messages. Humans and flowers are stimulated by one another, reacting to each other to nourish and grow. This special relationship is conveyed through the theme "symbiosis" in the two installations of *The Art of Bloom*. *https://theartofbloom.com/*

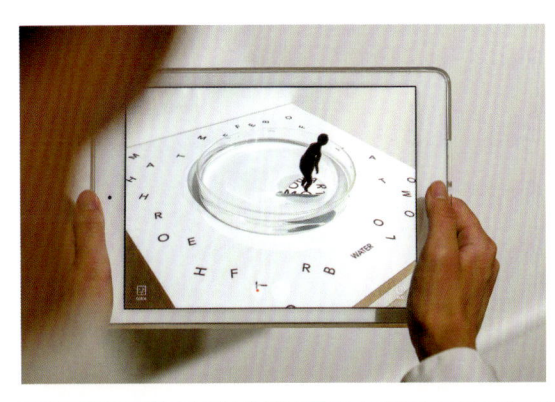

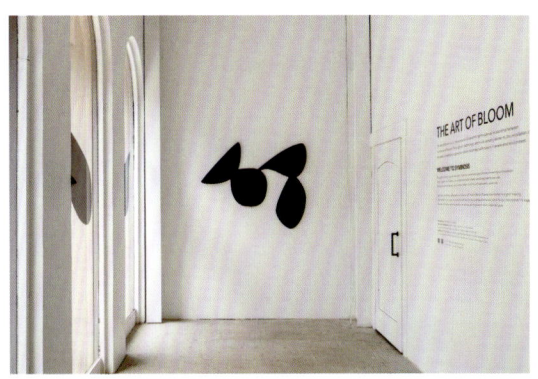

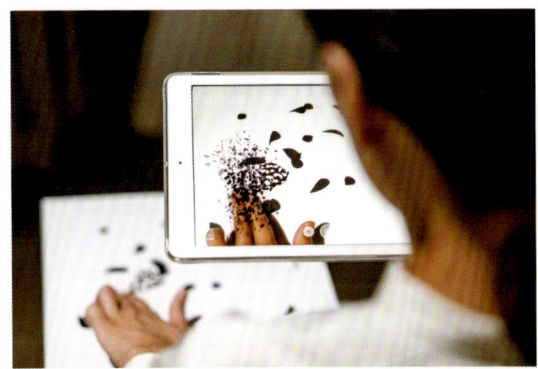

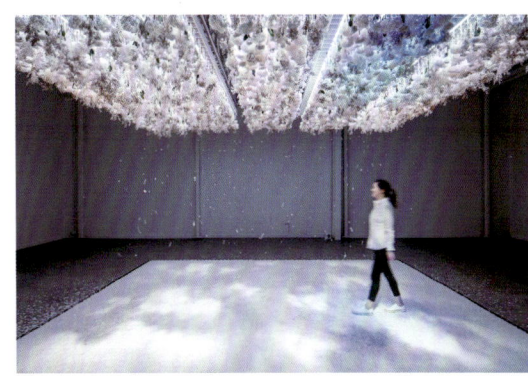

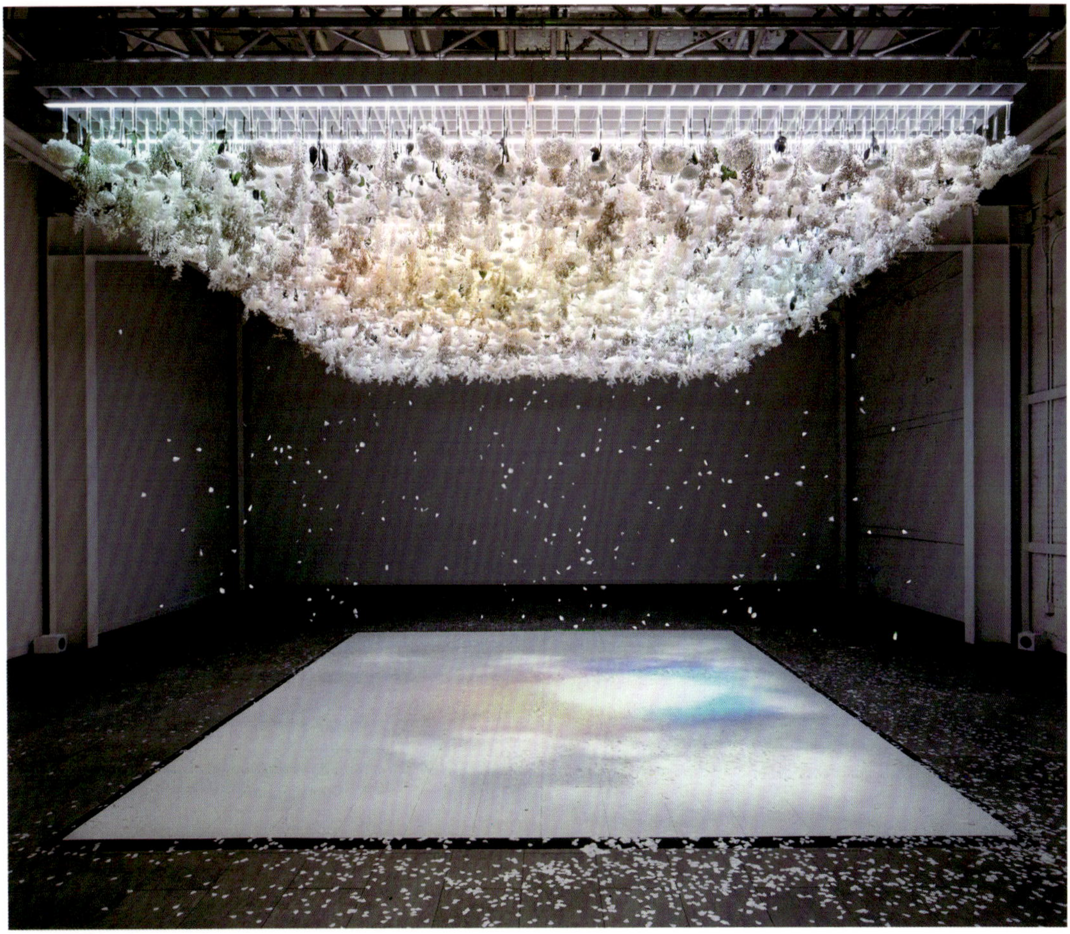

I believe that those who have an independent mentality from an early stage will become robust creators. Instead of working for companies' titles or personal benefits, one should think about how deep-rooted his or her power can be.

Atsushi Hirano

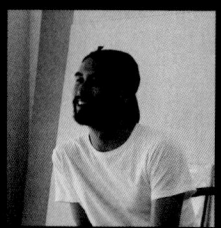

Atsushi Hirano is the founder of AFFORDANCE inc. With graphic design at the core of their work, AFFORDANCE inc. offers branding, VI & CI planning, signage planning, and space design. They aim to create designs with depth that encompass humor and coincidence, born from careful study, ranging from digital to analog expression.

Q Could you share your overall impression of Japanese graphic design?

A My impression of Japanese graphic design cannot be summed up in one word. The reason, I think, is the influence of the various values that abound in Japanese society. I think that values vary greatly from major to minor and the design quality also varies. However, my impression is that 30 years ago, the quality of design for mainstream jobs was very high and there was a lot of interesting work, even in commercials.

Q What do you think of the influence of the Japanese aesthetic heritage, social culture, and graphic design education? How do they work into your design philosophy and practice?

A Hard work and discipline are still appreciated. This is a very wonderful thing. But, at the same time, things like breaking the norm and having exclusive perspectives may be ignored. I want to express the middle ground between the values of innovation and tradition. This is also because of my interest in a kind of ambiguity.

Q How do you find inspiration daily? Before a design project begins, is there anything you do for preparation?

A My biggest source of inspiration is music. I like to listen to various genres. And I decide on what to listen to according to the job at hand. I get design ideas and inspiration from the music I choose. It is necessary to know about musical tunes as much as possible.

Q The materials and colors you used in the signage system of the tech company UNITEX are simple yet intriguing, aligning with the corporate's image. Could you share your design strategy with us?

A UNITEX is a company whose business is mainly based on magnetic tape, a recording medium. Therefore, in the renovation of the headquarters, we used the tape as a sign and worked to keep the elements as minimal as possible.

平野篤史

Q Compared with UNITEX, the visual language of the Yatsushiro City Center for Folk Performing Arts signage system is more inclusive. How do you achieve unity of function and aesthetics in this project?

A The Yatsushiro Myoken Festival includes traditional performing arts and has a unique atmosphere. When implementing the design, we researched the festival and chose to include gold, red, black, and wood colors in the end. The iconic pictograms and font needed to be decorative, ethnic, and old-fashioned to create this atmosphere. In addition, to create a new look for its future role, we tried to generate not only simple graphics but also dotted graphics, across the space.

Q The package for the pizza-flavor cookie Pizza Bear is intentionally designed to look like a pizza box. The design idea is refreshing. How did you make sure that customers knew about the content and got the trick you played?

A The client had already decided to use a pizza box as the highlight of the design and the mission left to me was to decide on the design and the name. The design was based on the idea of a pizza-loving bear and the problem was how to make the concept become casual and pop. In the end, we decided that a graffiti-like graphic with thick lines and multiple colors would best fit the product, so we just went straight for the cute bear.

Q The fonts used in your design go along with the design concept very well. What are some factors you consider when choosing or designing fonts for projects?

A It is essential to think about whether the font delivers the theme and its nuance. Then we will choose a suitable font or develop a new one. We will provide customers with different choices. Often, we create an original font for a unique expression. And this ends up with a design that is one-of-a-kind.

Q Do you think you have a specific design style?

A In terms of design style, I am not interested in being free from limitations in design expression. Rather, my style is to find out the appropriate method, presentation, and design for a project, and work on it.

Q You've shown your unique understanding of colors and graphics through the design approach of your creations. Could you share your exploration and experiment with visual language with us?

A We consider our clients' needs. When taking commissions, I do not want to think of my work as my creation. And I will decide on the presentation and design methods according to the content and feature of the project. However, I will always have some preferences for shapes and color combinations. I believe that these come from experiments and explorations, but the source of these elements is more often from things other than graphic design, such as fashion, architecture, music, and ethnic groups. I have always been particularly influenced by architecture, space, and three-dimensional expression.

Q In your opinion, what elements are needed to make a good piece of work?

A The ideas of the works should not be self-satisfied, have enough negative space, and are born from deep thought.

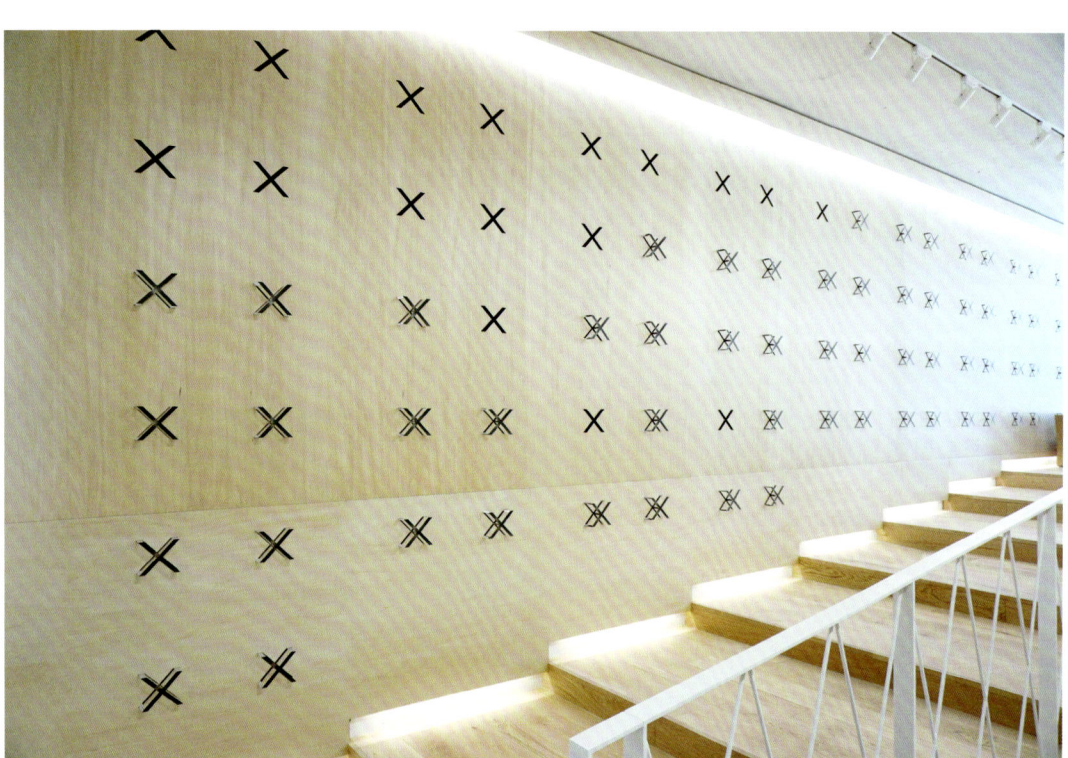

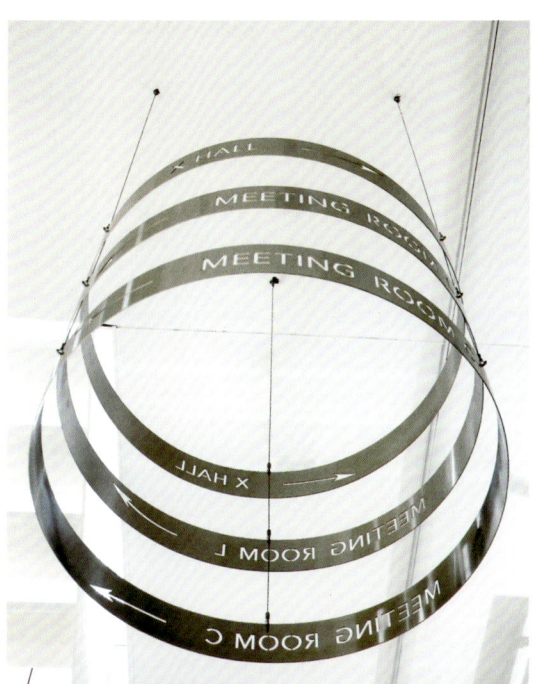

UNITEX

The designers created the logo, guidance sign, and room name sign by bending stainless steel, inspired by the magnetic tape used for recording, a commercial product of UNITEX. They attempted to promote the iconic role of the arrows and the flowing lines of the form by installing bent stainless steel signs. In the entrance hall, they installed a circular guide sign that can produce a 360-degree effect. In the step hall, removable acrylic objects in the shape of "X" are stuck on the wall, so that various products and exhibits can be displayed flexibly.

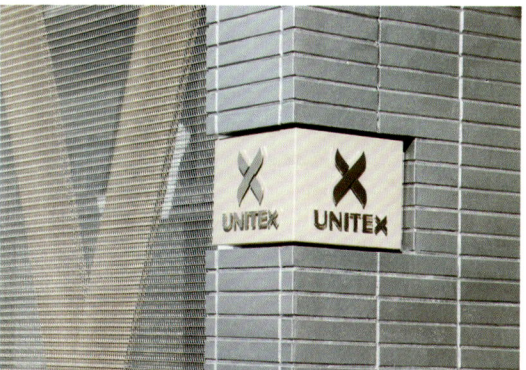

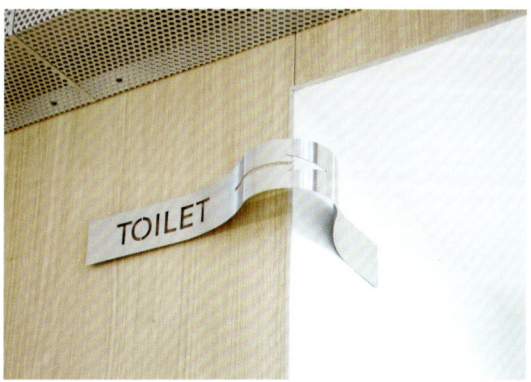

平野篤史

Q In addition to working as a designer, you also teach at Tama Art University. What should design students and designers of the younger generation be aware of?

A I think it requires remarkable fundamental skills, a flexible mindset, and a strong spirit to be a designer.

It is also important not to blindly follow trends. Without paradoxical thinking, it is impossible to cultivate one's individuality. And I believe that those who have an independent mentality from an early stage will become robust creators. Instead of working for companies' titles or personal benefits, one should think about how deep-rooted his or her power can be. This is vital for surviving in a world that will be severe in the future.

Q In recent years, many creations from Japan were presented through new media or forms. How do you look at contemporary graphic design in Japan and what is your expectation?

A I am not a person who can speak for the potential of Japanese graphics, but I think we need to be more tolerant, less closed-minded, and get rid of obsolete evaluations and standards. I think it is a good idea.

YATSUSHIRO CITY CENTER FOR FOLK PERFORMING ARTS

The logo of the center is composed of the Chinese character "八 (eight)," through which the designer put various meanings through shape and color. The character is reconstructed from cursive handwriting to geometric shapes to express the ambiguity of time.

Signs inside the art center also deliver a classical and folkloric feeling. The sign for the storeroom is a dot drawing of the restored items. The restroom's pictograms are made of thick wood to catch visitors' attention from a distance.

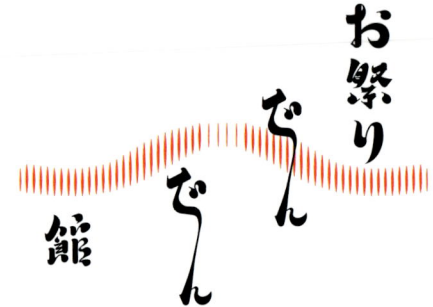

Yatsushiro City Center for Folk Performing Arts

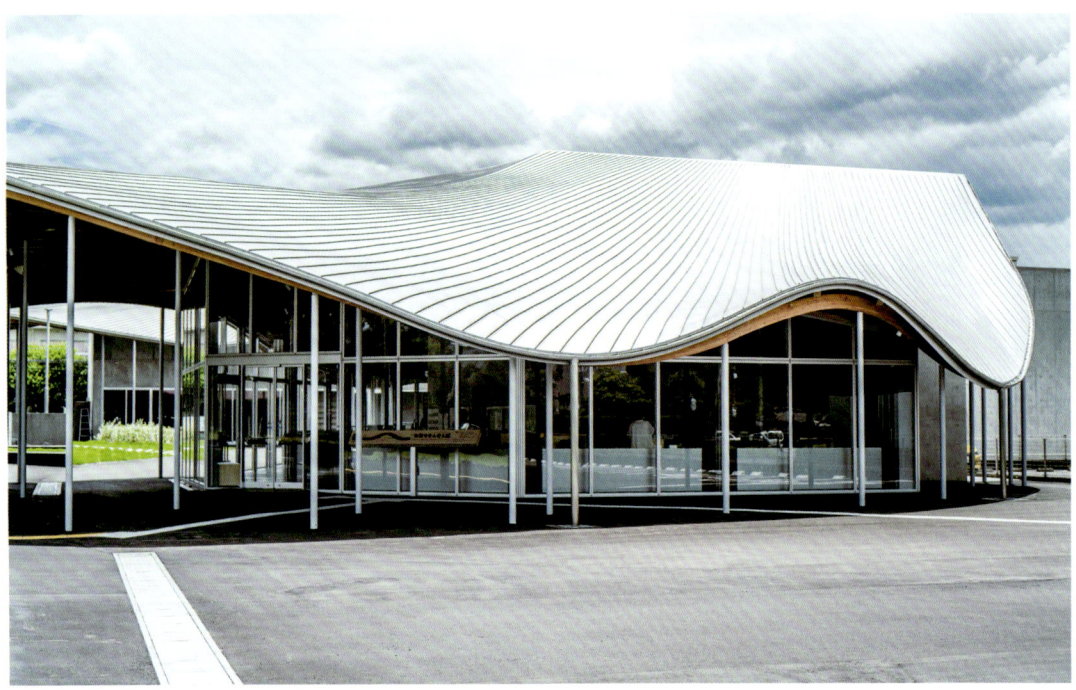

Atsushi Hirano

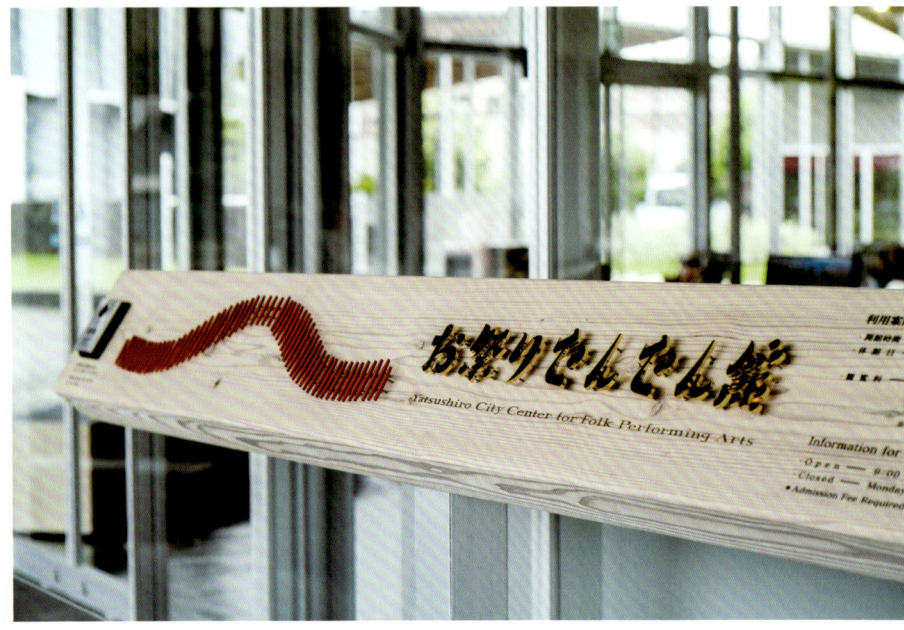

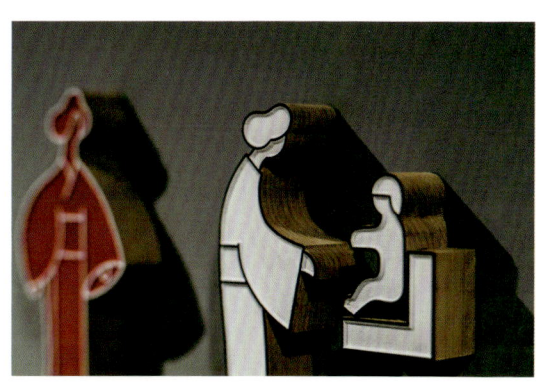

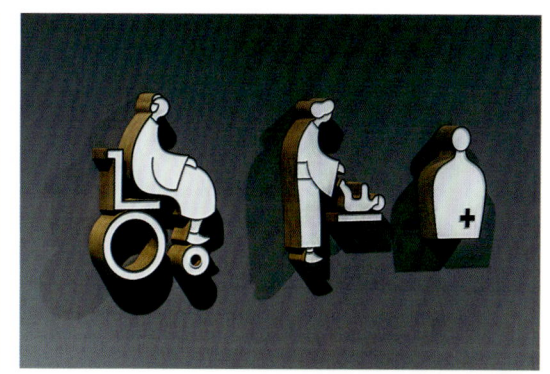

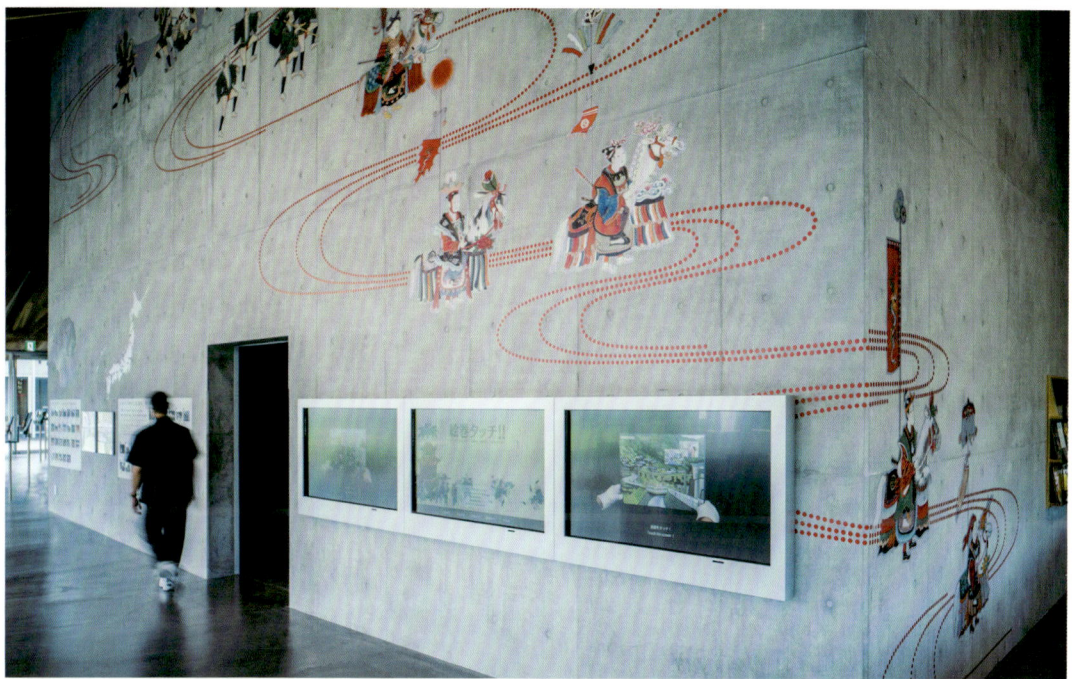

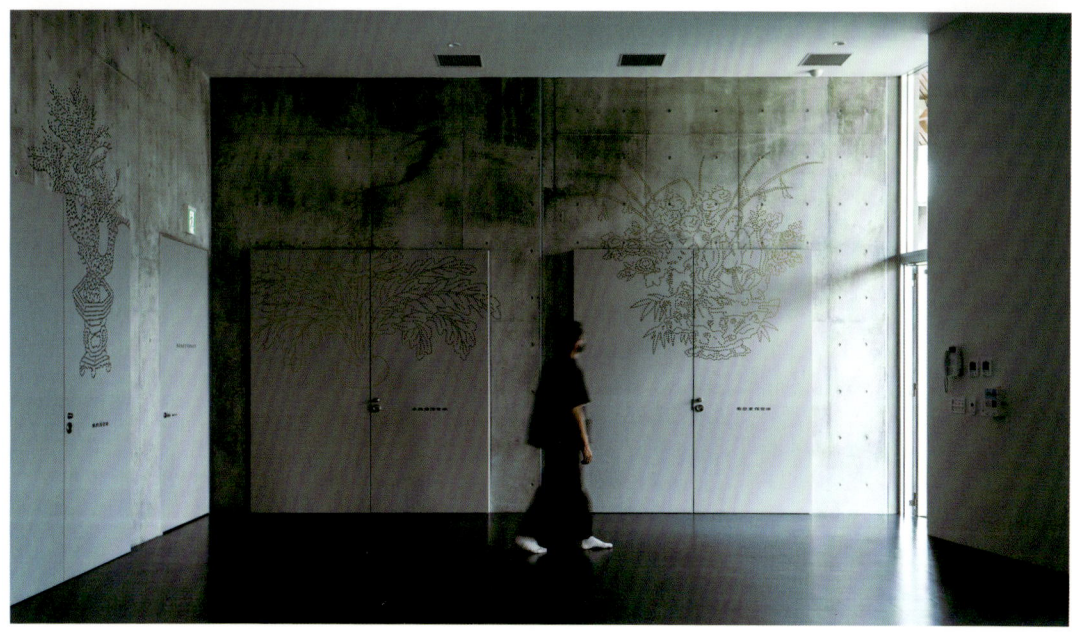

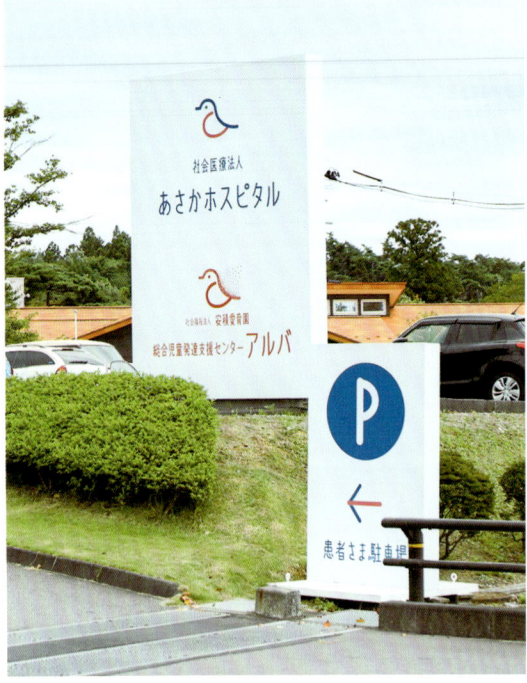

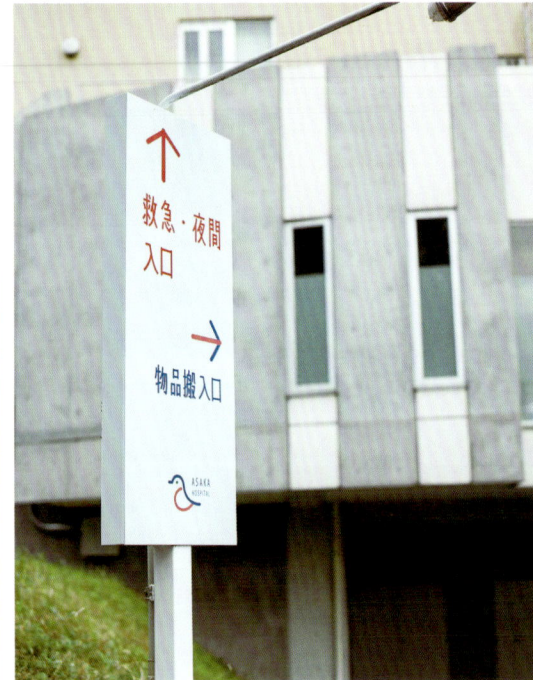

ASAKA HOSPITAL

The designers went through a trial and error process to create this work. They had a few questions in mind before the project started: "How can they create a simple and soft expression with only one line and a limited palette of colors?" "How much margin they should leave to achieve the balance of visibility and recognition?" "What is the best thickness and shape of the lines?" In the end, they finished the creation with three basic colors, including cobalt blue (the color of the sky), coral red (the color of the heart, kindness, and love), and evergreen (the color of immortality), along with original pictograms and fonts developed for the signage planning.

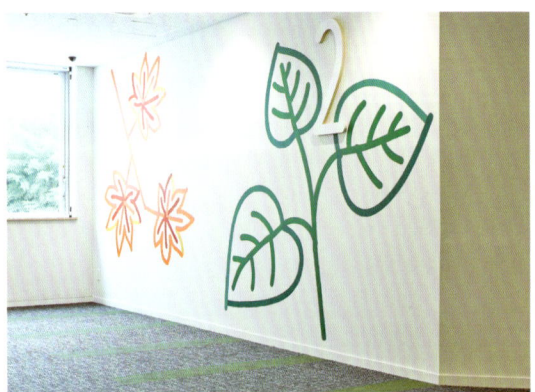

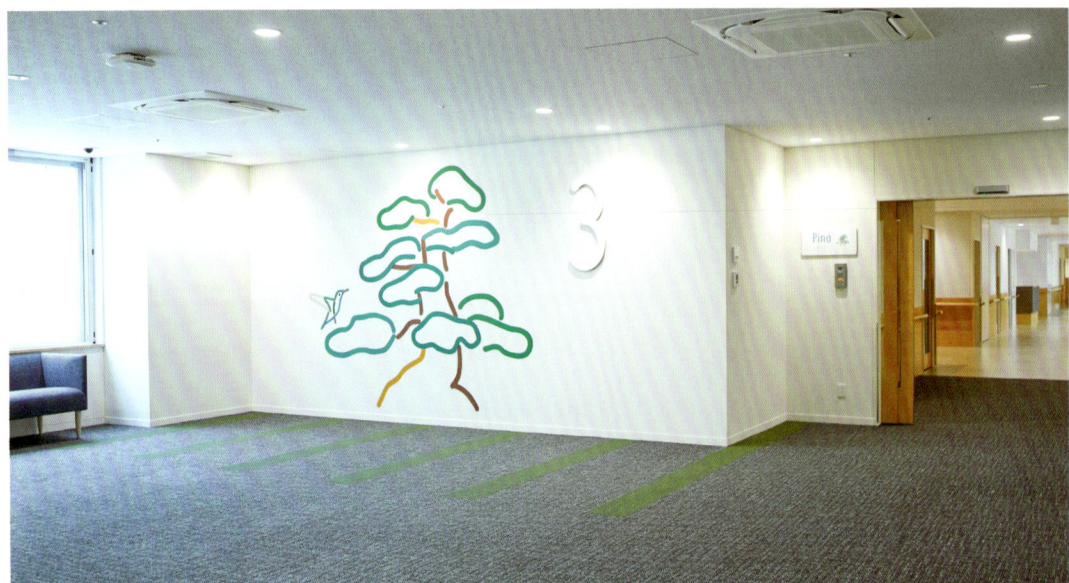

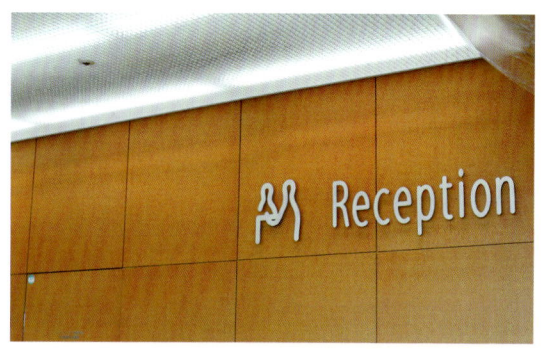

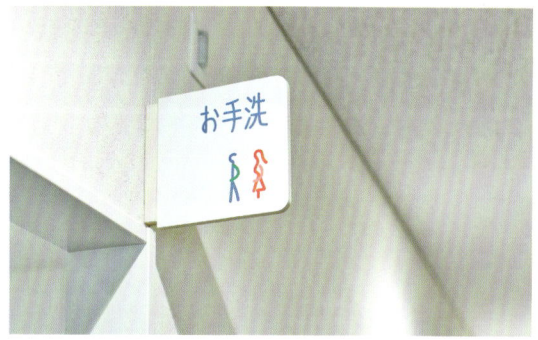

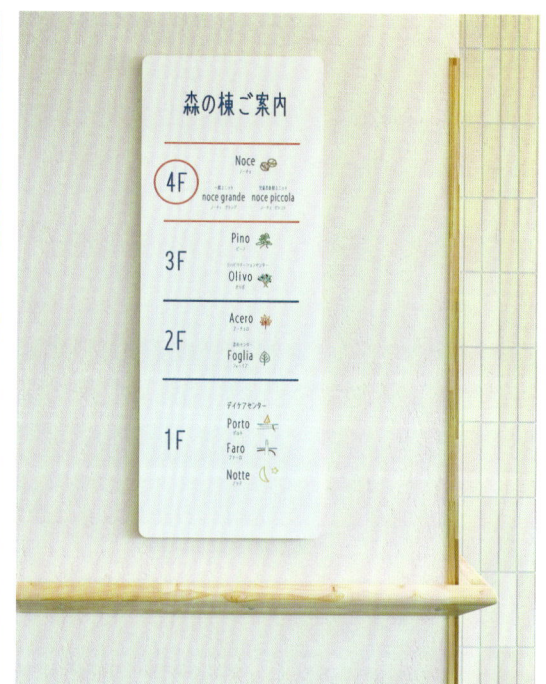

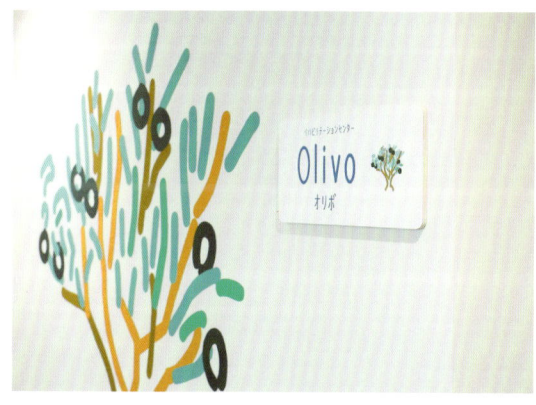

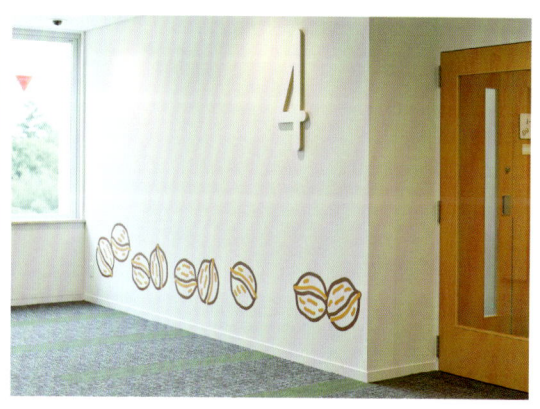

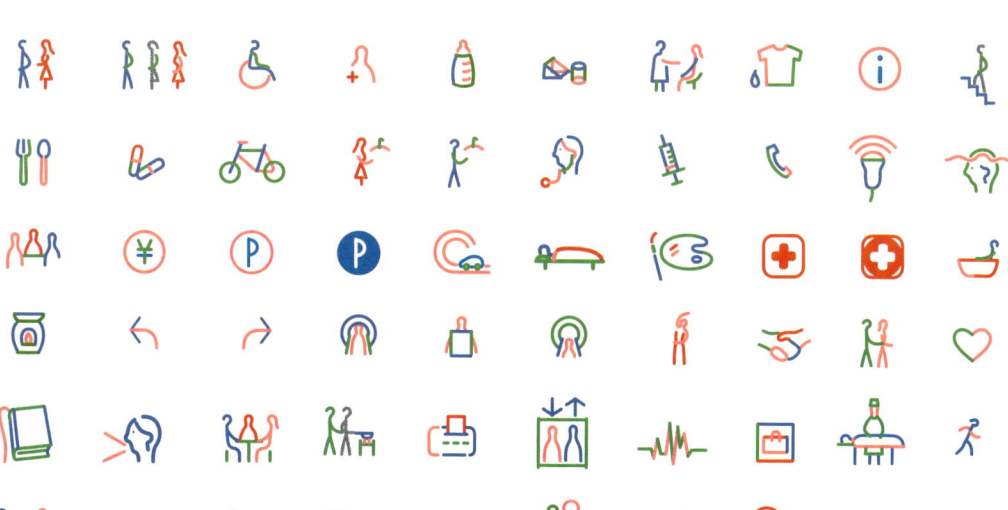

平野篤史

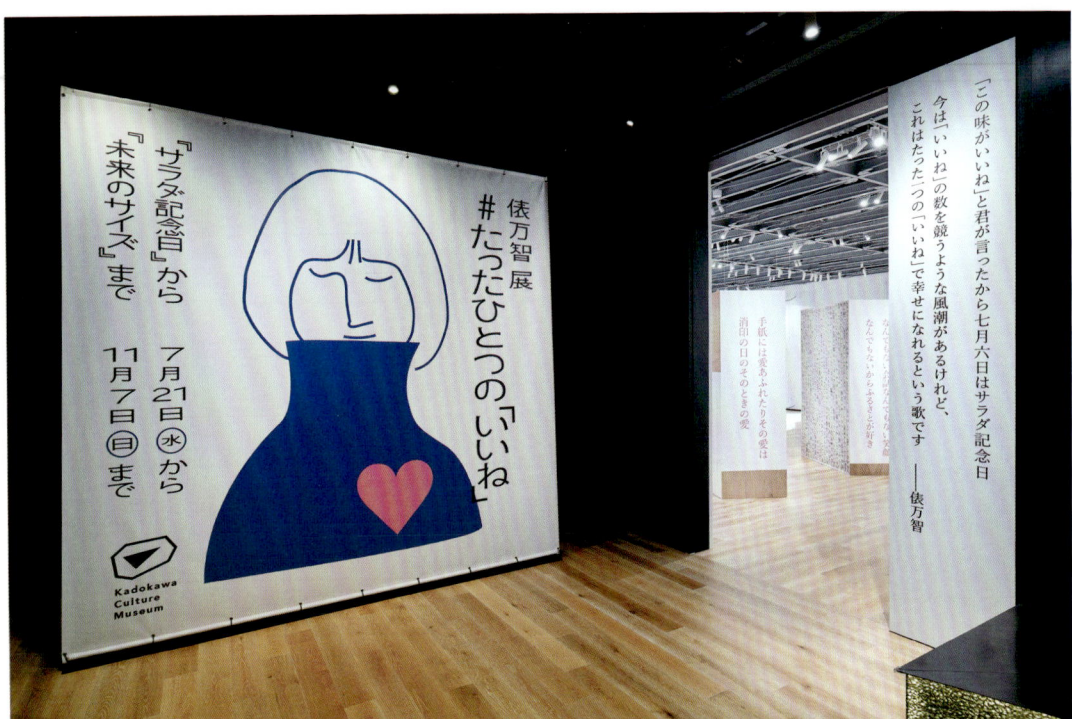

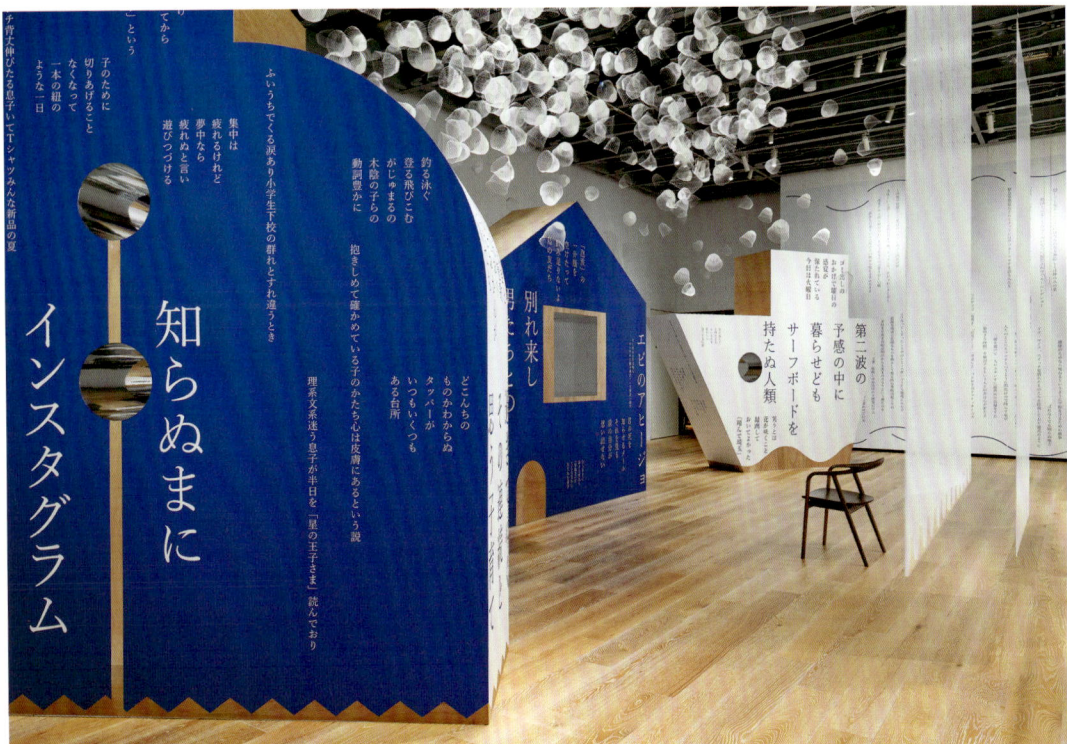

EXHIBITION OF MACHI TAWARA
The designer started by drawing Machi Tawara's face to get young people interested in the project. With two colors, blue and pink, he wanted to create a space where many poems were written on the wall and on transparent sheets of material.

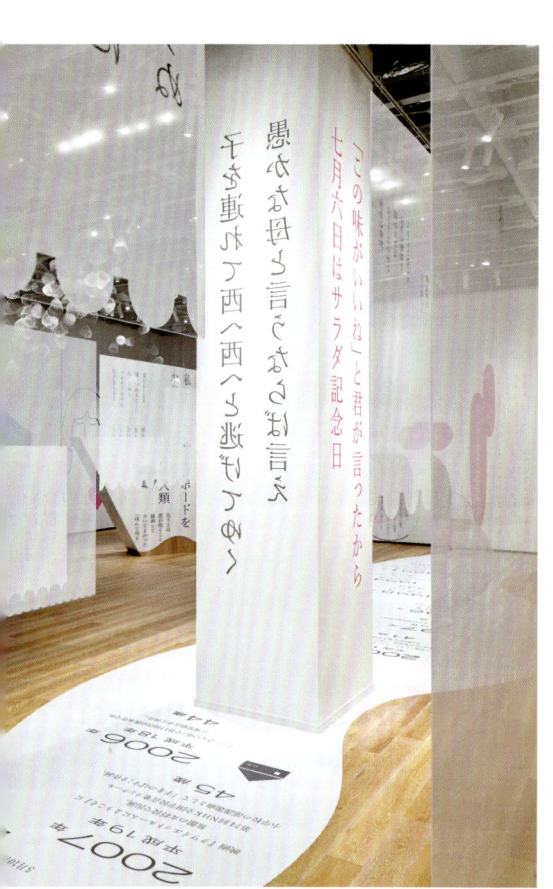

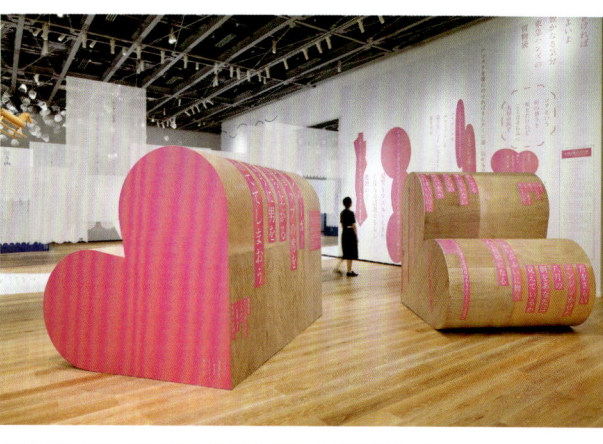

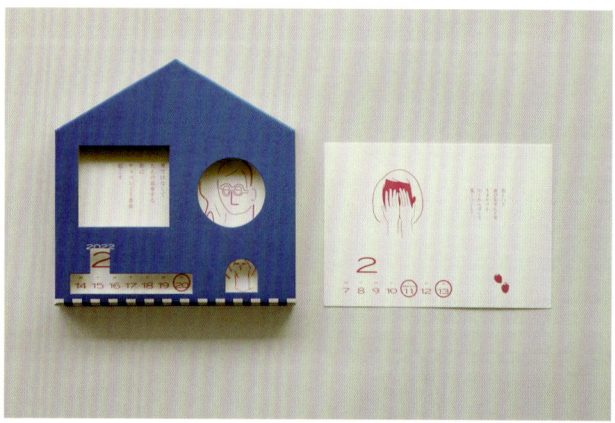

平野篤史

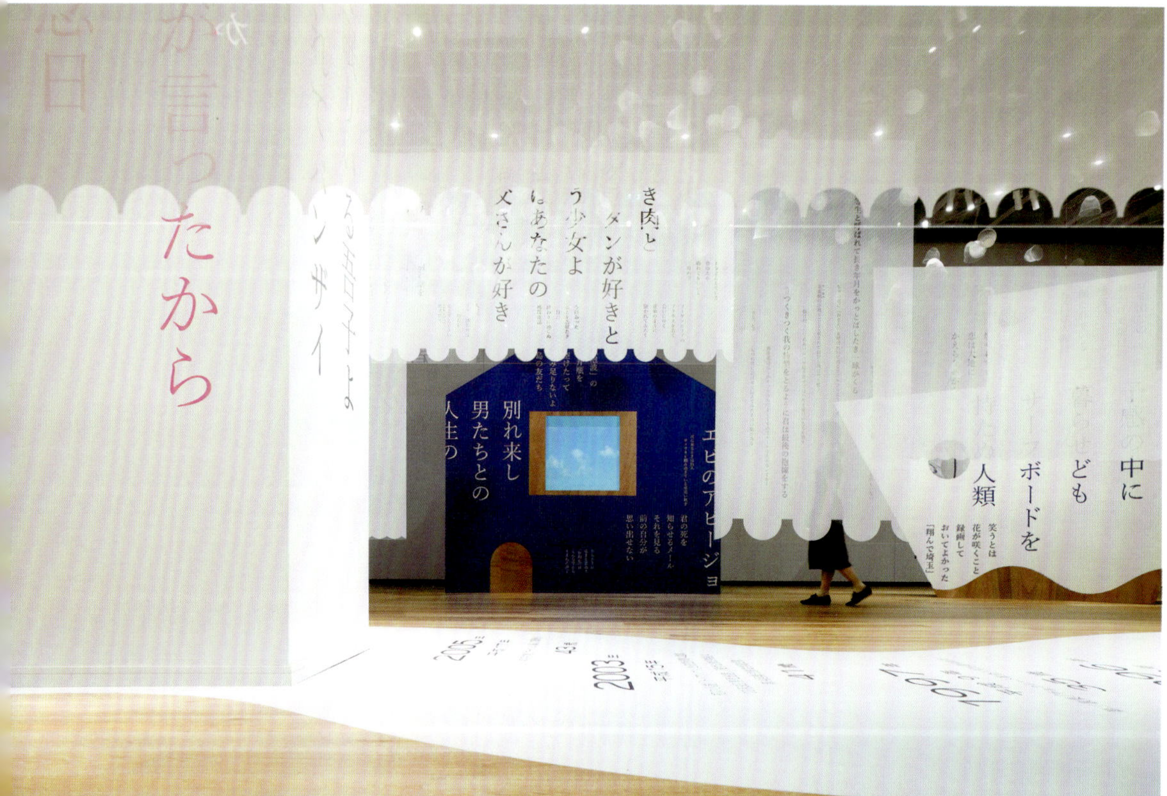

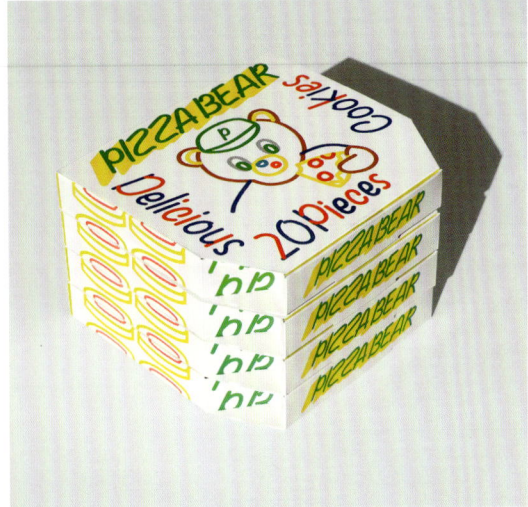

PIZZA BEAR

PIZZA BEAR is a new brand of cookies that tastes like delicious pizza. The designer created the character based on the concept of a pizza-loving bear. When the pizza delivery packages are put together one by one, the illustration on the side looks like the cookies are piled up.

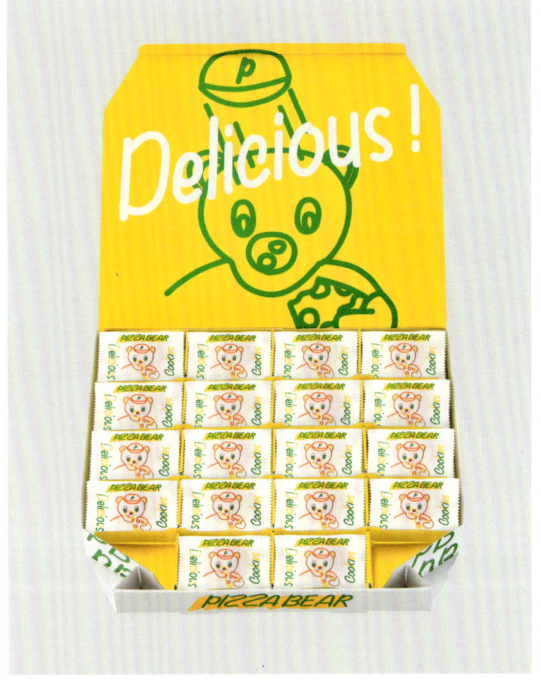

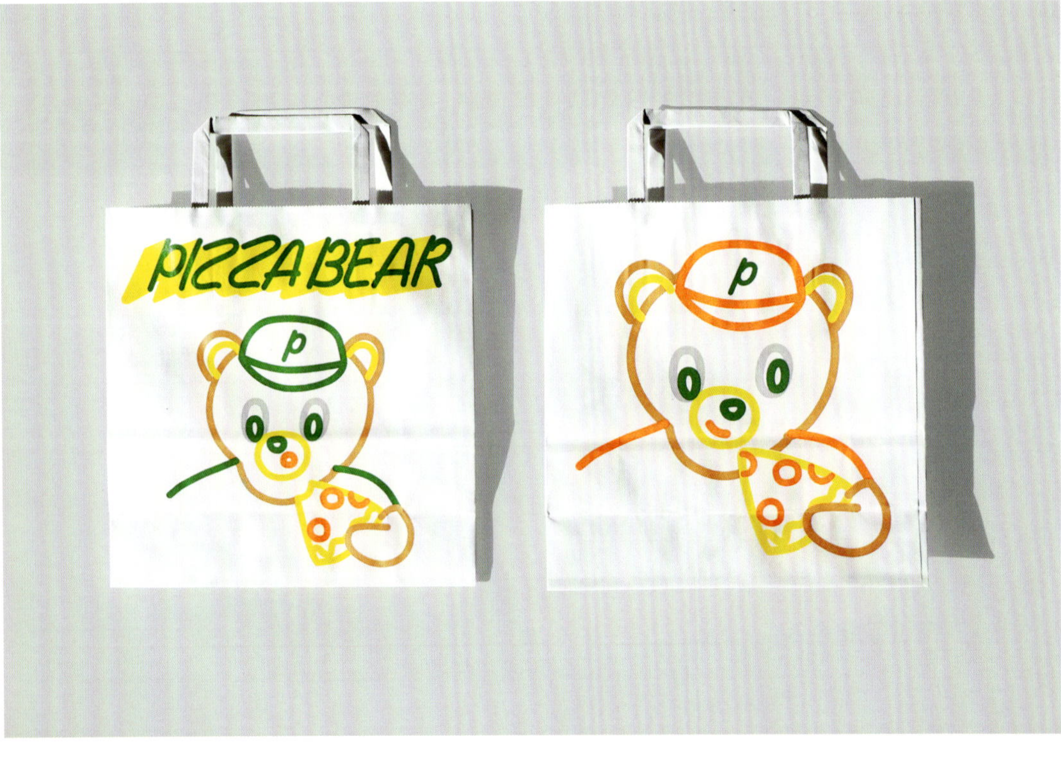

Atsushi Hirano

COOKIE UNION

The design of Cookie Union was created in honor of the British cookie culture and meant to be as colorful and pop as possible. The use of fairies is based on an old English myth and the coat-of-arms-like symbol represents the fact that each cookie is handmade by fairies. The detailed graphic patterns on the back of the shopping bag are a tribute to the English designer William Morris.

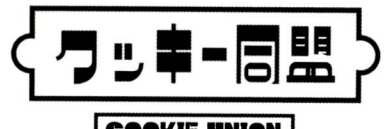

クッキー同盟

COOKIE UNION

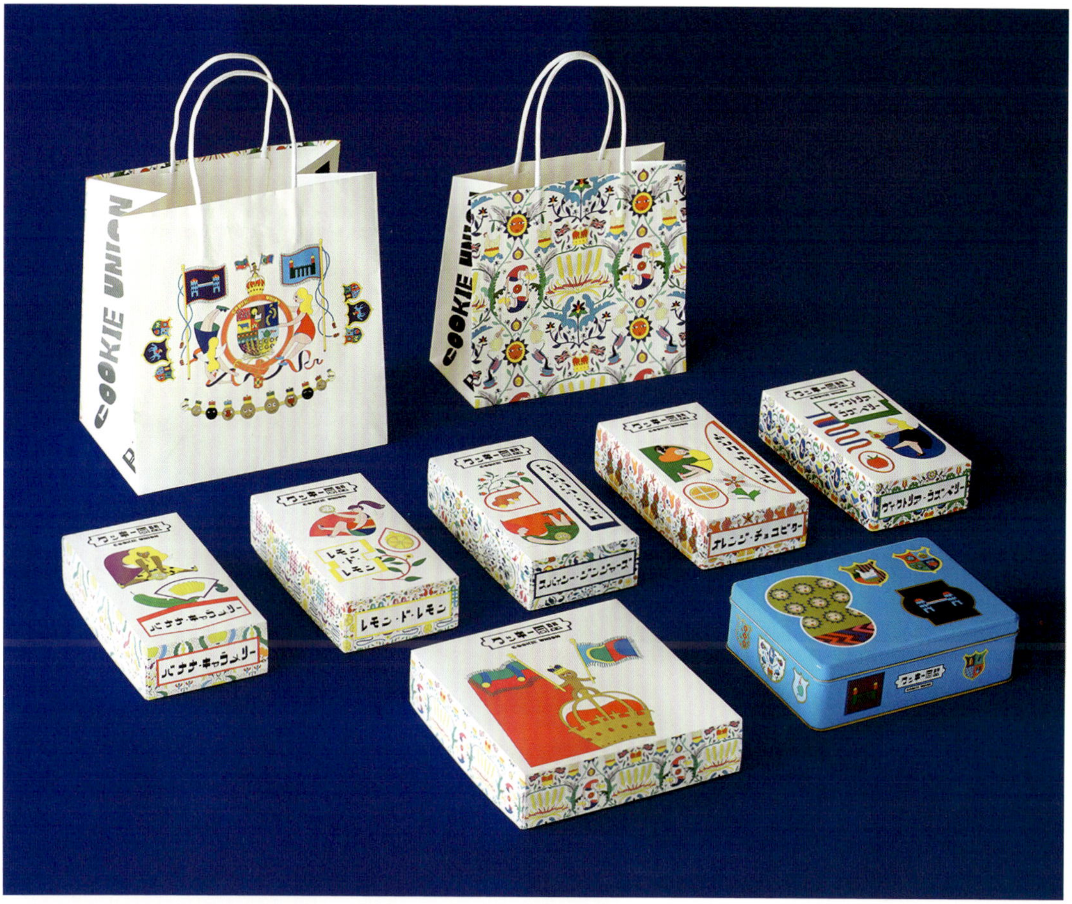

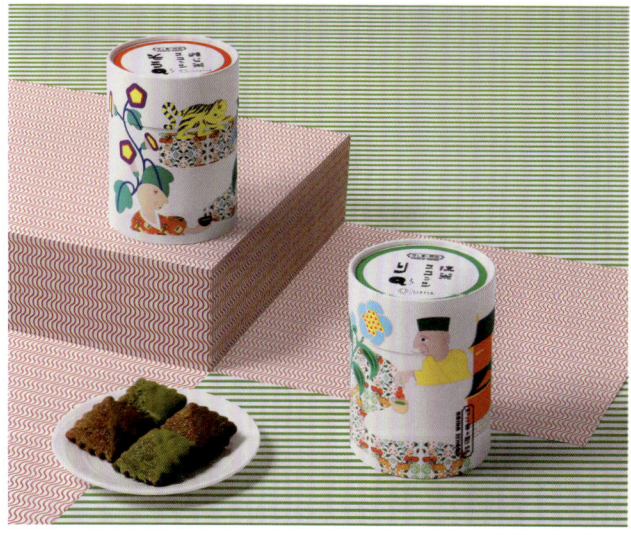

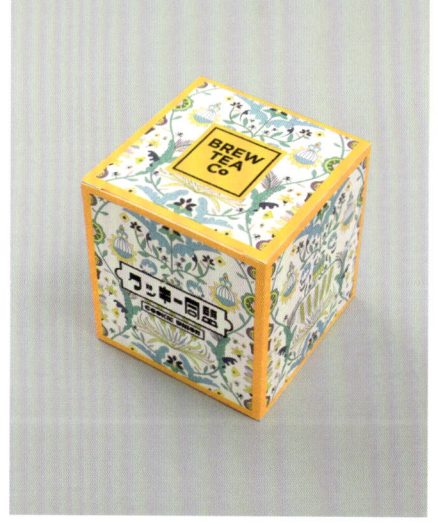

平野篤史

Many young people think
they know, feel like they
have done it, or avoid
failure even if they have
not yet tried it themselves,
but only your experience is
yours, and you should try
and fail.

Aya Codama

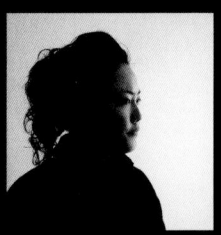

Aya Codama graduated from Tokyo Zokei University
and, after working at AWATSUJI design for seven years,
established BULLET Inc. in 2013. Fascinated by design
that can be touched and felt and that makes full use
of the texture of materials and printing processes, she
created works that transcend the boundaries of graphics.
She is the author of *Stepping Into Package Design*. Her
major awards include the One Show Design (gold), the
Pentawards (platinum), the Cannes Lions, the D&AD, the
iF Design Award, and the Good Design Award. She also
teaches at Tokyo Zokei University.

Q Could you share your overall impression of Japanese graphic design?

A I belong to several design associations of different genres. Three of them are the Japan Graphic Design Association (JAGDA), the Japan Package Design Association (JPDA), and the Japan Typography Association. This year I also served as a judge for the ACC Tokyo Creativity Awards.

Interestingly, the aesthetics of each organization and the points they emphasize in design are completely different. Although they cannot be summed up in one word, my impression is that JAGDA focuses on individual authorship and the pursuit of pure beauty in the form, while JPDA emphasizes design that resonates with the public and sells as a product. This diversity and the mixing of multiple schools of thought is evolving Japanese design in various directions.

Q What do you think of the influence of the Japanese aesthetic heritage, social culture, and graphic design education? How do they work into your design philosophy and practice?

A Japanese people are very sensitive to the sense of presence. Therefore, when designing packaging for daily necessities, I pay attention to the appearance of the product, such as trustworthiness, cleanliness, and not being overly pretentious.

On the other hand, for projects that strongly reflect my philosophy, I try to avoid "Japaneseness" and "Japan style" as much as possible. I want to create something that transcends borders, age, and time, something that instantly conveys interest. The design that first impressed me, Ross Lovegrove's Ty Nant mineral water bottle, is my goal.

Q You founded the design studio BULLET Inc. What was the reason for making this choice? And what is the philosophy of your design studio?

A I founded BULLET Inc. when I was 30 years old. Until then, I had worked in a design studio, AWATSUJI design. In the private office, work is commissioned by the boss, who directs and makes presentations to clients. I worked as a hand and foot of the boss for a few years, but after about five years, I felt the urge to interact directly with clients on my own and take the initiative in creating products, so I established my own company.

The company name "BULLET" has three meanings. The first is that it is the English translation of my name "Kodama (small ball)." The second is that our goal is to create a design that is as penetrating as a bullet. Third, when I paragraph sentences, I use the "·" and this is called a "bullet." Writing bullet points of ideas is to list vectors of different directions and be free from a single perspective. It is like writing a series of ideas with different directions.

Q When taking a commission, how do you communicate with the client to sort out and define their needs?

A I believe that communication is very important, so I prefer to work close to the person who has the final say in decision making. I am not a fan of working through agencies or competitions. I start every job with a meeting, and try to think like the executive of the company. In other words, I try to approach the job as if I were the person who wants to create it. In this way, questions naturally arise and we can engage in heated discussions. The client will give their opinions on the design I have proposed, and we will improve it over and over again to make it better for both of us. A design born from a good session is as strong as an iron sword that has been struck many times.

小玉文

The packages you designed for KOI are impressive. Could you share the design concept for KOI as well as KOI the Rising Sun?

A KOI is the flagship project of Bullet Inc. It all started about 10 years ago when we were involved in the rebranding of Imayotsukasa Sake Brewery. After all the basic designs were in place, we were asked to create a striking product to raise the brewery's profile. The brewery is located in Niigata Prefecture, a place where Nishikigoi or koi farming has long thrived.

One anecdote about this sake brewery remains. In the period of scarce supplies after World War II, many sake breweries sold sake diluted with water. People made fun of the sake that was so thin that goldfish could swim in it and called it goldfish sake. However, because the Imayotsukasa Brewery did not dilute its sake, the phrase "The sake of Imayotsukasa is not a goldfish sake, but a majestic Nishikigoi sake" remained. This design was born from the idea that Nishikigoi is the motif that expresses the brewery's ambition. The white bottle is made to look like a fish and the pattern is printed all over the bottle.

The Rising Sun design is based on the motif of a Nishikigoi called Tancho (a variety of Nishikigoi with a red circle pattern on its head). The red circle is reminiscent of the Japanese flag Hinomaru. The Rising Sun was created to support Japan, which has lost some of its vitality due to the COVID-19 pandemic.

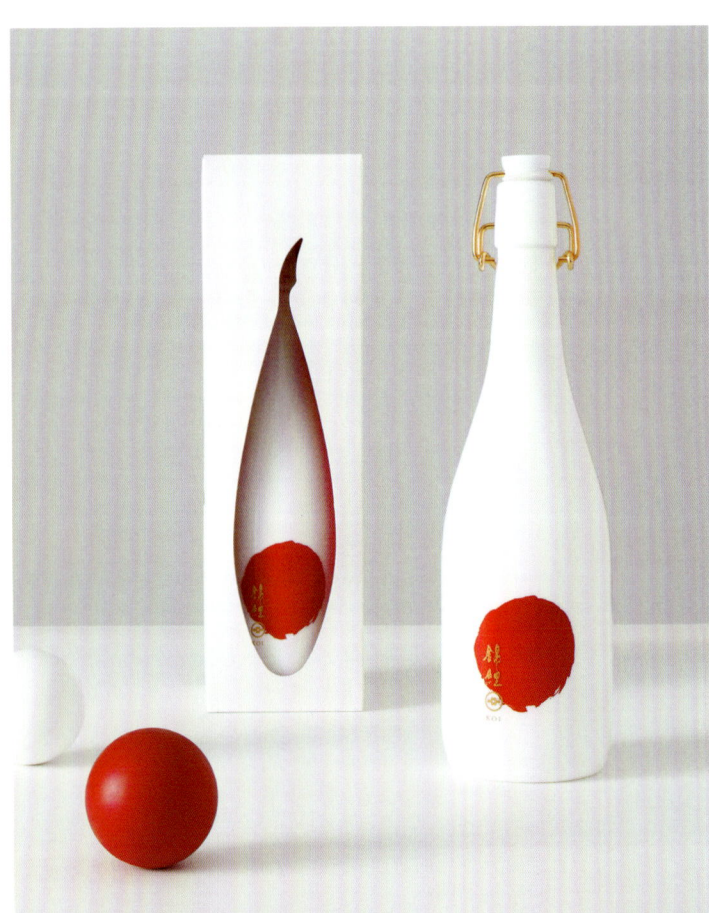

Aya Codama

KOI THE RISING SUN

This product belongs to the KOI sake series. The motif is based on the carp Tancho, which has a scarlet spot on its head like the Hinomaru (the Japanese national flag).

Due to the COVID-19 disaster, the Japanese are gradually losing their energy. In such circumstances, this product was born from the thought to give support to Japan. The red circle shape was designed to point slightly upwards with the hope that the sun will rise again and that things will get better.

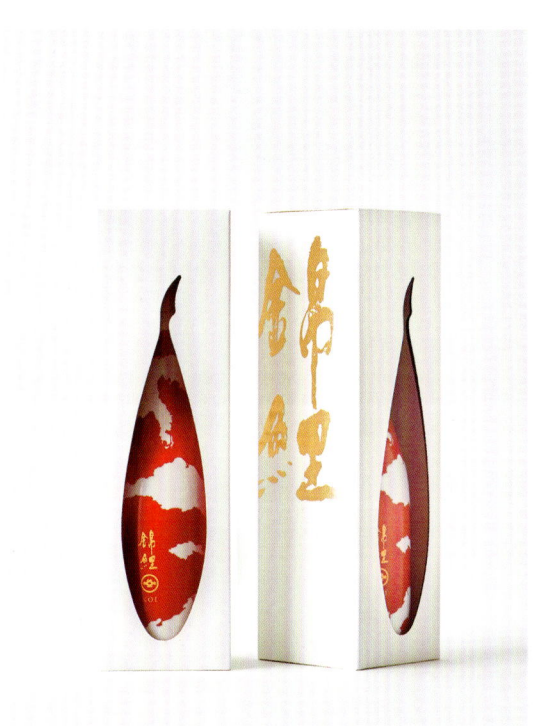

KOI

Around 10 years ago, Aya Codama was asked to create a product for the Imayo Tsukasa Sake Brewery. The design was born from the idea that Nishikigoi is a motif that expresses the aspirations of this brewery. The white bottle is made to look like a fish and the pattern is printed all over.

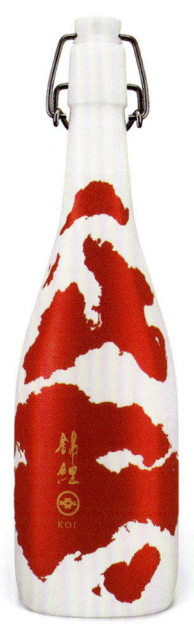

小玉文

Q What role does packaging play in the process of product distribution? How do designers deliver the characteristics of products and brands through packaging?

A Package design is similar to designing clothes that suit a person. The clothes a person wears may mislead people about his or her personality. When people who buy products at convenience stores and supermarkets look at the appearance of the package design, they instantly think "Does it look like a trustworthy company?" "Does it look good?" or "Does it look tasty?" Graphic design in packaging is communication that conveys the essence of a product tangibly and instantaneously.

Q Triangle Trial presents various printing techniques in the form of posters. How do you decide on the image to use in the poster? What was the idea behind this work?

A What I wanted to try in this trial was a conversation with the printing directors of Toppan (a printing company). Nowadays, with the development of printing technology, it is taken for granted that printing will be completed according to the data created on a PC. However, in such an age, I wanted to create an unknown work of art, the finished product of which I could not see. The final image would be completed by the addition of the directors' ideas and innovations, based on the images and graphics I presented.

First, I printed a simple triangle. By printing various layers of white and transparent ink on top of it, various images of smoke, fog, clouds, etc. were created.

Q In addition to taking commissions from clients, you also personally tried to explore the possibilities of design. Could you share your design practice and experiment with us using a specific project?

A I value the relationship with the printing and processing companies highly. They are the ones who give the final shape to my design.

This work, Cracked Paper, was born out of a joint project with Fukunaga Print, Paper Craft Perspective and the director is Tomohiro Okazaki. Various creators rethink the material of paper from their perspectives, create experimental products, and present them along with their thinking process in this project. Initially, I was looking for new ways to express the unique fraying characteristic of paper, but then I thought that showing paper cracking, would create a strange and interesting sense of discomfort.

The employees of Fukunaga Print were extremely energetic in taking on new challenges and worked hard to express the cracks and design the box. The experience of working together on difficult processing and design, which was different from our usual package design work, strengthened our bond. There is no doubt that Fukunaga Print has become a reliable presence in our subsequent work.

Q Your works are refined and restrained, yet full of fun and surprise. How does the daily inspiration work for your creations?

A I don't feel that I am reflecting my daily inspirations in my creations, but I want to create something that I want or find interesting. Perhaps I want to surprise even myself.

Aya Codama

CRACKED PAPER

This is a product produced by a paper processing company with a plan to capture the charm of paper from a new perspective. The designers explored the unique characteristic of paper by showing its "cracking" feature. To achieve this effect, elaborate paper crafting techniques are required to make this cracked product.

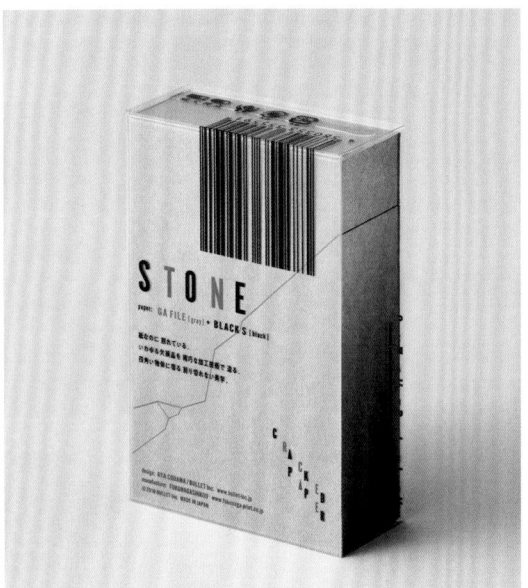

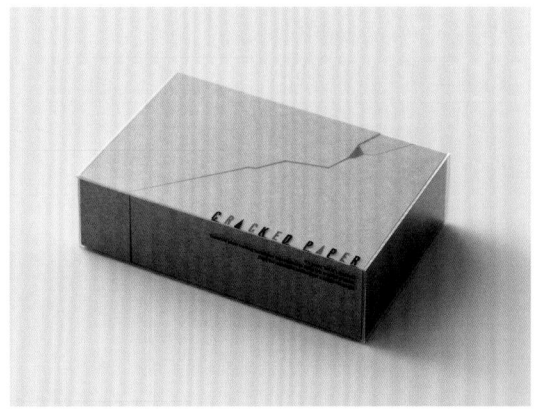

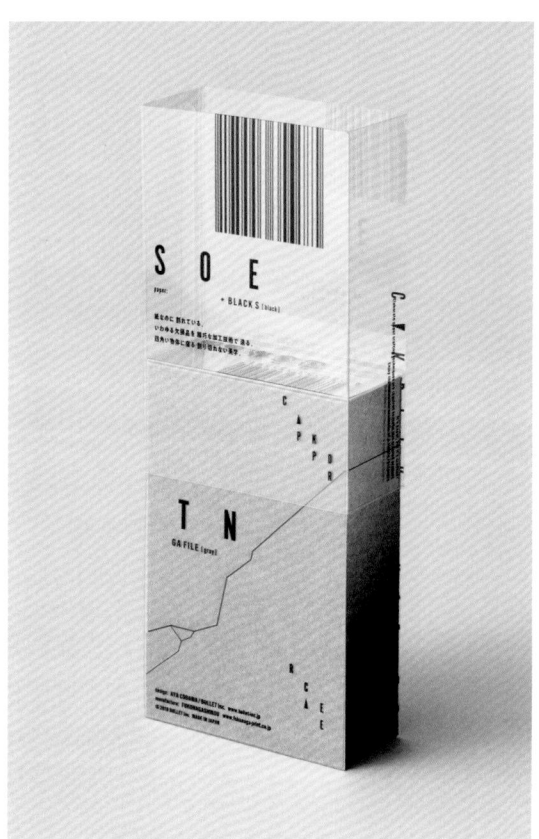

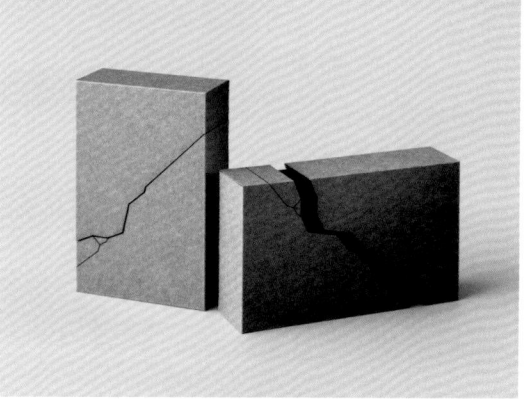

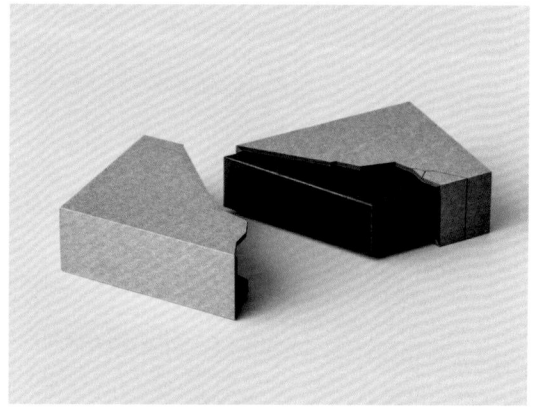

Q You have created many works using paper as a medium with a designer's keen sensibility. In today's world of electronic reading and online social platforms, what do you think is the unique appeal of print?

A The experience of seeing something digitally and the experience of actually holding it in one's hands are very different.

The design of the sake Hito to Ki to Hitotoki was born from this idea. This sake was born from the Imayotsukasa Sake Brewery's desire to preserve for future generations the culture of wooden bucket brewing which is dying out in Japan. They participated in the production of two new large, wooden vats to be installed in the brewery. Hito to Ki to Hitotoki is brewed in those vats. We traced the grain of the wooden vats and designed a three-dimensional, uneven white grain label.

People need to get this sake and experience it by drinking it. The importance of preserving the sake culture of large wooden vats for future generations is not something that should be just thought about in one's head, but something that should be experienced and understood. Sake brewed in wooden vats is characterized by a slightly yellow color and, interestingly, the color can show through the translucent grain of the wood. And the label can be seen through the sake from the back. This label design has an appeal that makes people want to touch and get their hands on it, and this invites many people to purchase it.

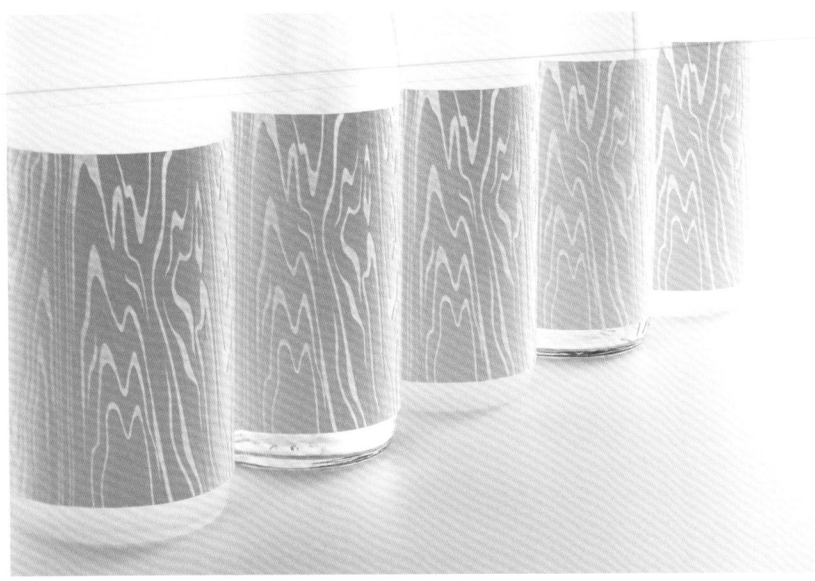

HITO TO KI TO HITOTOKI

This is the design for sake brewed in wooden vats. For the label design, the designers traced a part of the grain pattern from the cedar vats which the brewery's employees had poured their hearts into. Sake brewed in a wooden vat takes on a light yellow color, which can be seen through the translucent part of the wood grain pattern and it is also interesting to see the label through the liquid from the back.

Aya Codama

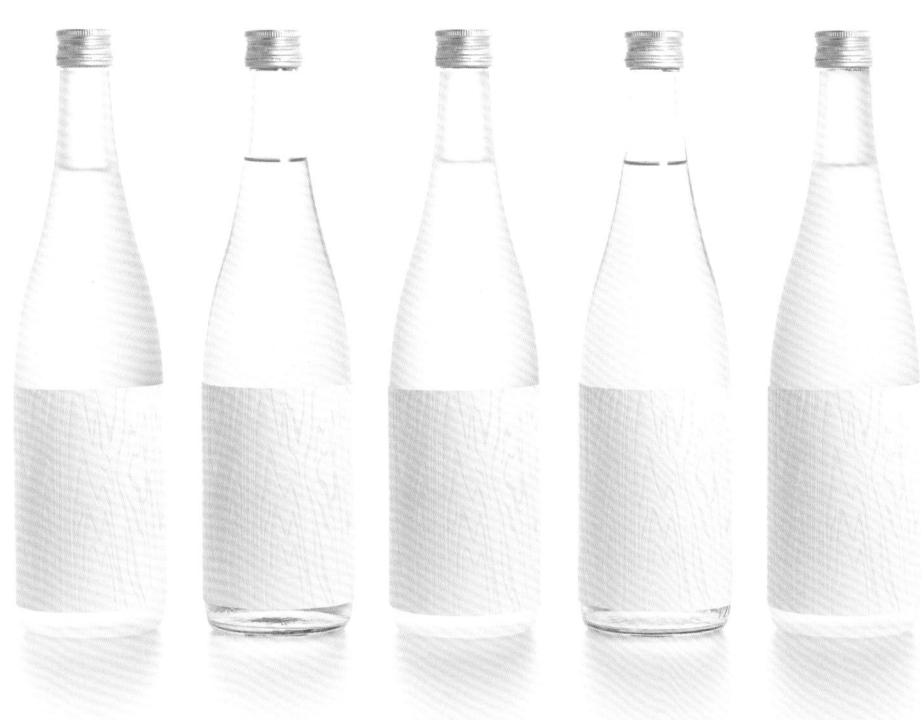

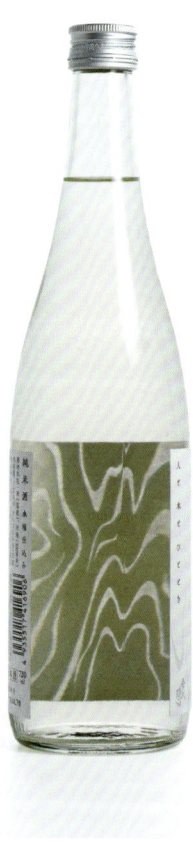

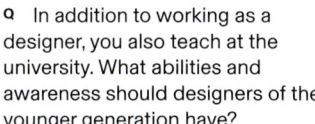

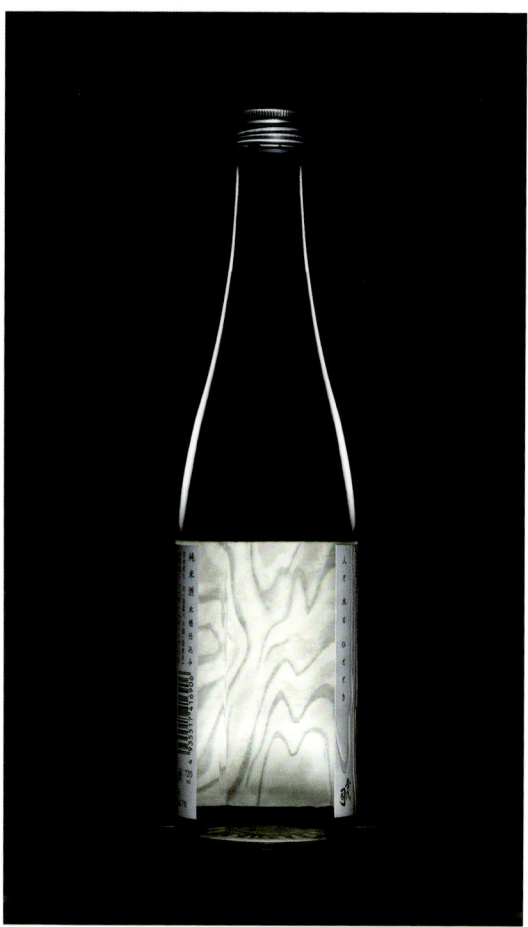

小王文

Q In addition to working as a designer, you also teach at the university. What abilities and awareness should designers of the younger generation have?

A We live in an age where a lot of information is coming in. Many young people think they know, feel like they have done it, or avoid failure even if they have not yet tried it themselves. But only your experience is yours and you should try and fail.

Q In recent years, many creations from Japan were presented through new media or forms. How do you look at contemporary graphic design in Japan and what is your expectation?

A Although I often use social media to present my work and look at other companies' designs, perhaps because I worked on so many packages, I still have a strong desire to value the real experience in the end.

The moment when you hold the design in your hands is something that cannot be shared and is unique to that person. I would like to explore the balance between disseminating the design widely around the world and having each person hold and feel it in their hands.

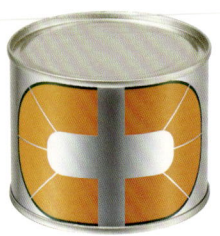
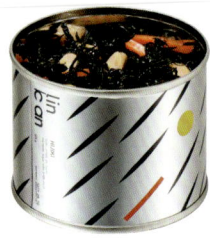
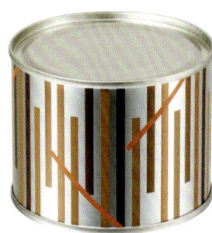
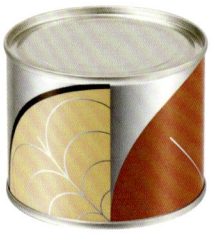
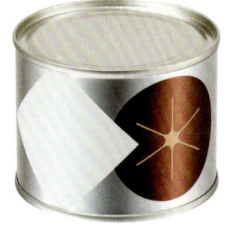
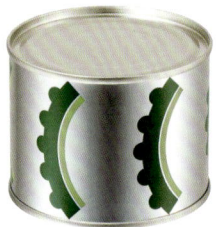
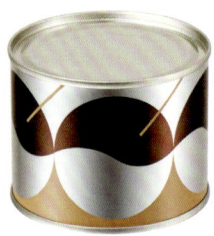
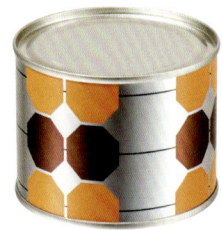
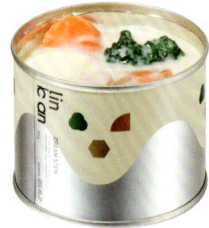
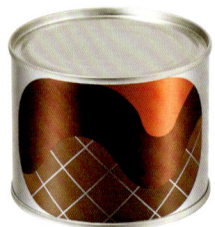
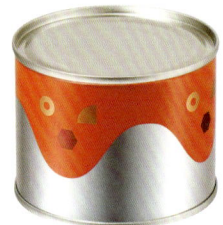
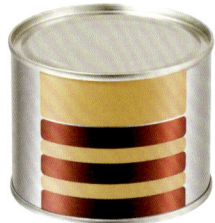

Aya Codama

LINKCAN

This packaging was created from a project to devise a new design using the technology of Japanese packaging manufacturer Fuji Seal and foil manufacturer KURZ. The design concept is a package that links the every day with the extraordinary. The term "linkcan" was coined by combining the words "link" and "can."

Emergency food, which is only needed occasionally, is often tucked away, forgotten until it expires. The designers approached the project with the idea that the place for emergency food can be a comfortable part of everyday life and that stock cases could be used as stools. The fun design, with its graphical representation of food, will give people a bit of ease and joy, especially in times of disaster.

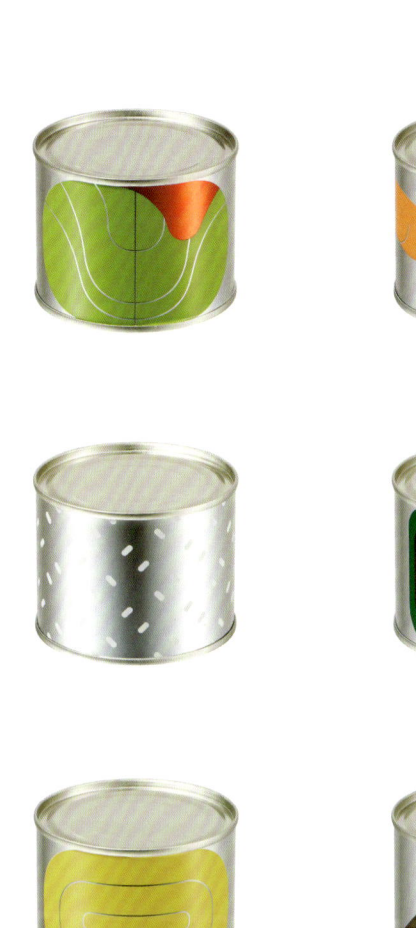
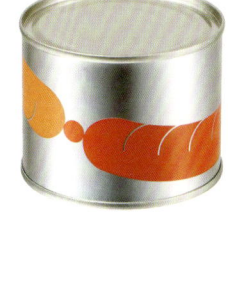
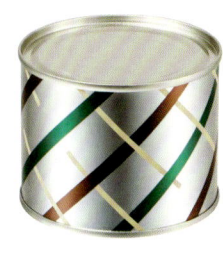
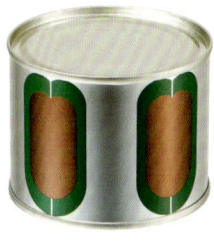
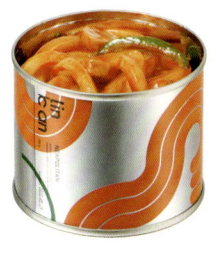
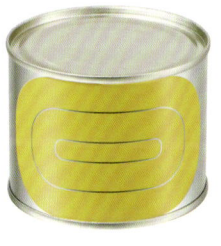
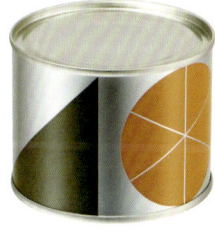
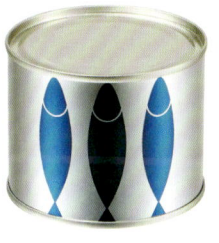
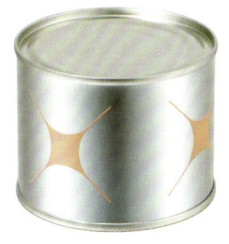
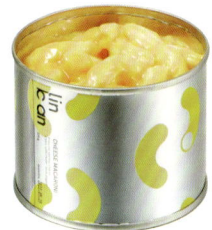
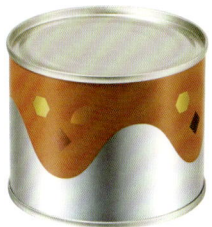

small小王文

99

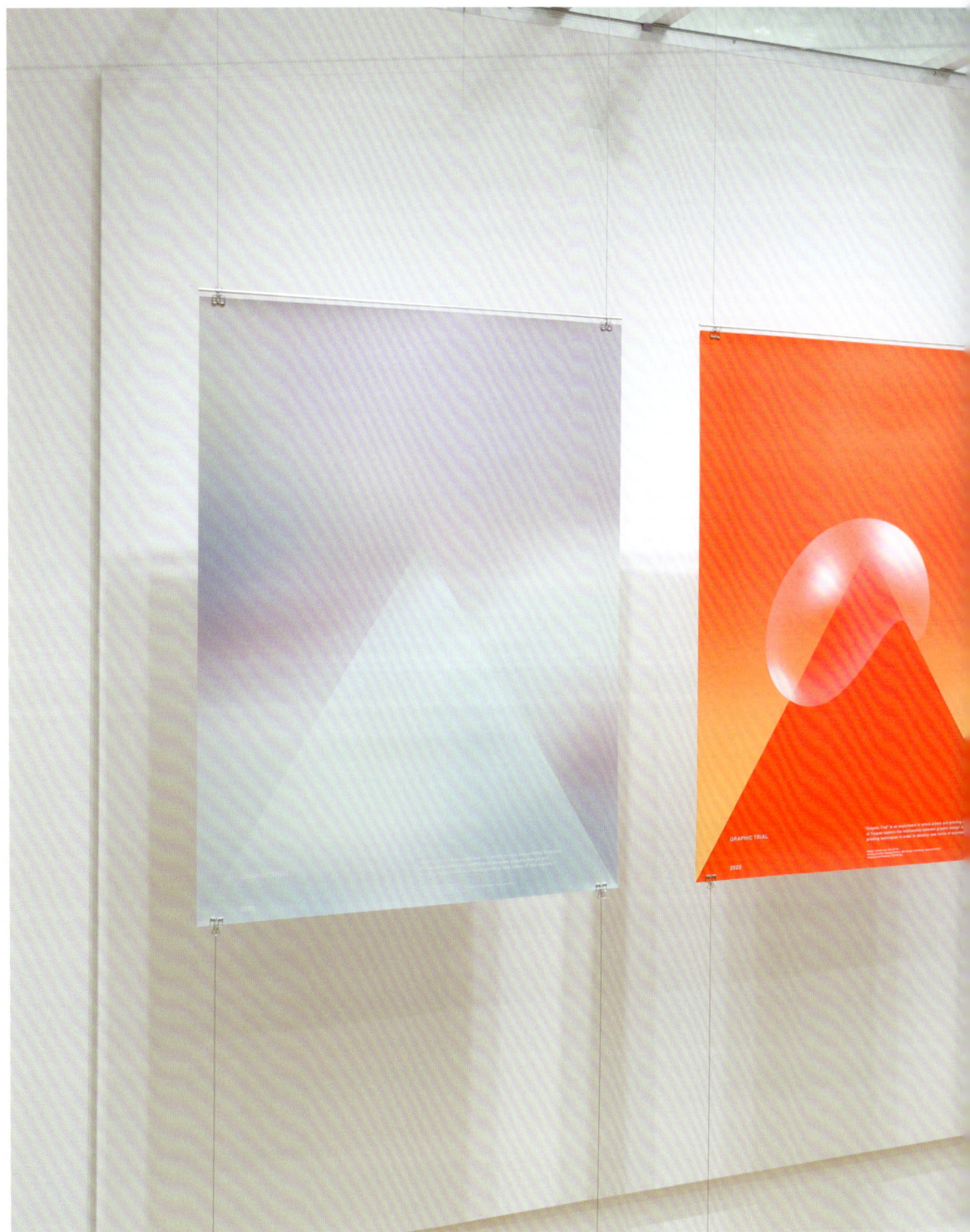

TRIANGLE TRIAL

Aya Codama produced 10 B1-sized posters as part of an experimental printing project conducted by Toppan. Her intention was to explore new and creative expressions, applying her idea of gases. She created various artworks employing fog, smoke, and clouds and then printed them over triangles, using different printing techniques.

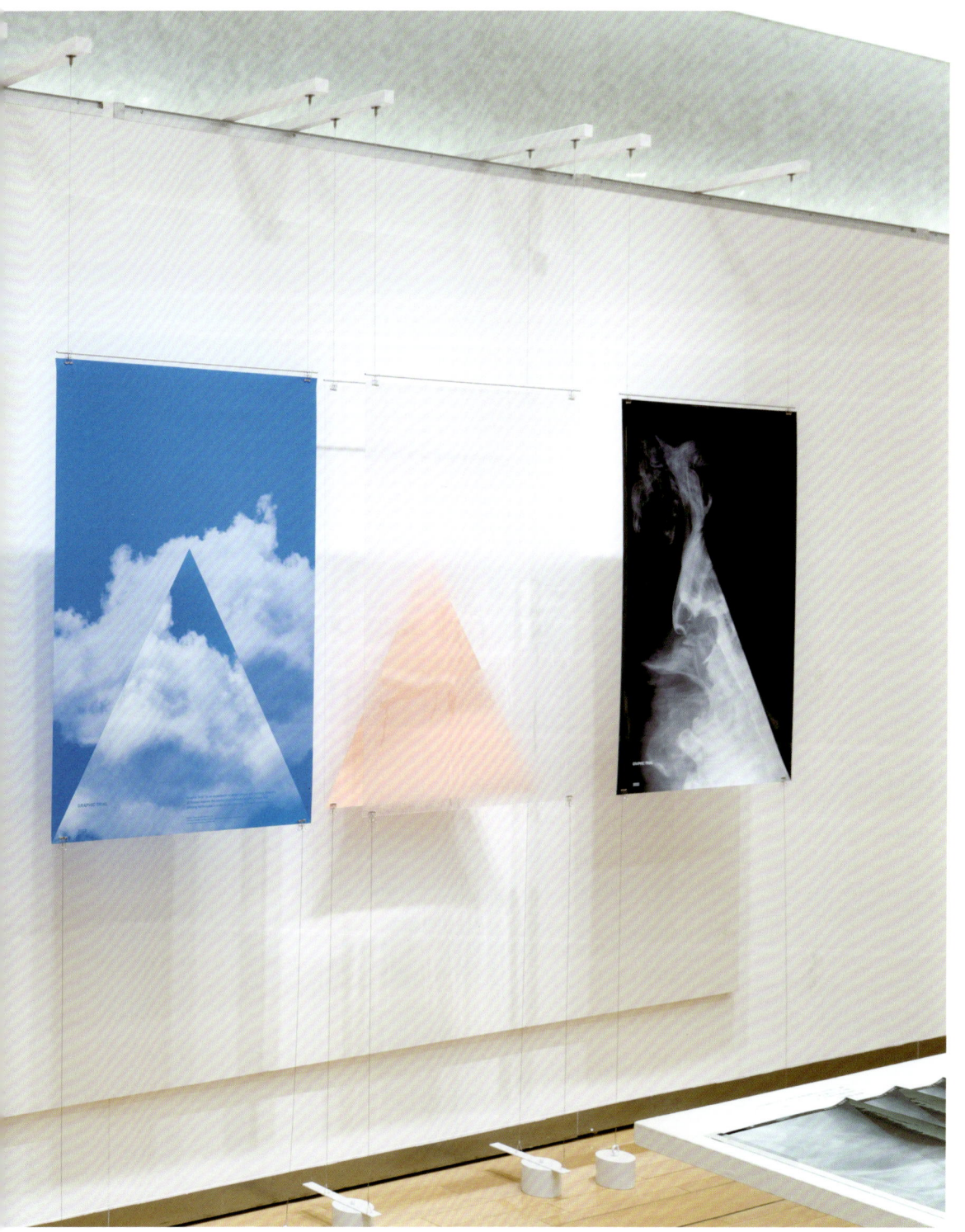

It is important to learn
from the various aspects
of context and wisdom
that have grown up in our
history and to repeatedly
devise ways to apply them
to the future.

Taku Sasaki

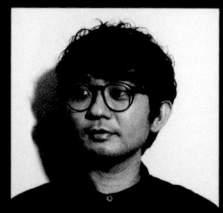

Taku Sasaki is an art director and product designer
based in Tokyo. Born in 1985, he studied product design
at Tama Art University and graduated in 2008 and then
joined KOKUYO Co., Ltd. His works focus on design that
crosses the plane and the solid, such as planning and
design of product brands, spatial signage planning, and
corporate branding. Taku won the JAGDA New Designer
Award in 2022, the Tokyo ADC Award, the Good Design
Award Gold Prize and Best 100, the Red Dot Design
Award, the KOKUYO Design Award, etc.

Q Could you share your overall impression of Japanese graphic design?

A I had never been aware of my being a designer from Japan or of Japanese graphic design until I was asked this question. I have always been attracted by something that is seemingly unidentifiable when it was created or an expression that does not evoke a sense of nationality or gender. This is because the objects being designed are becoming more diverse in increasingly diverse circumstances.

Q What do you think of the influence of the Japanese aesthetic heritage, social culture, and graphic design education? How do they work into your design philosophy and practice?

A The environment in which I grew up was not with a strong Japanese culture or climate. But the sensations I considered normal in my daily life were uniquely Japanese. In the process of designing, I place great importance on the act of discovering new aspects of the land and things that are unique and previously unseen.

In addition, when thinking about design, I often start thinking in terms of words to find the purpose and meaning of the design and I strongly feel the influence of language. When I find something that cannot be expressed in words, I am happy and try to verbalize it to create a new expression. The repetitive acts of visualization and verbalization always makes me think that if the language were different, I would arrive at a completely different expression.

Q You were trained as a product designer. What made you start doing graphic design?

A I studied product design and only did product design for three years after joining the company. I started working in graphic design because the products I designed were often communicated in a way that was different from my imagination and I became interested in how to convey that image.

Gradually, I was allowed to work in that part of the company as well. I also received much help on various tasks from a classmate at the company, Aki Kanai, with whom I have been working on many projects recently. It was an environment where I could learn graphic design, although not intentionally.

Q How do you draw inspiration from daily life and use them in your creations?

A I have multiple projects going on at the same time, so I have projects in the back of my mind all the time. I live my life looking for inspiration, regardless of what I am doing and the time.

It is hard to find inspiration. I keep thinking and working with my hands and sometimes find a small inspiration. The design is created through the accumulation of these inspirations.

佐々木拓

Q The project EX- is very refreshing. Could you share your design idea with us?

A "EX-" is a preposition, which is both the origin of the work's name and its concept. By eliminating the graphics and materials of KOKUYO's familiar products, this series aims to bring to light the essence of tools that we usually do not pay attention to, such as the beauty of form, detailed design, and fresh coloring, and to encourage users to create new ways of using these products. In addition, by utilizing conventional production methods, this initiative is based on the concept of industrial production, which is high-quality and easily affordable, while considering new ways of making tools.

The visuals were created in collaboration with photographer Gottingham. The products piled on top of each other are treated like sculptural works to show that the products are mass-produced, that they look more beautiful when stocked, and that the tools look different from what they used to be after their original information and uses were taken away.

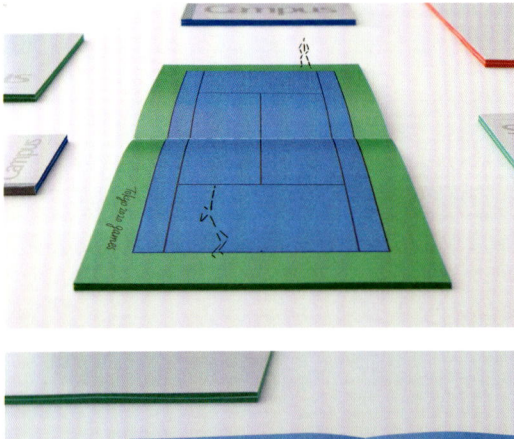

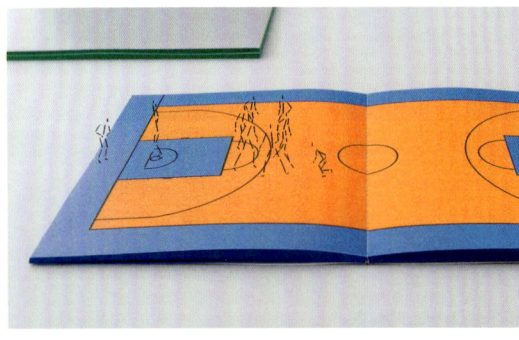

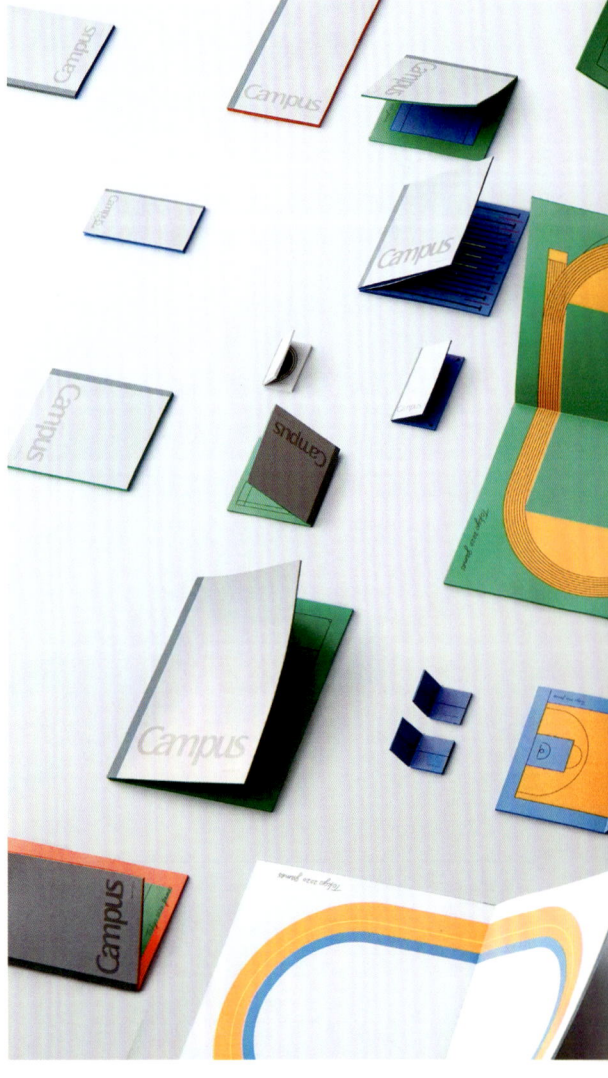

OPENING A NEW PAGE FOR TOKYO

This branding movie was created by KOKUYO, a Japanese stationery and office supplies manufacturer and official supporter of the Olympic Games Tokyo 2020. It features KOKUYO's Campus notebooks, with the message "Open a New Page for Tokyo." The movie shows the movement of opening notebooks, drawing a line, forming the court, and people playing games. Every time a new page is opened, it expresses the situation of the Games like a welling up of various sports. Notebooks and sports aren't obviously connected, but the designers think sports might have begun with someone drawing the court. Their hope is that the Games will fill Tokyo with people's passion, wisdom, and creativity, and bring a vibrant future.

THE CAMPUS was a large-scale project including branding materials, products, and a website. What was the design idea and logic of the project?

A THE CAMPUS is a renewal project of the building that originally housed KOKUYO's offices. It was redesigned as a place for employees and people in the city to create a diverse and rich mix for the coming era. In this project, we focused on how to create a new image of THE CAMPUS, a place that is at once an office, a store, and a park, and how to make that image permeate the building while dispelling the conventional image of an office. There was a lot of design work, but we also spent an enormous amount of time on team building and coordination.

The key visual is a three-dimensional shape of the initial letter "C" of the facility's name, which indicates the expanse of space and place, and it changes into various shapes to express the diverse activities that will be generated from this place. The concept of this key visual is reflected in the signage, merchandise, website, etc. so that it can be embodied not only on a flat surface but also in the entire space and outside of the city.

These developments and the intent of the place— diverse mixing, were made possible through collaborations with various artists and brands. It has been a very exciting project because what we have interpreted continues to be interpreted in ways beyond our imagination.

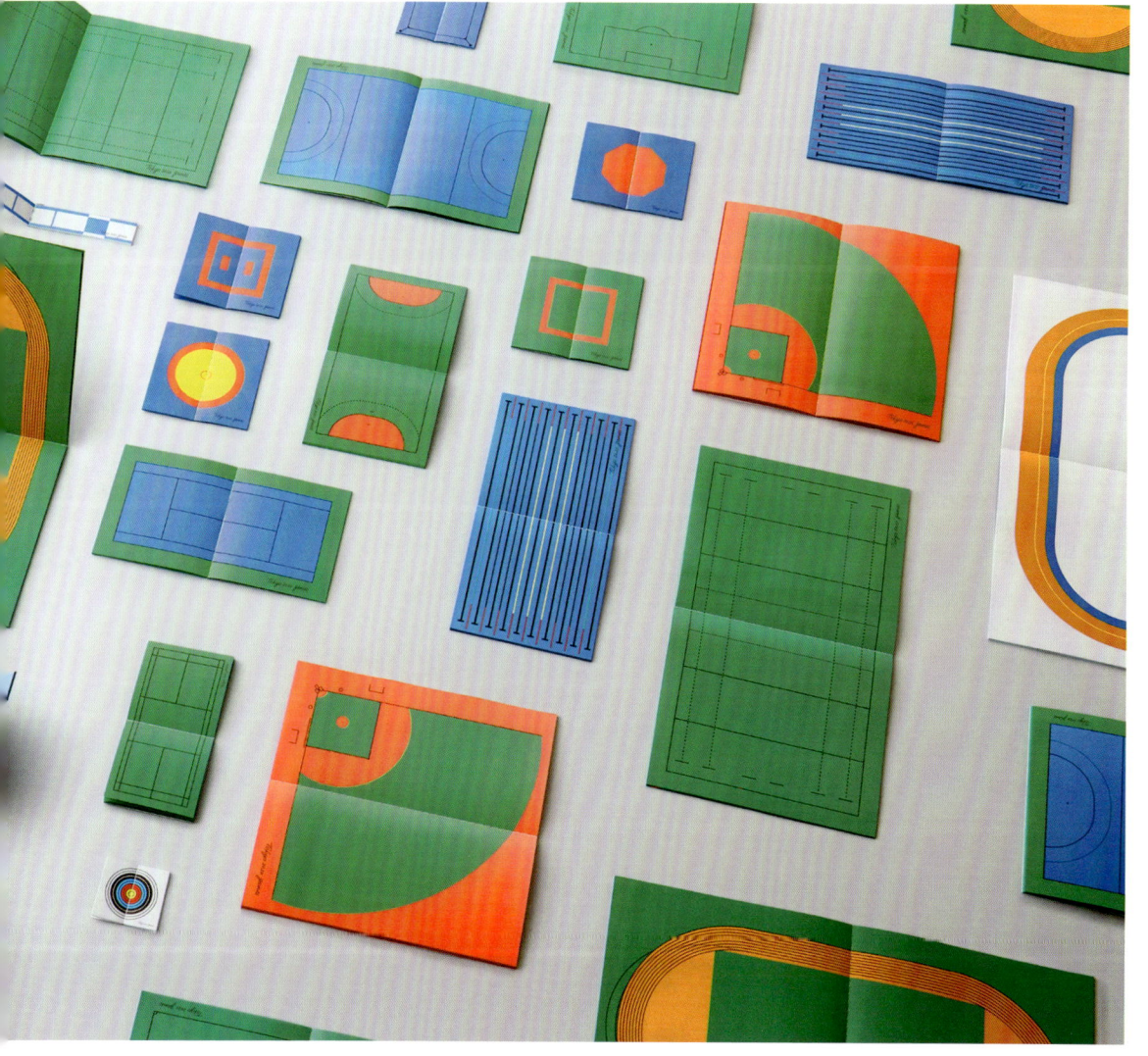

佐々木拓

Q YOHAK DESIGN STUDIO is a design collective at the service of KOKUYO. As a member of the team, what do you think is the key to developing innovative design constantly for a time-honored brand like KOKUYO?

A KOKUYO's YOHAK DESIGN STUDIO brings together creators of different genres, including in-house space designers, graphic designers, and product designers, to engage in cross-disciplinary design. The work is done through a combination of independent projects and client work, and the designers are expanding the scope of both activities while constantly learning.

Being originally from KOKUYO, we often work on how to carry on the existing image rather than creating an image from scratch. If an image is already established, it means there are elements that people have been familiar with and loved for many years, and when those elements are reviewed again in a flat way, we consider what meaning and points of contact they can have in our lives and society today. It is important to learn from the various aspects of context and wisdom that have grown up in our history and to repeatedly devise ways to apply them to the future.

Q You work as an art director as well as a product designer on the team. How does the process and idea of designing the product influence the thinking to present the product graphically?

A When planning a new product brand, we always keep both product and promotion in mind from the planning stage. We do not just express the product through graphic design, but create the product according to the intention and image we want to convey in the final product. Depending on the project, we may start creating a website or key visuals before the product is finished.

In the past, when I showed a product I had designed to my acquaintances, the product designers responded enthusiastically, but this is not the case with graphic designers and space designers. The final output is not just for the designer to see. It is important to make decisions based on a variety of perspectives and values.

Taku Sasaki

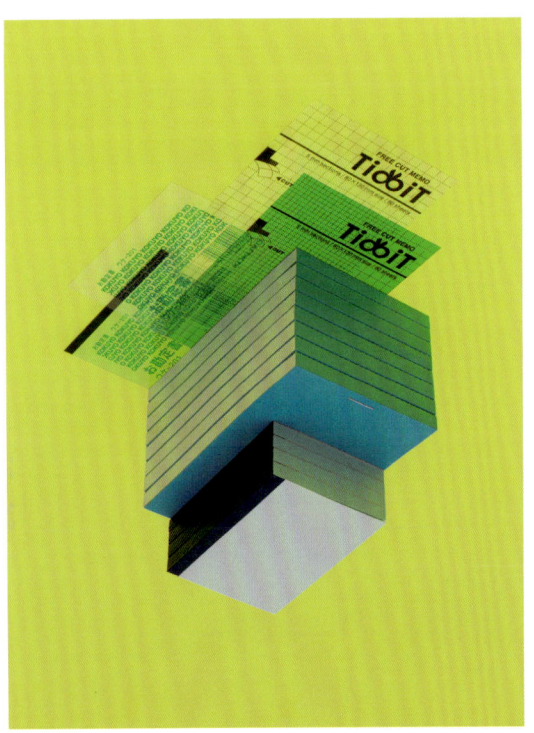
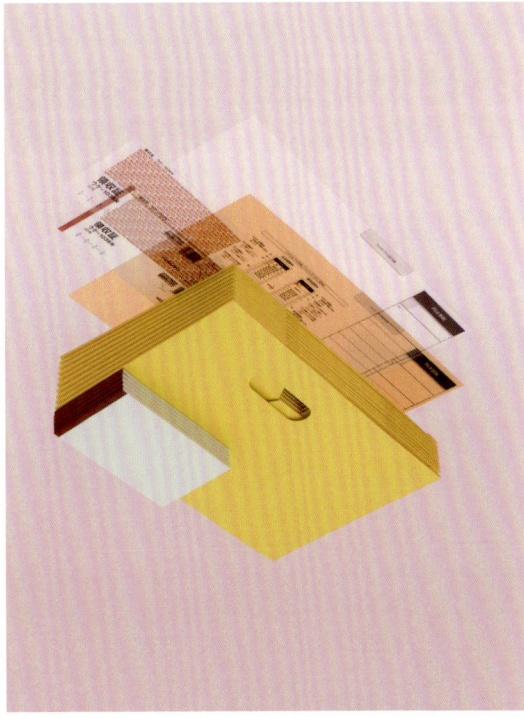

EX-

A series of products by KOKUYO's THINK OF THINGS offering stationery and everyday tools along with new ways to work and live. The series' name "EX-" means "former." It strays from KOKUYO's signature graphics and materials and emphasizes properties that make up the true essence of tools, such as aesthetic shapes, meticulous designs, and vibrant colors—things people often take for granted. It's a stationary series that inspires new ways to create. The designers are also thinking about new approaches to create while sticking to the idea of inexpensive, high-quality, conventional industrial production.

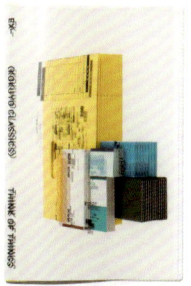

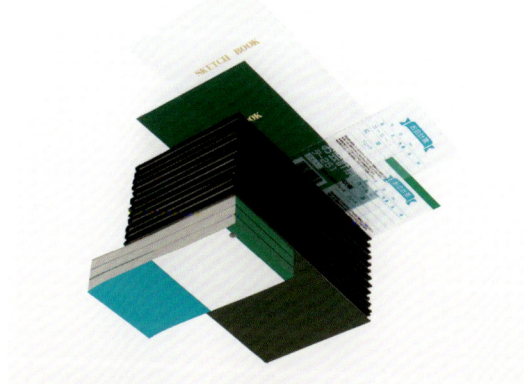

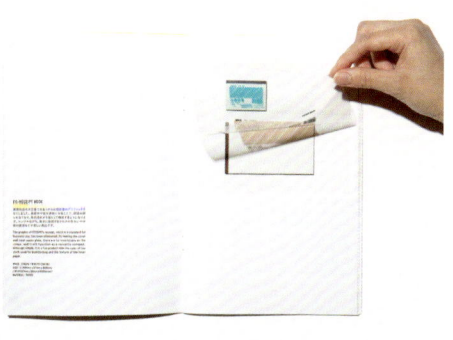

Q Do you favor a particular kind of visual language? Are there any explorations you have been conducting on design language?

A Currently, I like to use expressions that have a visual play that can be perceived as both three-dimensional and two-dimensional. Visual language is something I explore with each project and I am constantly lost in the process.

Q Design is the coordination of many sub-fields. What are some practices in the design mindset that can motivate designers' interdisciplinary thinking?

A I have always loved looking at the work of designers and artists, even more than designing. No matter the field, I find people who have arrived at and achieved things that I could never have thought of and I wonder why they were able to do it. It is important to find something you like or something that interests you, to explore it, and keep learning.

Q In your opinion, what elements are needed to make a good piece of work?

A Good work is sincere, captures the essence of things, shows an inquiring mind and thought, and invokes hope and awareness.

Q In recent years, many creations from Japan have been presented through new media or forms. How do you look at contemporary graphic design in Japan and what is your expectation?

A Society as a whole, not only in the design world, but also in Japan, is still undergoing a whirlwind of major changes. Designers are also members of this society and, in designing, the relationship with society is inseparable. In this context, there may be little that graphic design alone can do, or that Japan alone can do but I believe that by overlapping, influencing, and collaborating with diverse values, designs that give us hope for the future will continue to emerge. I would like to continue designing as a member of this group and as an activity to maintain my hope.

佐々木拓

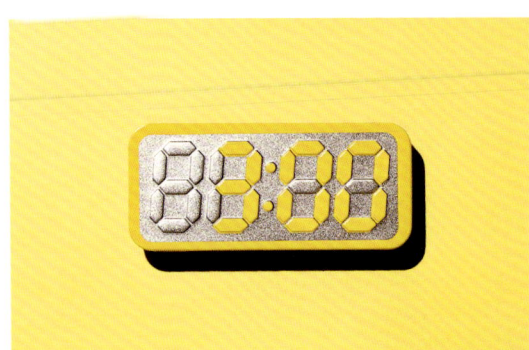

MINUTE MINT

Minute Mint is a mint candy designed to dissolve in a certain amount of time. The tablets dissolve in the time on the package. This snack offers a new experience for people when they want to switch work mode on or off, or want to take a break. To visually express the concept of "measuring time by eating time," the packaging features a hexagonal tablet shape that resembles the segments of a digital clock and "1:30" and "3:00" are embossed on the package. It's a joint creation by confectionery maker UHA Mikakuto, stationery and furniture maker KOKUYO, and creative studio Whatever.

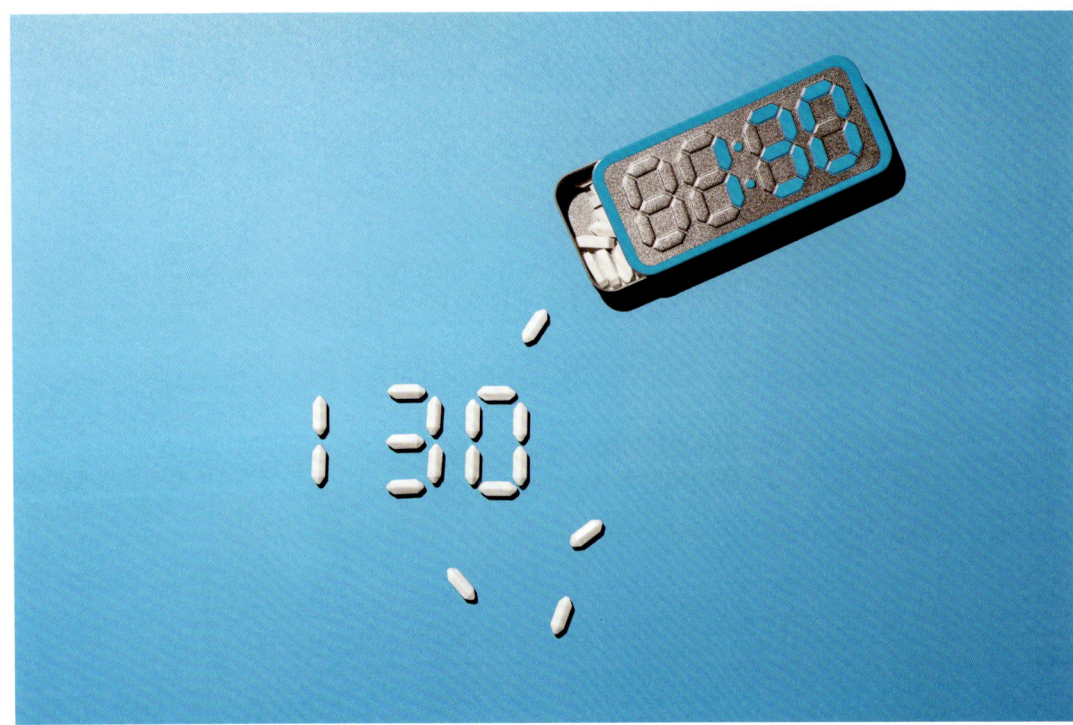

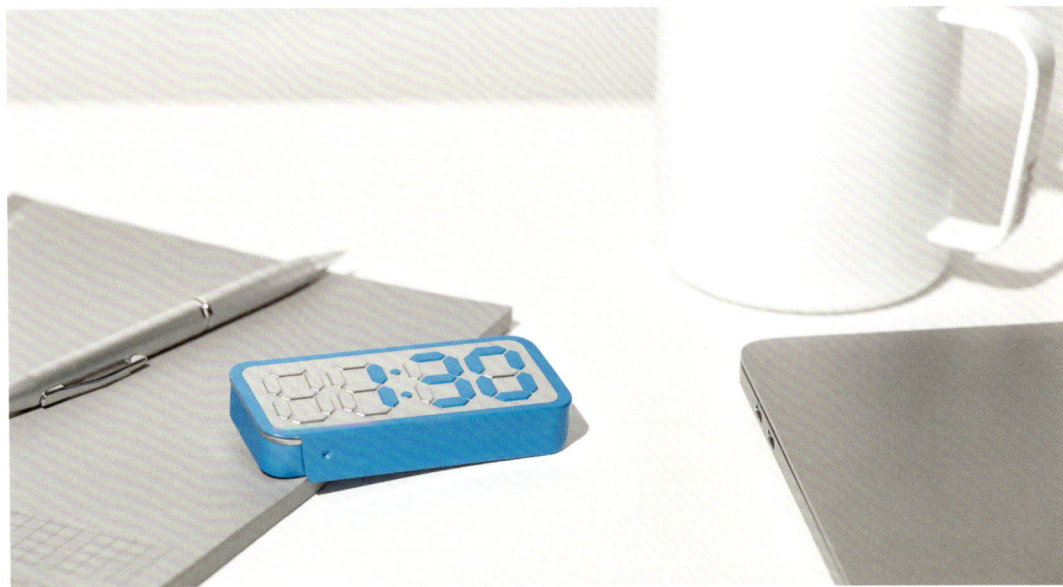

Taku Sasaki

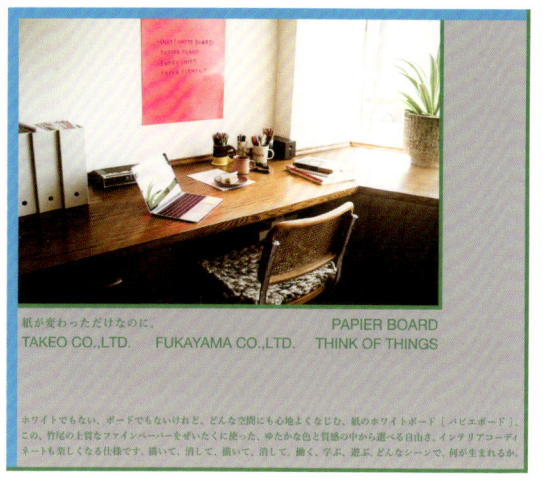

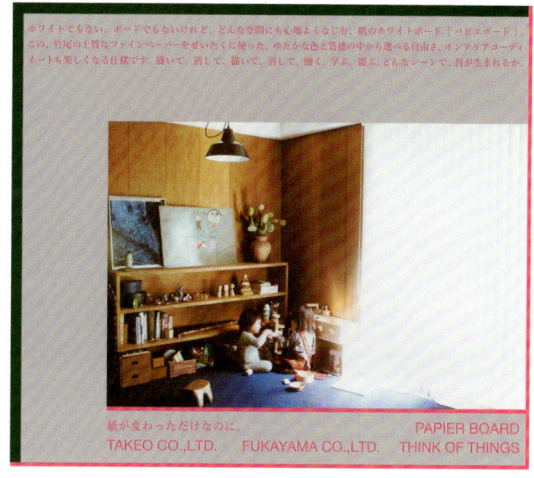

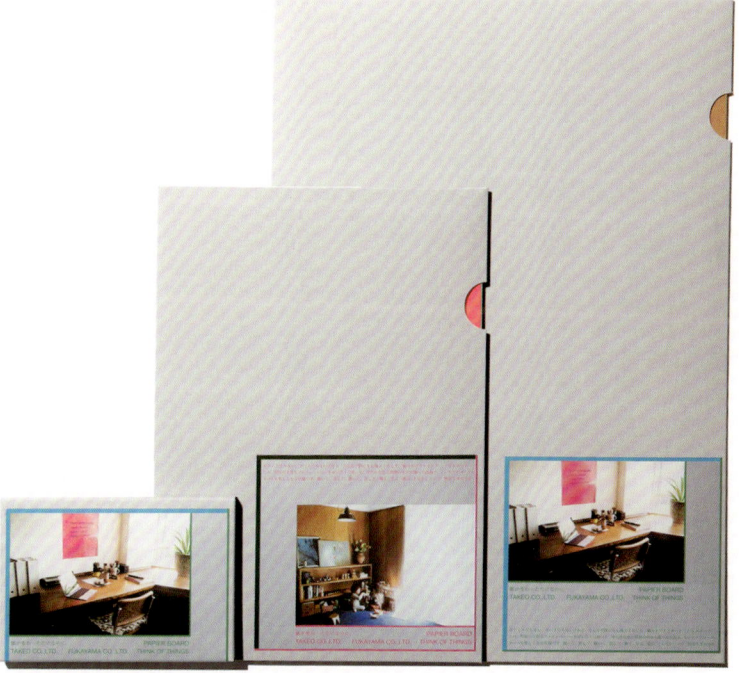

佐々木拓

PAPIER BOARD

It's neither white nor a board, but a paper whiteboard made of 100% pulp. Created from Takeo's high-quality fine paper, it comes in various colors and textures. It's fun to use for interior decoration, too. Because it's paper, users can choose their favorite color and stick it up like a poster, clip it onto a wall, or cut it. They can also customize it for their own spaces and lifestyles. This product brand was developed jointly by KOKUYO's THINK OF THINGS and paper trading companies Takeo and Fukayama to provide the optimal experience when writing or drawing, whether for work, school, or fun.

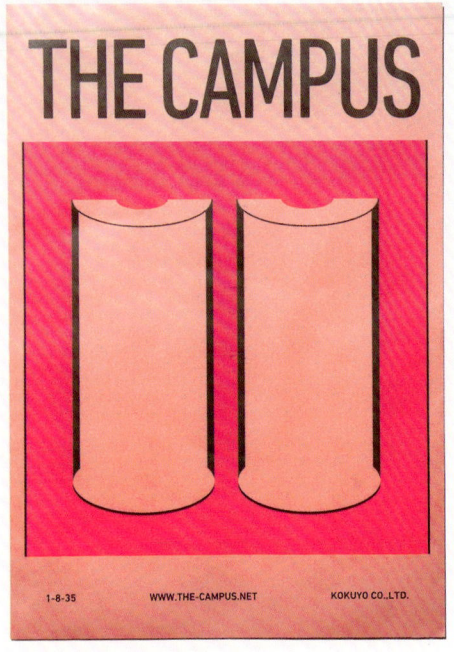

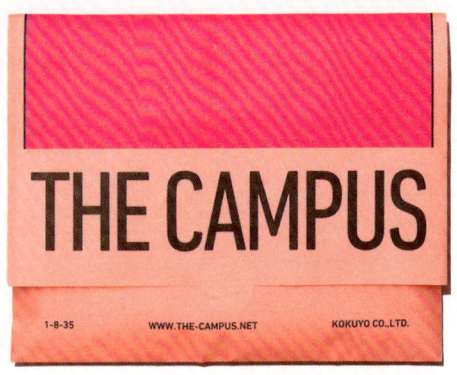

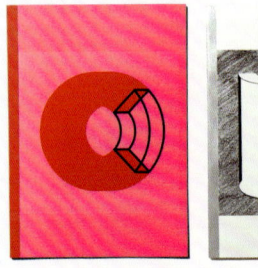
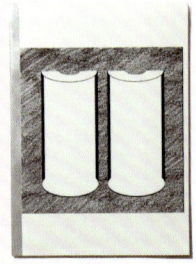

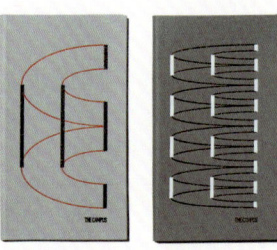

THE CAMPUS

THE CAMPUS is a laboratory from KOKUYO with the theme of "Work and Live." It has been redesigned as a living space not just for its staff, but for the whole public, creating a rich, diverse mix for the future generation. This graphic is the facility's new icon and the first letter of its name, "C." The transforming shape gives a sense of expansive space and symbolizes diverse activities. The pink similarly represents diversity, while having a warm, gentle feel that brings the people and the town closer to the company and reminds them of new beginnings.

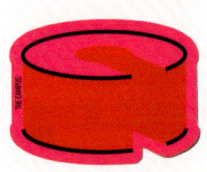

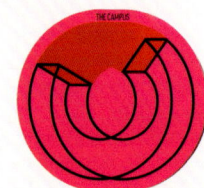

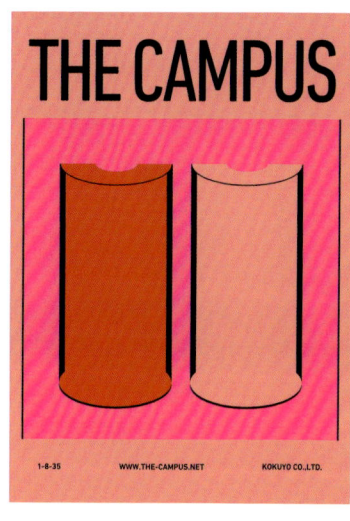

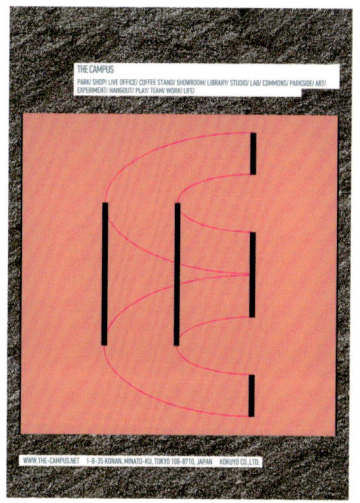

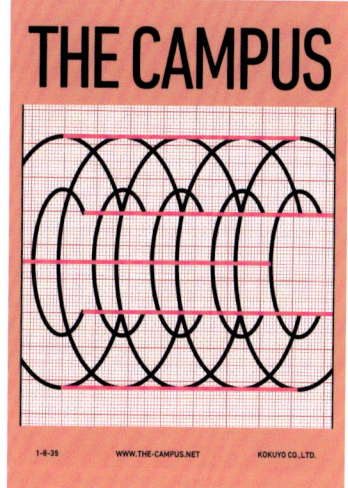

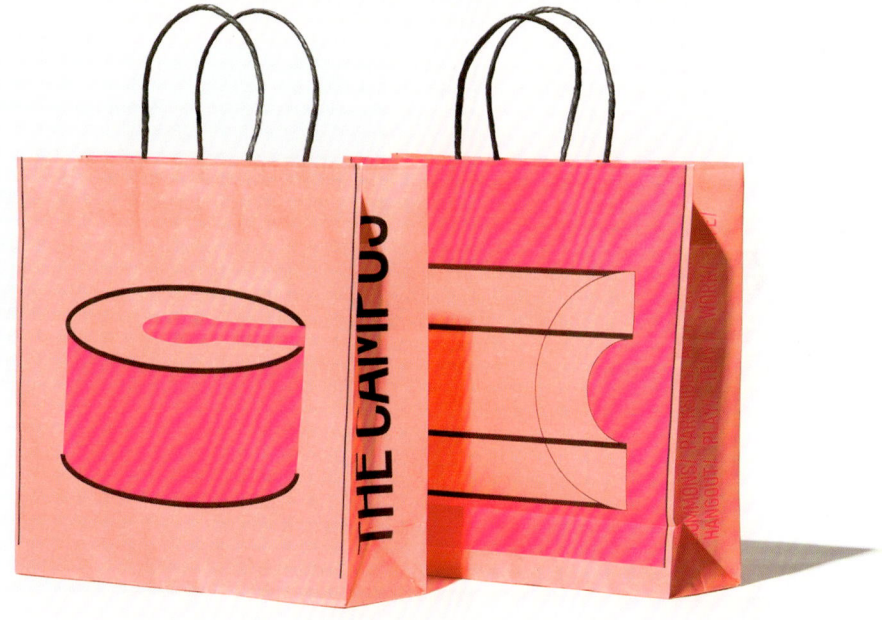

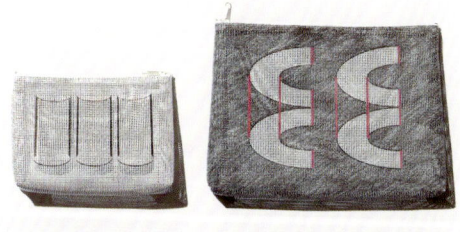

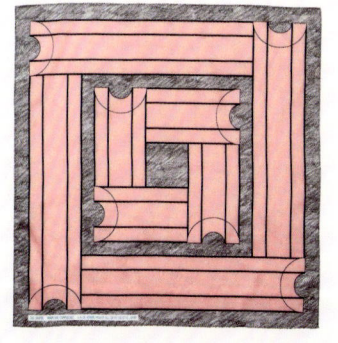

Inspiration will not come to
a sleep-deprived designer.

Shun Sasaki

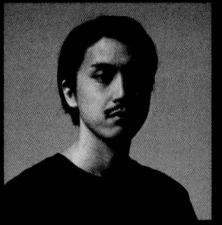

Shun Sasaki is a graphic designer and art director. He
was born in Sendai, Japan in 1985. He studied graphic
design at Tama Art University and graduated in 2010
and founded his graphic design office AYOND in 2016.
In 2020, he was selected for the JAGDA New Designer
Award.

Q Could you share your overall impression of Japanese graphic design?

A For Japanese graphic design, be it a good or bad work, there is a lightness to it.

Q What do you think of the influence of the Japanese aesthetic heritage, social culture and graphic design education? How do they work into your design philosophy and practice?

A I am not aware of any influence of something like traditional "Japanese-ness" for me. My goal is to be free from the spell of such aesthetics as much as possible.

Q Do you think your design has a personal style? How do you keep a balance between your design expression and clients' preferences?

A I do not think I have a specific style. I want to create the most appropriate graphic answers to both commercial and personal work.

Q What do you do when you run low on inspiration and have difficulties progressing on the project?

A Getting away from your desk and taking a walk outside will bring you good ideas. It is important to move.

Q Human is your personal project and it presents the image of a human in motion. Why did you choose the theme of human? Any thoughts behind the creation?

A Because human is the most familiar and easy motif. There is no deep reason. I just wanted to have fun creating a shape that was on the edge of looking human. What is special about the graphic is the strange balance between the head that looks like a dot and the body that fills the paper.

Q The design you've done for Tahi Saihate is distinctive. How do you maintain the overall style while keeping each work unique?

A To read poetry is also to face oneself. In my work with Tahi Saihate, I am honest about what colors and shapes I imagine for the words she writes and I use them instinctively in my graphic design. It is like designing by instinct rather than thought.

Q Could you share your design idea of Tahi Saihate exhibition posters with us?

A The design illustrates that various cells of poetry come together, connecting with and relating to each other like gears. It is also an image of the moment when words are chained together to form a poem.

Q What is the message you are trying to deliver with the poster Nature Is Not Your Household?

A This is based on the language of philosophy. However, I dared to do the wild thing, going out of my way to turn the language of philosophy into an illustrative visual.

Q How can a designer create works that are peculiar and thought-provoking?

A I think it is about getting a good night's sleep. Inspiration will not come to a sleep-deprived designer.

佐々木俊

Q You mentioned that life provides the nutrients to design. How does daily inspiration work for your creations?

A It is important to really be interested in it, but not observing it for the purpose of reflecting it in your work.

Q Are there any explorations you have been conducting on design language?

A The tension between form and color.

Q How do you look at contemporary graphic design in Japan and what is your expectation?

A I believe that we will be more influenced by graphic design in China and other Asian countries.
Japan's unique philosophy will fade away and blend in with the rest of the world.

Shun Sasaki

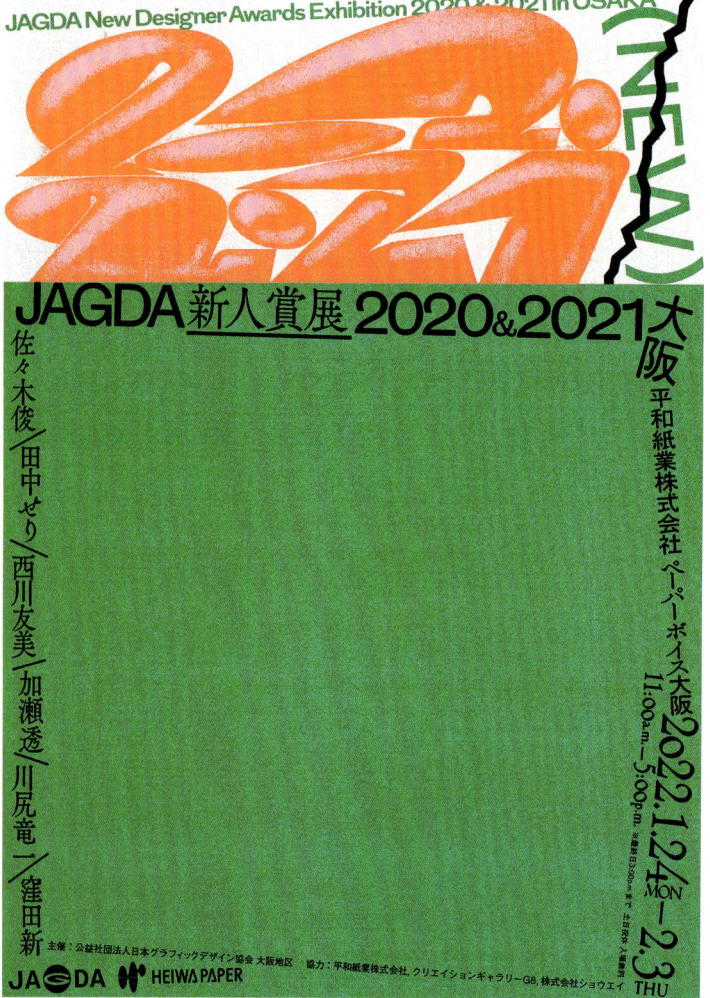

JAGDA NEW DESIGNER AWARDS EXHIBITION
This is an exhibition poster for the designers who received the JAGDA New Designer Award in 2020 and 2021. The exaggerated and deformed numbers at the top of the poster indicate the year of the award, while the bottom half of the poster presents the names of the winners, the organizers, the exhibition schedule, etc. This information is presented in a rectangular-like manner around the poster, with the center left blank, like the great possibilities in the designers' works. The poster is in bright orange and steady green. The two colors collide with each other and are full of tension.

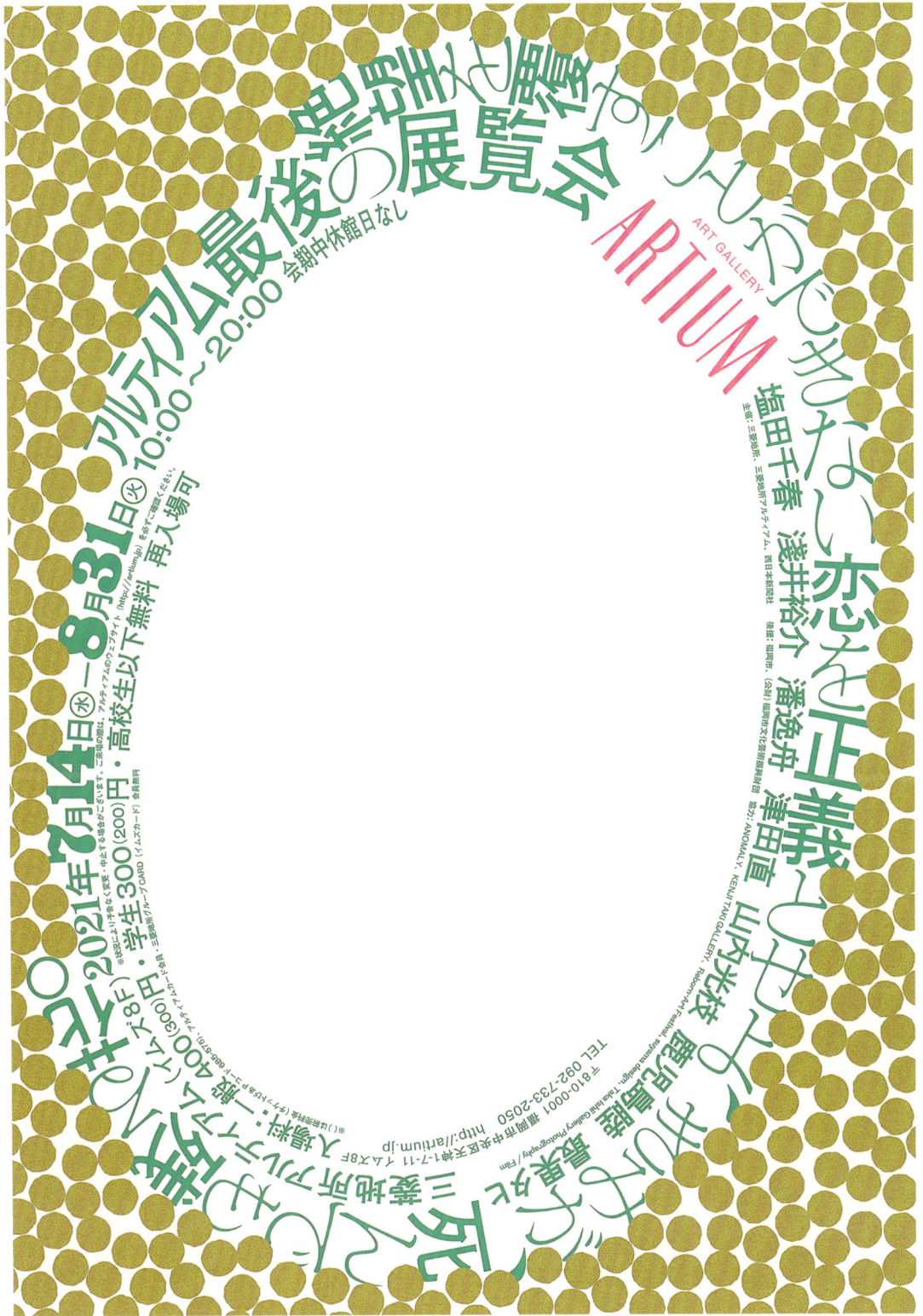

THE LAST EXHIBITION OF ARTIUM

Shun Sasaki designed a poster for the final exhibition of the Mitsubishi Estate Artium, filling the poster's outer perimeter with a circular shape that expresses the splendor and richness of the work of the designers who exhibited at the Artium. The theme and message of the exhibition are enclosed in an oval shape, leaving a blank space in the middle, allowing room for the viewer's imagination.

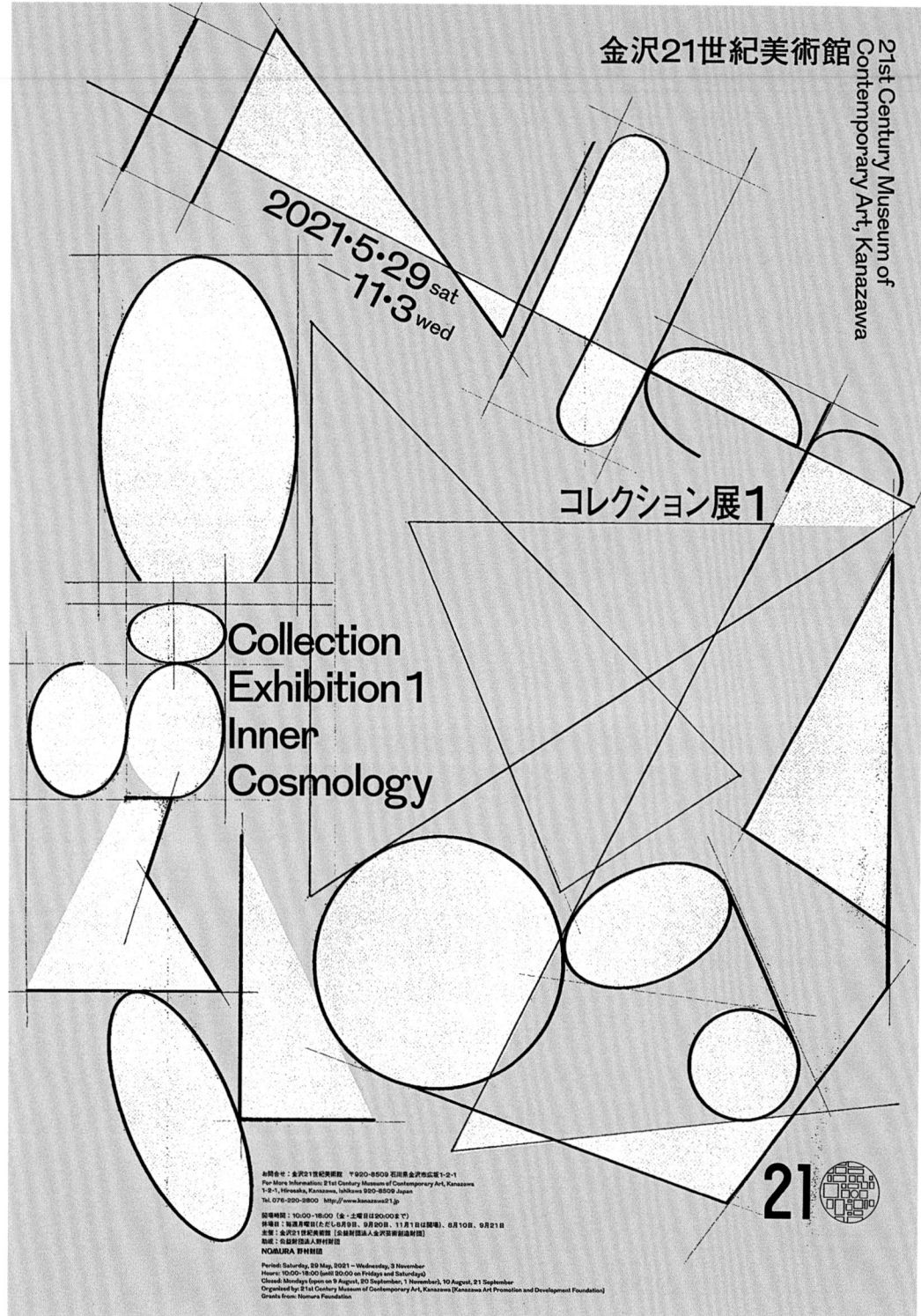

Shun Sasaki

金沢21世紀美術館

21st Century Museum of Contemporary Art, Kanazawa

2021・5・29 sat — 11・3 wed

コレクション展1

Collection
Exhibition 1
Inner
Cosmology

お問合せ：金沢21世紀美術館 〒920-8509 石川県金沢市広坂1-2-1
For More Information: 21st Century Museum of Contemporary Art, Kanazawa
1-2-1, Hirosaka, Kanazawa, Ishikawa 920-8509 Japan
Tel. 076-220-2800 http://www.kanazawa21.jp

開館時間：10:00-18:00（金・土曜日は20:00まで）
休館日：毎週月曜日（ただし8月9日、9月20日、11月1日は開館）、8月10日、9月21日
主催：金沢21世紀美術館［公益財団法人金沢芸術創造財団］
助成：公益財団法人野村財団

NOMURA 野村財団

Period: Saturday, 29 May, 2021 – Wednesday, 3 November
Hours: 10:00-18:00 (until 20:00 on Fridays and Saturdays)
Closed: Mondays (open on 9 August, 20 September, 1 November), 10 August, 21 September
Organised by: 21st Century Museum of Contemporary Art, Kanazawa (Kanazawa Art Promotion and Development Foundation)
Grants from: Nomura Foundation

21

INNER COSMOLOGY

Inner Cosmology explores the power and comfort of artworks like an endless universe through the collection of the 21st Century Museum of Contemporary Art, Kanazawa. Shun Sasaki used gray and white as the main colors of the poster. Geometric shapes and auxiliary lines are scattered on the surface of the painting, seemingly irregular, but forming some kind of inner pattern and the lines have the texture of hand-painted lines, achieving a subtle balance of delicacy and warmth.

TAHI SAIHATE EXHIBITION IN NAGOYA

In the exhibition poster designed for poet Tahi Saihate, Shun Sasaki used a large number of circular elements and contrasting colors to symbolize the interconnection of poetic cells like gears and the moment when words are linked together to become poetry.

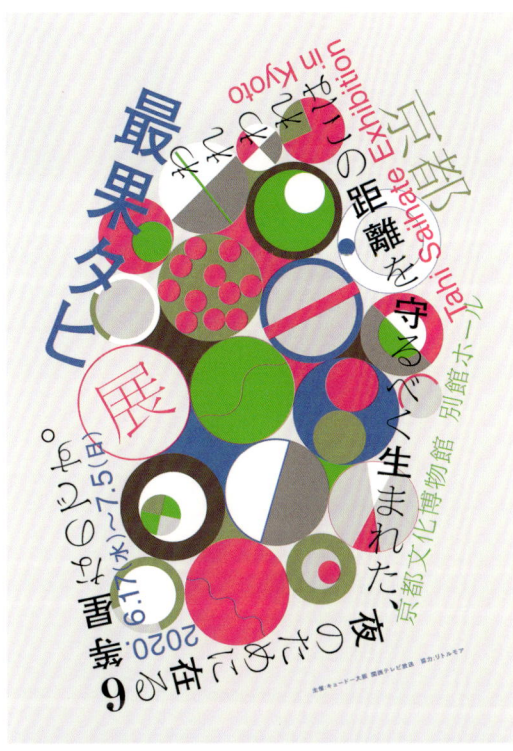

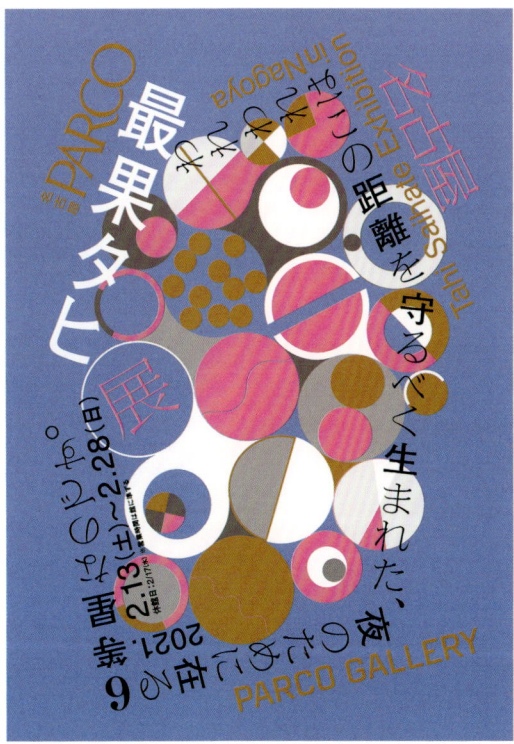

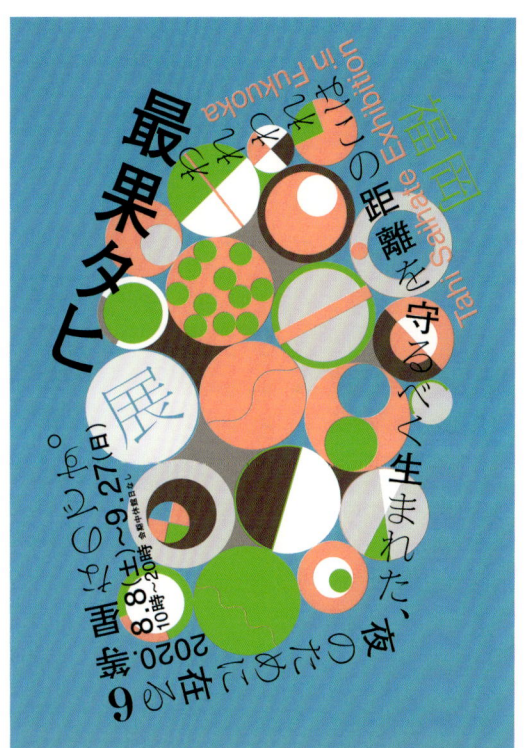

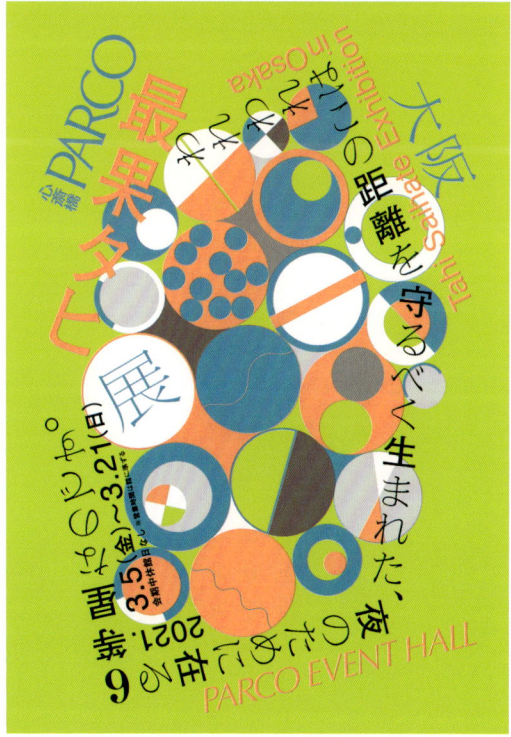

佐々木俊

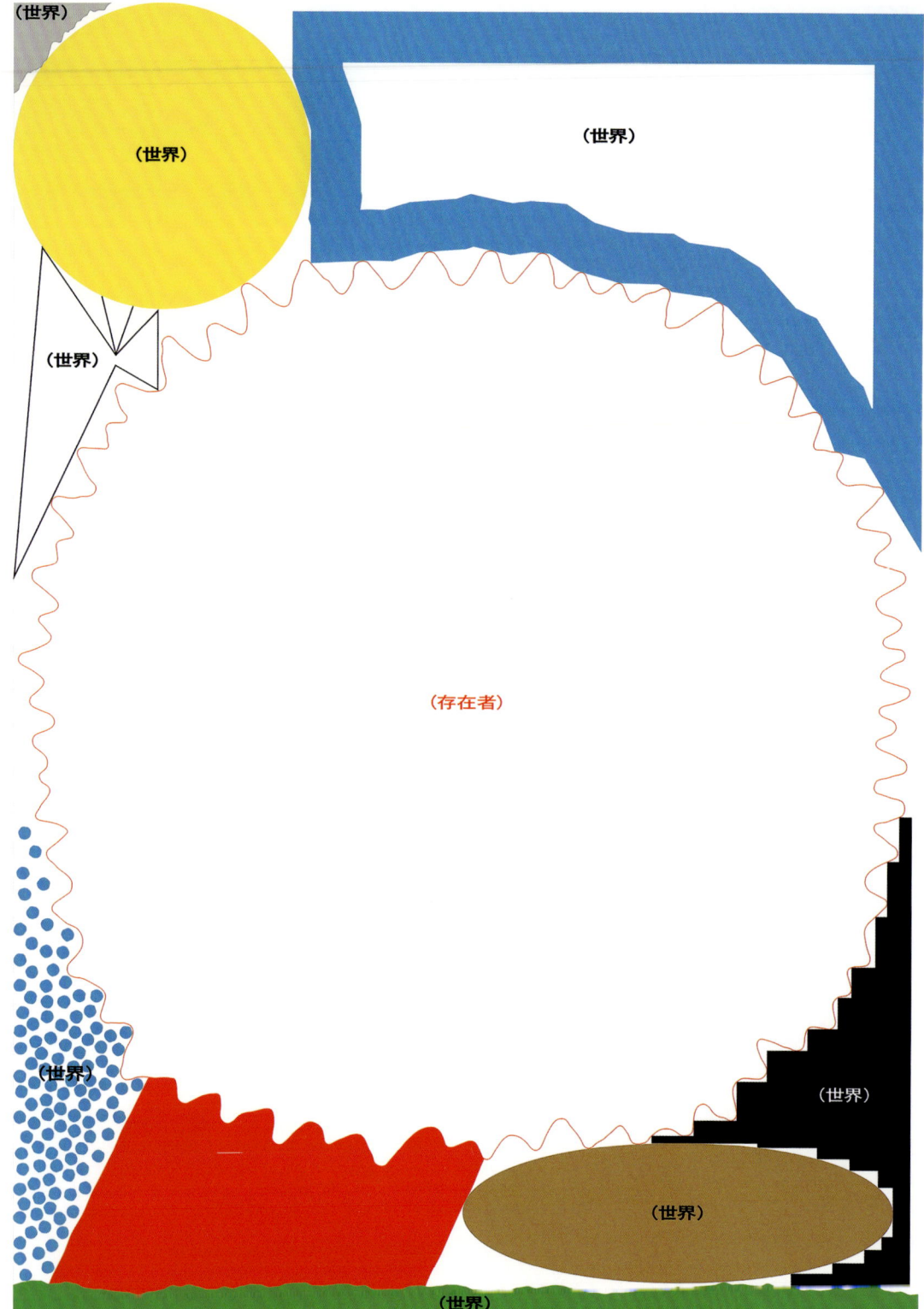

Shun Sasaki

NATURE IS NOT YOUR HOUSEHOLD
This poster presents the state between "world" and
"entity," using visual patterns to present the philosophical
language, which is a fresh and interesting collision.

SUPER DUPER PAPER DRIVER

This is a small book using digital screen printing, filled with all kinds of small cars. Since the creator himself is not used to driving cars, he can use the car as a simple container for his wild imagination.

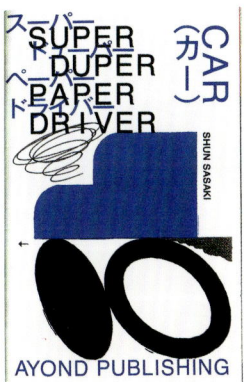

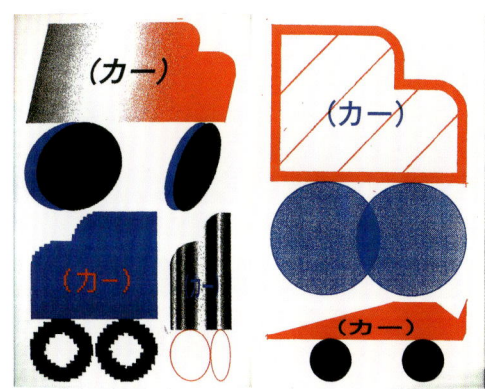

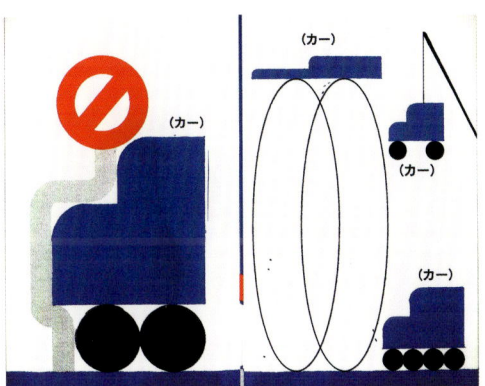

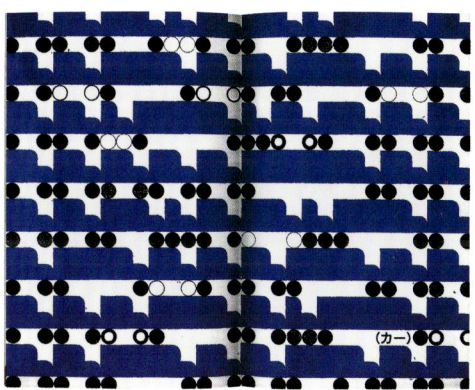

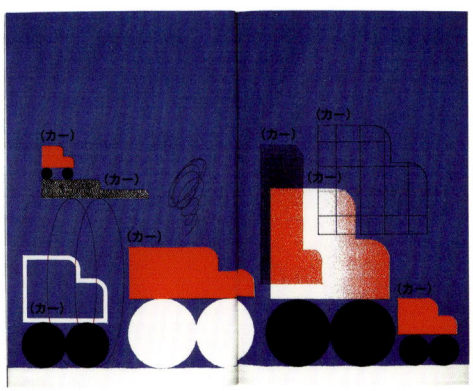

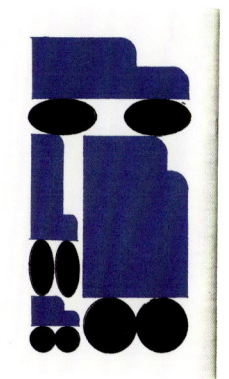

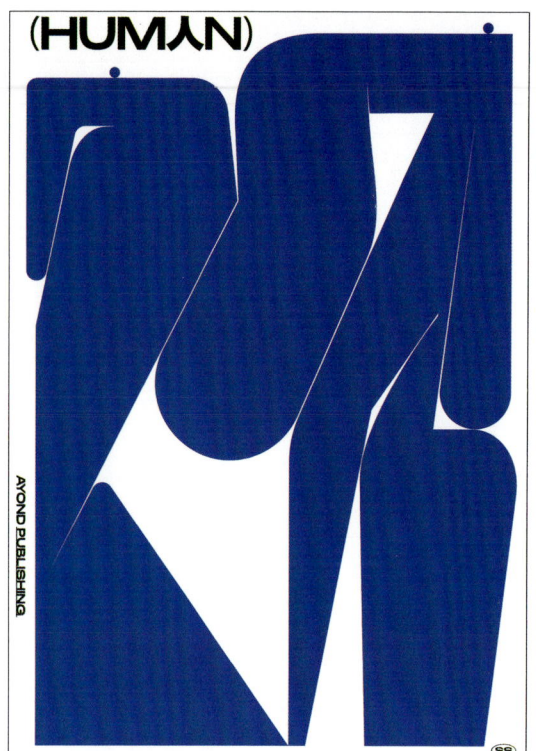

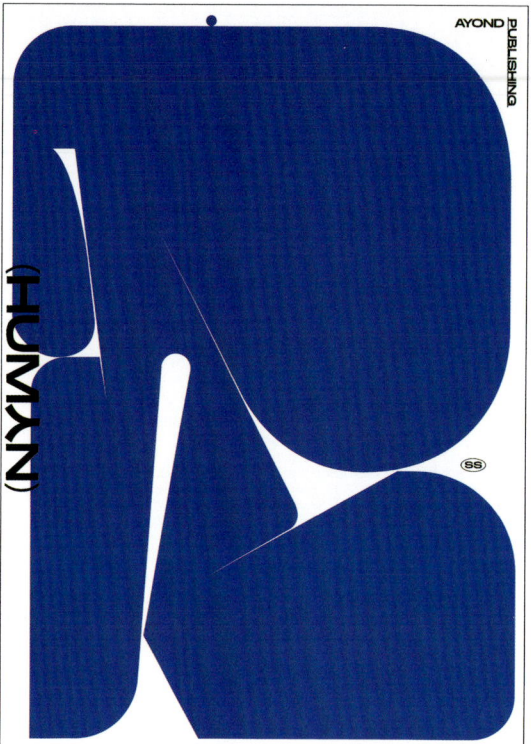

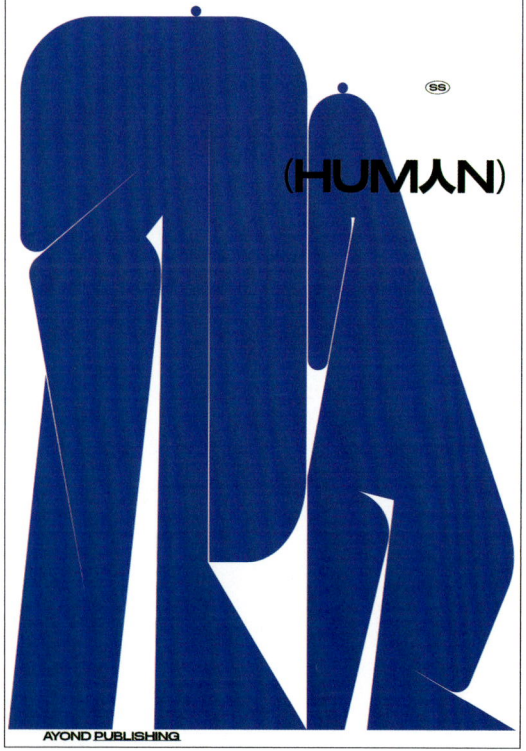

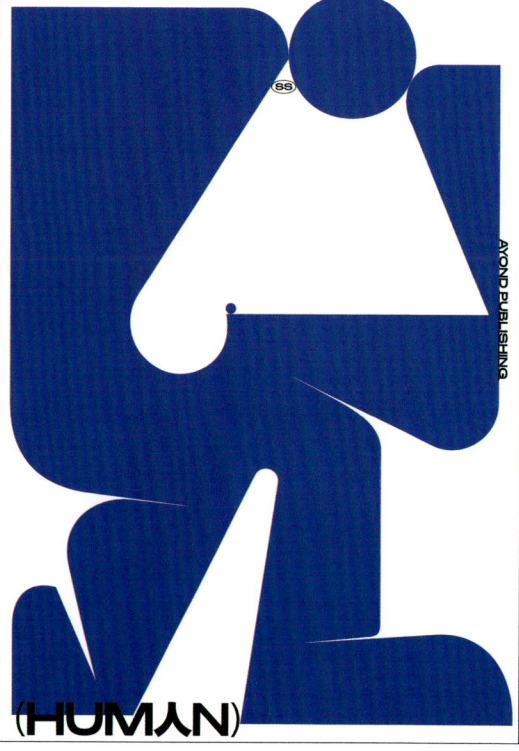

HUMAN

Shun Sasaki chose human—a theme that is the most familiar to people—for his work. The head, which is as big as a dot and the body, which covers almost the entire page, create a delicate balance and the human form is barely visible. This is a free and original attempt at creation.

Explore More Projects

その他のプロジェクトを見る

■ Branding／ブランディング

■ Environmental Graphics／環境グラフィックス

■ Poster Design／ポスターデザイン

■ Print／プリント

■ Package Design／パッケージデザイン

3

Branding

This is the identity design for Hearth Kitchen, an event to learn, talk, and think about food.

The logo in italics, arranged in a circle, was conceived as a symbol of Hearth Kitchen, which is operated by Hearth, named in the sense that it aims to be a community that connects individuals across organizational, corporate, and field boundaries and domains, just like people having a conversation around a fire.

In addition, the designer developed a schematic representation of the crop rotation as the initial visual.

D   Mariko Okazaki
CL   Hearth

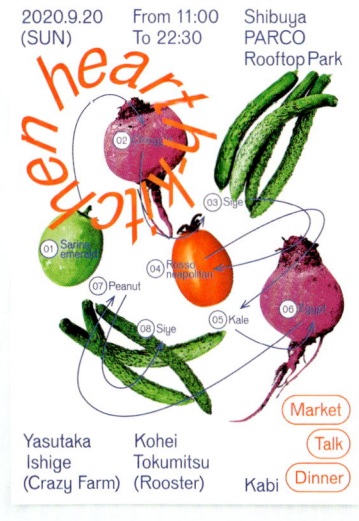

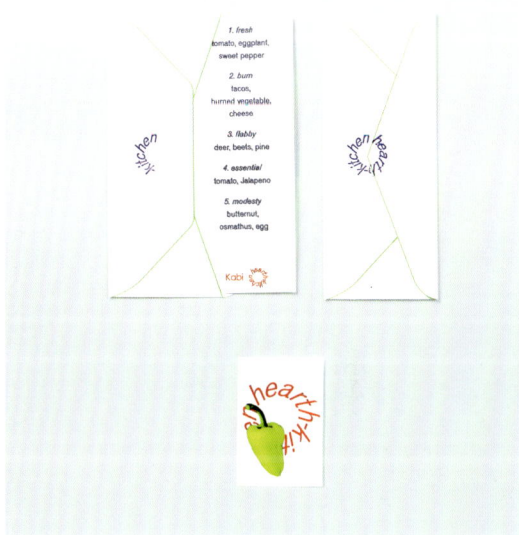

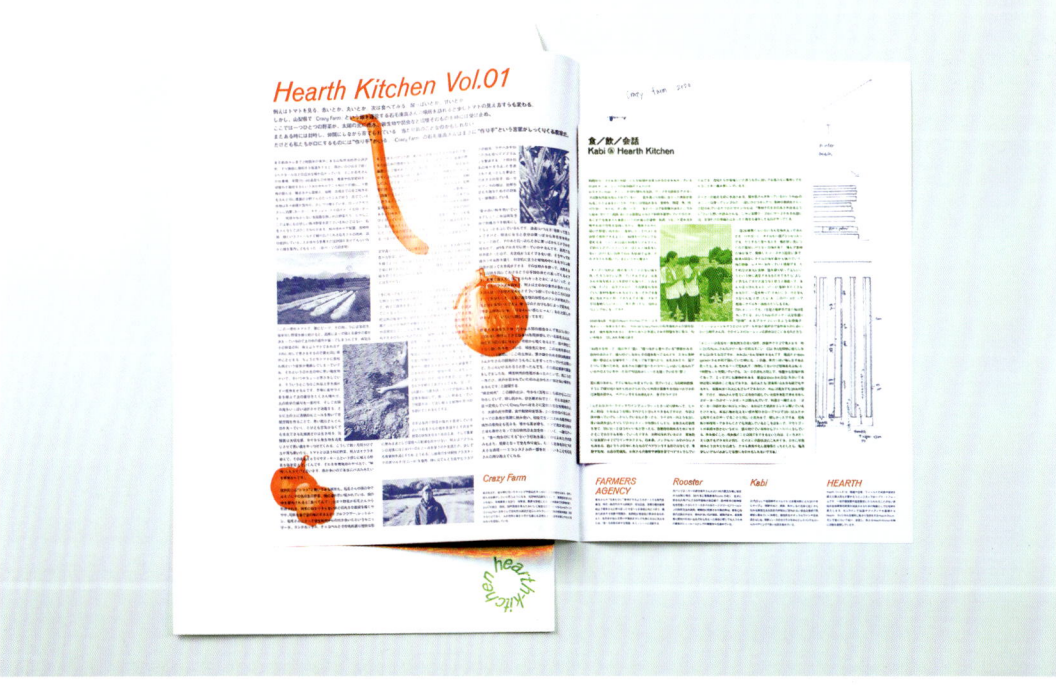

This is the package design for the collaboration between JINS and FUJISUBARU, a limited edition gift given to car purchasers. The package includes an original cleaning cloth, JINS drive lenses, and a certificate for buyers to get eyeglass frames at the store.

The driving glasses provide people with clear sight while driving. Inspired by the idea, the designer developed a concept where the color saturation and brightness are improved inside the circle. When displayed, the package can be rotated every 90 degrees or flipped back for a different look.

AD	Keiji Yano
D	Keiji Yano
CD	RCKT/Rocket Company*
CL	JINS, FUJISUBARU

JINS × FUJISUBARU

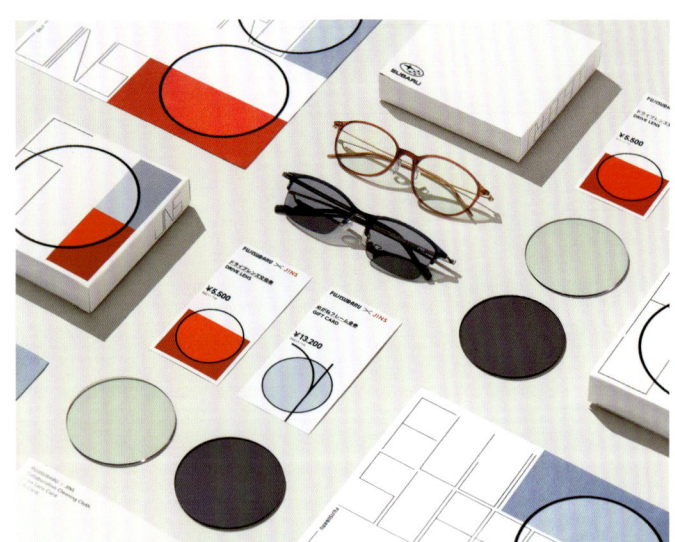

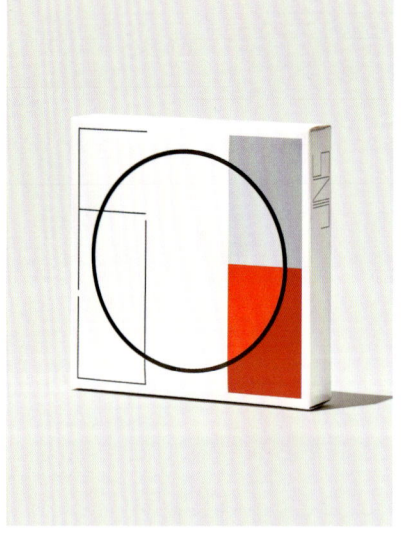

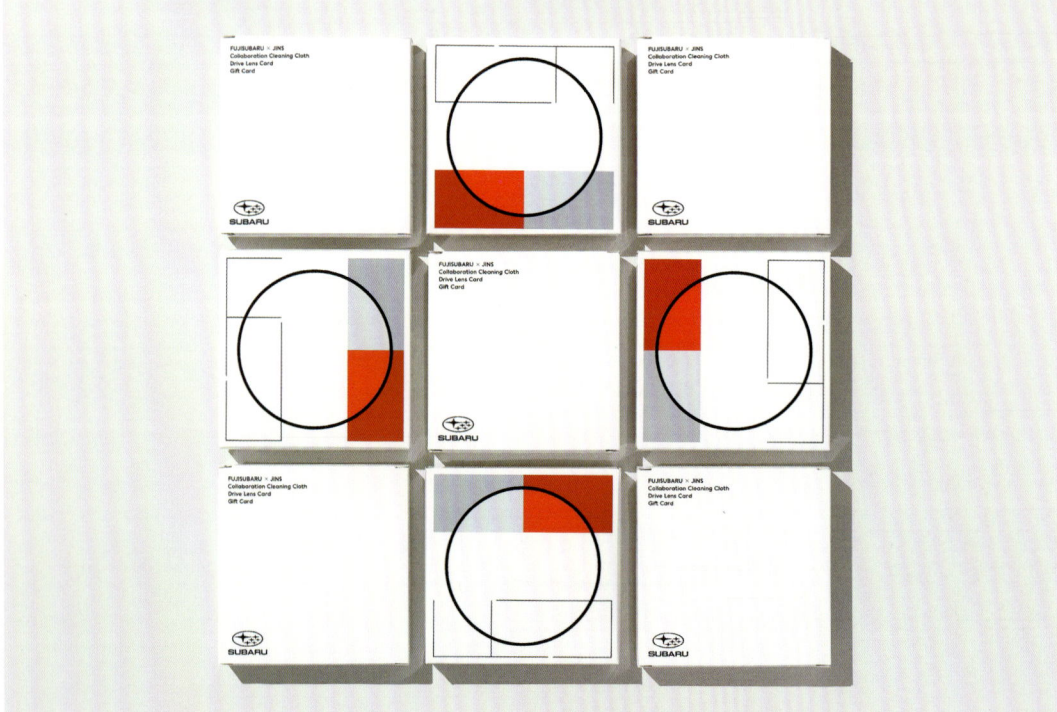

KIZASHI LLC. encourages adaptive reuse of empty
houses and facilities to create local kitchens and working
spaces. The logo design is inspired by a denominator
in mathematics, which represents the company's
philosophy to invigorate Japan by contributing to an
inclusive society and solving local issues.

CD   Kyohei Ohwa (MUSUBI inc.)
AD   Mayuko Kanazawa (KOKON Inc.)
D   Mayuko Kanazawa (KOKON Inc.)
CL   KIZASHI LLC.

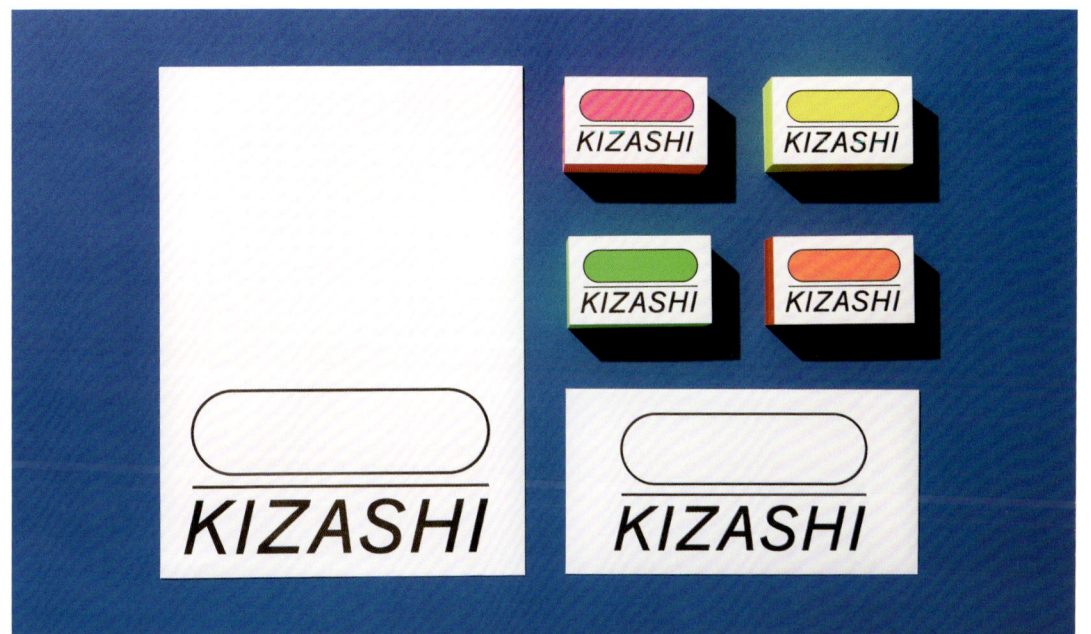

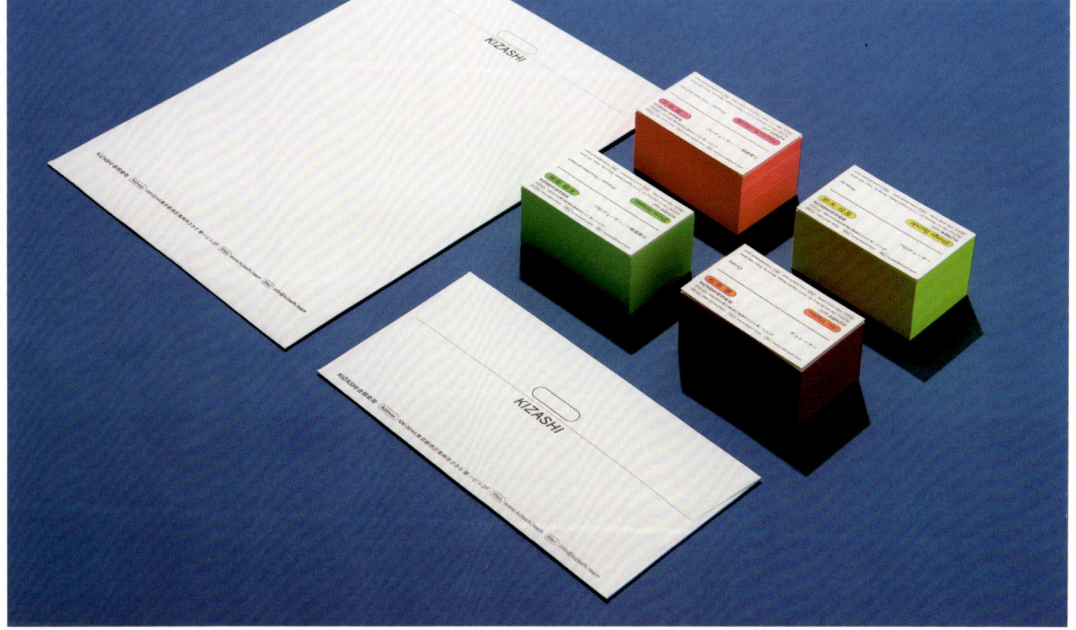

KIZASHI LLC.

This is the rebranding design for för ägg, a company that sells chiffon cakes and other western-style confections, while running a poultry farm. The design concept is the integrated production process from the poultry farm to the cake factory and the change and development from eggs to chiffon cakes. When designing the logotype, the designer took the raw egg as a double circle, put the cracked egg in the grid, and showed the process of making chiffon cake. The typography allows for individualistic change within the constraints of the divided double circle.

DA   Sitoh inc.
D   Motoi Shito
CL   för ägg

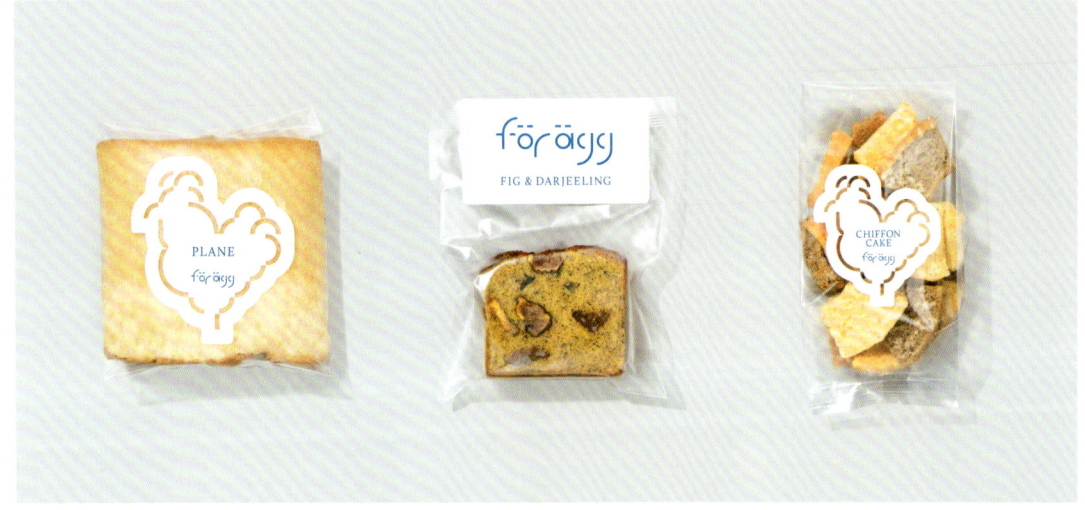

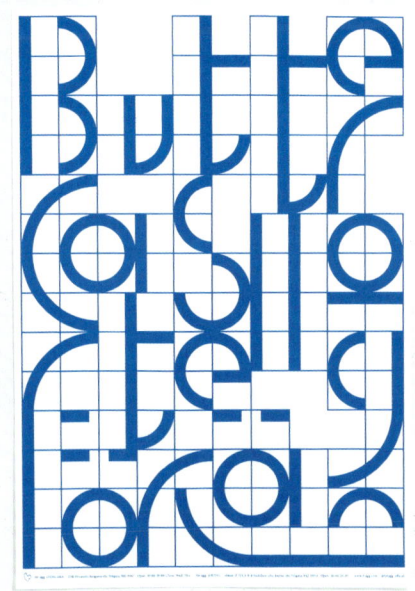

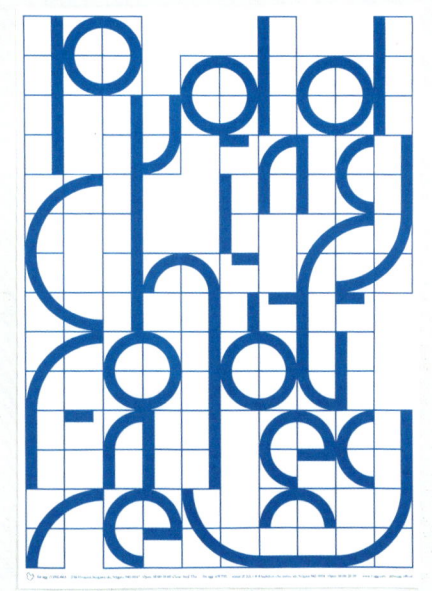

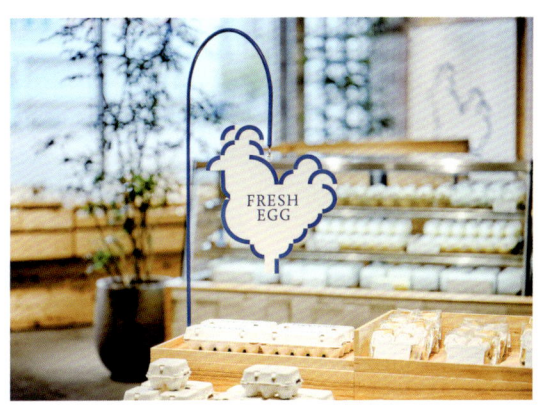

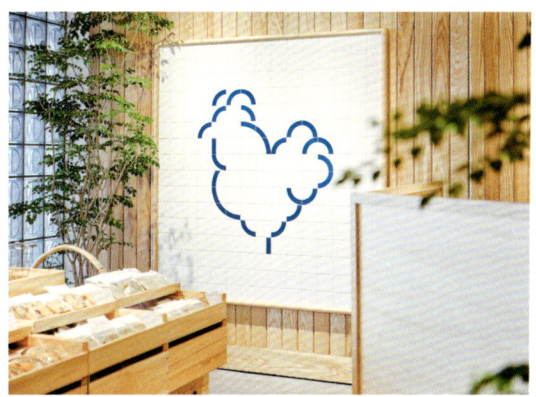

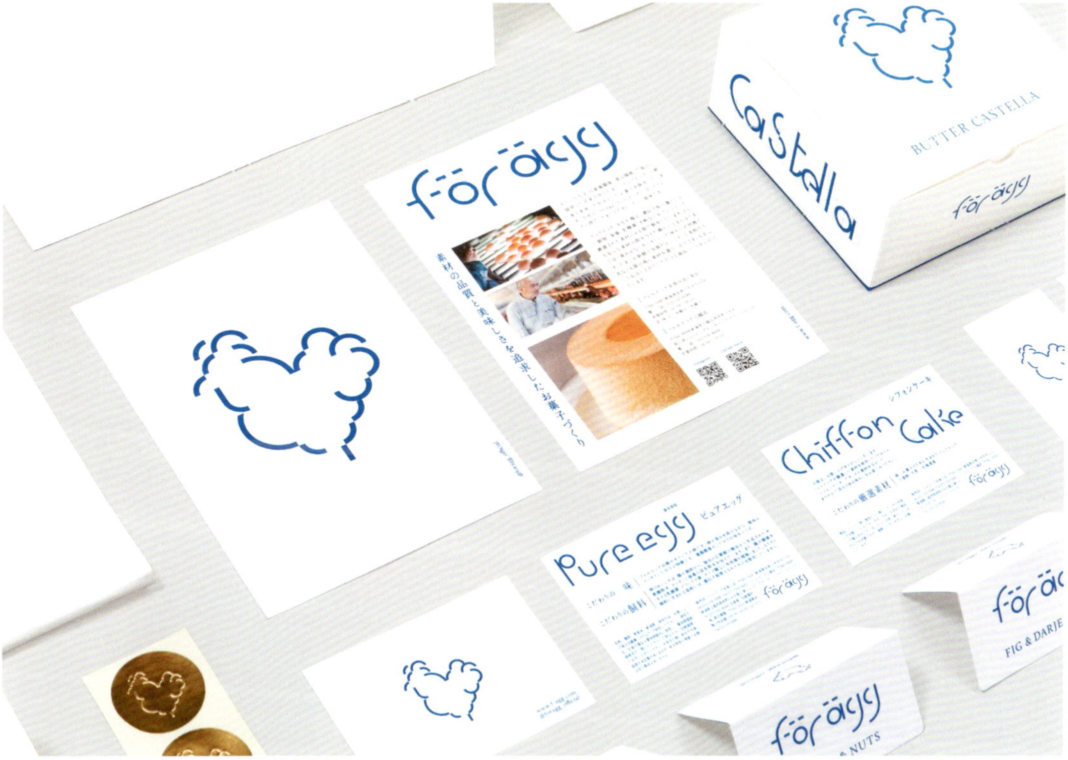

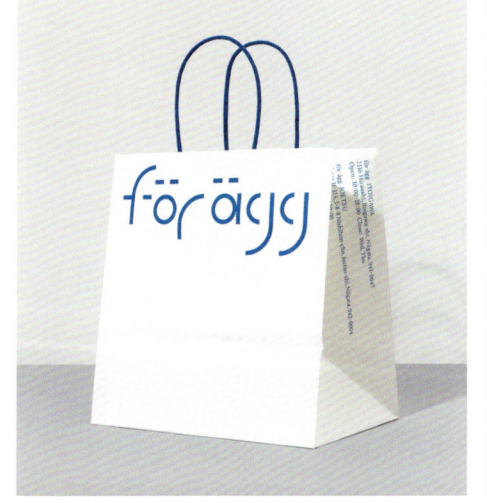

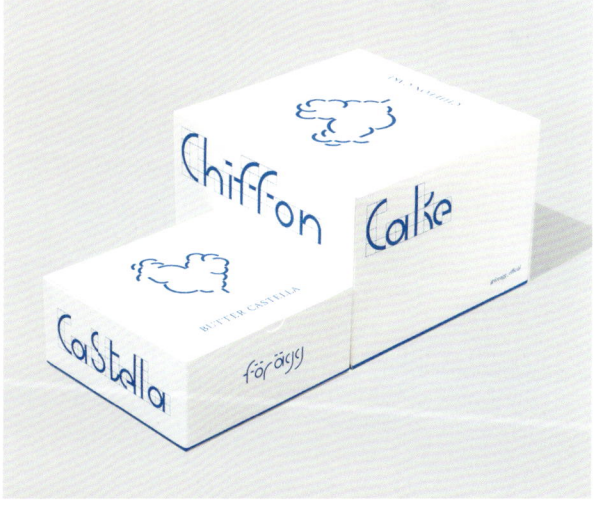

Akiko Sekimoto designed the exhibition for the renewal of
MERMAID with the inspiration that the paper of MERMAID is
manufactured at the foot of Mount Fuji.

The name MERMAID is inspired by the paper texture
that feels like the calm sea where mermaids live and the logo
describes the shape of the initial "M" of "MERMAID" together
with the "W" shape of "wave," and the reversed "W"—"M" of
Mount Fuji. Akiko Sekimoto has created works to be used
consequently, hoping that paper will be loved like the ever-
flowing ripples.

While the MERMAID portfolio was renewed with
additional heavier weights and fluorescent colors, the
properties of higher saturation and density were presented
through punched paper and kumi-bako (a solid box) in the
exhibition.

AD   Akiko Sekimoto
D   Akiko Sekimoto
CL   TAKEO CO., LTD.

Mermaid Wave

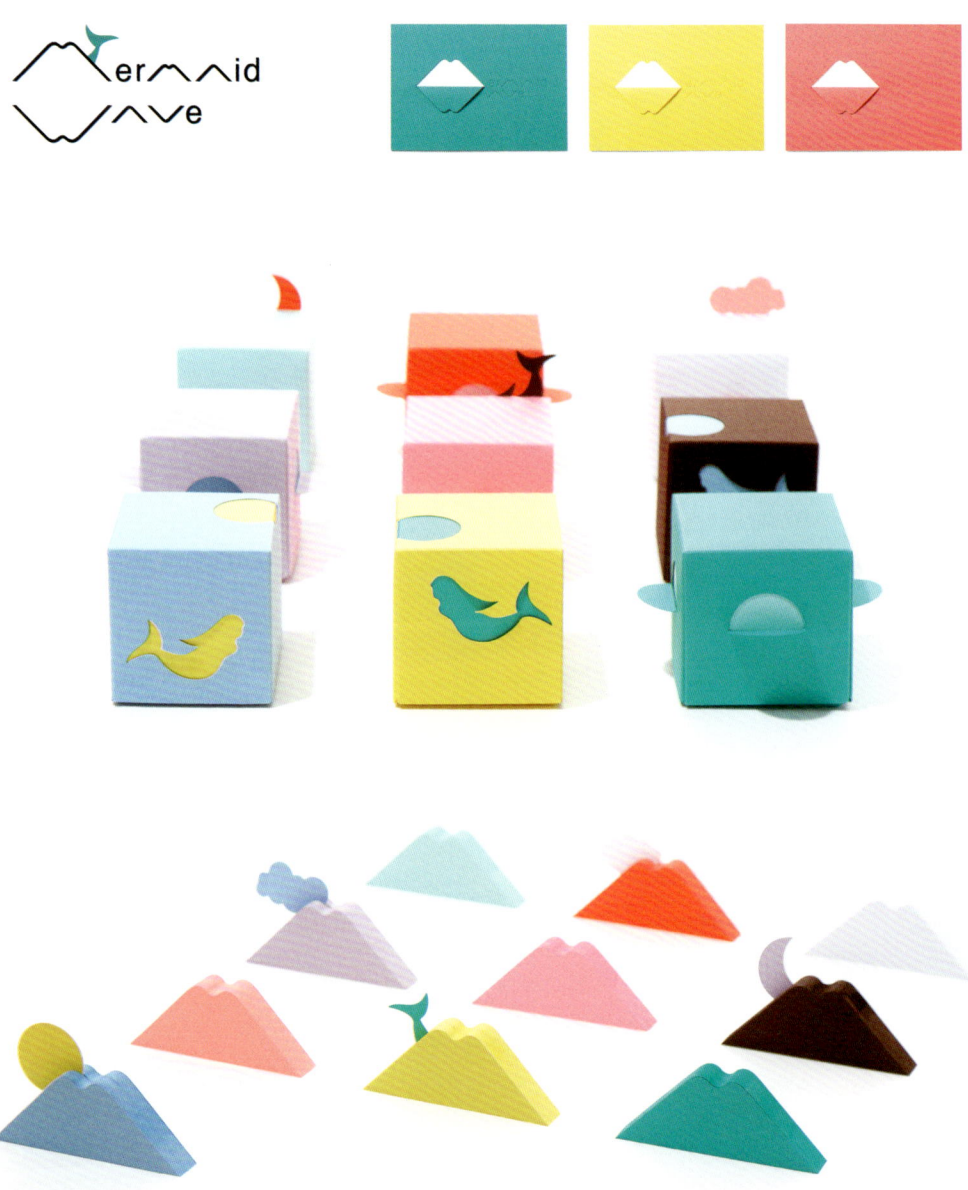

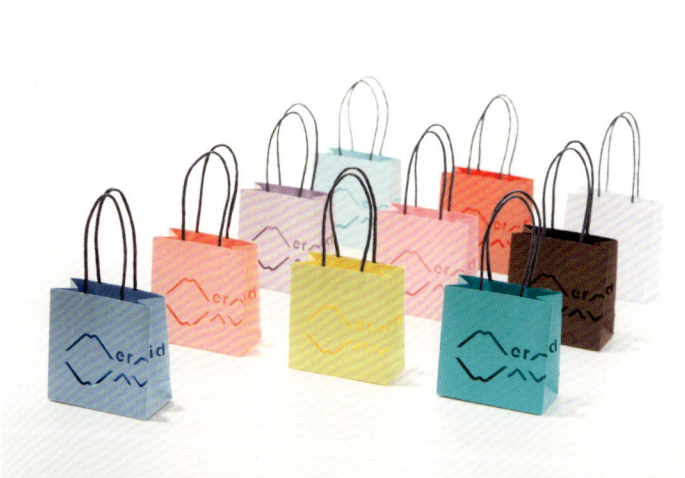
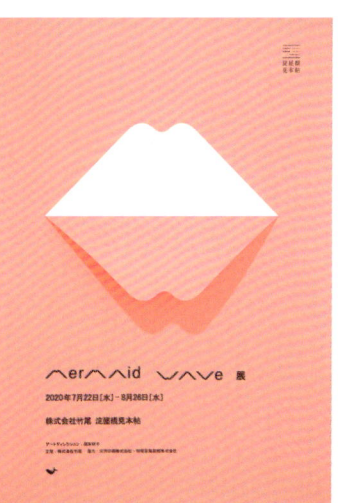
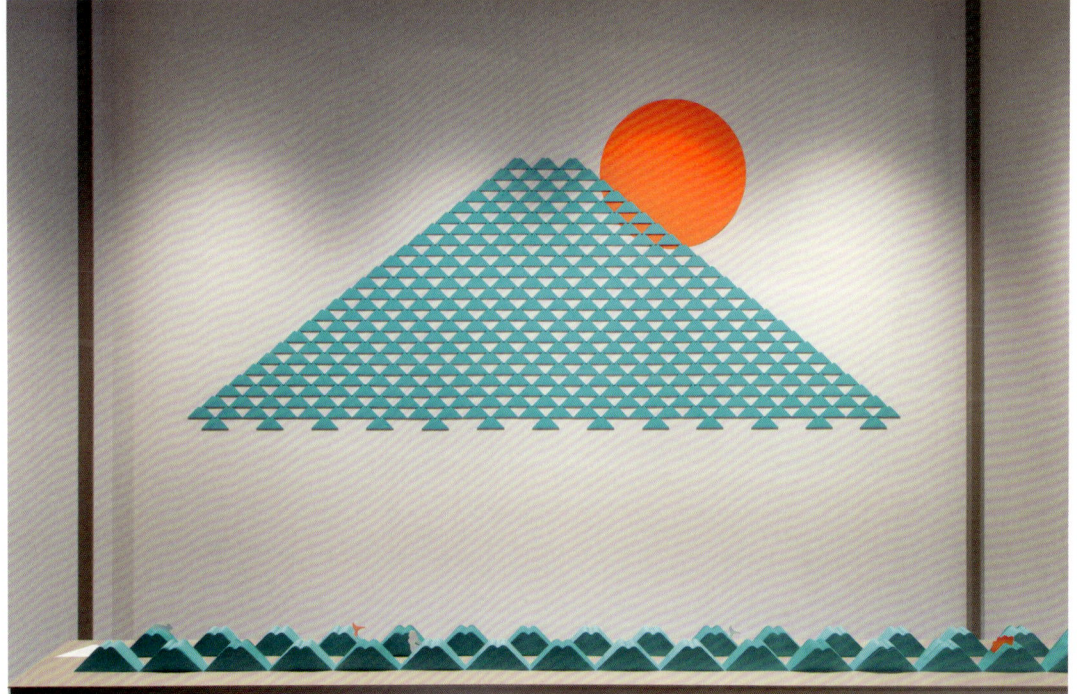
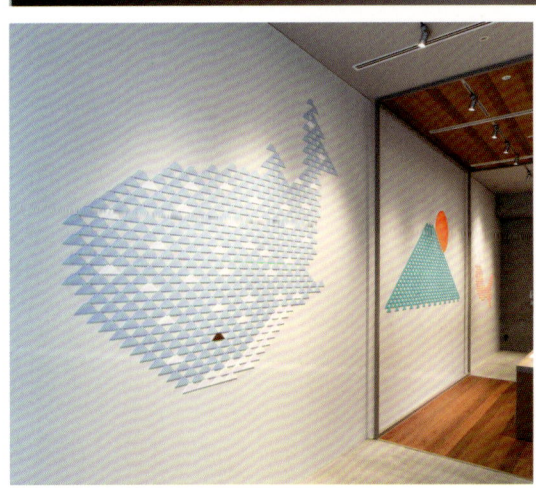
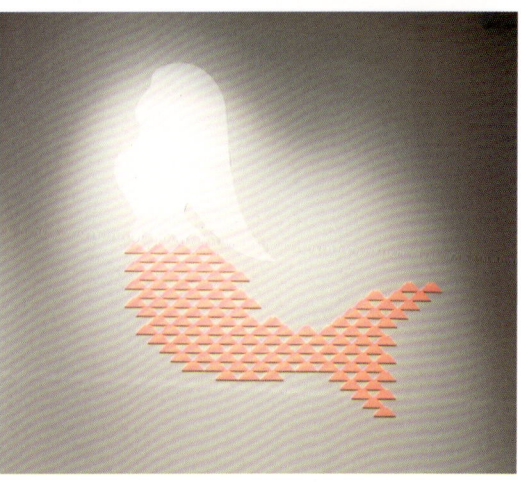

This is a branding design for a lemon cake specialty store in Komae City, Tokyo. The store specializes in lemon cakes made from domestically grown lemons. When Akiko Sekimoto went to the local lemon farm for research, she was impressed to learn that lemon trees have many large thorns. Inspired by the powerful wildness and the sharp acid flavor of lemons, she developed a design based on the motif of thorns of lemon trees for the logo and other materials.

AD	Akiko Sekimoto
D	Akiko Sekimoto
CW	Mika Kunii
PH	Kohei Yamamoto
CL	Lemon Noki

Lemon Noki

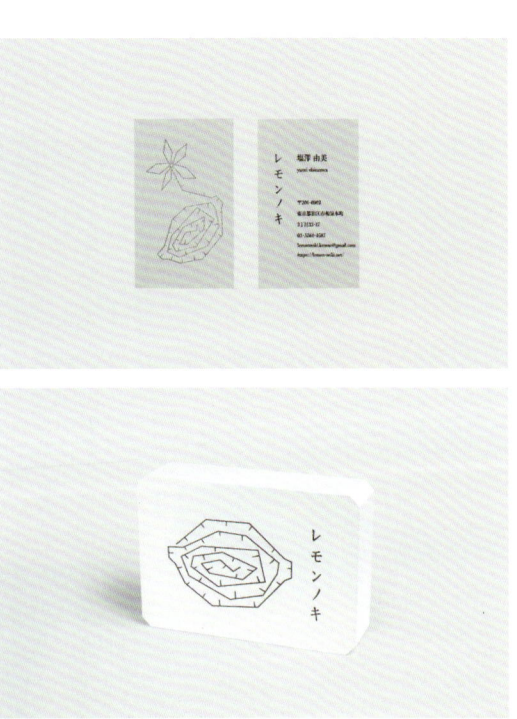

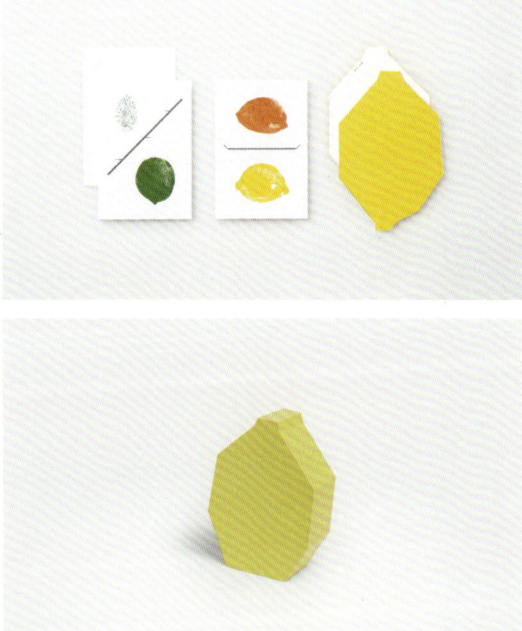

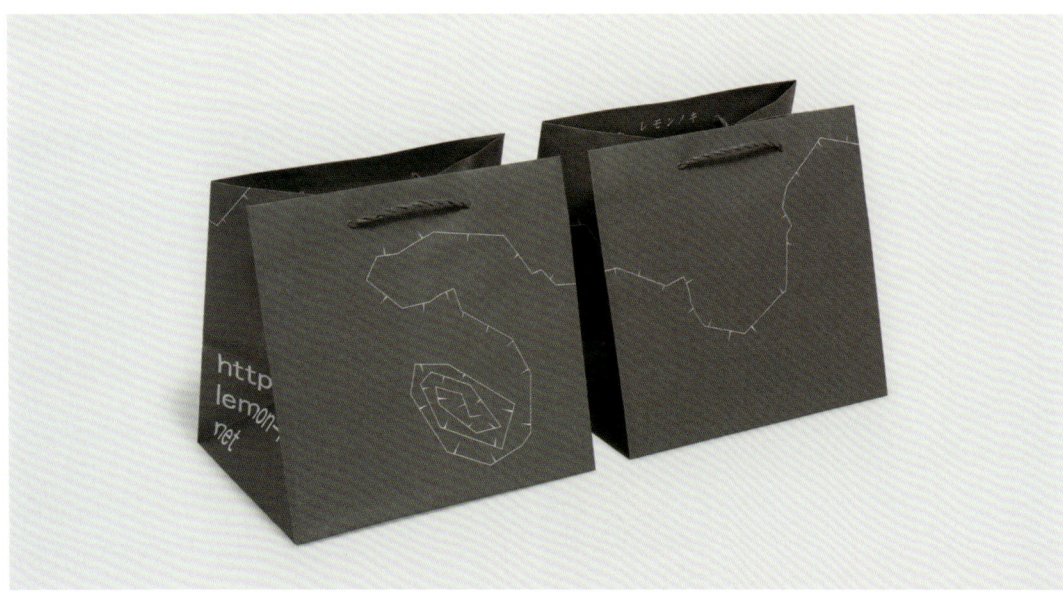

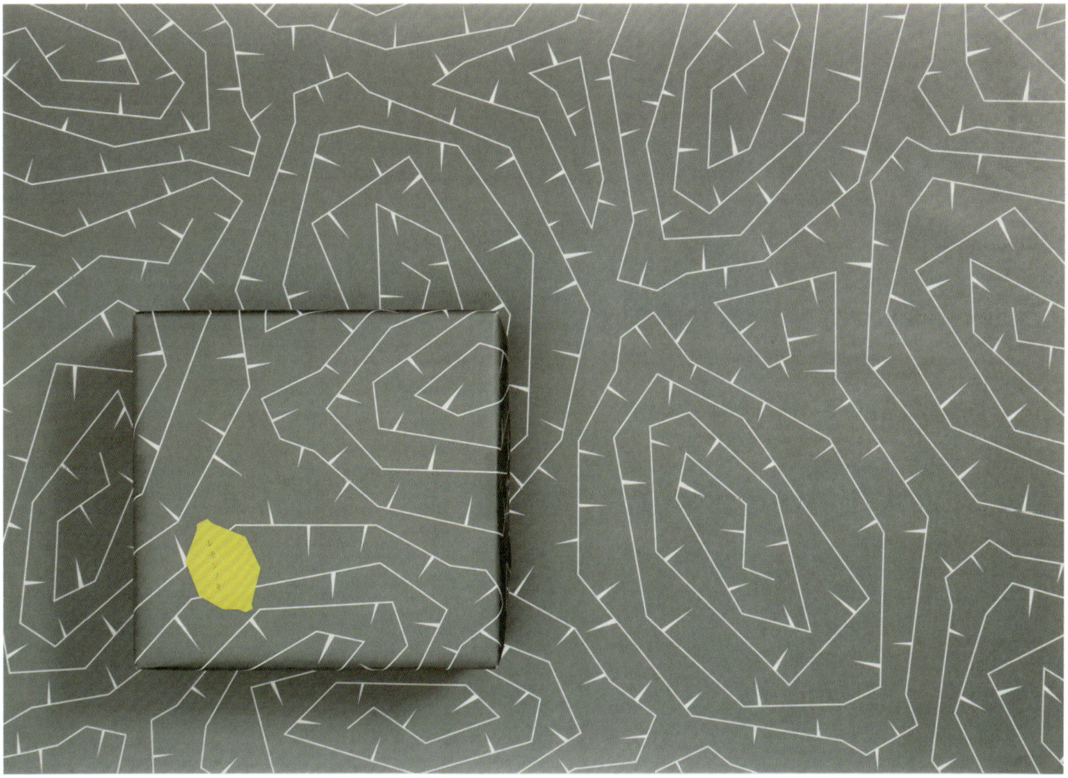

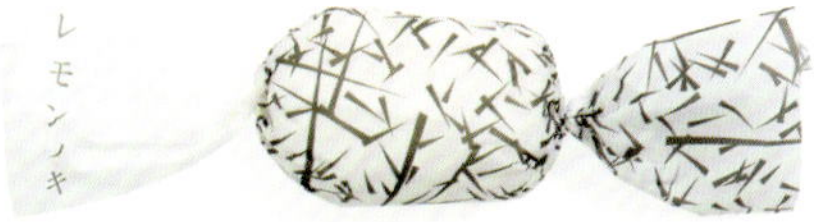

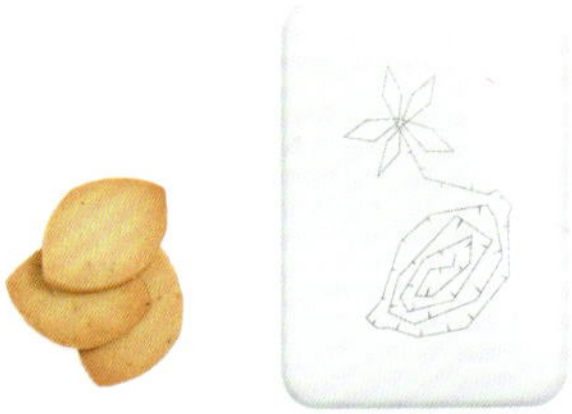

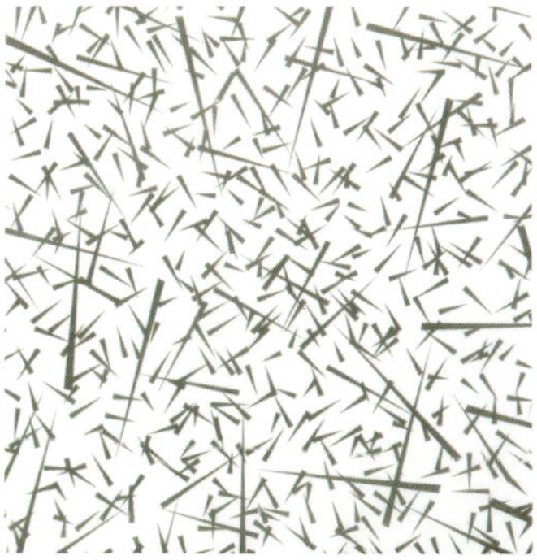

レモンノキ

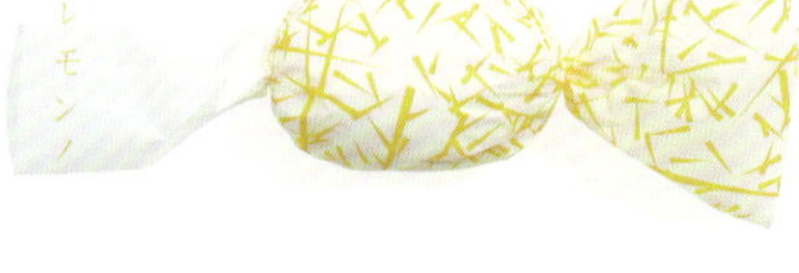

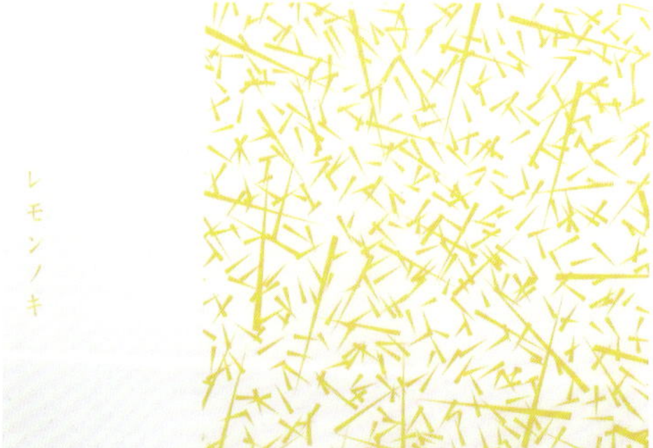

レモンノキ

レモン

レモンノキ

This project is the corporate identity and visual identity development for pratya, a brand that works on solving social issues by utilizing artificial intelligence or AI and data science. The concept of the logo is the coexistence of AI and humans. The square on the left embodies AI and the organic shape on the right represents humans. In addition, the logo also reminds Agata Yamaguchi of the everyday feeling he gets from a park.

DA   collé
D   Agata Yamaguchi
CL   pratya

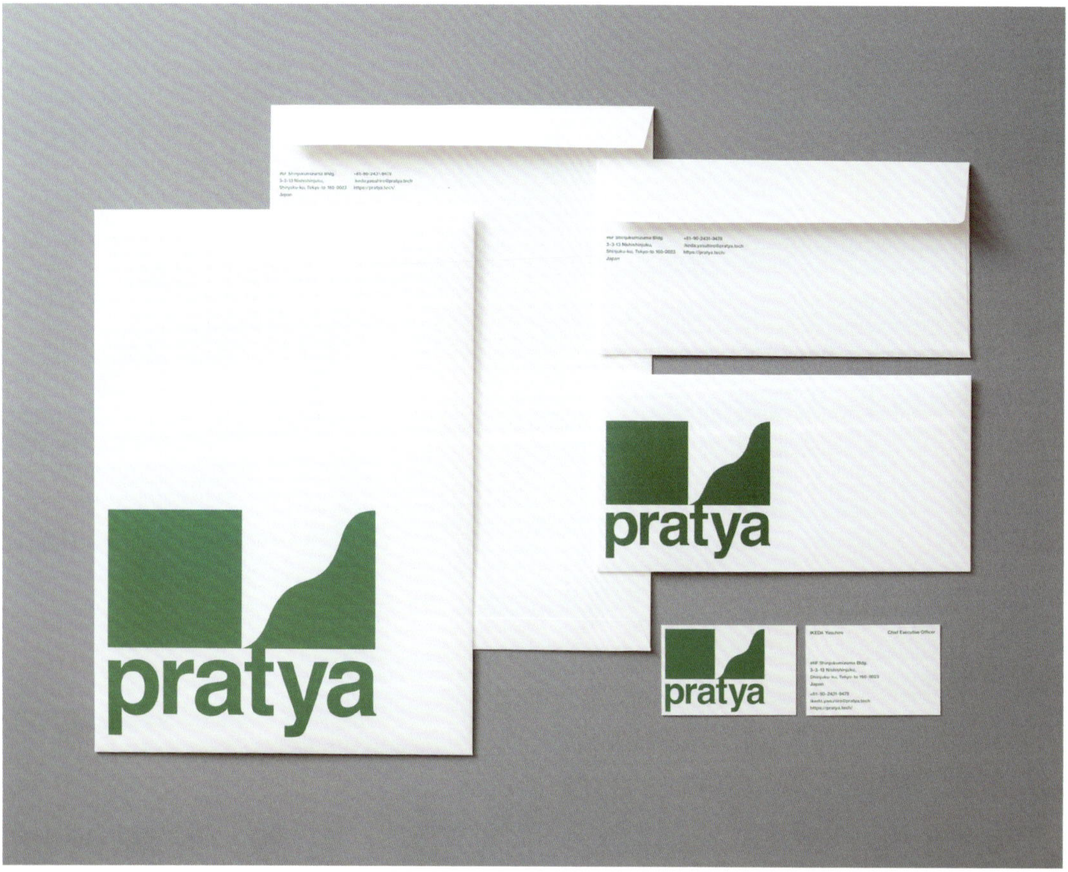

pratya

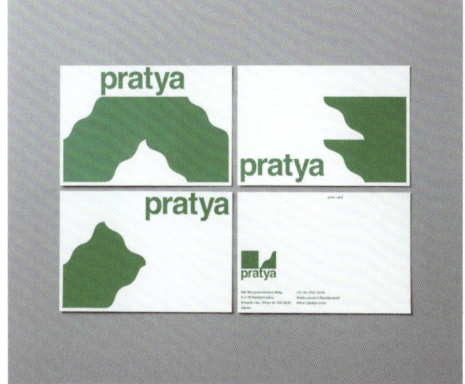

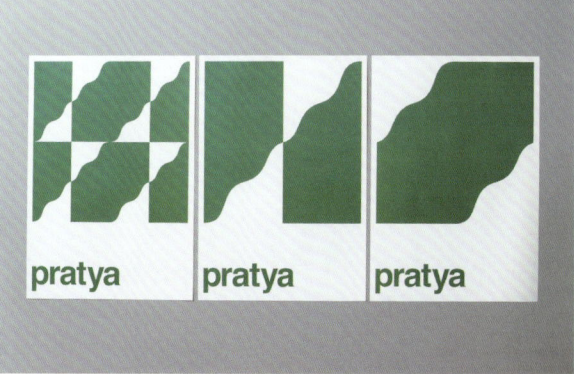

132

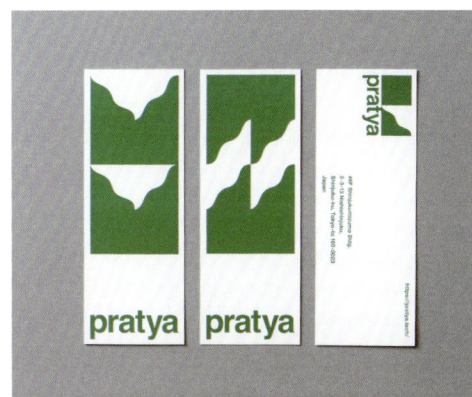

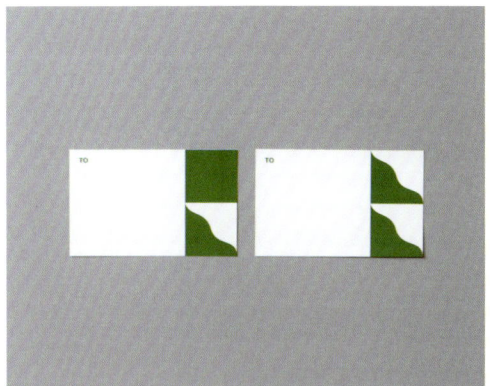

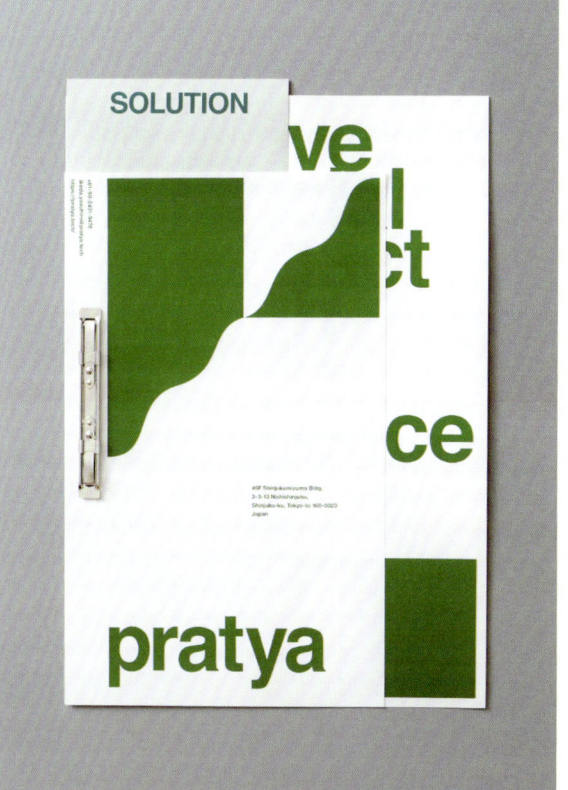

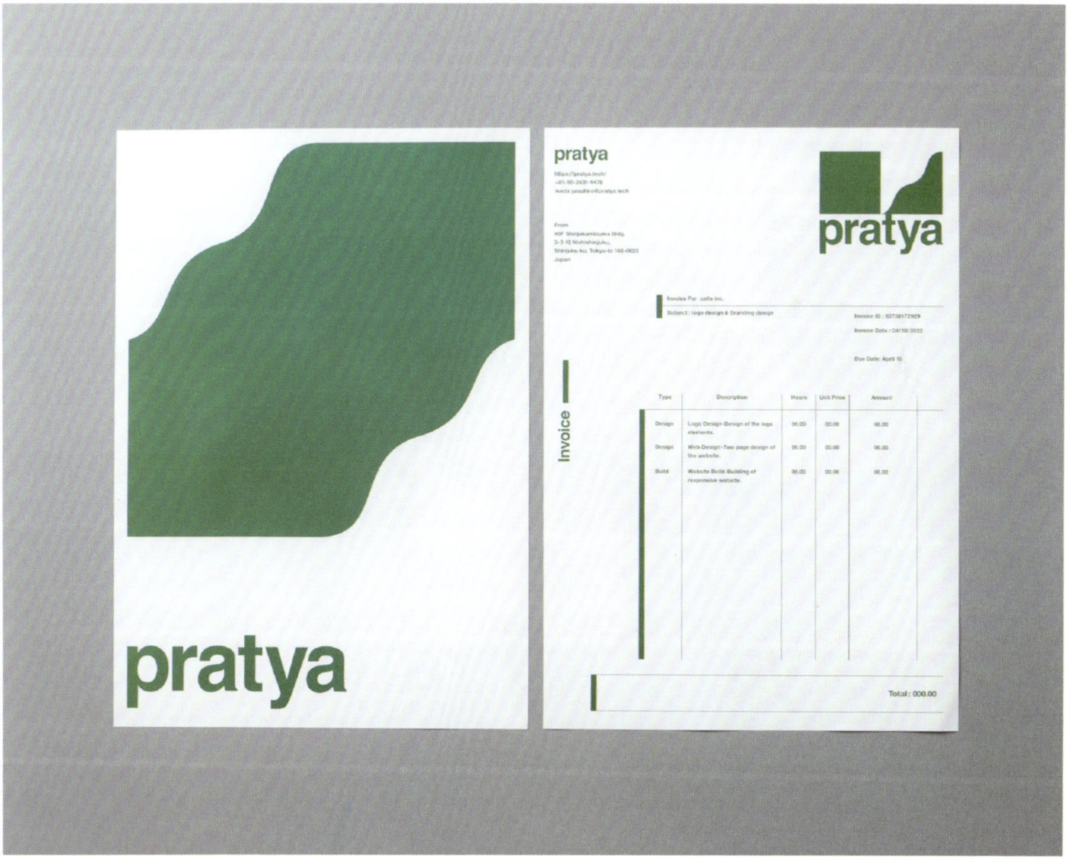

This is the branding design for the outdoor lifestyle store THE GATE. The key visual reflects the store's name, "GATE," which means the point of interaction between people in the city center and the countryside, as well as the "gate" through which people pass when they experience the outdoors for the first time. The designers identified the three elements that make up THE GATE's key visual: products, outdoors, and gate. They were graphically transformed into a tent, a gradient sky, and a semicircle of tunnels and were combined to create a visual looking outdoors from the inside of the tent, representing the concept of contact points and boundaries with nature.

DA   Sitoh inc.
D   Motoi Shito
CL   THE GATE

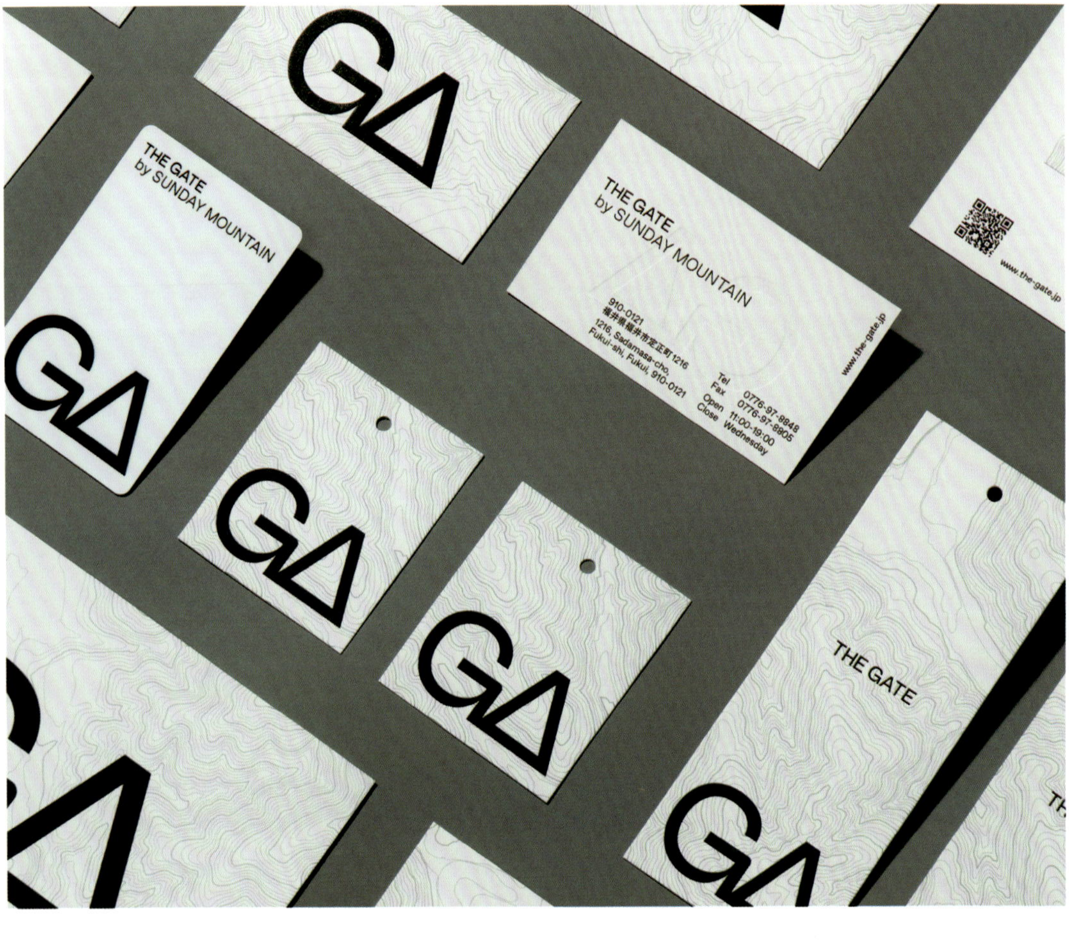

THE GATE

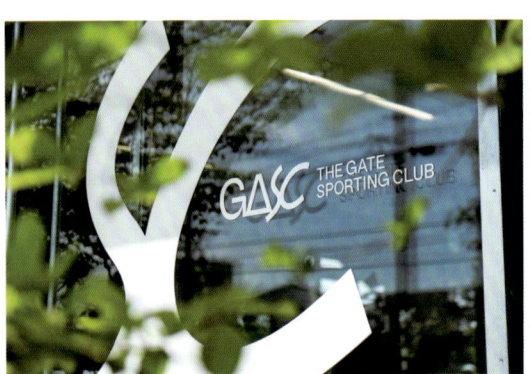

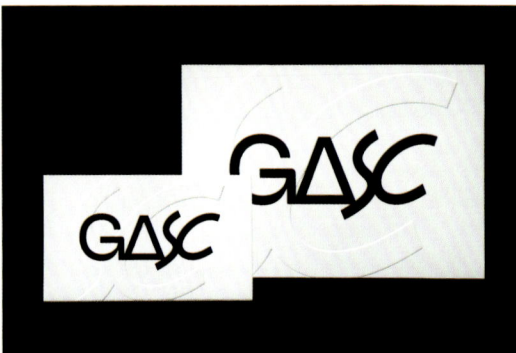

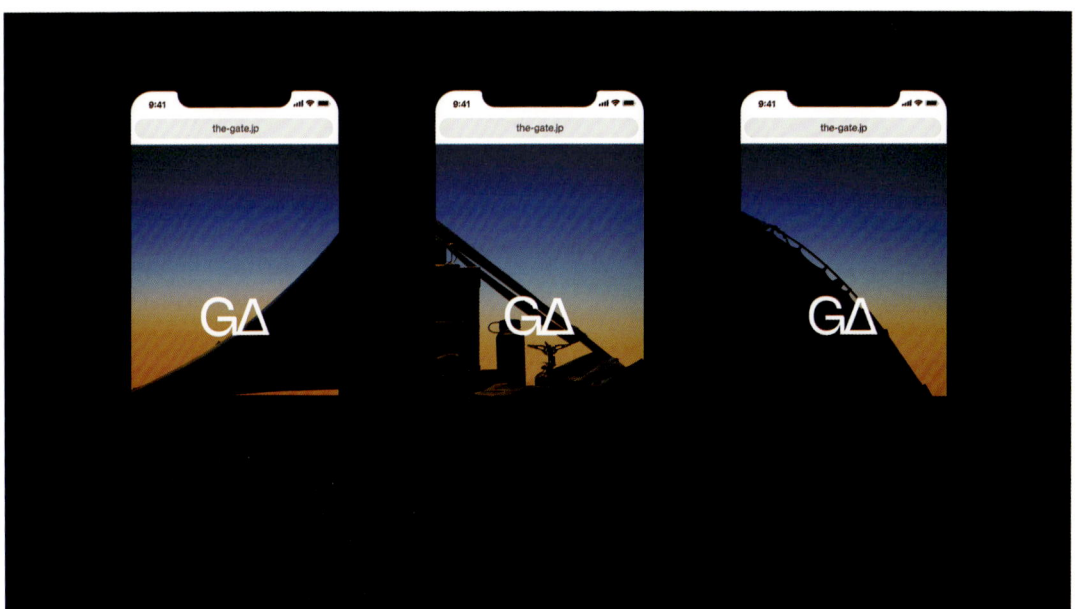

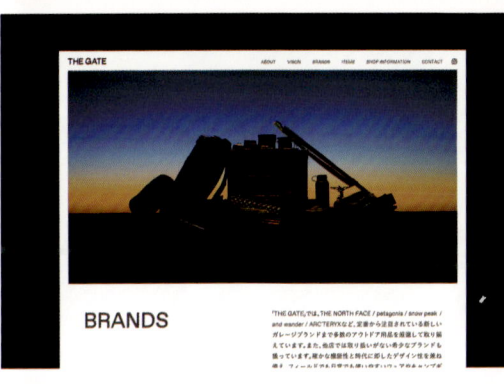

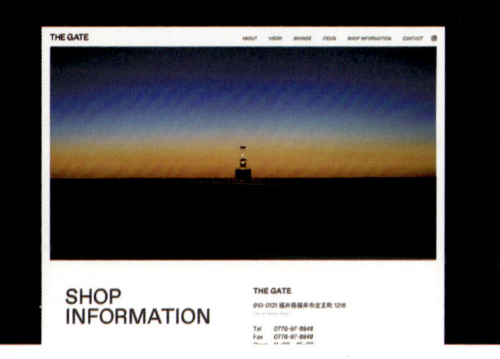

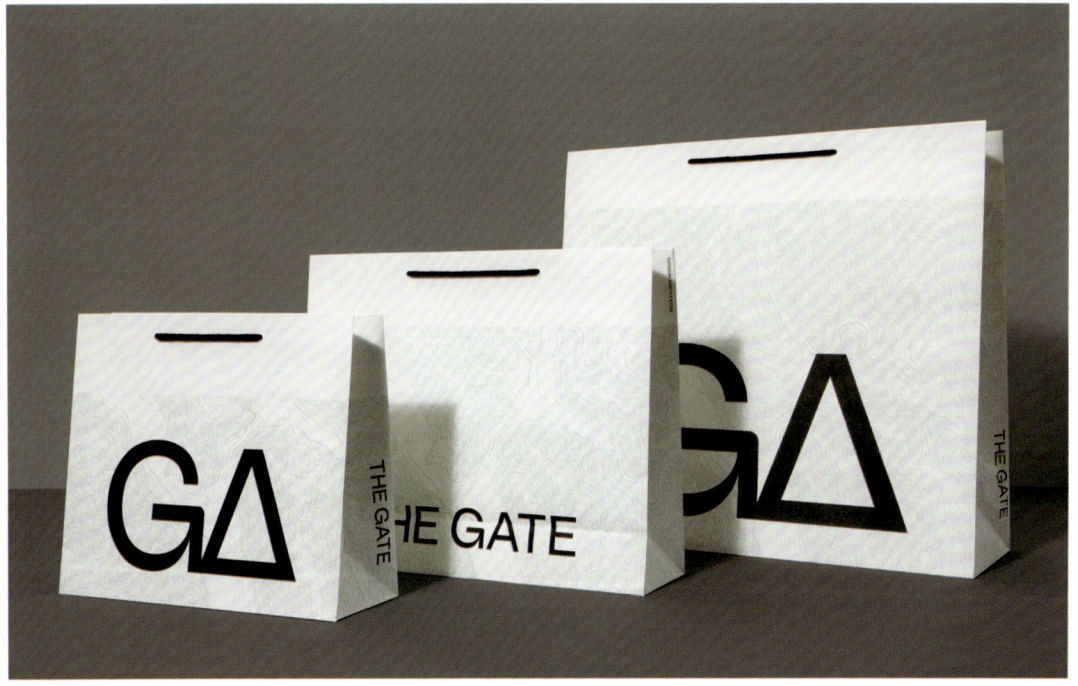

Fujimidai Tunnel is a shared kitchen for people who want to have a small shop or who want to do experimental business.

    With the concept of "digging your potential," the logo of the Fujimidai Tunnel includes a katakana "to" and an English alphabet "T" with a pickaxe motif. Moe Furuya thought that finding what a person wanted to do and raising the level was like a role-playing game, so he created a design like a video game with rough pixels.

AD   Moe Furuya
D   Moe Furuya
AR   Junpei Nousaku
CW   Tomoyuki Torisu
CL   Fujimidai Tunnel

Fujimidai Tunnel

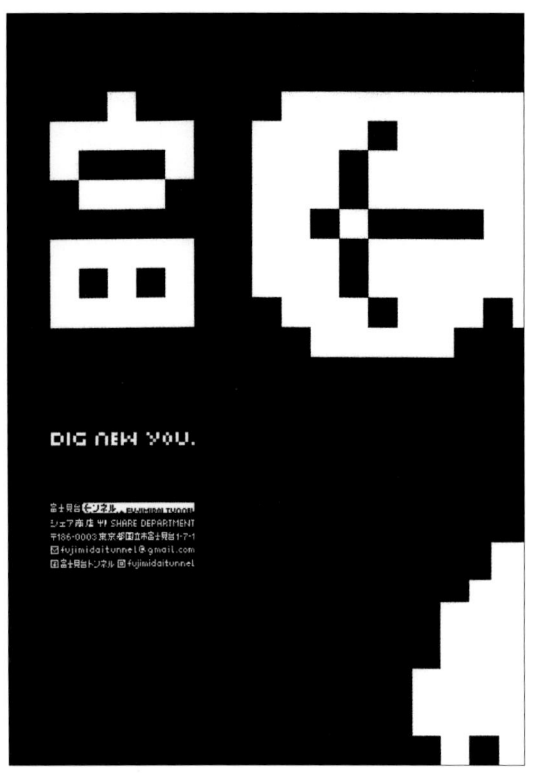

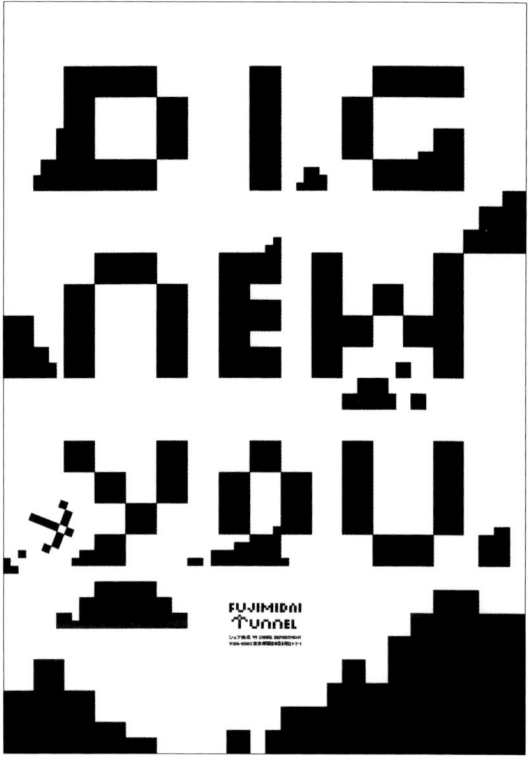

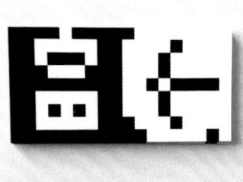

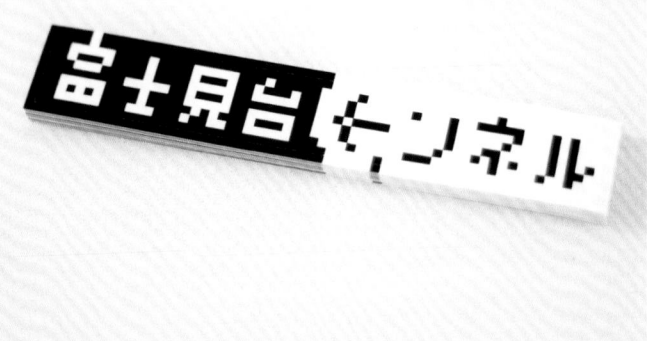

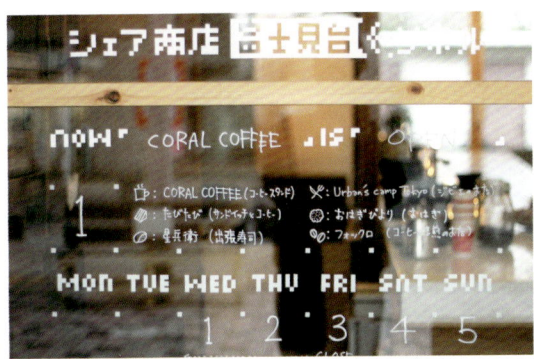

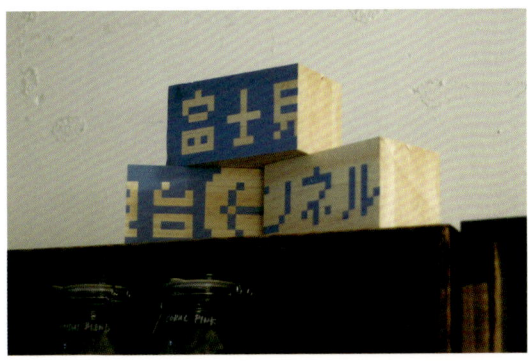

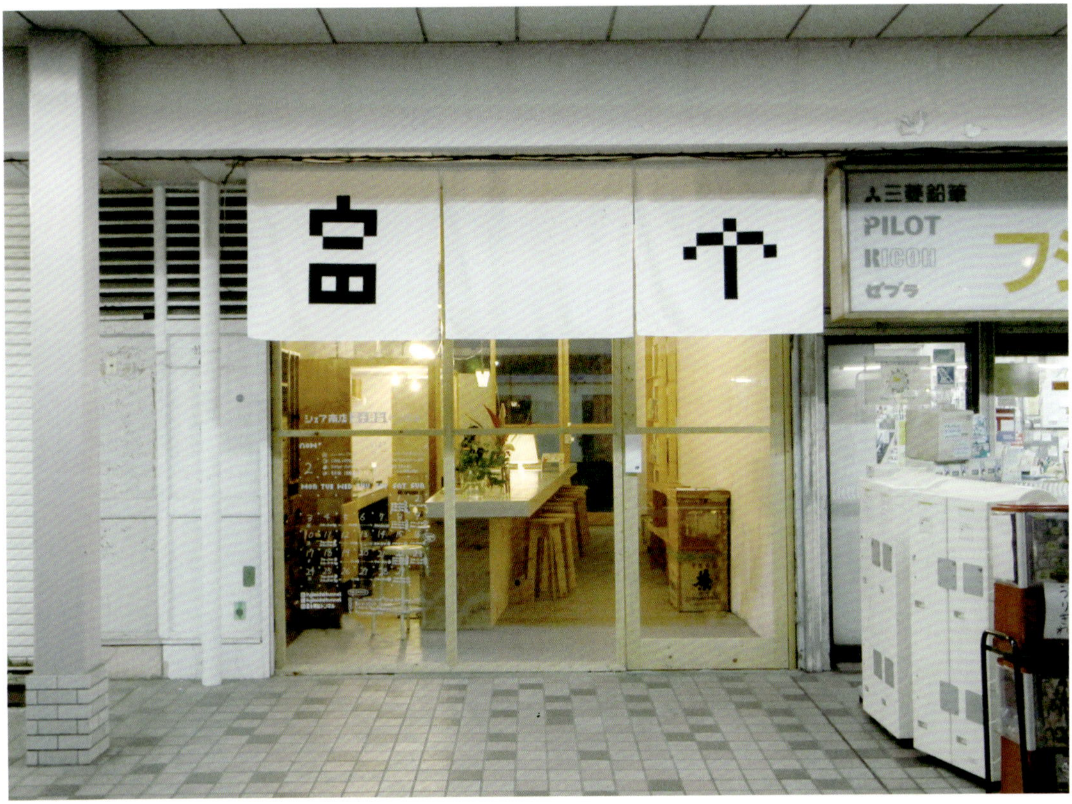

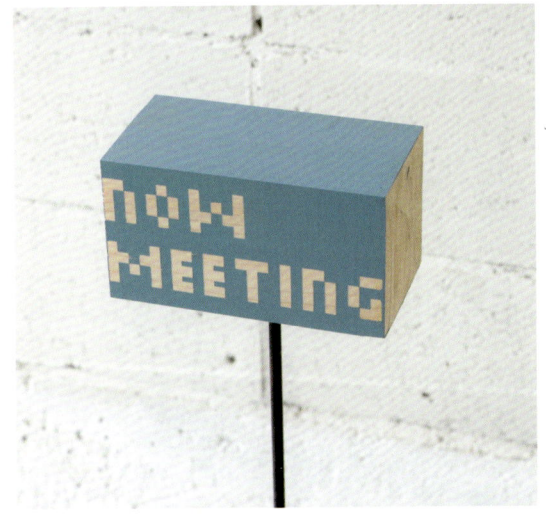

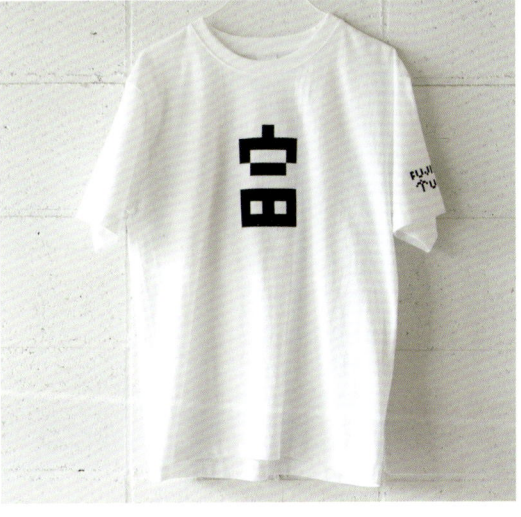

This is the brand design for a Chinese medicinal herbal lifestyle brand. Yakuzen, which is rooted in Eastern medicine, is a way of accumulating "養生 (yojo)," or adjusting one's lifestyle, including diet and routines, to maintain one's health. To express this visually, the designers created the logo and other graphics using pencil lines. The plant drawn in the same way is a precious ingredient used in Chinese herbal medicine called jujube. It was also combined into the brand graphics.

AD   Akiko Sekimoto
D   Akiko Sekimoto, Mako Sato
CW   Atsuko Fujishiro
PH   Shinichi Kaneko
CL   Inagawa Yakuzen

Inagawa Yakuzen

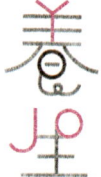

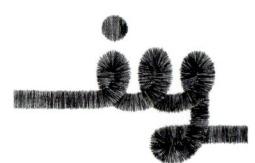

inagawa
yakuzen

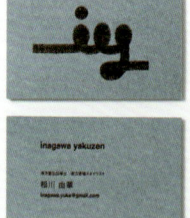

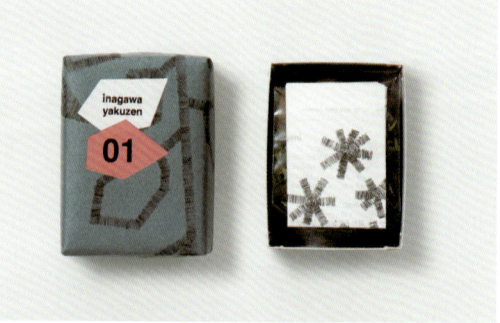

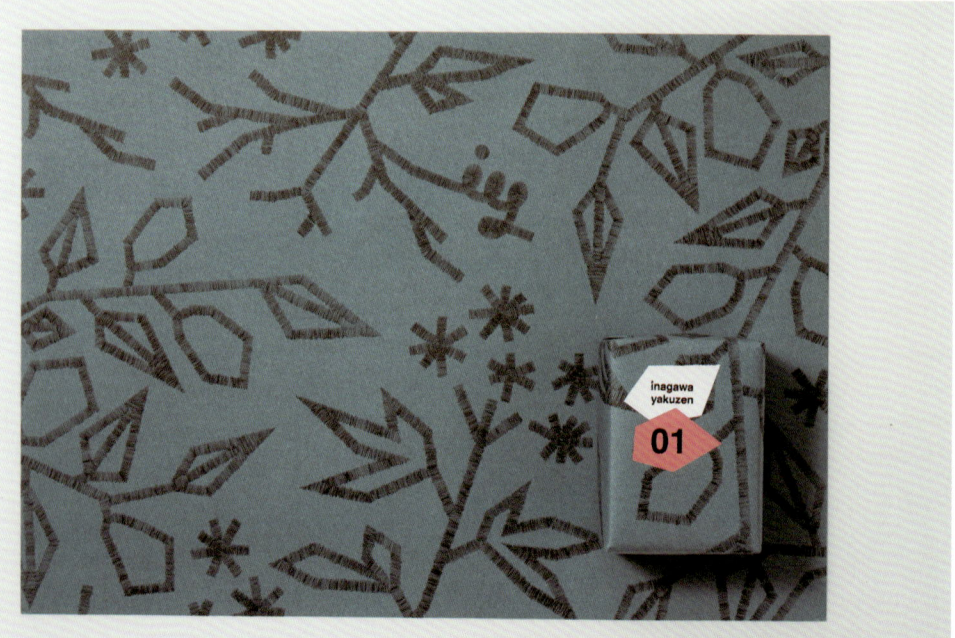

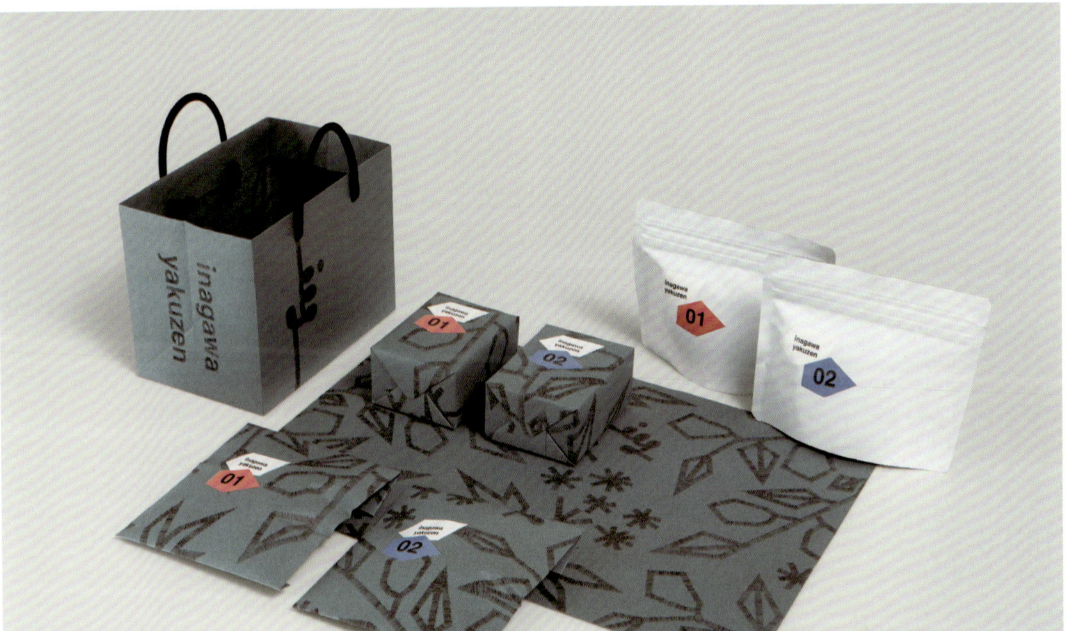

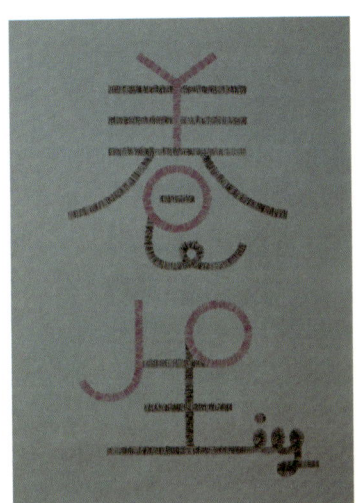
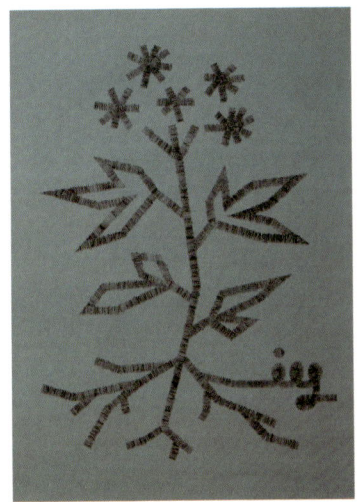
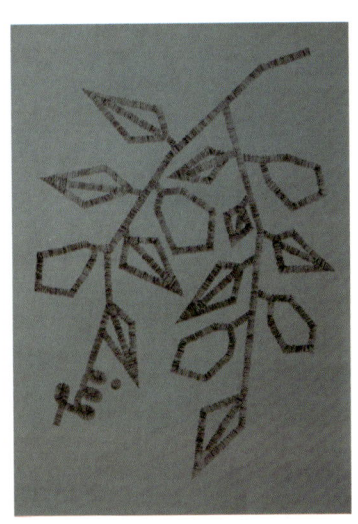
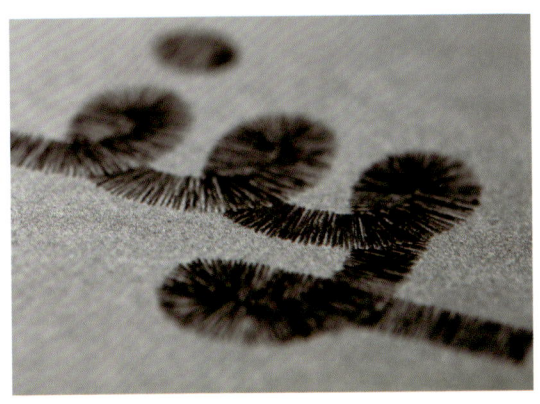
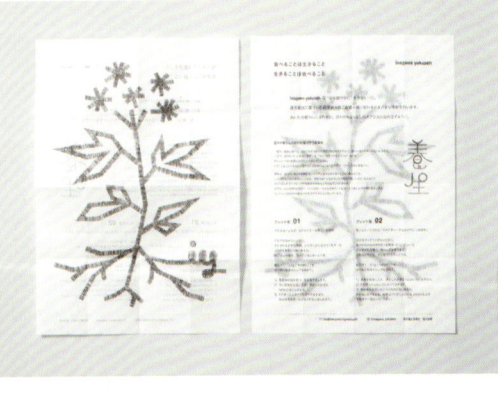

Ayari Nakamura is the art director for a parade by three local governments—Kushiro Town, Mata City, and Matsumae Town—with their abundant agricultural and marine products.

The local specialty products were wrapped in paper that depicts the producer's anecdotes and production process. When visitors purchase and take these products home, they bring the stories with them as well.

CD   Moto Takagi
AD   Ayari Nakamura
D   Rikito Fujitani
IL   Yasuhiro Suzuki
CL   TOKYU LAND CORPORATION

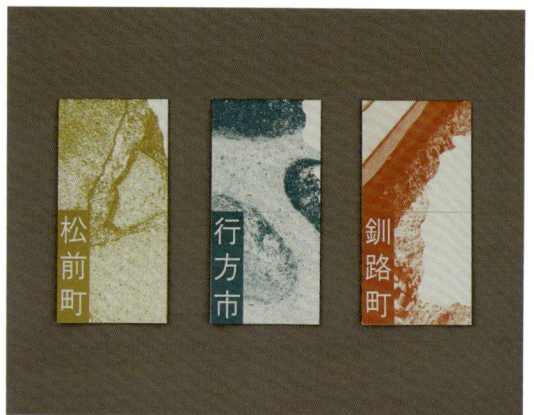
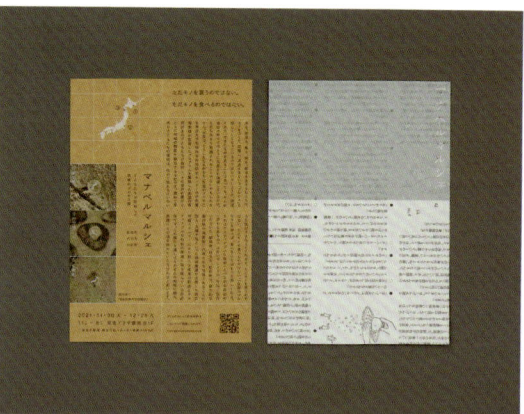

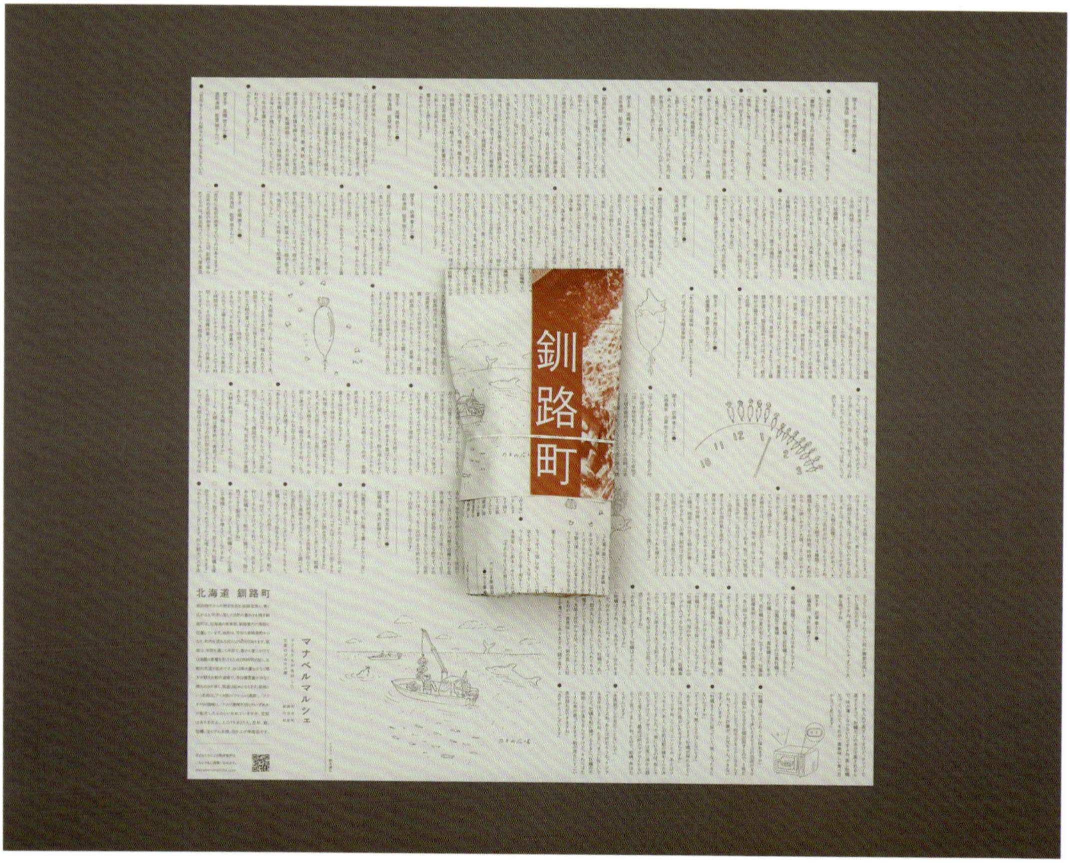

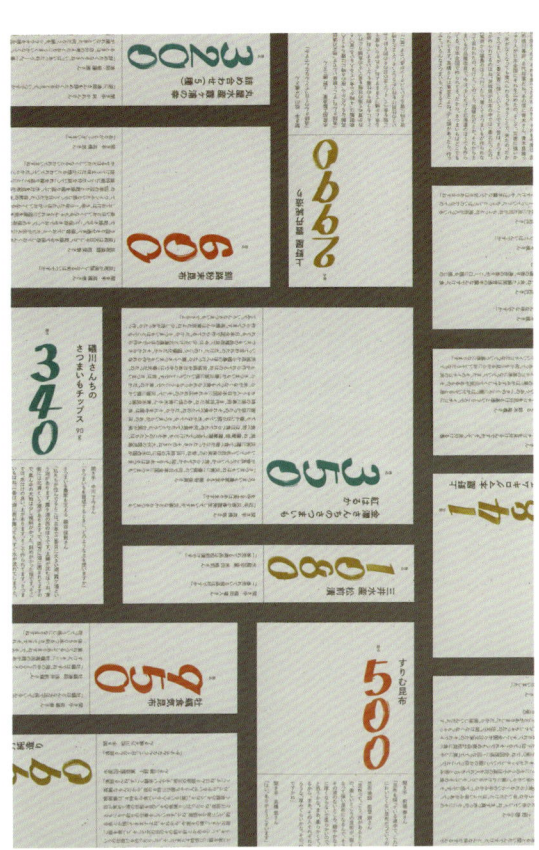

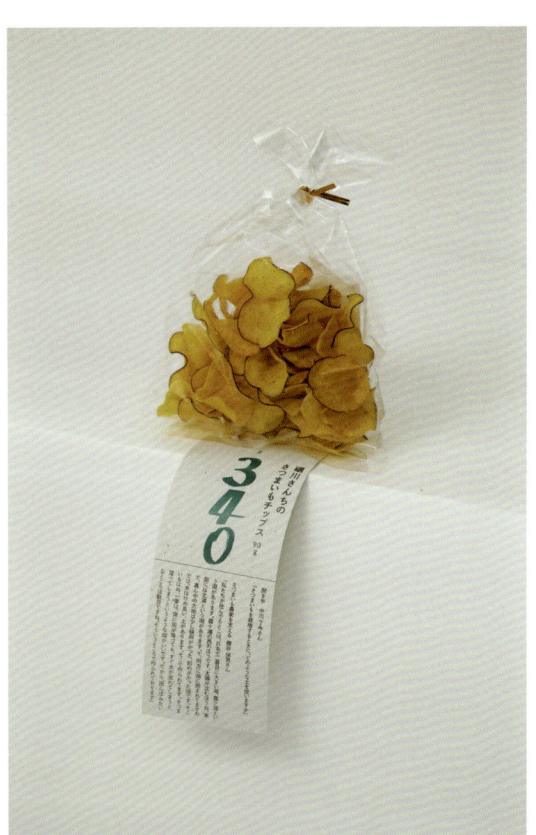

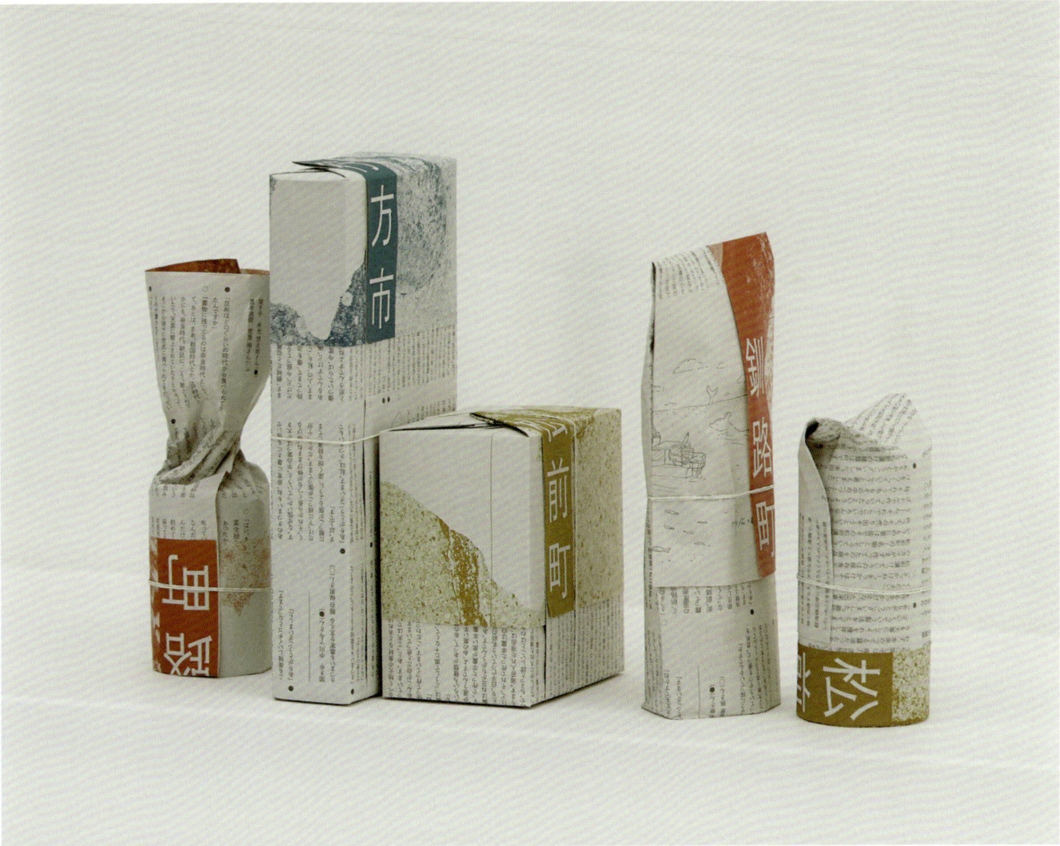

S.Labo is a shop and workshop space with the concept of a laboratory to enjoy socks. It was built in 2021 by a long-established socks factory in Koryo-cho, Nara, which is said to be the "town of socks." The shop was born from the desire to let everyone know more about the appeal of socks and think about the future of socks. It is a facility that allows people to think about the sustainability of the socks industry. Based on the concept of a laboratory, the designer created the project using a sock knitting machine and thread as the motif.

DA   Hi! Design
CD   Kengo Morita, Hitomi Morita
AD   Kengo Morita
D   Kengo Morita
ID   Yutaro Ishida
IL   Shinichi Nakayama
PH   Masakazu Hirata
CL   SOUKI CO., LTD.

S.Labo

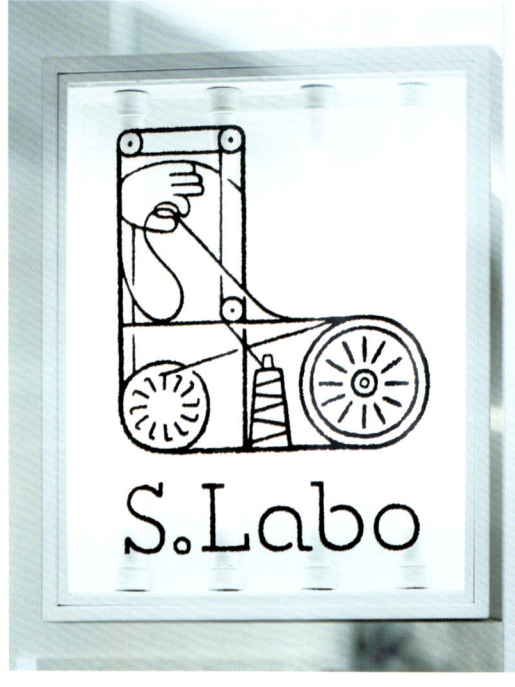

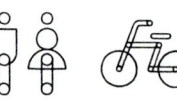
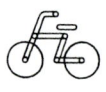
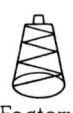
Factory
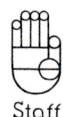
Staff Only

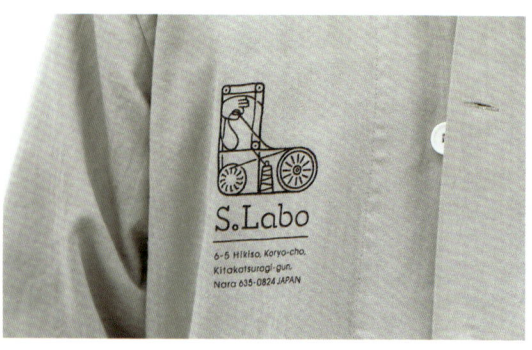

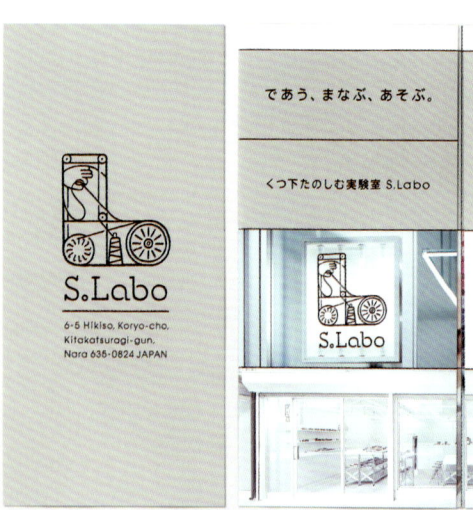

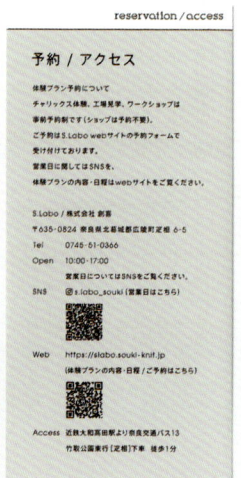

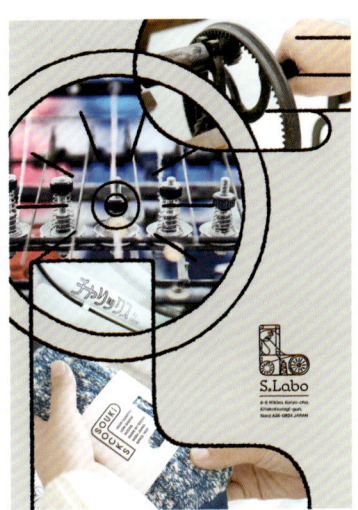
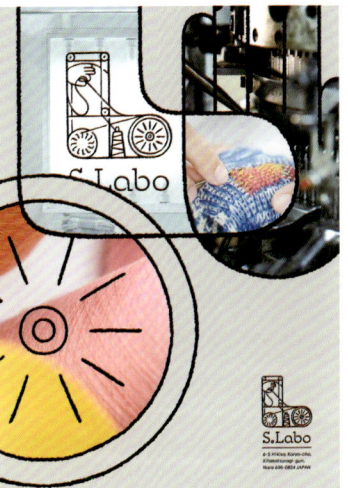
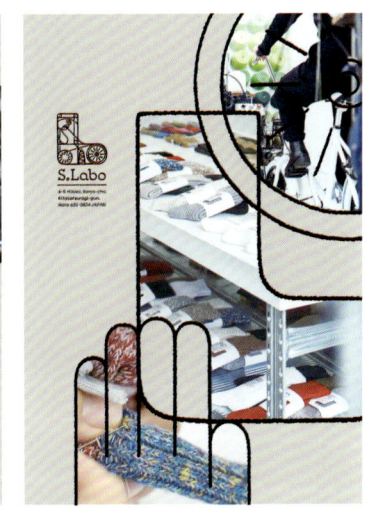

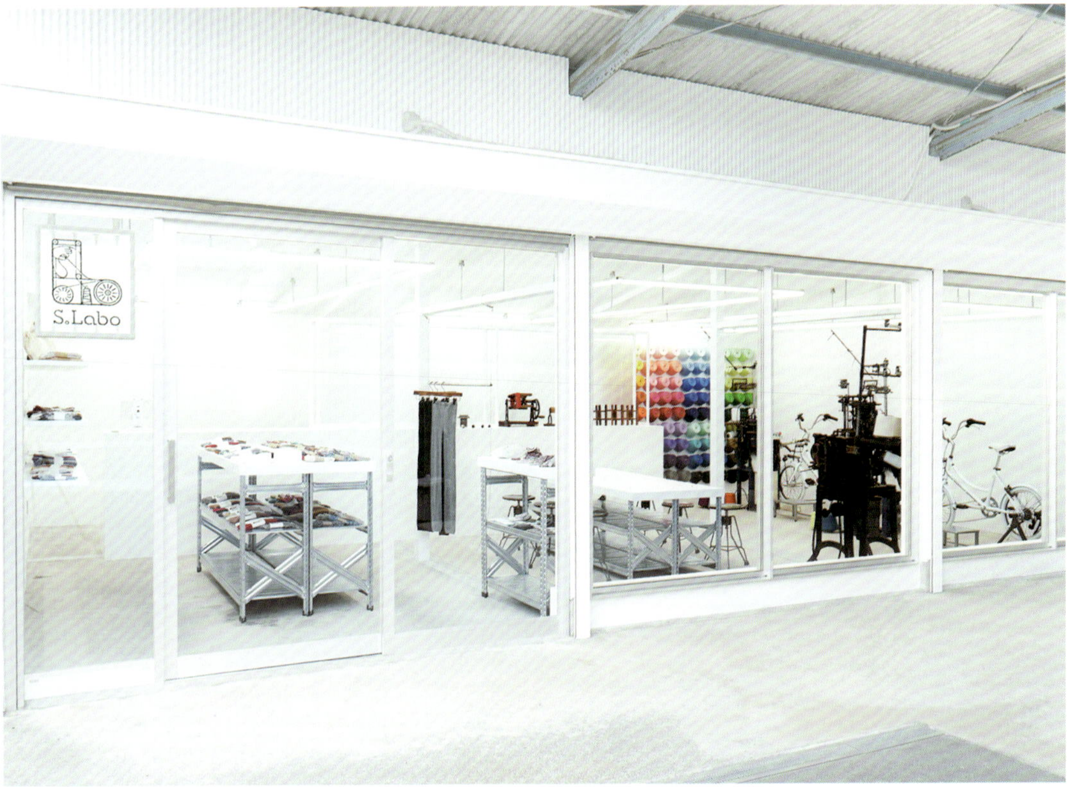

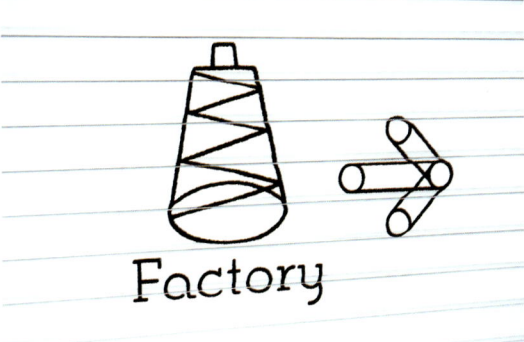

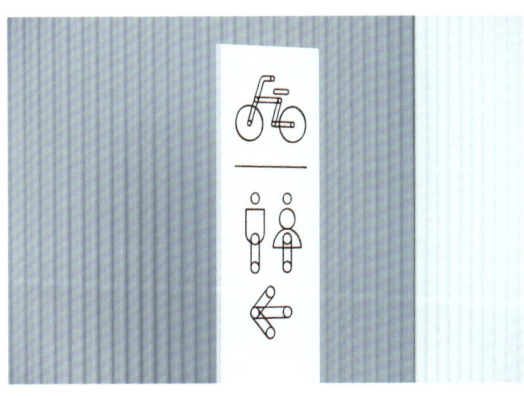

Shiseido is a company that considers conveying modern Japanese beauty as a key strategy for winning in global markets. Based on Shiseido's own font that had been used for over 100 years, the designers created a new font and logos with components of the Japanese Kanji "美 (beauty)" in Shiseido's font. The attempt was to convey Japanese-ness to global consumers by using the font, though it was challenging to make the design look modern, while preserving the essence of the original font. The design that embodies Japanese-ness has attracted great attention not only from Japanese people, but also from global consumers.

DA   SOAR NY
CD   Masaki Hanahara
AD   Masaki Hanahara
D   Ikki Kobayashi, kontrapunkt
CL   Shiseido Co., Ltd.

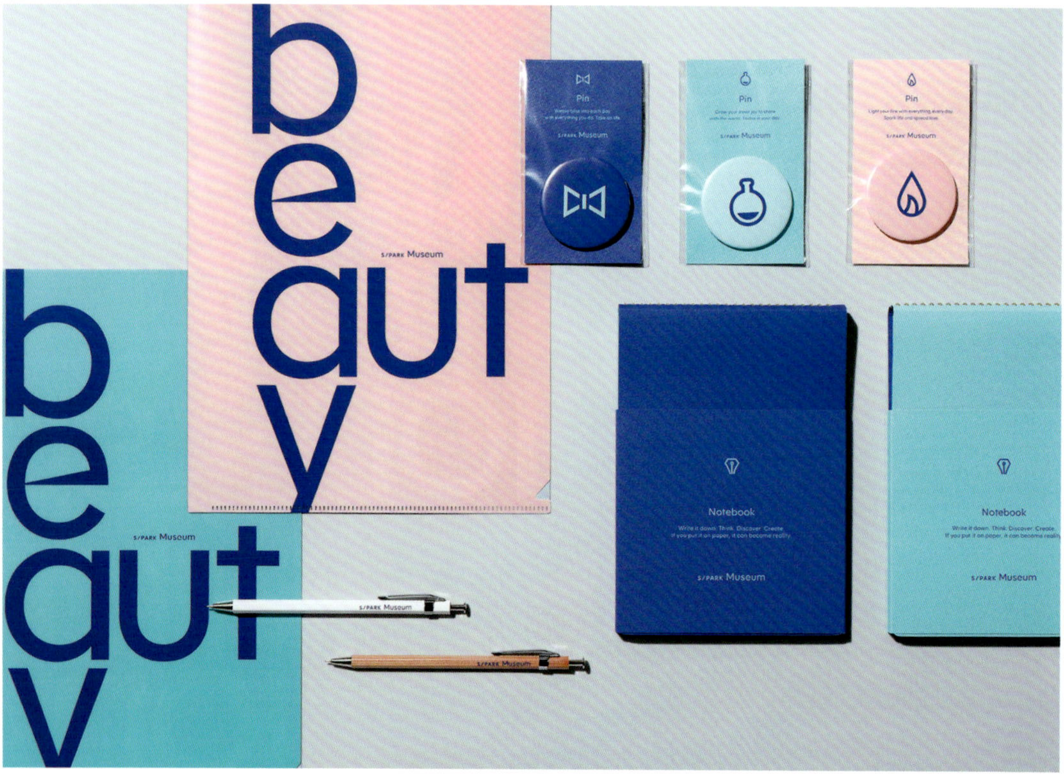

S/PARK GOODS

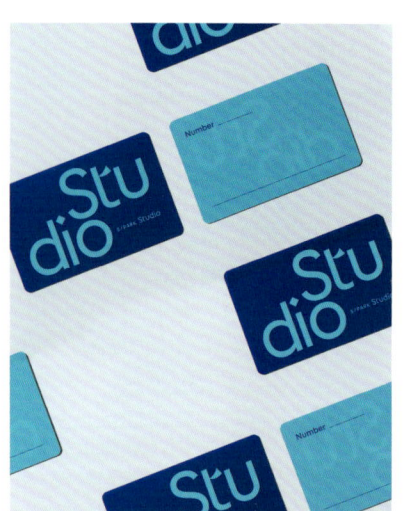
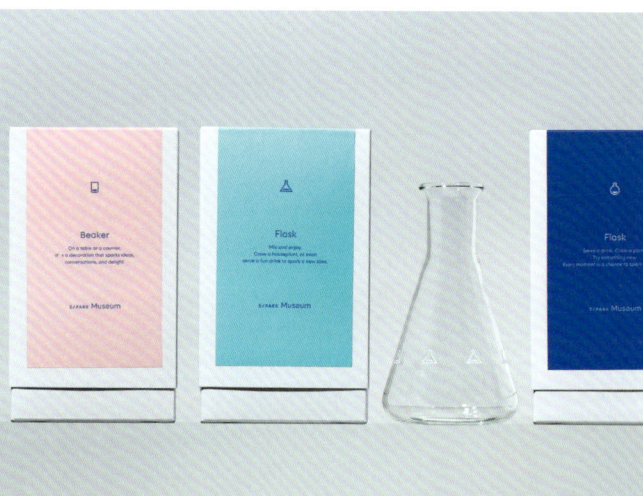

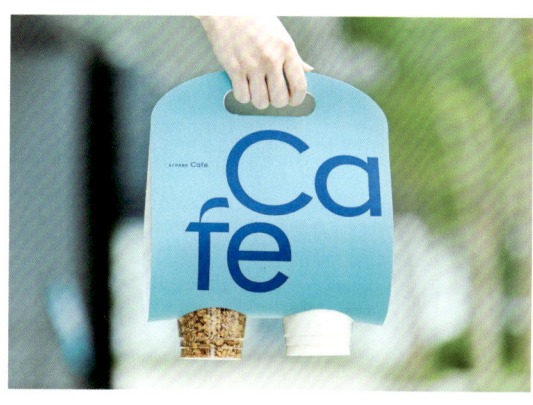

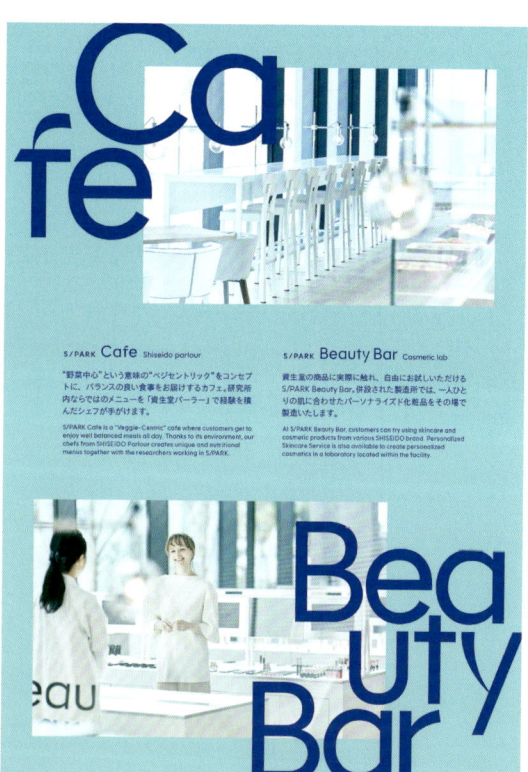

Cafe

S/PARK Cafe Shiseido parlour

"野菜中心"という意味の"ベジセントリック"をコンセプトに、バランスの良い食事をお届けするカフェ。研究所内ならではのメニューを「資生堂パーラー」で経験を積んだシェフが手がけます。

S/PARK Cafe is a "Veggie-Centric" cafe where customers get to enjoy well balanced meals all day. Thanks to its environment, our chefs from SHISEIDO Parlour creates unique and nutritional menus together with the researchers working in S/PARK.

S/PARK Beauty Bar Cosmetic lab

資生堂の商品に実際に触れ、自由にお試しいただけるS/PARK Beauty Bar。併設された製造所では、一人ひとりの肌に合わせたパーソナライズド化粧品をその場で製造いたします。

At S/PARK Beauty Bar, customers can try using skincare and cosmetic products from various SHISEIDO brand. Personalized Skincare Service is also available to create personalized cosmetics in a laboratory located within the facility.

Beauty Bar

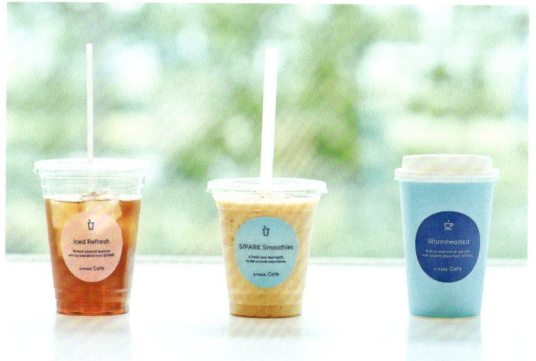

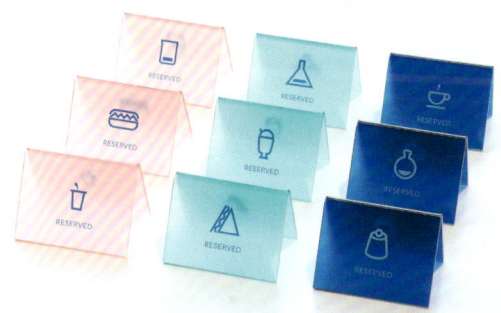

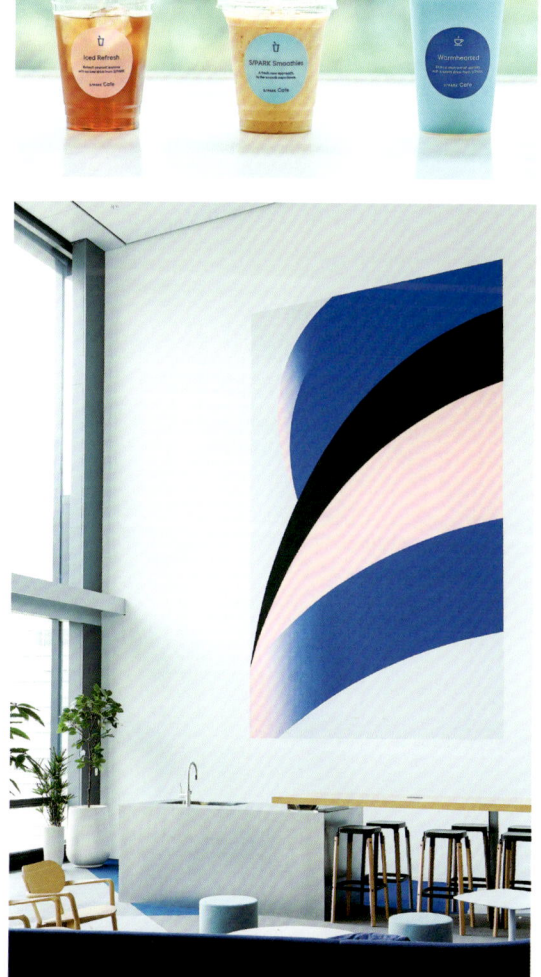

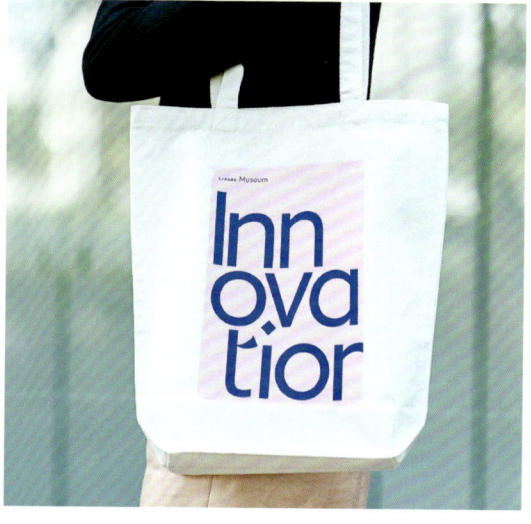

Innovation

This is the design for publicity materials for ARTISTS'
FAIR KYOTO, an art fair for younger artists curated by
Japan's leading artists.

The aim was to create the impression that "purple,"
a classic and elegant image used in Kyoto for centuries,
could be perceived as a modern and energetic "purple."
In this graphic system, people can have a glimpse of this
year's exhibits in a layer at the back of the visual that
looks as if the purple surface has been wiped away. The
works are replaced each year to create a main visual that
is unique to the year of the exhibition, while retaining the
same impression of "purple" each year.

DA   UMA/design farm
AD   Yuma Harada
D   Keisuke Yamazoe
CL   Kyoto Prefecture,
        Kyoto Shimbun,
        Artists' Fair Kyoto Organizing
        Committee

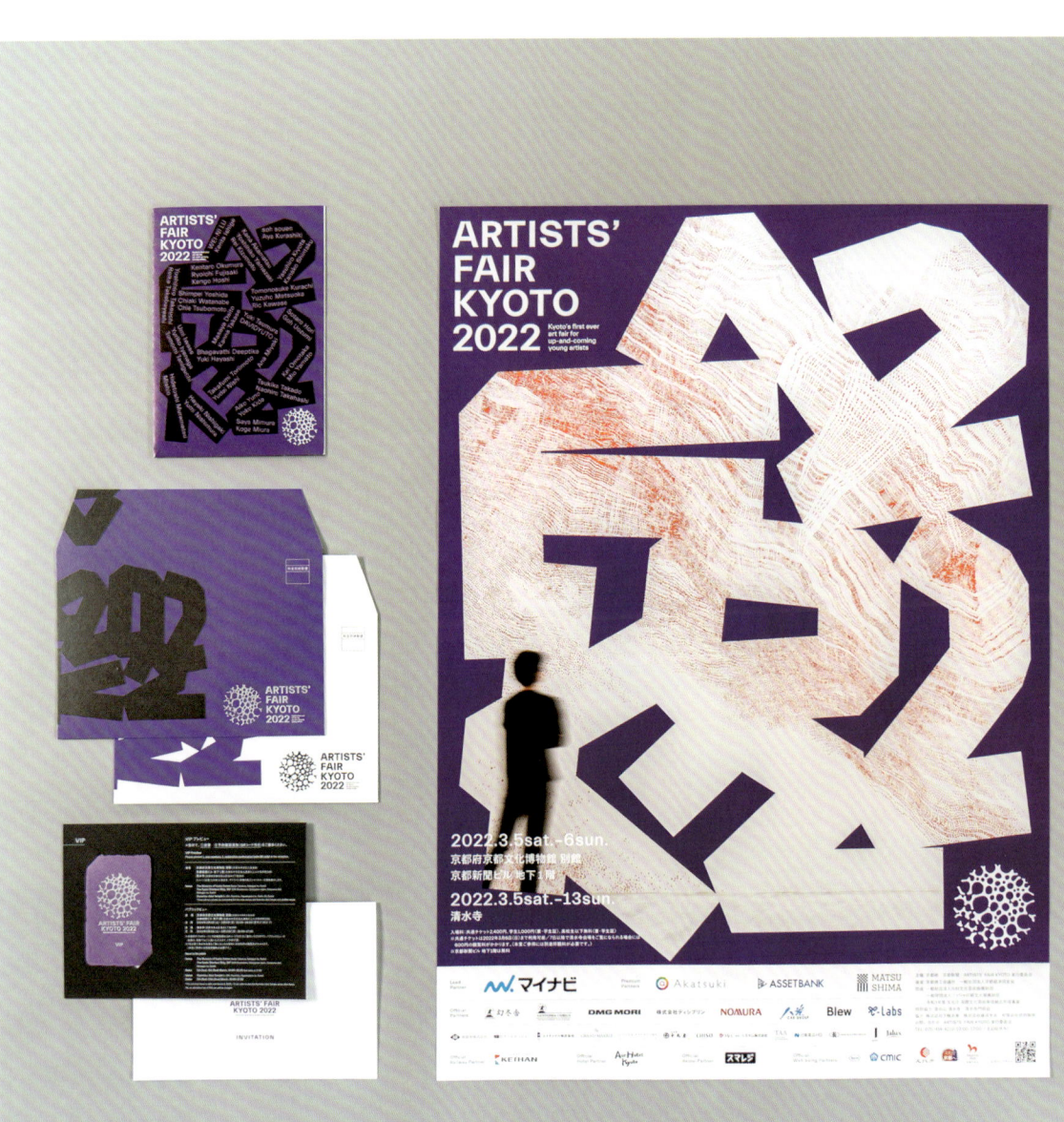

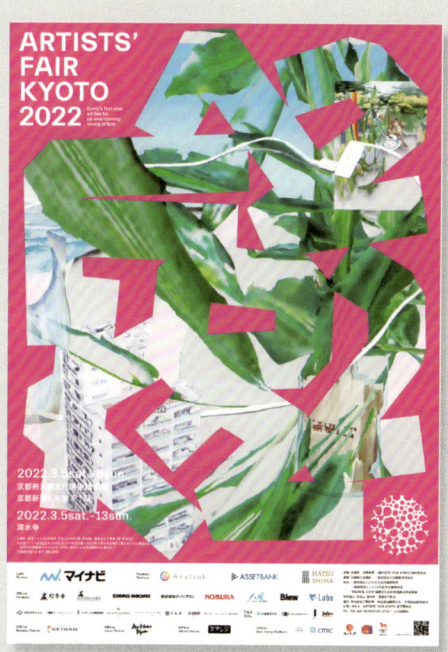

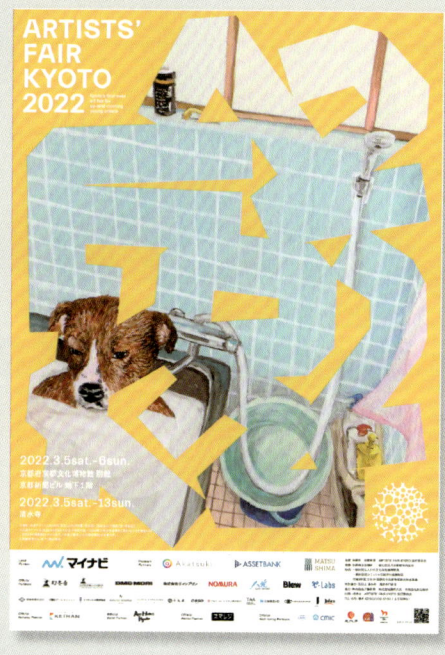

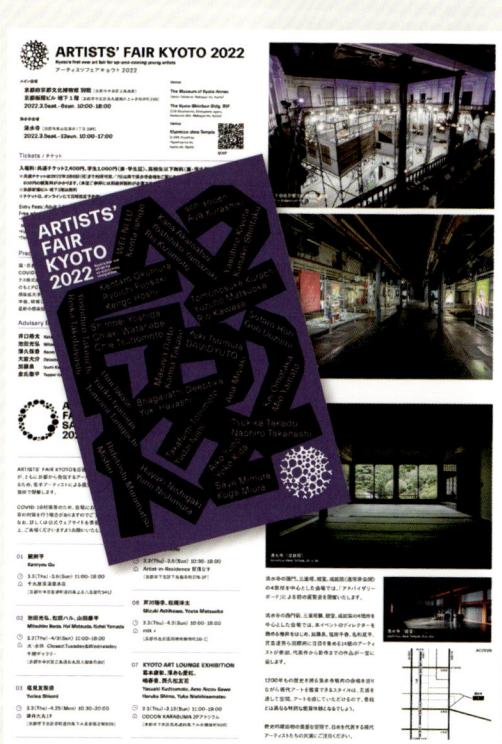

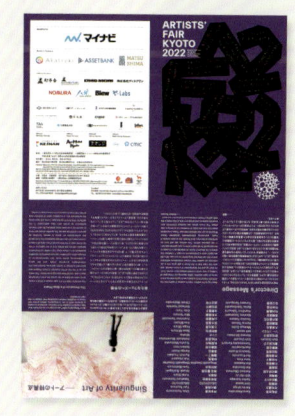

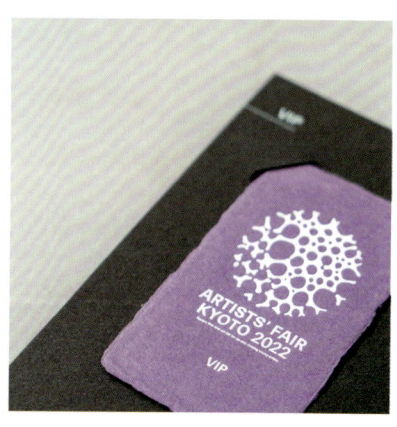

Hirosaki Arts Pollination is a local exhibition that encourages citizens to rediscover the land of Tsugaru and Hirosaki. The logo, made up of joined dots, expresses the connection between people, things, and ideas through the medium of art. Like the exhibition, the logo is a design element to be combined in diverse ways.

AD   Arata Kubota
D   Arata Kubota, Hiroki Uranaka
CL   HIROSAKI_AIR

Hirosaki Arts Pollination

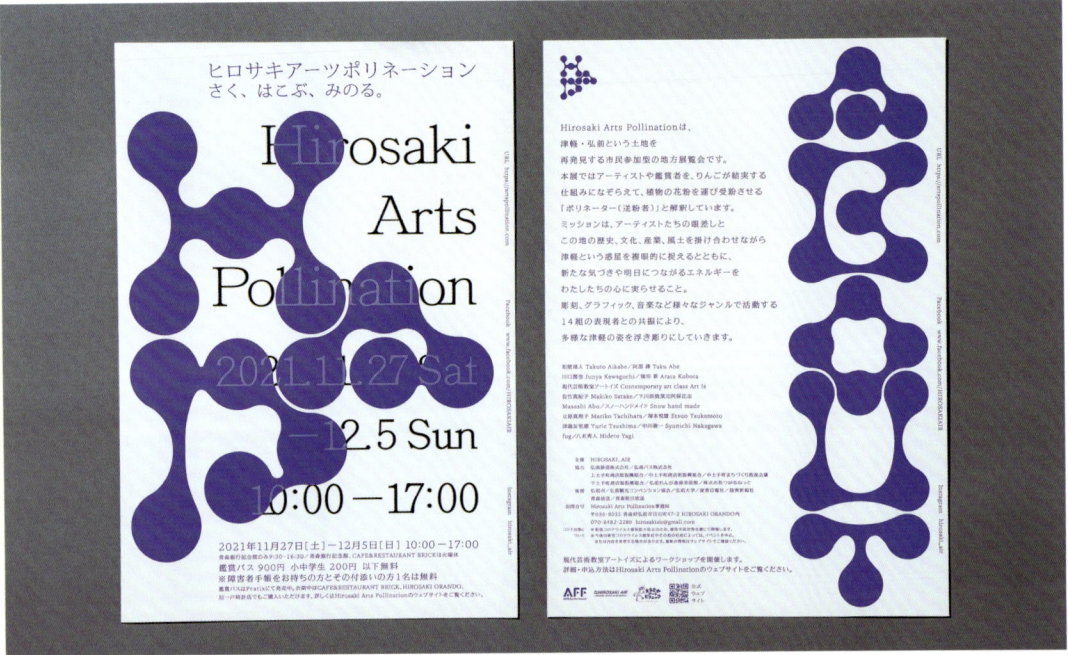

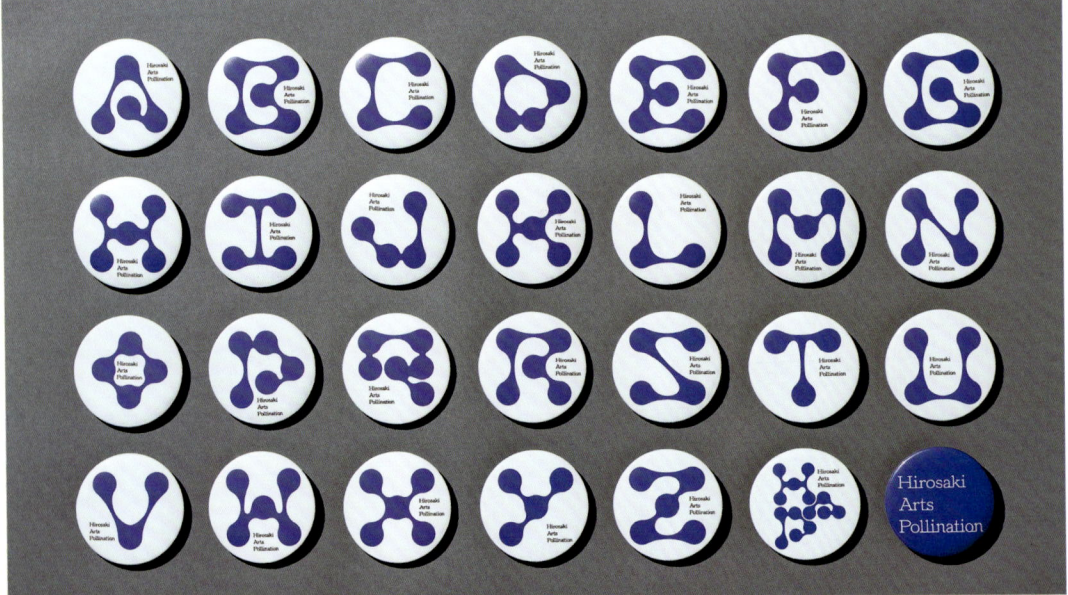

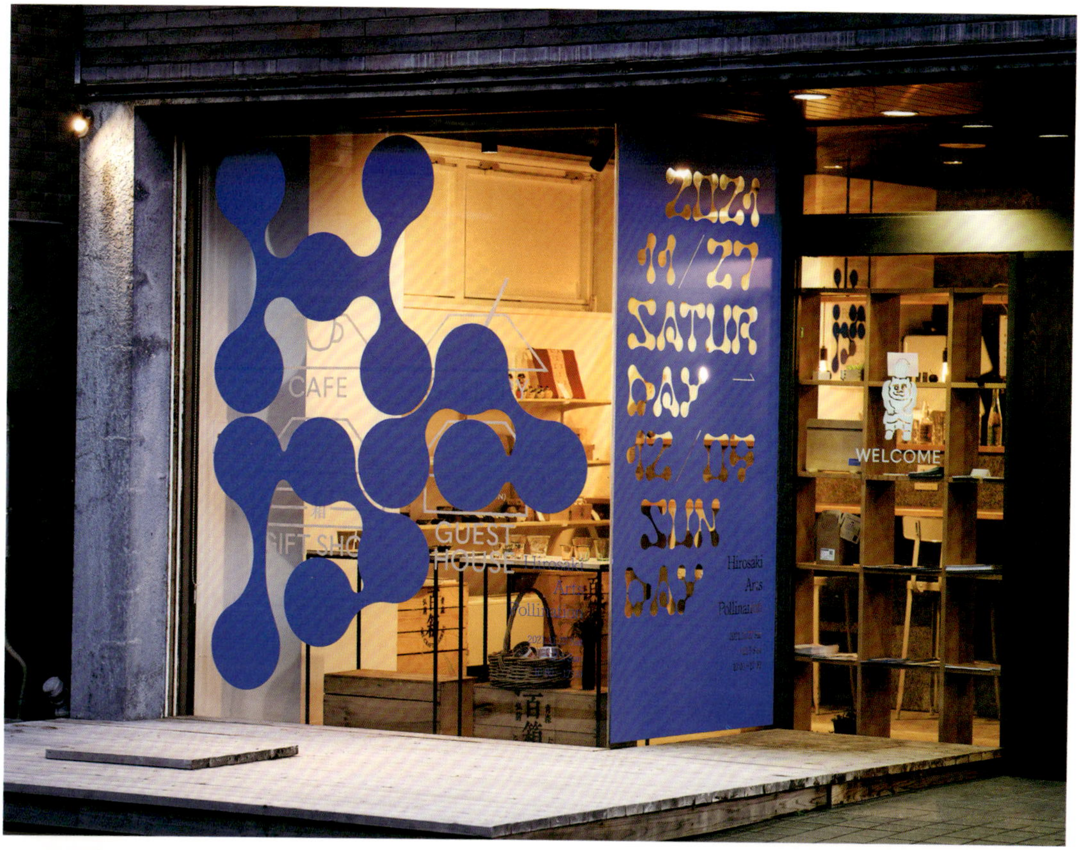
CAFE
GUEST HOUSE
Hirosaki
Arts
Pollination
WELCOME

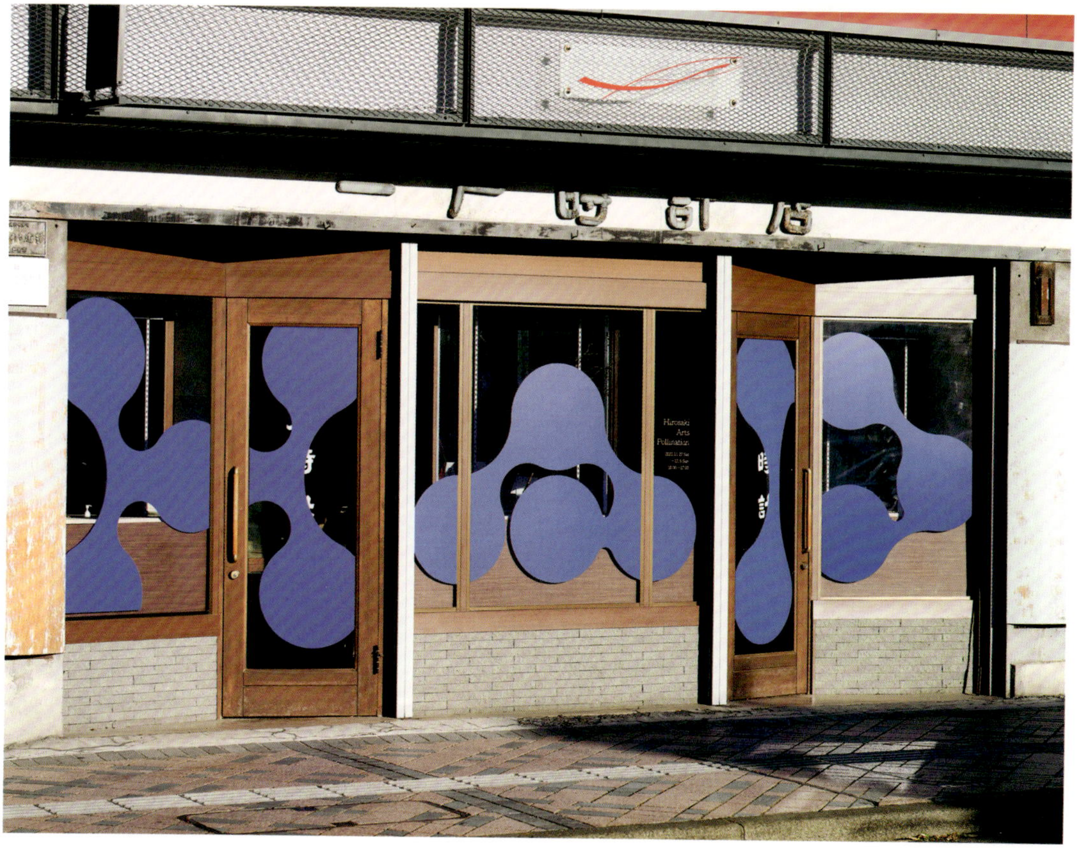
Hirosaki
Arts
Pollination

The Japanese word for rice ball is "omusubi." "Musubi" means to unite, like the way sticky Japanese rice is united in the hands of the cook. As Moe Furuya was thinking about that word (and maybe also eating omosubi), he came up with this idea: Give rice balls a new role—to unite people. This is also the goal of United Rice Ball.

CD   Hidetoshi Kuranari
AD   Moe Furuya
D   Moe Furuya
CL   United Rice Ball

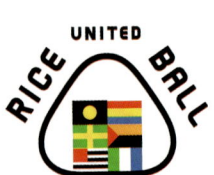

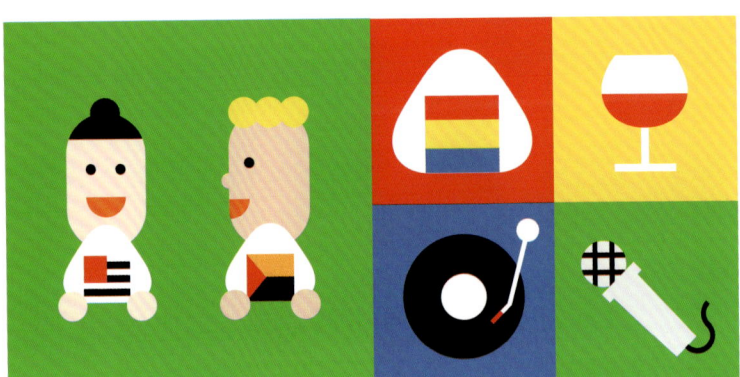

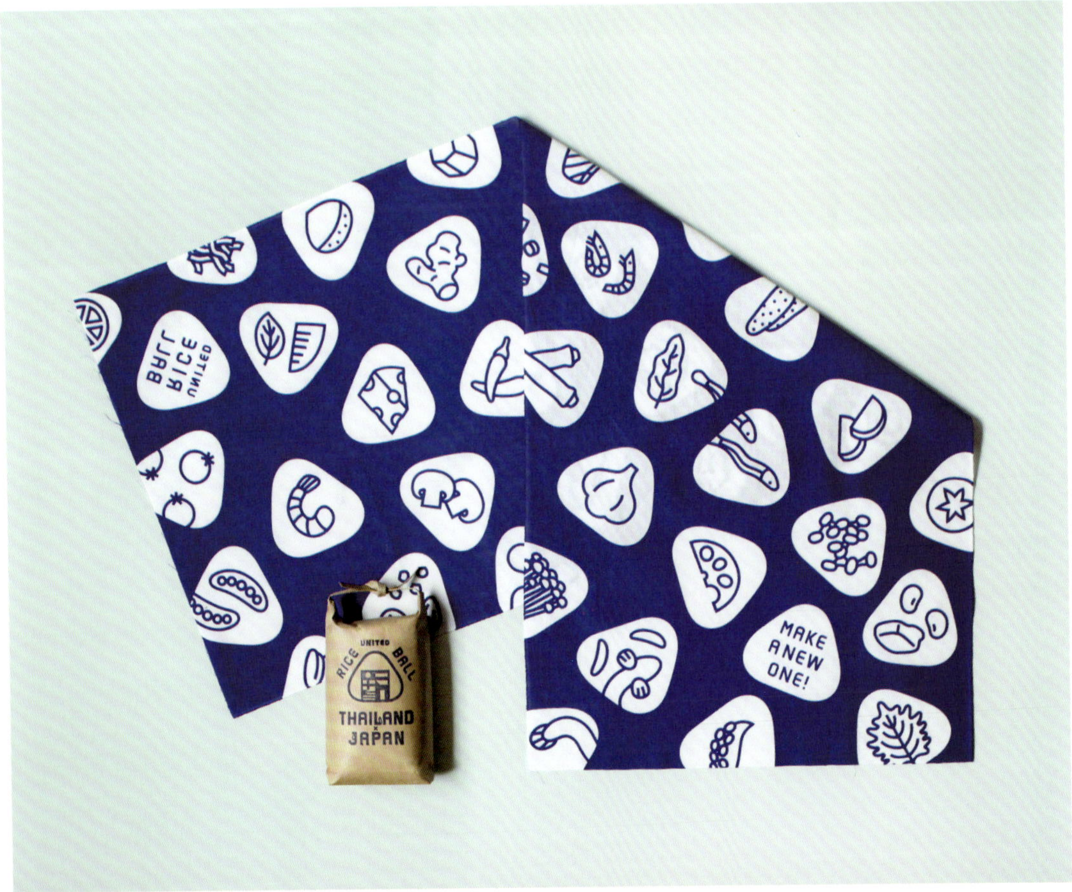

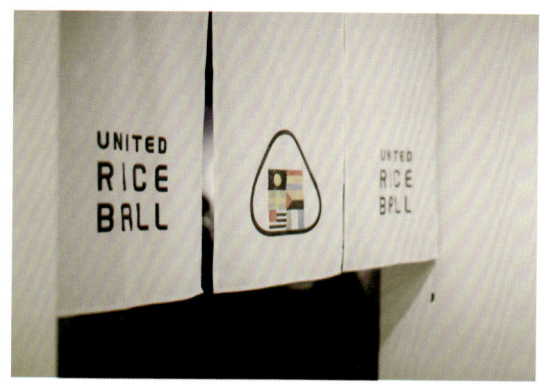

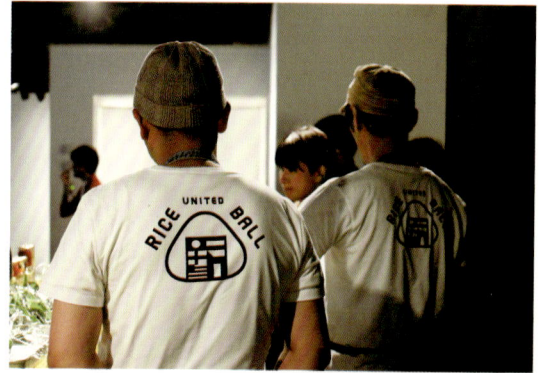

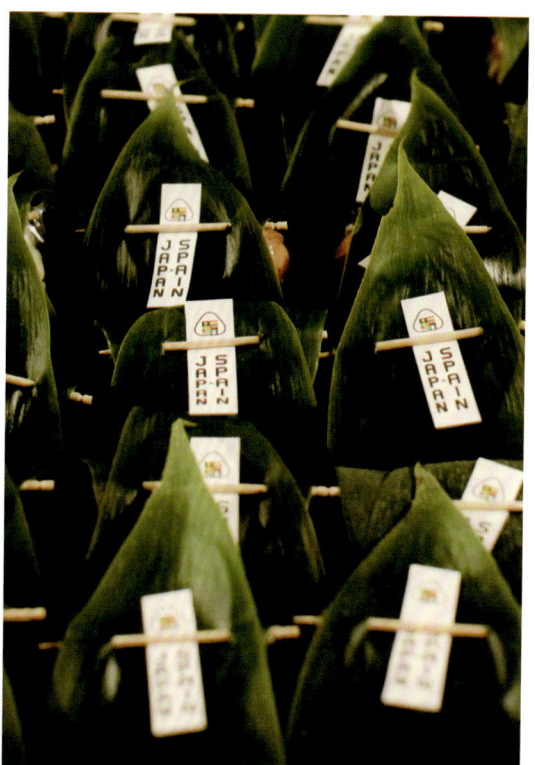

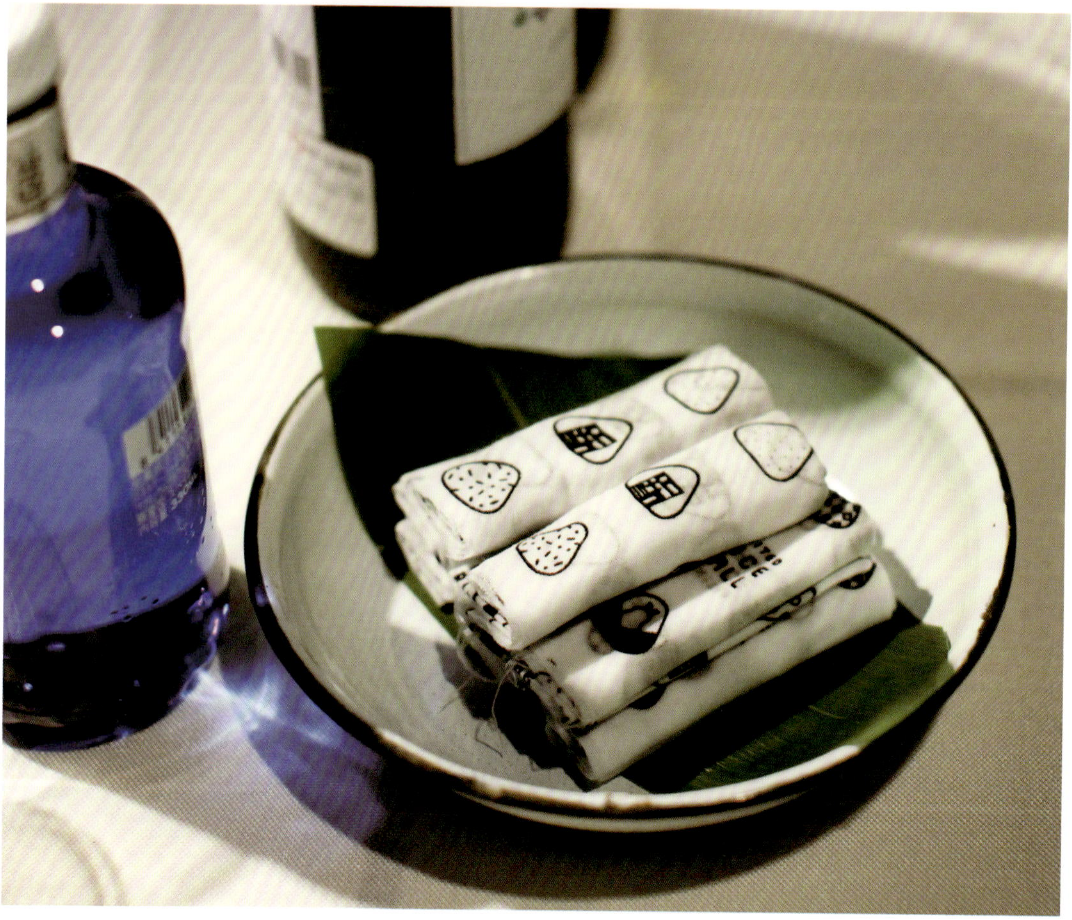

UMA/design farm created the logo, signage, and pamphlets for the relocation of the Kobe International Community Center.

Using green and blue as key colors, reminiscent of the mountains and sea of Kobe, the logo, signage, and pamphlets were developed to make the center more friendly and open to the public. The abbreviated logo uses a vertical format, a characteristic of Asian languages and incorporates elements of Slavic typefaces to create something neutral that cannot be identified with any one country. In addition, the greeting patterns in 11 languages on the glass facing the shopping street create a lively atmosphere.

DA   UMA/design farm
AD   Yuma Harada
D   Mariko Kishiki
CL   Kobe International Community
      Center

Kobe International Community Center

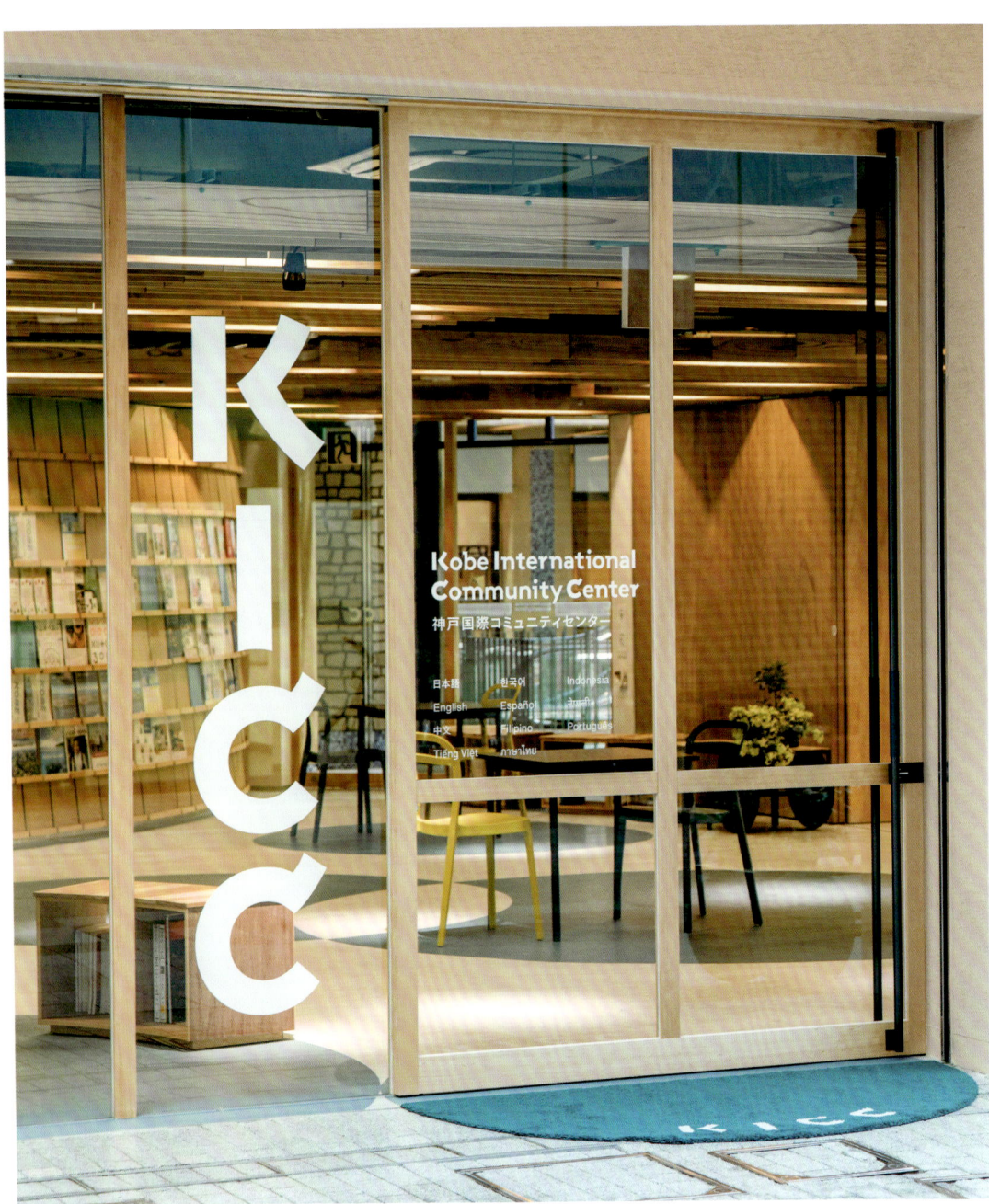

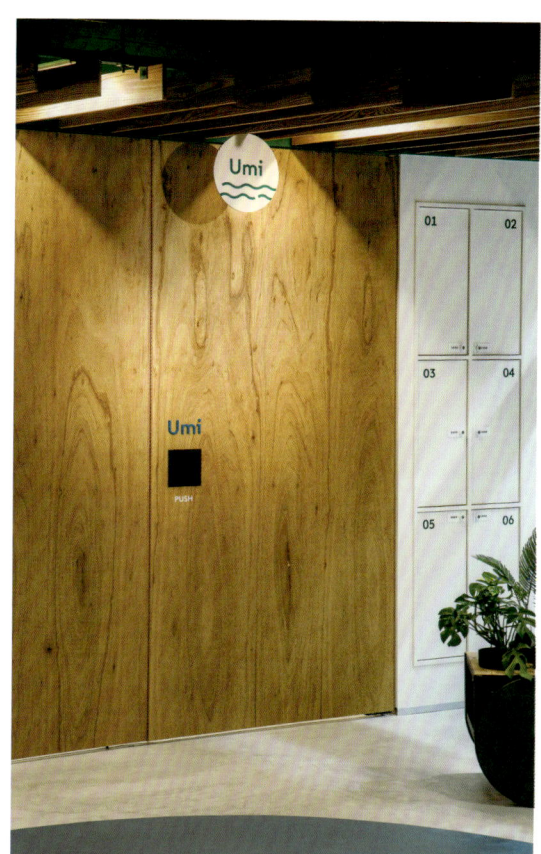

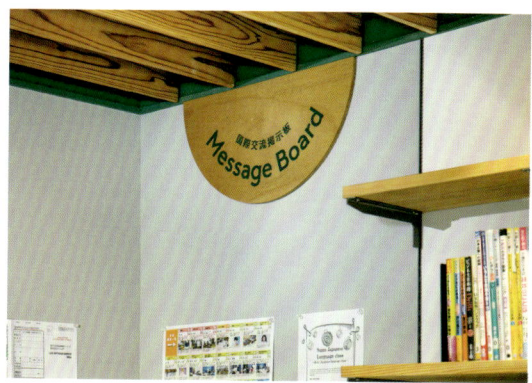

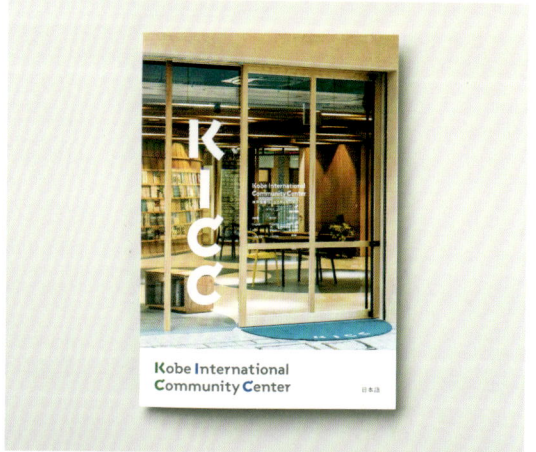

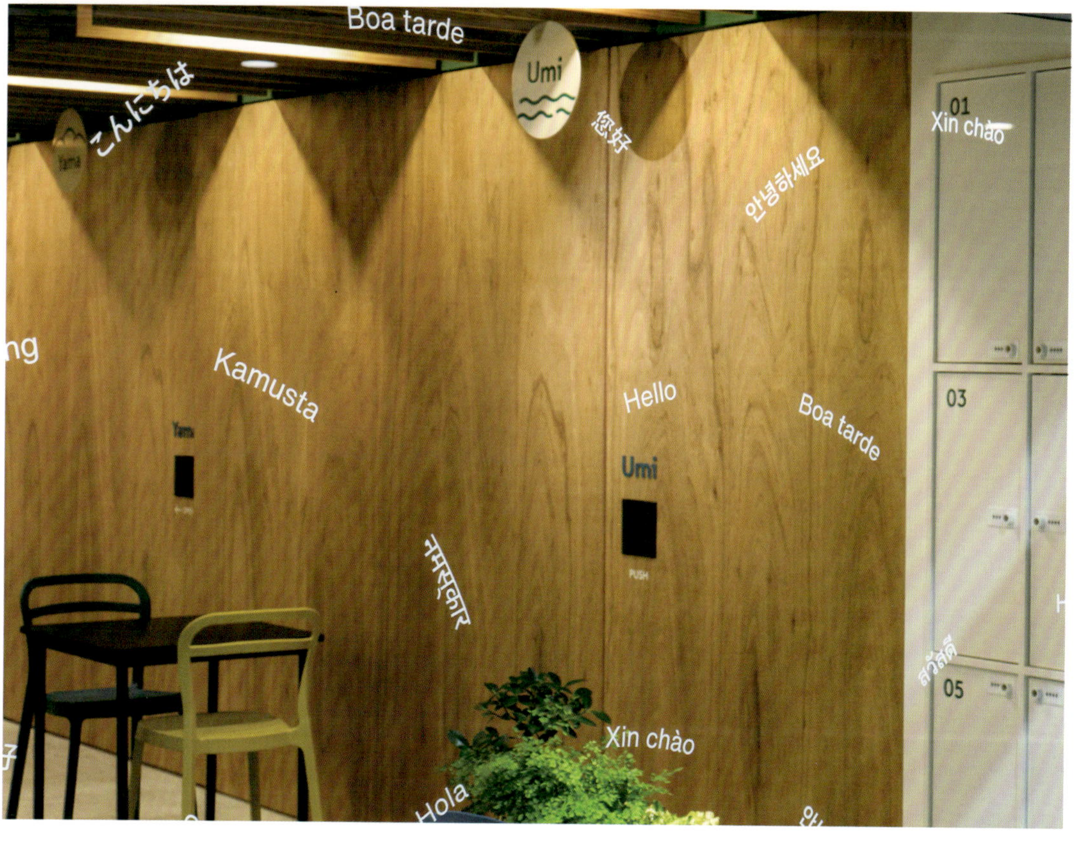

Hakone is a famous hot springs resort in Japan. This is the branding of cu-mo, a space for a short rest in the Sounsan station building. It is a relay point for the mountain railroad and cableway that pass through Hakone. Inspired by the design of marquetry—a traditional Hakone craft, KAAKA Inc. created a logo that is composed of squares to form a cloud. Based on this, KAAKA Inc. deconstructed the logo and developed patterns on various items.

DA   KAAKA Inc.
D   Ryosuke Kato
ID   UDS Ltd.
CL   Hakone Ropeway Co., Ltd.

cu-mo

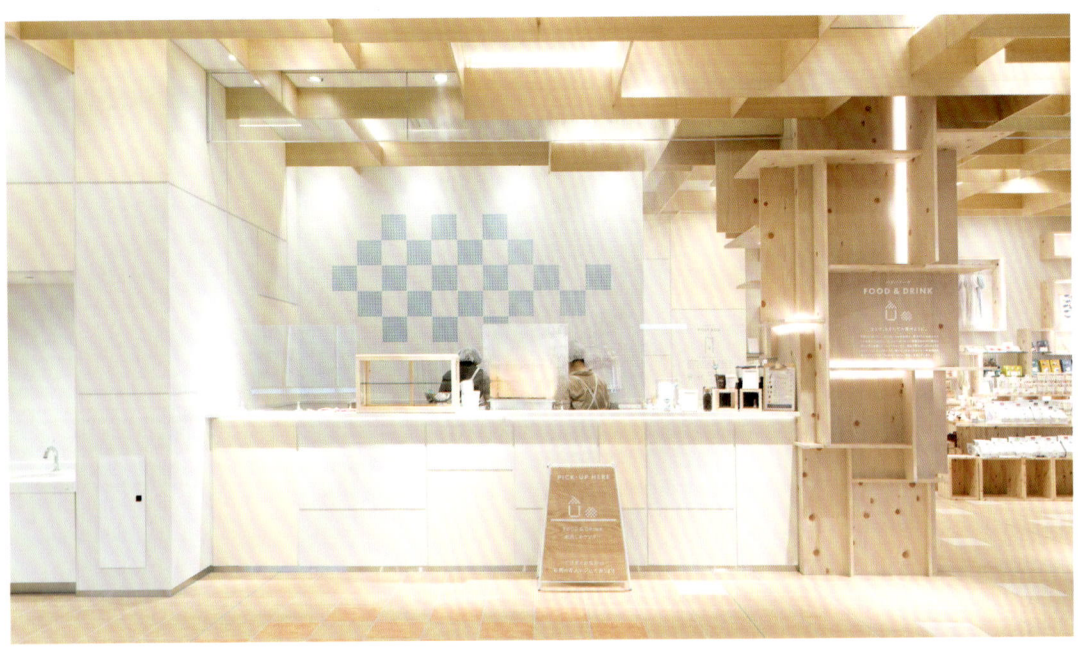

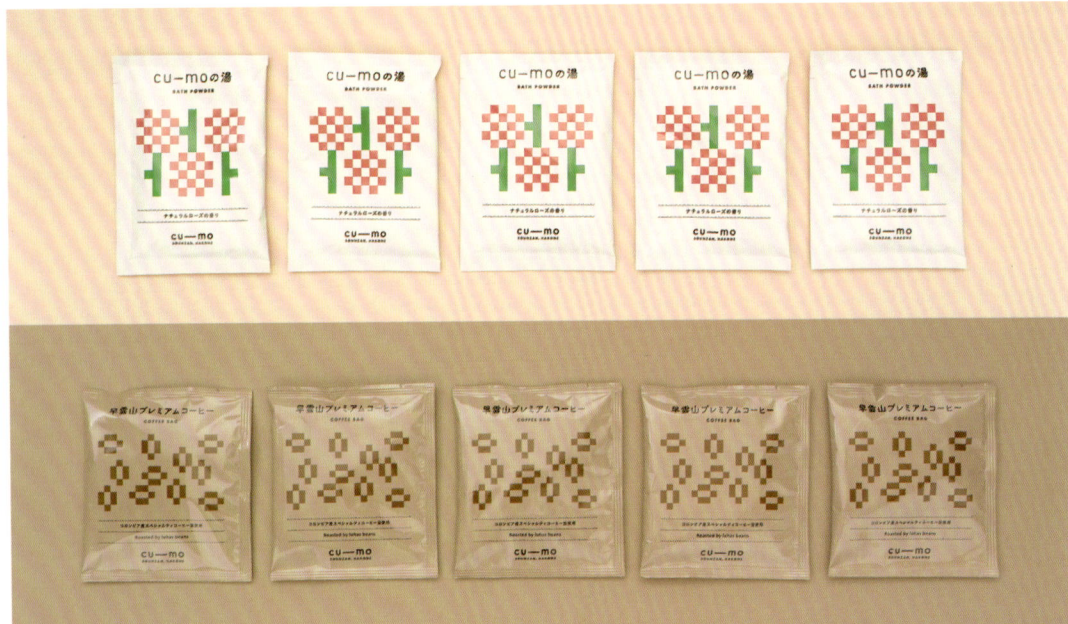

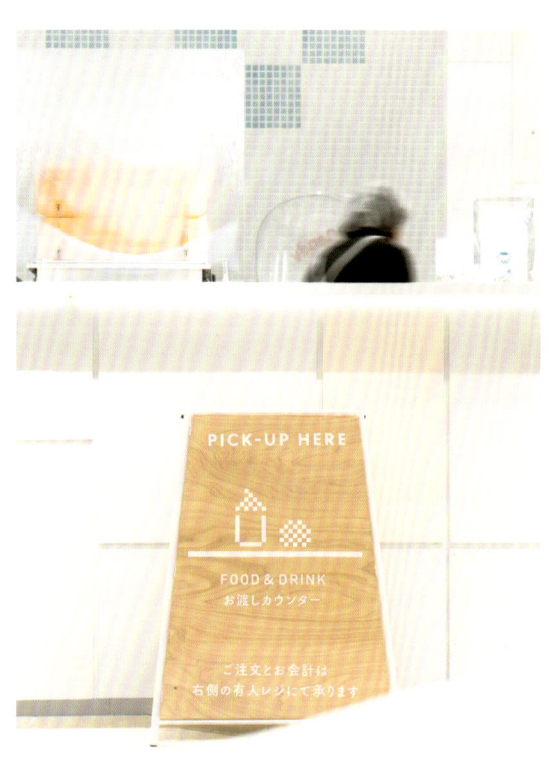

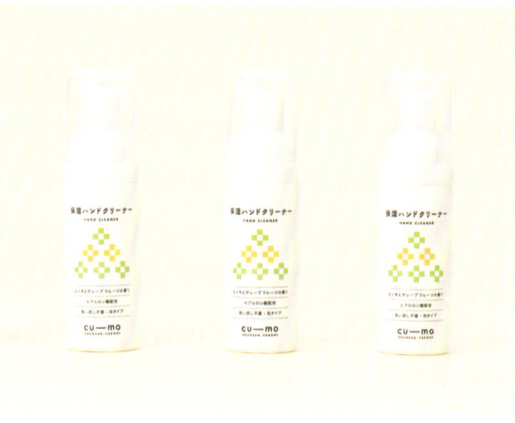

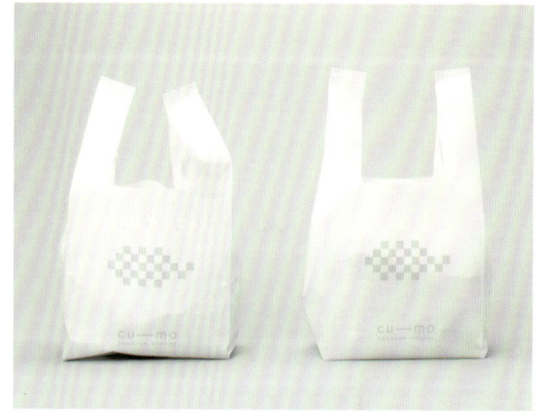

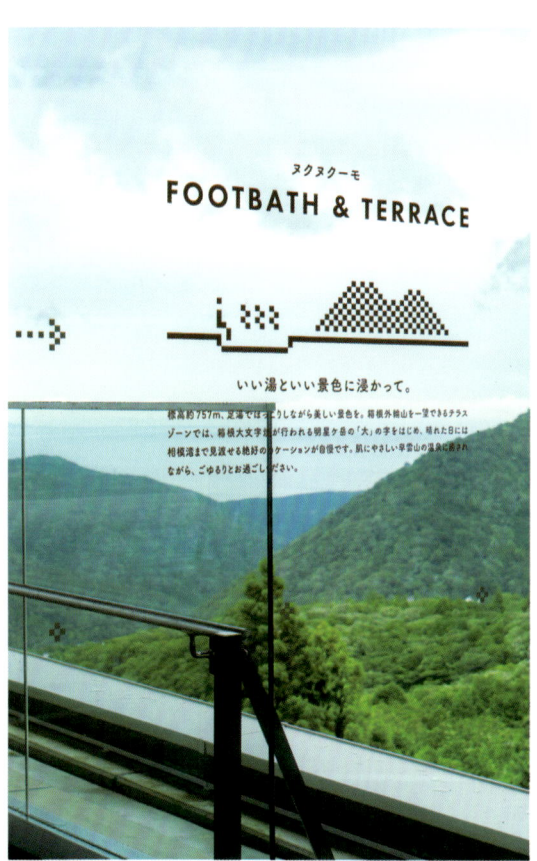

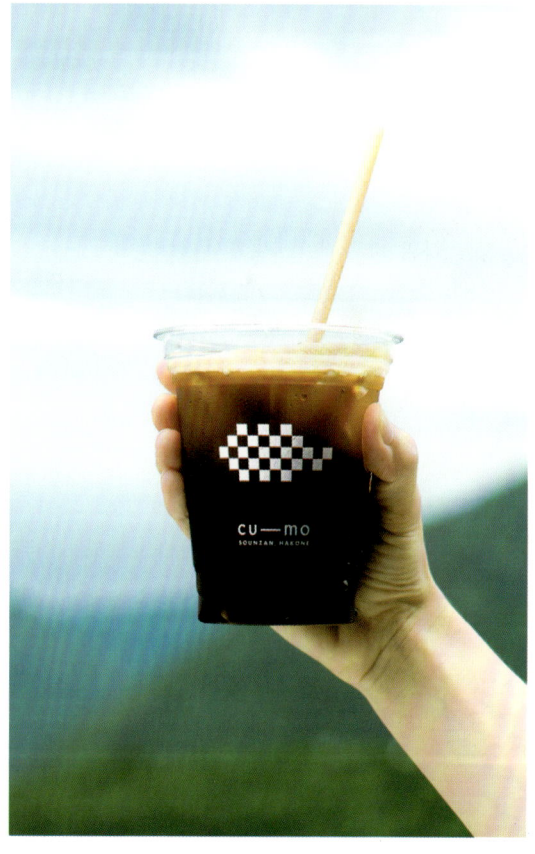

This is the art direction for a souvenir store opened in conjunction with the renovation of the Kyushu Saga International Airport terminal building.

The logo, which gives the impression of an airplane lightly taking off from Saga, was designed to convey both "saga" and "air" by using different shapes of the lowercase letter "a." The store card is in the shape of a boarding card. The sign for the bar inside the shop is inspired by the image of a window pane fogged up with breath when people look through an airplane window, or clouds seen through a window, adding an essence of lightness and friendliness to the refined space.

DA   UMA/design farm
AD   Yuma Harada
D   Yuka Tsuda
PH   Koichiro Fujimoto
CL   Saga Products Promotion
        Public Corporation

Sagair

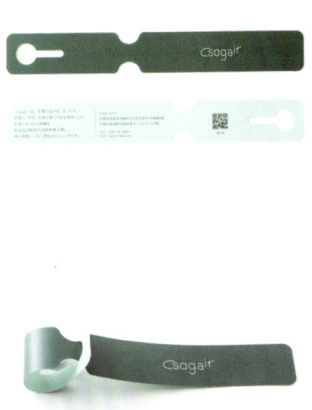

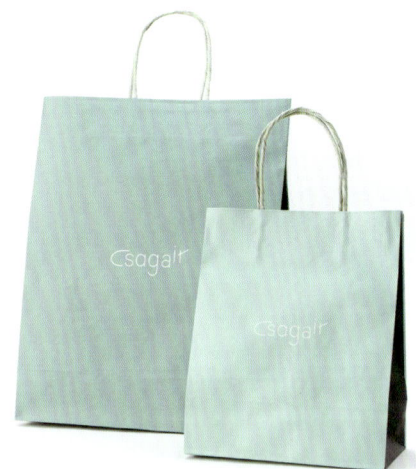

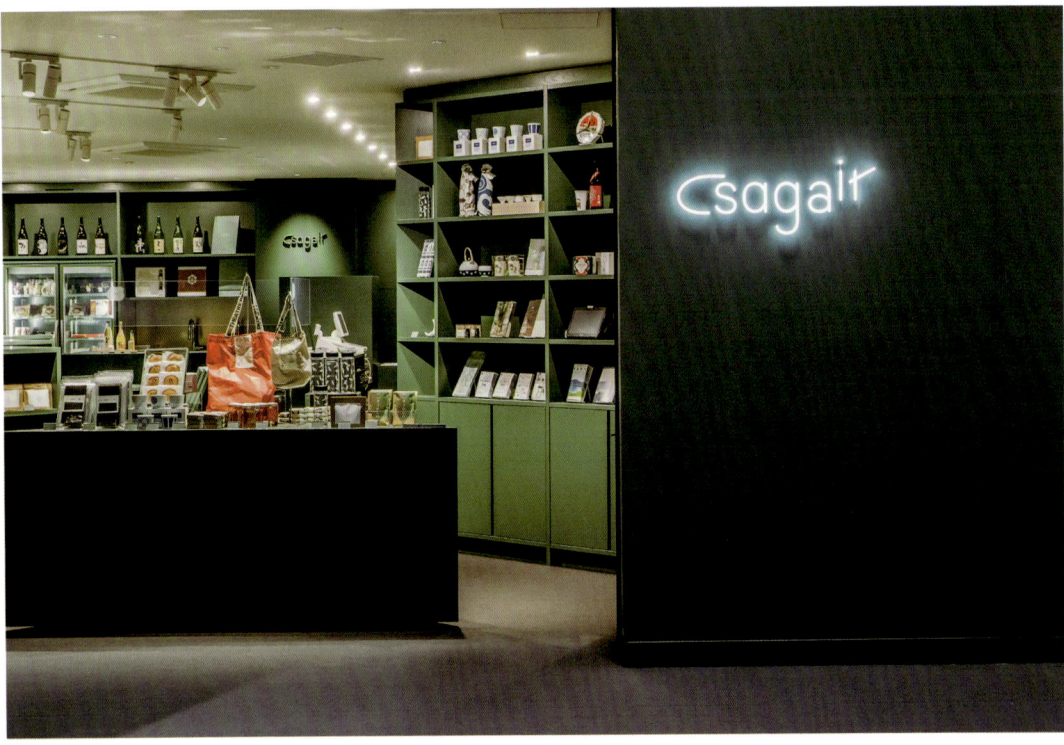

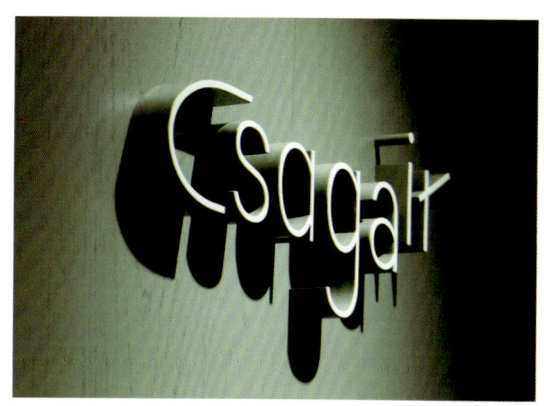

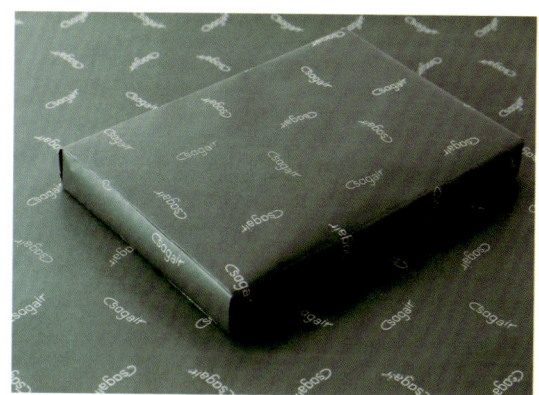

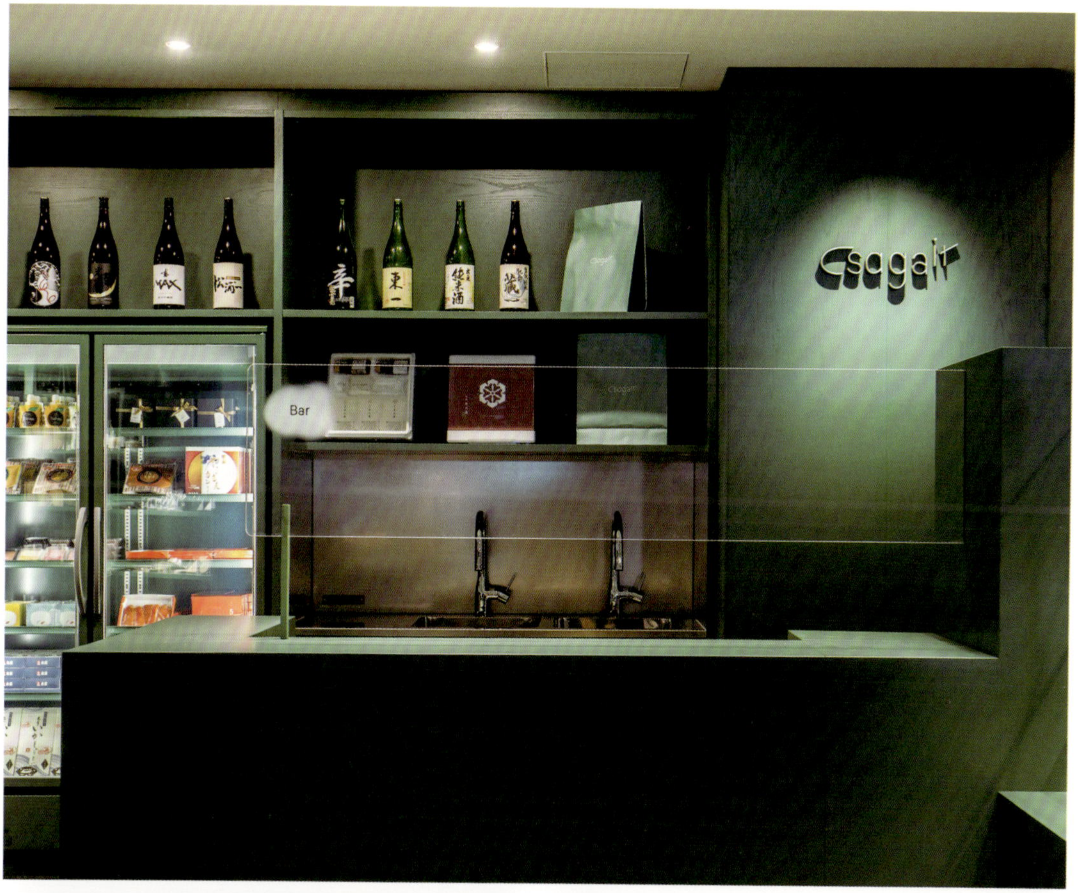

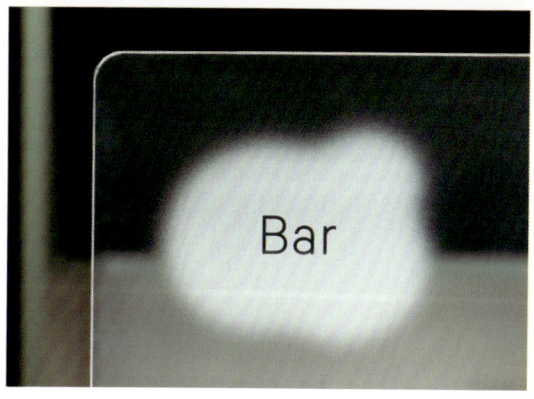

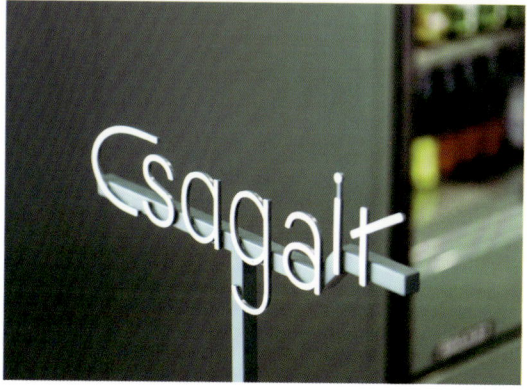

KAMADO, a web magazine in the art field, celebrated its first anniversary with an exhibition to launch two new services, "KUJI" and "FUMI." To make art more accessible to the public, the design centers on a simplified motif of the shapes of lottery and letter from which the names KUJI and FUMI were derived. The motifs are recombined to form various patterns for different media. The sub-theme of the exhibition is to change the perspective of familiar things.

AD   Keiji Yano
D   Keiji Yano
PR   Naomi Kakiuchi
CL   KAMADO

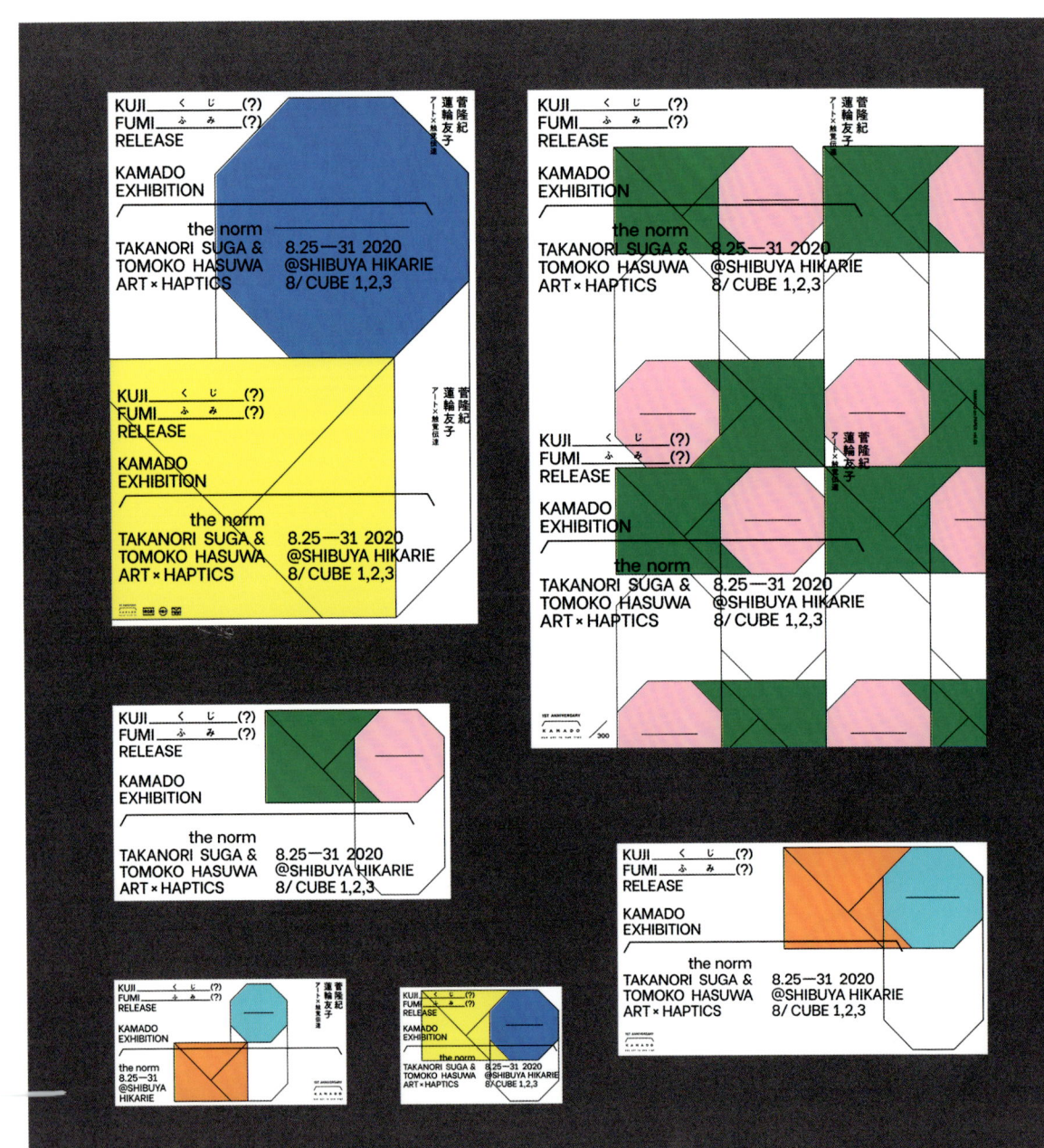

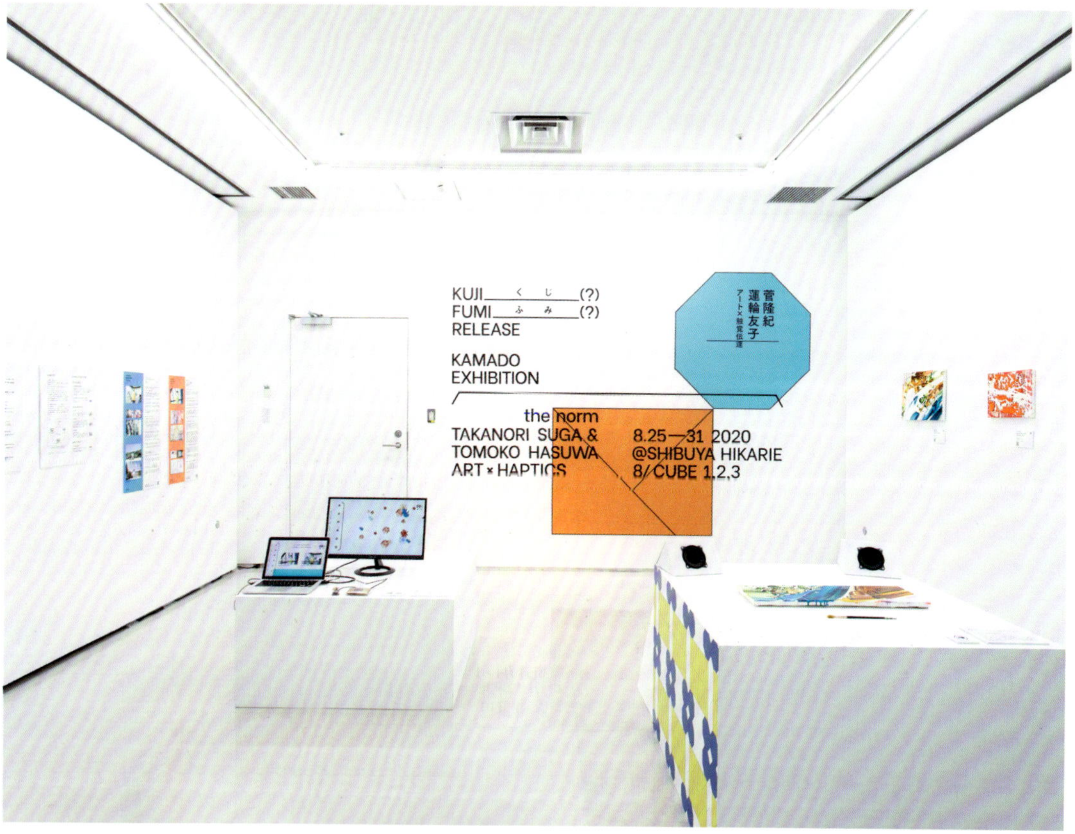

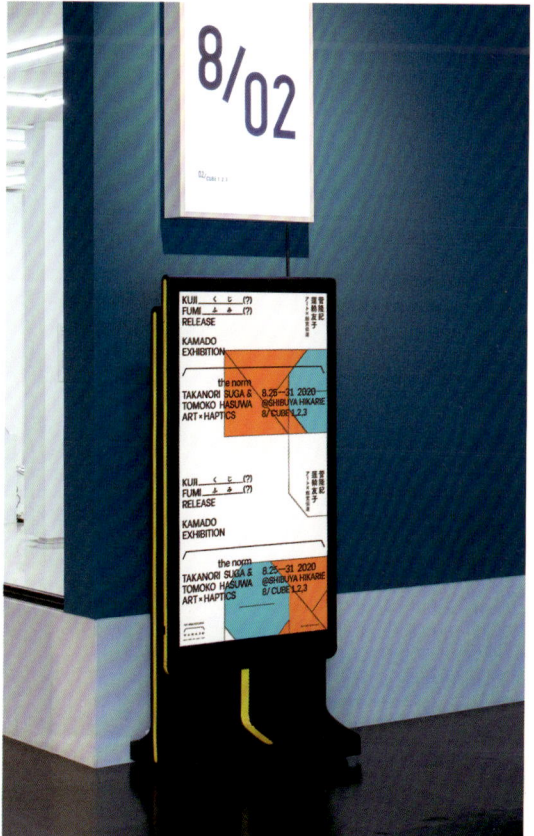

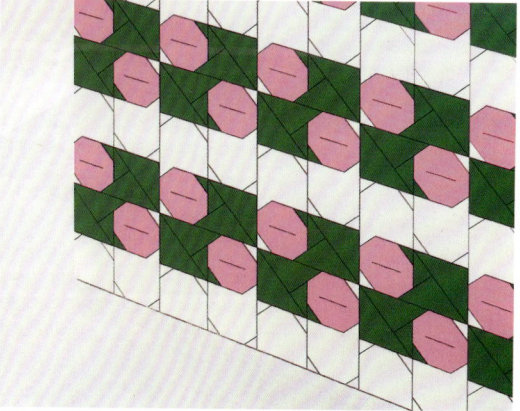

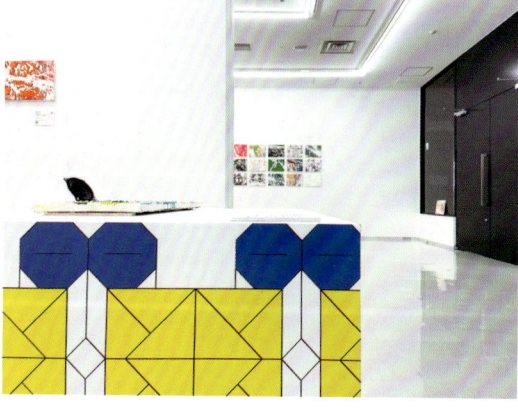

Keiji Yano designed advertising arts at an exhibition, which is a part of Setouchi Triennale 2019. The client, Takamatsu Art Museum, required visualizing the theme of Dissect the Society on posters, flyers, captions, and an art book. To illustrate the theme, Keiji Yano chose the concept of "incision" for the main visual. The visual looks like an entrance, which means inviting people to the exhibition. In addition, Keiji Yano set a rule about visuals and typography to distinguish the outside and inside of the exhibition. The font switches from serif to sans-serif at the ruled lines and this applies to the caption. The visuals, although free from images, became more efficient.

AD   Keiji Yano
D   Keiji Yano
CL   Takamatsu Art Museum

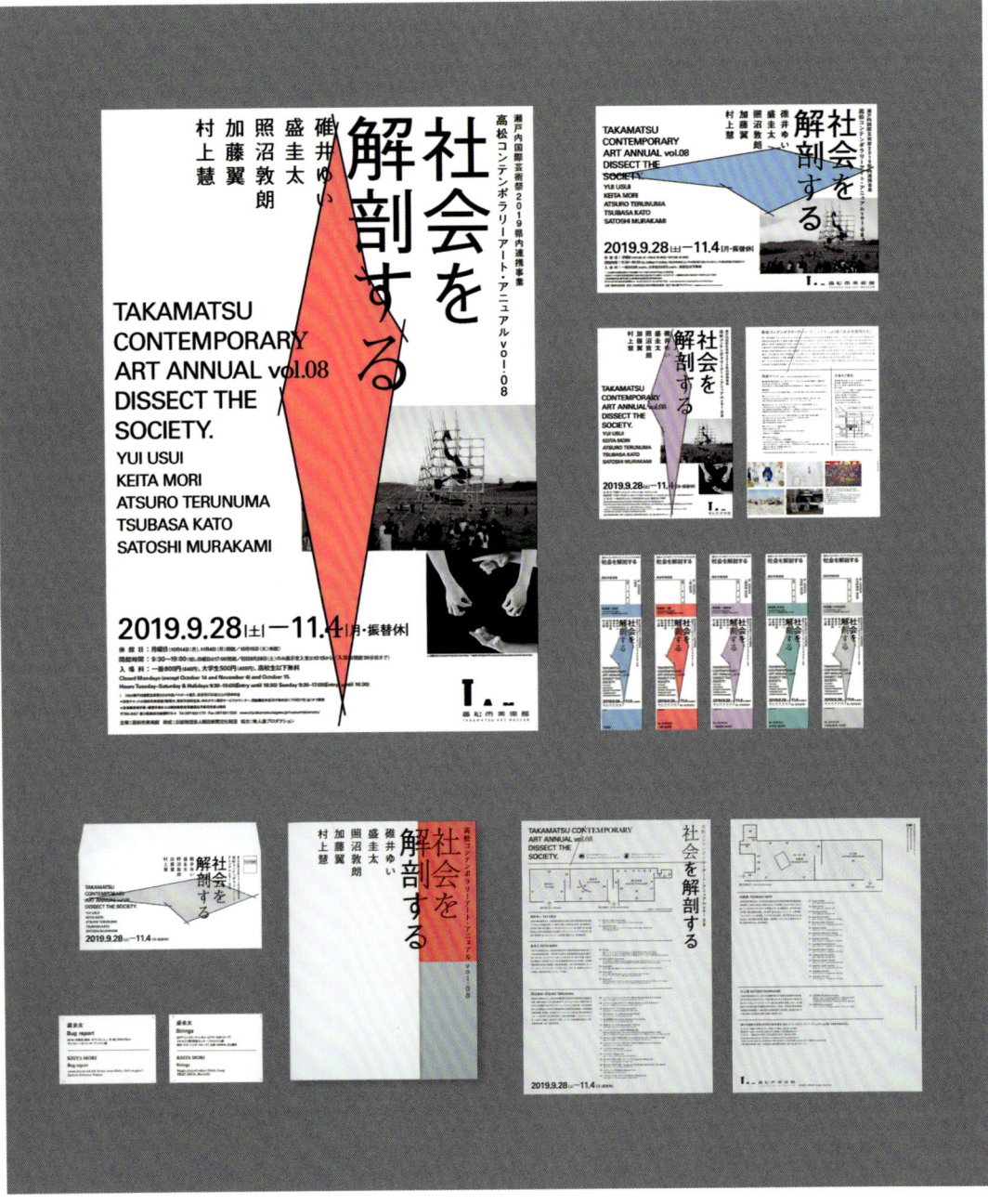

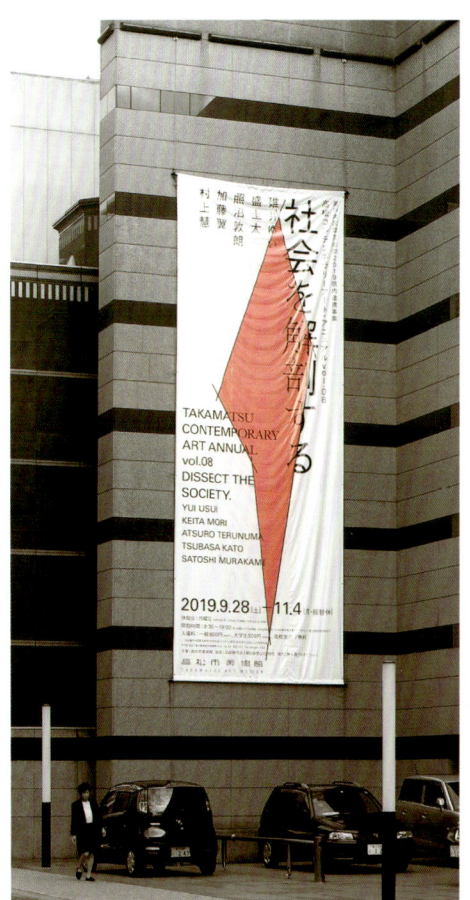

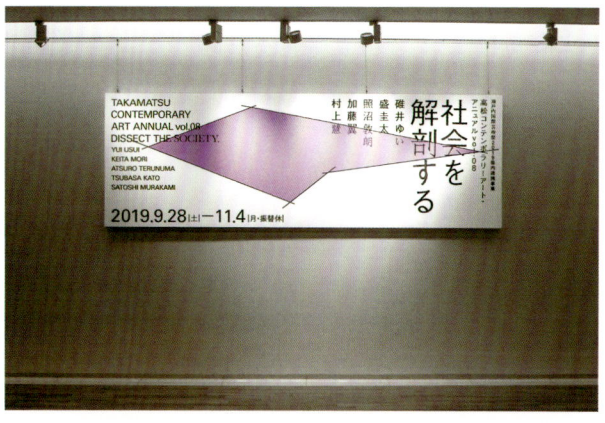

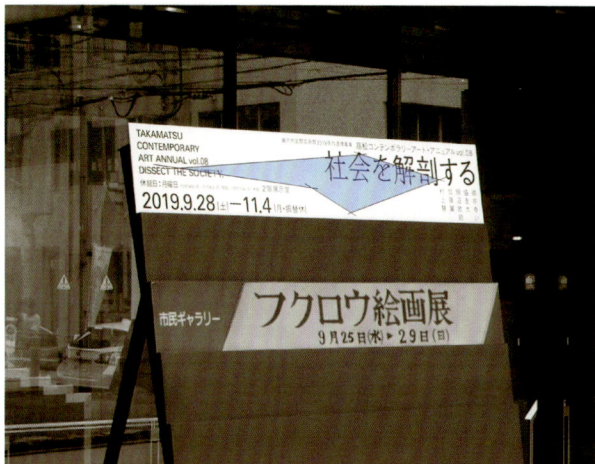

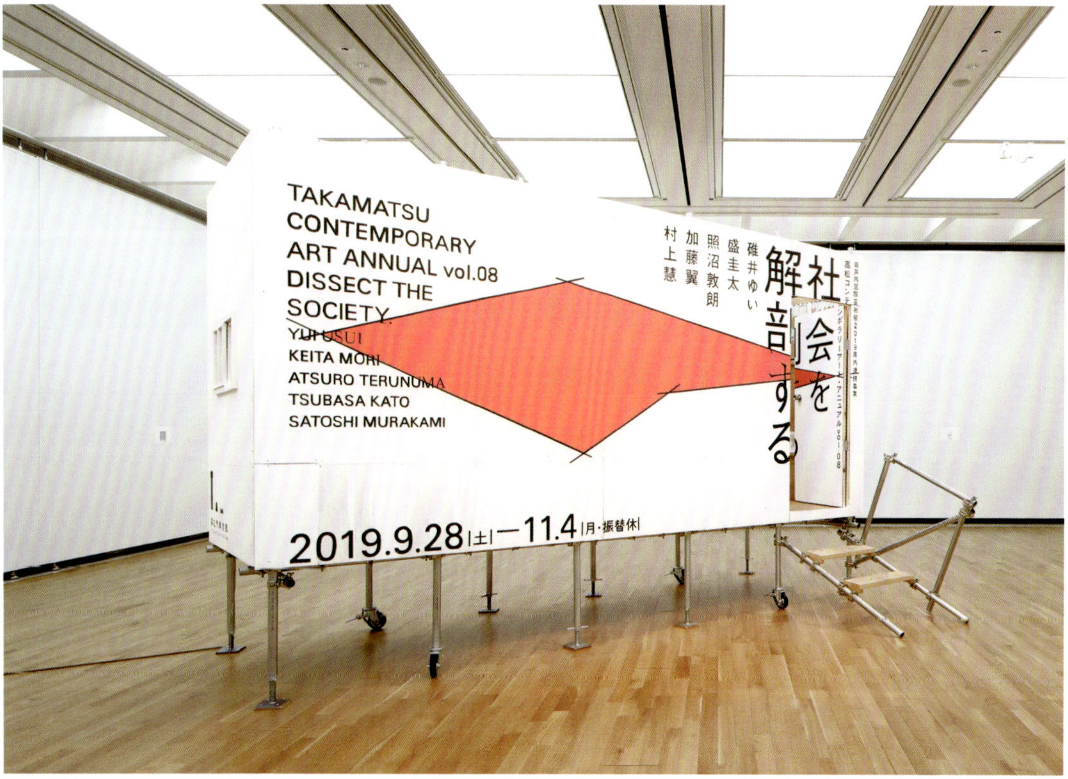

Studio Wonder created a design for SOMESAND, a brand that sells "something" and "sandwiches" for a wide range of age groups to enjoy. SOMESAND runs with a business model that can change its products along with trends and store locations. The graphic is a broccoli-like lettuce with the concept of "a sandwich and something." It could be an octopus like a grape or cheese like an orange. Customers can expect a rich lineup of sandwiches from this.

Studio Wonder also created 3D sandwiches, called "polygon sandwiches" to express newness and fun on various media and different tools. They also produced motion graphics that enliven the brand opening.

DA   Studio Wonder
D   Sou Nomura, Momoka Kato, Mayu Sugihara
ID   Natsumi Mori
CL   WONDER CREW

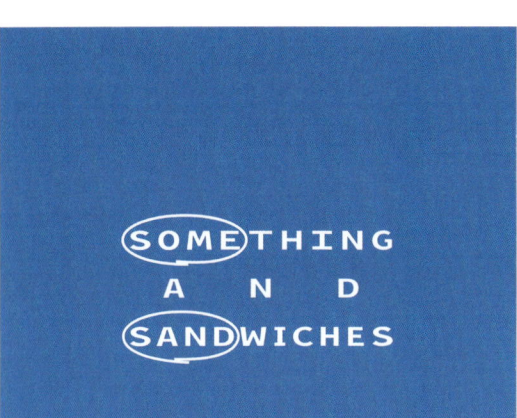

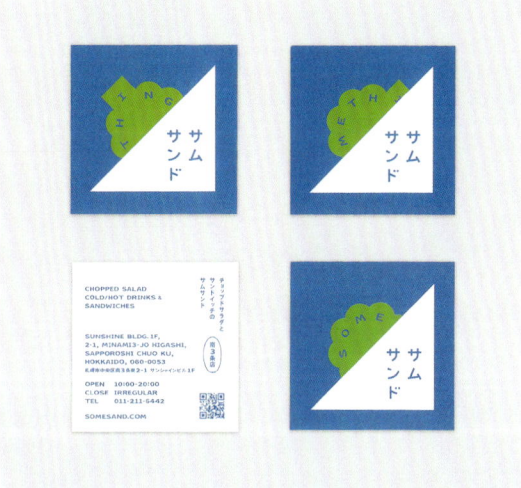

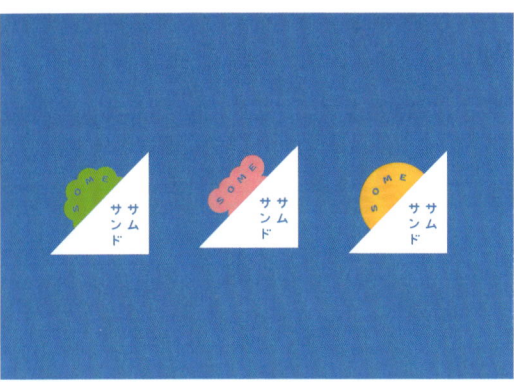

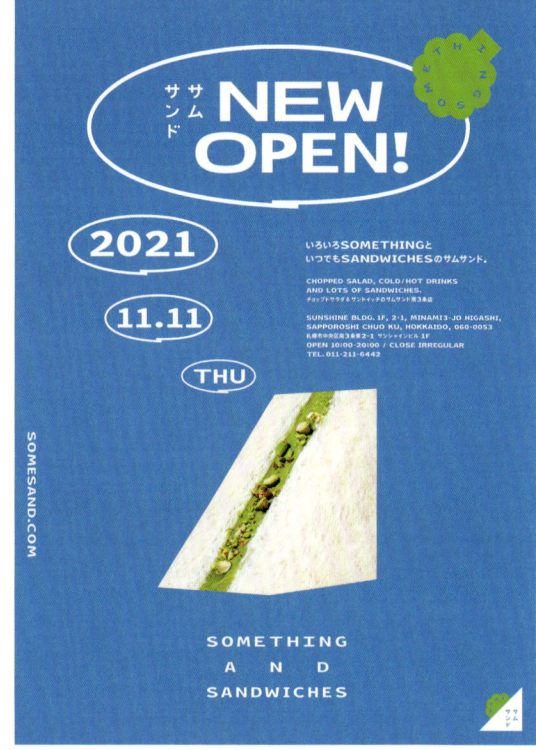

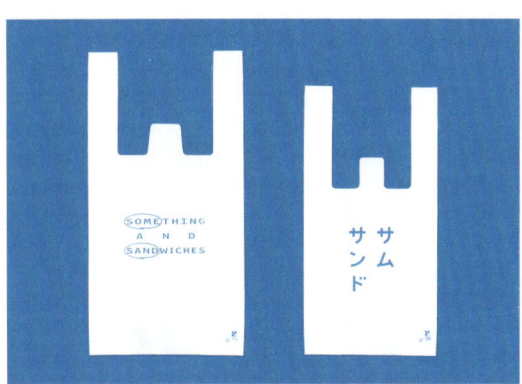

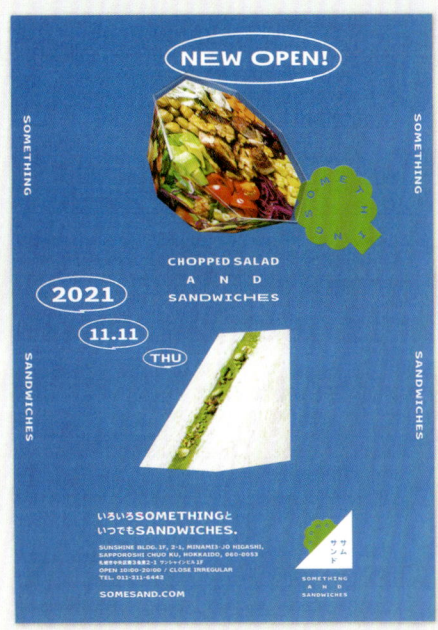

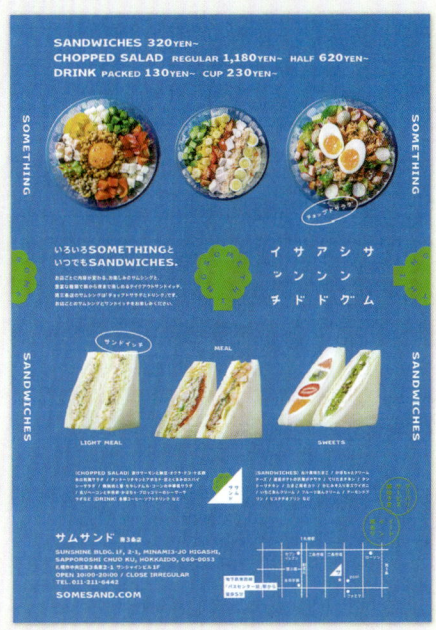

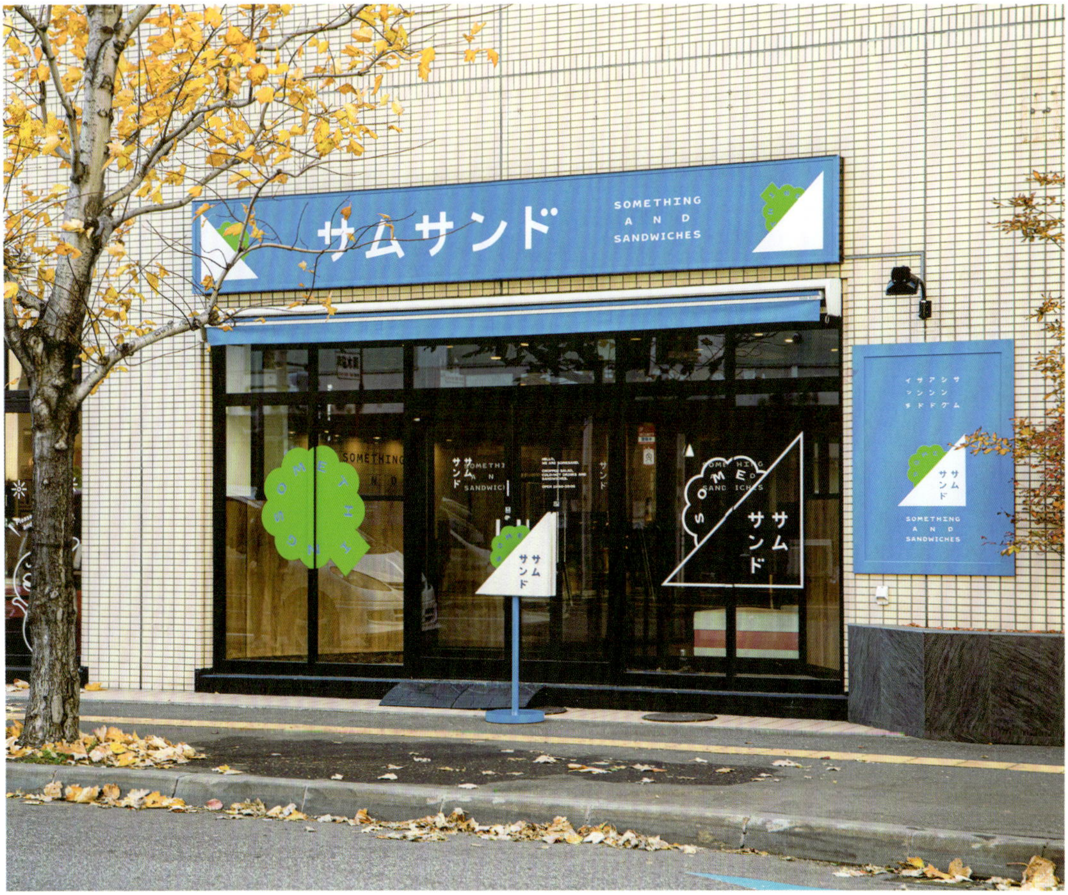

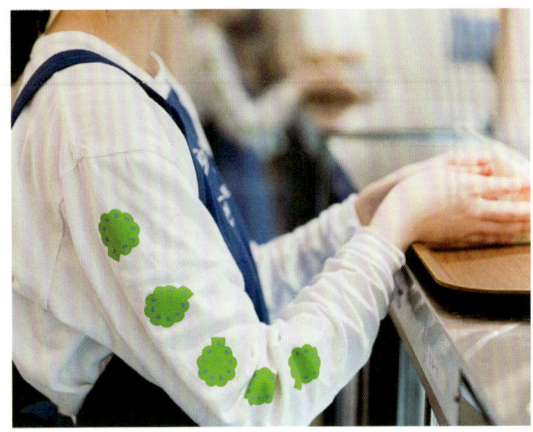

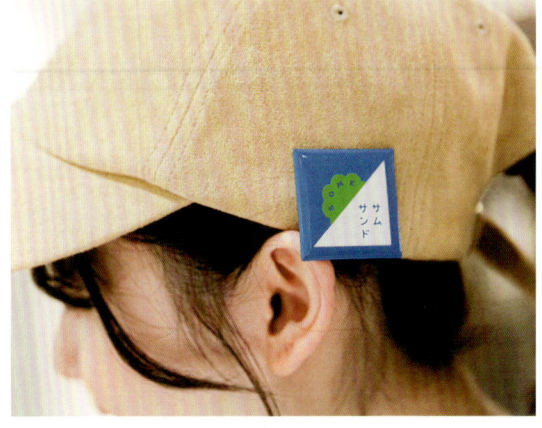

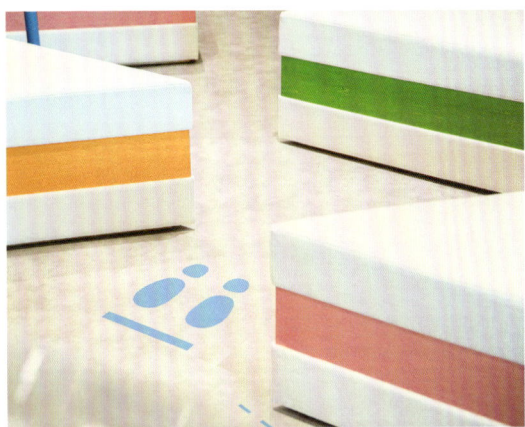

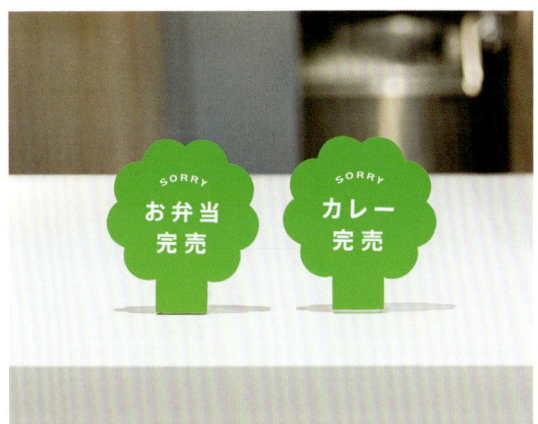

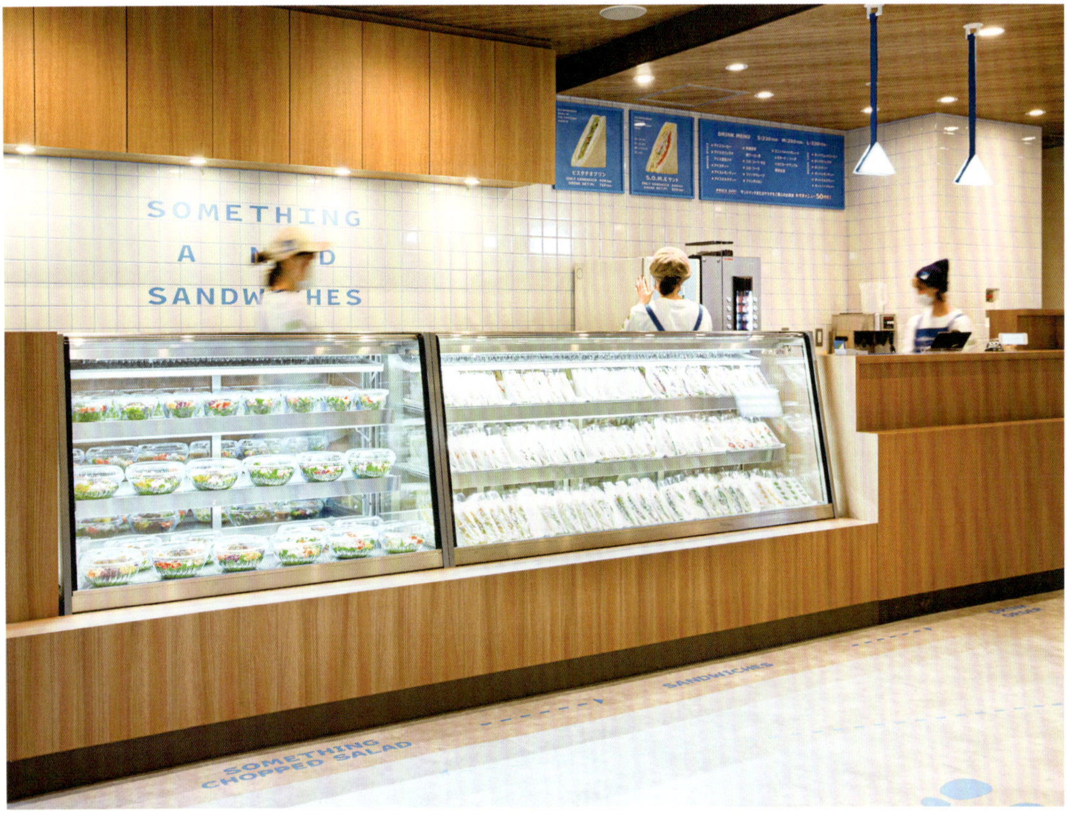

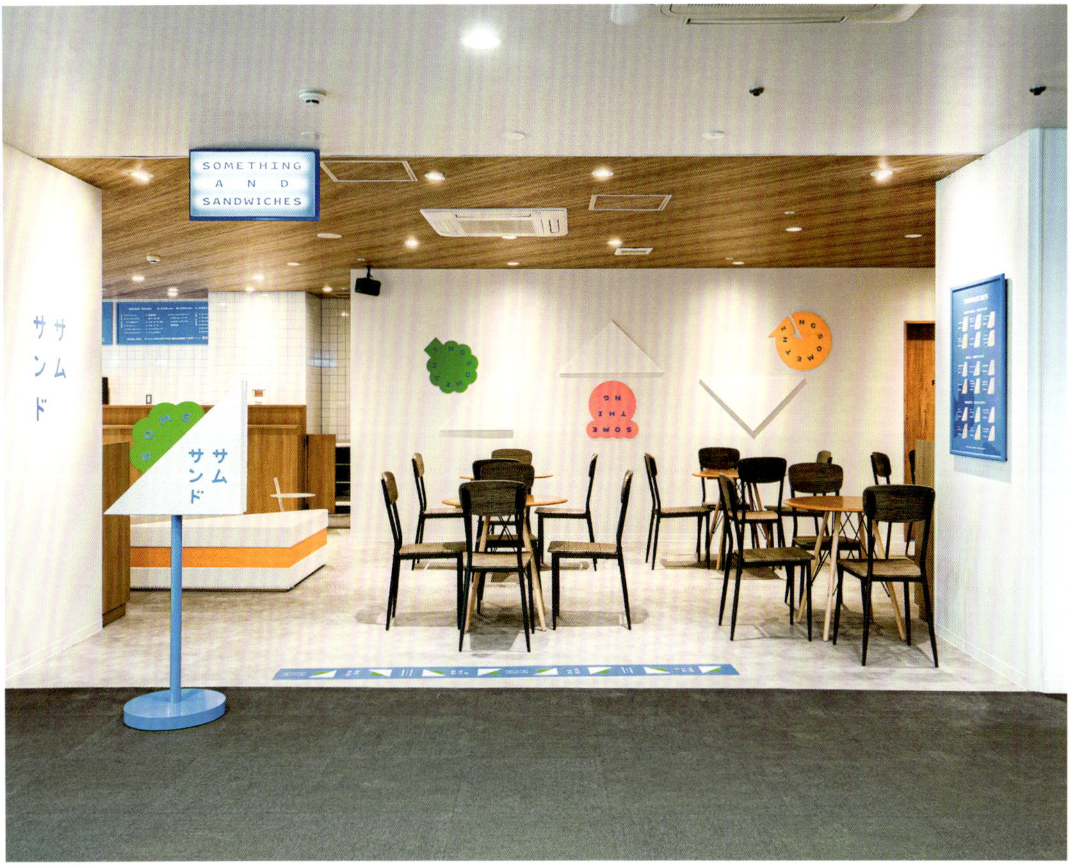

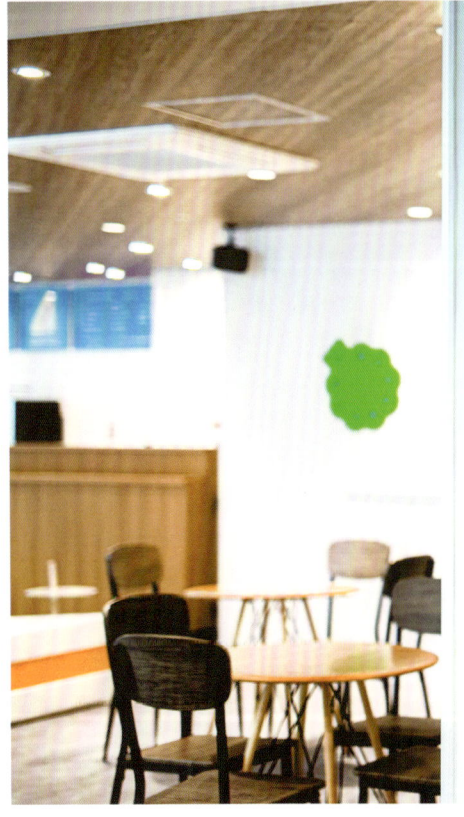

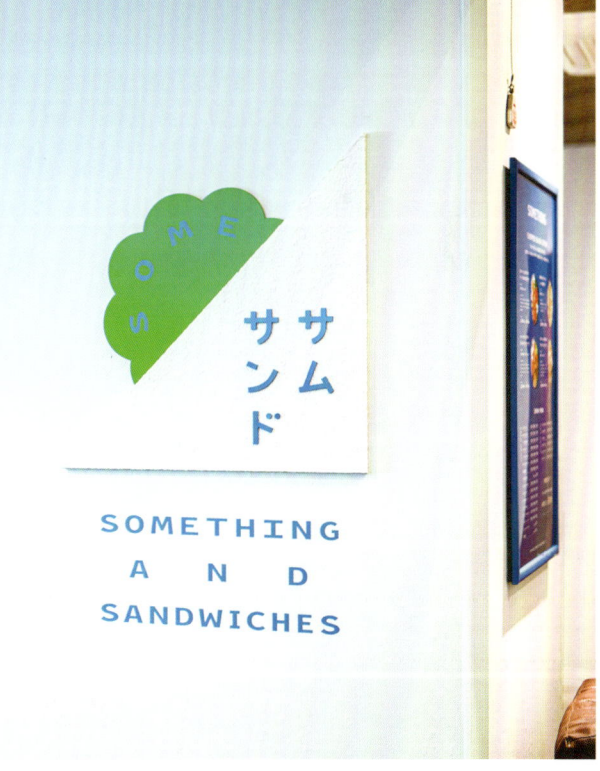

S/PARK is a complex built for Japanese beauty company Shiseido. The company has been trying to win in the global market with the key strategy of "modern Japanese beauty." Based on Shiseido's own font that had been used for over 100 years, the designers created a new font and logo with components of the Japanese Kanji "美 (beauty)" in Shiseido's font. Therefore, the design of the CI and signage system of S/PARK was able to present modernity, while preserving the essence of the original typeface, which conveyed Japanese-ness to global consumers.

DA   SOAR NY
CD   Masaki Hanahara
AD   Masaki Hanahara
D   Ikki Kobayashi, kontrapunkt
CL   Shiseido Co., Ltd.

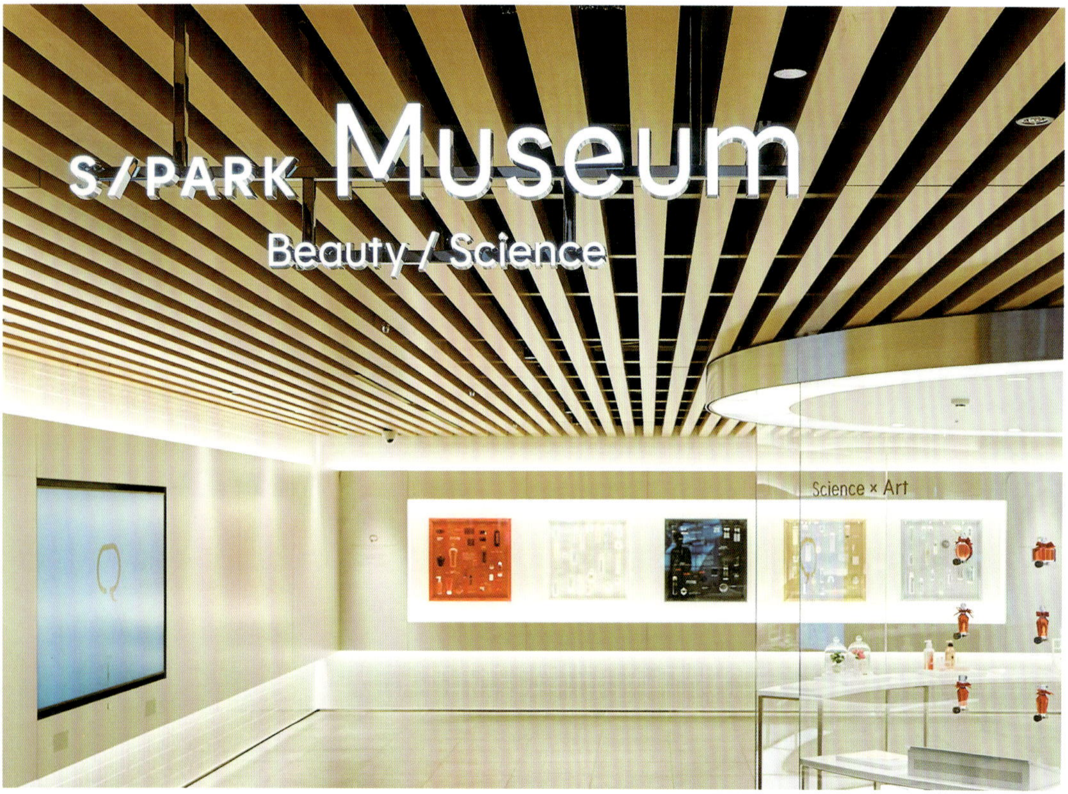

S/PARK CI & Signage

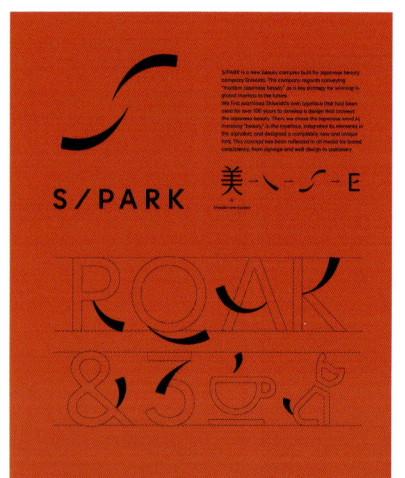

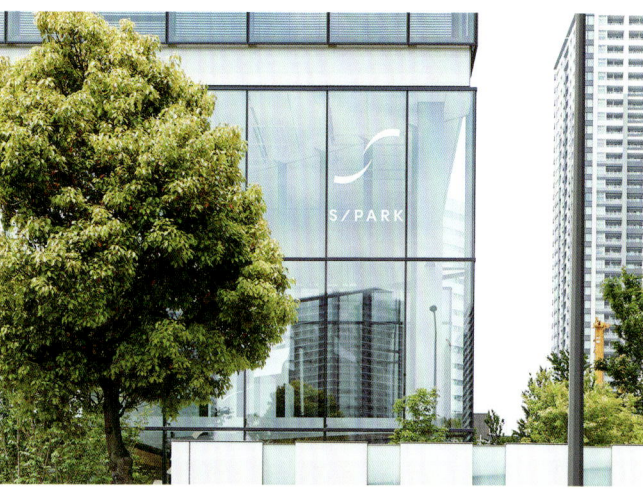

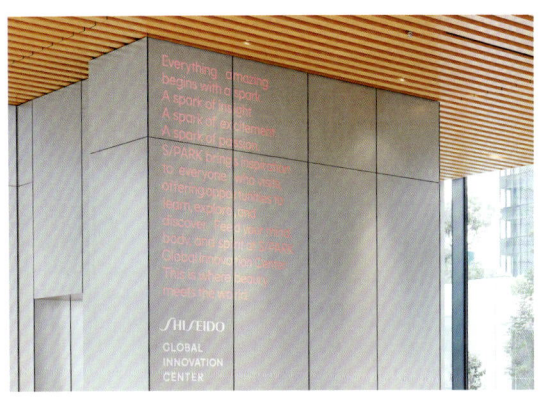

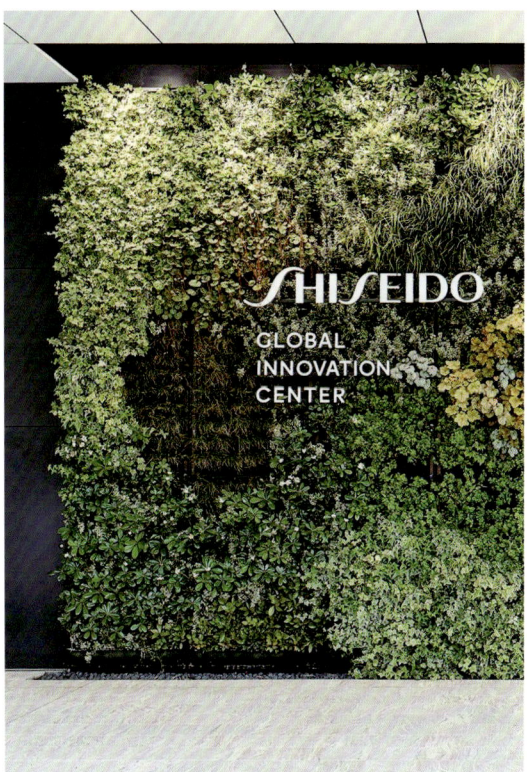

↖

2f s/park Museum
3f s/park Hall

SHISEIDO
GLOBAL
INNOVATION
CENTER

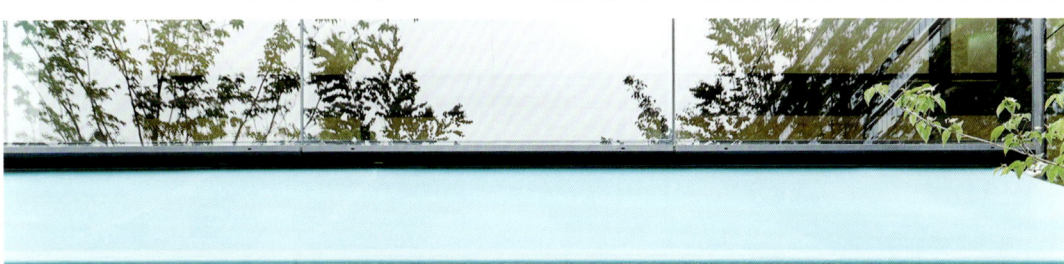

S/PARK Café

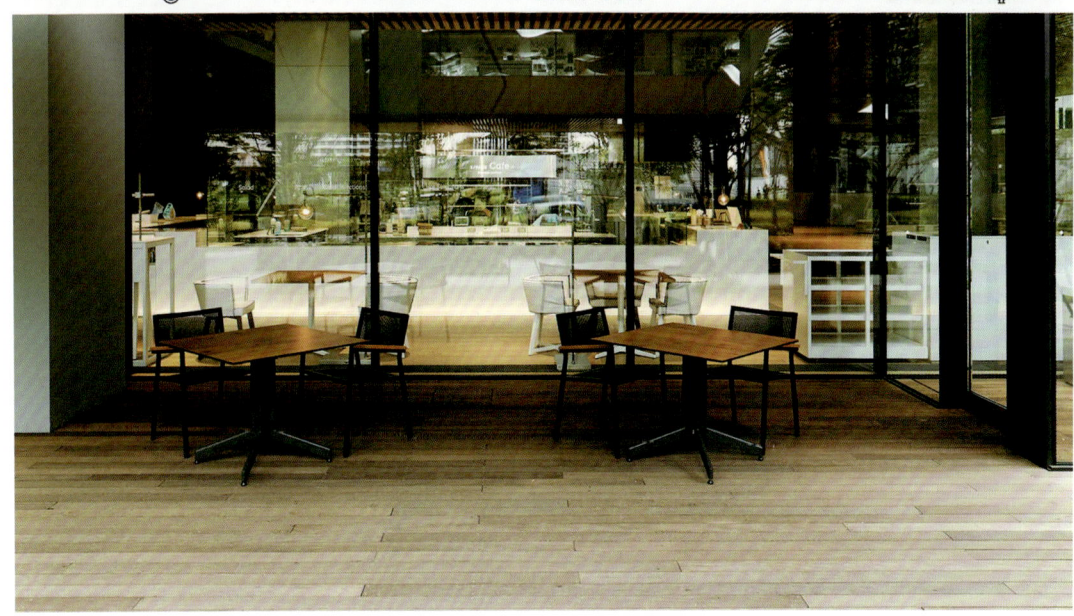

Environmental Graphics

This is the visual identity and signage design for Muni Nursery School in Katsushika-ku, Tokyo. The parent organization of Muni Nursery School is Jofukuji Temple in Ibaraki Prefecture. To create a new nursery school, the designers wanted to incorporate elements from Jofukuji into the VI and signage, and they developed the design based on the theme of light. The pictograms and signs were created with a combination of circles. Plants and animals in the form of simple circles leave a vivid impression.

AD   Takahiro Eto
D   Takahiro Eto, Ayumi Sato
PH   Sohei Oya
      (Nacasa & Partners Inc.)
AR   Tatsuya Nagao
CL   MUNI Nursery

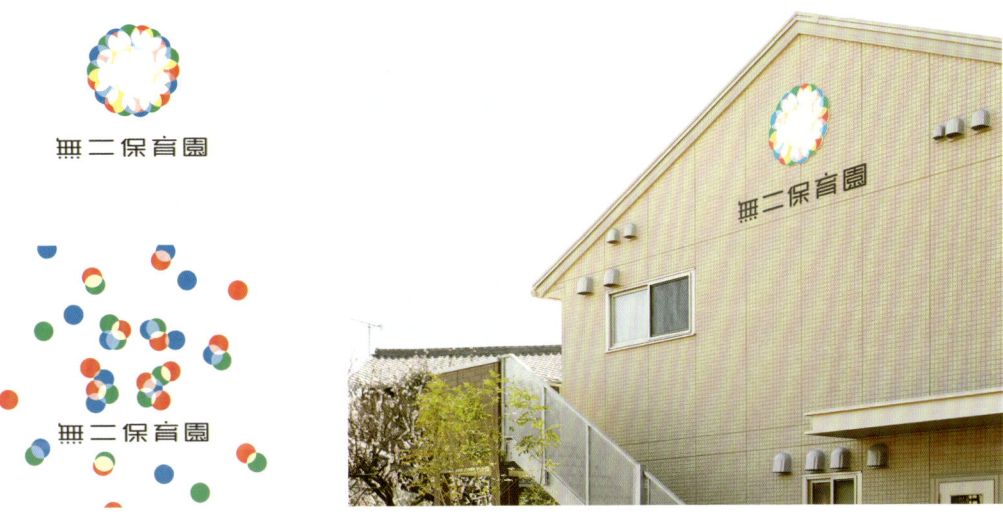

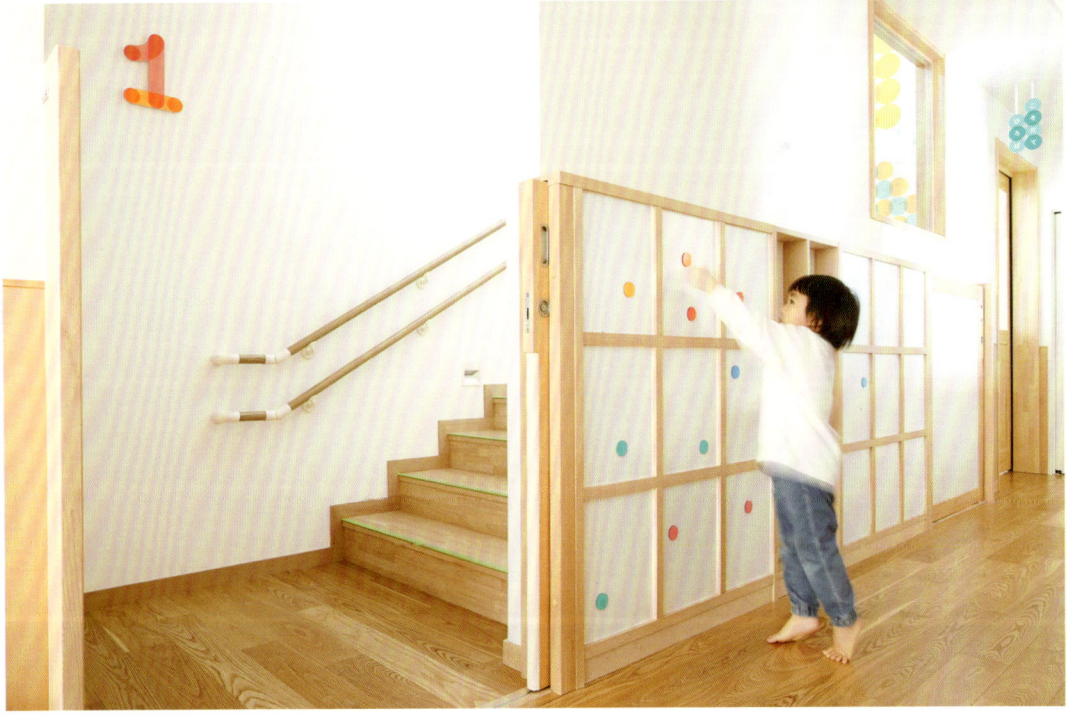

MUNI Nursery

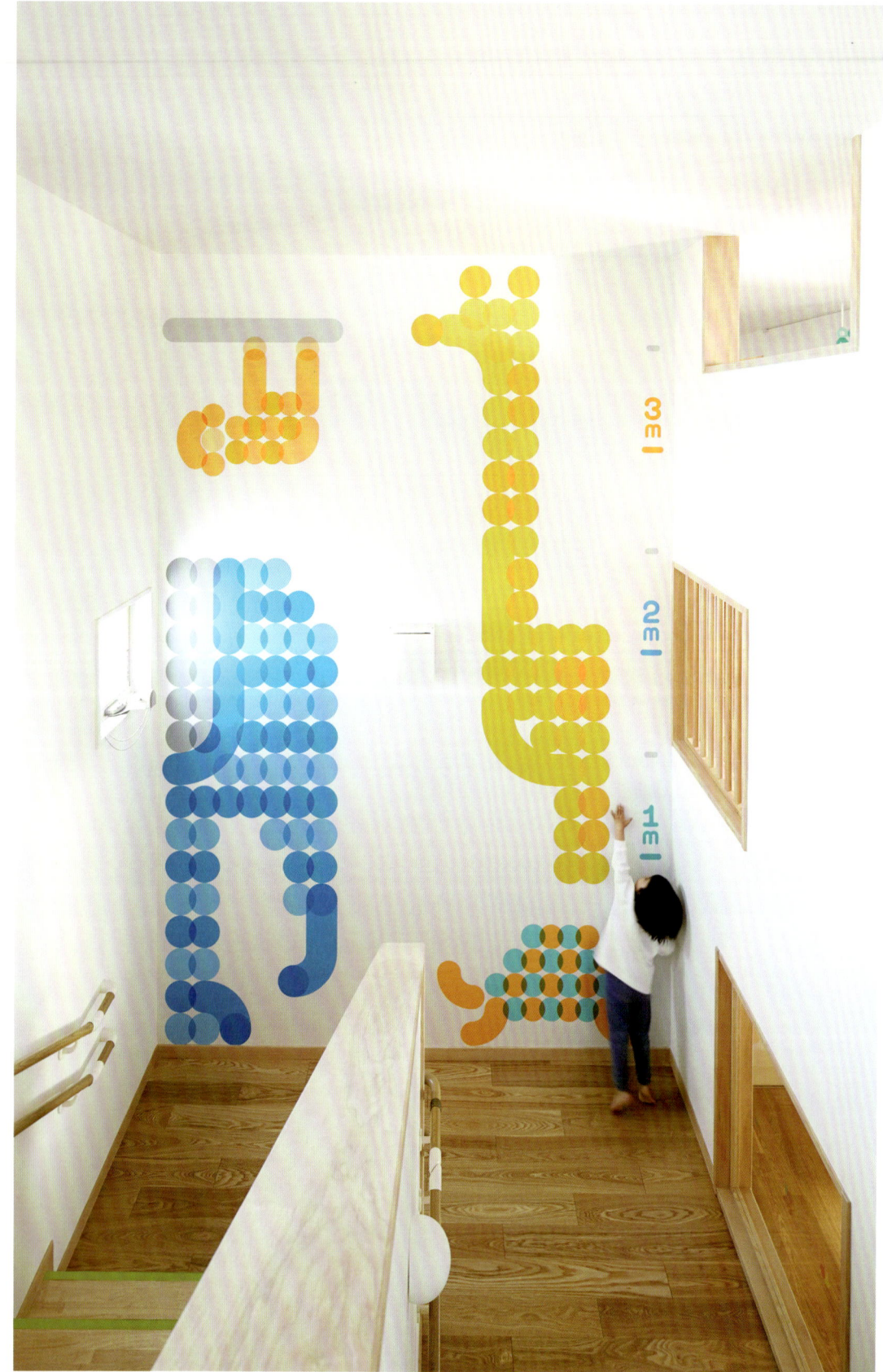

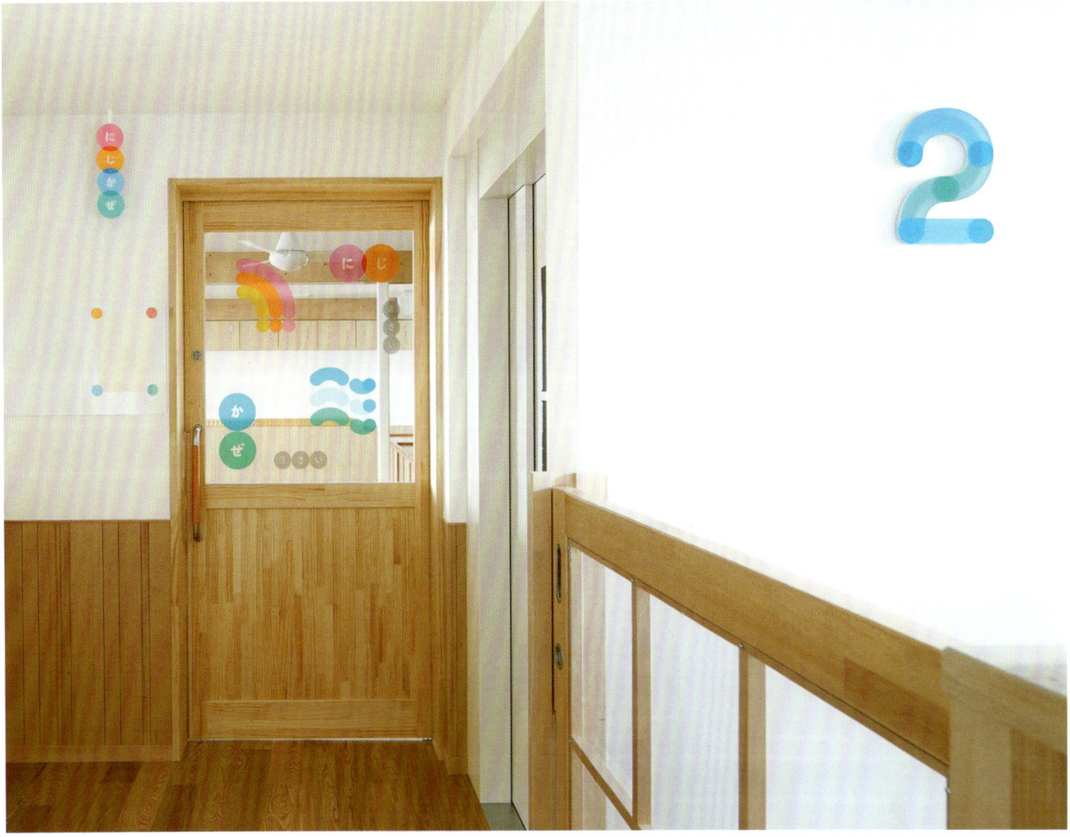
にじかぜ
にじ
かぜ
2

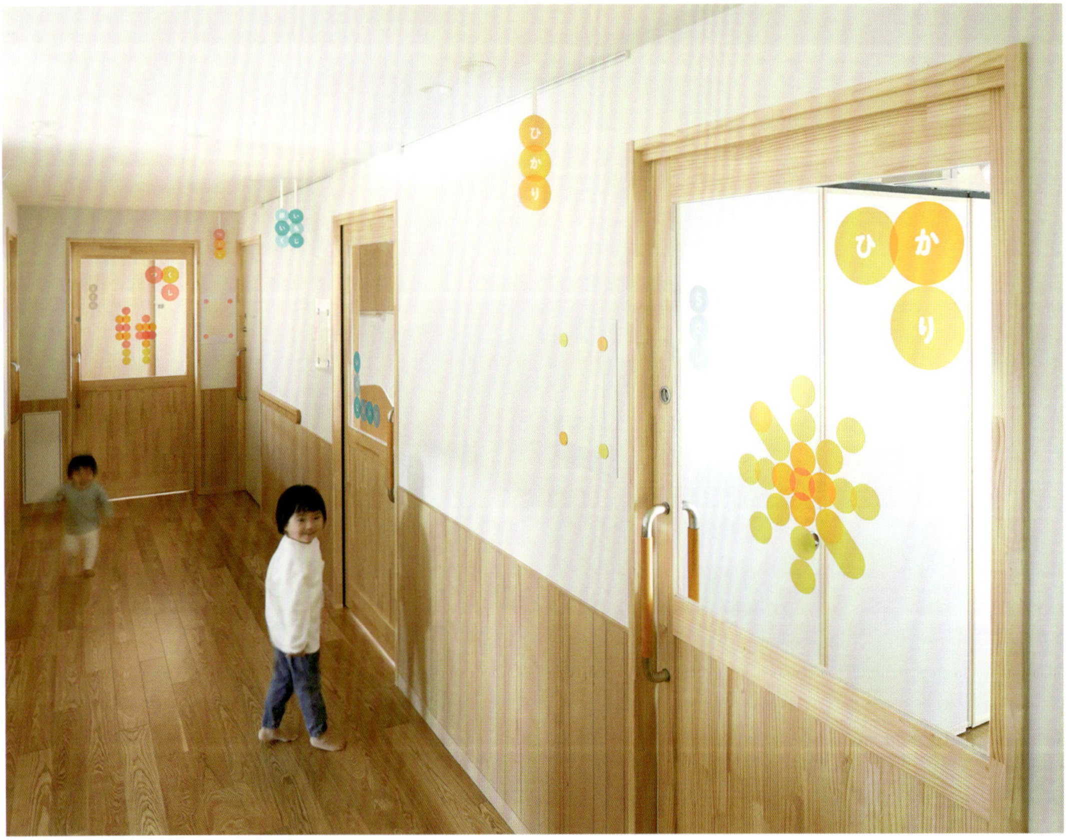
ひかり
ひかり

Midorigaoka Center in Itami City is a 7.8-hectare area with two ponds at its center and is known for its suitability for observing a variety of wild birds. hokkyok used bird icons and their colors in each room to attract children to use the facility because it is faster to identify creatures in nature and their species by color than by shape.

The motif of the first floor is a water bird floating in a pond and that of the second floor is a wild bird perching on a tree. By simplifying the shapes and eliminating the classfications, hokkyok not only made the colors stand out, but also encouraged the children to learn about the actual shapes, sizes, sounds, and other aspects of bird ecology.

DA	hokkyok
AD	Hokuto Fujii
D	Hokuto Fujii, Shohji Kawazakai
AR	TOMOTAKA KYO + KYT ARCHITETCS
PH	Nobutada Omote
CL	Itami City

Itami City Share Facility Midorigaoka Center

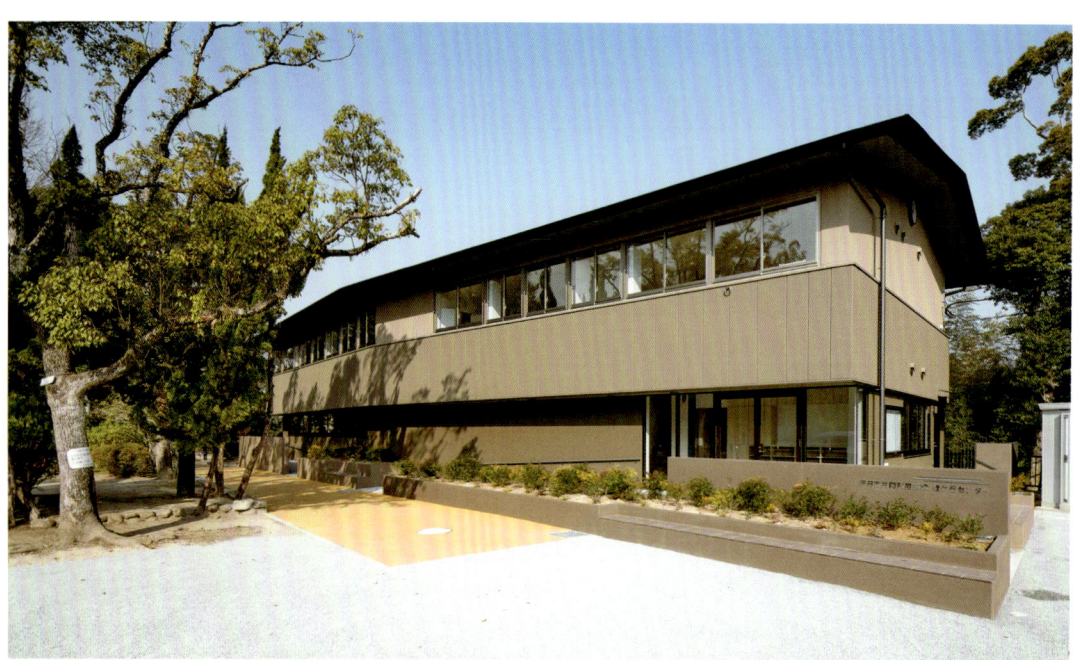

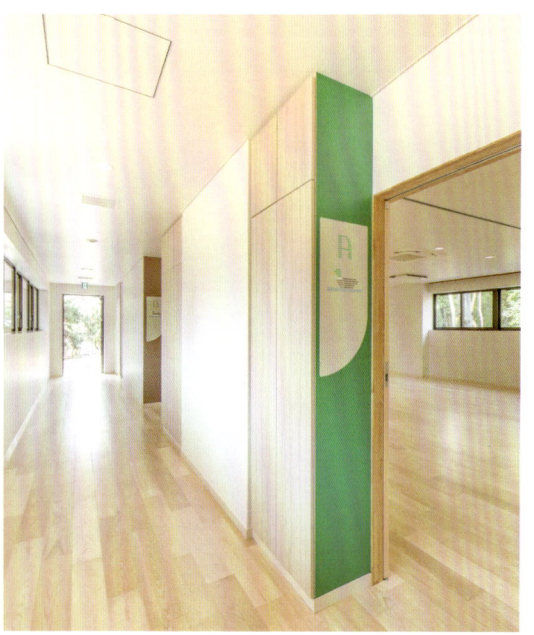

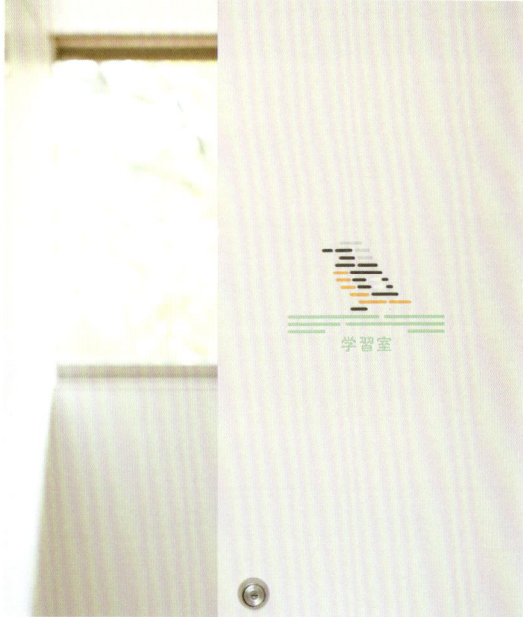

学習室

172

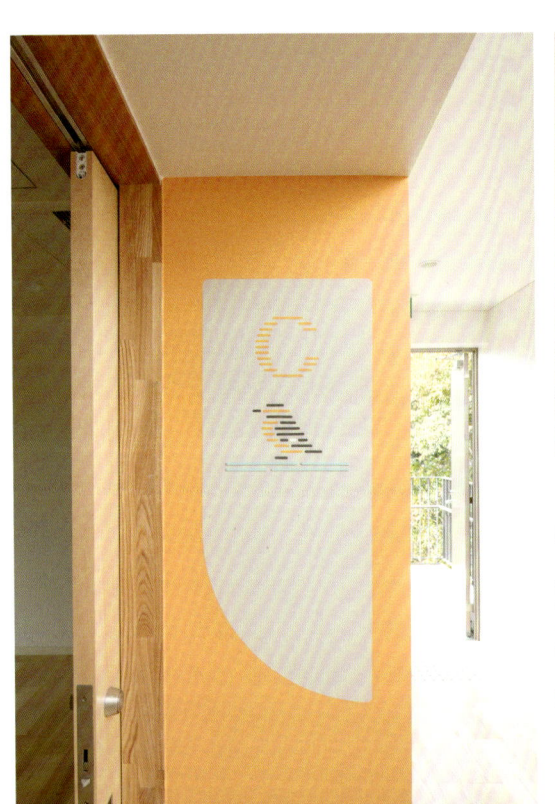

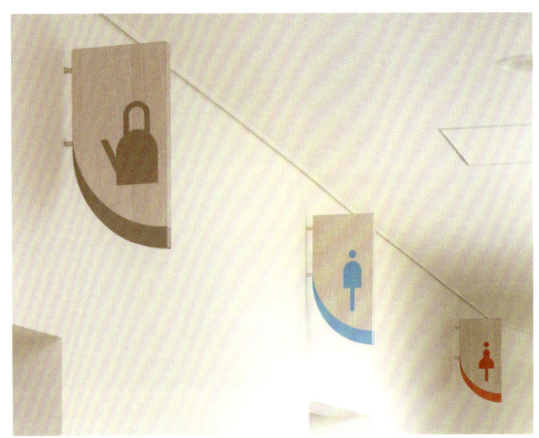

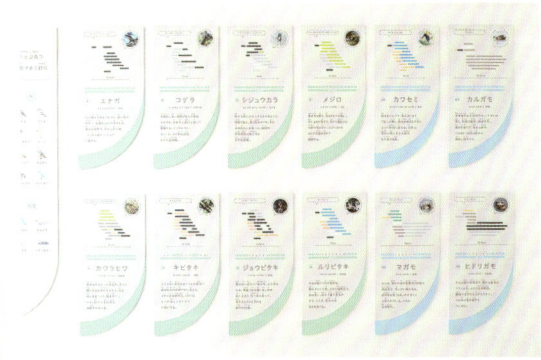

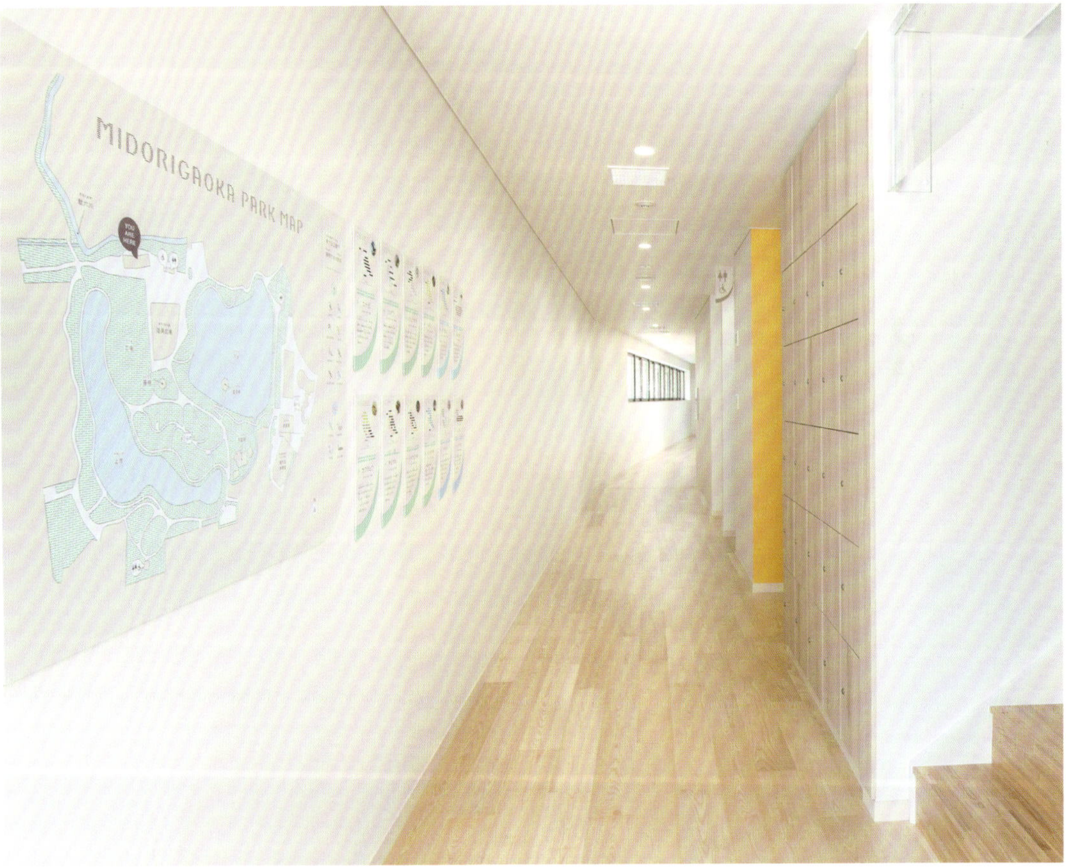

Leonardo da Vinci's Vitruvian Man, anatomical sketches of the human body, had a large influence on modern anatomy and formed one of the cornerstones in the development of medicine. Referring to these anatomical charts, the identity and signage of the medical education institution were established. The moving pictograms express the students' active engagements in the discussions, research, and richness of their student life.

With the theme of the light of life, the north and south zoning employ a culturally and intuitively recognizable pair of colors—red and blue, the same as the representation of arteries and veins, north and south poles, warm and cold colors.

DA	OK design Inc.
D	Kayo Ouchi
AR	SHIMIZU CORPORATION
PH	Ooki Jingu
CL	Chiba University

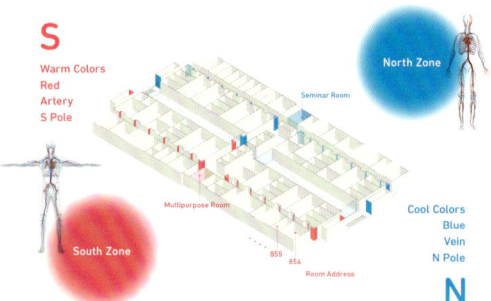

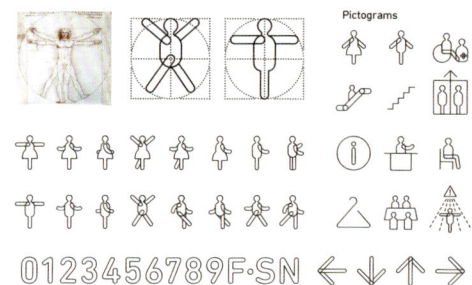

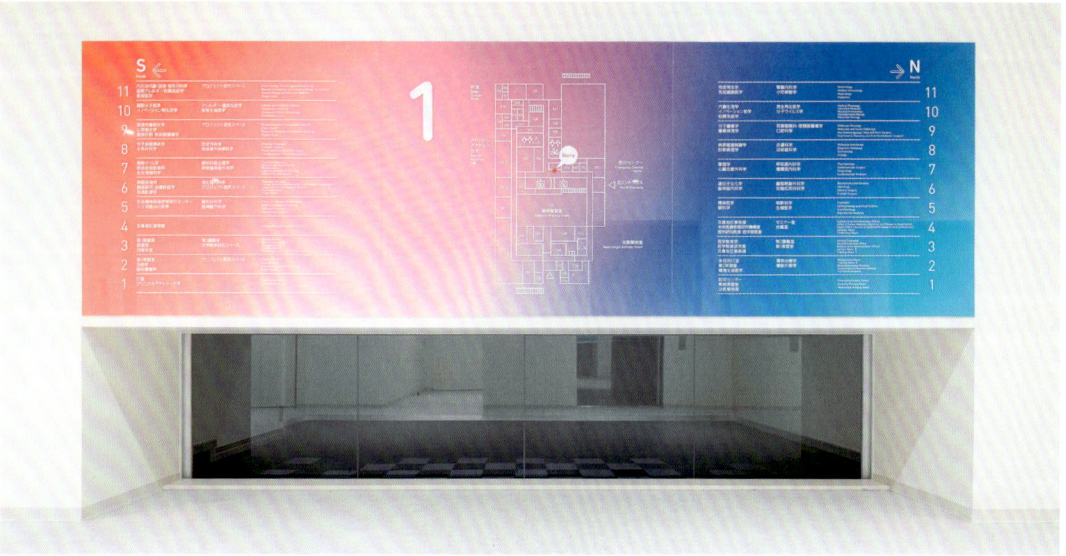

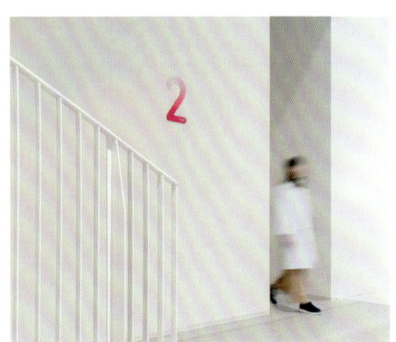

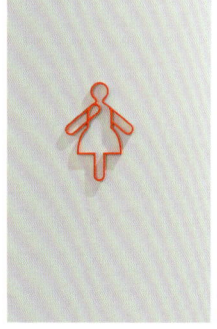

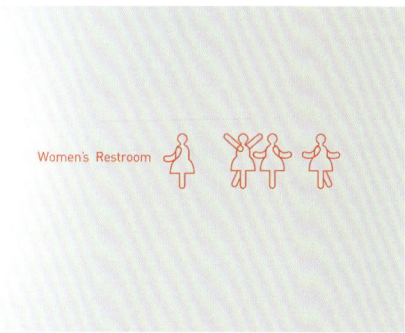

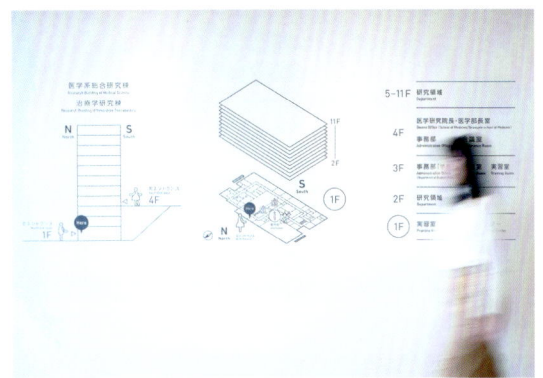

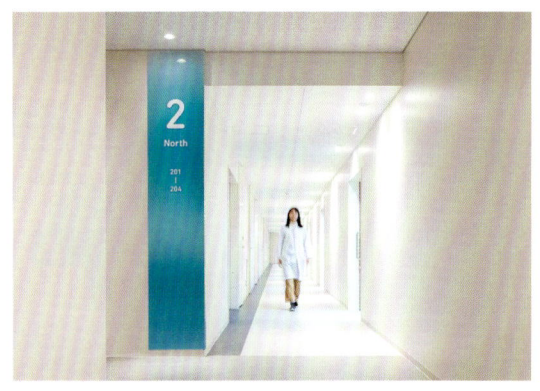

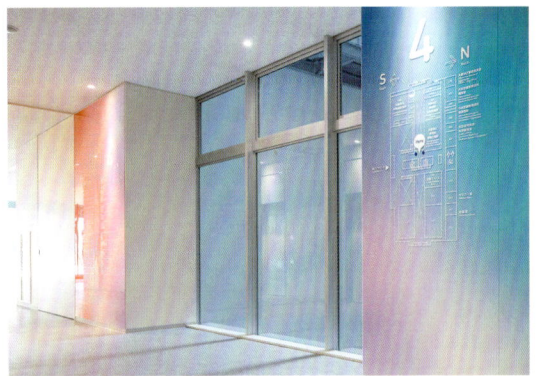

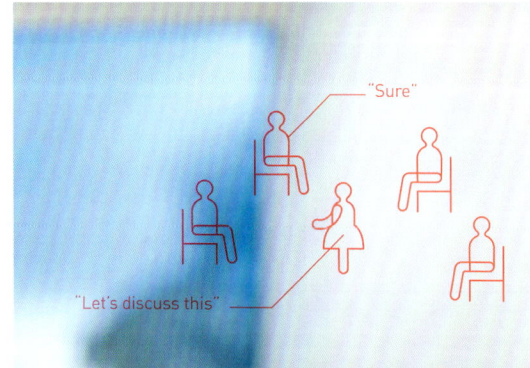

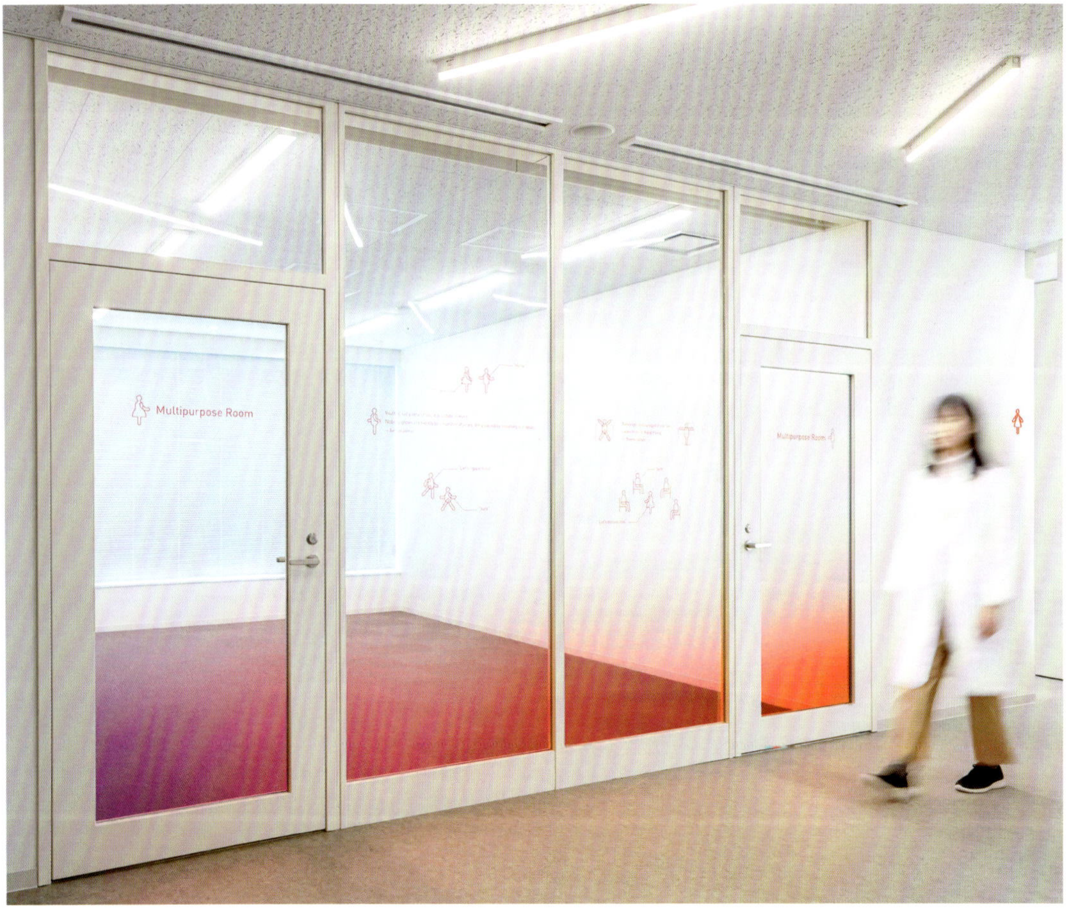

Museum Tower Kyobashi is a skyscraper consisting of a museum and offices. This is a signage plan for the area centered around the offices. The designers aimed to visualize the identity of the architecture and the owner of the building in the signage, while fully satisfying the functions of guidance and information. The signage area was planned to be as small as possible. The pictogram combines straight lines taken from the louvers on the exterior of the building with the organic curves of the AXIS font. The arrows and letters were painted directly on the wall, and the pictogram was floated off the wall to create a slight layering.

CD   Masanori Yano
        (Nikken Sekkei Ltd.)
AD   Takahiro Eto
D   Takahiro Eto
PH   Sohei Oya
        (Nacasa & Partners Inc.)
CL   Nagasaka Co., Ltd.,
        Ishibashi Foundation

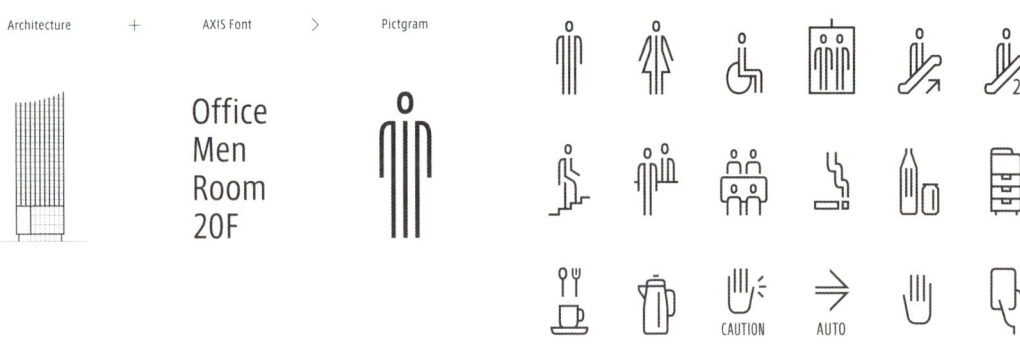

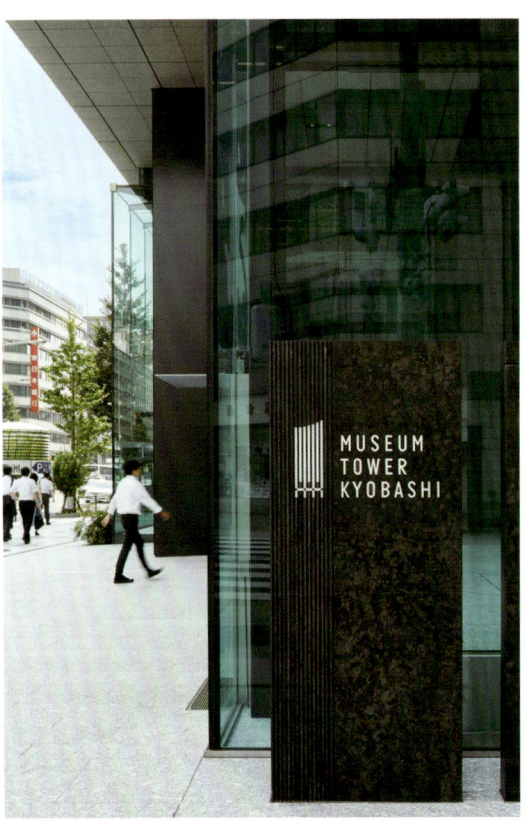

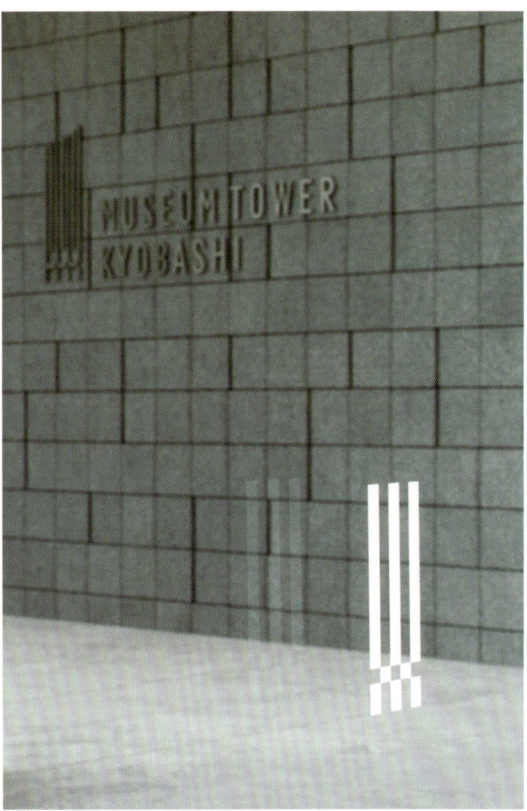

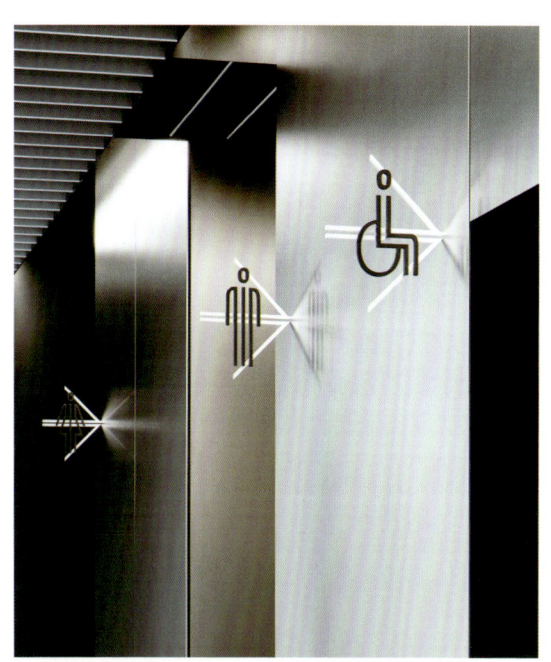

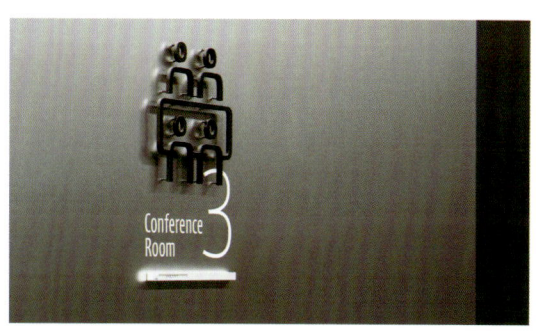

Conference Room 3

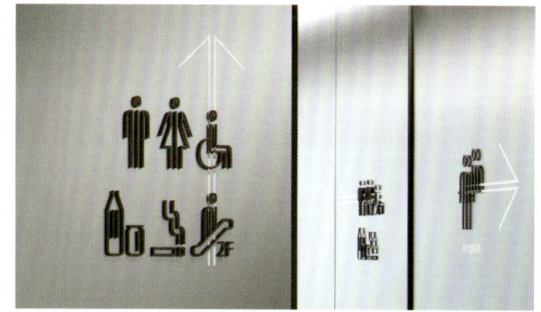

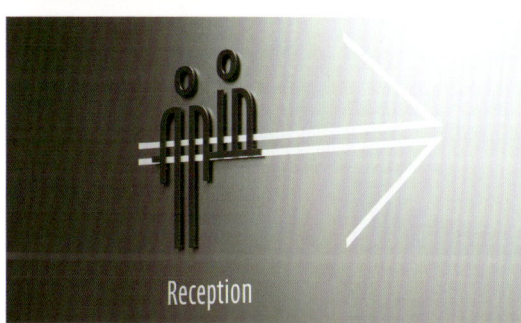

Reception

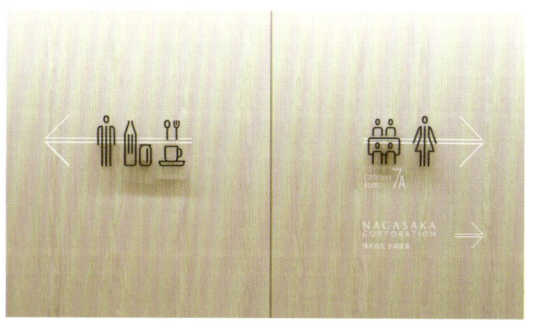

NAGASAKA
CORPORATION

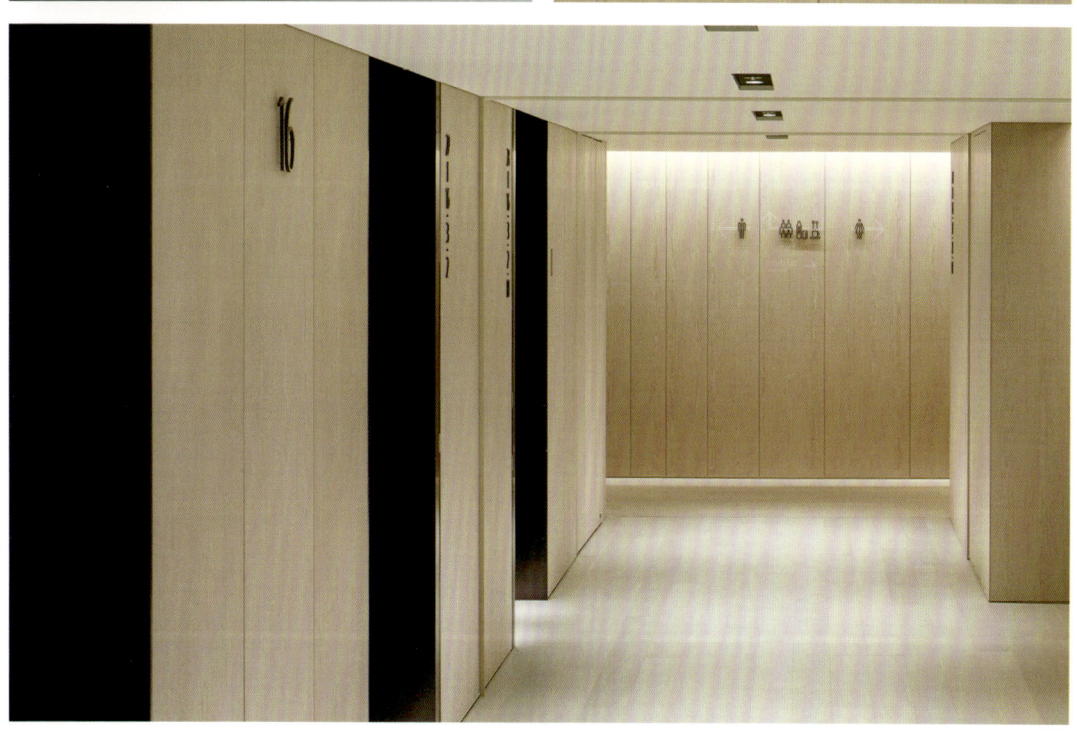

BETTER BODIES HI is a workout studio. Its goal is to change the bodies and lives of its users through short, high-impact workouts. The designers needed to create an environment where users after work could gradually prepare their bodies and minds for exercise. Therefore, they designed a font that transforms into three stages. As users move from the reception to the workout area, the signs become thicker and larger, encouraging the user to do the workout. In addition, the font was also used in the logo, the website, and products to develop a brand identity.

CD	Takaaki Nakamura
AD	Takahiro Eto
D	Takahiro Eto
PH	Sohei Oya
	(Nacasa & Partners Inc.)
CL	RENAISSANCE
	INCORPORATED

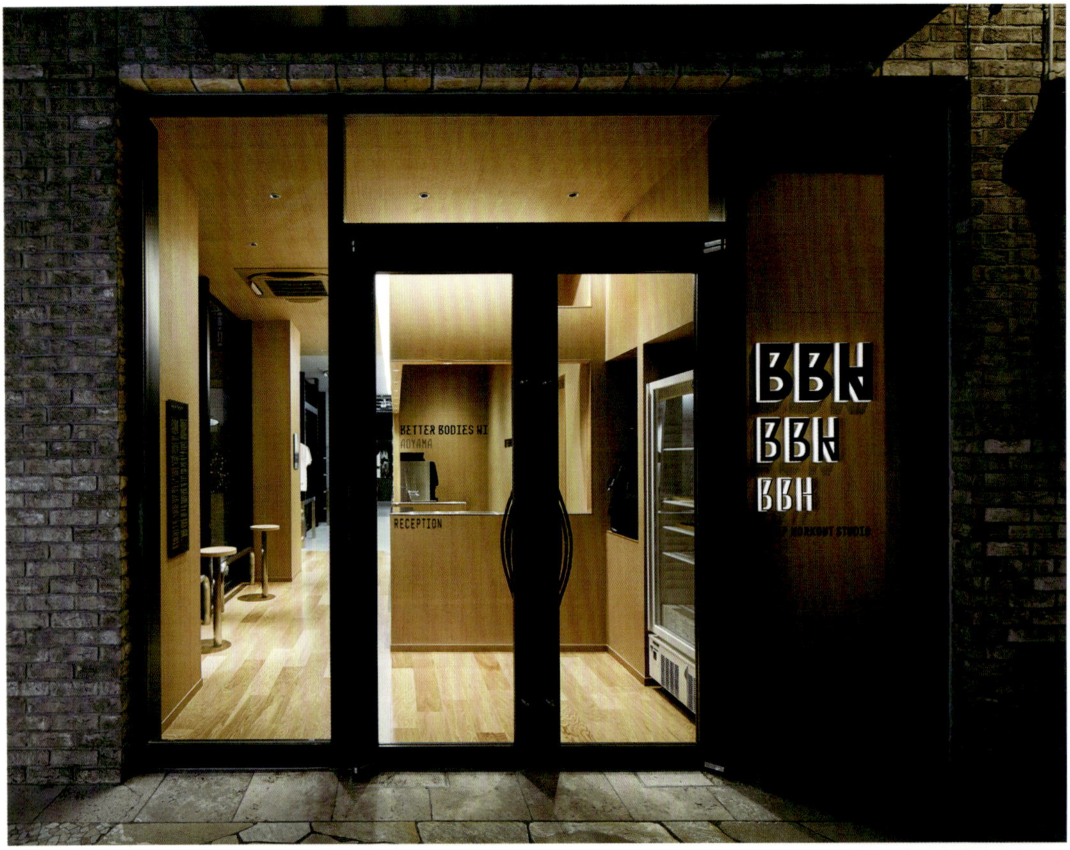

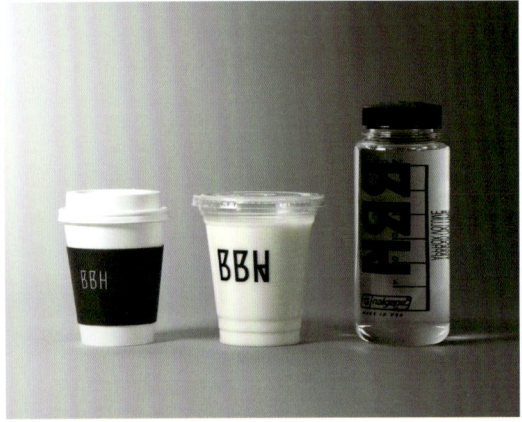

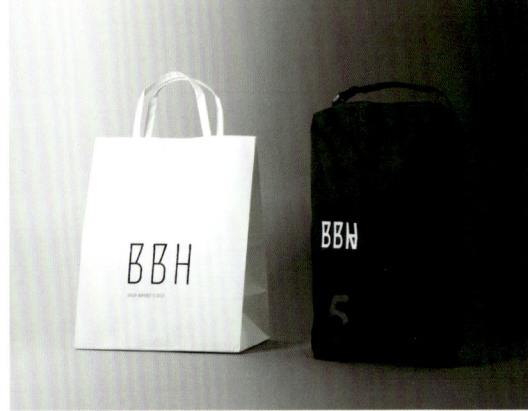

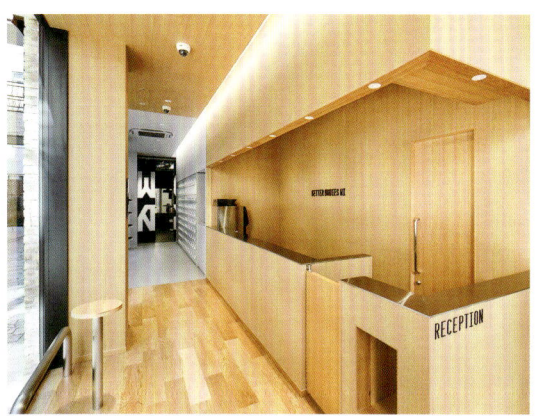

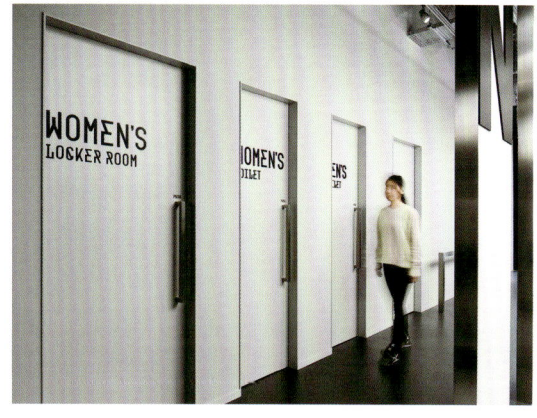

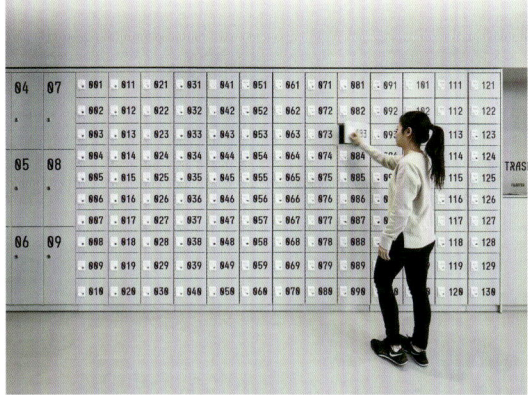

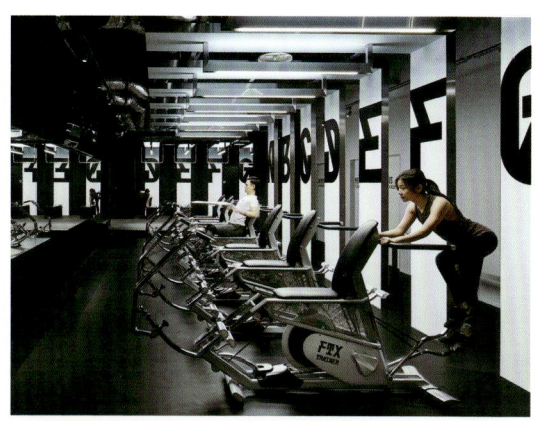

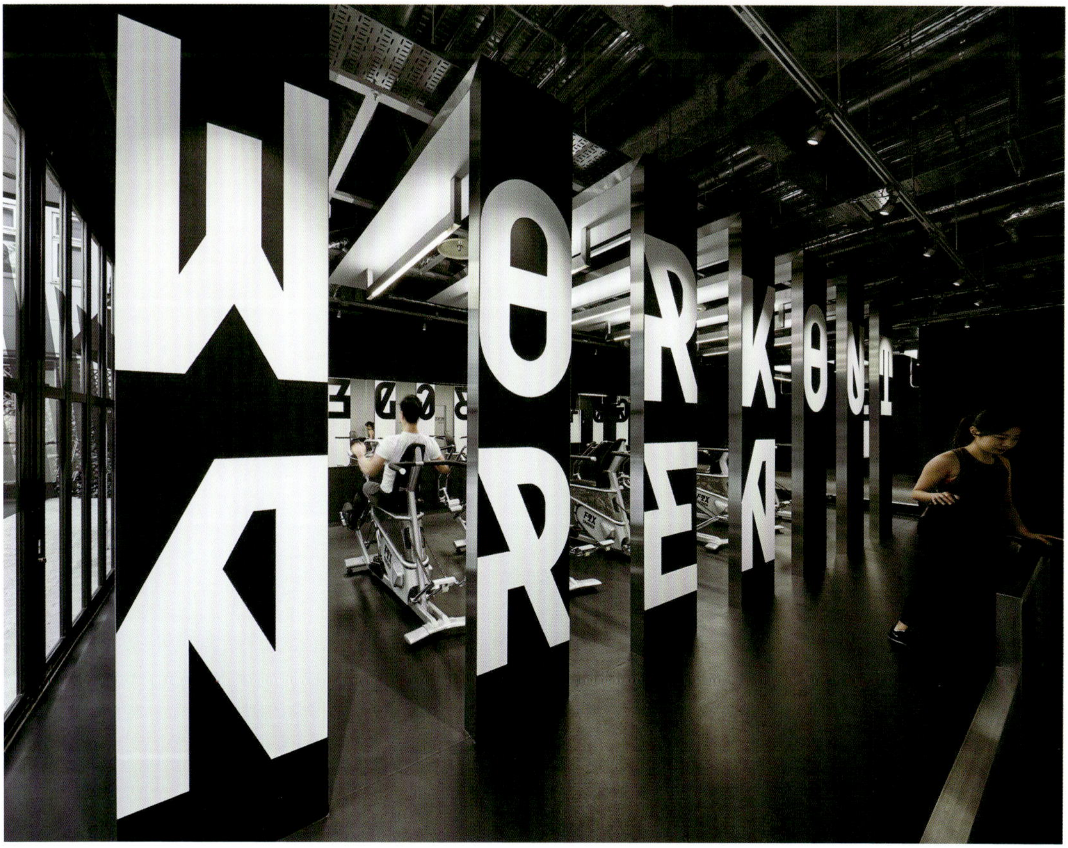

The bicycle garage in the common area of the condominium is a space for people who love cycling. OK design Inc. created a graphic design with a motif of the bicycle. In the garage shared by residents, they printed a large bicycle map on the wall for residents to freely explore their hometown of Koganei by bike.

DA   OK design Inc.
D   Kayo Ouchi
ID   FIELD FOUR DESIGN OFFICE
PH   Ooki Jingu
CL   Musashi-koganei Station
      South Entrance 2nd District
      Urban Redevelopment
      Cooprative

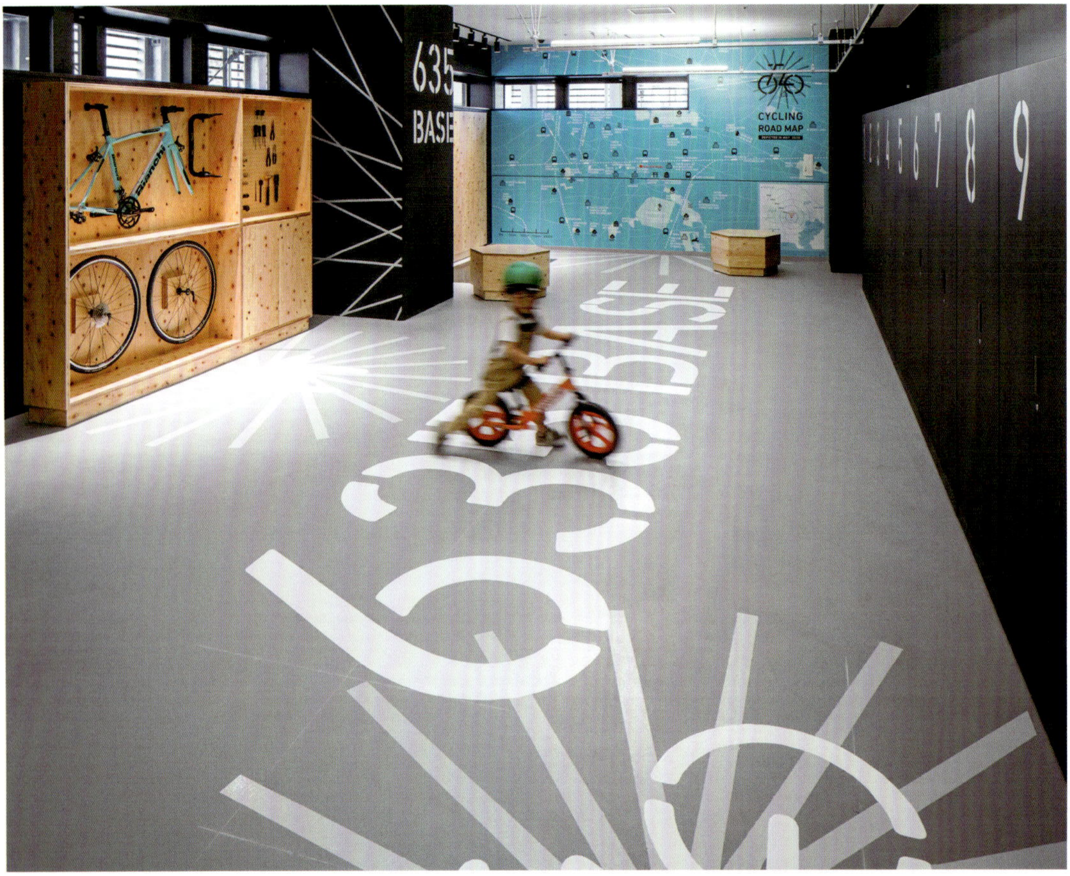

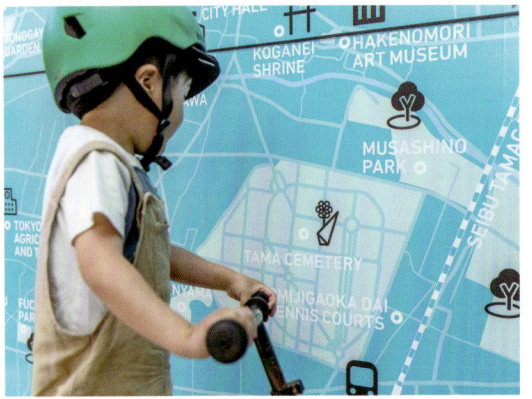

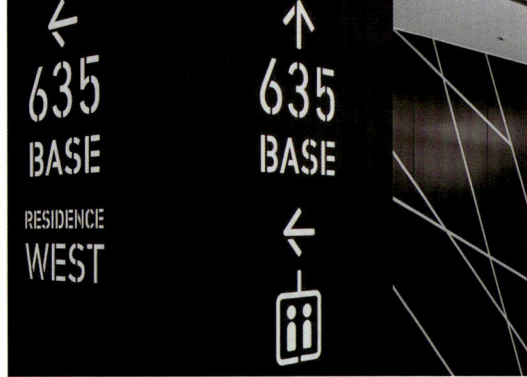

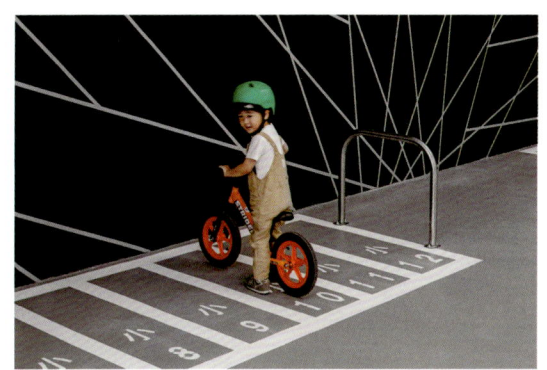

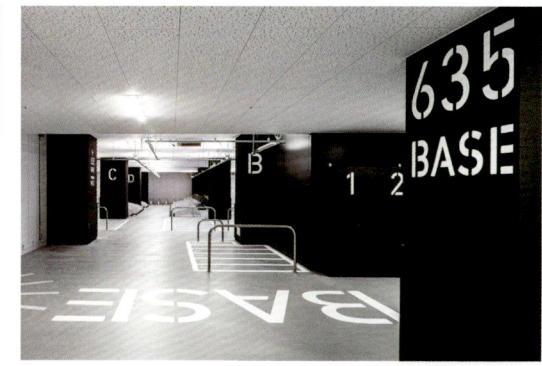

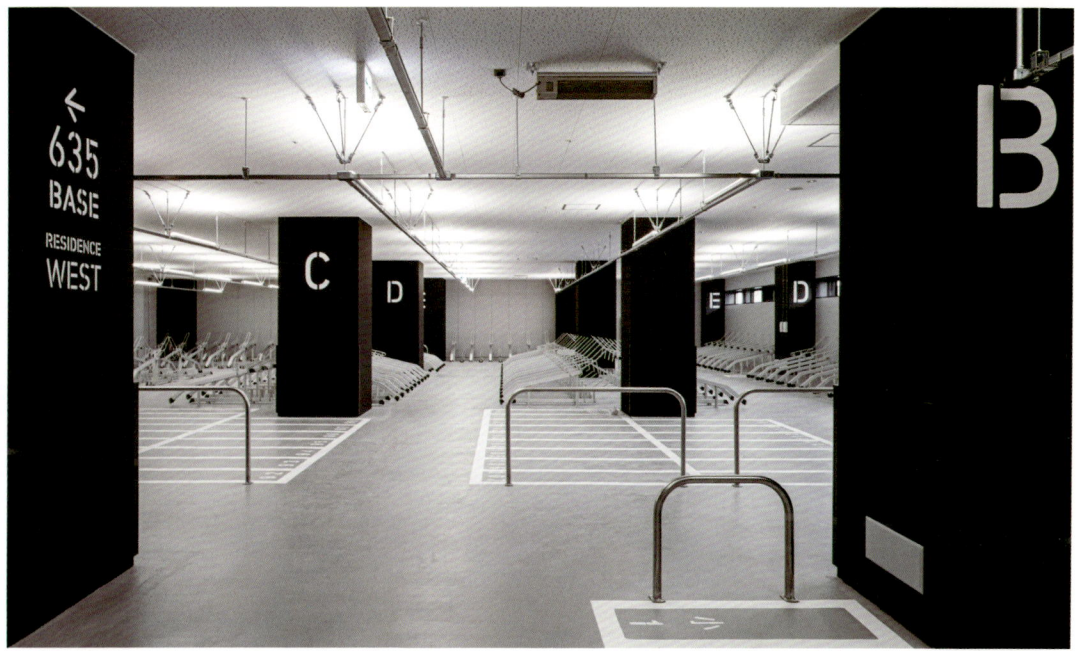

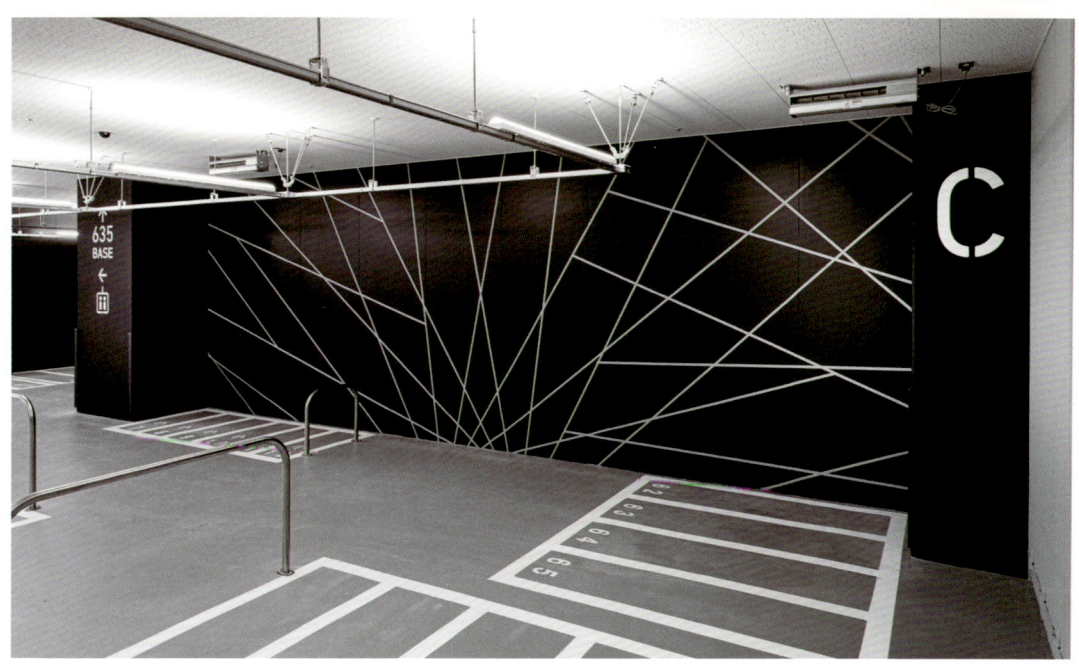

Koganei City is surrounded by nature, including springs, the Tama River water supply, and parks. It also has the Kokubunji Cliff Line where cliffs and slopes vary in height. The design theme of the project is "hake," a word that depicts the characteristics of the Musashino Plateau. And the architecture, interior, and signage work together to create a space. The interior and architectural design incorporates gentle curves that symbolize the geological formation of the hake. To create a space with the same theme, the signage in the common areas also follows the same curvilinear design.

DA   OK design Inc.
D   Kayo Ouchi
ID   FIELD FOUR DESIGN OFFICE
PH   Ooki Jingu
CL   Musashi-koganei Station
      South Entrance 2nd District
      Urban Redevelopment
      Cooperative

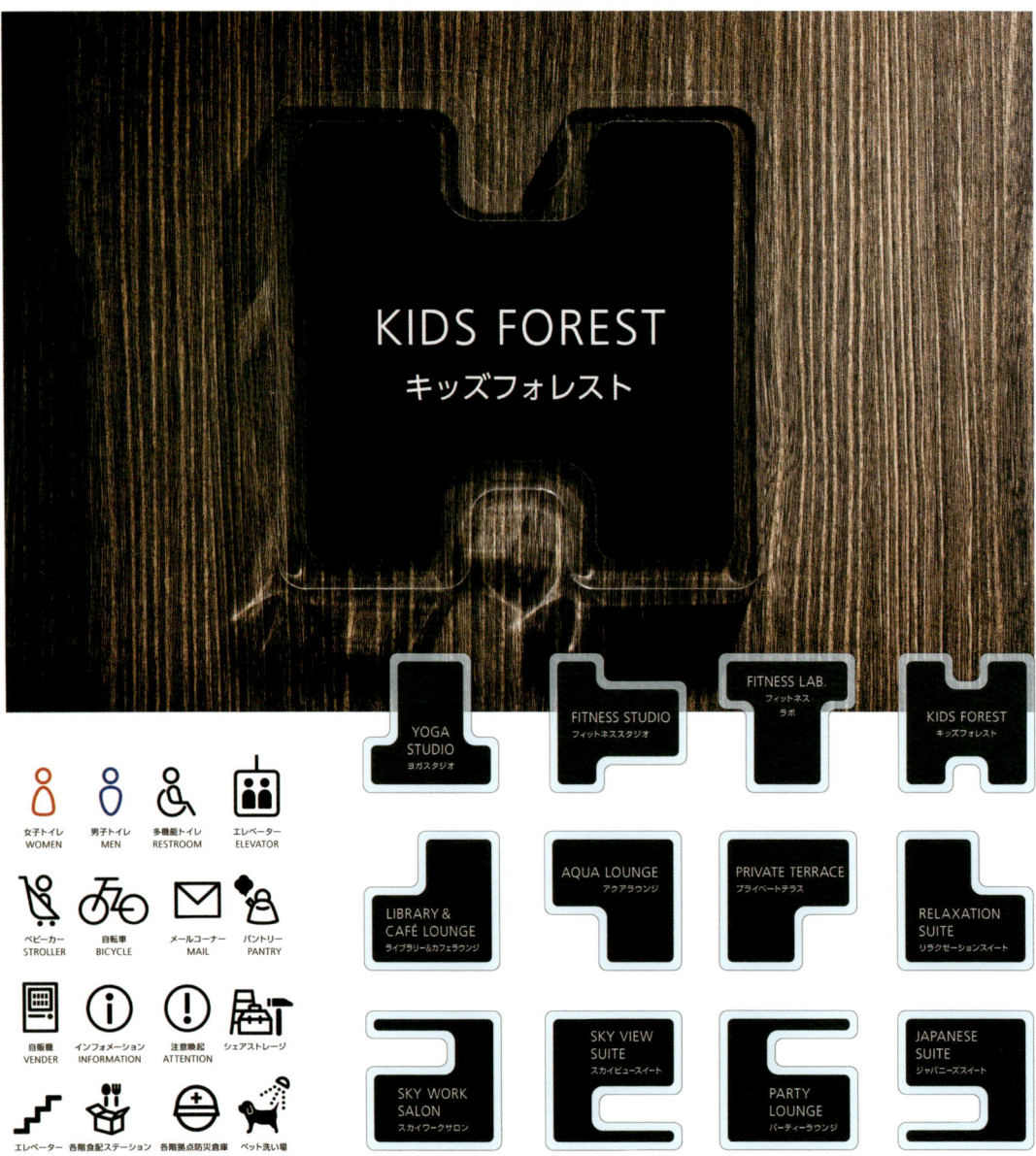

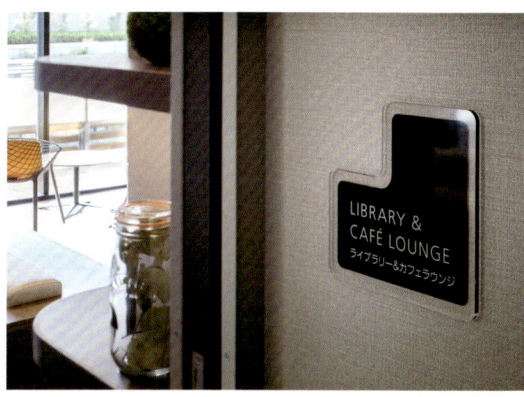

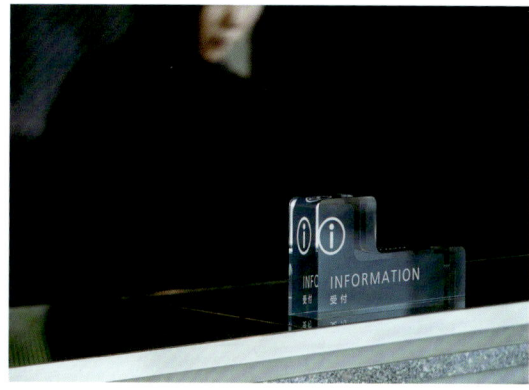

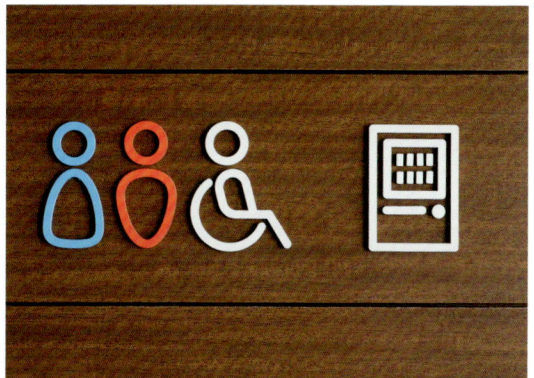

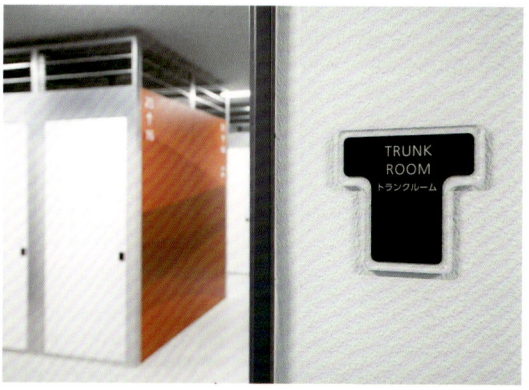

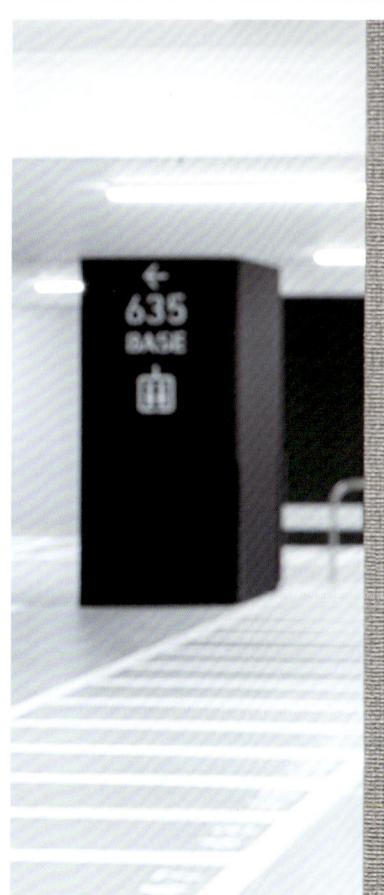

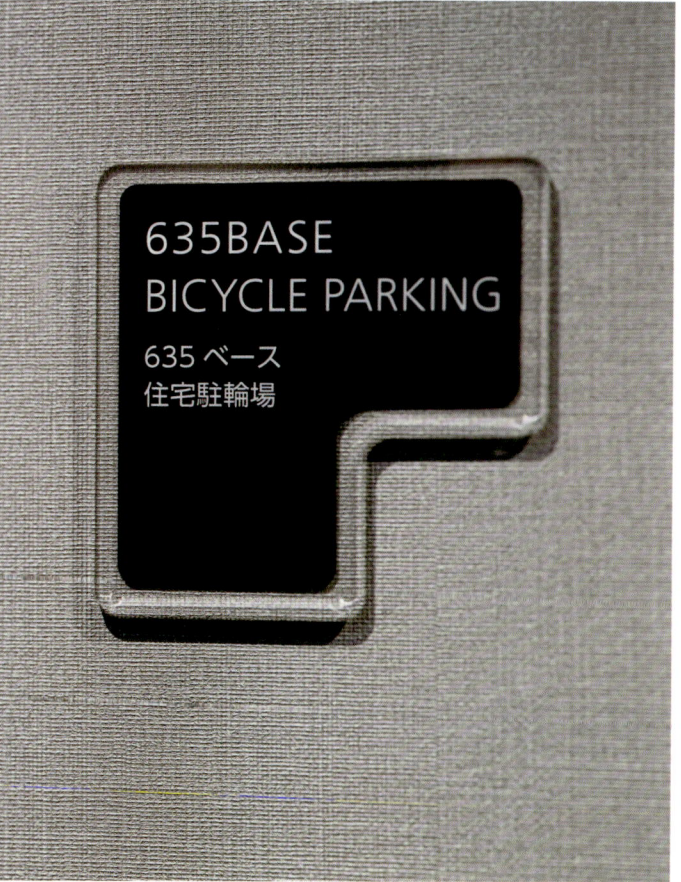

Located in a commercial facility in Makinohara, Inzai City, Makinohara Table is a place that offers various experiences to enrich people's lives with local foods and goods in a shared kitchen, co-working space, and shop.

The logo, consisting of an "M" and a "T," looks like a table, while the greenery above the table represents the Makinohara area. The signage plan was also developed from the motif of a table. Each icon in the shape of a table indicates a different experience. The design demonstrates Makinohara Table's intention, which is to create opportunities for visitors to interact with the staff and the community.

DA   hokkyok
AD   Hokuto Fujii
D   Hokuto Fujii, Shohji Kawazakai
ID   Shinsuke Yokoyama
PH   Takuya Yamauchi
CL   Chiba Newtown Center Co., Ltd.

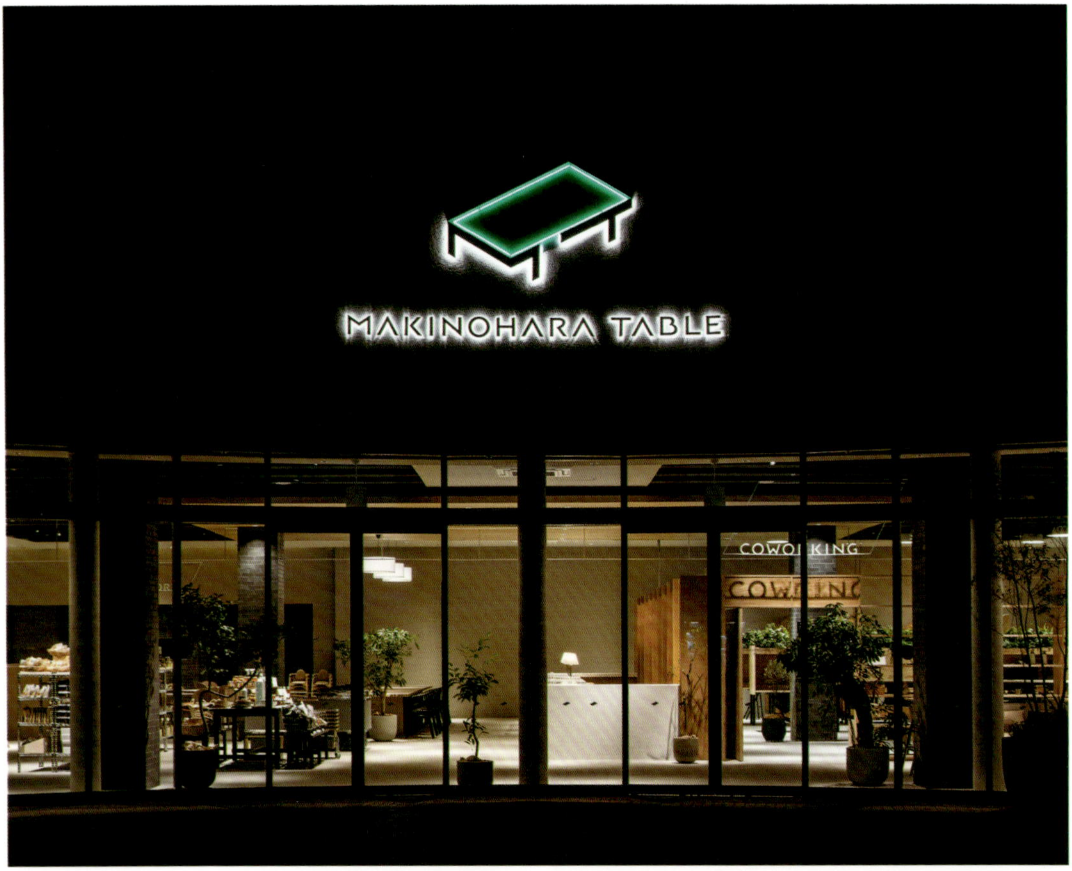

Makinohara Table

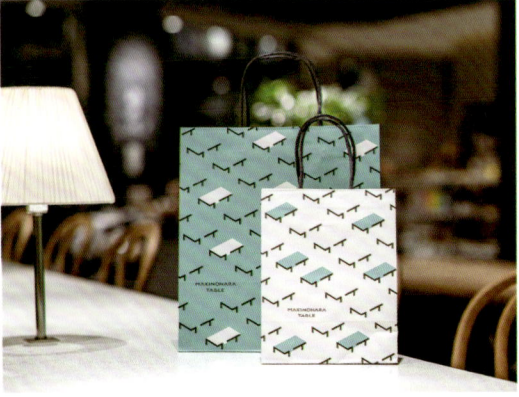
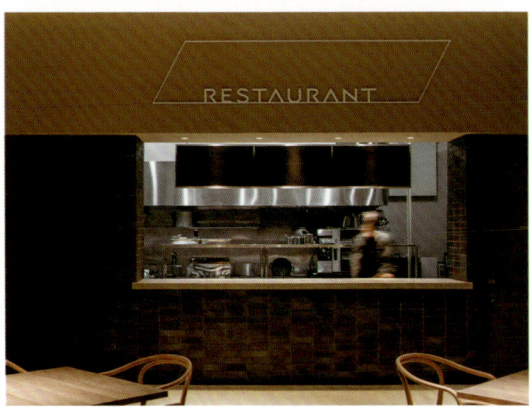

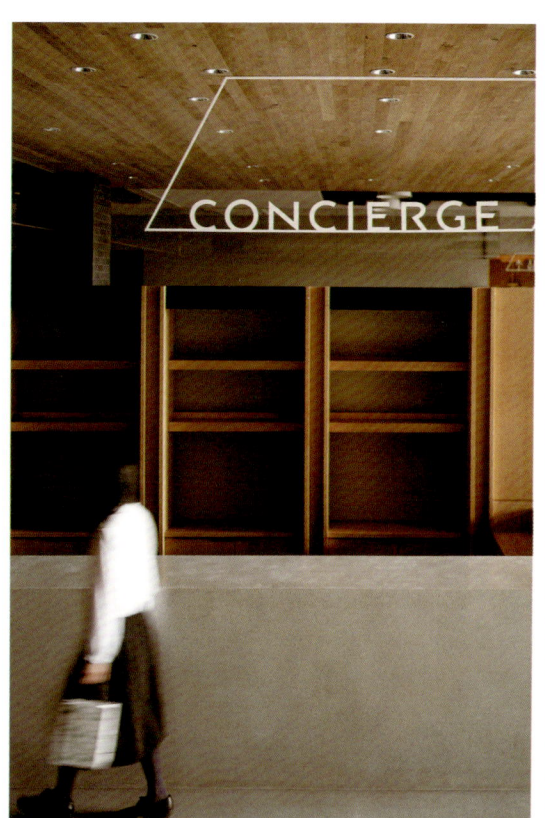

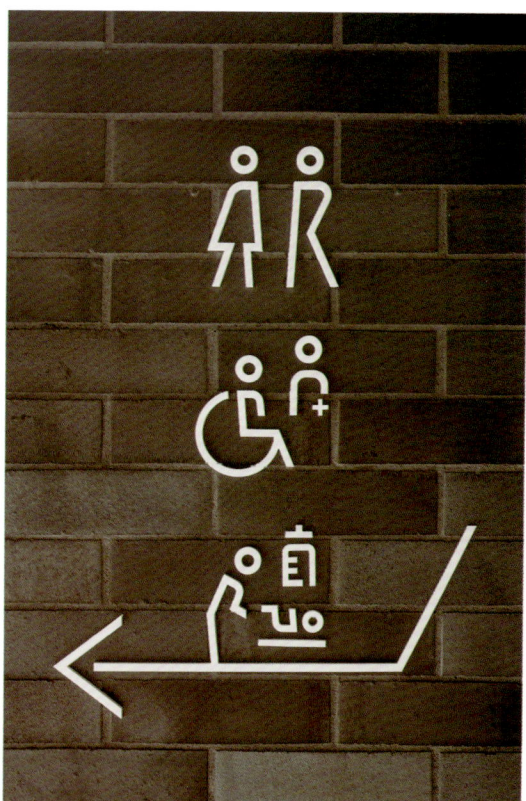

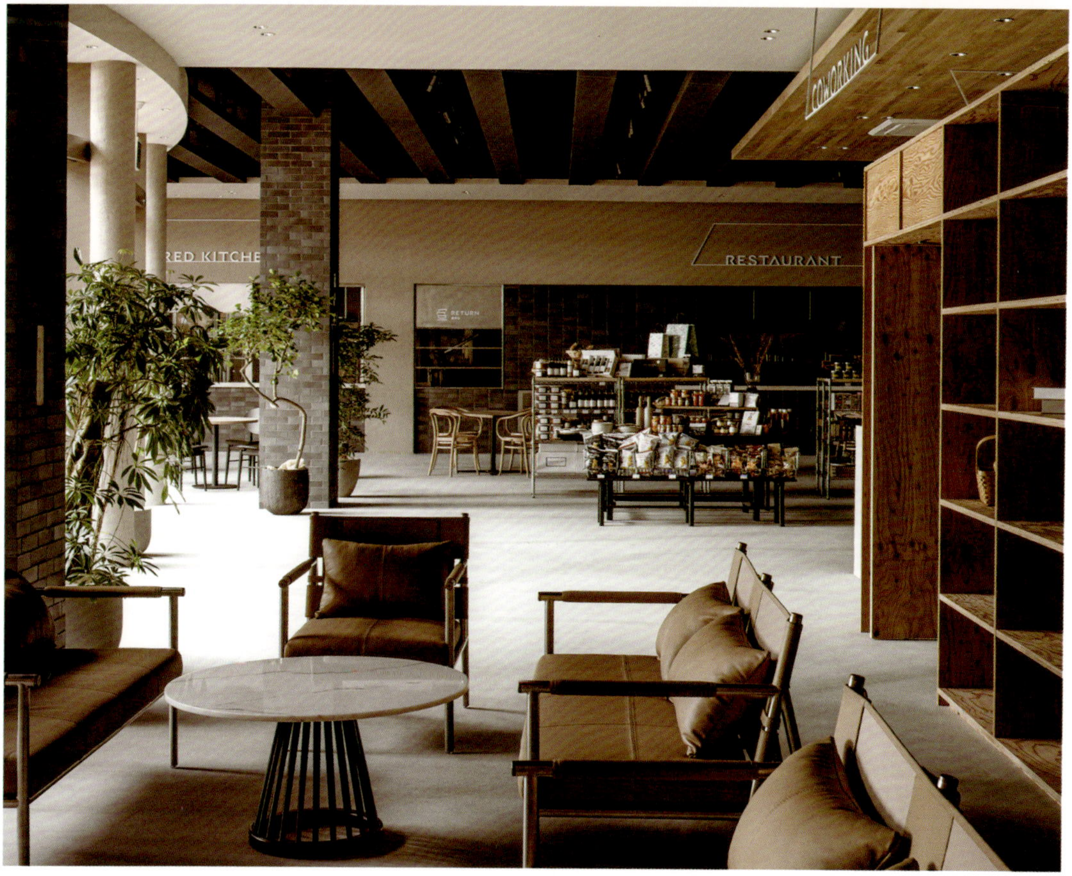

In the kids' space in the common area of the condominium, OK design Inc. used familiar objects and creatures in nature and daily life to create a fun wall for children to learn how to measure. They can compare their heights, count the number of leaves, and learn how much they weigh. The design is closely related to nature and even a casual anti-collision sign is a hidden pictogram of creatures in nature.

DA   OK design Inc.
D   Kayo Ouchi
ID   FIELD FOUR DESIGN OFFICE
PH   Ooki Jingu
CL   Musashi-koganei Station
      South Entrance 2nd District
      Urban Redevelopment
      Cooperative

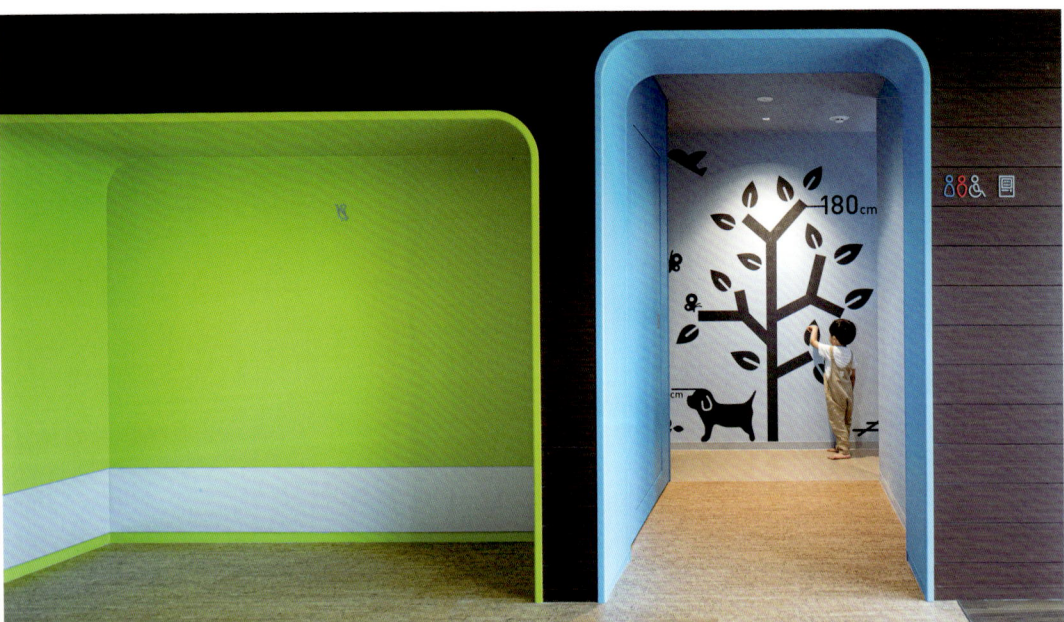

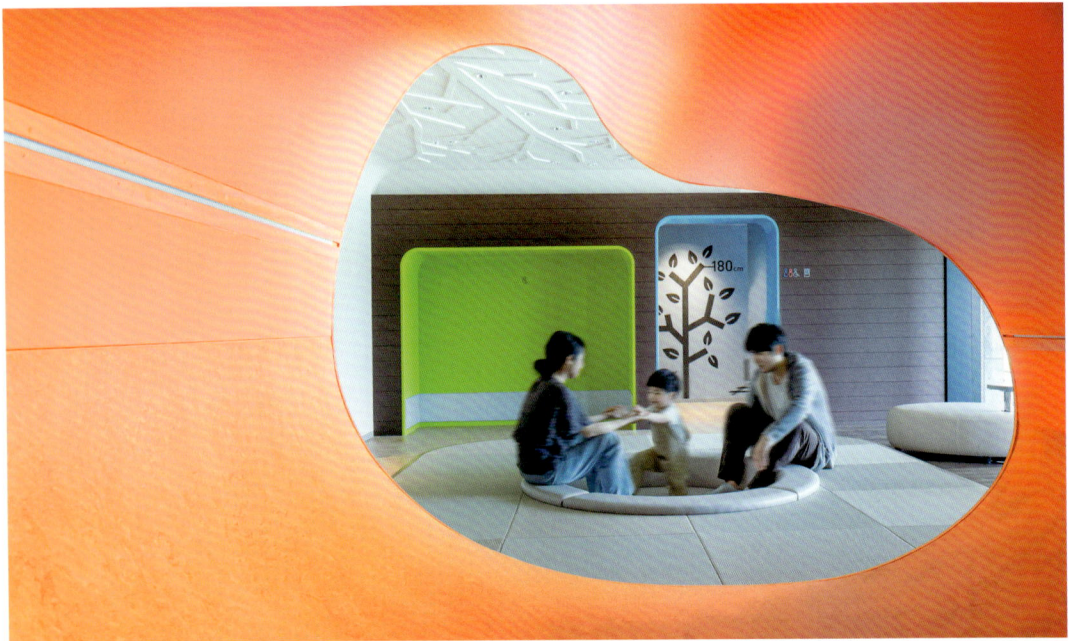

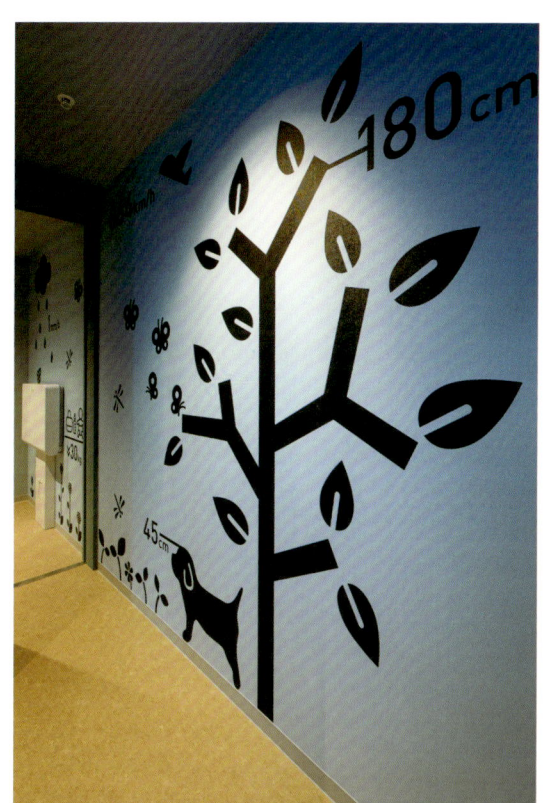
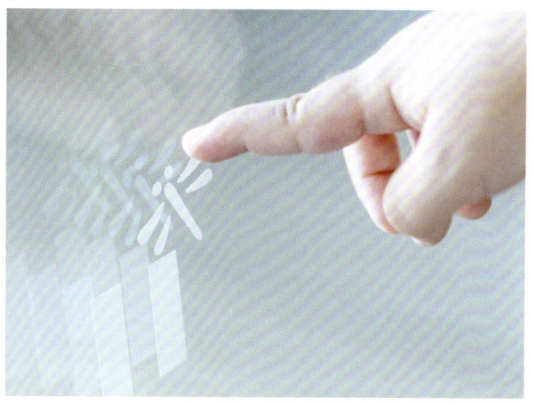
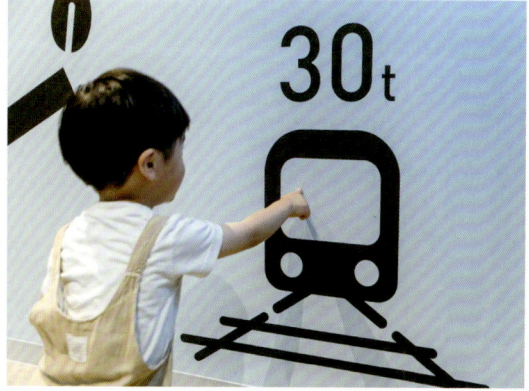

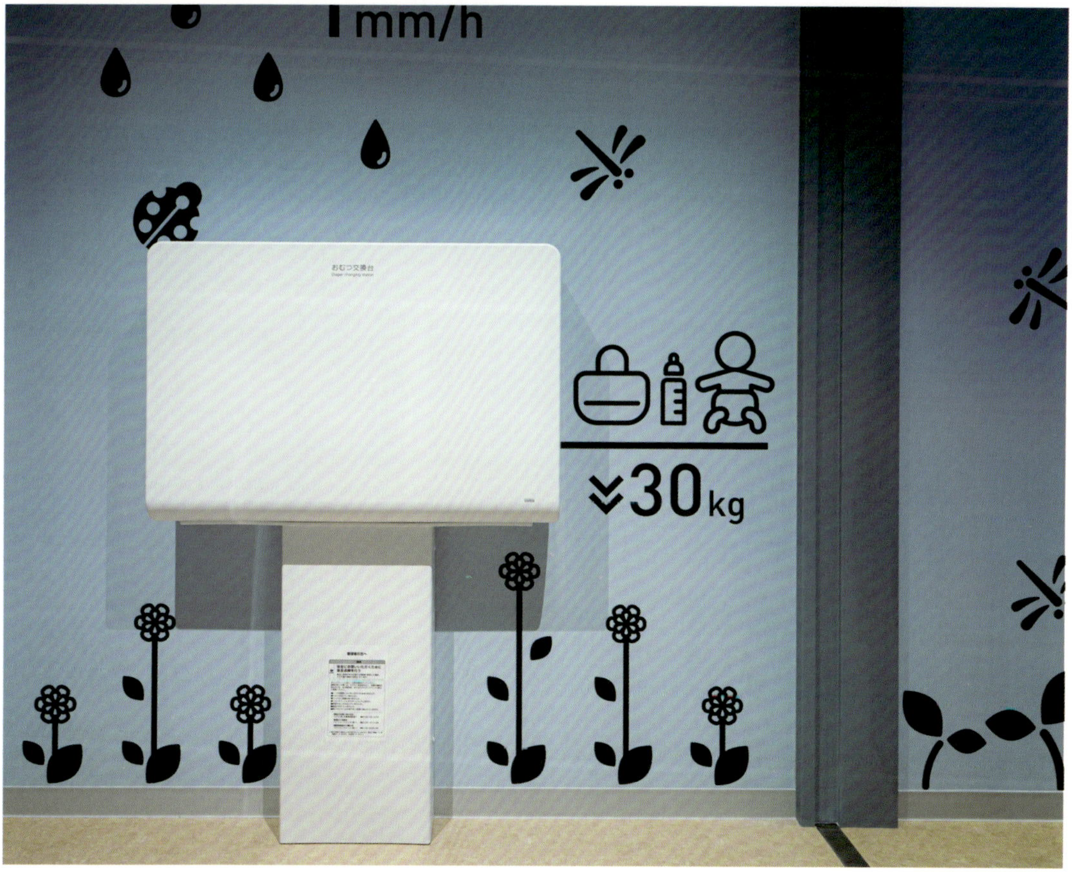

Kameido is a town that combines the traditions of Edo craftsmanship with modernity. For the signage design of the commercial facility in front of Kameido Station, an original crest was designed to enliven the town, symbolizing a familiar commercial facility with deep roots in the local community.

The design concept was a crest for the feast. The original pattern, based on the traditional Japanese tortoiseshell pattern, changes its colors and patterns for each zone within the facility and creates a lively atmosphere.

DA	OK design Inc.
CD	Kayo Ouchi
AD	Kayo Ouchi
D	Kayo Ouchi, Yumi Hasebe
PH	Ooki Jingu
CL	Nomura Real Estate Development Co., Ltd.

Kameido Clock

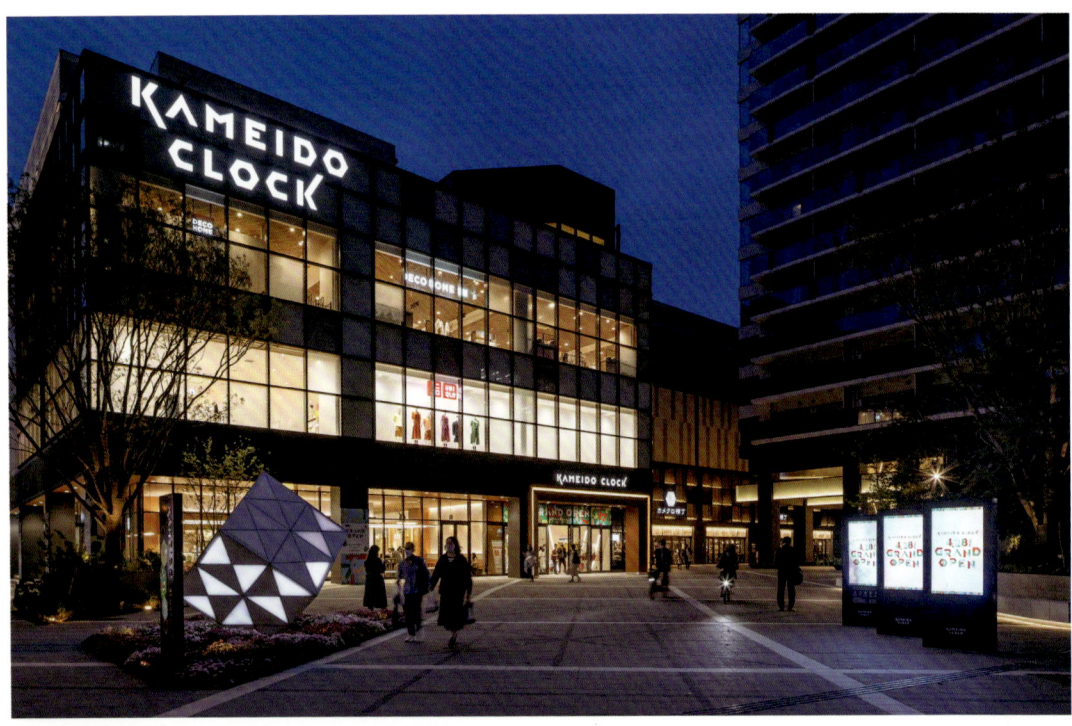

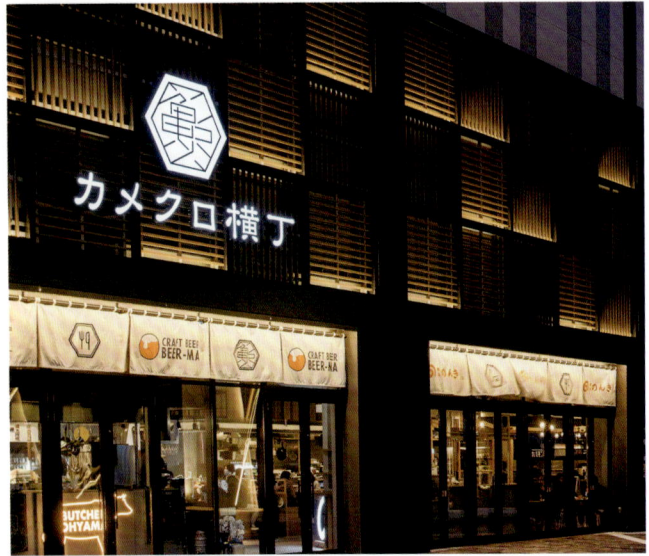

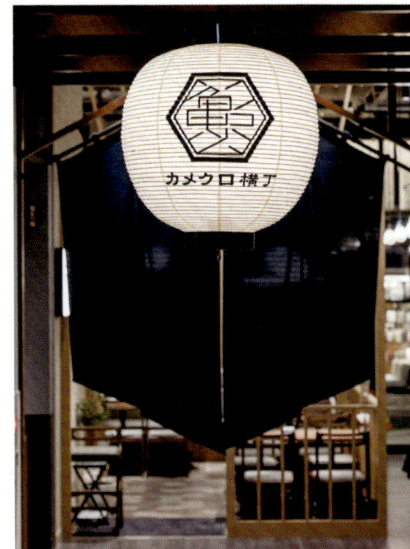

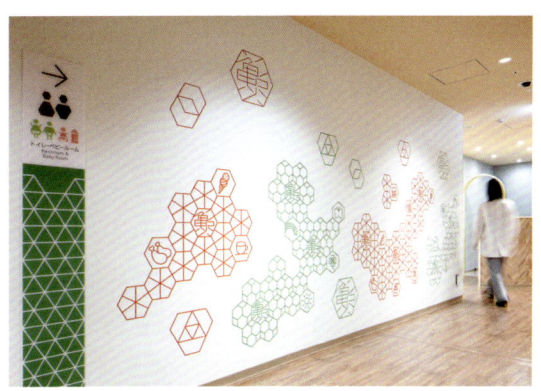

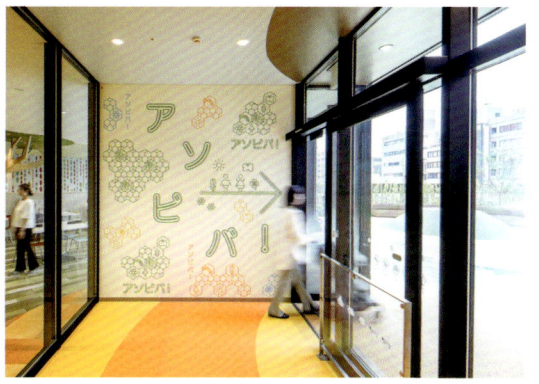

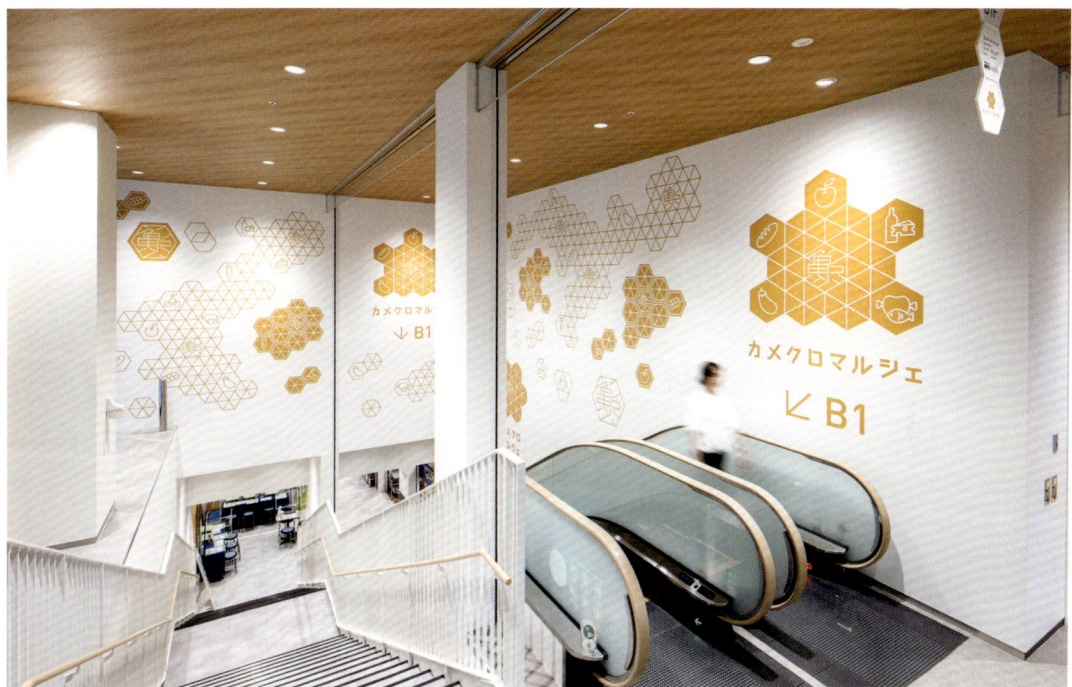

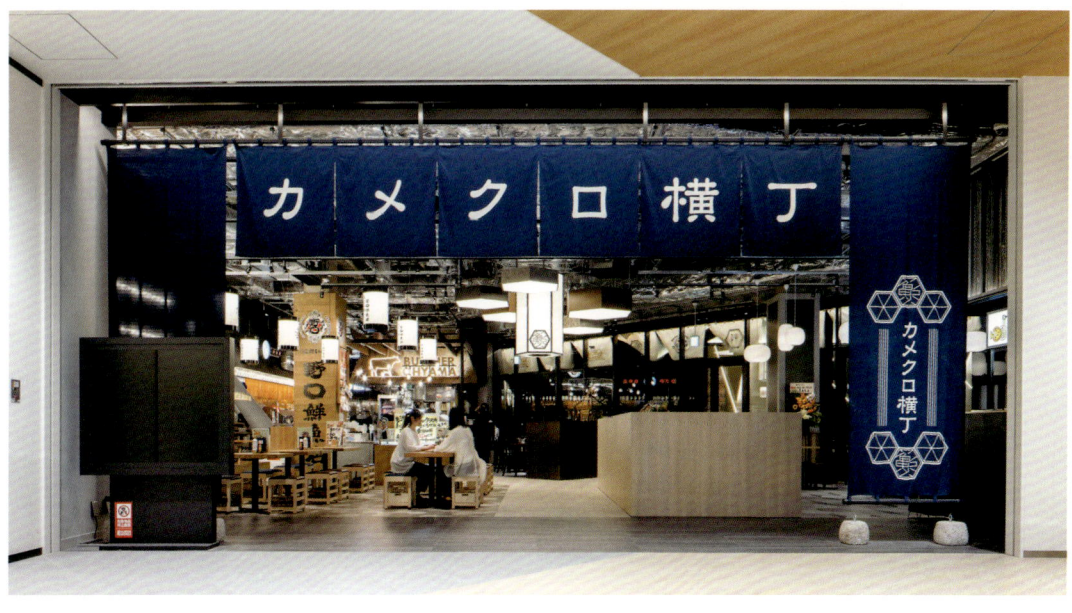

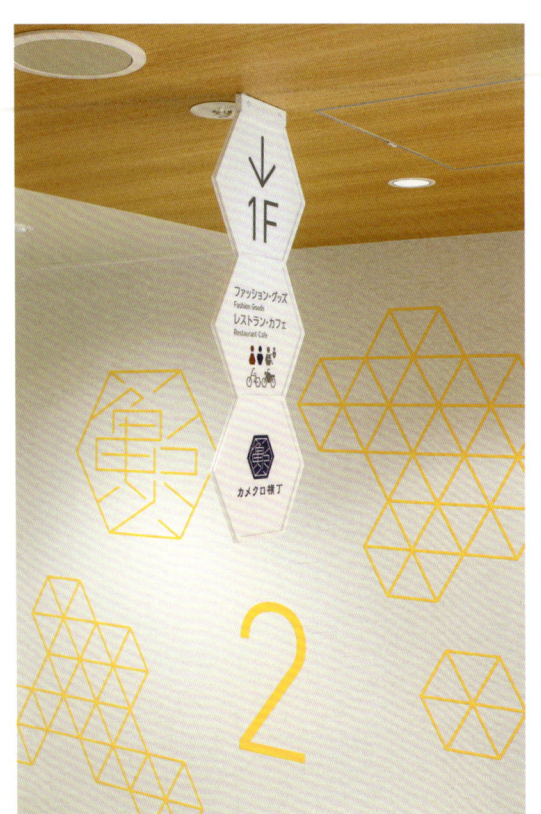

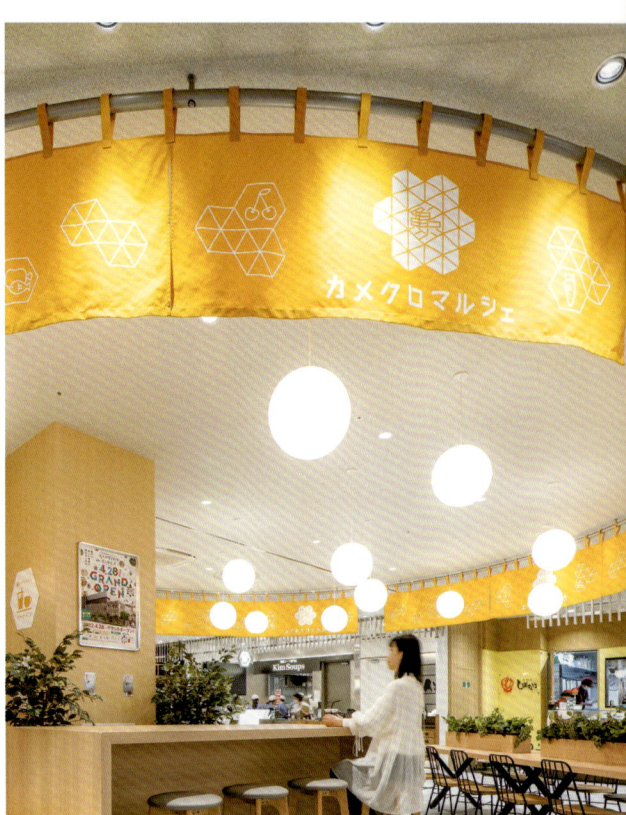

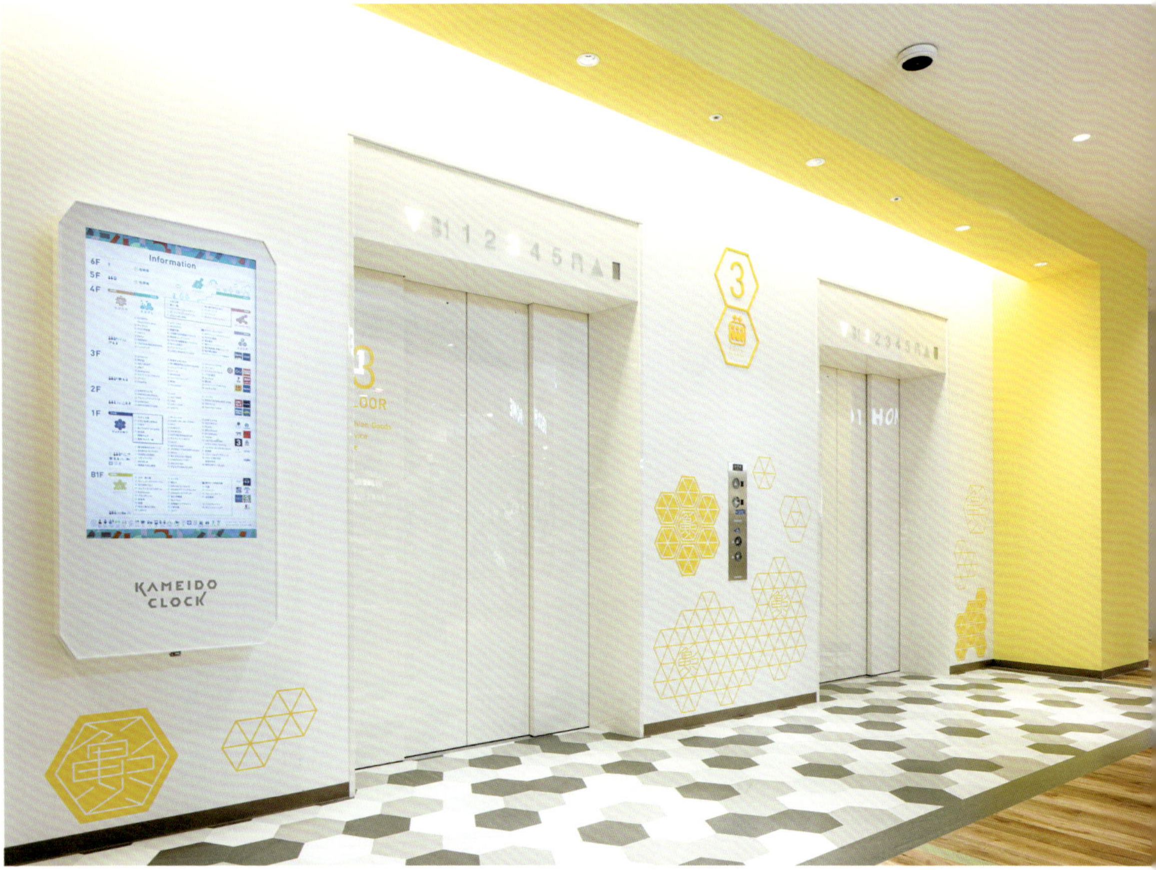

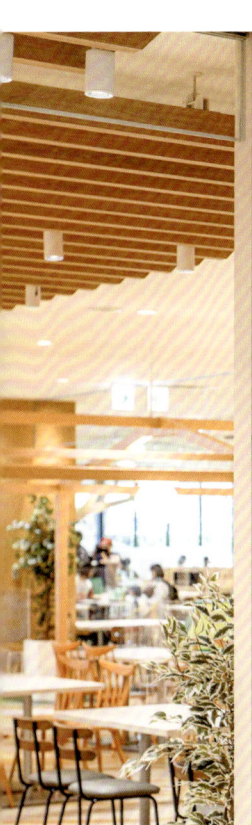
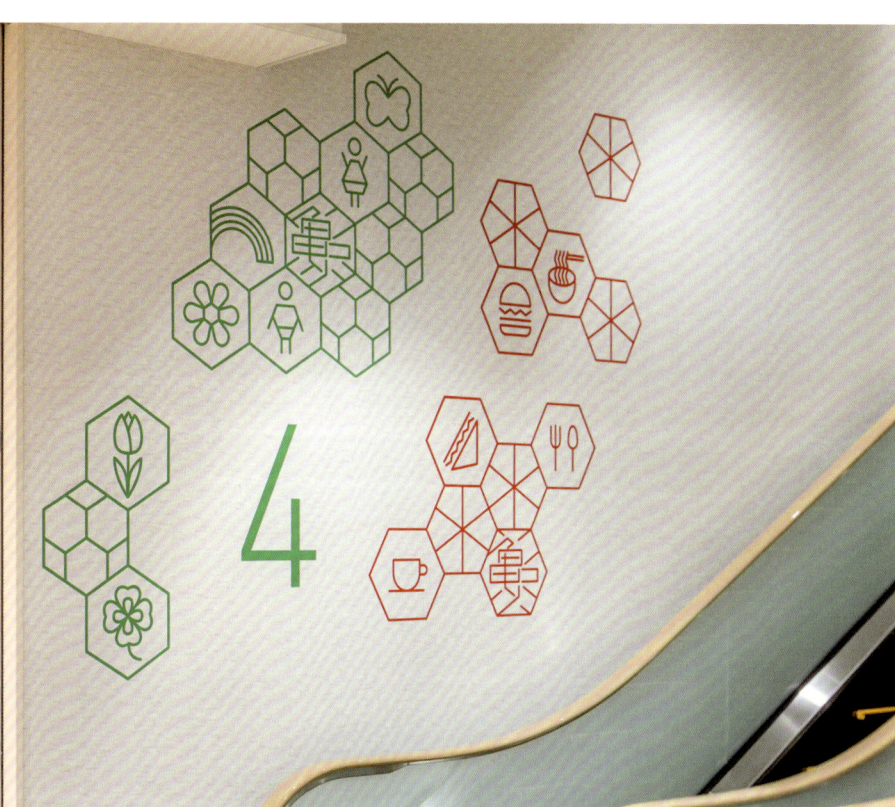
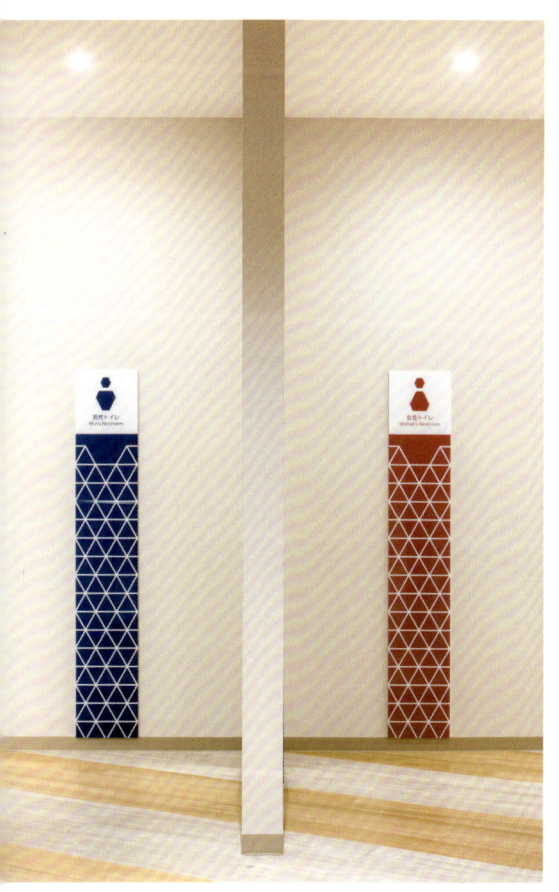
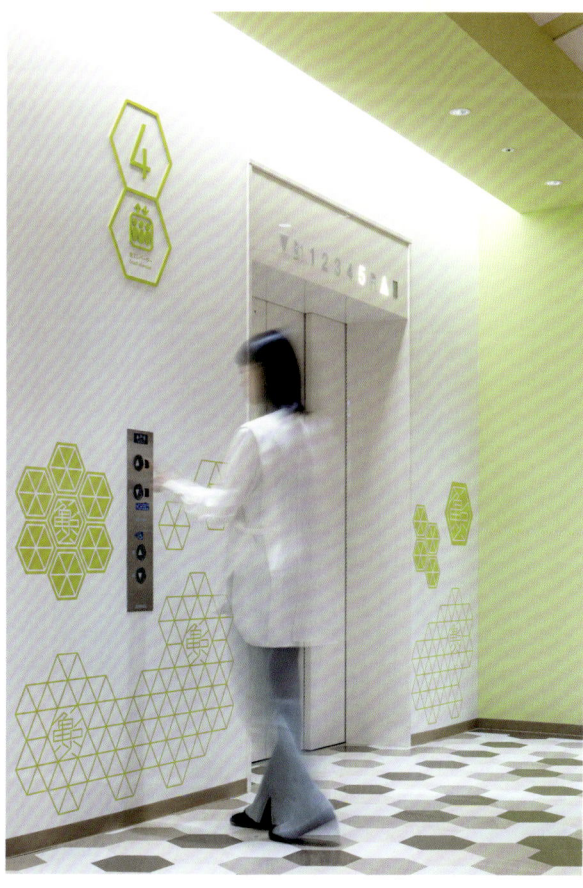

The new school building for the Beauty and Bridal School is characterized by softly arched corner walls and a north-south stairwell that can be seen from the outside through the glass. The students are always conscious of beauty here, and the signage was designed to create a high-quality space that is more like a salon than a school.

OK design Inc. created the visual identity of the school with the letter "B" as a motif. The "B" and "B" facing each other represent a butterfly fluttering its wings and the blossoming of students' skills and talents. The symbol floating from the first to the fifth floor delivers support for the students as they flap their wings toward the future.

DA   OK design Inc.
CD   Kayo Ouchi
AD   Kayo Ouchi
D   Kayo Ouchi, Yumi Hasebe
ID   FIELD FOUR DESIGN OFFICE
PH   Ooki Jingu
CL   Tokyo Bunkyo Gakuen

Tokyo Bunka Beauty College/Tokyo Bunka Bridal College

Visual Identity

The symbol is based on the letter "B"

Bunka
Beauty
Bridal

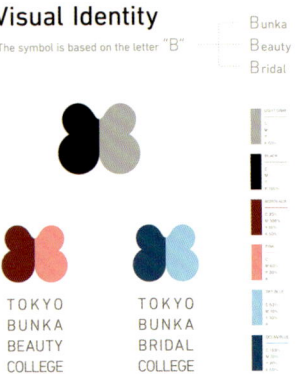

TOKYO
BUNKA
BEAUTY
COLLEGE

TOKYO
BUNKA
BRIDAL
COLLEGE

Color Scheme

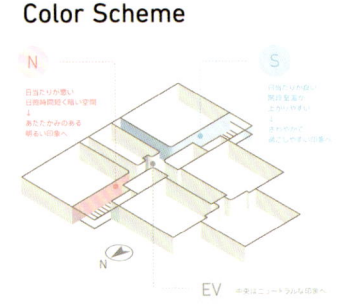

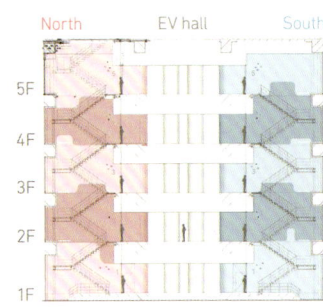

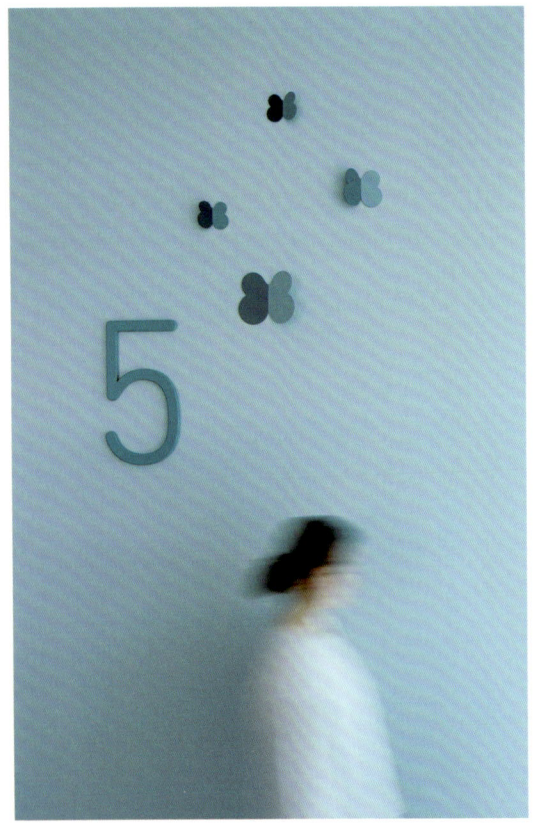

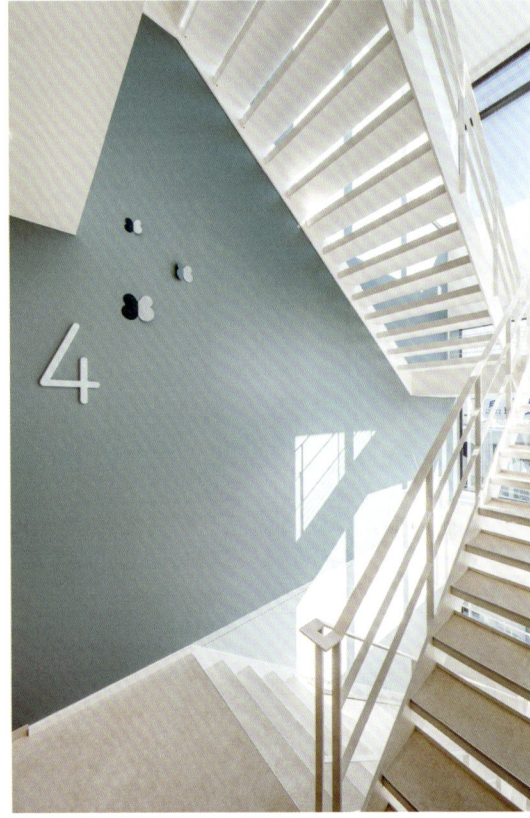

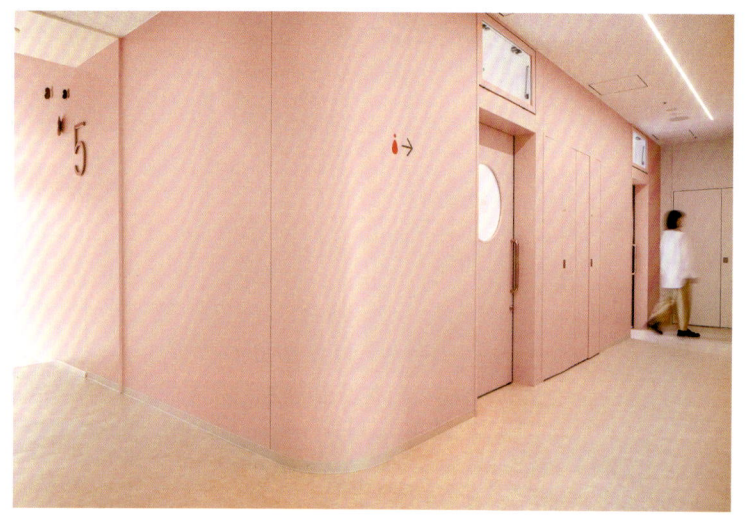
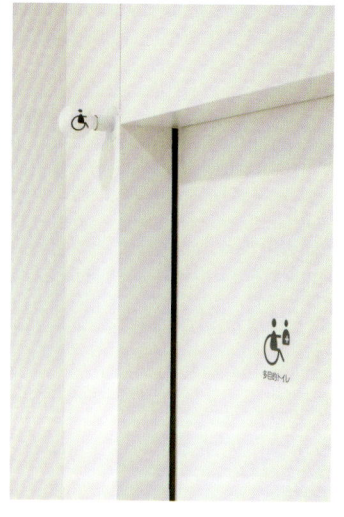
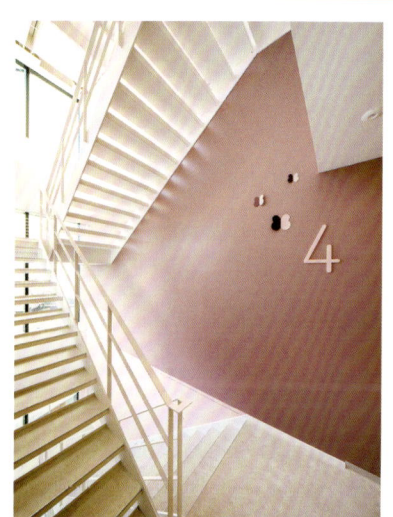
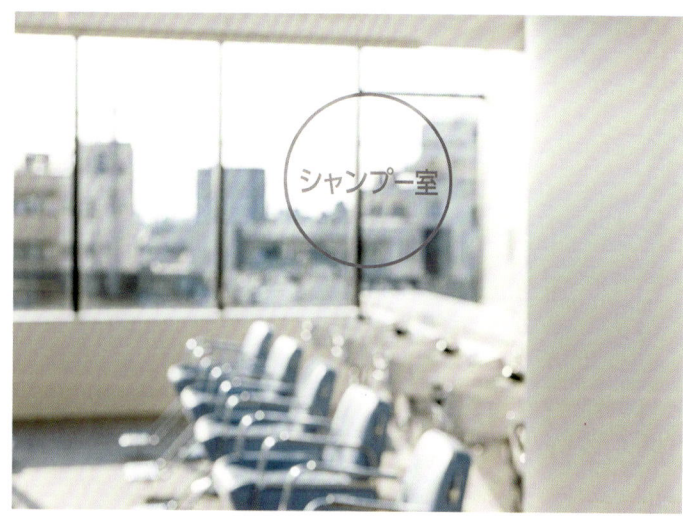

シャンプー室

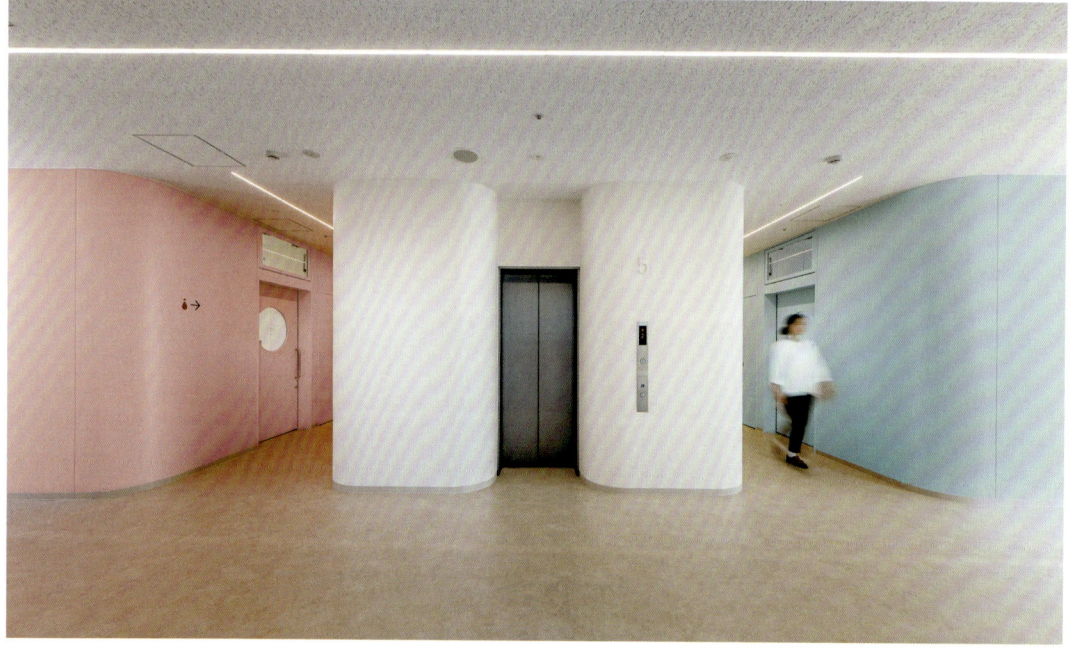

This is a signage design for the new MS LAB building of Sankyo Frontier, a leading modular space provider in Japan. The new MS LAB is built with the company's modular space solution Mobile Space. Mobile Space features high flexibility and is designed to be relocated and expanded easily.

For the signage plan to embody the flexibility and creativity of Mobile Space, the designers proposed to use magnetic bars to display letters and pictograms, a design that can flexibly respond to changes in space. A magnetic sheet is applied on the back of each plate, allowing the plates to be attached to and detached from a steel wall surface. It is up to users' creativity in how they are used.

DA   Arata Takemoto Design Office
ID   Inter Office
PH   Tomooki Kengaku
CL   SANKYO FRONTIER

MS LAB

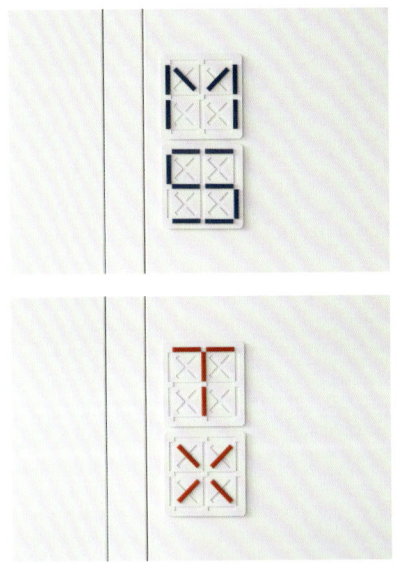

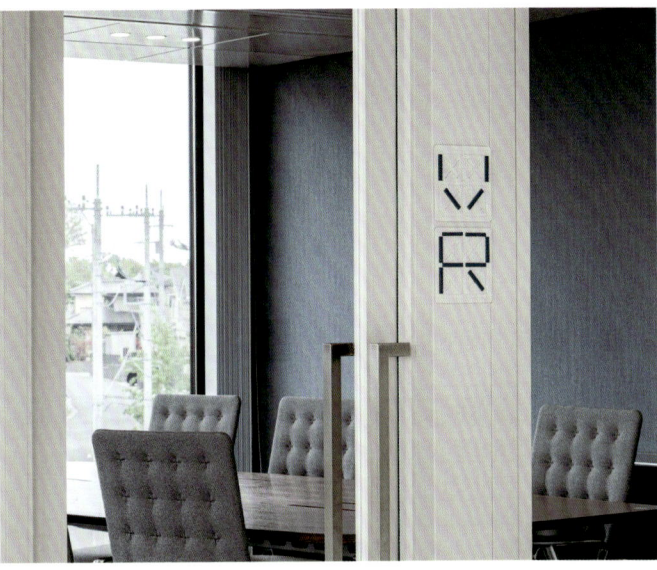

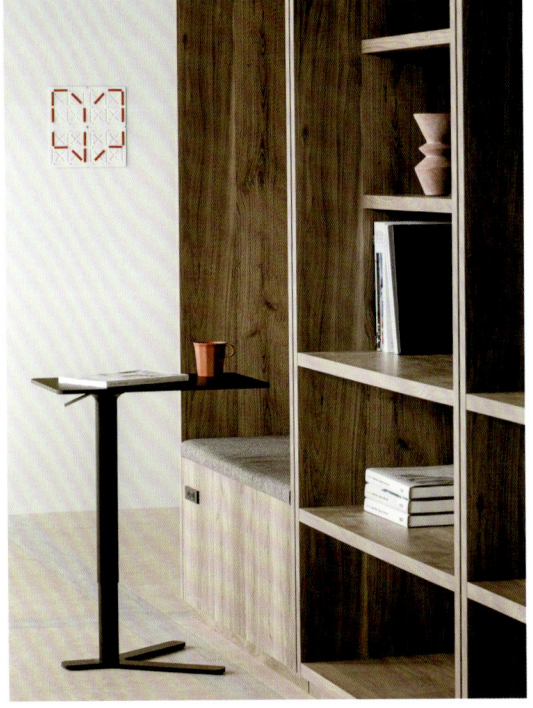

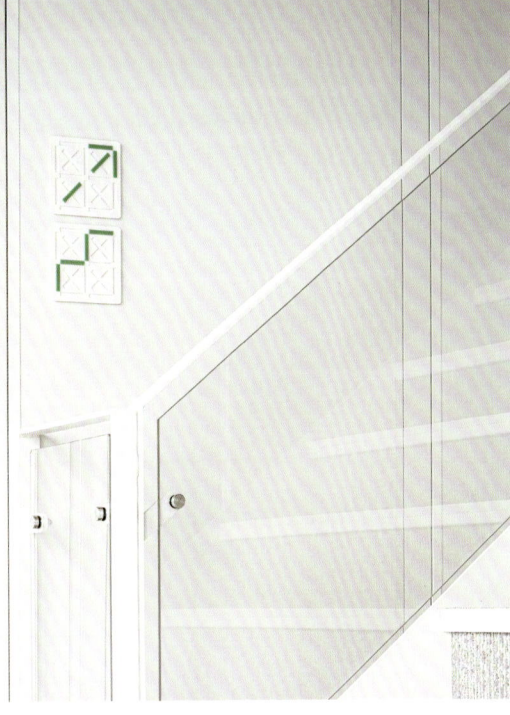

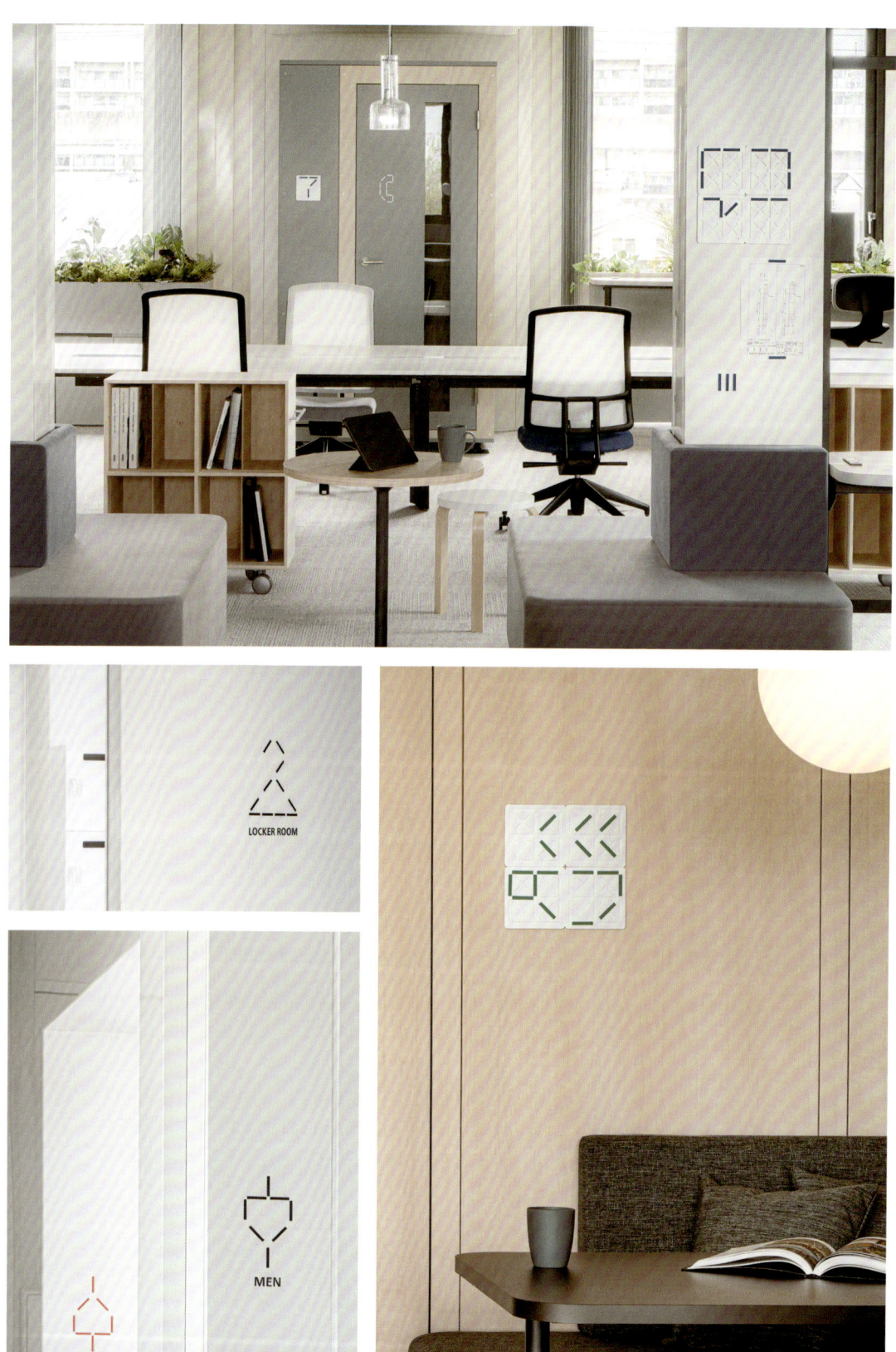

LOCKER ROOM

WOMEN

MEN

This is the signage planning for Chuo University's new school building. The building boasts an atrium spanning four floors. Taking advantage of the bridges over the atrium, the designers drew out a signage scheme that integrated space and information.

Signage letters are installed on the bridges with a background of white arrows that gradually turn transparent. Hence, the letters are highly visible and easy for users to understand. The building accommodates various types of space, so the designers used pictograms to symbolize the spatial character of each classroom. Instead of using motifs of people for facilities' pictograms, the designers used abstract expressions so that they will not limit the activities of users.

DA   Arata Takemoto Design Office
AR   TAKENAKA CORPORATION
PH   Tomooki Kengaku
CL   Chuo University

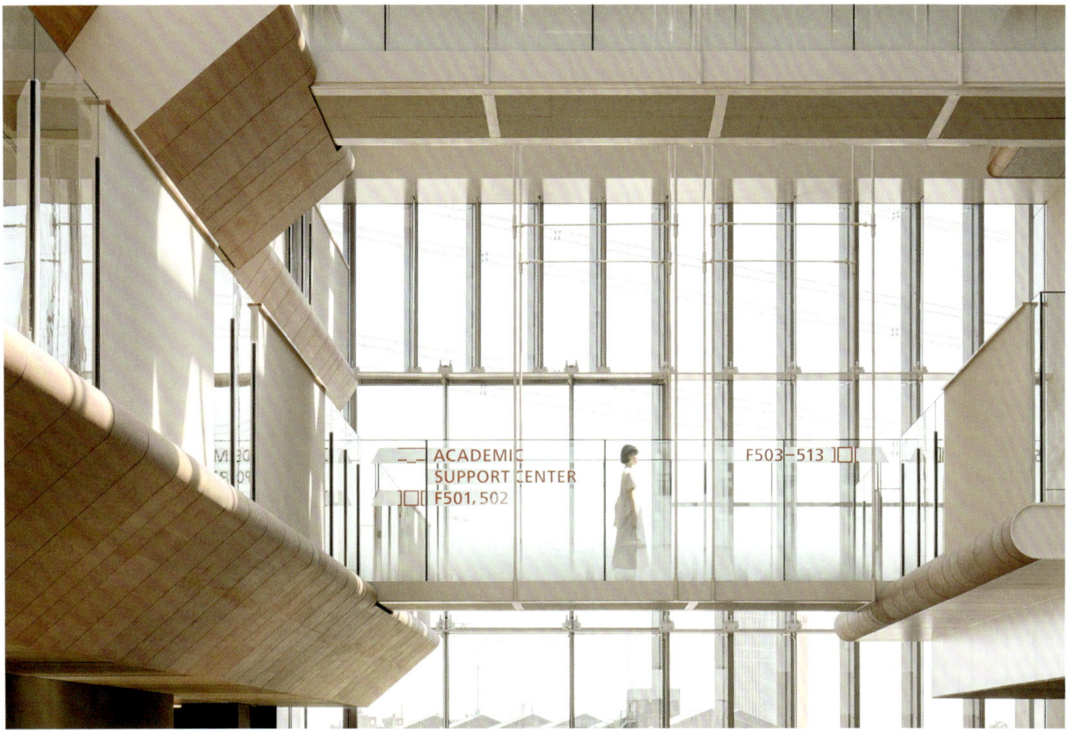

FOREST GATEWAY CHUO

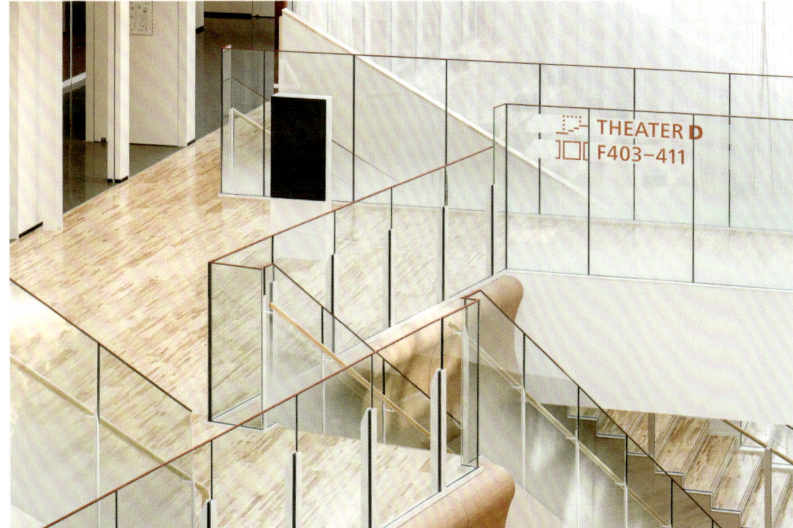

⊐⊐ HALL

⊐⊐ THEATER **A–D**

⊐⊐ ACADEMIC
     SUPPORT CENTER

]☐[F101–608

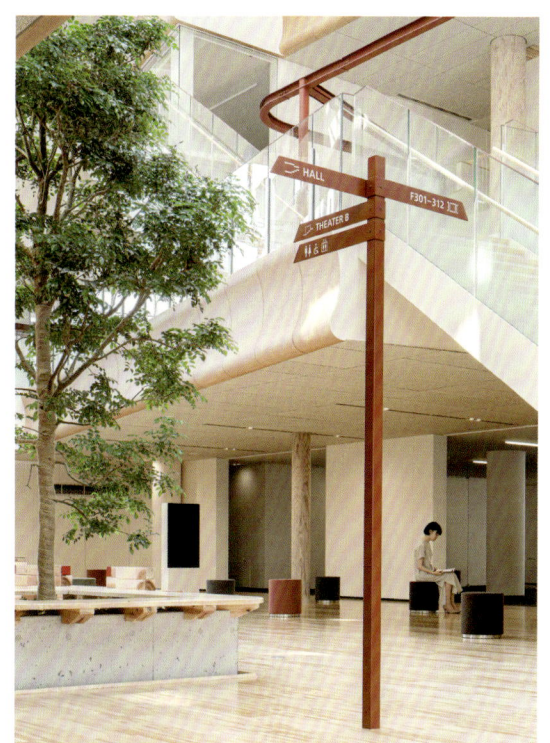

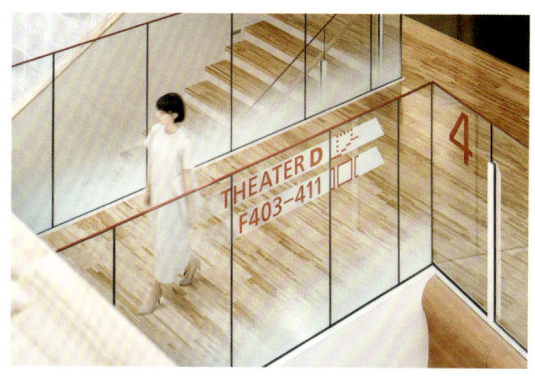

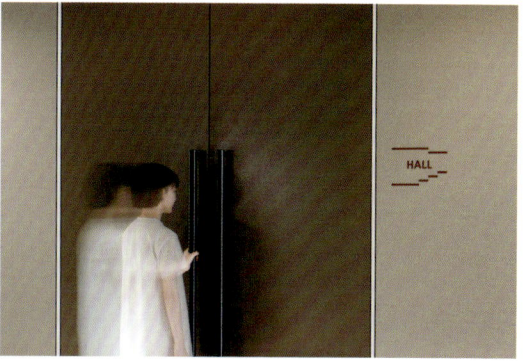

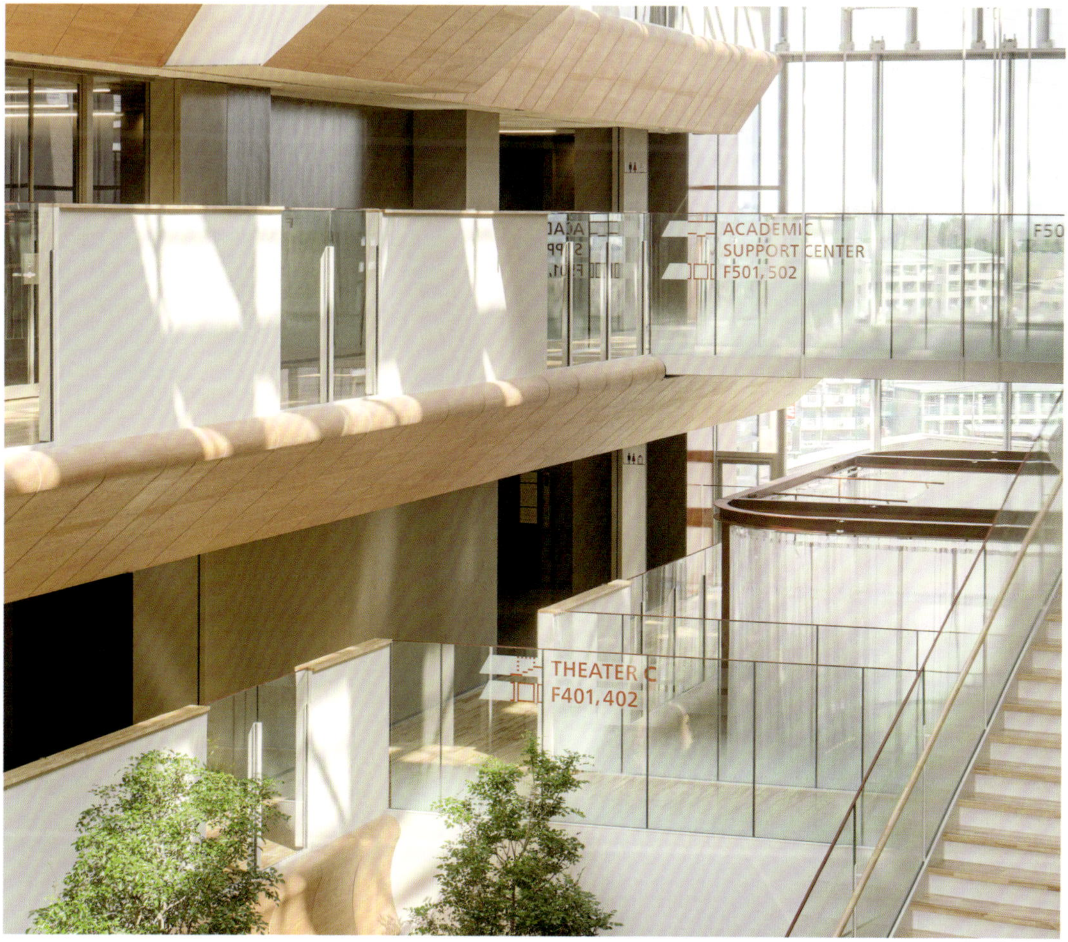

SAGA FURUYU CAMP, a renovated four-story school building, was reborn as a complex facility. It is expected to be used in a wide range of ways.

With the building surrounded by rich nature, the logo and signage were designed based on the concept of "incorporating elements of the surrounding environment," and mirror materials are used to blend these landscapes into the space within the building. The mirror sheets used for the room numbers allow for the inclusion of shimmering ambient color and light, which stainless steel mirrors are unable to express. To evoke the atmosphere of the old days, the color of each floor is carefully selected and coordinated.

DA   UMA/design farm
AD   Yuma Harada
D   Yuka Tsuda
CL   SAGA FURUYU CAMP

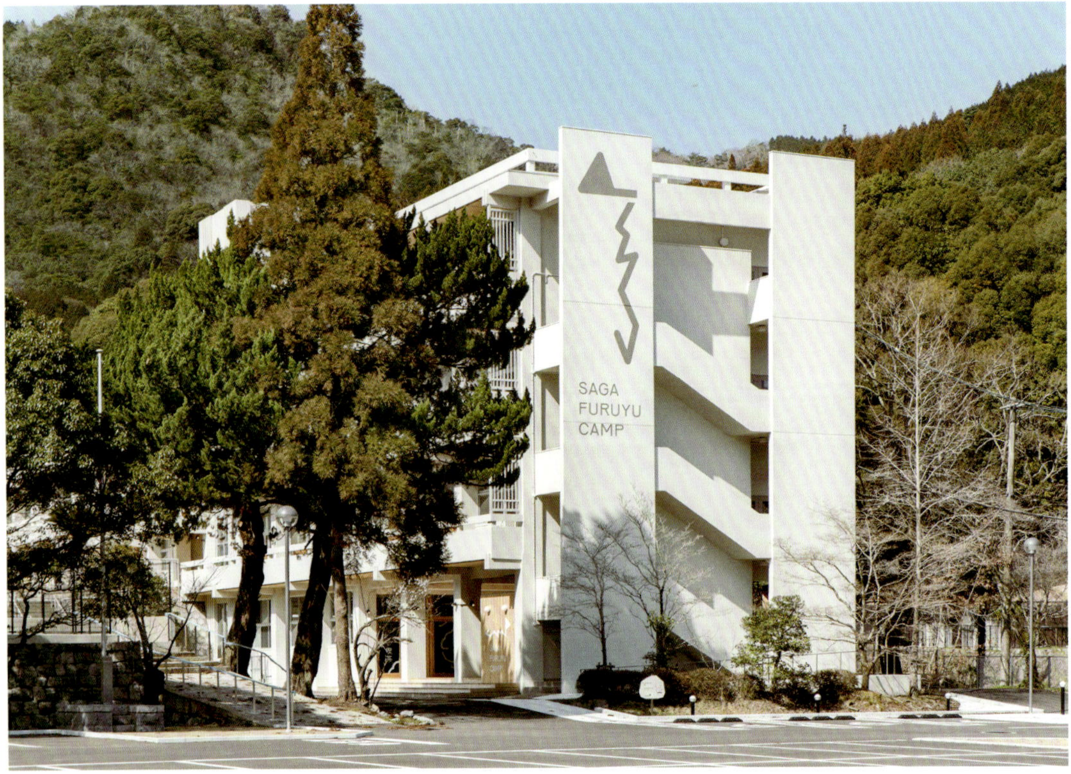

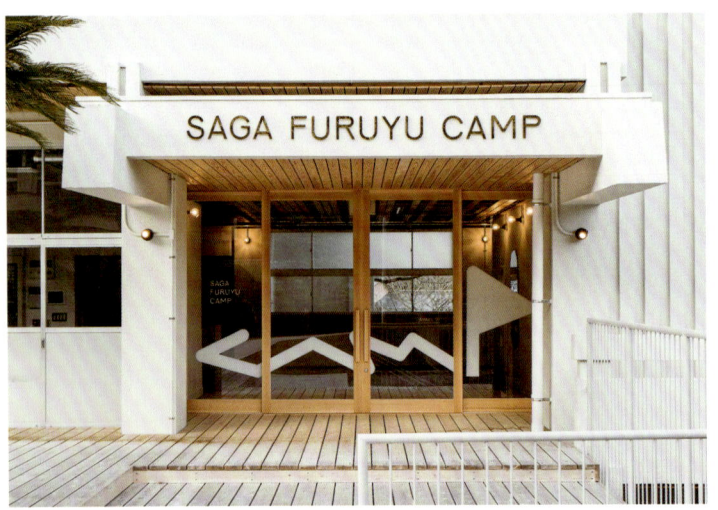

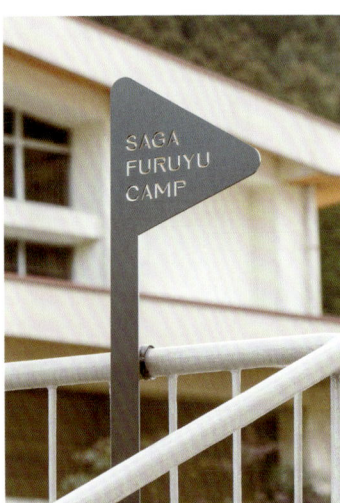

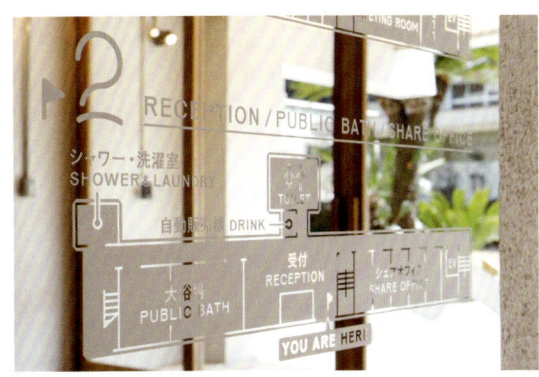

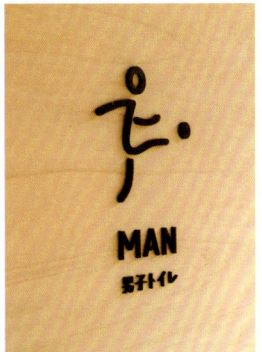

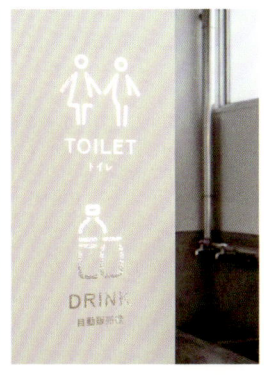

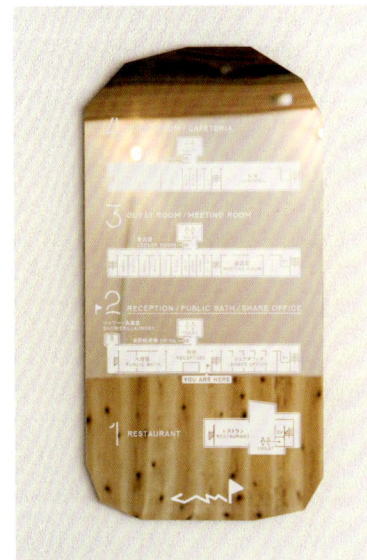

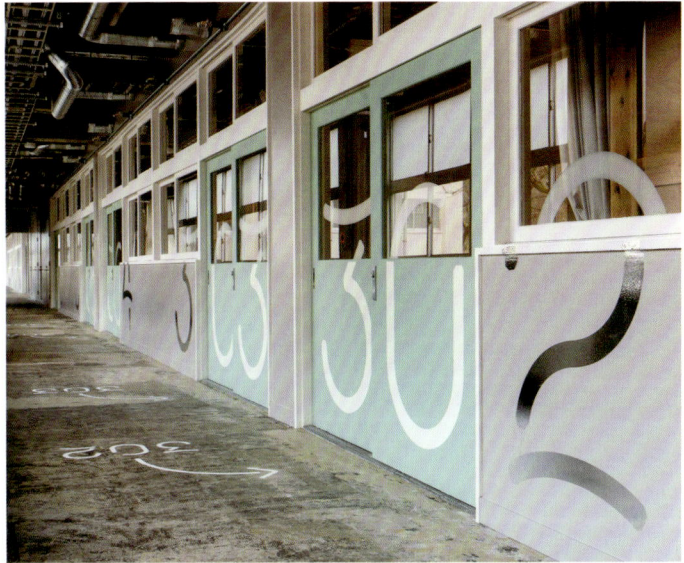

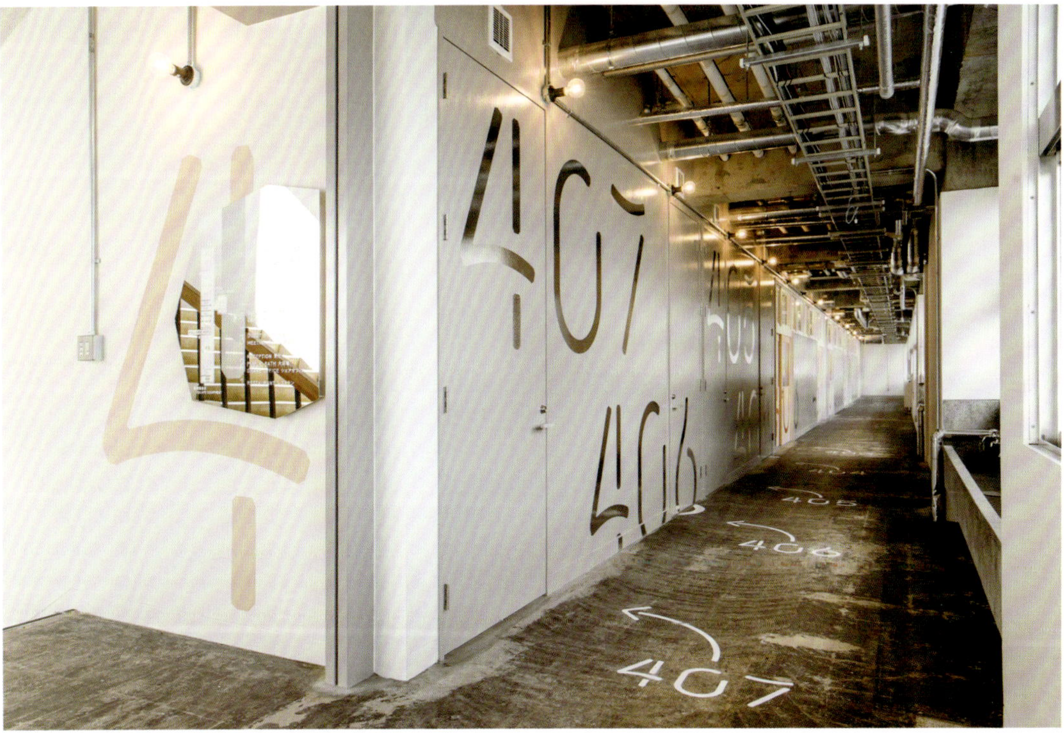

The prefectural swimming pool is in the SAGA Sunrise Park, the Saga Prefectural Sports Complex.

Inspired by the name Sunrise Park, the design consists of round dots and is based on the motif of the sun and light, aiming to form a major sports base that will generate local vitality. The visual expression was designed to evoke the trajectory of a movement with the hope that people in the facility will take Sunrise Park as their starting point and start running.

The signs, which serve as a catalyst for various forms of communication, are expected to ensure visibility and have a light and charming visual effect when dynamically deployed in the space.

DA	UMA/design farm
AD	Yuma Harada
D	Yuka Tsuda
CL	SAGA AQUA
PH	Yoshiro Masuda

SAGA AQUA

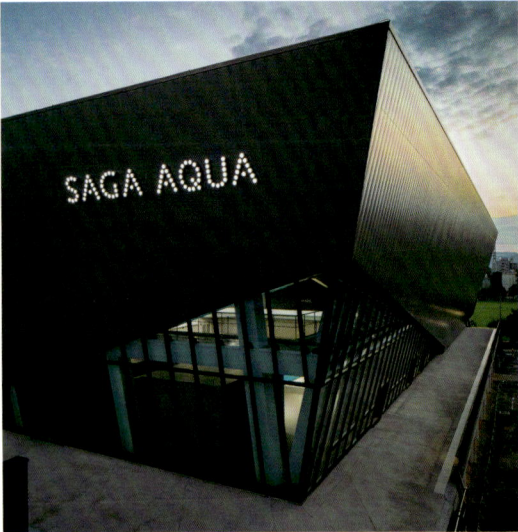
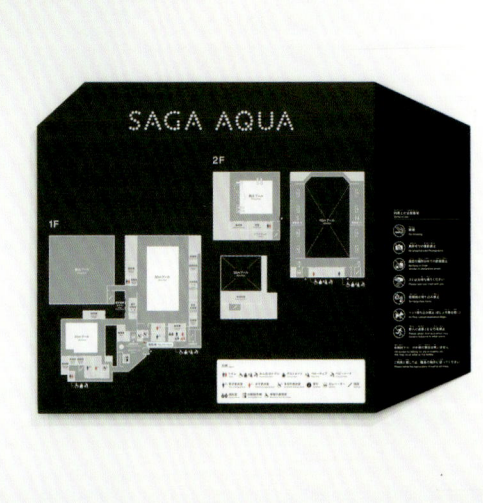
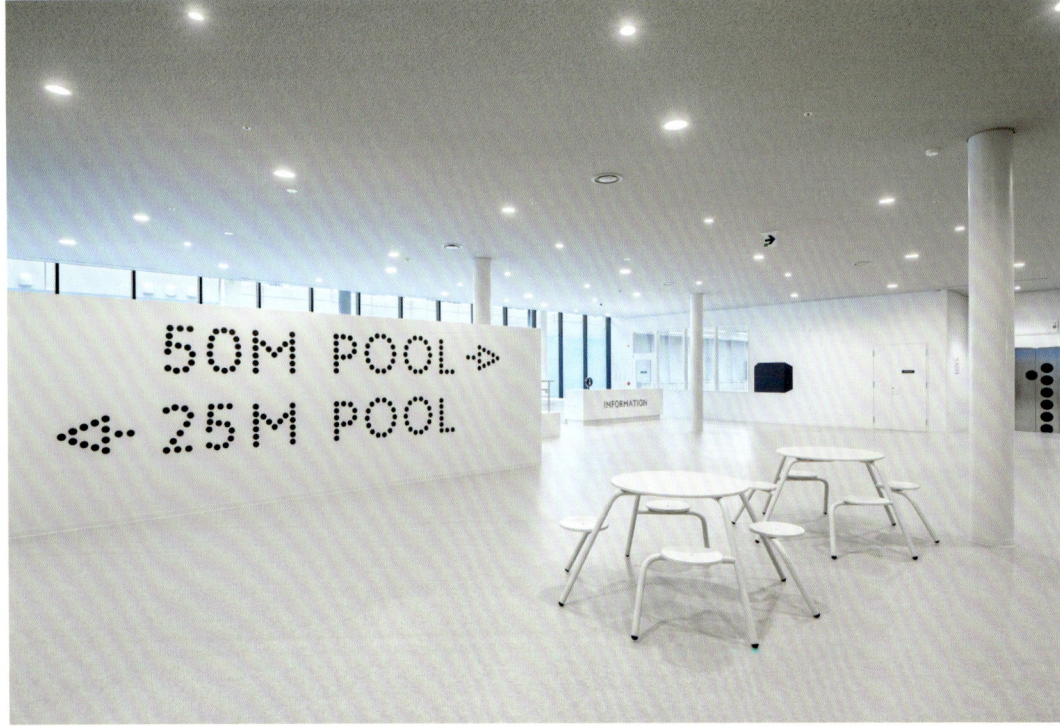

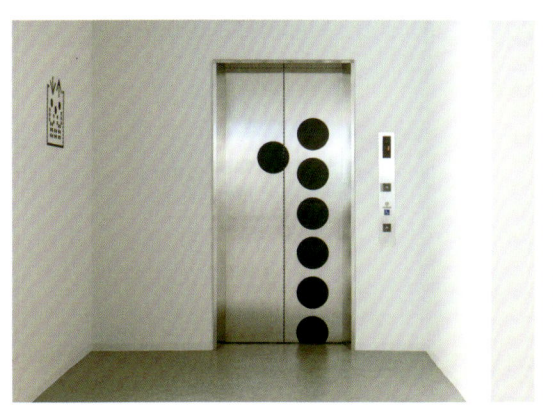

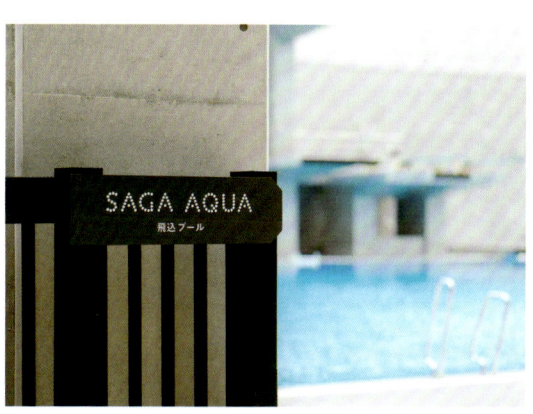

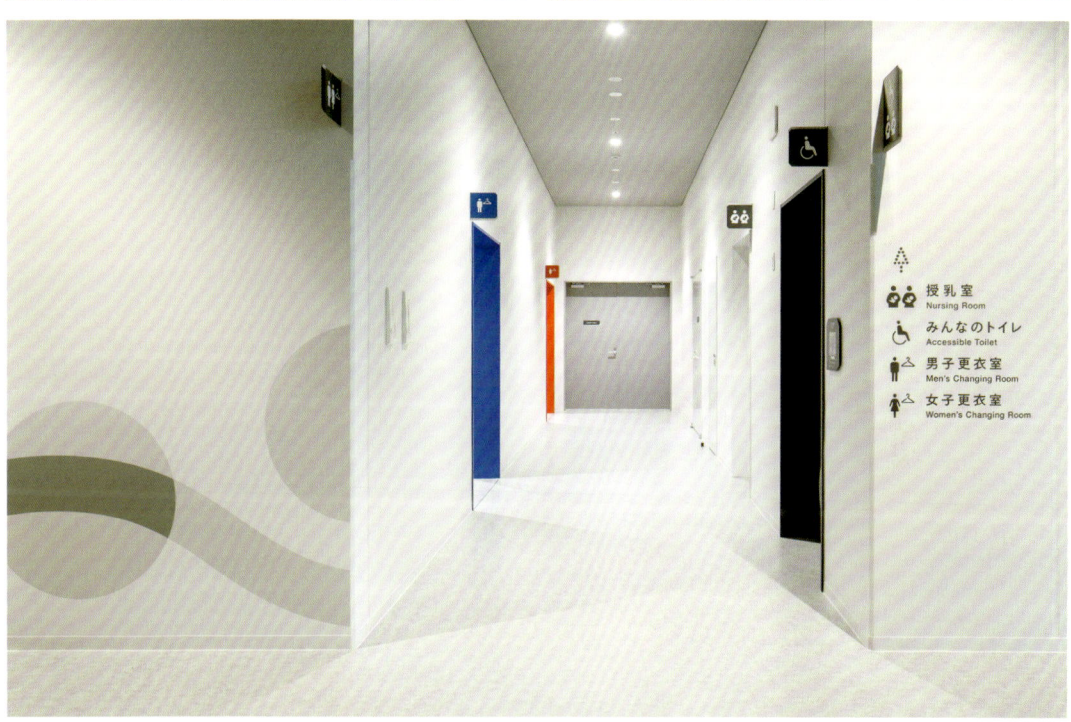

授乳室
Nursing Room

みんなのトイレ
Accessible Toilet

男子更衣室
Men's Changing Room

女子更衣室
Women's Changing Room

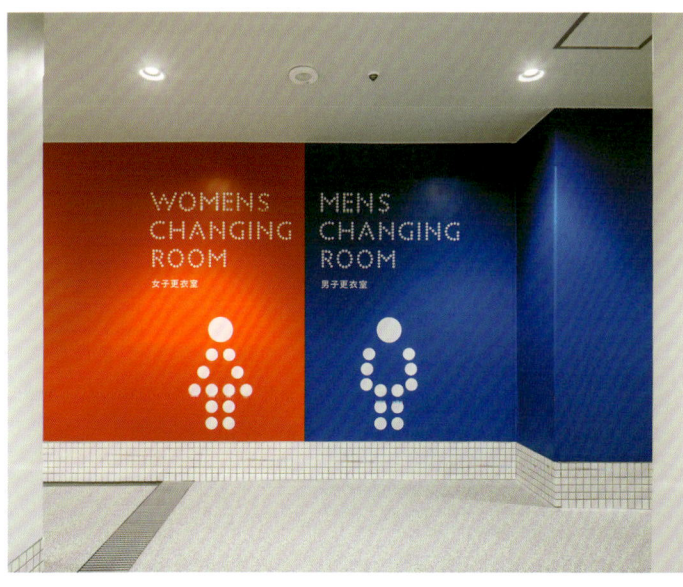

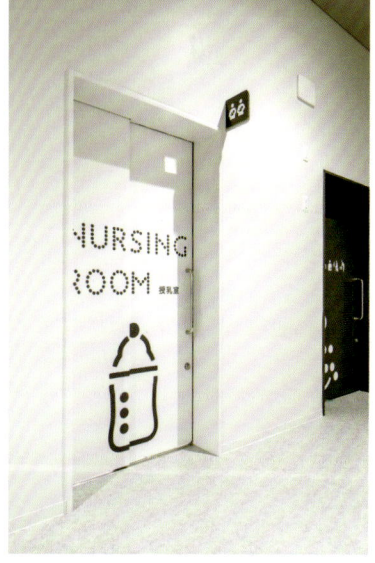

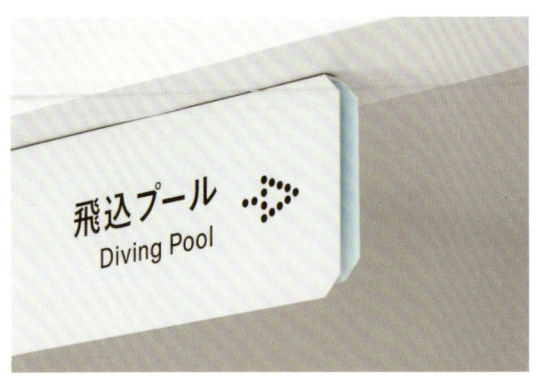

飛込プール
Diving Pool

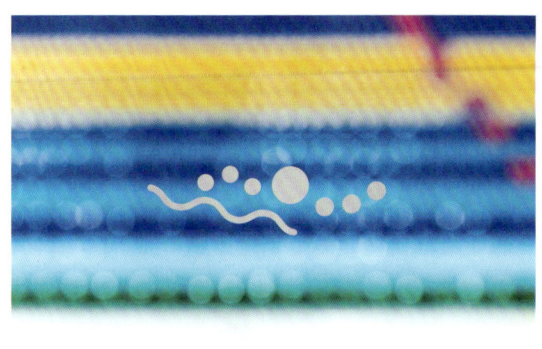

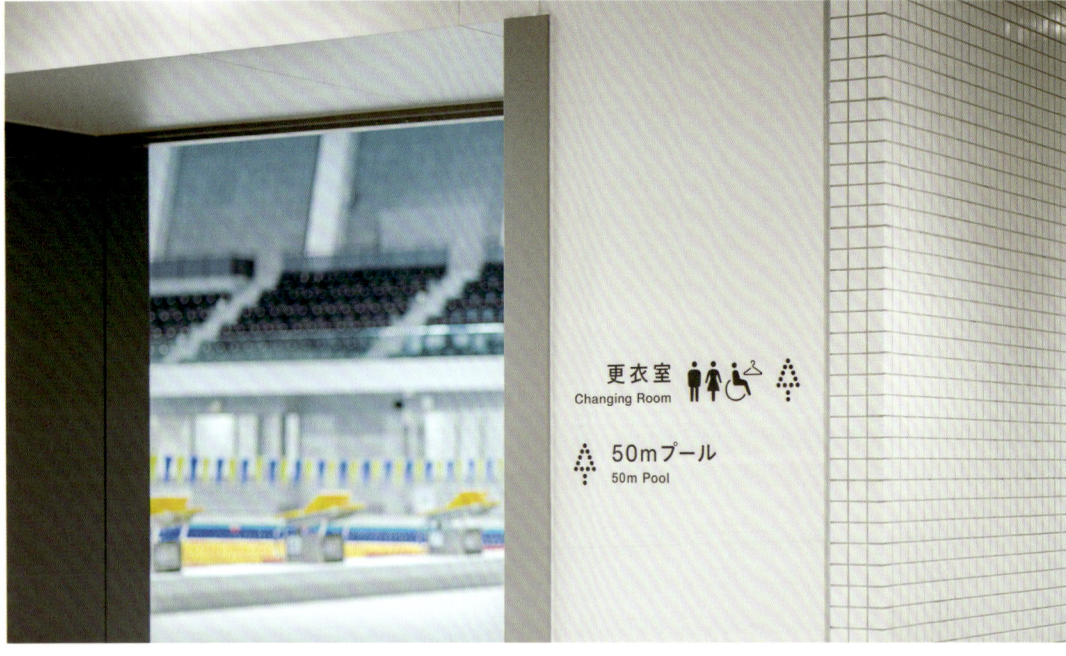

更衣室
Changing Room

50mプール
50m Pool

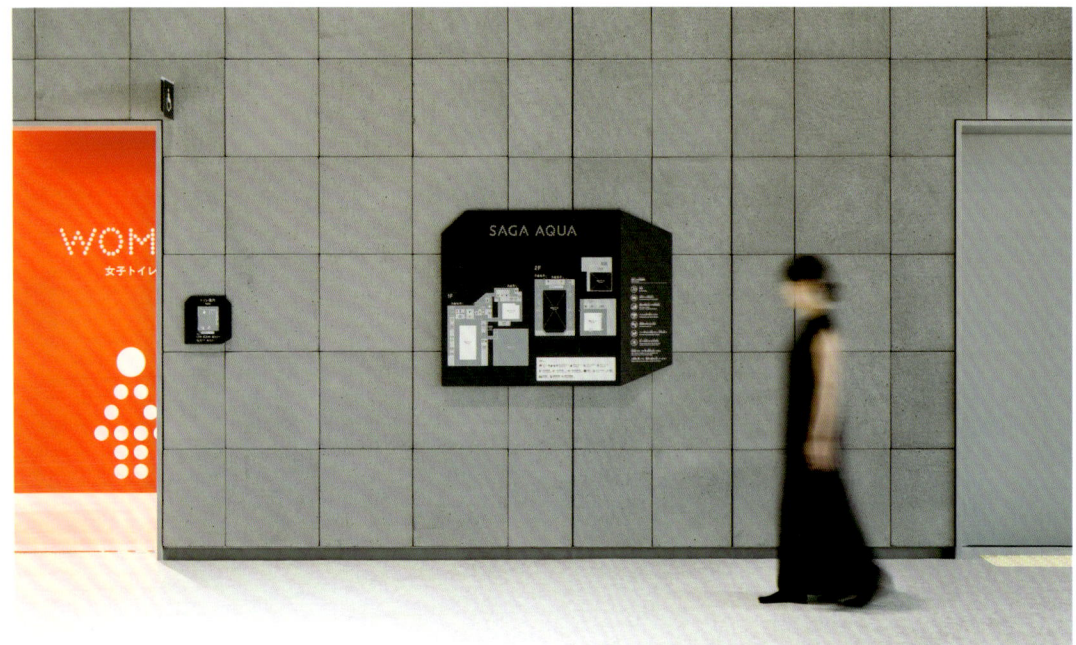

WOM
女子トイレ

SAGA AQUA

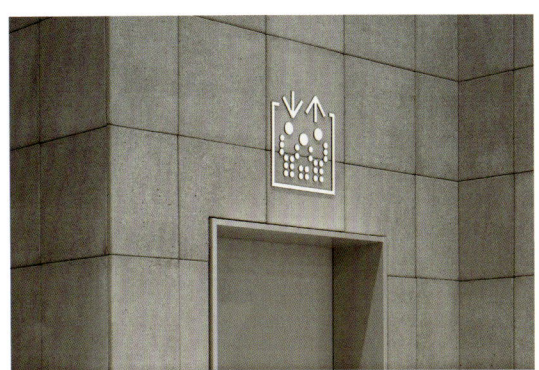

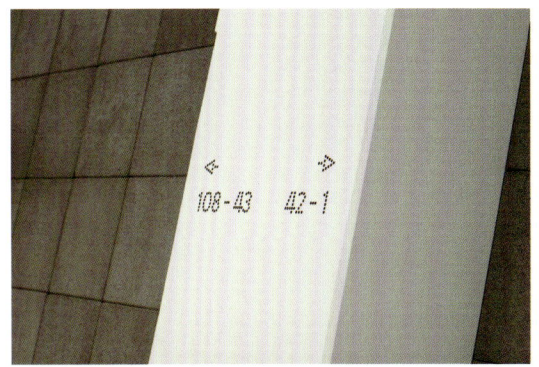

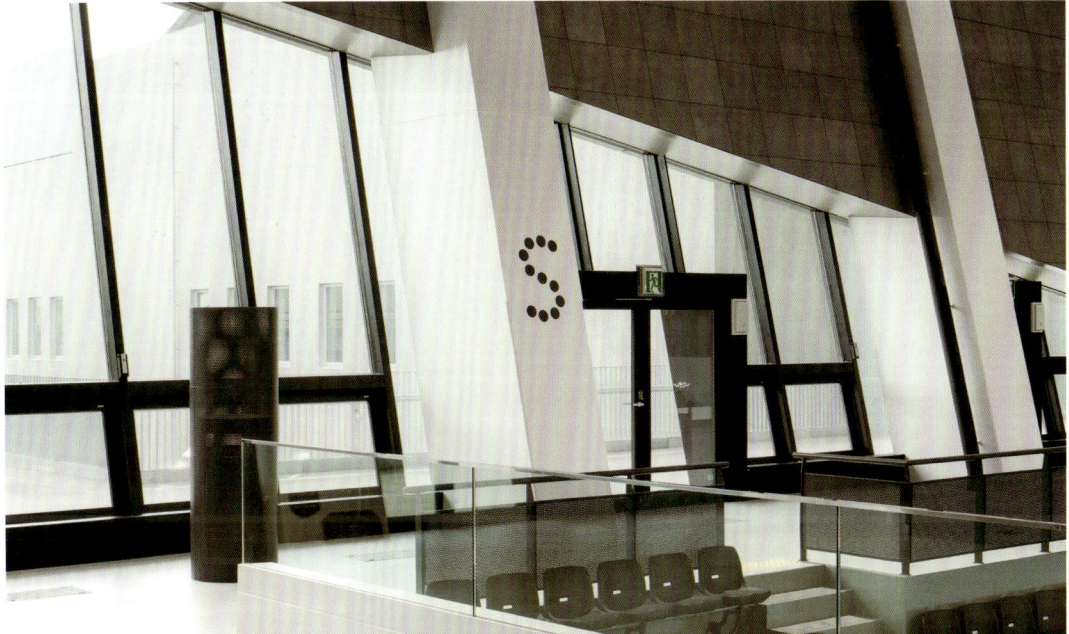

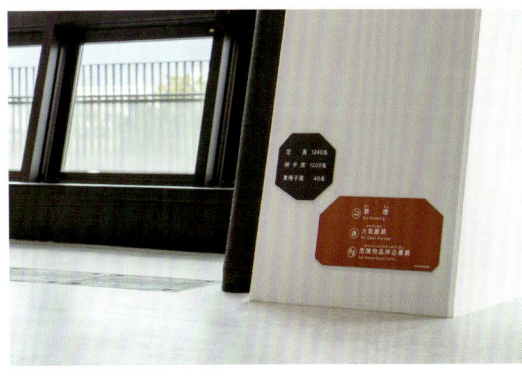

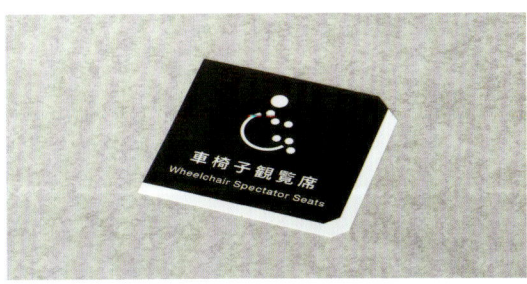

車椅子観覧席
Wheelchair Spectator Seats

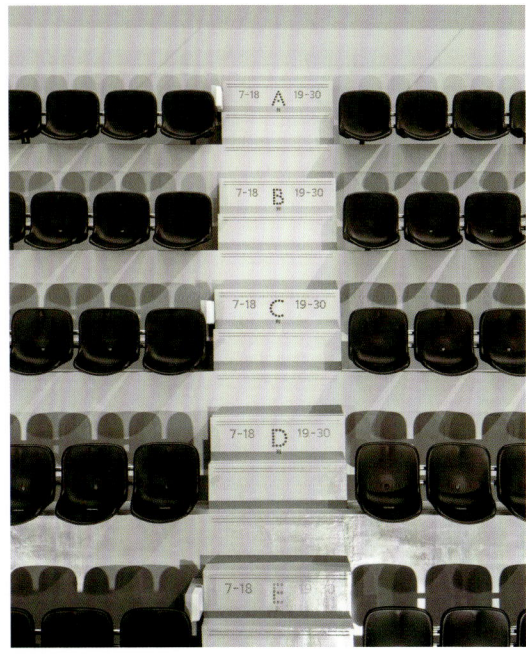

HOTEL ANTEROOM currently has three locations in Kyoto, Seoul, and Naha, each with its own graphic design. And UMA/design farm created the hotel logo, restaurant logo, signage design, and tool design for HOTEL ANTEROOM NAHA.

The geometric, yet angular, stylistic font design and illustrative pictograms, which were inherited from the first hotel in Kyoto, were used to unify the design. The identity is inspired by the striking blue of the crystal clear sea and sky visible from the hotel and the signage design is intended to convey the high quality luxury of an art hotel with a playful resort feel.

DA   UMA/design farm
AD   Yuma Harada
D   Keisuke Yamazoe
CL   UDS Ltd.

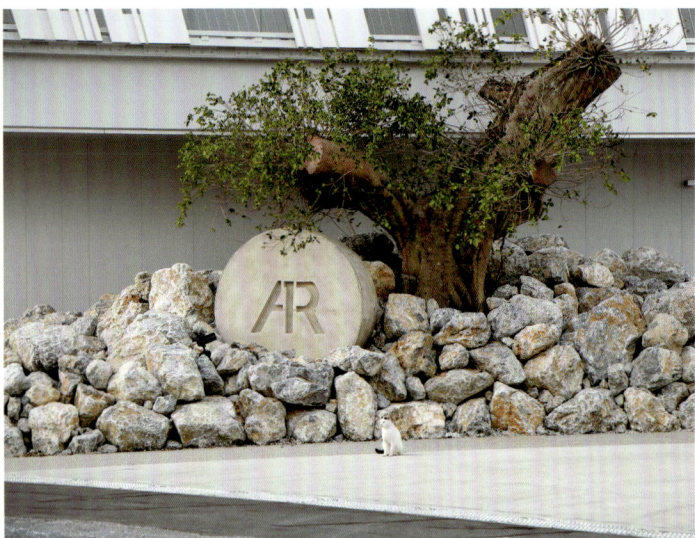

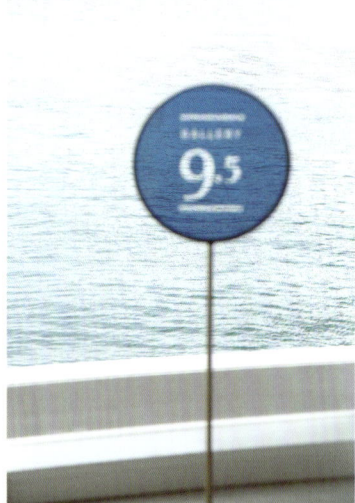

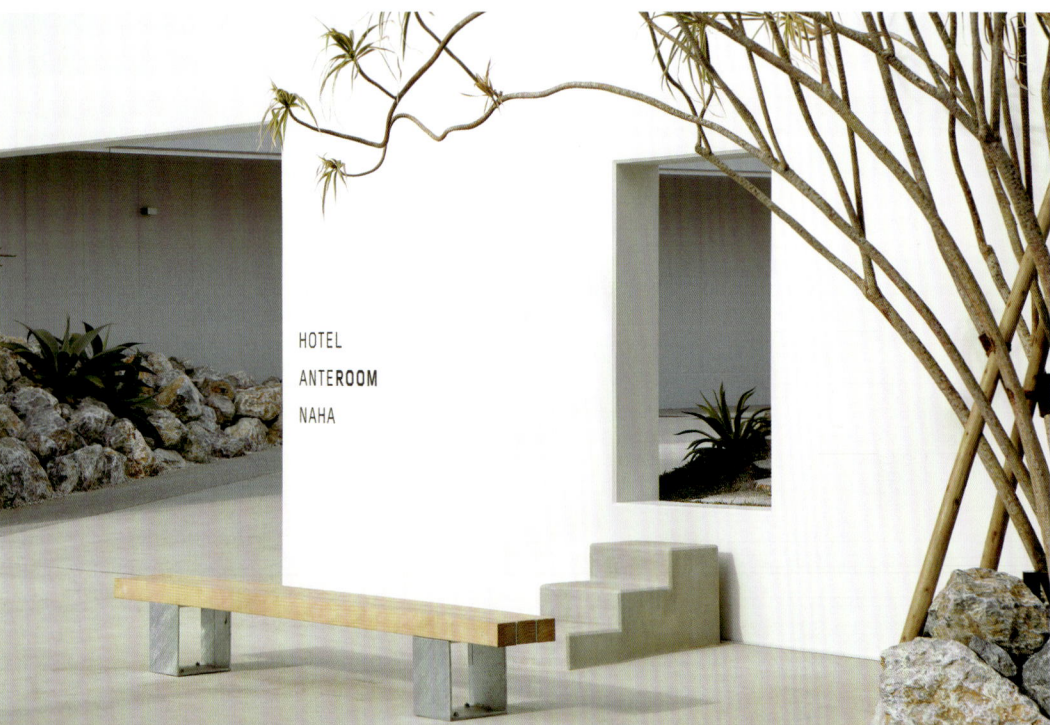

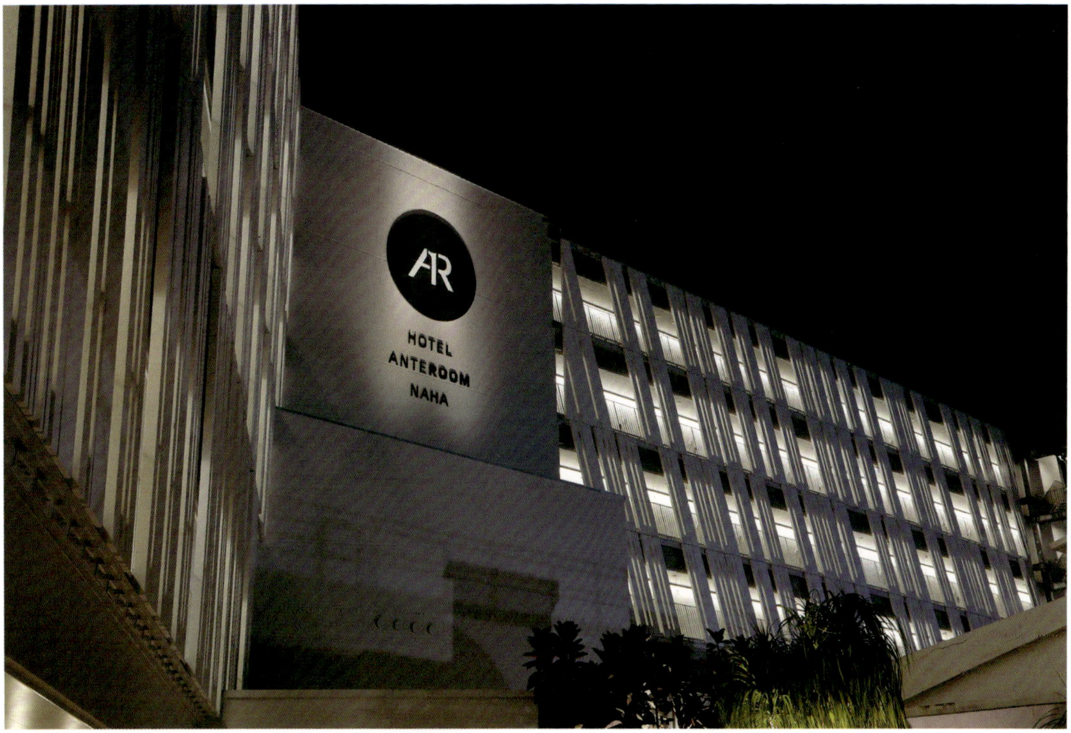

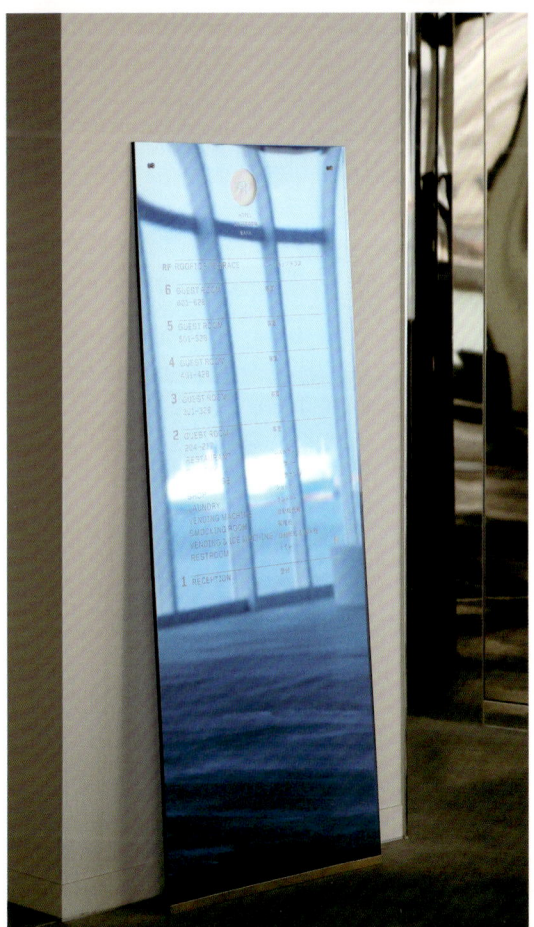

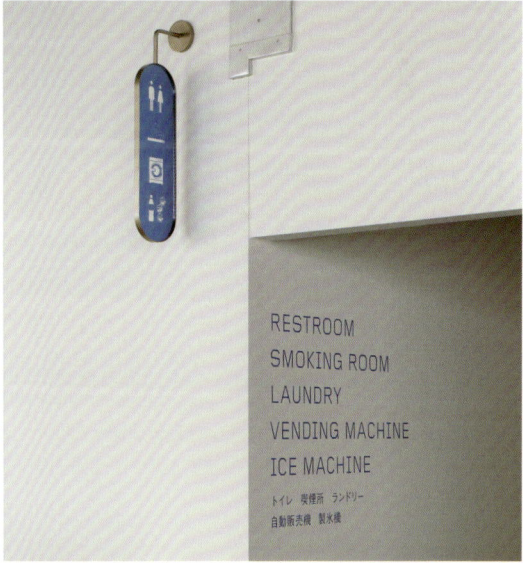

RESTROOM
SMOKING ROOM
LAUNDRY
VENDING MACHINE
ICE MACHINE

トイレ 喫煙所 ランドリー
自動販売機 製氷機

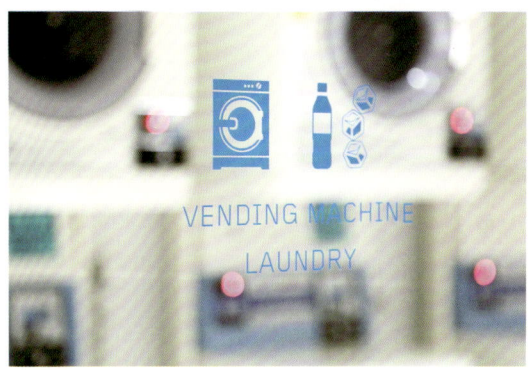

VENDING MACHINE
LAUNDRY

This is the signage design for the new office, 101 BASE, of the advertising agency Nakachika. The designers have renovated a distribution warehouse into an office for people to work in a new way. The concept is a secret base because the place is surrounded by walls on four sides. An original font made up of white circles allows employees to leave cryptic messages in various places.

D   Moe Furuya
AR   Junpei Nousaku, Ikumi Shumuta
PH   MEGUMI
CL   Nakachika Co., Ltd.

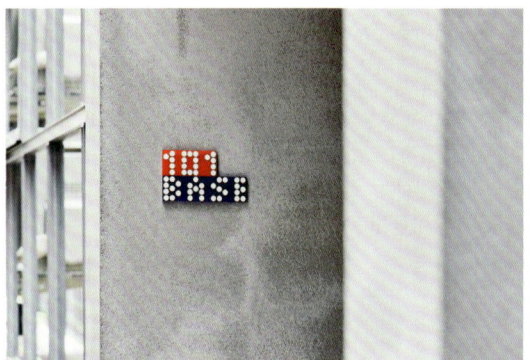
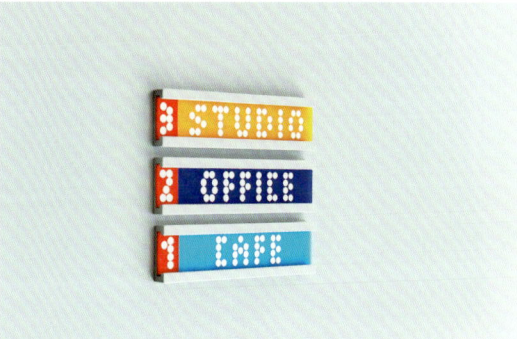

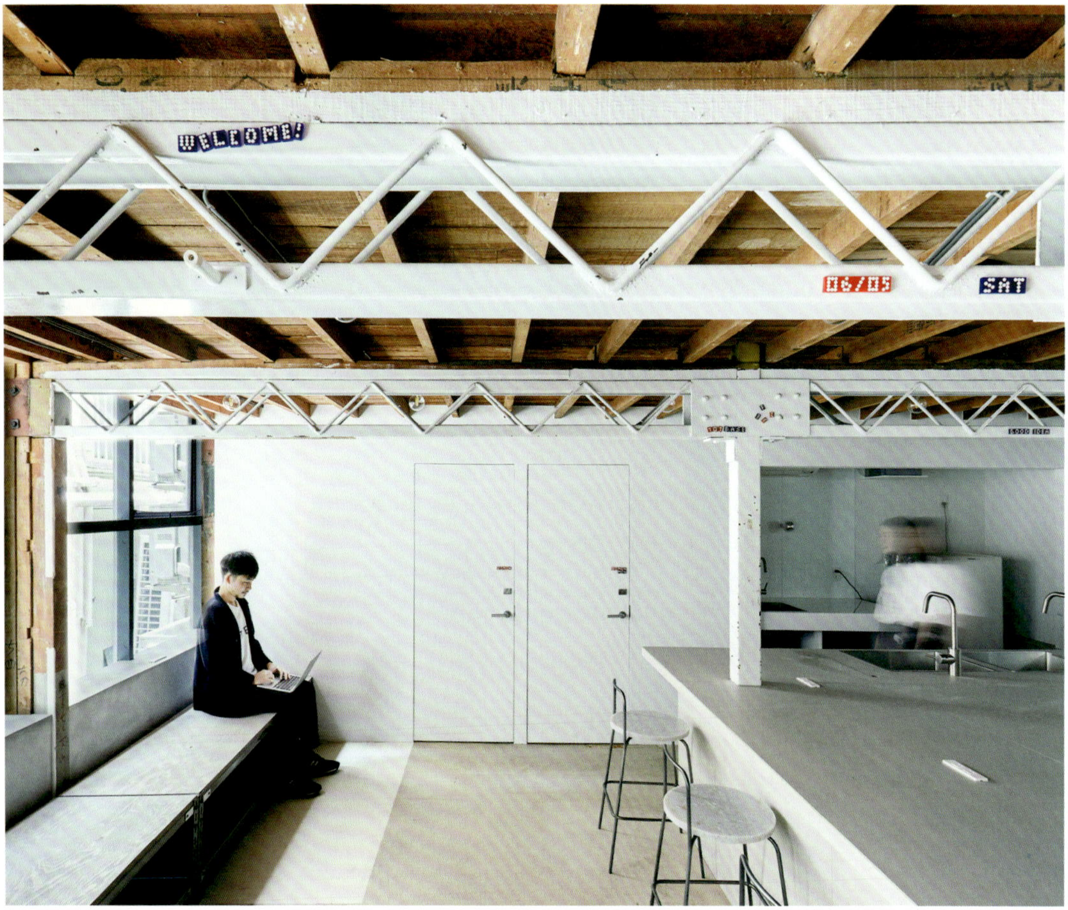

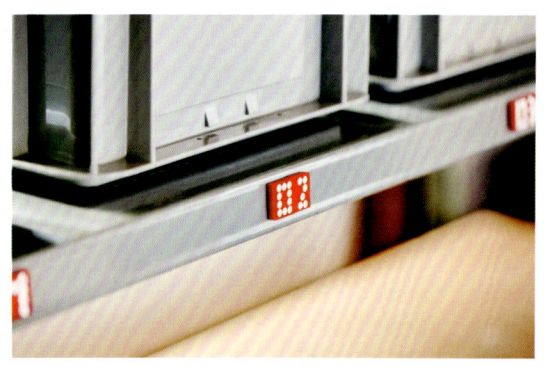

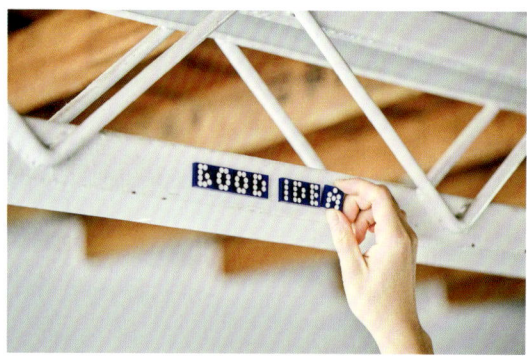

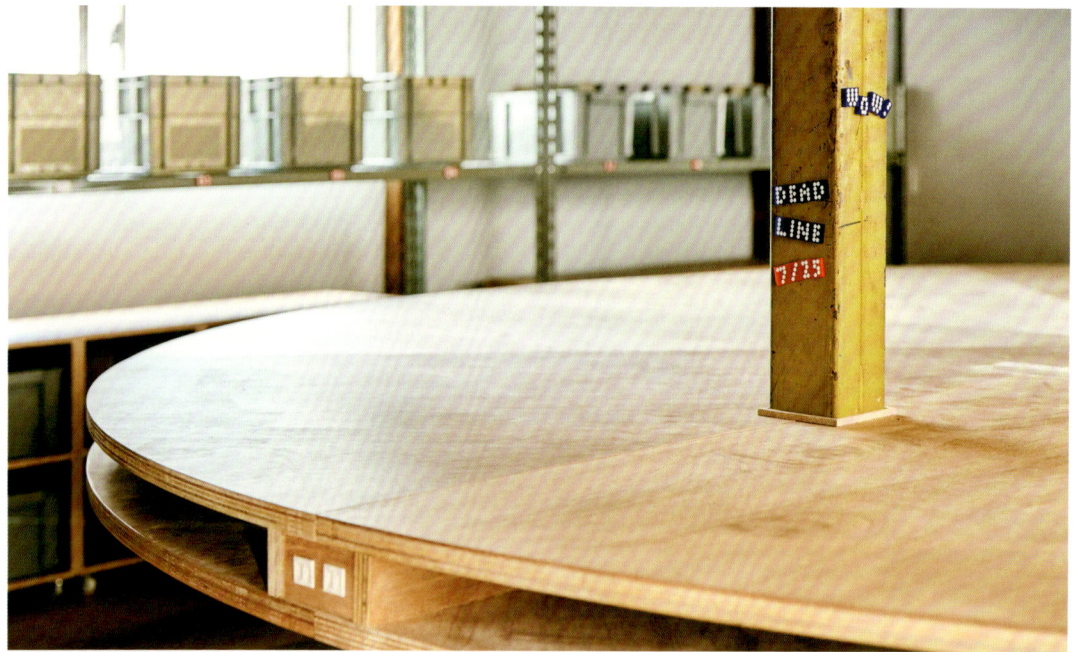

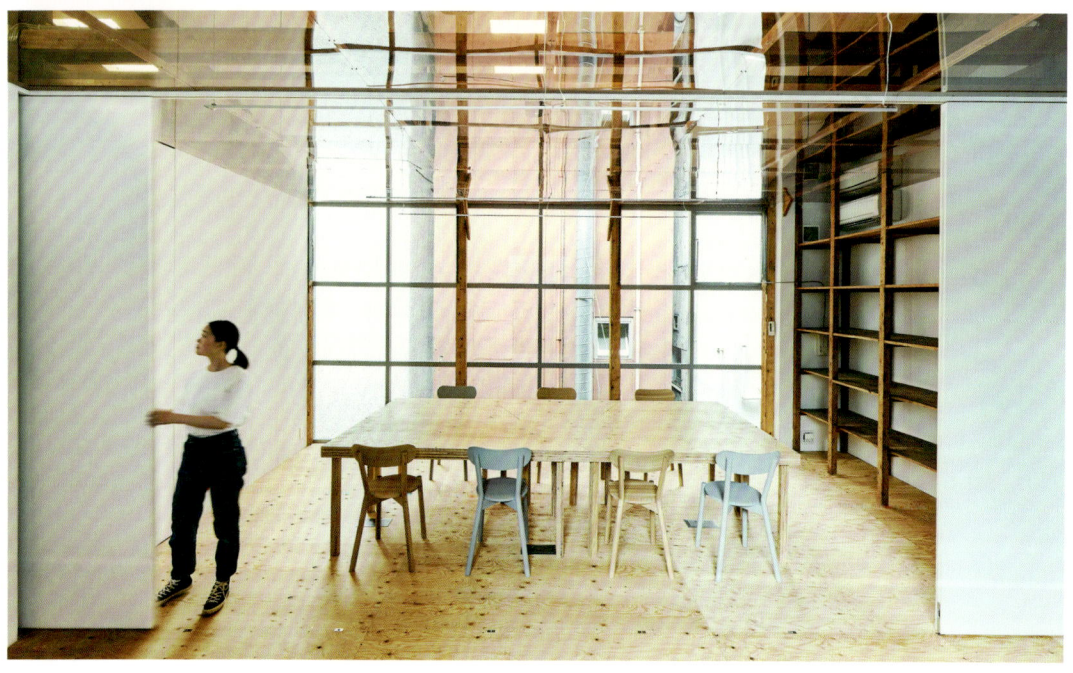

Poster Design

This is the corporate advertisement of Shizuoka Shimbun. It was posted in March 2022 to reflect the wars taking place around the world. Noticing that there is a character "爭 (fight)" in the name "靜冈 (Shizuoka)," the designers created an advertisement that triggered people to think about peace.

CD   Yoshimitsu Sawamoto
AD   Arata Kubota
D   Arata Kubota, Yoh Kitanaka
CW   Hirokazu Ueda
CL   Shizuoka Shinbun

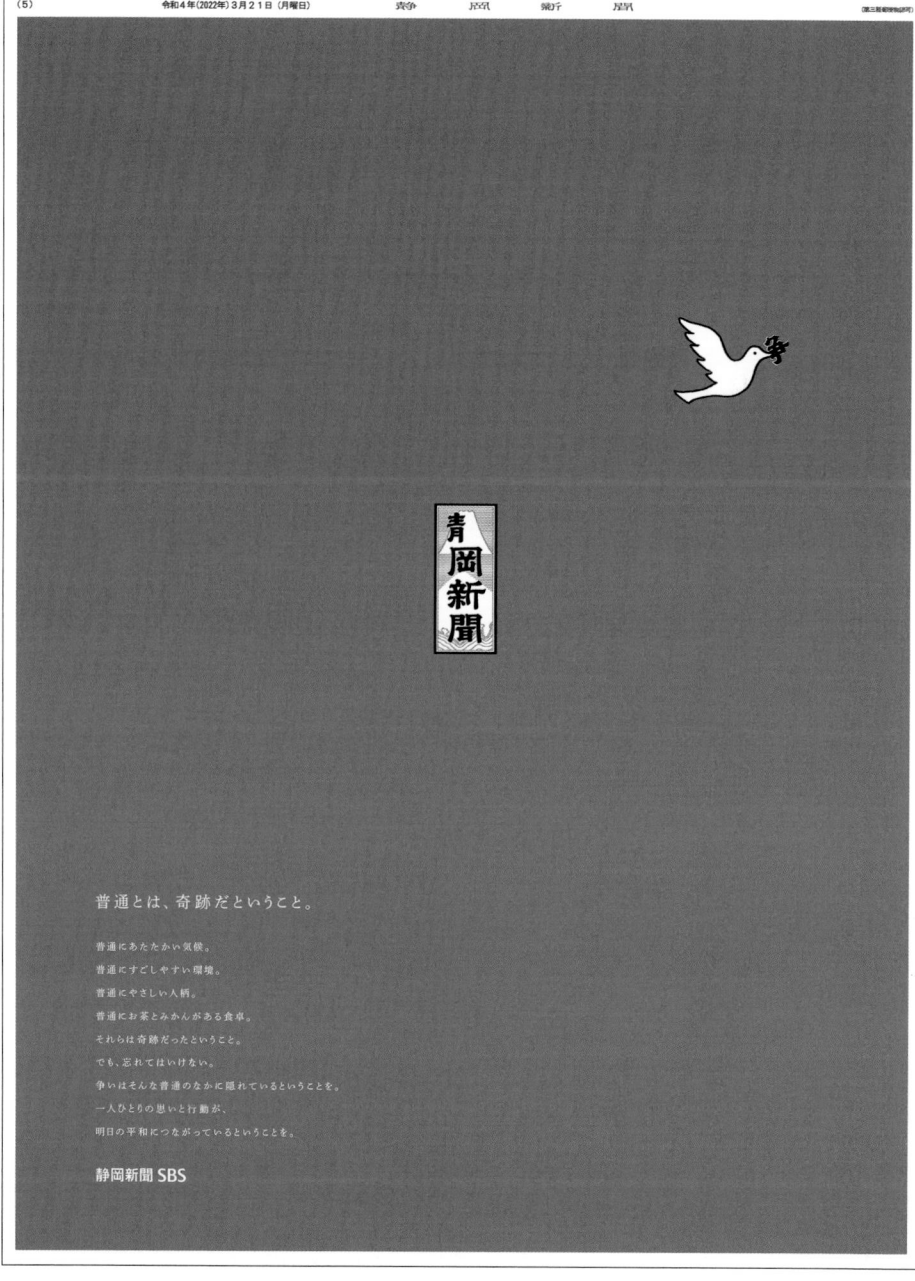

This is the key visual for the Japan Graphic Design Exhibition—I'M POSSIBLE. The designer wanted to express the contradictory relationship between the possible and the impossible. The form is in the shape of "可 (possible)," and the unbalanced typography of "I'M POSSIBLE" as well as the small squares represent the entrance to the possibilities. In addition, the designer created visual anxiety to present the contradiction of possible and impossible by combining blue and orange halation colors and low-resolution processing.

DA   Sitoh inc.
D   Motoi Shito
CL   At Design

I' M POSSIBLE

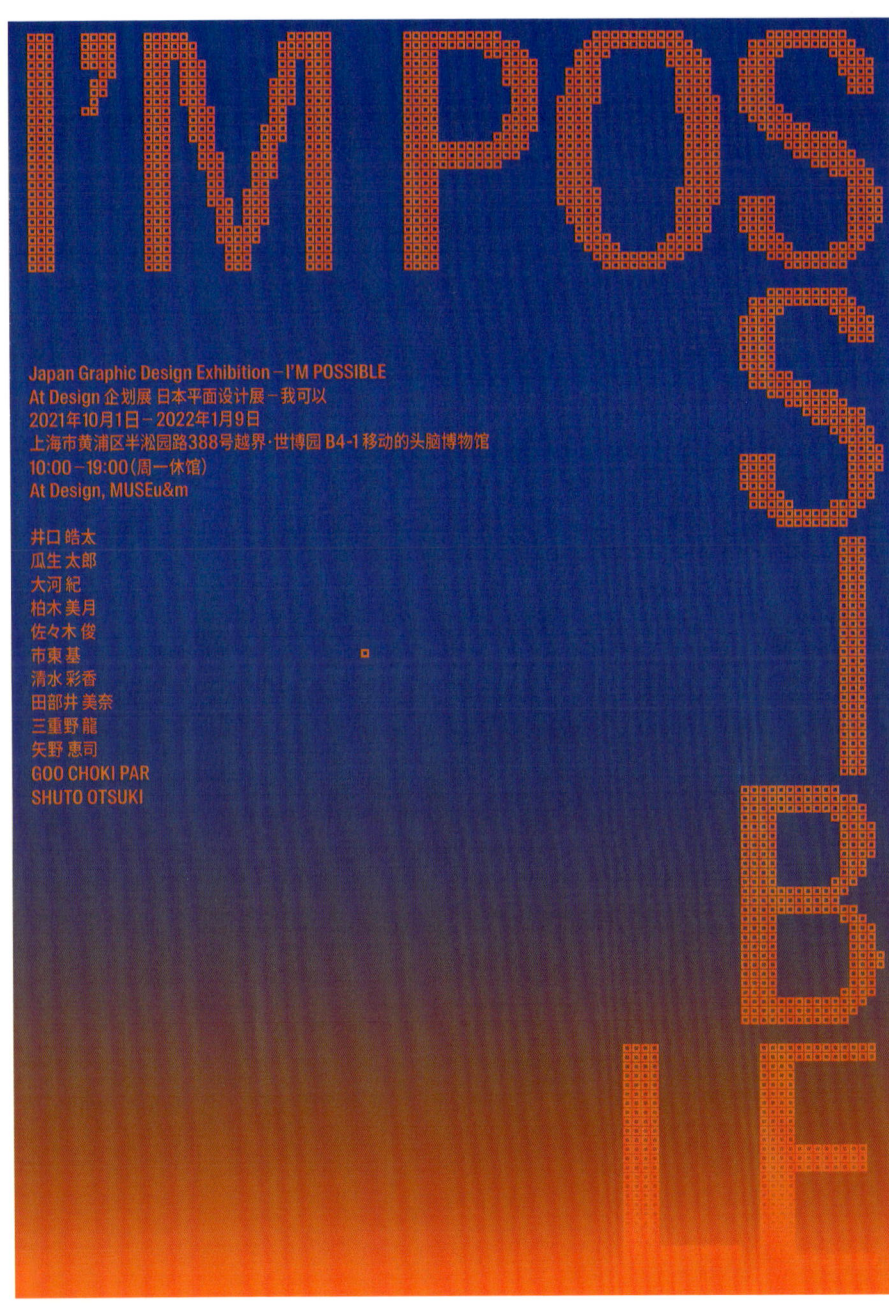

This is a corporate advertisement for Shizuoka Shimbun.
When the newspaper is folded, it becomes a square
and the Chinese characters "人生 (life)" emerge. The
illustration on paper means that life has its ups and
downs like mountains and valleys.

CD   Yoshimitsu Sawamoto
AD   Arata Kubota
D   Arata Kubota, Yoh Kitanaka
IL   Keiji Yano
CL   Shizuoka shinbun

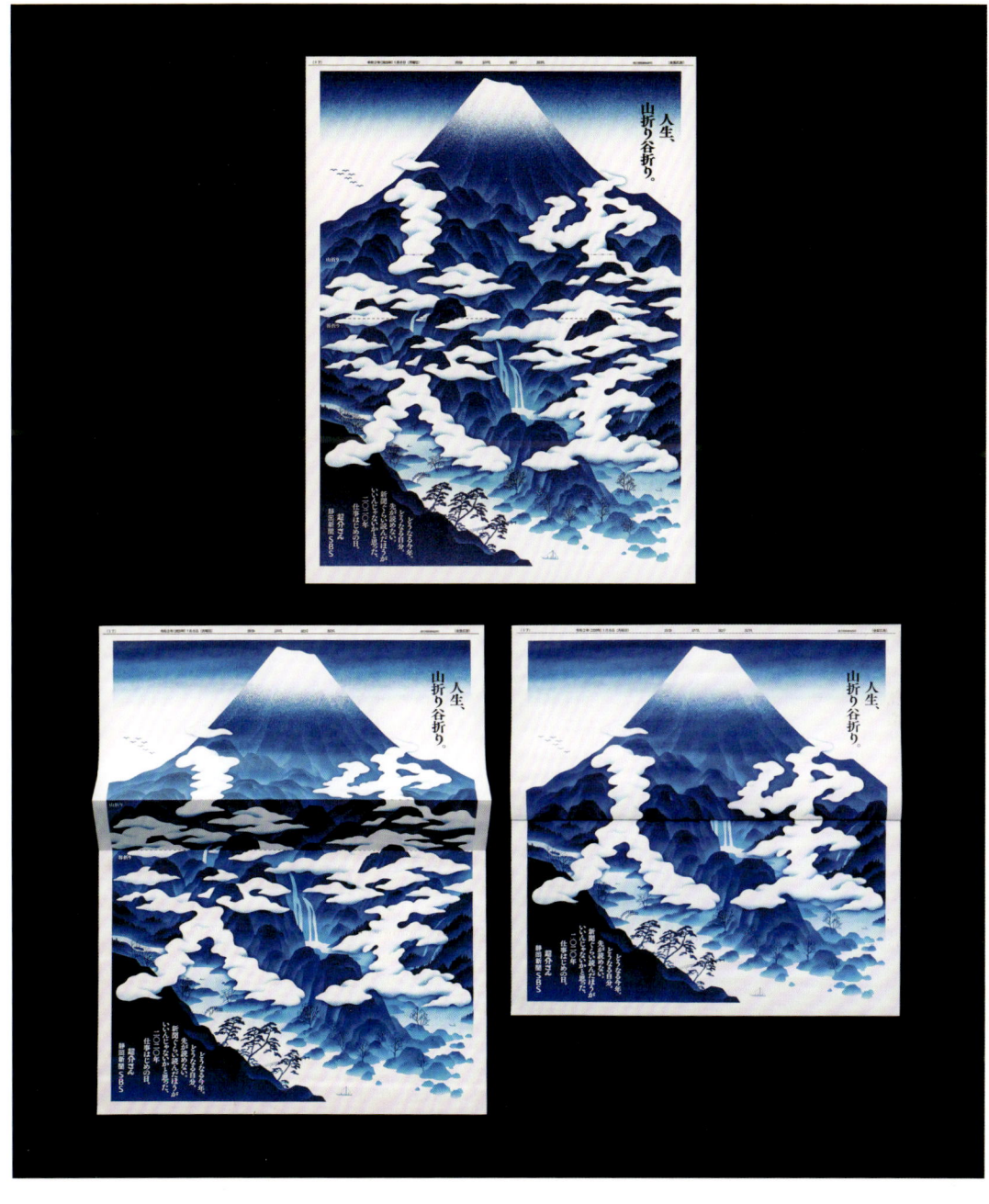

Life Has Its Ups and Downs

This is a poster created by employees of the advertising agency Nakatika using the new office 101 BASE and the magnet of the original font. The designers thought about the slogan for the new office and used scenes in the office to take photos that reflect the slogans' ideas.

D   Moe Furuya
PH   MEGUMI
CL   Nakachika Co., Ltd.

101 BASE Poster

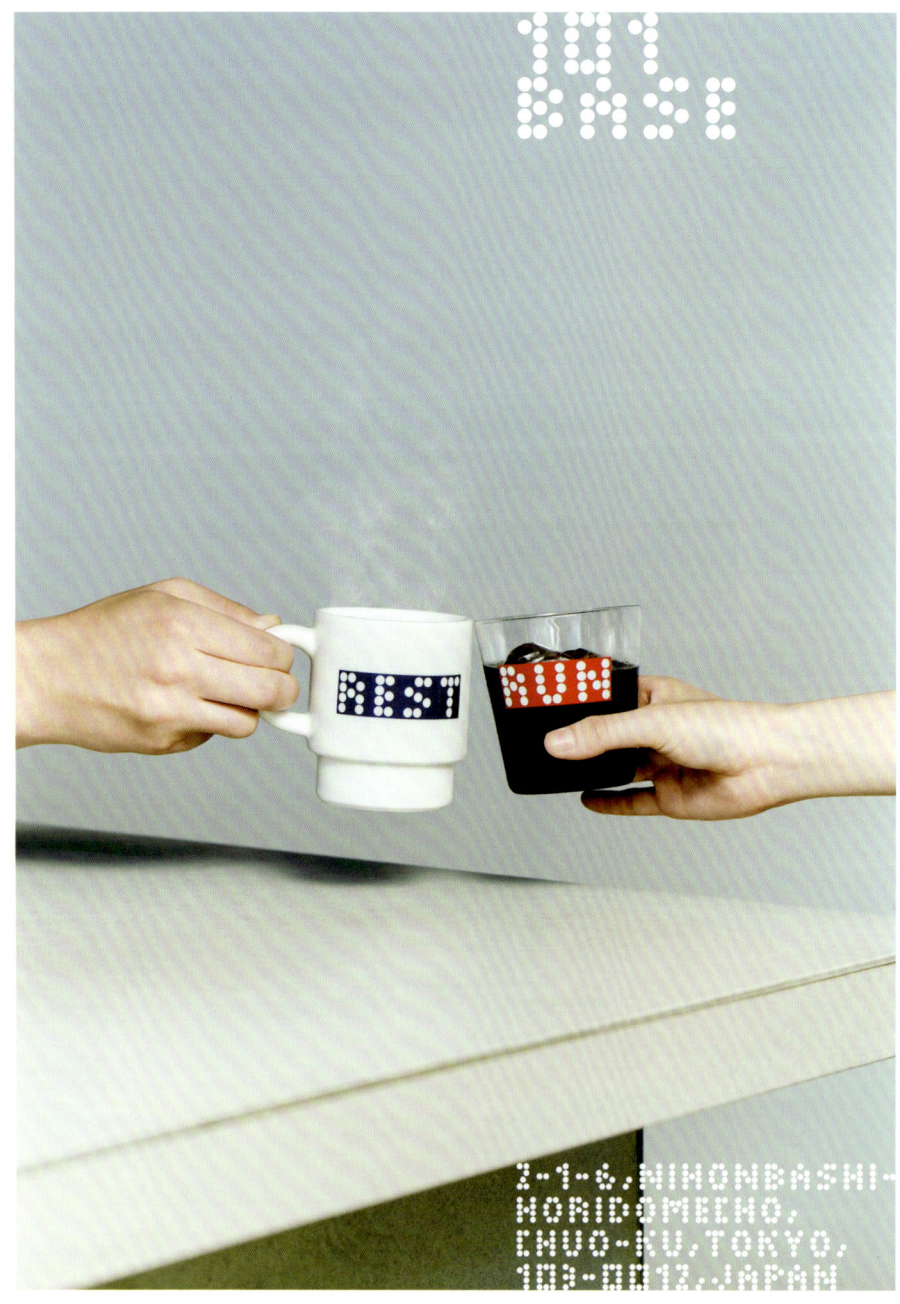

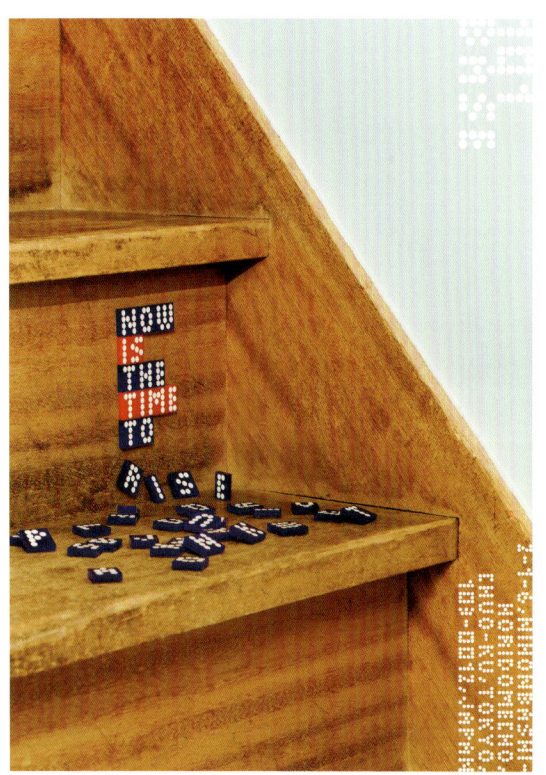

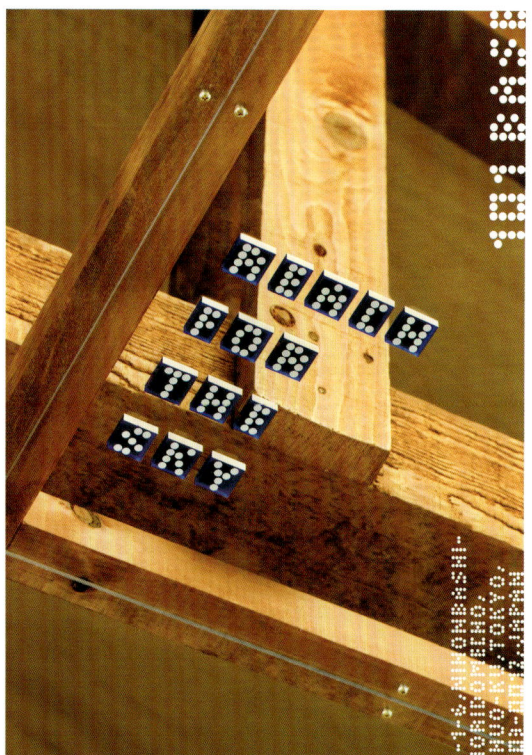

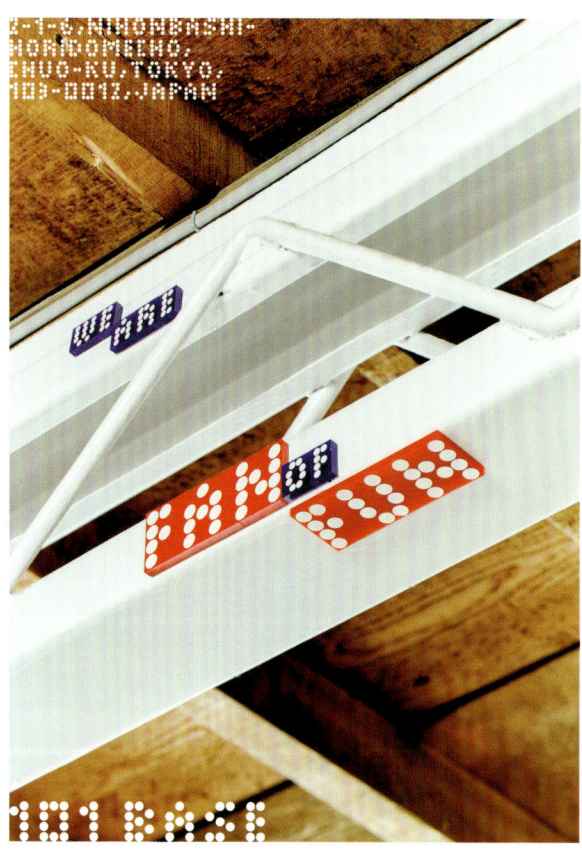

This is a series of seasonal posters for PARCO, made in collaboration with photographer Go Itami. It is a challenge to deconstruct the conventional commercial poster formula with three simple elements: photographs, the PARCO logo, and the name of the season. Multiple B-size white rectangles (which look like posters within posters) are stacked on top of each other within B1 vertical and B3 horizontal paper. Each rectangle contains a photo without cropping and the PARCO logo is placed in the poster within a poster.

AD	Mariko Okazaki
D	Mariko Okazaki
PH	Go Itami
PR	RCKT/Rocket Company*
CL	PARCO

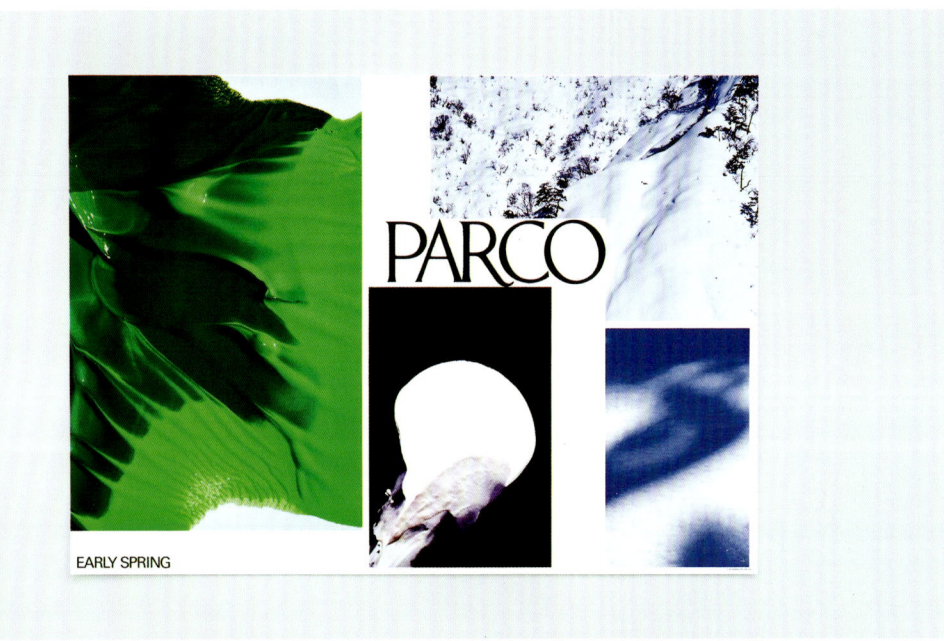

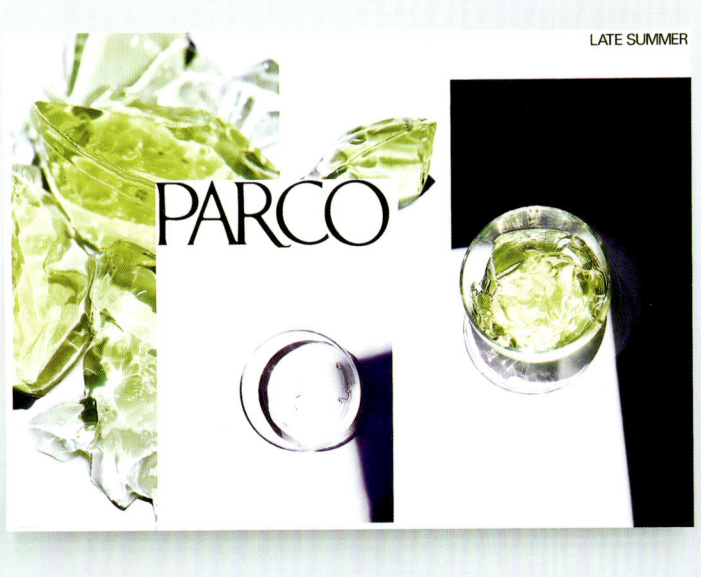

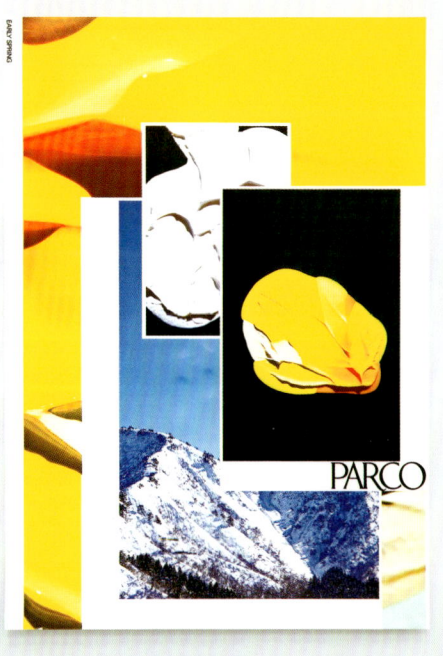

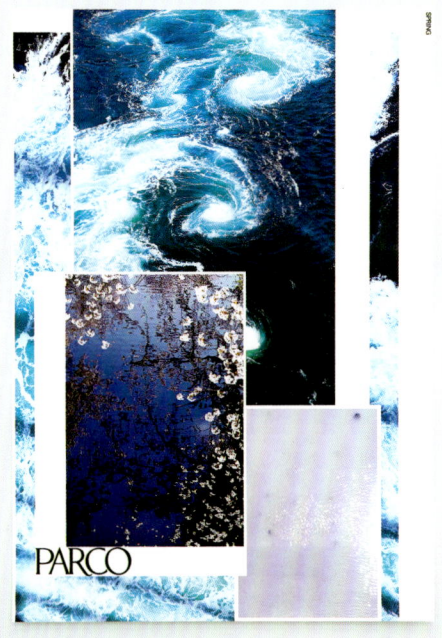

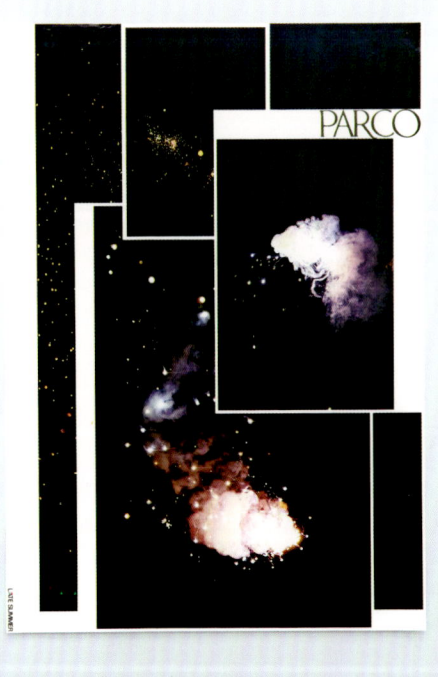

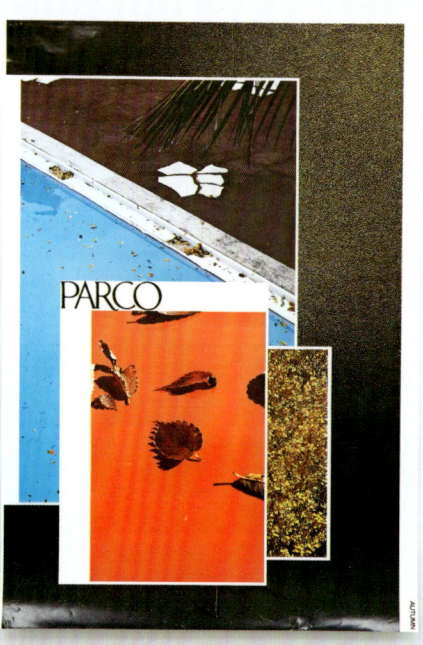

As people casually spend their days, they're overcome by the sudden craving to eat. These posters for an udon restaurant visualize people's unexpected craving for a feast.

DA   OUWN
D   Atsushi Ishiguro
CL   People and Thought

BUZENBOH

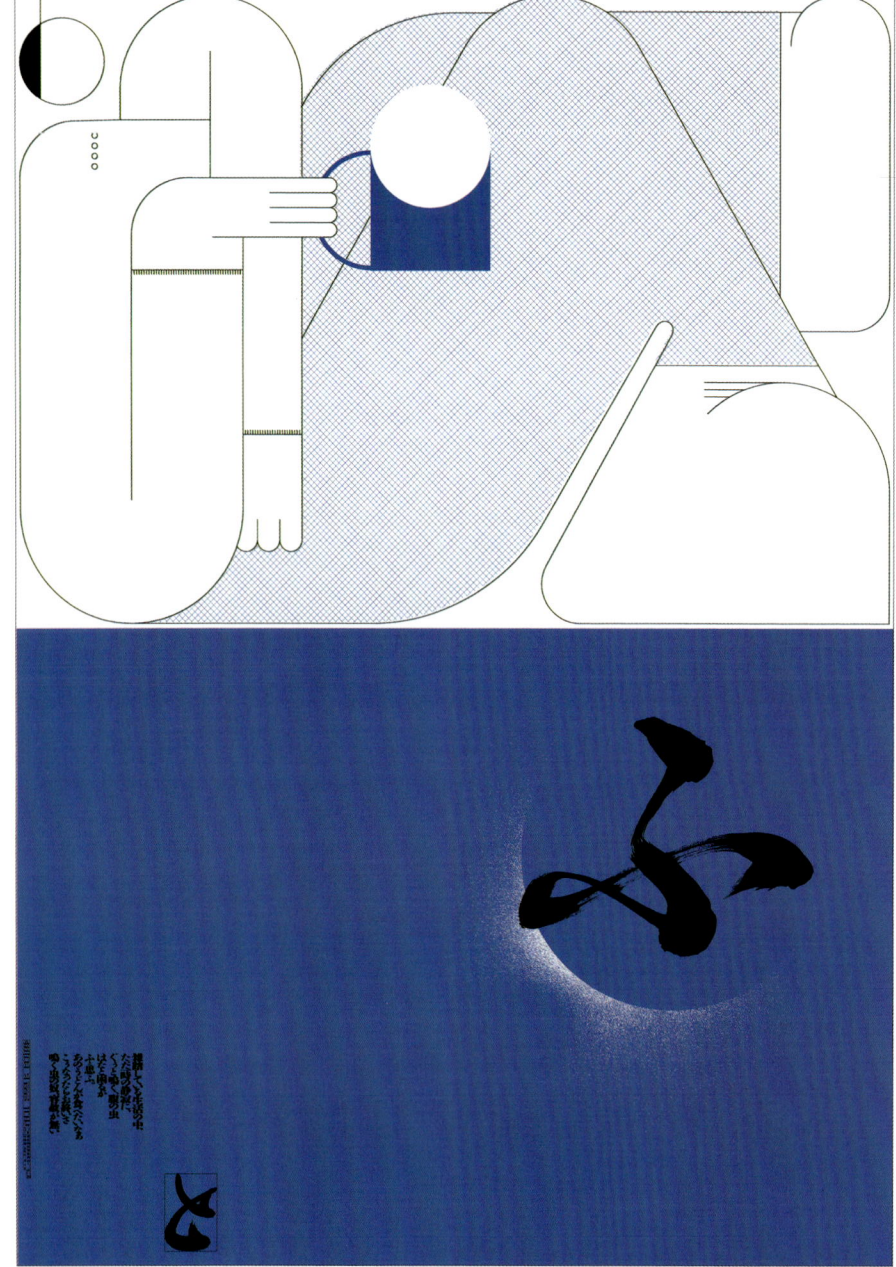

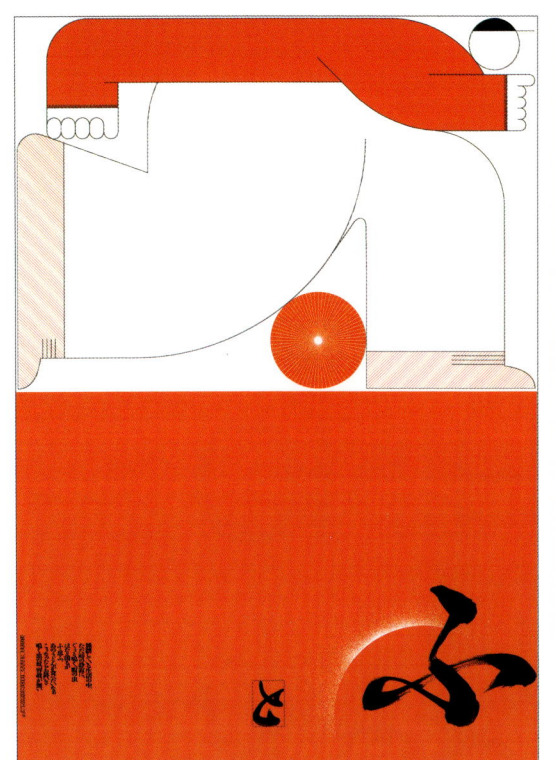

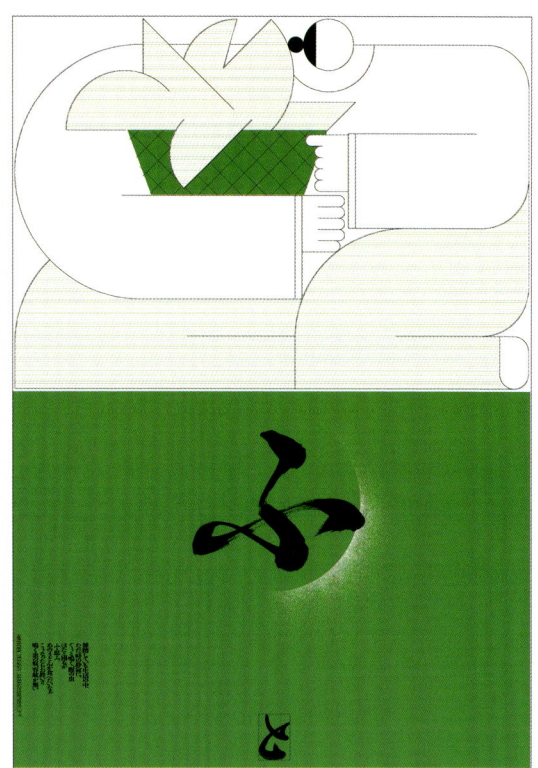

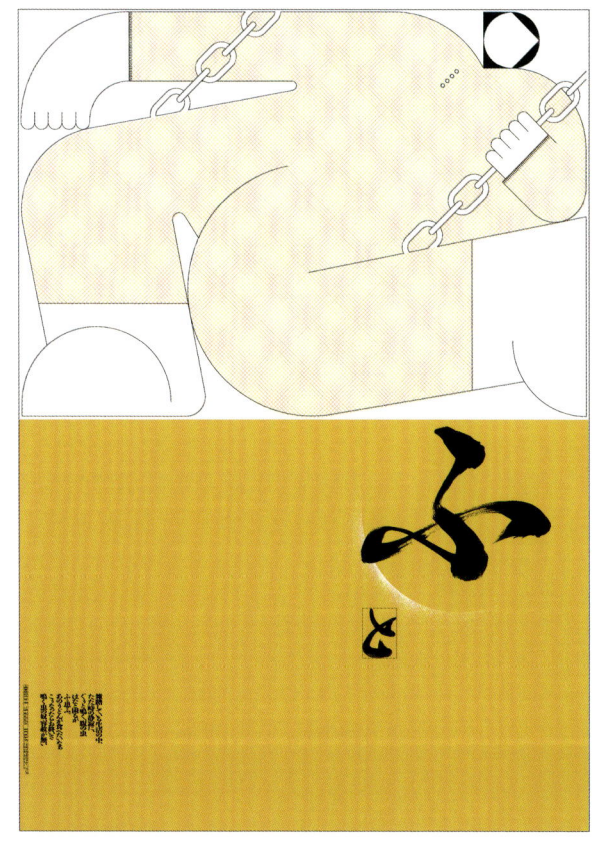

This is a visual for Musashino Art University. The composition of abstract color composition is inspired by the theme of the eye. The eye on the poster symbolizes the desire to absorb things voraciously. It looks like a circle that is about to protrude out of the screen. Each of the three patterns is a combination of highly saturated special colors and silver color.

D   Mina Tabei
CL   Musashino Art University

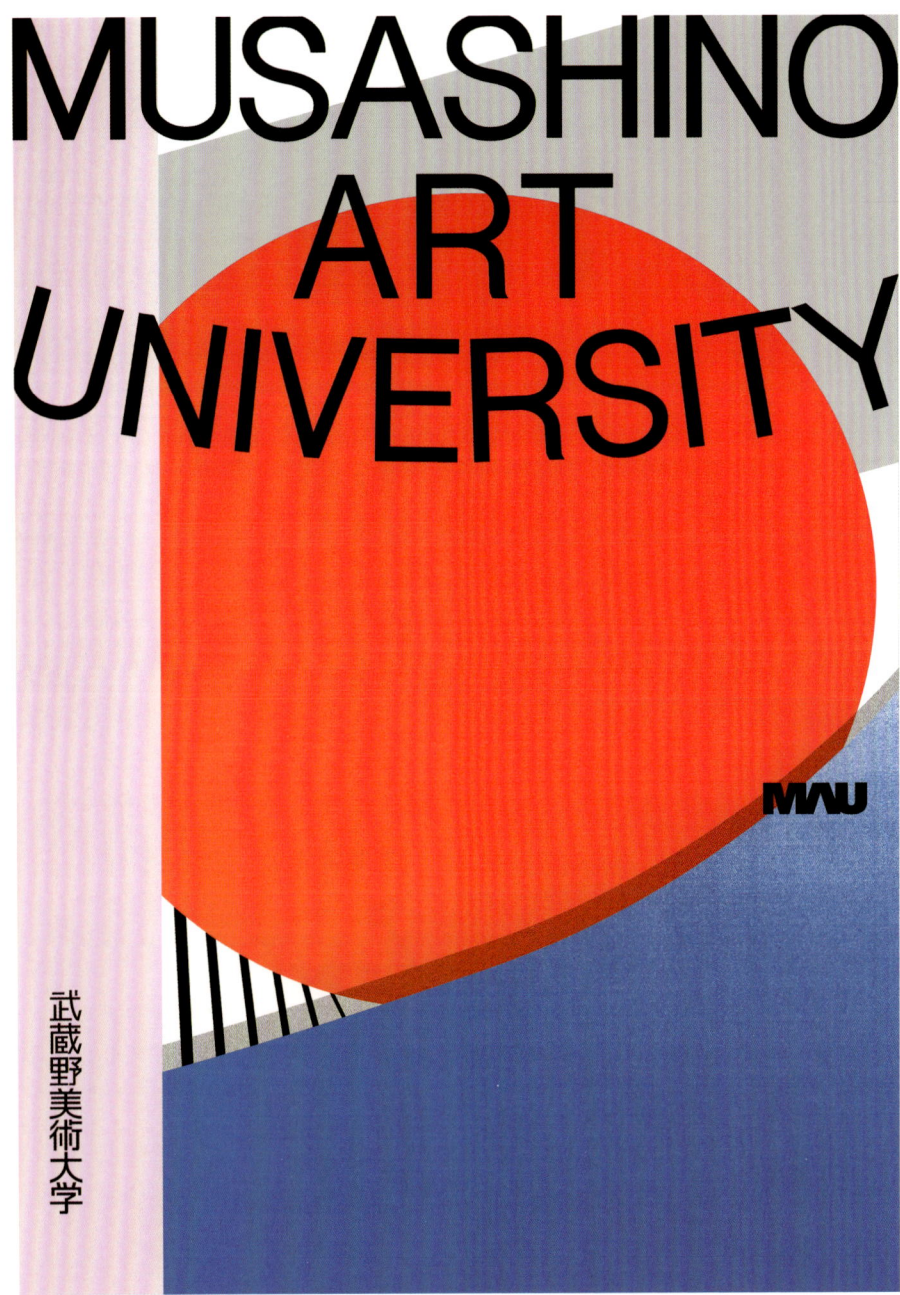

武蔵野美術大学

Musashino Art University 2019

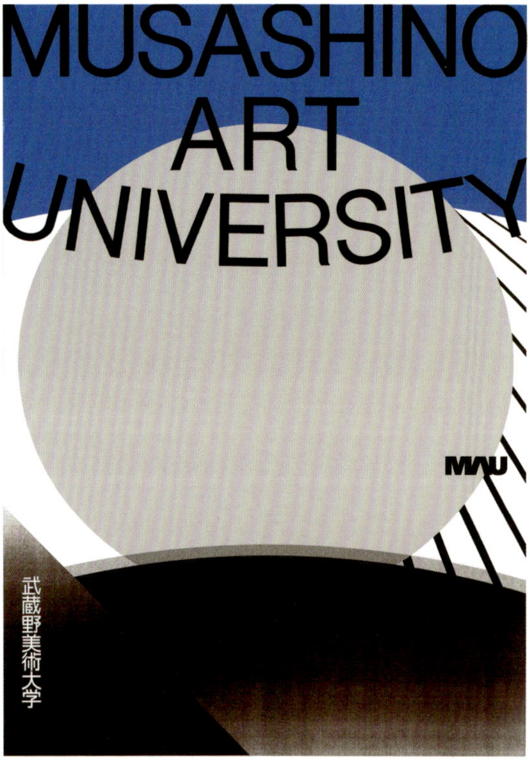
MUSASHINO
ART
UNIVERSITY
MAU
武蔵野美術大学

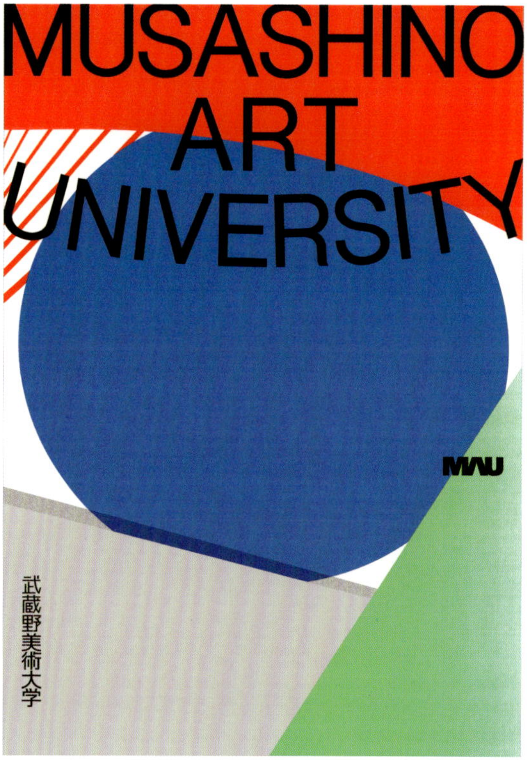
MUSASHINO
ART
UNIVERSITY
MAU
武蔵野美術大学

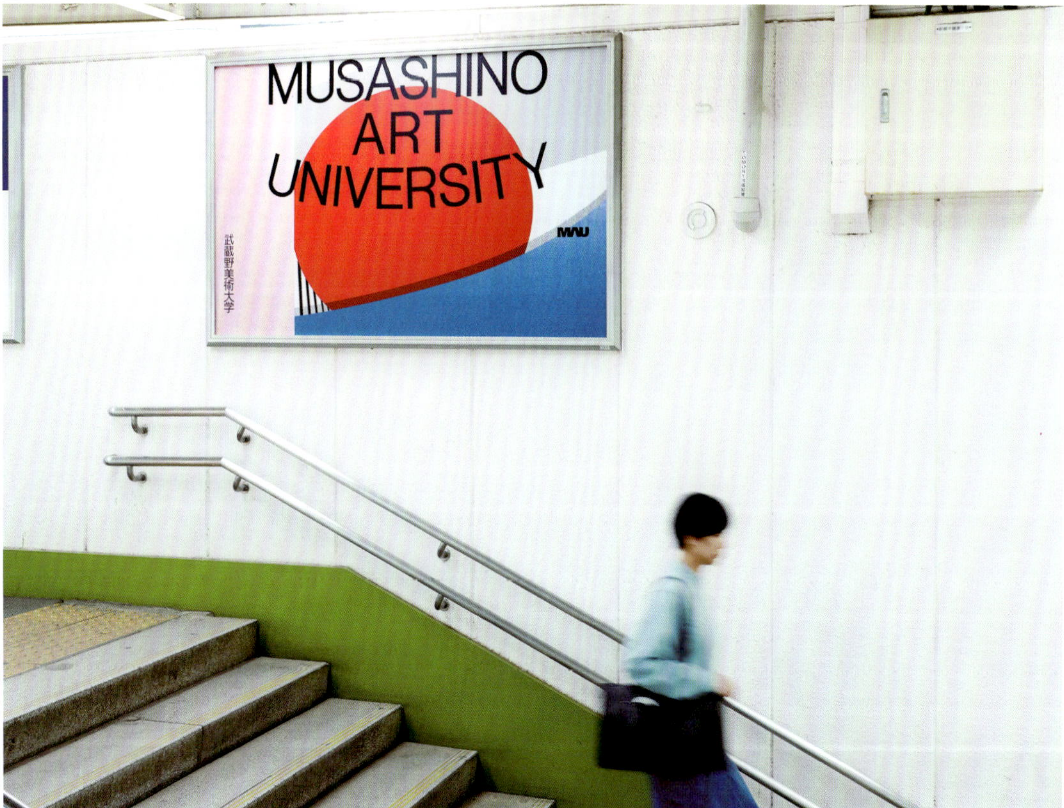
MUSASHINO
ART
UNIVERSITY
MAU
武蔵野美術大学

This is a visual for Musashino Art University. It combines paper, mirrors, ubiquitous objects, and light and shadow with photographic expression. The graphics were created along with the theme of circle and water, square and wind, as well as triangle and flame.

D   Mina Tabei
CL   Musashino Art University

Musashino Art University 2020

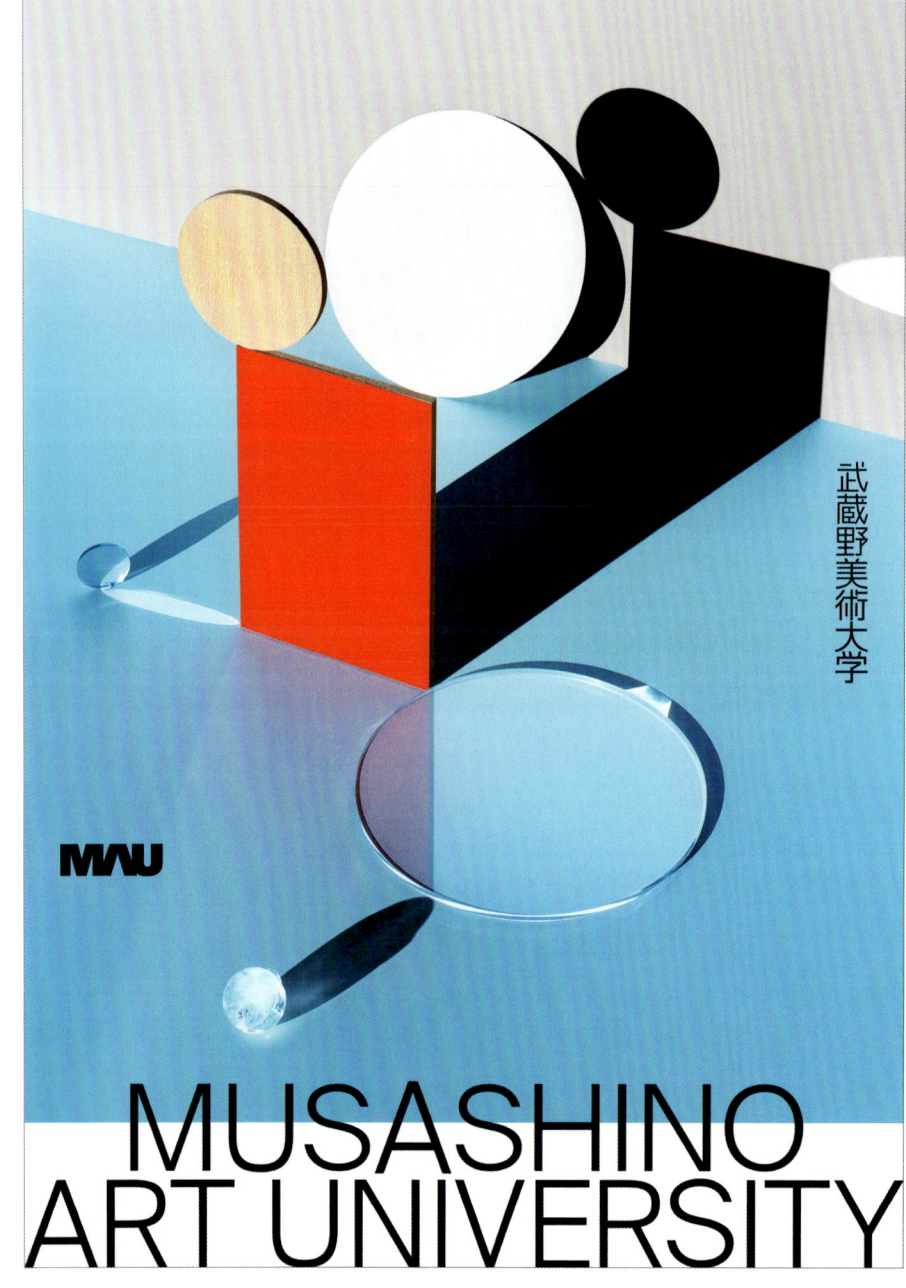

武蔵野美術大学

MUSASHINO
ART UNIVERSITY

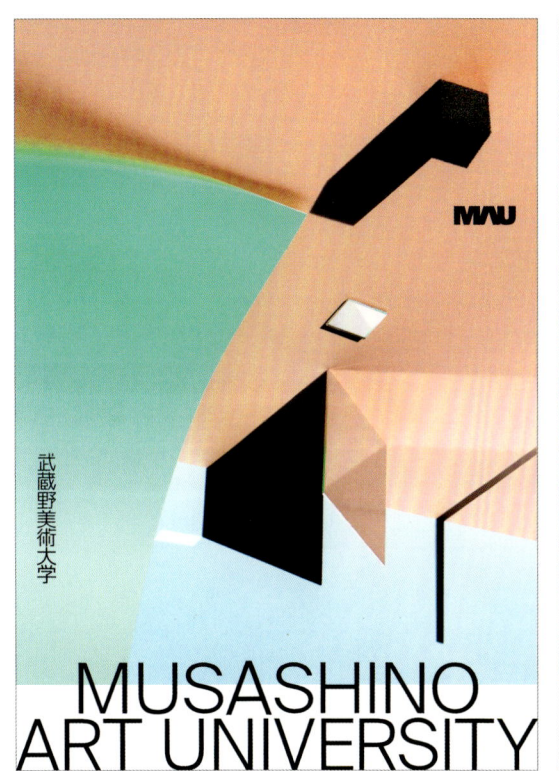

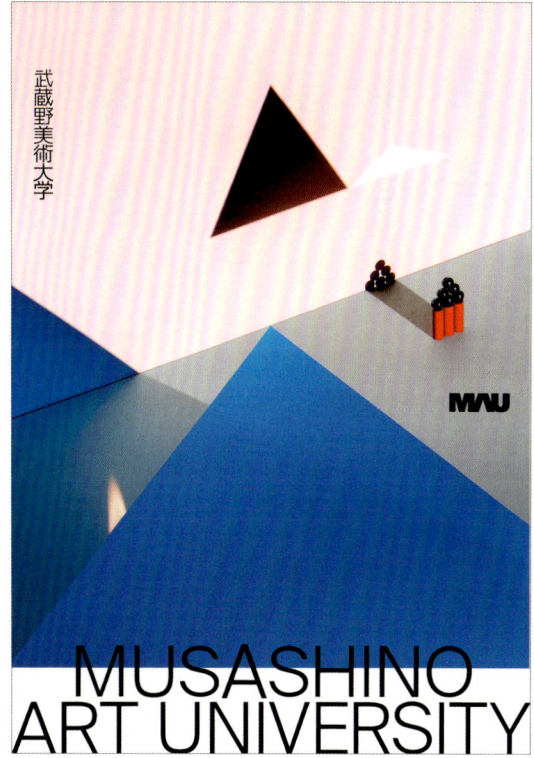

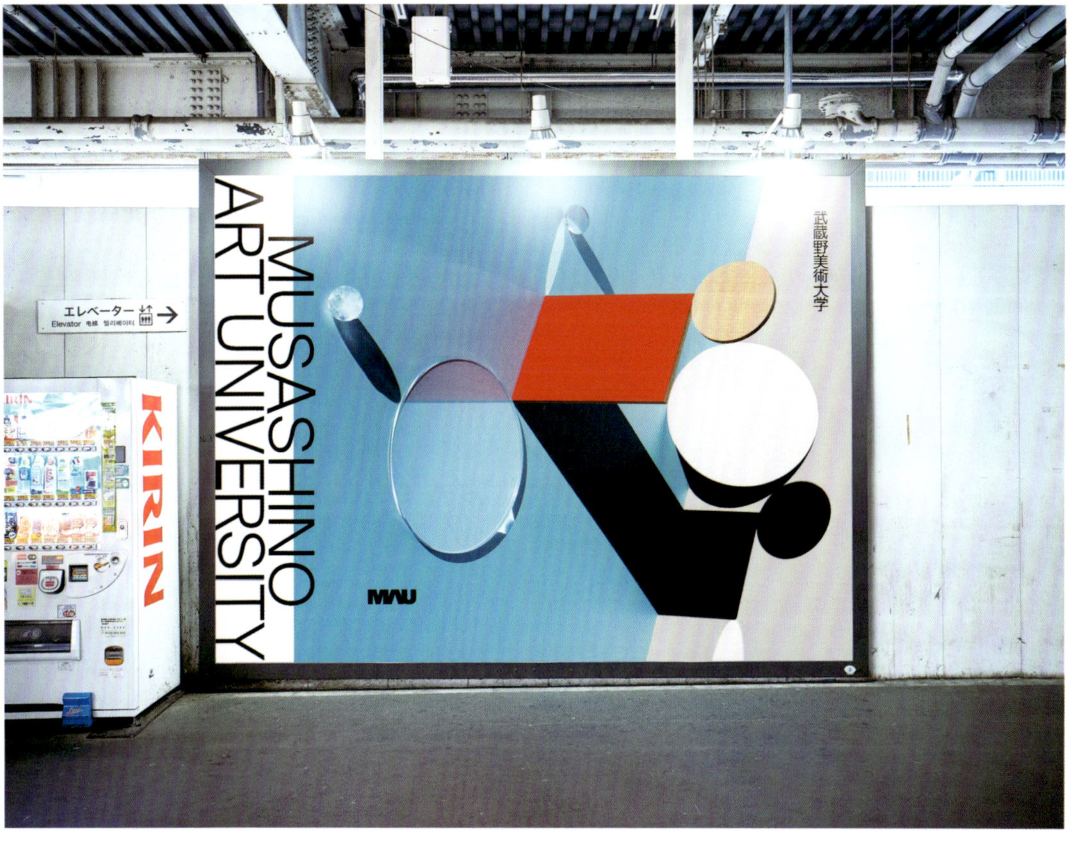

This is a visual for Musashino Art University. This visual, which looks like an actual room, is a one-tenth size model. The designer put the model on colored surface paper and took several test shots with an iPhone to decide on the screen composition. The creation was finished with the help of the photographer. They looked through the viewfinder and found out the ideal spot and content for shooting. The visual of the single poster was extended into five different ones to put on the magazine advertisements.

D   Mina Tabei
CL   Musashino Art University

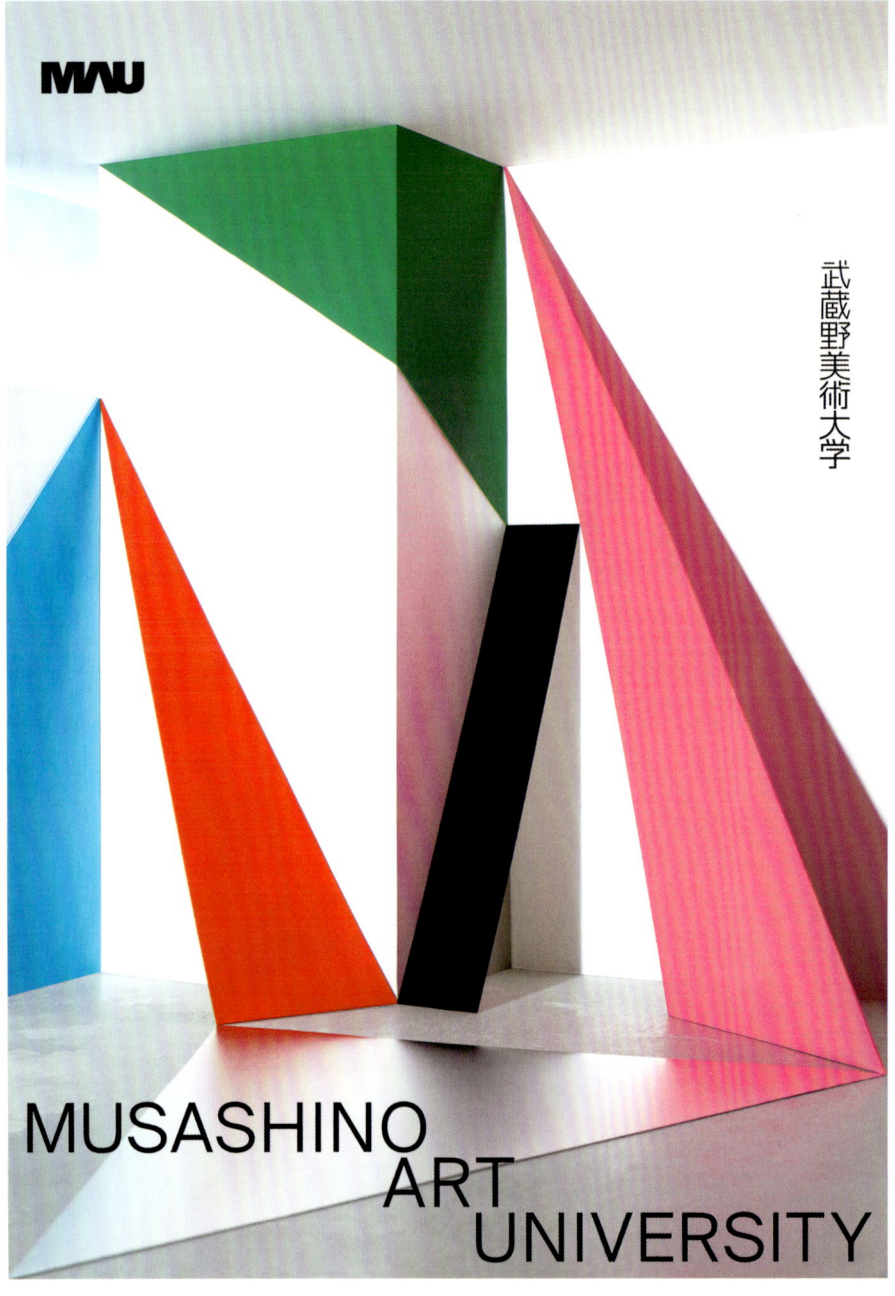

MUSASHINO ART UNIVERSITY

武蔵野美術大学

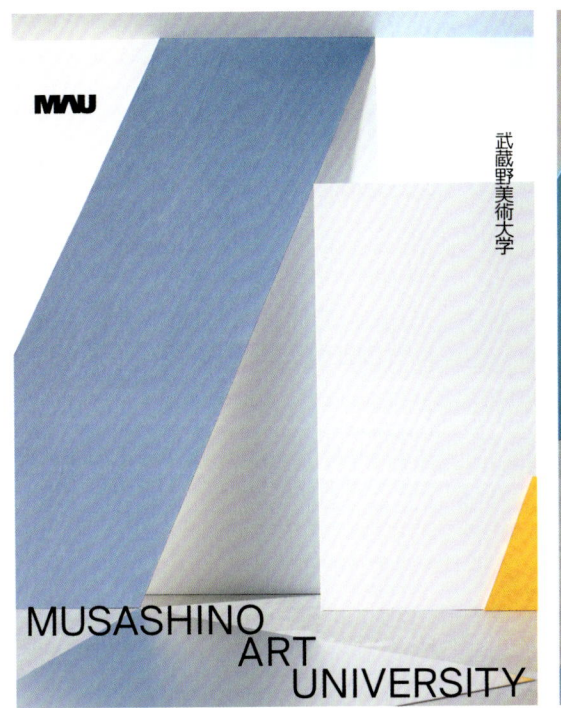

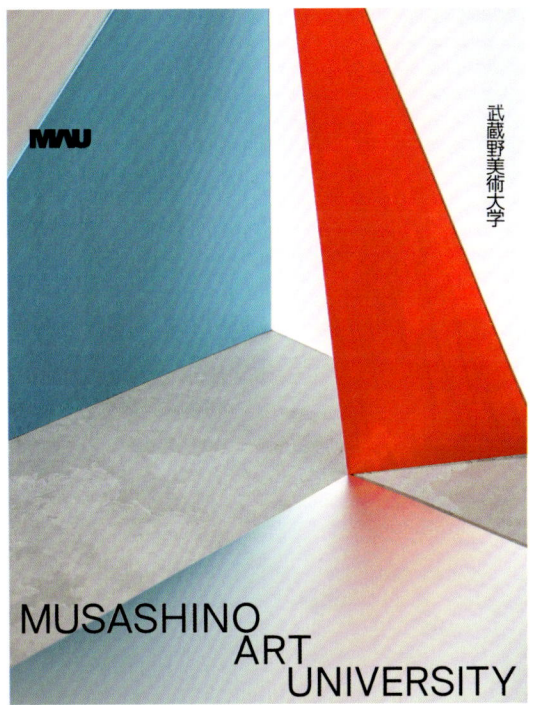

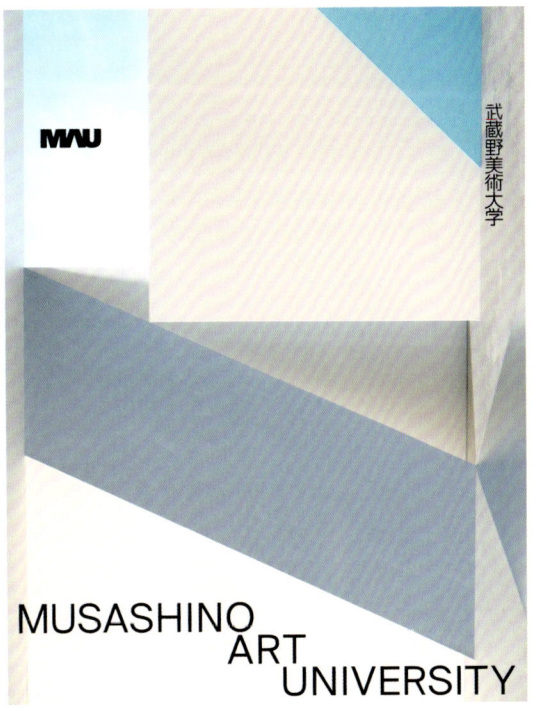

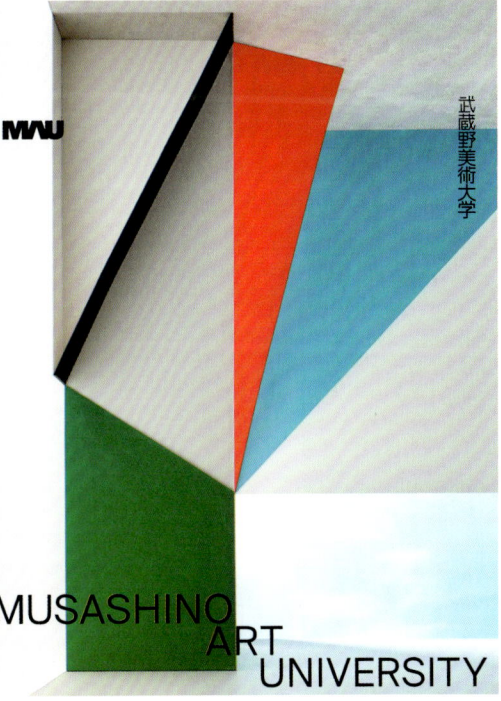

This is a poster made for the JAGDA New Designer Award. Established in 1978, the Japan Graphic Designers Association (JAGDA) is one of Asia's largest design organizations with its current membership of 3,000 designers. JAGDA undertakes a variety of activities to enhance communication. The poster was developed with iconic graphics with the motif of K, a letter shared by the names of the three winners.

D   Arata Kubota
CL   Japan Graphic Design
Association Inc.

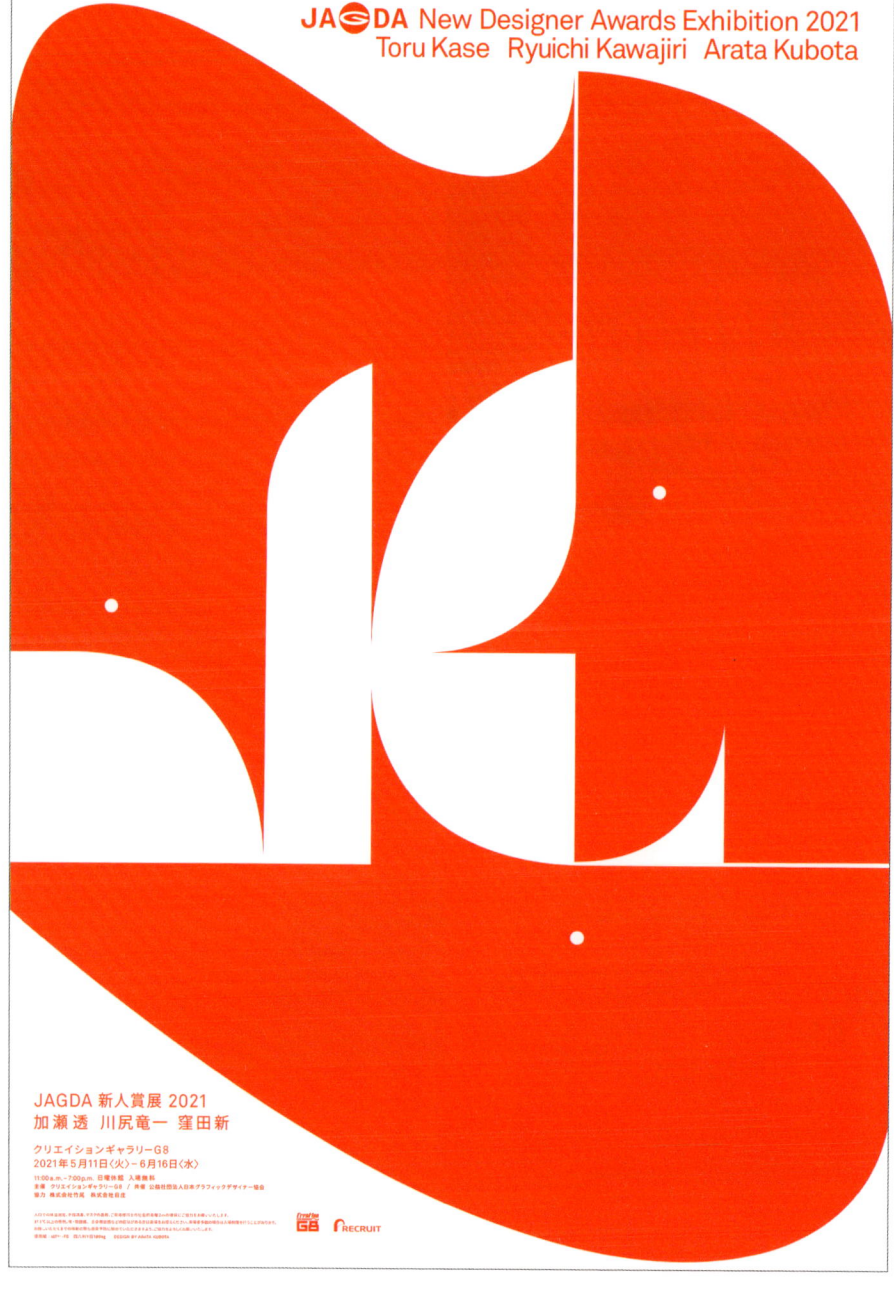

These are posters for a plant reuse brand. In the posters, the veins of plants depict the Chinese character "未來 (future)" and the philosophy of a brand that cares about the future of plants.

D   Arata Kubota
CL   Nijiiro Green

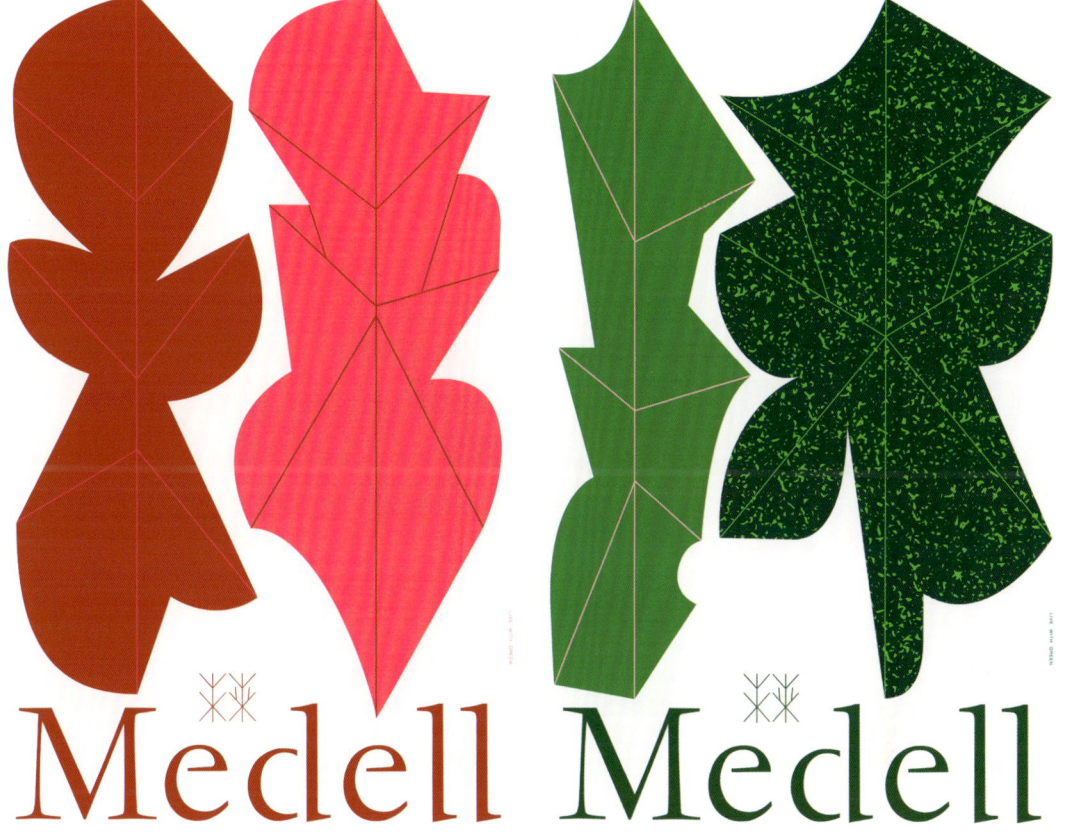

This is an advertisement recognizing the activities of the Gifu Mokuiku Association. The Gifu Mokuiku Association is an organization that communicates a wide range of information about trees, from the mountains to everyday tools. To show that tree knowledge grows around Gifu, Yu Inoue used a graphic of trees growing out of the word "岐阜 (Gifu)" as the main visual. It is designed for people to understand the location of the activities and what they do at a glance.

AD   Yu Inoue
D   Yu Inoue
CW   Ryosuke Irie
CL   Gifu Mokuiku Association

Gifu Mokuiku Association

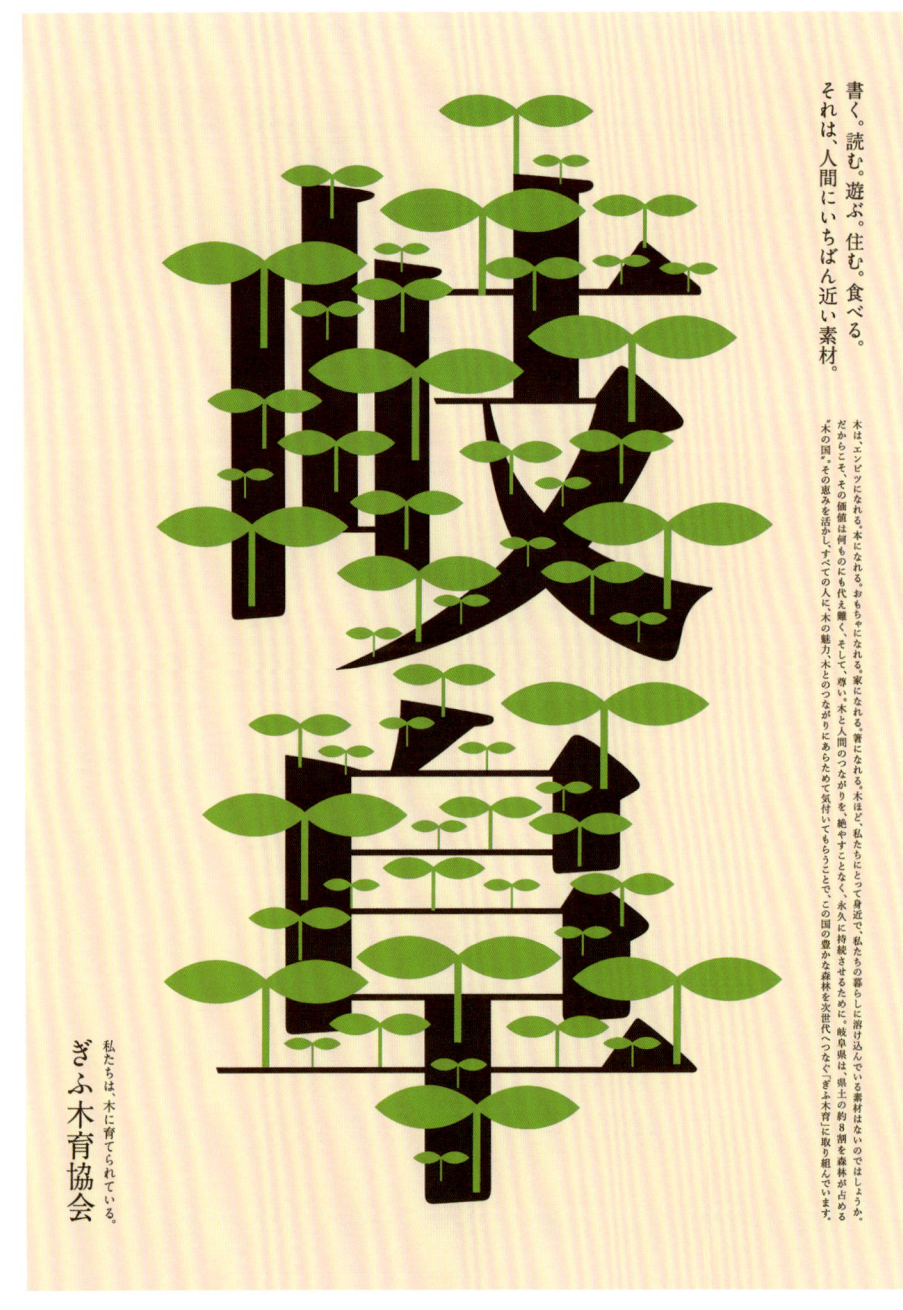

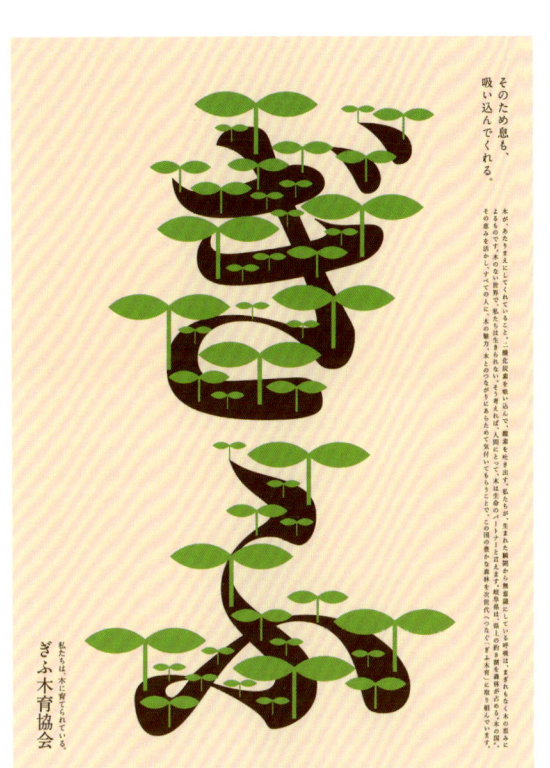

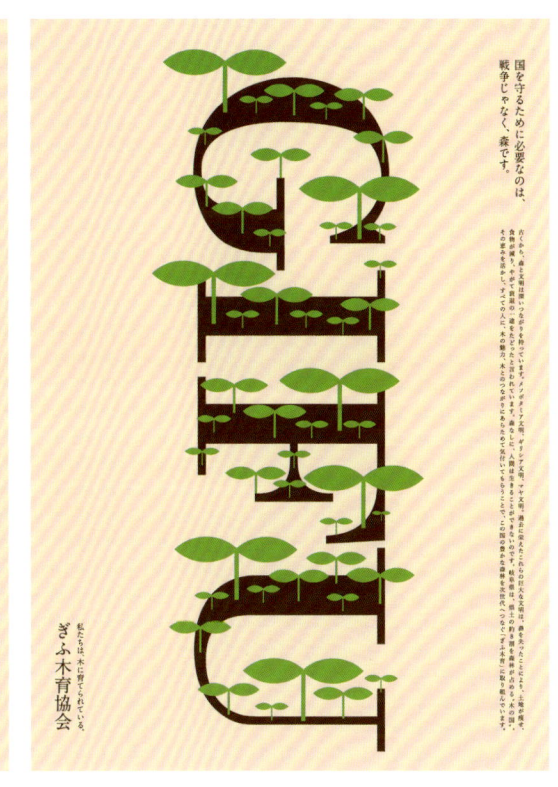

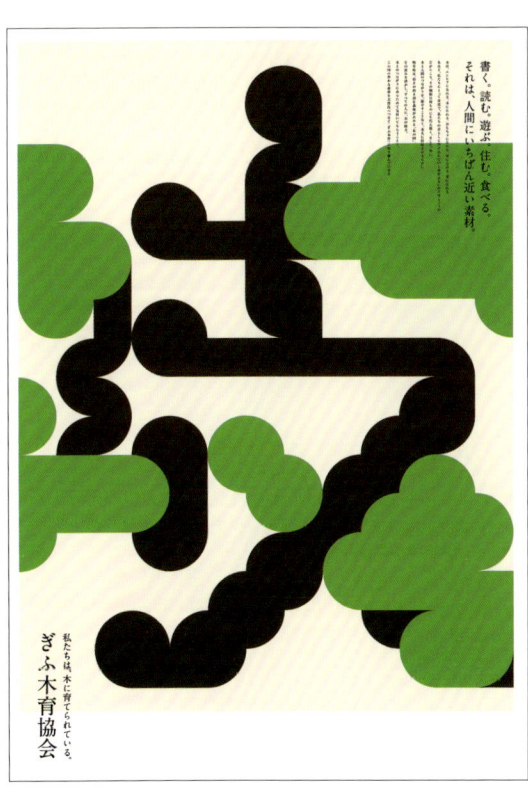

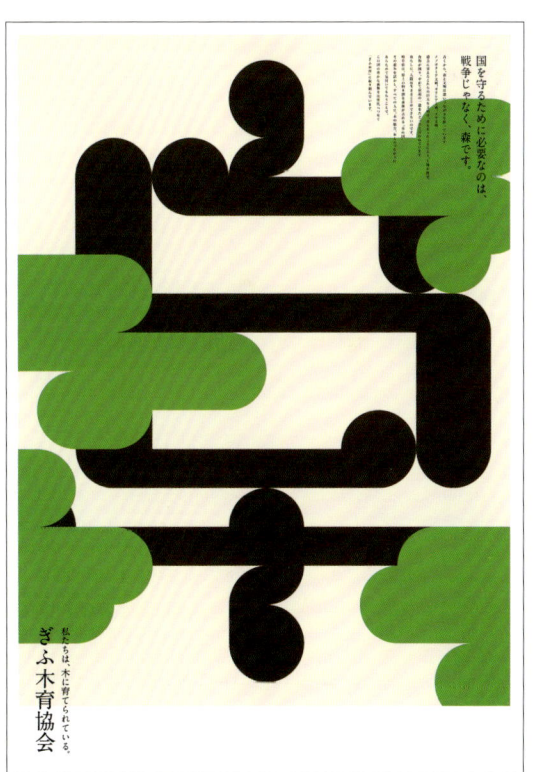

This is a graphic collateral for Dai Fujiwara, a Japanese
artist. He held his exhibition in 2021 in Chigasaki, Japan.

DA   SOAR NY
D   Masaki Hanahara
CL   Chigasaki City Museum of Art

Human Nature

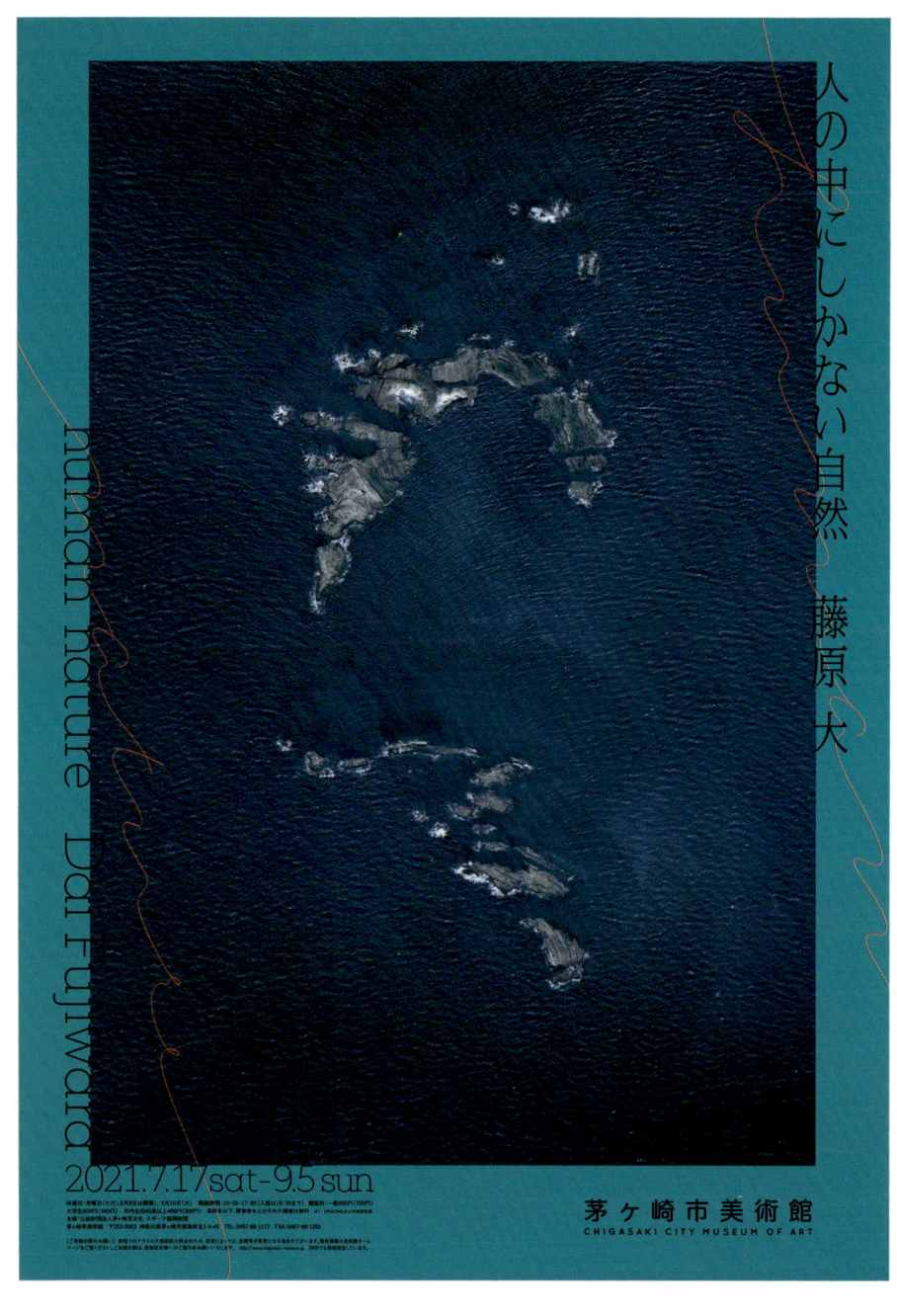

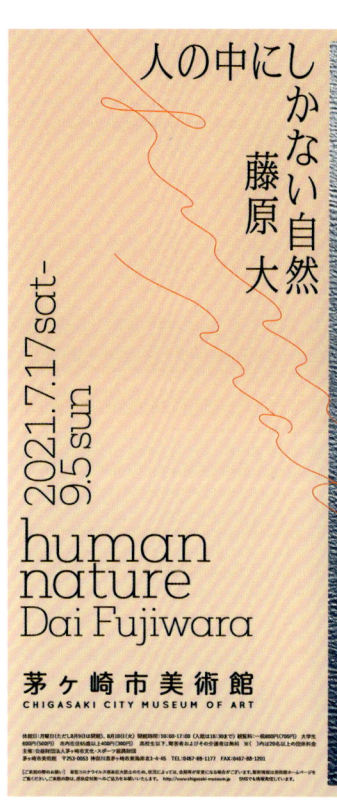
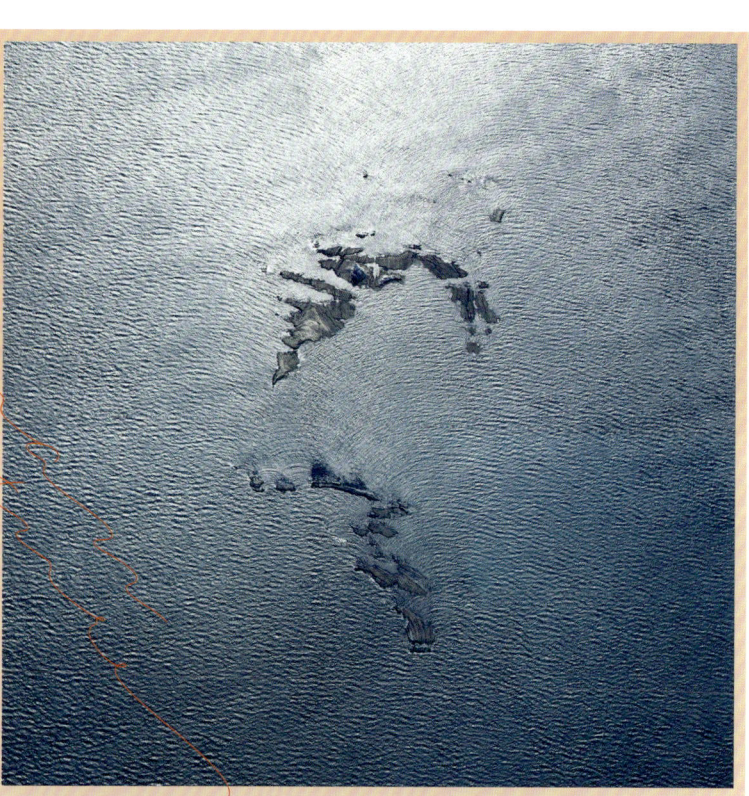

人の中にしかない自然
藤原 大

2021.7.17 sat-
9.5 sun

human
nature
Dai Fujiwara

茅ヶ崎市美術館
CHIGASAKI CITY MUSEUM OF ART

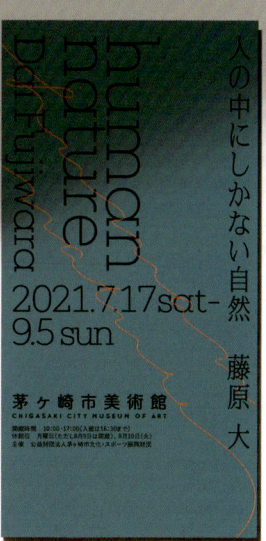
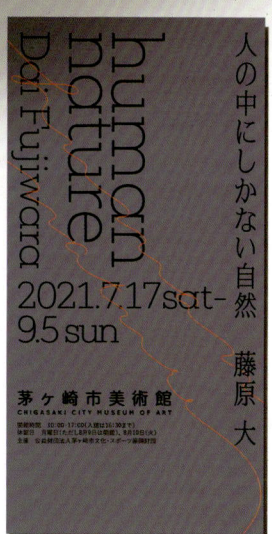
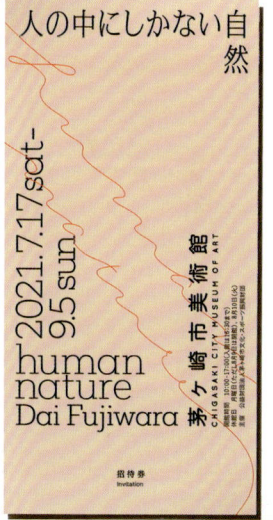

Syndicate was established in December 2021 as a studio and gallery by photographer Tomoya Fujii and illustrator noisy_eye.

The design was created to show only the information by taking advantage of the similarity of information between the reception and the exhibition. The gallery space is a white cube and Keiji Yano tried to create a curatorial mood that is unique to Syndicate, which deals with contemporary art and photography and is not found in other galleries. The ruled lines surrounding the address trace the shape of the gallery space.

AD   Keiji Yano
D   Keiji Yano
CL   Syndicate

Syndicate (Gallery Open)

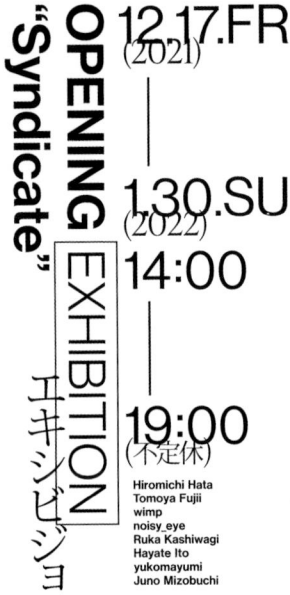

OPENING "Syndicate"

EXHIBITION エキシビジョン

12.17.FRI (2021)
—
1.30.SUN (2022)
14:00
—
19:00
(不定休)

Hiromichi Hata
Tomoya Fujii
wimp
noisy_eye
Ruka Kashiwagi
Hayate Ito
yukomayumi
Juno Mizobuchi

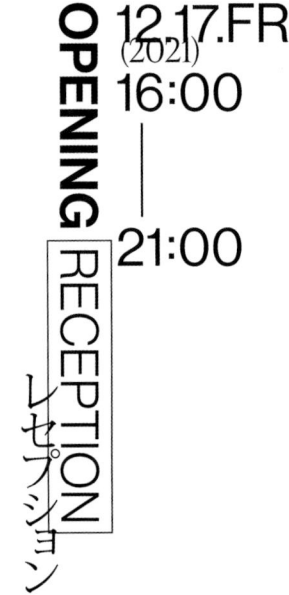

OPENING RECEPTION レセプション

12.17.FRI (2021)
16:00
—
21:00

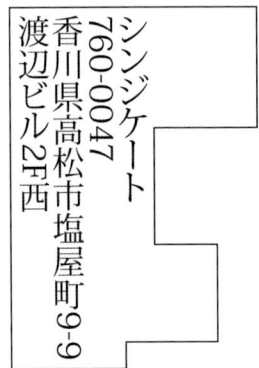

シンジケート
760-0047
香川県高松市塩屋町9-9
渡辺ビル2F西

https://syndicate-tak.com

2021年12月、Syndicateは写真家Tomoya Fujii、イラストレーターnoisy_eyeのスタジオ兼ギャラリーとして設立されました。
国内外を問わず、現代写真、ペインティングなど平面作品を軸に、企画展の開催／作品集の販売を行います。
この度オープニングに際し、設立者及び、交流のあるアーティスト8名によるグループ展を開催いたします。

OPENING EXHIBITION "Syndicate" エキシビジョン

12.17.FRI (2021)
—
1.30.SUN (2022)
14:00
—
19:00 (不定休)

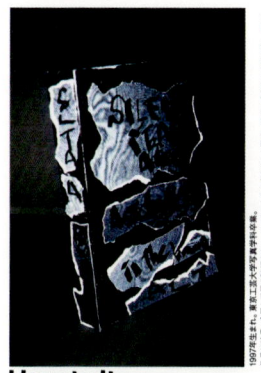

Hiromichi Hata

1981年生まれ。
写真は私の中にあり、例えばやがての自分や世界中の楽しさという概念を更新させてくれるもの
だと思っている。作品として成立するイメージは話らこう描かったと思い撮影しているものの
ほとんどなど、行動や過ゆや瞬間ときが作品になることから…写真には、結論には至るのと思う。
ある意味表現しない、写真自体も本意、概要更新や像像を超えてくる事が大切だと思っている。
2019年 JAPAN PHOTO AWARD Patricia Karallis賞（Paper Journal 編集長）
2018年 TOKYO FRONTLINE PHOTOAWARD ファイナリスト
2018年 Athens Photo Festival ショートリスト
https://hiromichihata.com/

Juno Mizobuchi

1992年、香川県生まれ、京都精華大学デザイン学科イラスト専攻。作品を制作する、作品販売、アートワークの制作、装画の制作などを
行う。主に線画での制作により、既石の社会や言葉、概念の分化を表す作品を制作する。
Designed by Keiji Yano
https://junomb.blogspot.com/?m=1

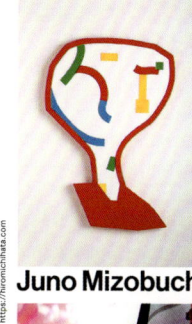

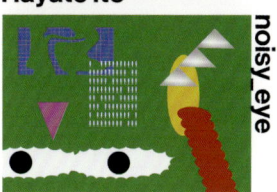

wimp

1992年生まれ。
wimpはアニメーションや寓話における、キャラクターの同一性や物語が伝聞される
たびに生じる変化に着目し、「ループ」や「亡霊」をテーマに制作している。ペイントを
主に立体やビデオなど様々な表現方法を扱う。
2019 ART START UP 100 リワード受賞
2018 メトロ文化財団賞受賞
2017 第16回グラフィック「1_WALL」ファイナリスト
https://www.wimp423.org/

Tomoya Fujii

1984年 香川県生まれ。ヘリット・リートフェルト・アカデミー写真科中退。
イメージ、物質、記憶との関係性を起点に、制作過程や様々なデバイス、
メディア遠通させることで、再構築を行い、写真を生成している。主な展
示として「NEW VISIONS #03」（G/P gallery Shinonome）、隈同 もしく
はその四子（Basement GINZA）、KYOTOGRAPHIE KG+ 2021 特別展
「JAPAN PHOTO AWARD + INTUITION」など。
2021年 JAPAN PHOTO AWARD Charlotte Cotton賞（キュレーター／
ライター）、Xiaopeng Yuan賞（写真家／Samepaper ファウンダー）
2017年 TOKYO FRONTLINE PHOTOAWARD ファイナリスト
2016年 TOKYO FRONTLINE PHOTOAWARD ファイナリスト
https://tomoyafujii.com

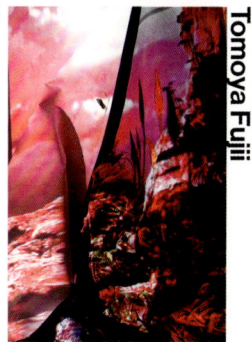

Hayate Ito

1997年生まれ。東京工芸大学写真学科卒業。
作品集制作、自己と世界の認識やコードの不之さを扱った作品や壁面などの制作を行っている。
2020年 TOKYO FRONTLINE PHOTO AWARD 東ブブリ
2020年 アートタワーミトーキョーネグパ2020／ノネート
https://fractionmagazinejapan.asia/portfolio/Hayatelto.html

yukomayumi

1992年生まれ。多摩美術大学情報デザイン学科メディア芸術コース卒業。
2018年、渡独。2019年、日本にて活動を開始。
まなざしを通して、景色や風景、情景を結晶化している。
2019年 第21回 グラフィック「1_WALL」ファイナリスト
https://www.instagram.com/yukomayumi/

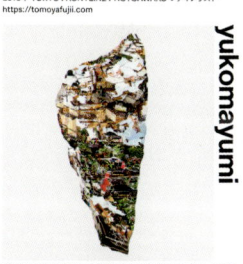

noisy_eye

1987年生まれ。
デンマーク、オランダ等への留学後、帰国。自身のイラストにインターネット上
で見つけた画像などを制作・発表している。
2020年 グラフィック 1_WALL 入選
2019年 グラフィック 1_WALL 都製奨励賞受賞
https://noisyeye.com/

Ruka Kashiwagi

1991年 東京都生まれ。
柏木は、この世の中にある様々な空無を、区別する事なく混ぜ合わせるような作業を
している。一度流失する様に変えたらその中間部で新たらしいな想を呼び生む。イメー
ジを見た判断を通して正規を得られた情報を解放される。
展示に「BYPASS」表参山展マロン」、KYOTOGRAPHIE KG＋2021 特別展「JAPAN
PHOTO AWARD EXHIBITION＋INTUITION」がある。
2021年 JAPAN PHOTO AWARD 太田 幸子賞（IMA エディトリアルディレクター）
https://rukakashiwagi.com/

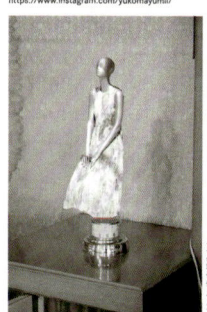

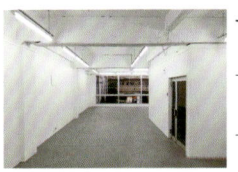

Syndicate

〒760-0047 香川県高松市塩屋町9-9 渡辺ビル2F西
Open：14:00～19:00 Close：不定休 @Instagramにてご確認ください。
Watanabe Bld 2Fwest, 9-9 Shioyamachi, Takamatsu, Kagawa, Japan 760-0047
https://syndicate.tak.com syndicate.tak@gmail.com

Instagram
@syndicate_tak

This is a design for an exhibition themed shiten or viewpoint. In the exhibition graphics, the diversity of the four participants' eyes, each looking in a different direction, is expressed through icons. The logo also combines the word "SHiTEN" in four different ways. Under the theme of viewpoint, the exhibited works combined printed and textual expressions to create a variety of graphics expressing the theme. Sometimes the text and sometimes the graphics alone are used to express the viewpoints.

AD   Yu Inoue
D   Yu Inoue
CL   SI IiTEN

SHITEN

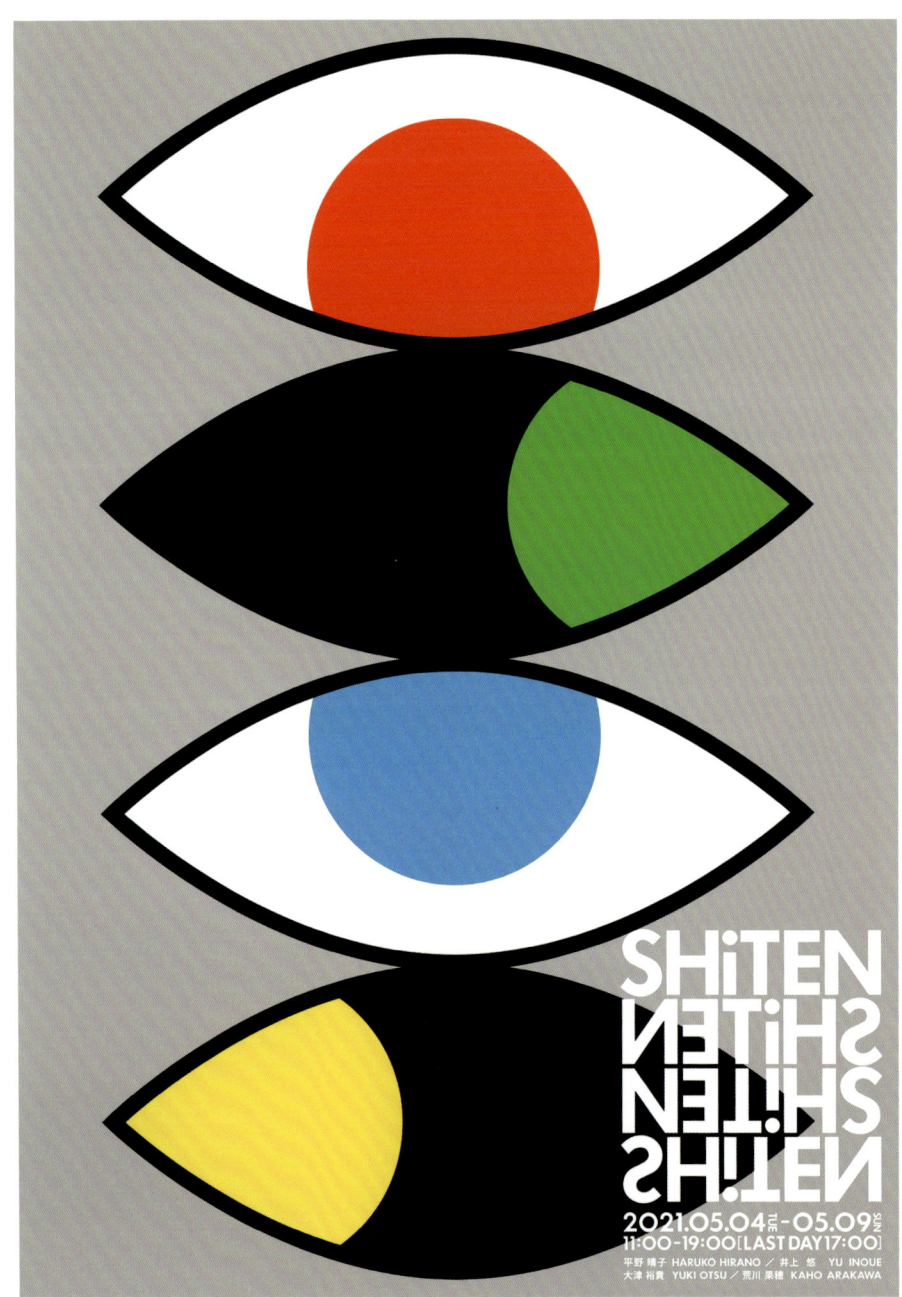

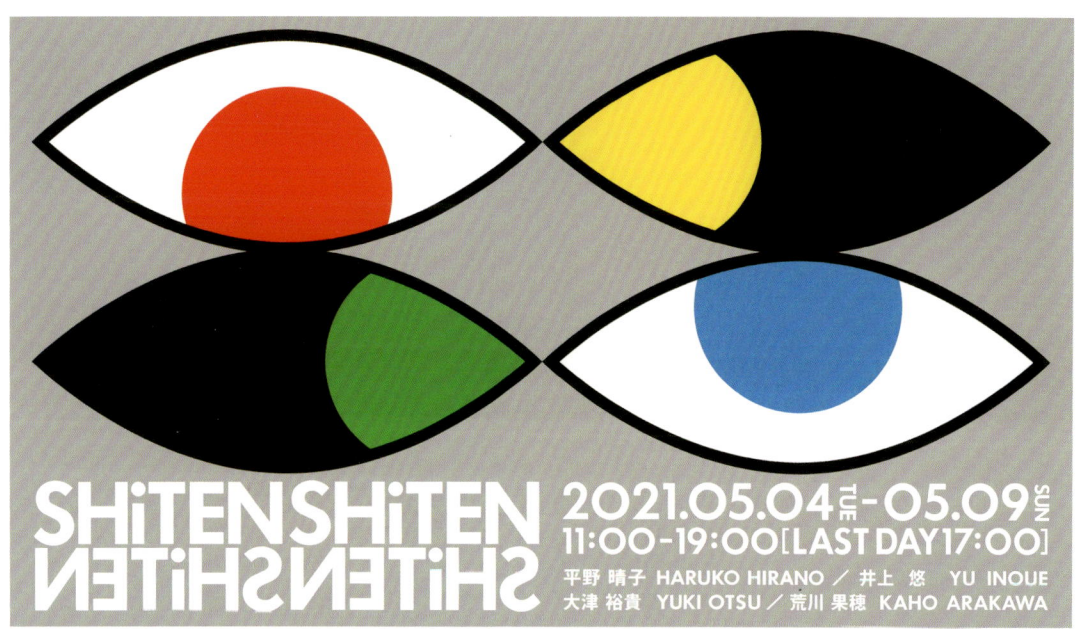

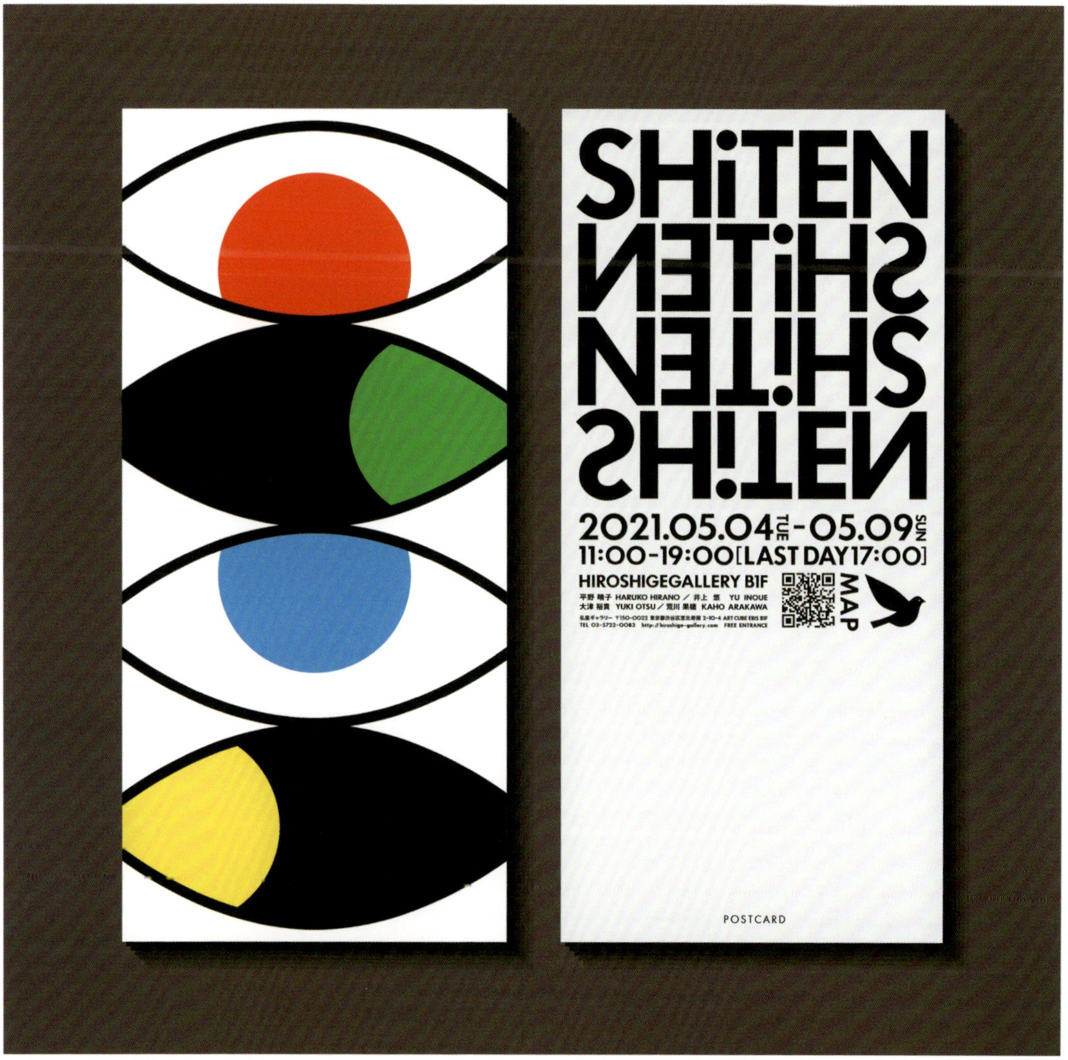

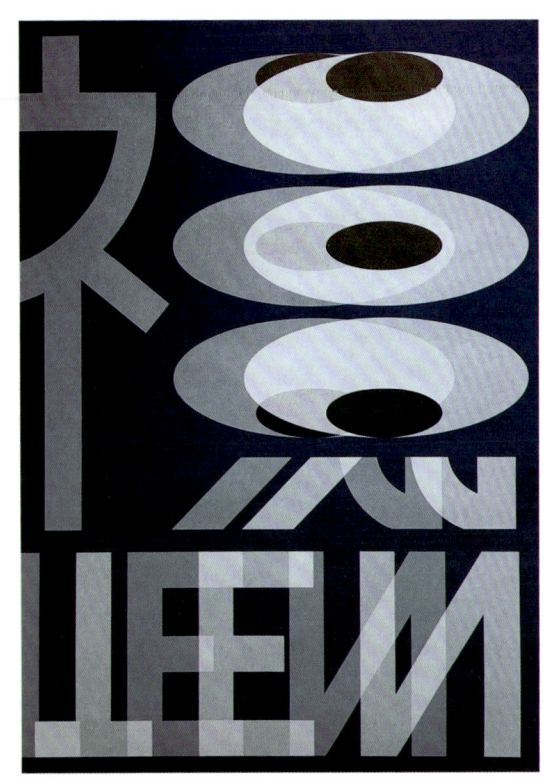

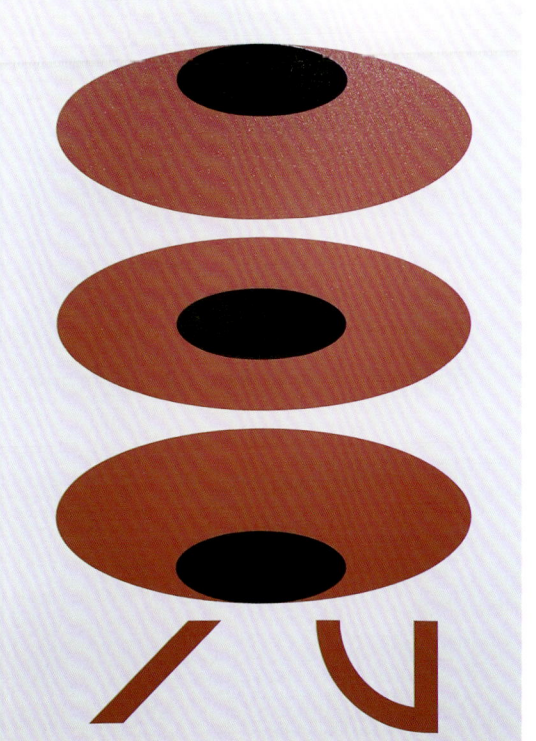

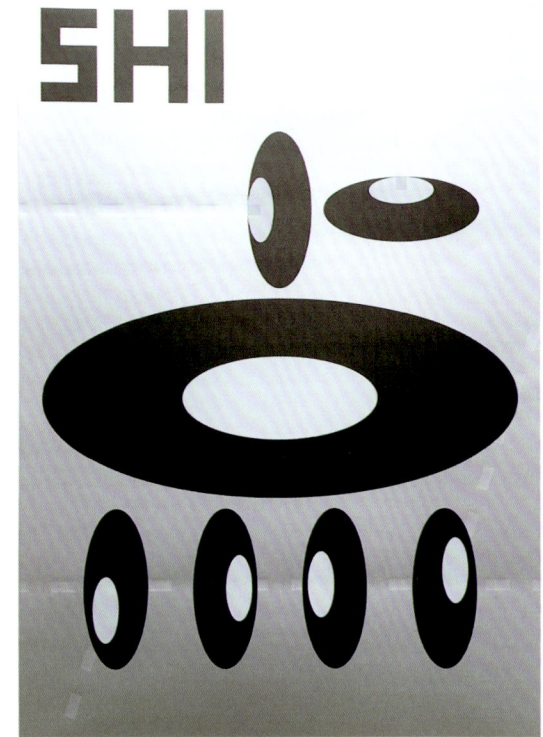

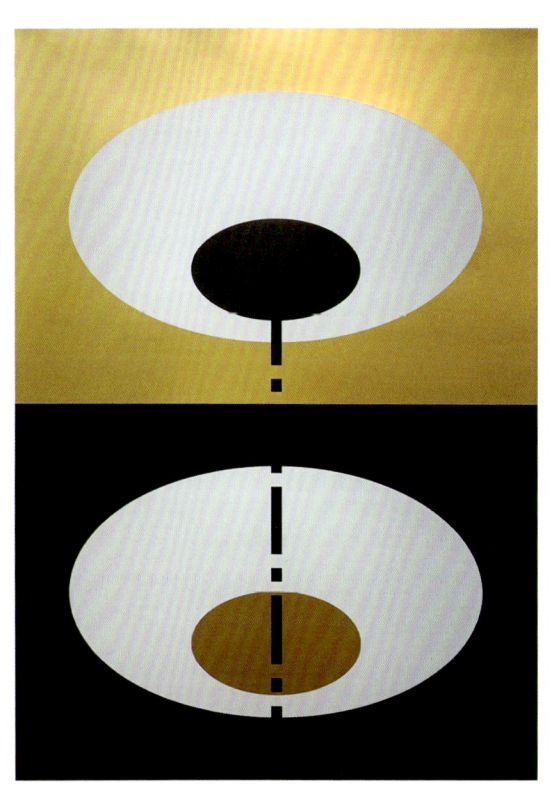

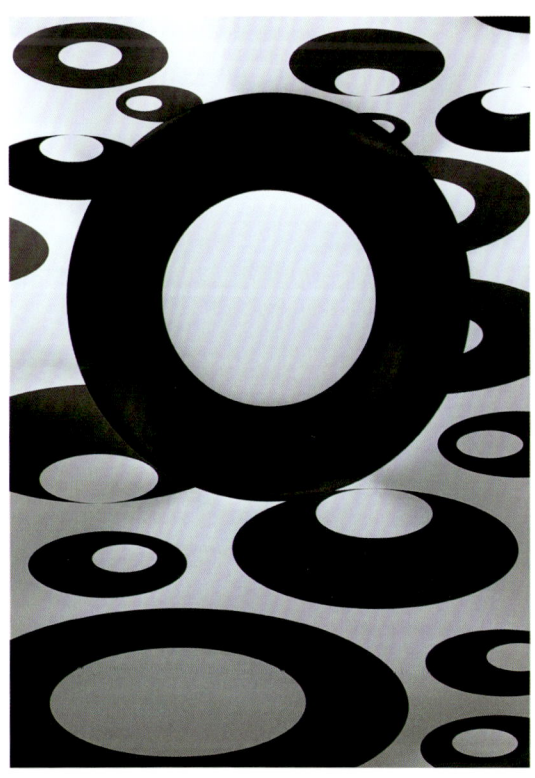

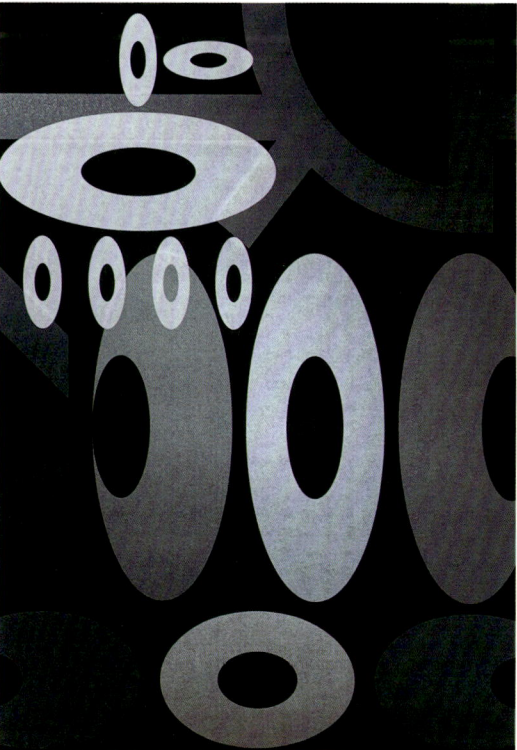

This design is meant to appeal to the caring for athletes' mental health. People tend to see weakness as negative, but everyone has both weak and strong tendencies, including athletes whose images are always powerful. By placing both "弱 (weak)" and "強 (strong)" on the same plane, the designer delivered a message to support people without judgement.

CD   Goro Yoshitani
AD   Arata Kubota
D   Arata Kubota
CL   Japan Rugby Players
        Association & CMHL &
        CBT Center in NCNP

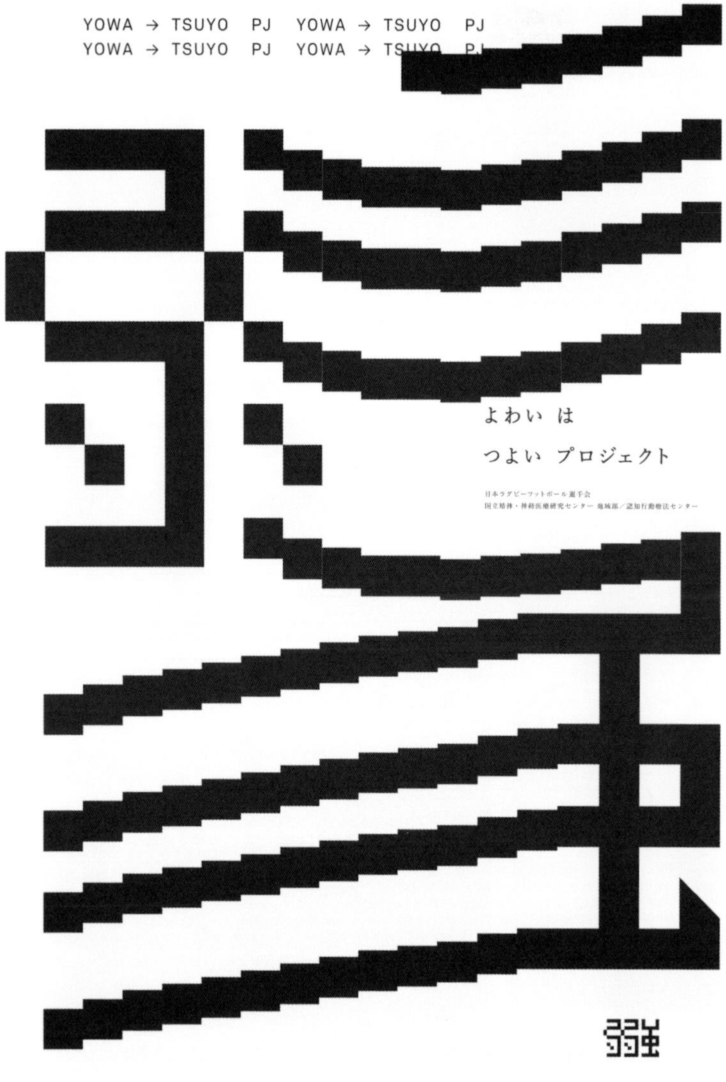

Weak Is Strong

YOWA → TSUYO PJ   YOWA → TSUYO PJ
YOWA → TSUYO PJ   YOWA → TSUYO PJ

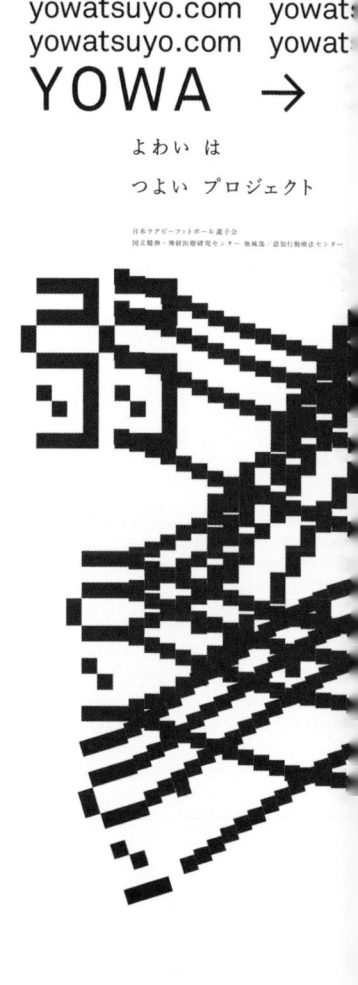

よわい は
つよい プロジェクト

日本ラグビーフットボール選手会
国立精神・神経医療研究センター 地域部／認知行動療法センター

yowatsuyo.com   yowat:
yowatsuyo.com   yowat:

YOWA →

よわい は
つよい プロジェクト

日本ラグビーフットボール選手会
国立精神・神経医療研究センター 地域部／認知行動療法センター

SUYQ   PJ

YOWA → TSUYO PJ   YOWA → TSUYO PJ
YOWA → TSUYO PJ   YOWA → TSUYO PJ
YOWA → TSUYO PJ   YOWA → TSUYO PJ

よわい　は　強
つよい　プロジェクト

日本ラグビーフットボール選手会
同志機構・美唄医療経友センター 鬼城郡、認知行動療法センター

17 Works

9 Contributors

61 Images

P 239 - P 263

Print

Inspired by the Japanese tradition to send New Year's cards to each other and the word "enmusubi (bonding good relationships)," the creative team designed this greeting card. The card can be a yearly calendar when different layers of paper are turned.

CD   Kyohei Ohwa (MUSUBI Inc.)
AD   Mayuko Kanazawa (KOKON Inc.)
D   Mayuko Kanazawa (KOKON Inc.)
CL   MUSUBI Inc.

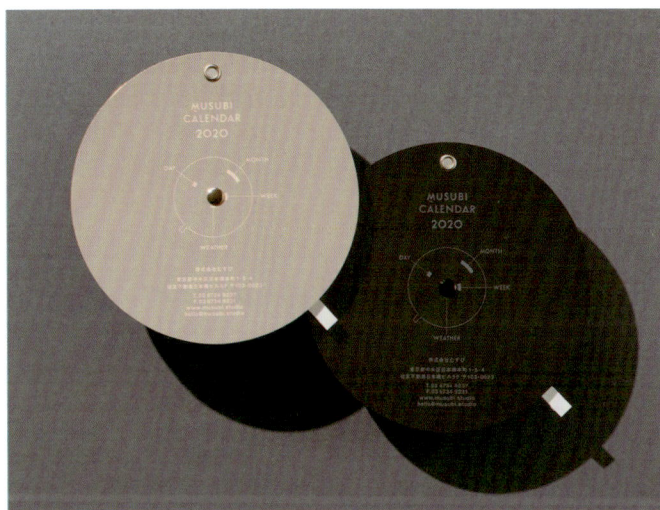

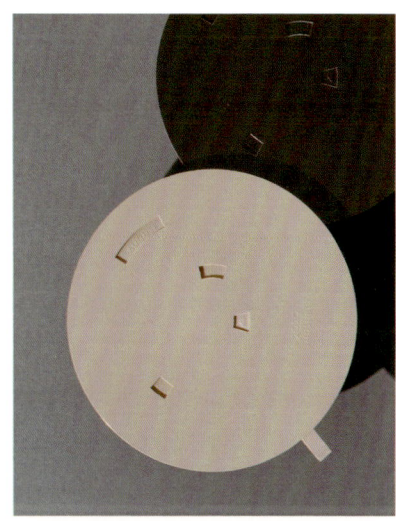

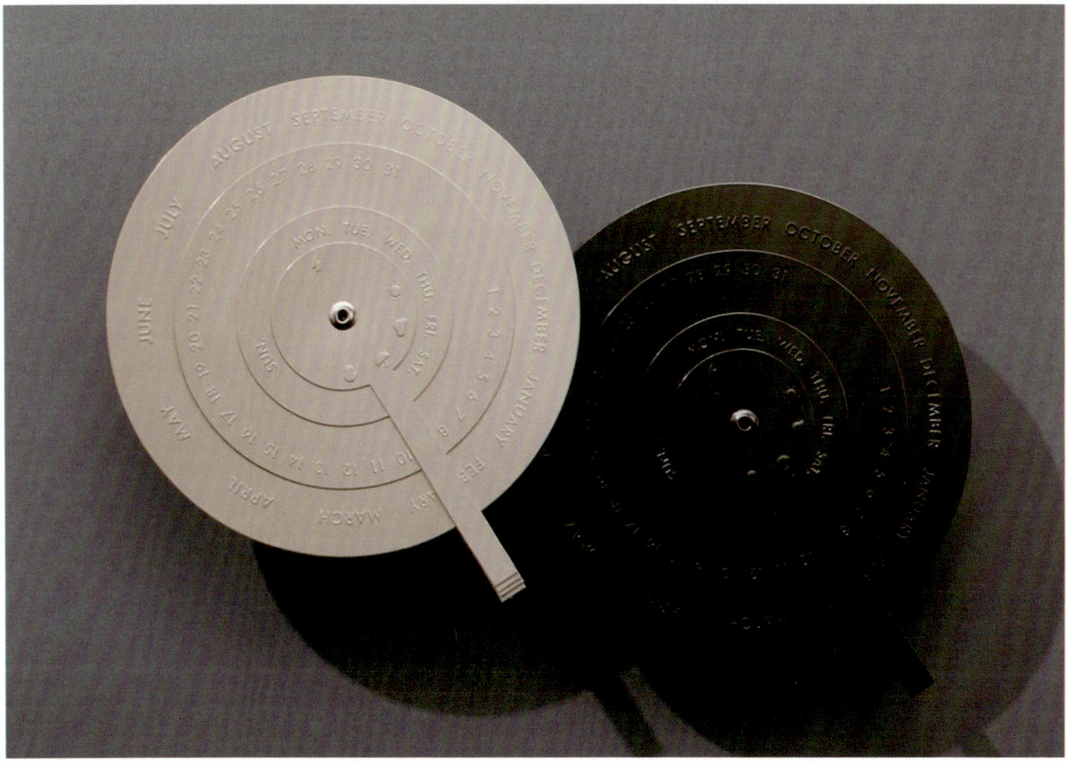

BXG CO., LTD. is a graphic design office. EP is a printing service specializing in special processing operated by BXG CO., LTD. This is a work that summarized the result of an experiment on foil stamping. KAAKA Inc. presented the design office's attitude of not being afraid of failure in foil printing attempts by the saying "No pain, no gain" and delivered the idea by stamping foil on various kinds of materials.

DA   KAAKA Inc.
D   Ryosuke Kato, Chihiro Kato
CL   BXG CO., LTD.

No pain, no gain

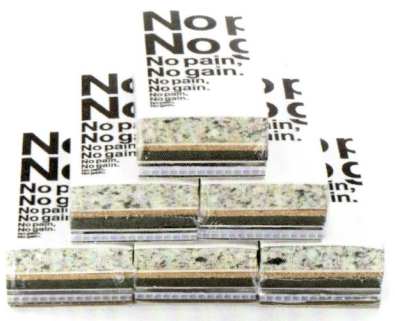

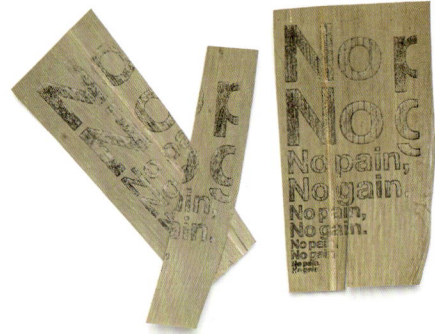

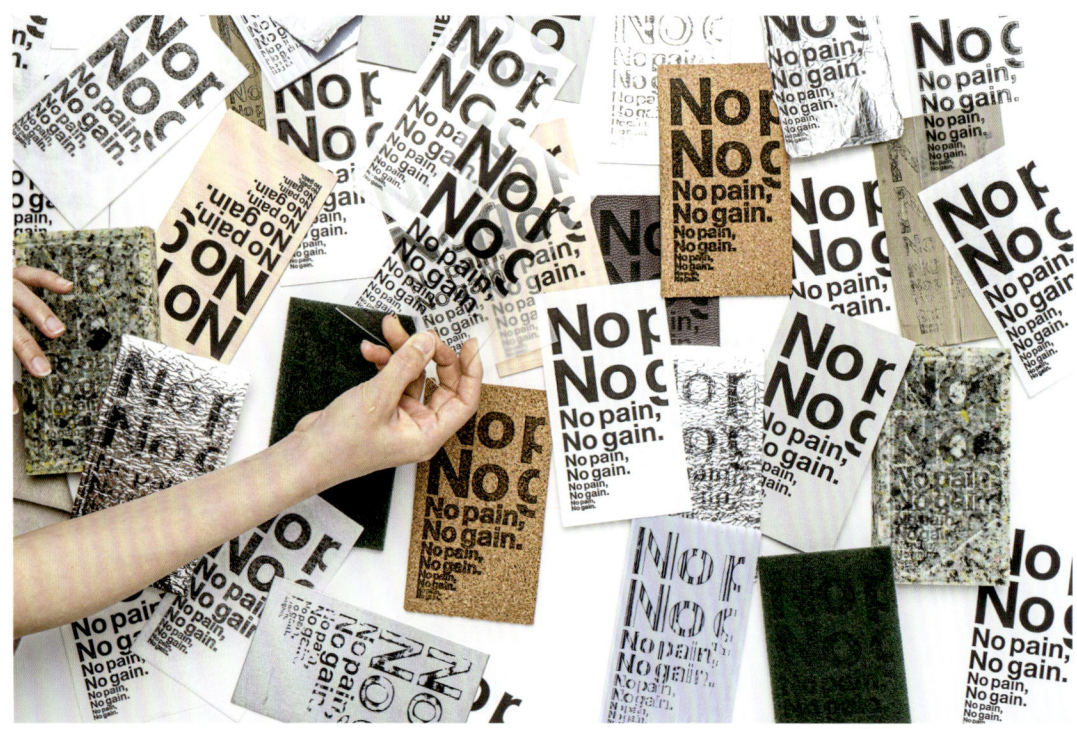

Designing Programmes is a design methodology from legendary Swiss designer Karl Gerstner, who believed the process of design is what should be designed. The design of the Japanese edition combines the design process explained in this book with bold and organized Japanese notation without compromising the design of the original version.

DA Sitoh inc.
D   Motoi Shito
CL BNN

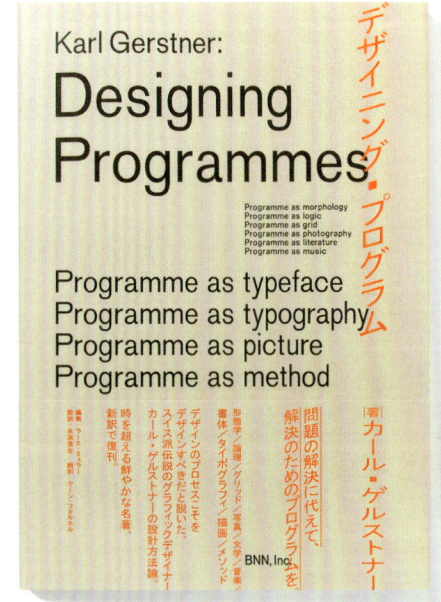

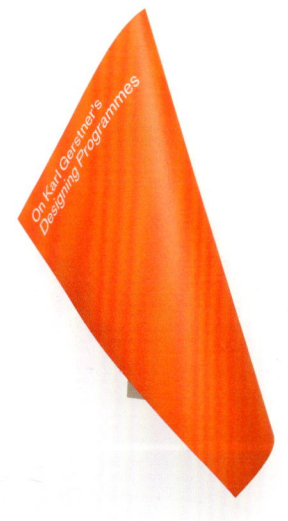

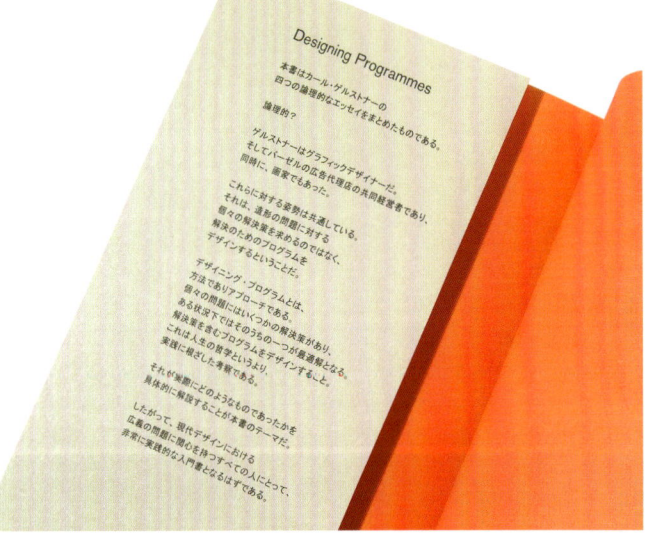

The book features 91 new generation designers recommended by 14 leading art directors in Japan. MdN's *New Generation Designers File* is a design yearbook that introduces their works and profiles with insights from the nominees. For the cover design, the meaning of ushering in a new era was delivered through an eclipse, and the passion and strong will of the new generation were revealed in the colors and typography.

DA   Sitoh inc.
D   Motoi Shito
CL   MdN Corporation

New Generation Designers File

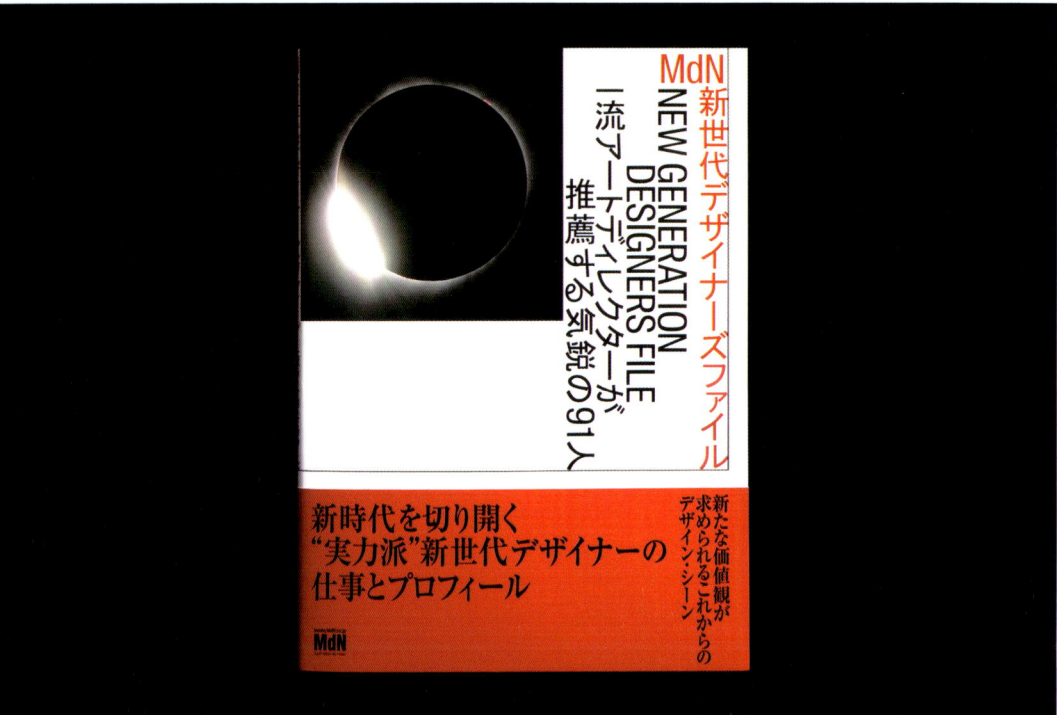

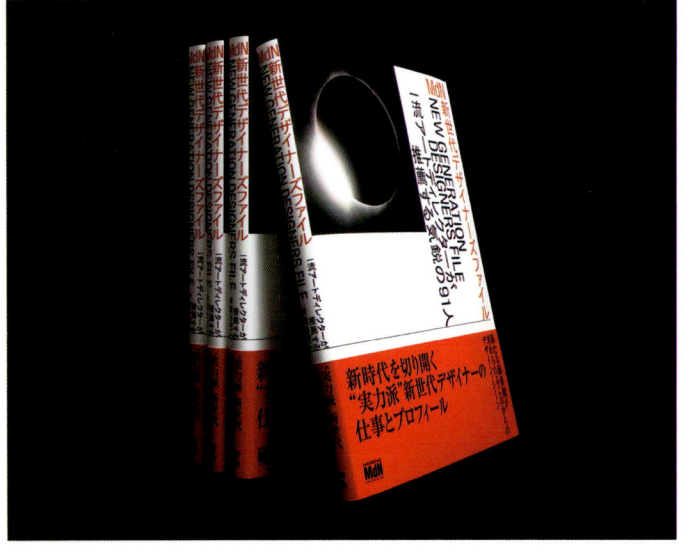

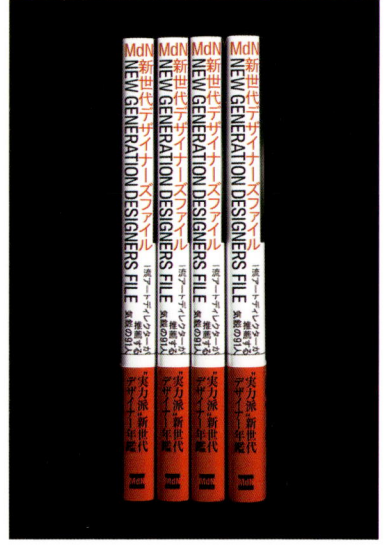

This book introduces various dessert brand designs sold in Japan today in Japanese and foreign categories.

The book wrapped with a band looks like a strawberry cake in the front, simple and lovely. But after removing the band, it shows the pattern of a strawberry and cream, creative and fun. Upon closer inspection, the shape of each cream is different, adding details and depth to the design.

The cover and the band are made of embossed paper with stripes and printed in a special silver color. The color, paper selection, and visual elements are in harmony with each other to create an editorial design with a natural touch and charm.

DA   paragram
D   Yusuke Akai, Miho Aoyagi
CL   Graphic-Sha

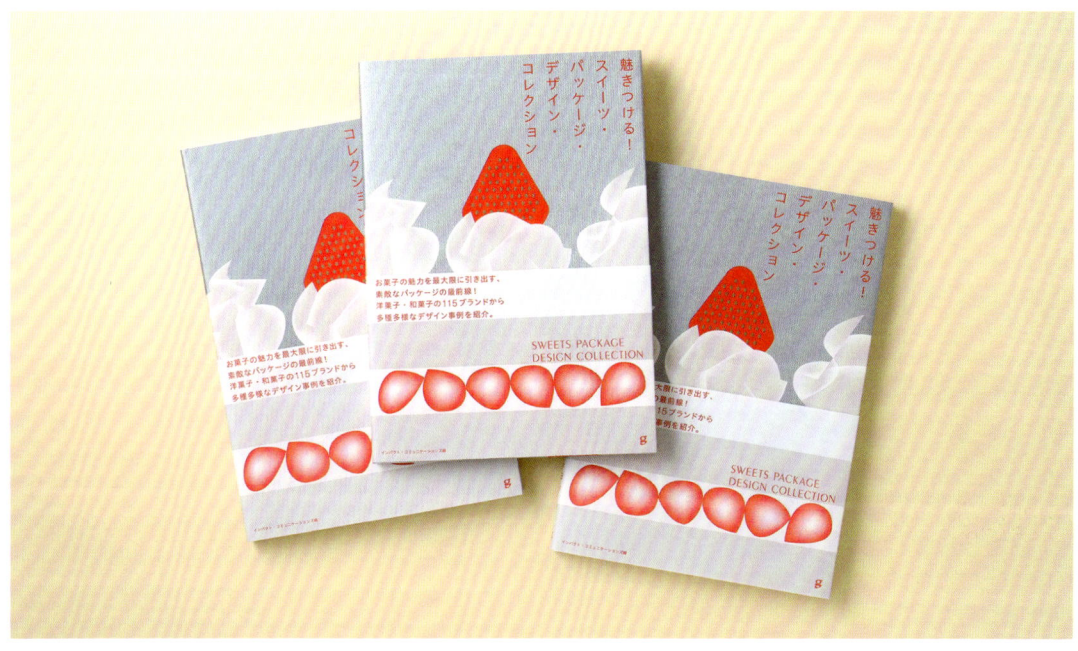

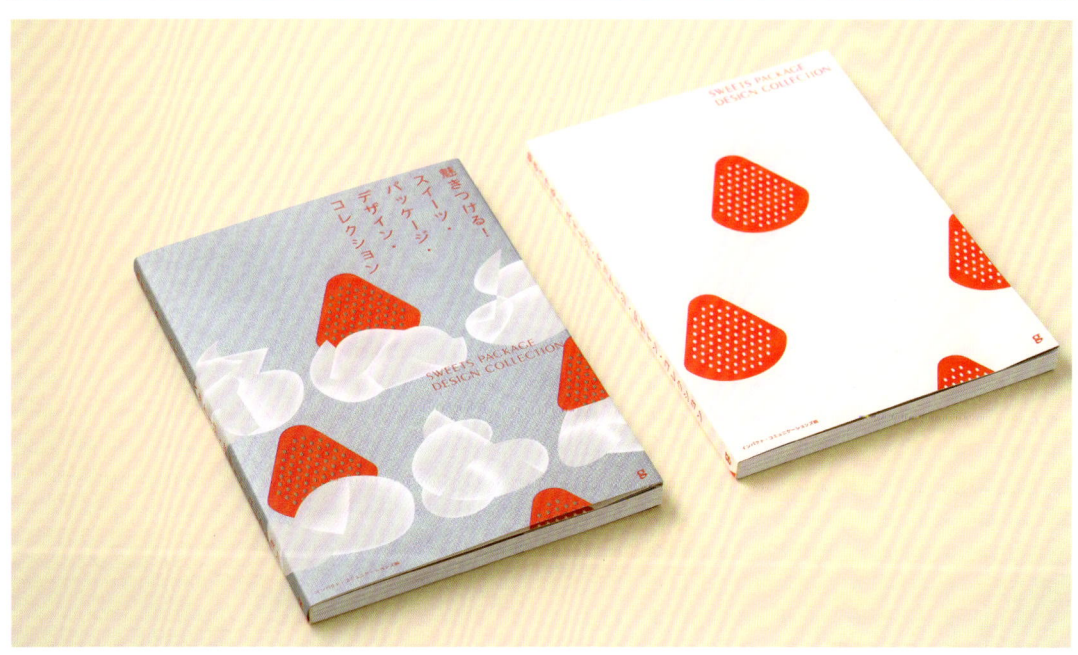

Sweets Package Design Collection

Arts and Media is a publication that focuses on the primordial relationship between art and media.

Hisaki Matsumoto created the book design of the 11th volume with the concept of "pursuing diversity, multi-layers, and multi-dimensionality." The printing and binding method is designed in such a way that the final form cannot be predicted, and the binding process is complicated. By making an unpredictable book that incorporates accidental beauty and ugliness, Hisaki Matsumoto tried to embody the genre ambiguity of the book and intellectual tension of the research area.

D   Hisaki Matsumoto
CL   Osaka University

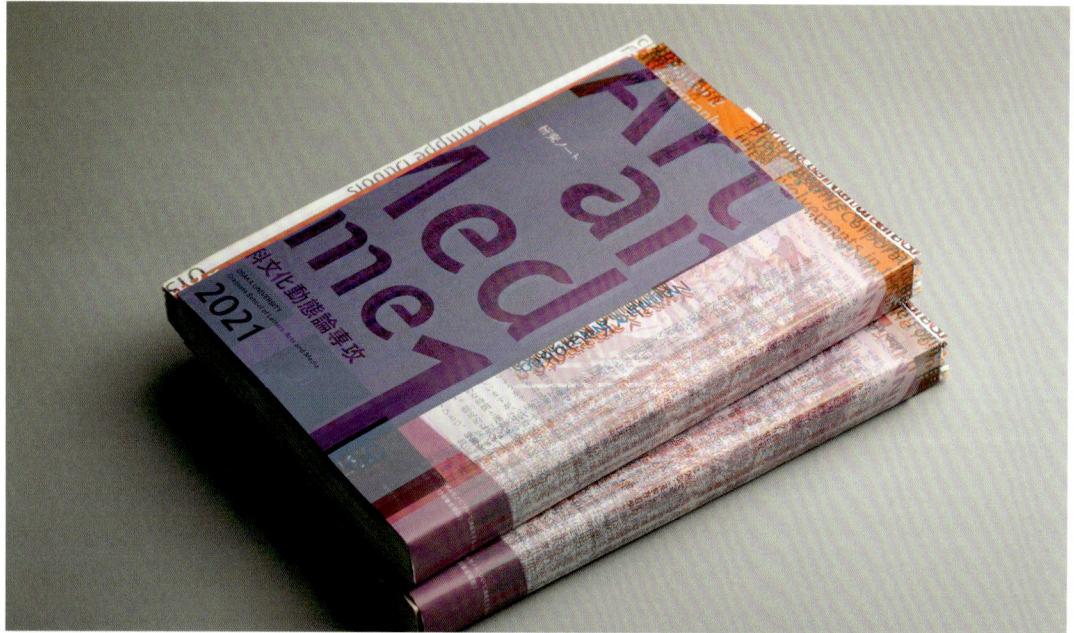

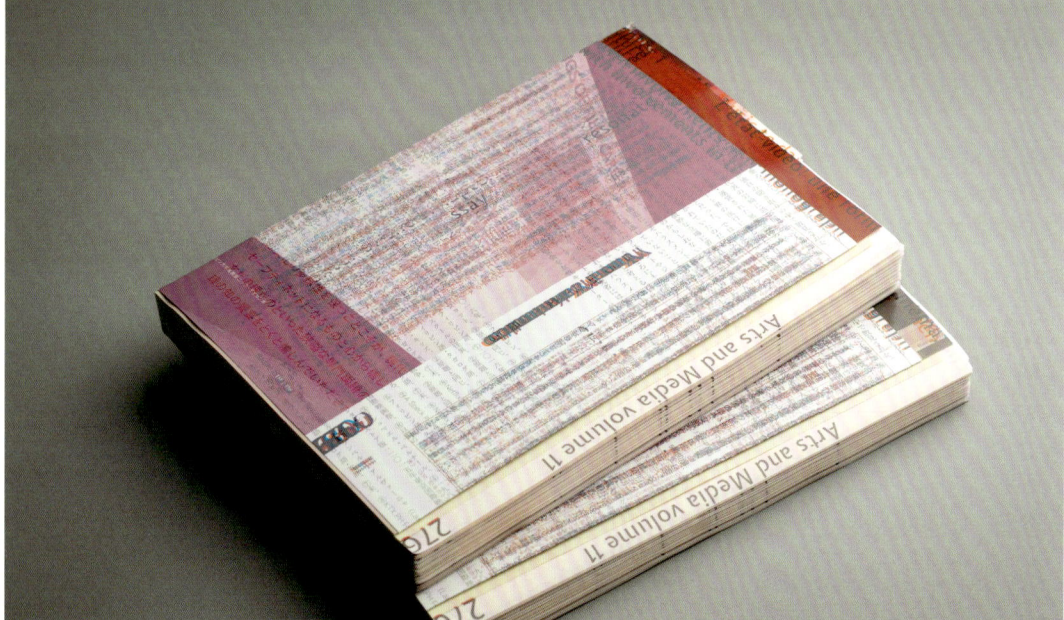

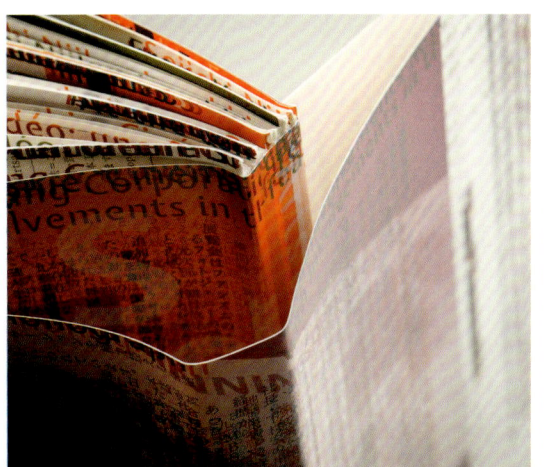

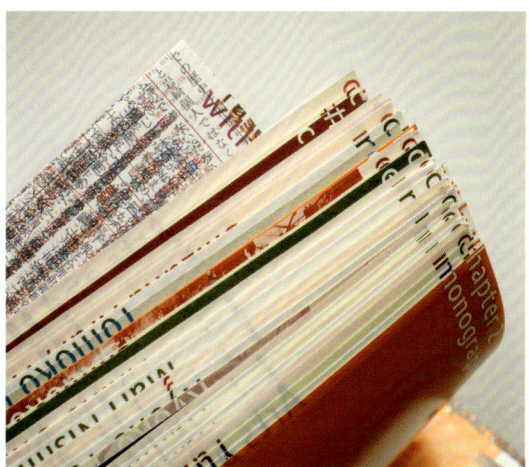

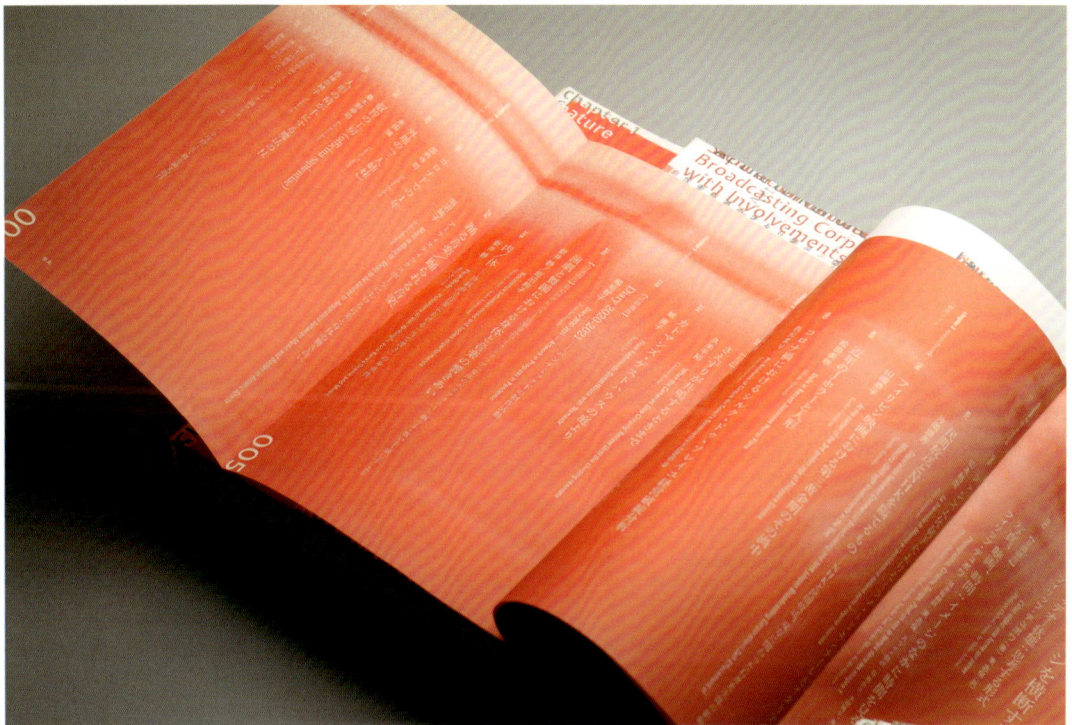

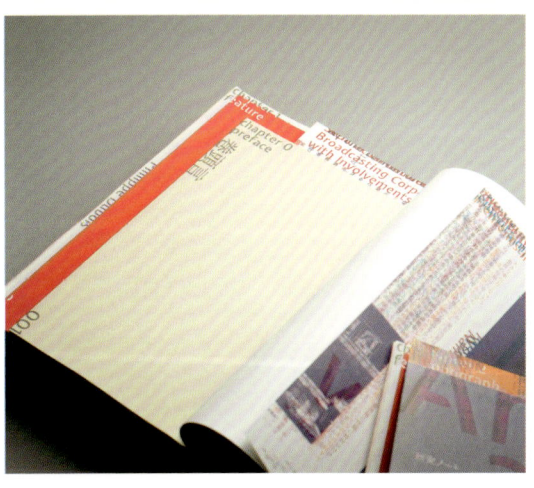

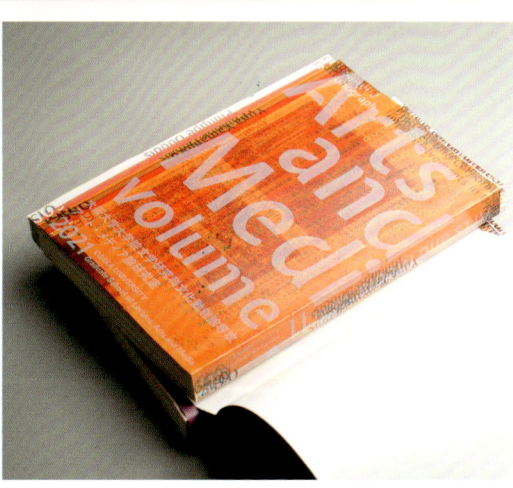

Tangite me is a record book of an exhibition that aims to introduce artworks in Keio University's collection from the viewpoint of conservation and restoration and to examine restoration work from the perspective of touching and contact.

Restoration work involving contact is a contradictory act of healing and destruction, requiring a high level of skill, extensive knowledge, and a great deal of experience from the restorer. The book design is based on the motif of deterioration and damage, restoration and protection of the exhibition's group of works. And the book is bound with a variety of materials and processed with surface treatment techniques to maximize the diversity of tactile sensations.

D   Hisaki Matsumoto
CL   Keio University Art Center,
      Keio Museum Commons

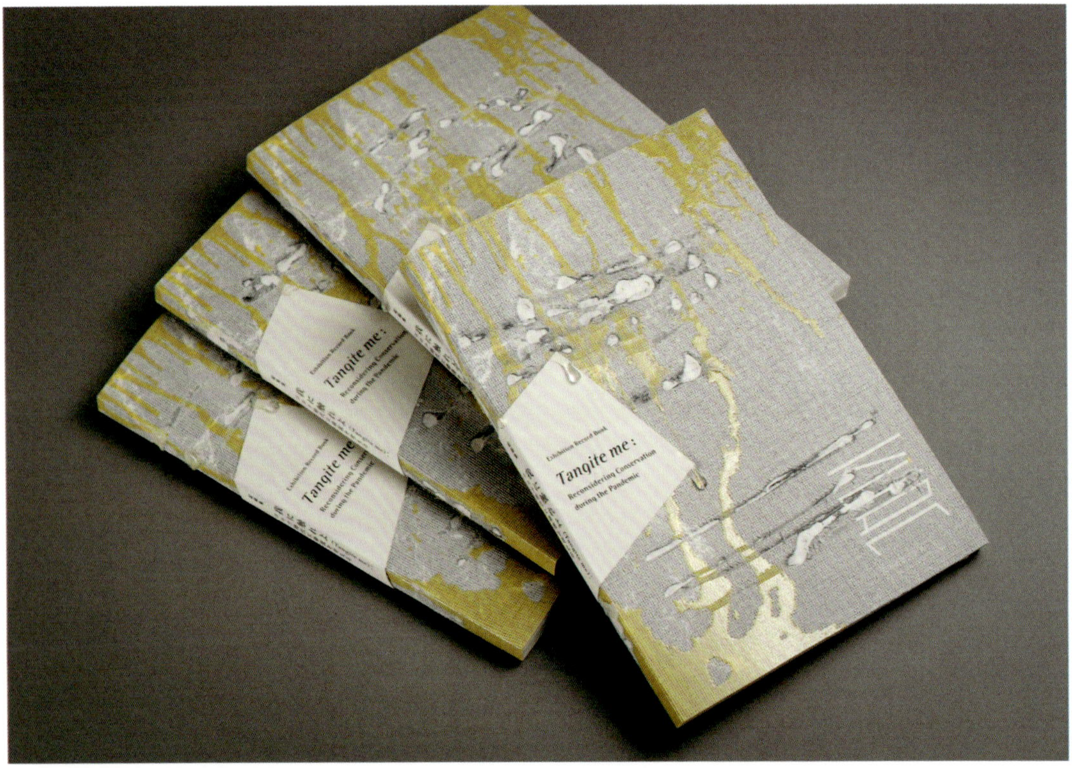

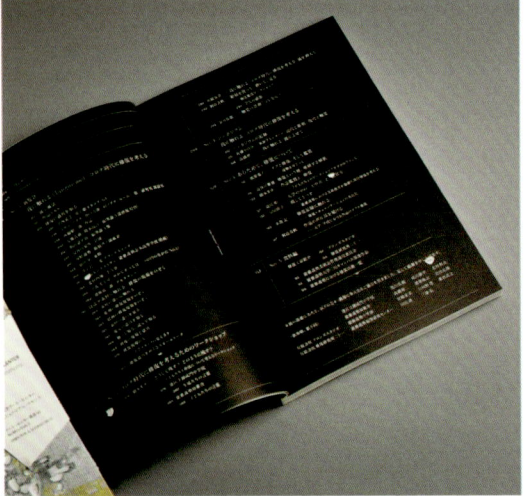

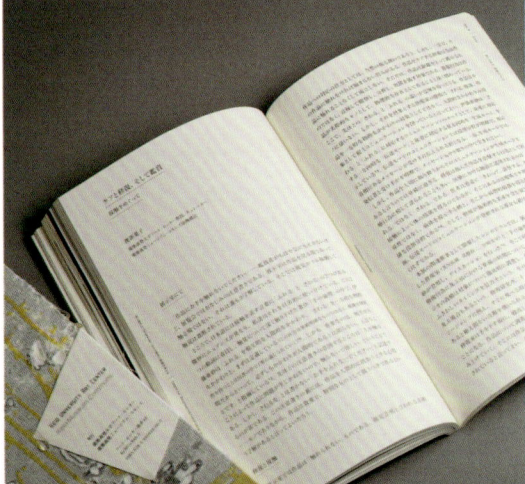

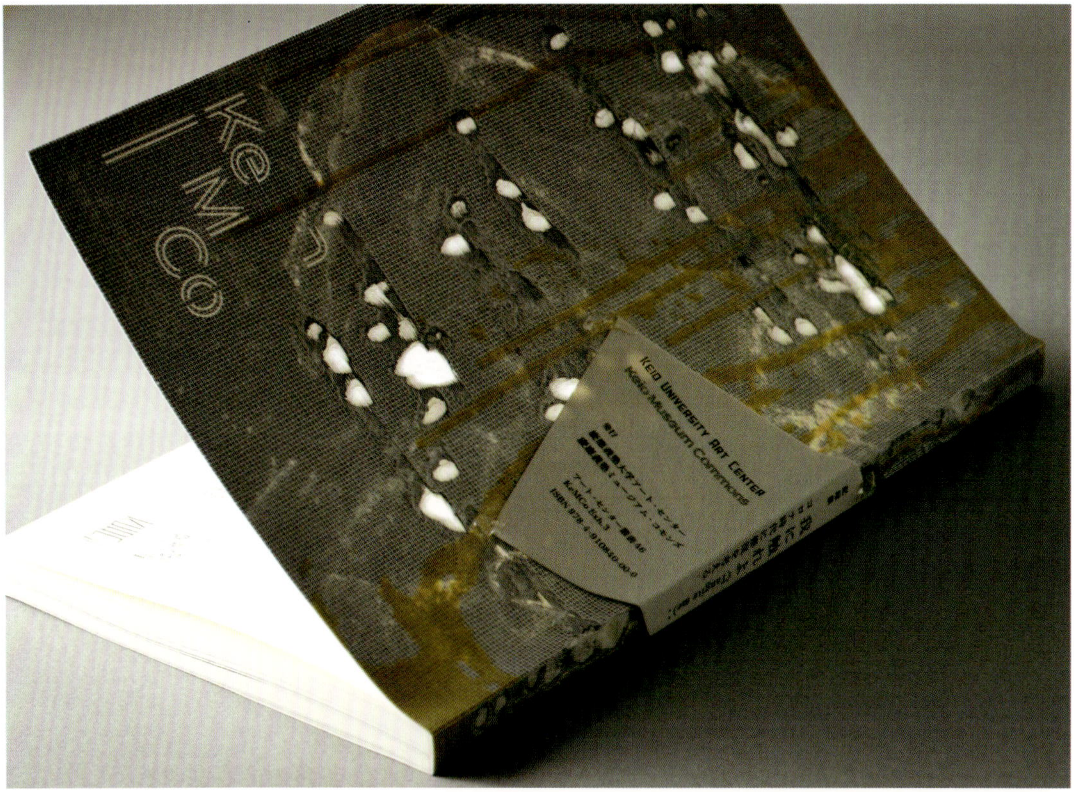

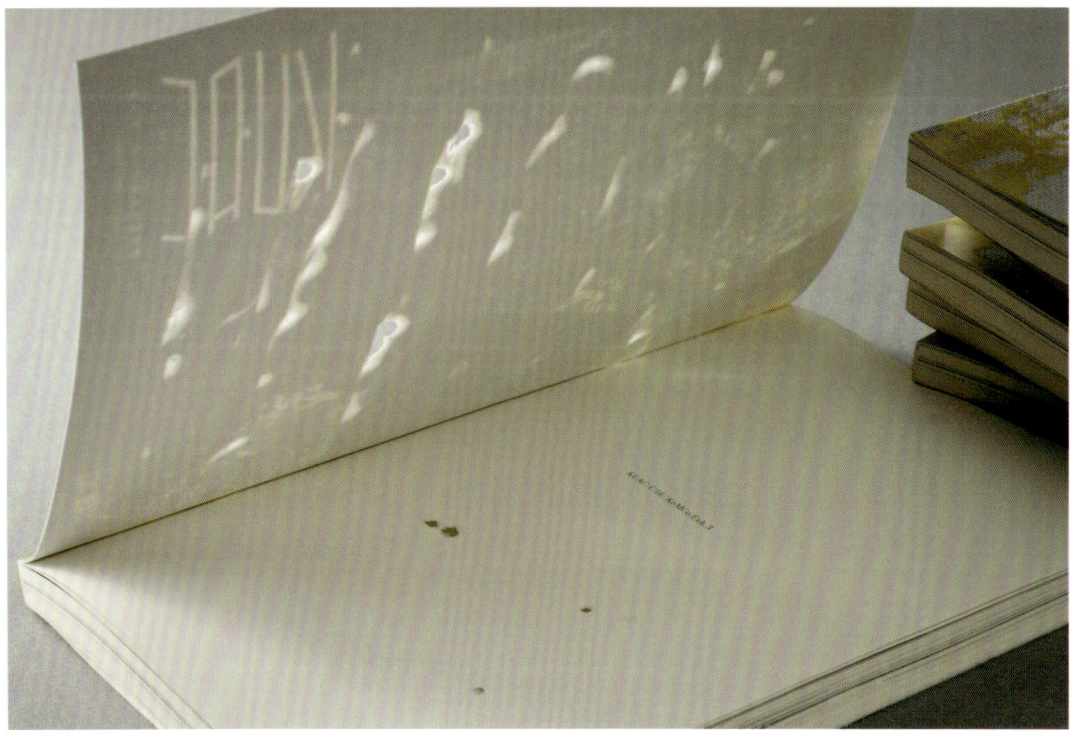

Arts and Media is a publication that focuses on the primordial relationship between art and media.

The concept of the 12th volume is orbis or circularity. Hisaki Matsumoto aimed to embody the mechanical characteristics of contraction and convergence, radiation and expansion, and swirling and circulating motion by inserting the disc sculpture work of Peter van der Doort into complex folded paperwork.

D   Hisaki Matsumoto
CL   Osaka University

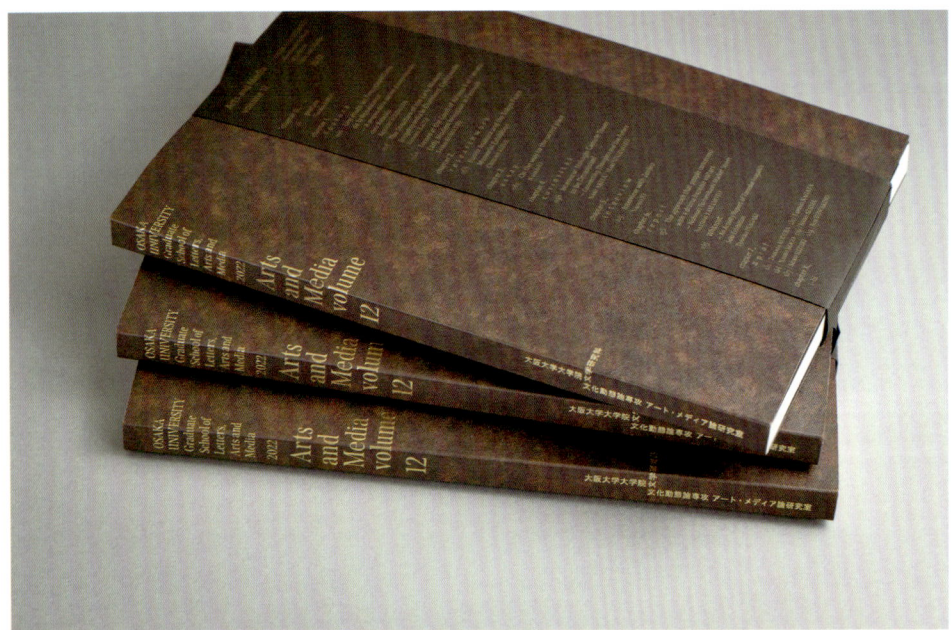

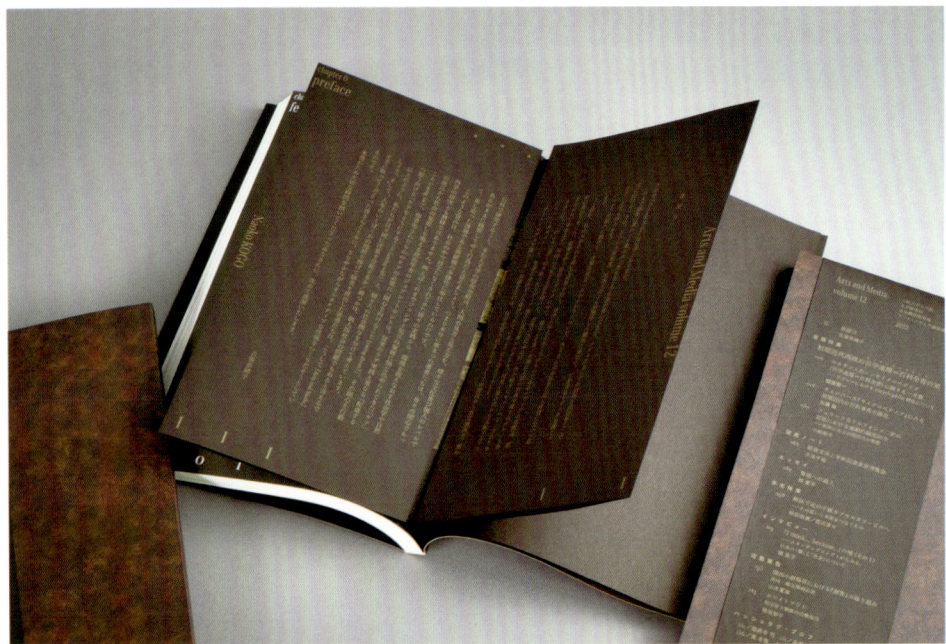

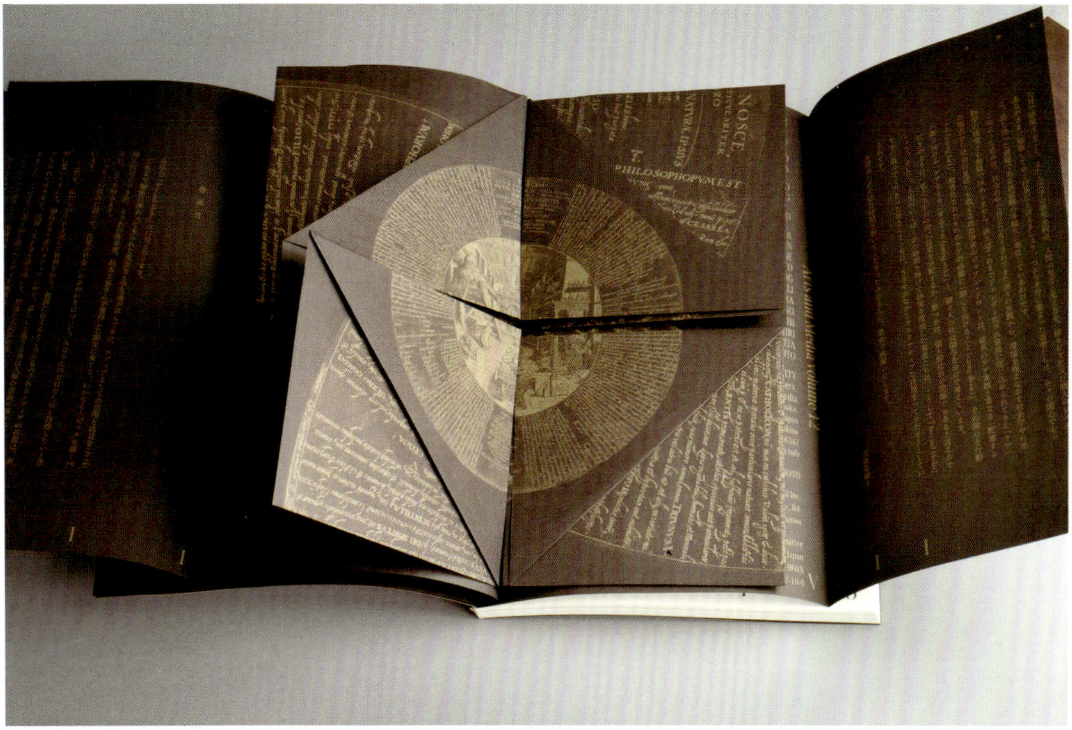

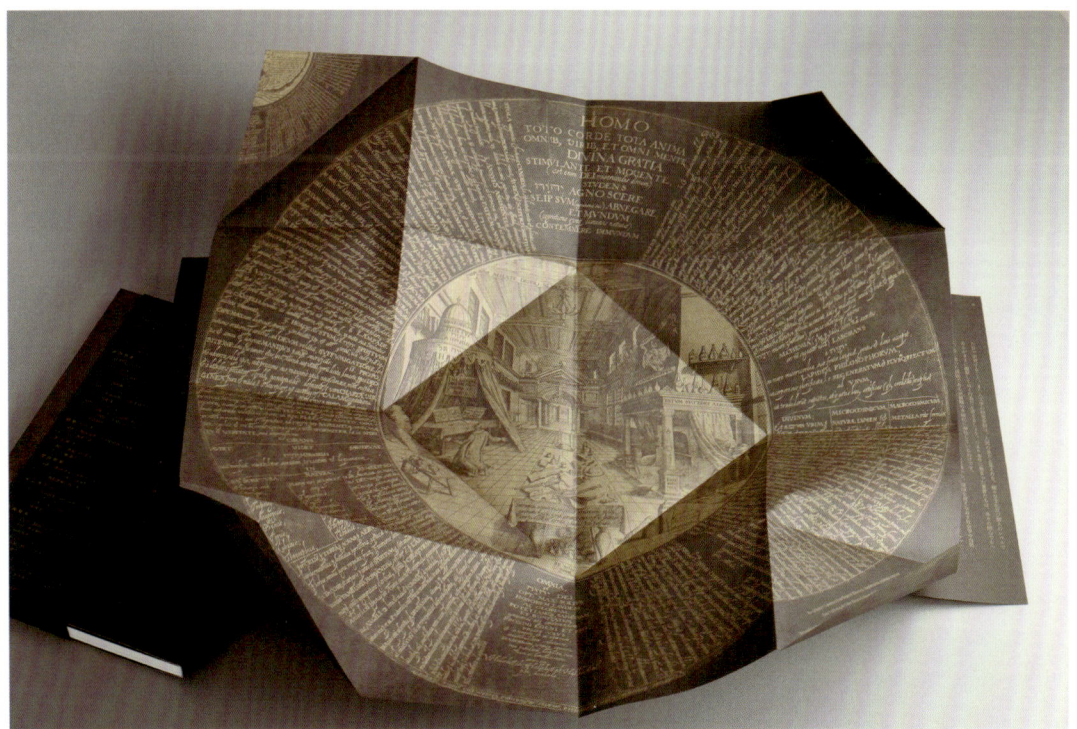

Stanislaw Lem was a Polish novelist and science fiction writer. He is considered one of the greatest writers of 20th century science fiction. *The Magellanic Cloud* is a story that Lem refused to reprint in Poland or to translate into foreign languages until his later years. The series consists of three books, and Isao Mitobe chose a pattern and jacket with geometric shapes for each cover. When readers take off the semi-transparent book jacket, the book cover appears and this leads them closer to the book and the writer's idea.

D   Isao Mitobe
CL   KOKUSHOKANKOKAI INC.

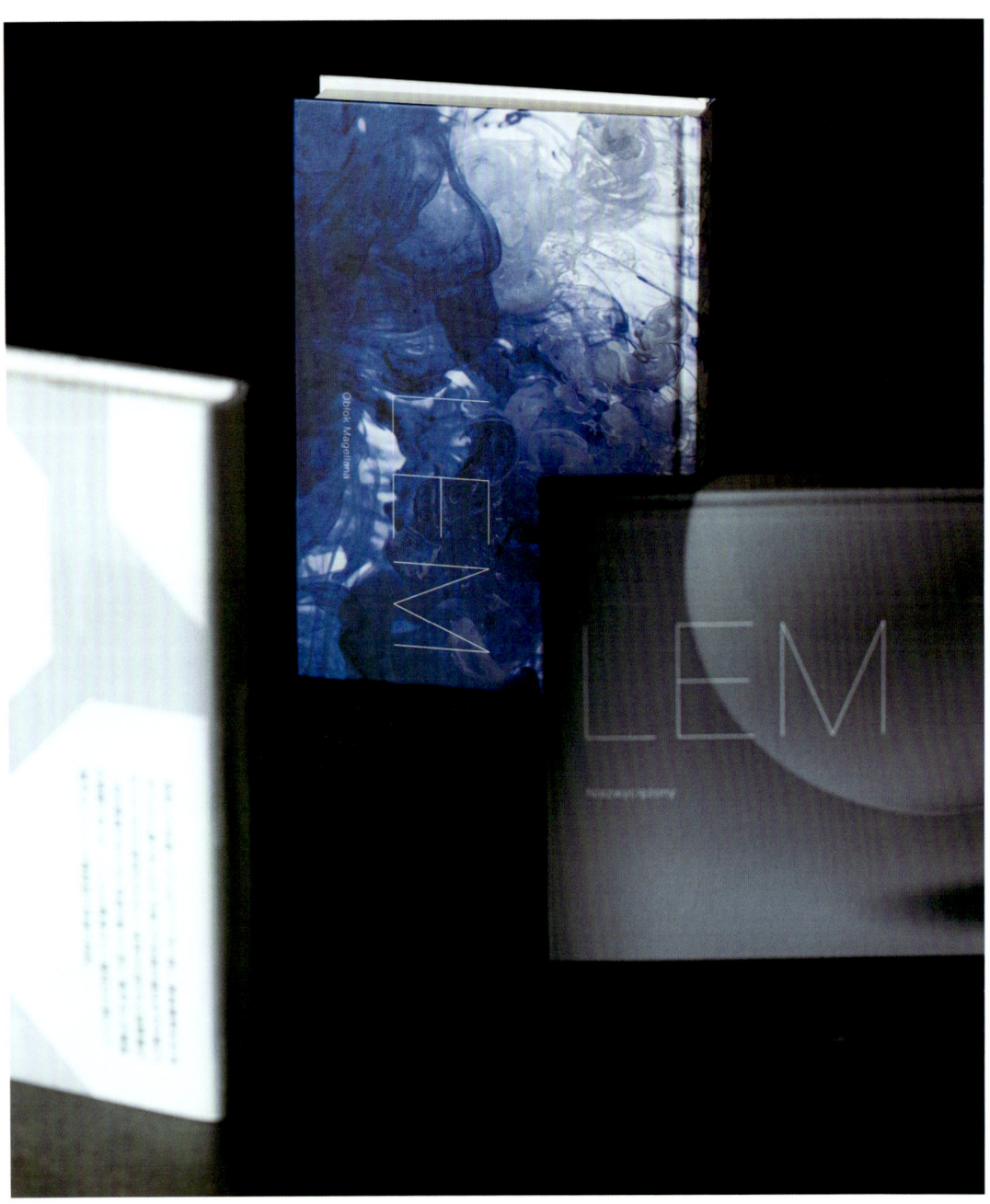

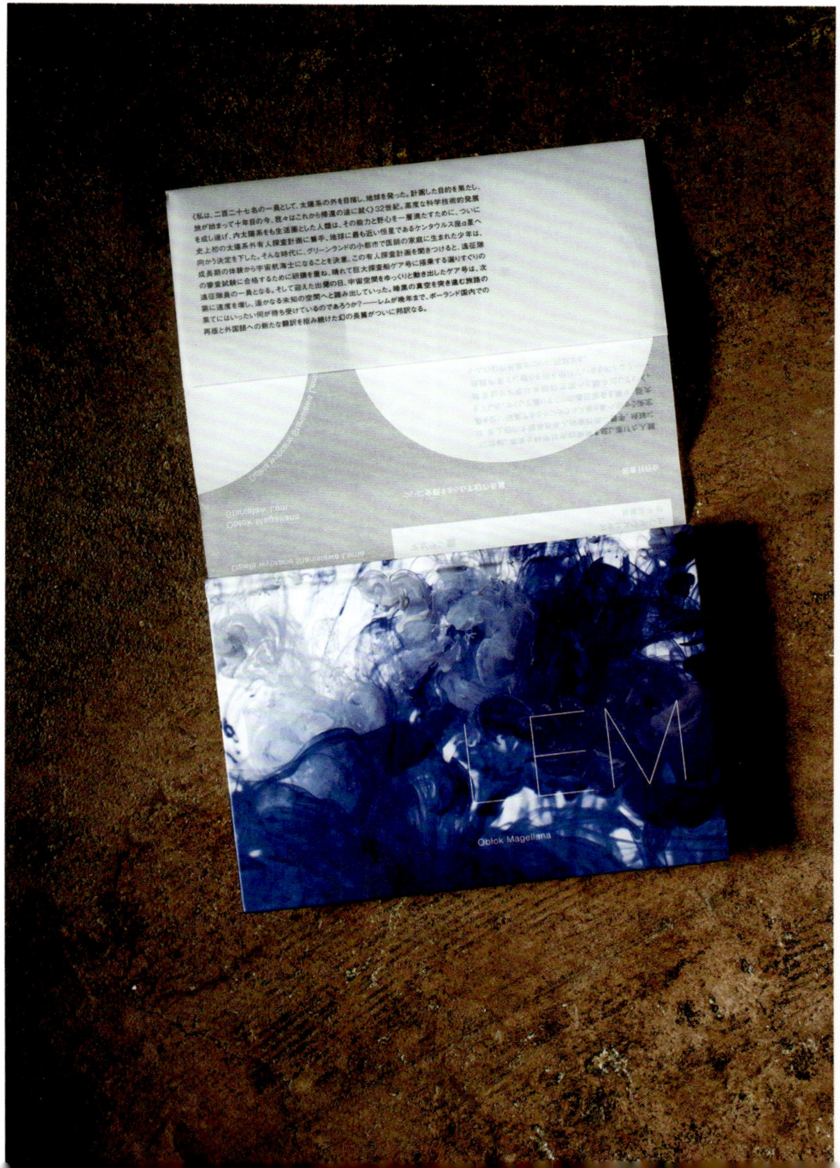
〈私は、二百二十七名の一員として、太陽系の外を目指し、地球を発った。計画した目的を果たし、
再版と外国語への新たな翻訳を拒み続けた幻の長篇がついに邦訳なる。
LEM
Obłok Magellana

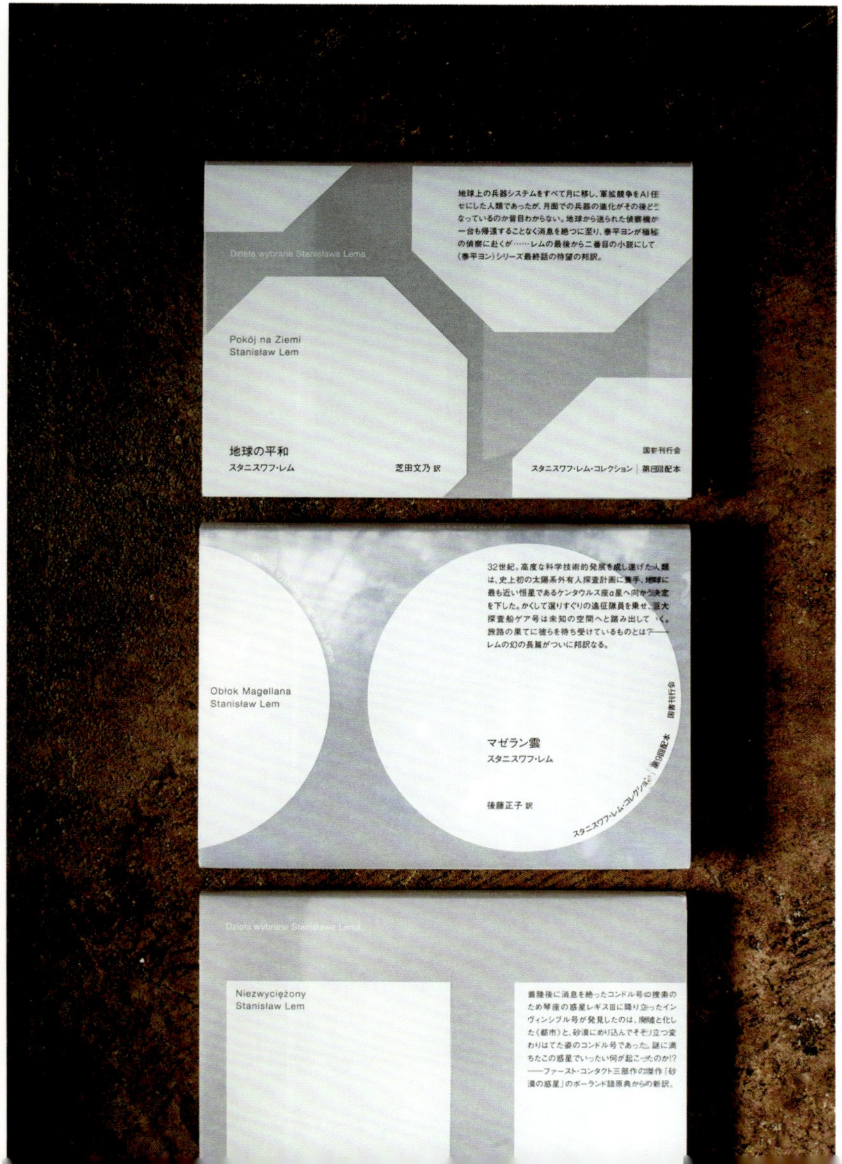
Dzieła wybrane Stanisława Lema
Pokój na Ziemi
Stanisław Lem
地球の平和
スタニスワフ・レム
芝田文乃 訳
国書刊行会
スタニスワフ・レム・コレクション｜第8回配本
32世紀。高度な科学技術的発展を成し遂げた人類
レムの幻の長篇がついに邦訳なる。
Obłok Magellana
Stanisław Lem
マゼラン雲
スタニスワフ・レム
後藤正子 訳
国書刊行会
Niezwyciężony
Stanisław Lem

Hirotaka Tobi is a science fiction writer who represents modern Japan. This book covers his valuable non-novel works, including theories, book reviews, essays, talks about his works, dialogues, interviews, and recommendations. The cover is a combination of pure black and white, and the title is arranged vertically. A part of the cover is blurred in contrast with the rest, implying that the book is a rare revelation of the author's thoughts.

D   Isao Mitobe
CL   Kawade Shobo Shinsha

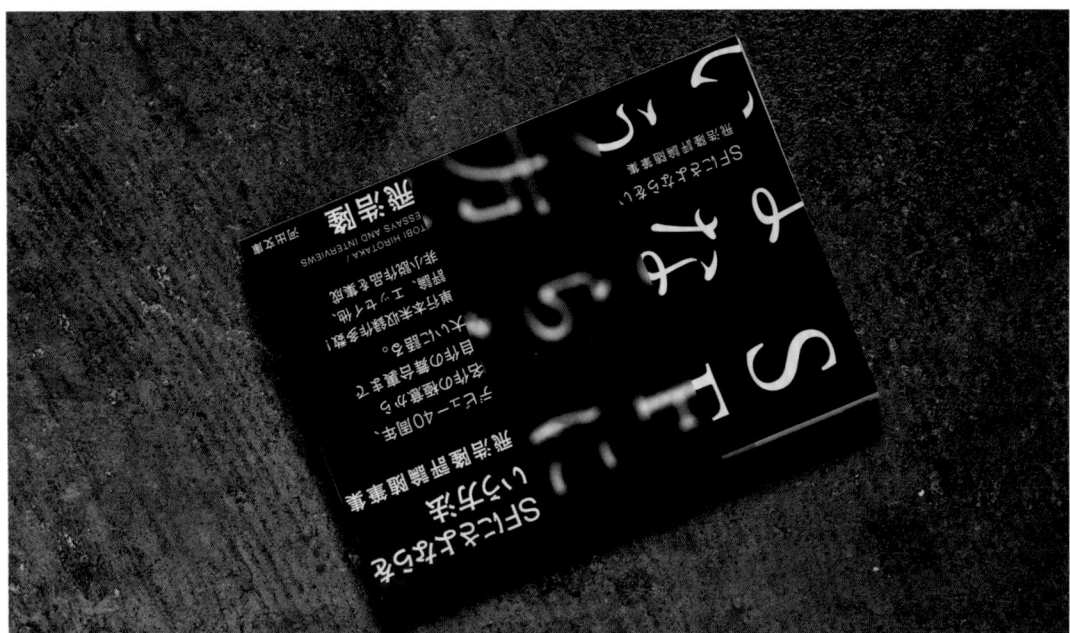

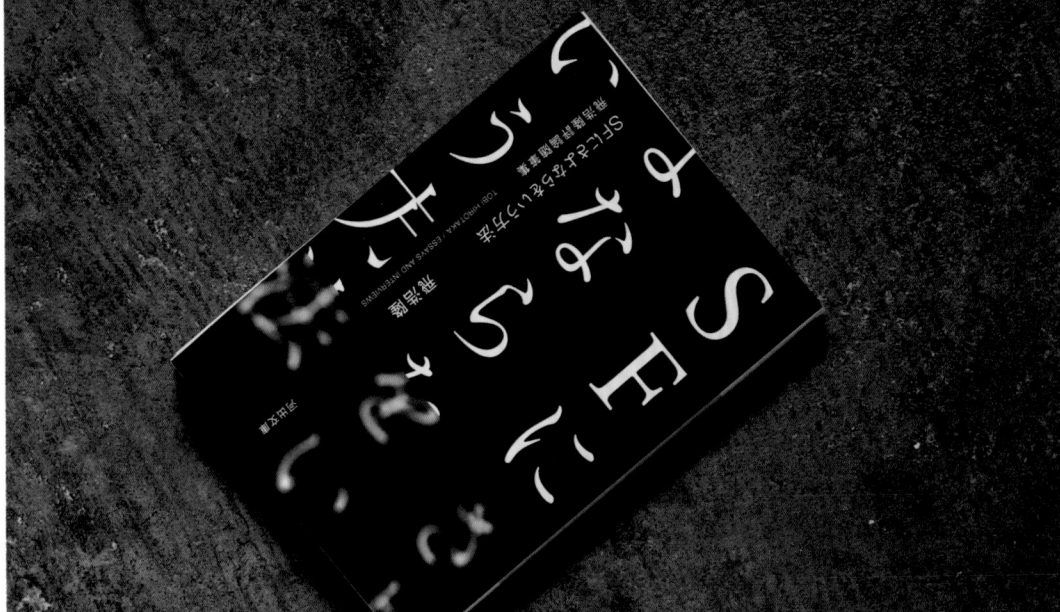

The book is a cruel story of mothers and daughters written by a Korean. On the cover, the Kanji characters of the title stay in the middle. To balance the composition, the Korean title, as well as another Chinese title is arranged with book edges as the baseline. The colors, white and green, create a feeling of solitude and sorrow that is rooted in the plots.

D   Isao Mitobe
CL   Kawade Shobo Shinsha

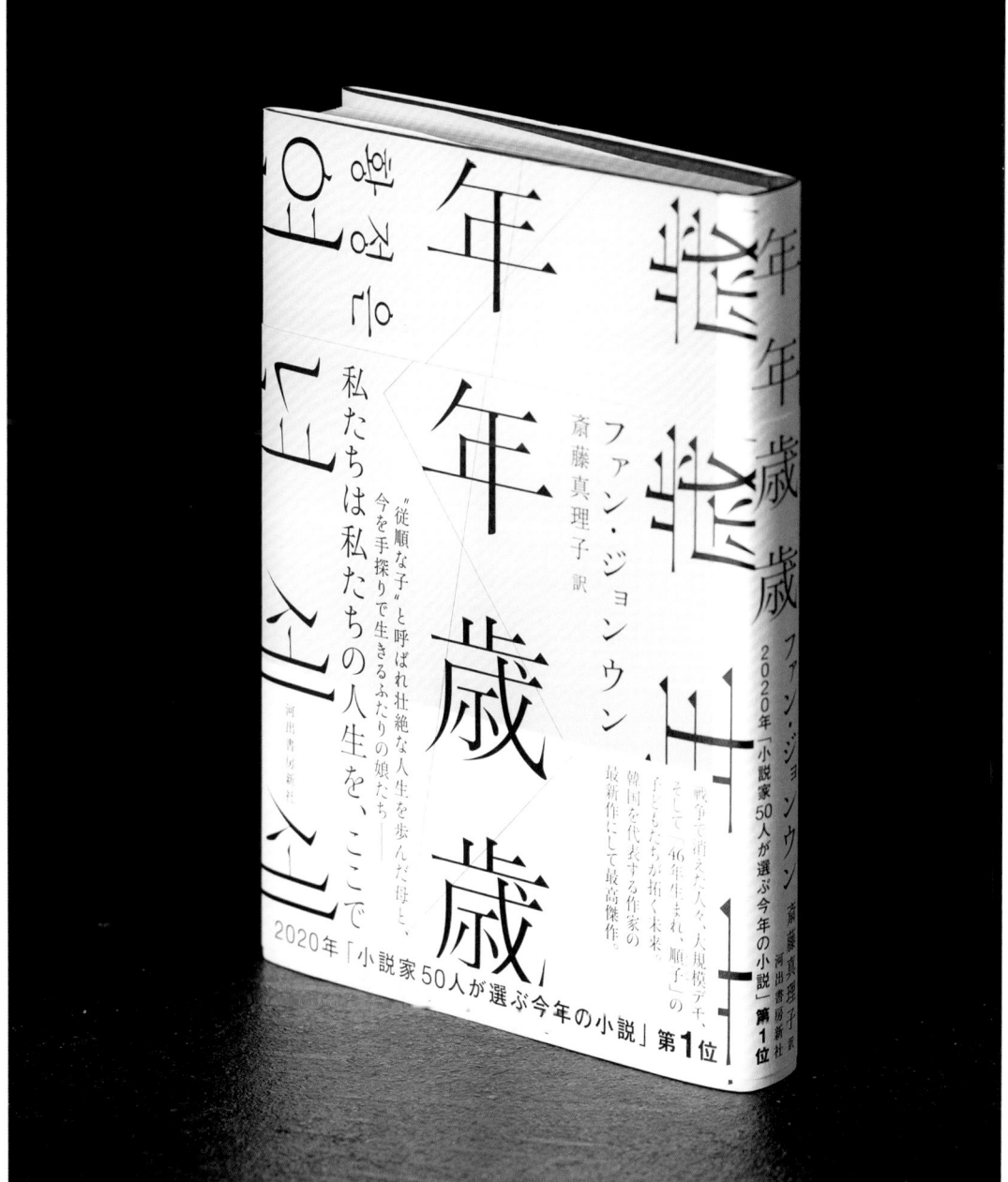

Year after Year

This is the design of a book of rough sketches by various designers. The process of sharpening a pencil, drawing a picture, and rounding the lead is captured in photo engraving, and the cover and inside pages express the enthusiasm of the designers as they drew the rough sketches.

AD   Masashi Murakami
D   Masashi Murakami, Moe Shibata
CL   MdN Corporation

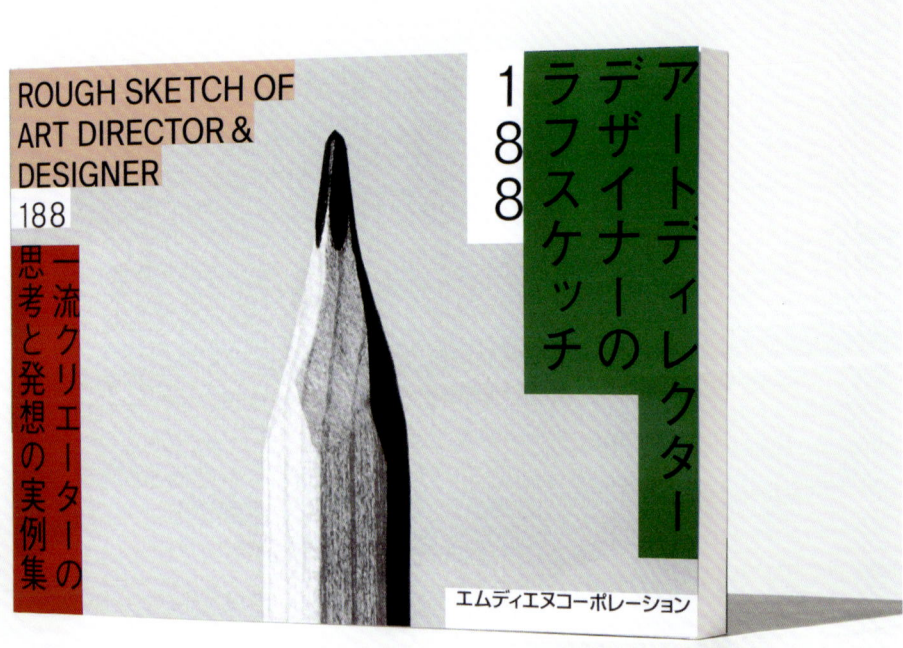

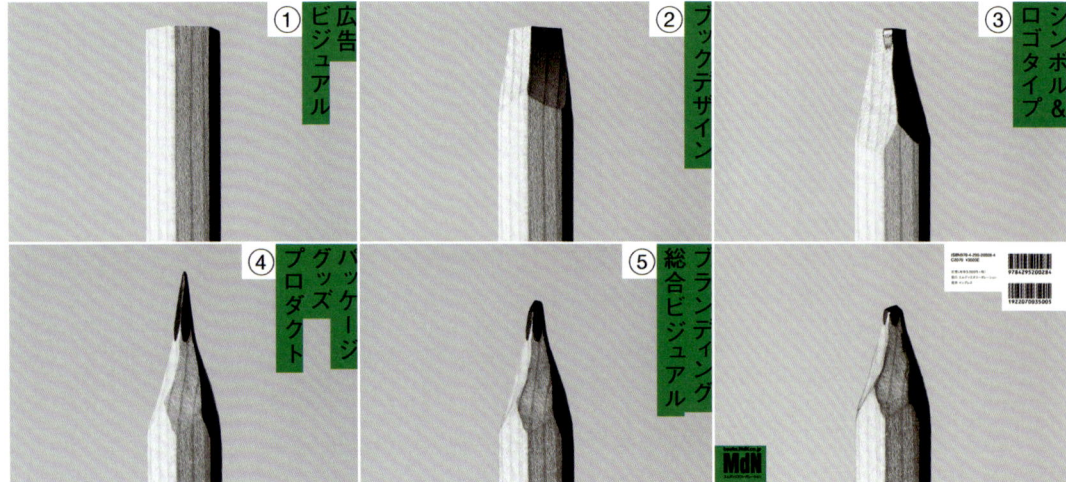

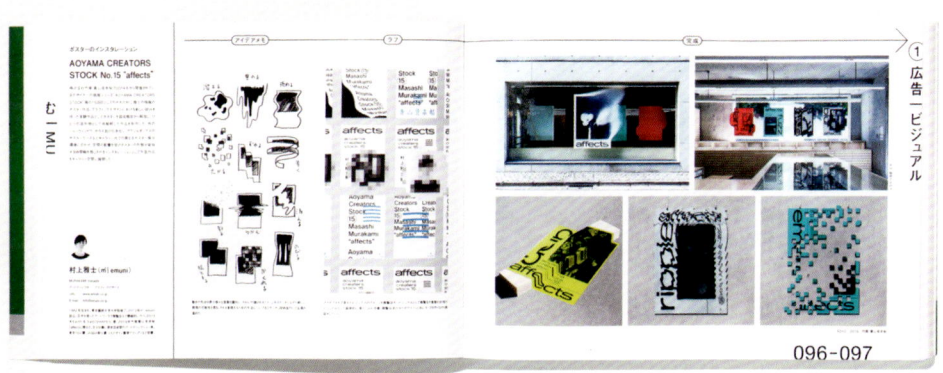

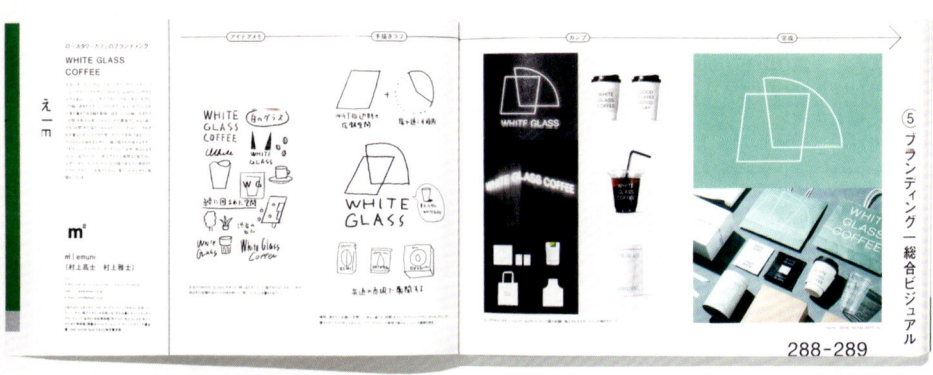

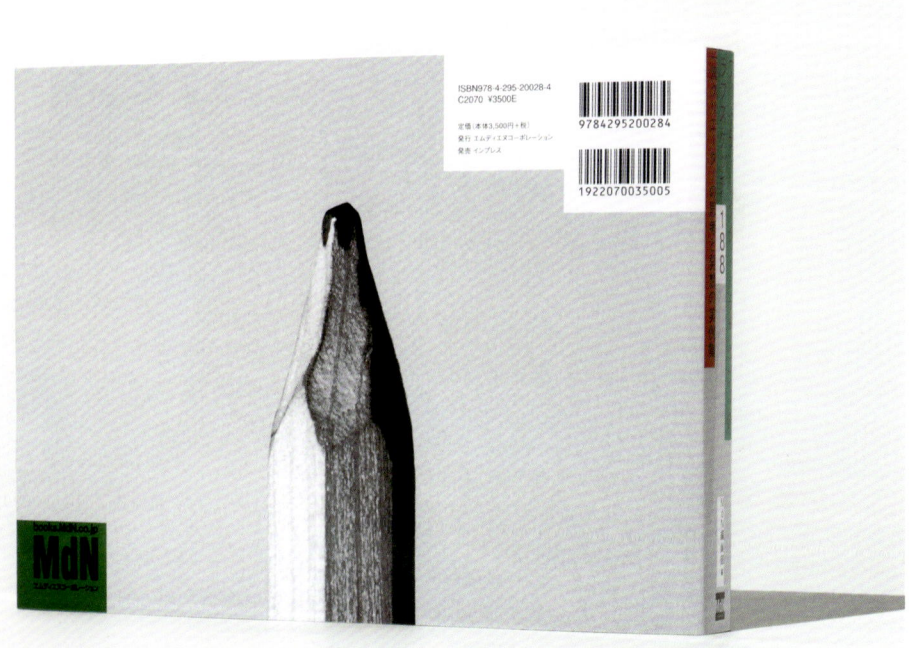

ISBN978-4-295-20028-4
C2070 ¥3500E

9784295200284

1922070035005

The artbook *Delusion to Hedi Slimane* is a poetry anthology. The stories are sequenced with the order from A to Z. The unique folding poetry anthology is placed within a mailable box. The motif and the text were developed with the idea of People and Thought.

DA   OUWN
D   Atsushi Ishiguro
CL   People and Thought

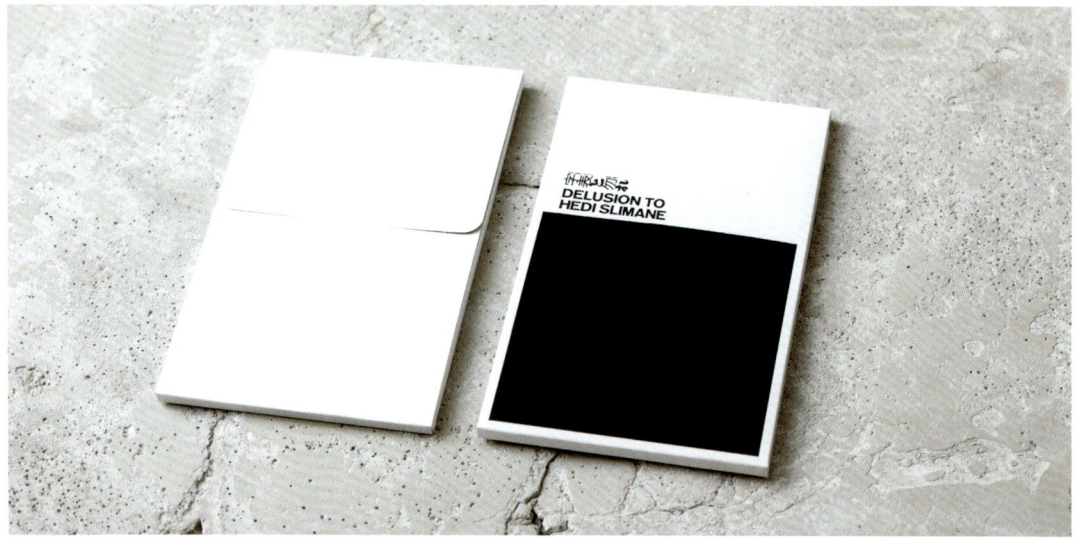

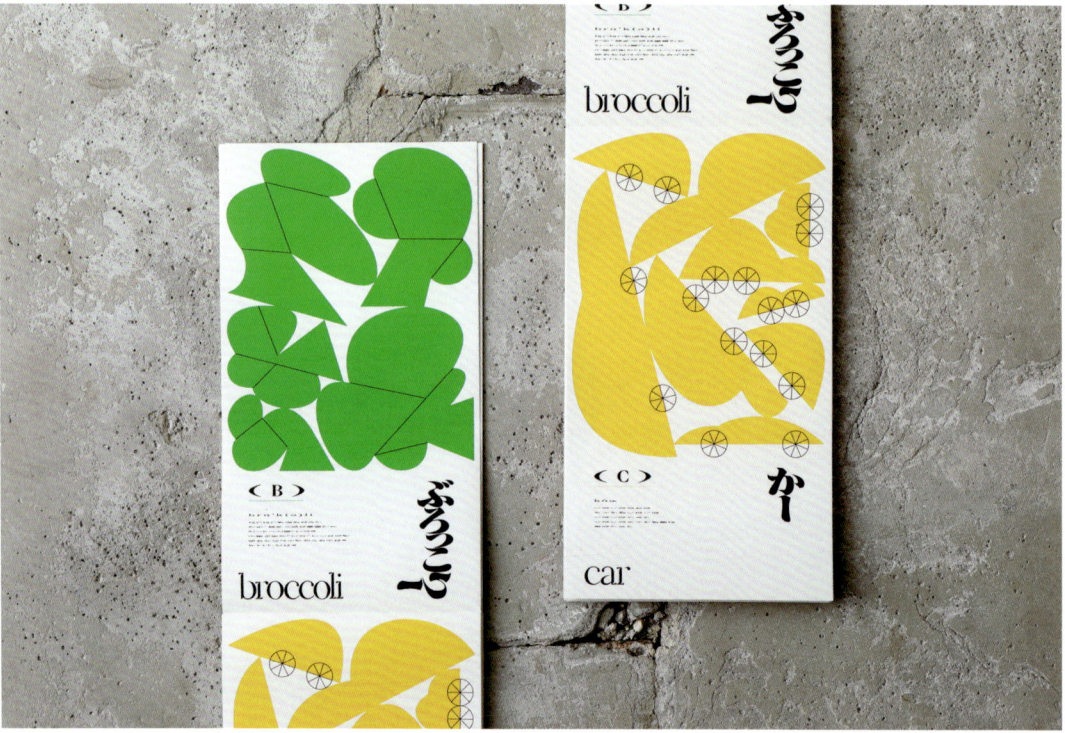

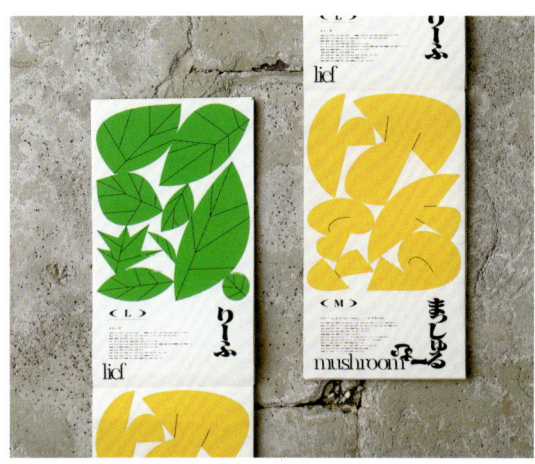

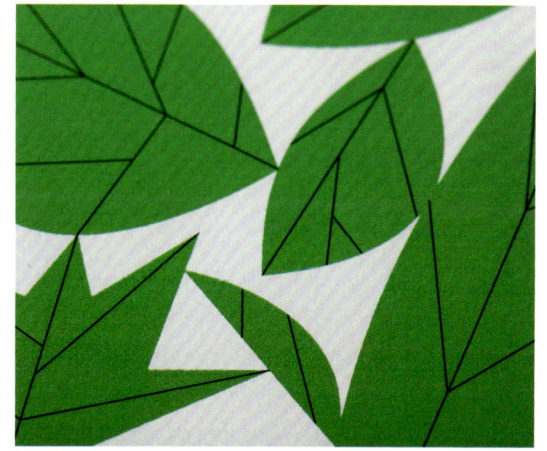

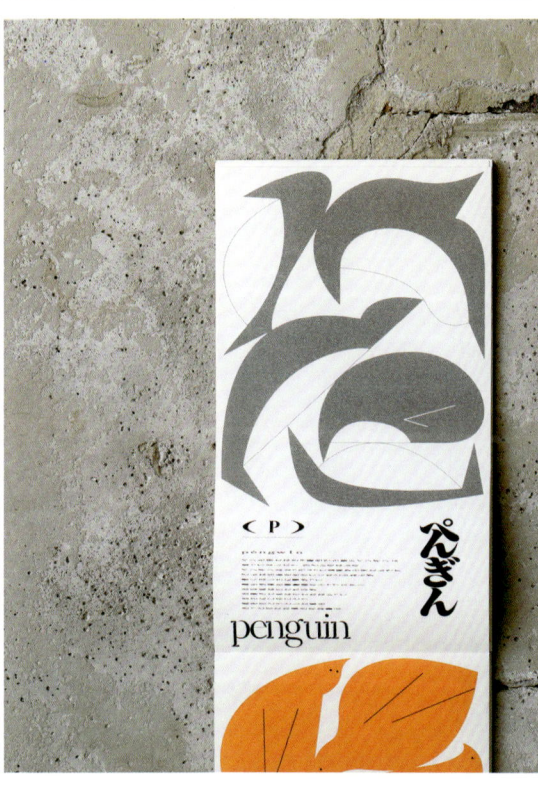

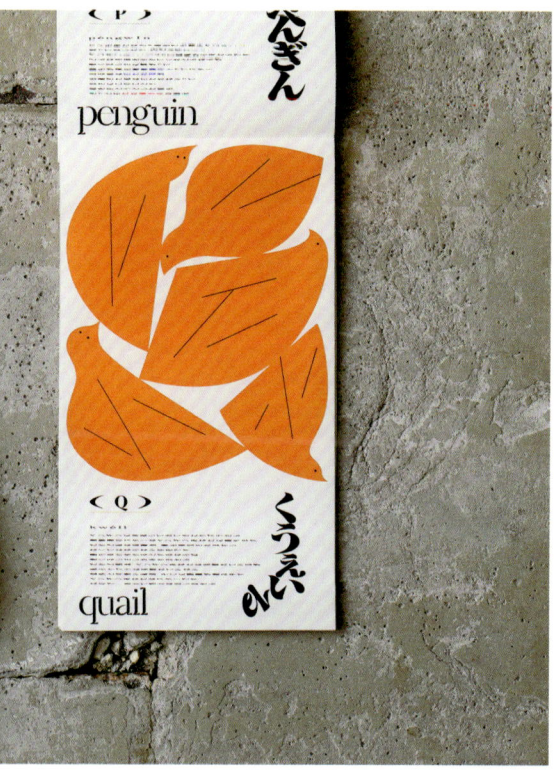

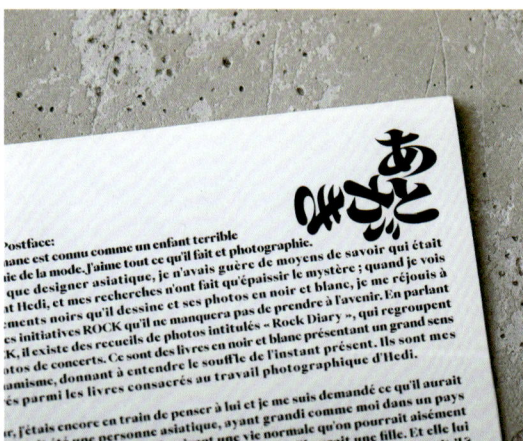

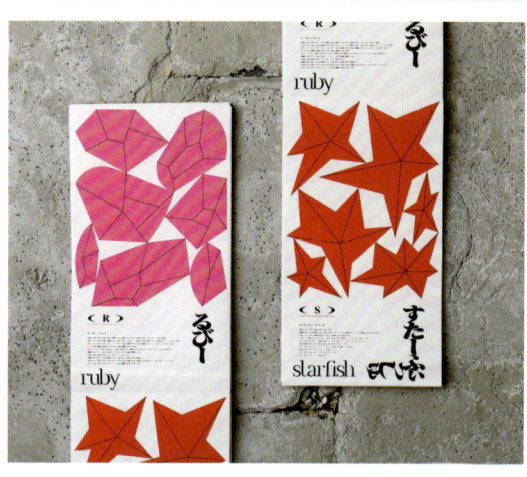

This greeting card is designed to look as if it were a single card that has been divided and reconstituted from various printed materials. The designers aimed for a design that transcends national borders by conveying a sense of diversity from the various hues of the two types of paper and by composing the card with elements that are not limited by languages.

AD   Masashi Murakami
D   Masashi Murakami, Sou Nagai
CL   TAKEO Co., Ltd.

Seasons Greetings

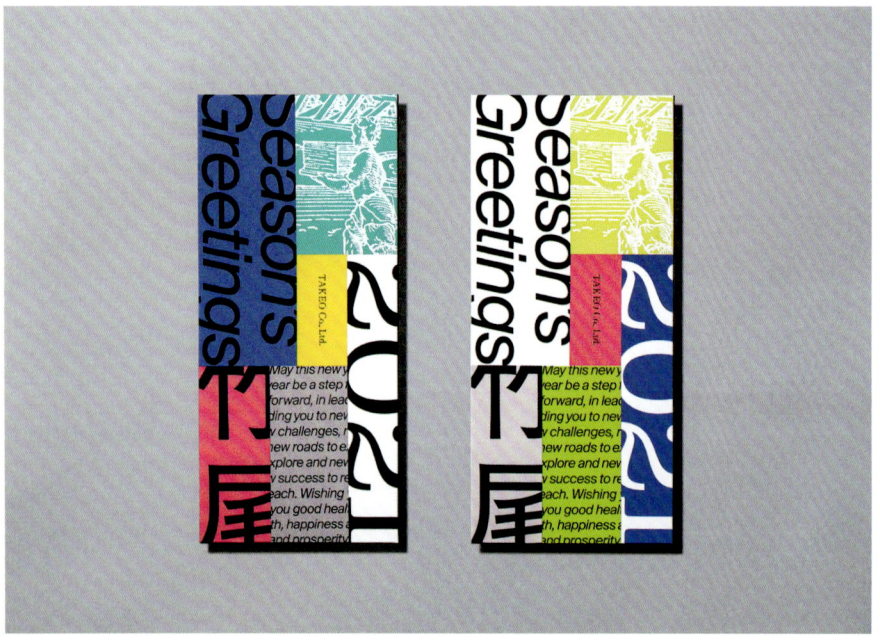

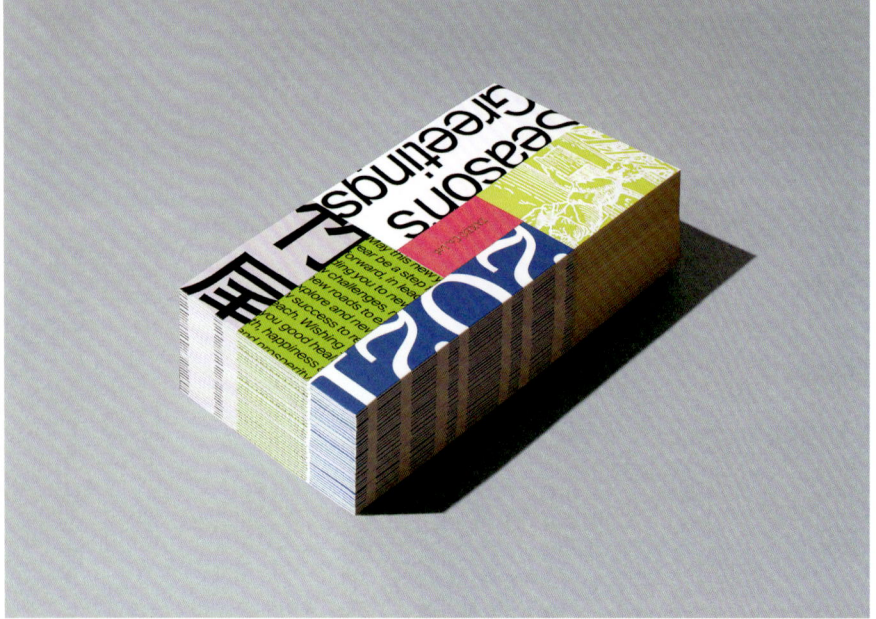

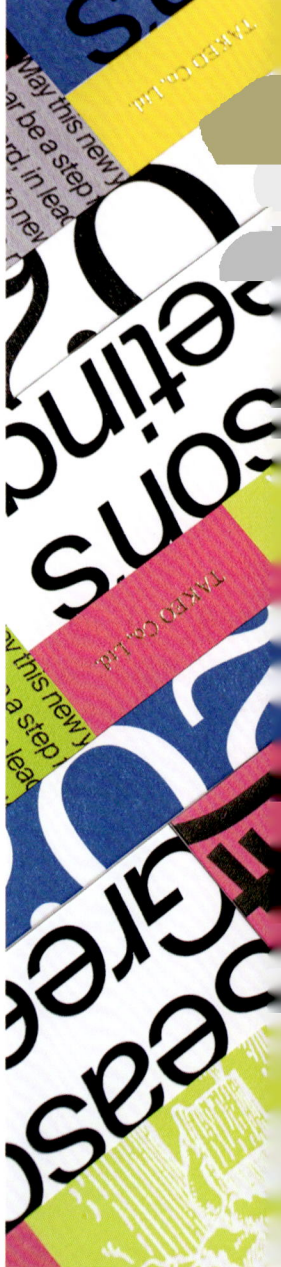

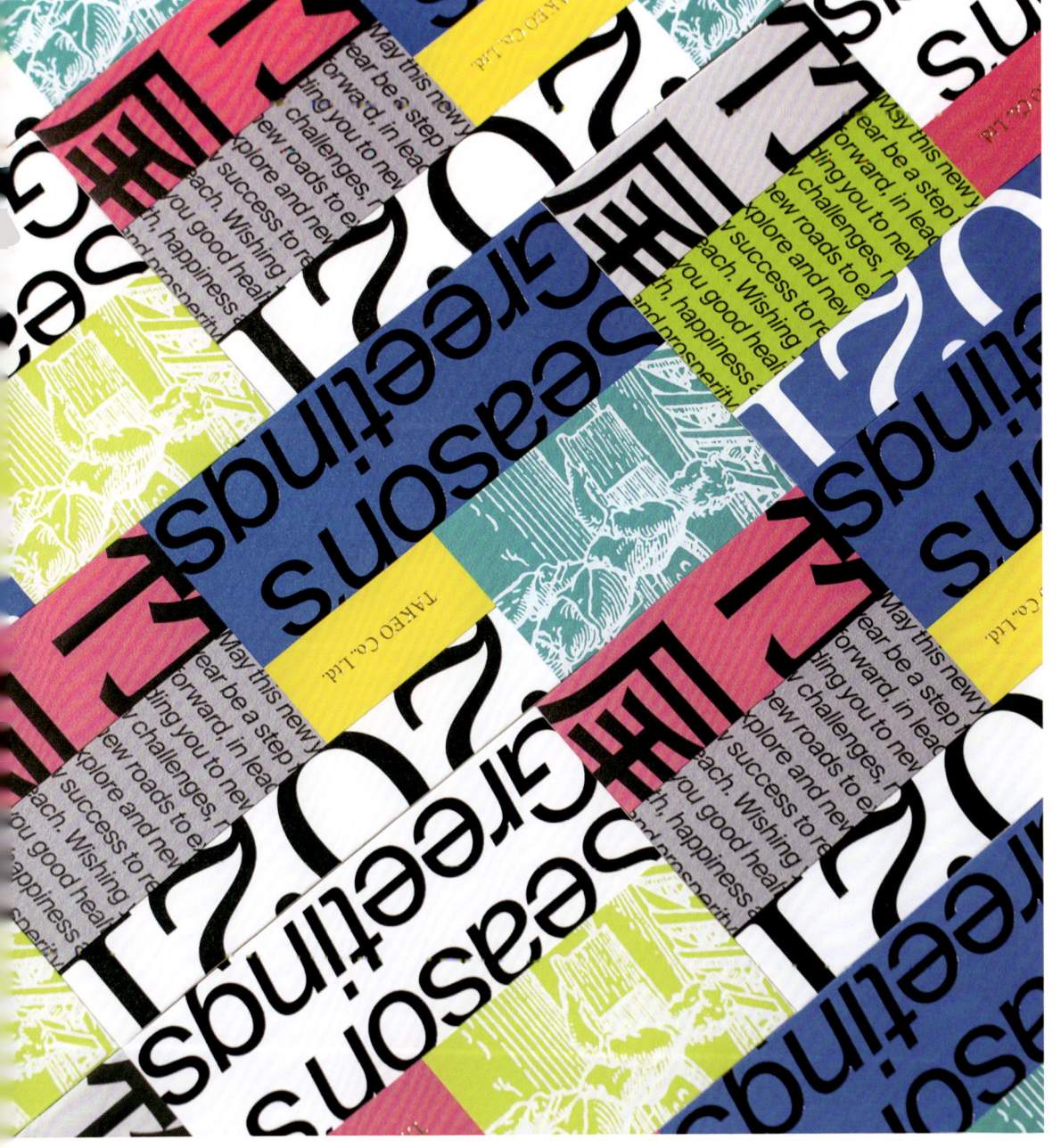

This is a design for fushigi design. Fushigi means "unthinkable" in Japanese.

This Japanese logo was broken down into a simple structure to create a natural visual form. As for the business card and envelope, paragram wanted to express the three-dimensionality of product design on the two-dimensional graphic design interestingly. Therefore, two extra borders were printed to create an effect of stacked paper. The envelope is printed with the color block when the die-cut pattern is spread out, and the flaps that are usually on the inside are glued to the outside. This also produced an unexpected splitting effect for the envelope.

DA   paragram
D   Yusuke Akai
CL   Fushigi Design

fushigi design Inc.

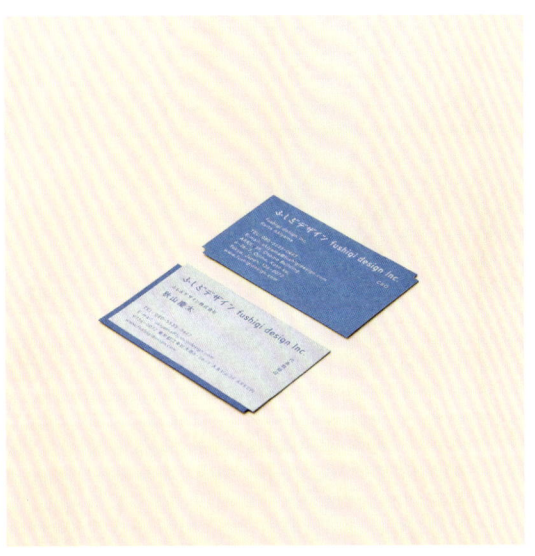

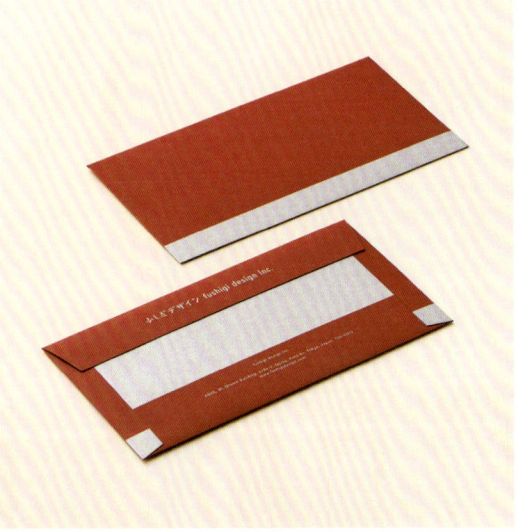

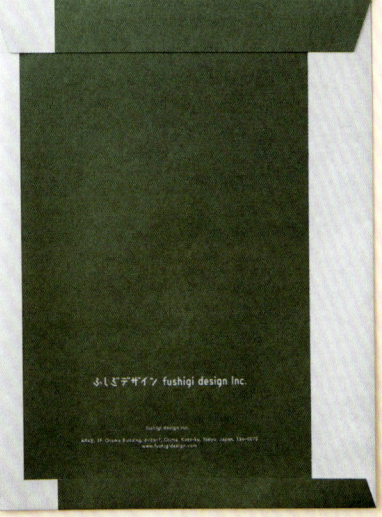

This is a card set created for an exhibition with the theme of paper as physical material, not as a medium for information. The exhibition proposed paper product prototypes that demonstrate new forms of paper like paper umbrellas, paper walls, and paper tables. Based on the concept to show never-before-seen paper landscapes, the works were photographed as if they were landscapes and were presented on the card, as well.

CD   Takuya Hoda, Yuuri Mikami
AD   Yuuri Mikami
D   Yuuri Mikami
PH   Yosuke Suzuki
CL   Heiwa Paper Co., Ltd.

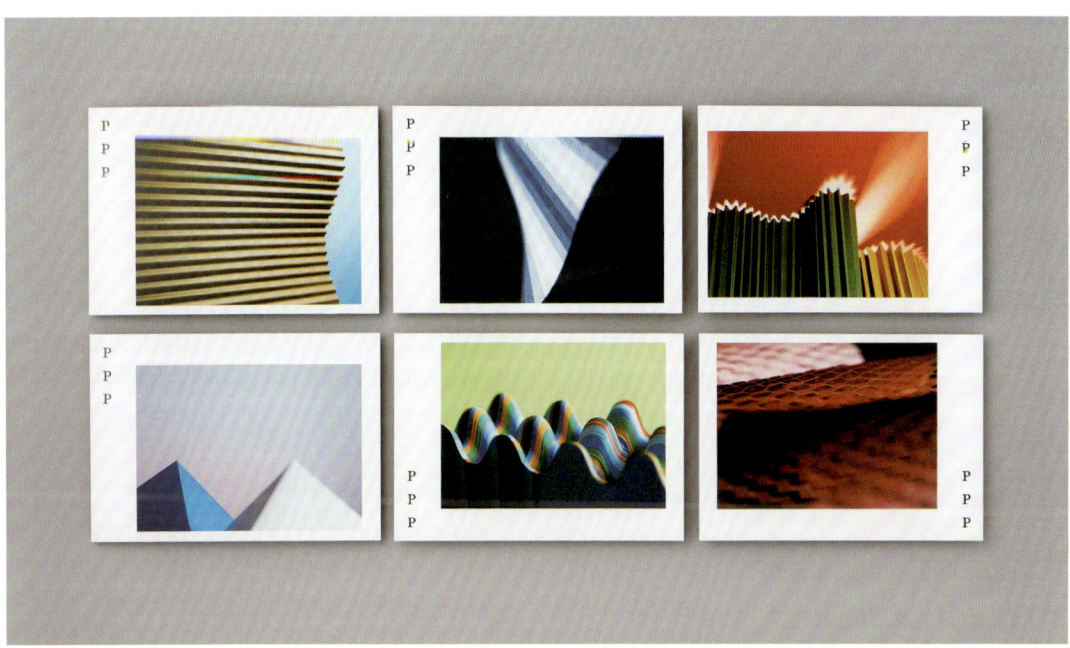

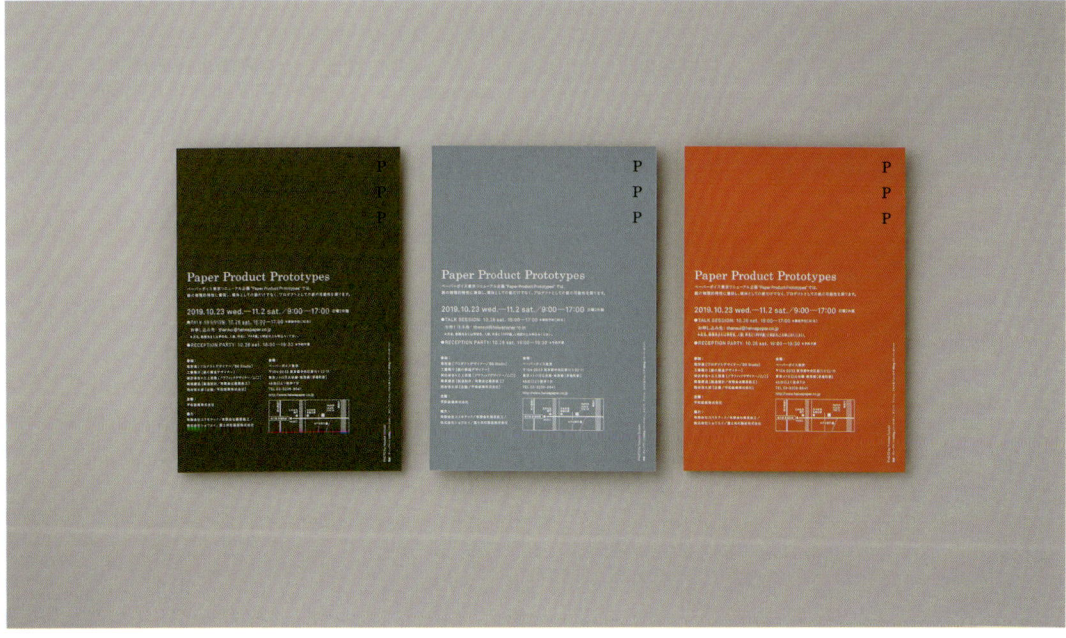

PPP—Paper Product Prototypes

TOKYOKOKKYO—Beyond Invisible Borders is a project aiming to form a community that generates opportunities for foreign residents of Japan and local people. Yuuri Mikami designed the project's logo and documentation booklet. The project explores the distance, points of contact, and commonality among different cultures, starting from the question of whether invisible borders exist in Tokyo, where many foreign residents live. The booklets, with words printed in contrasting colors on the spines, were also created based on this concept.

D   Yuuri Mikami
CL   Arts Council Tokyo

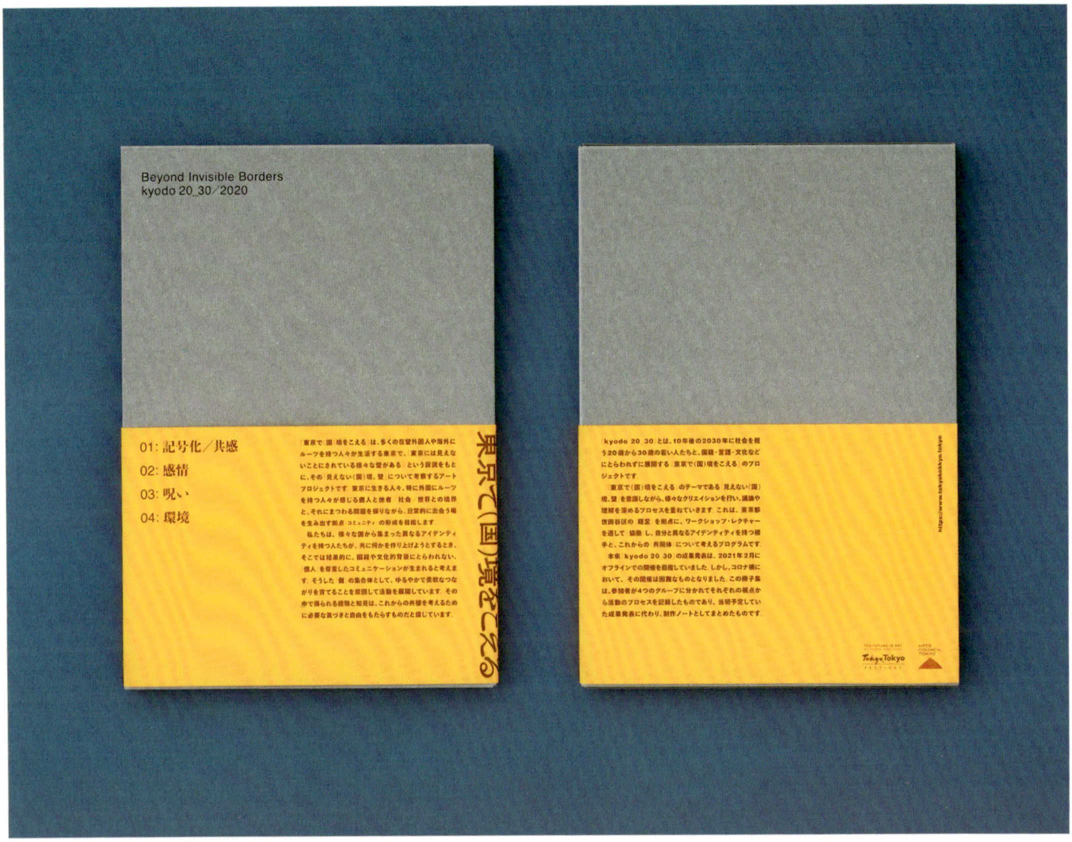

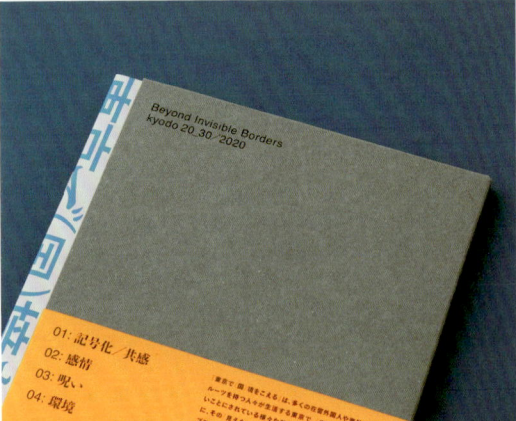

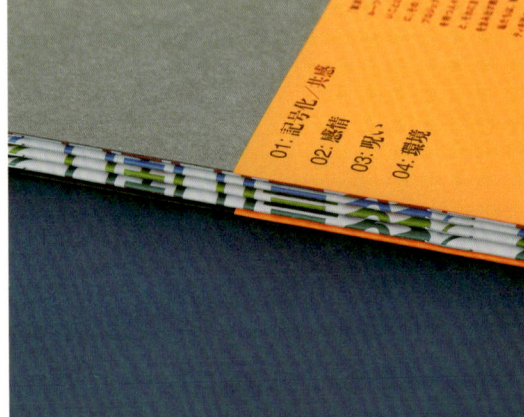

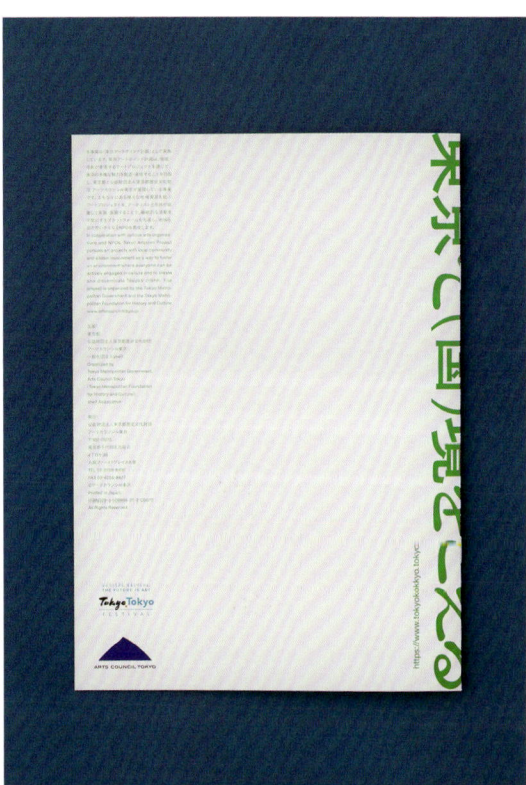
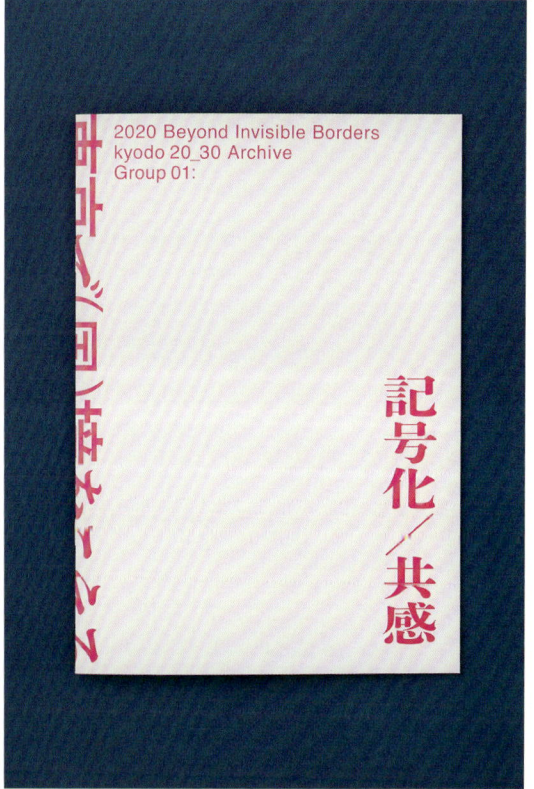

2020 Beyond Invisible Borders
kyodo 20_30 Archive
Group 01:

記号化／共感

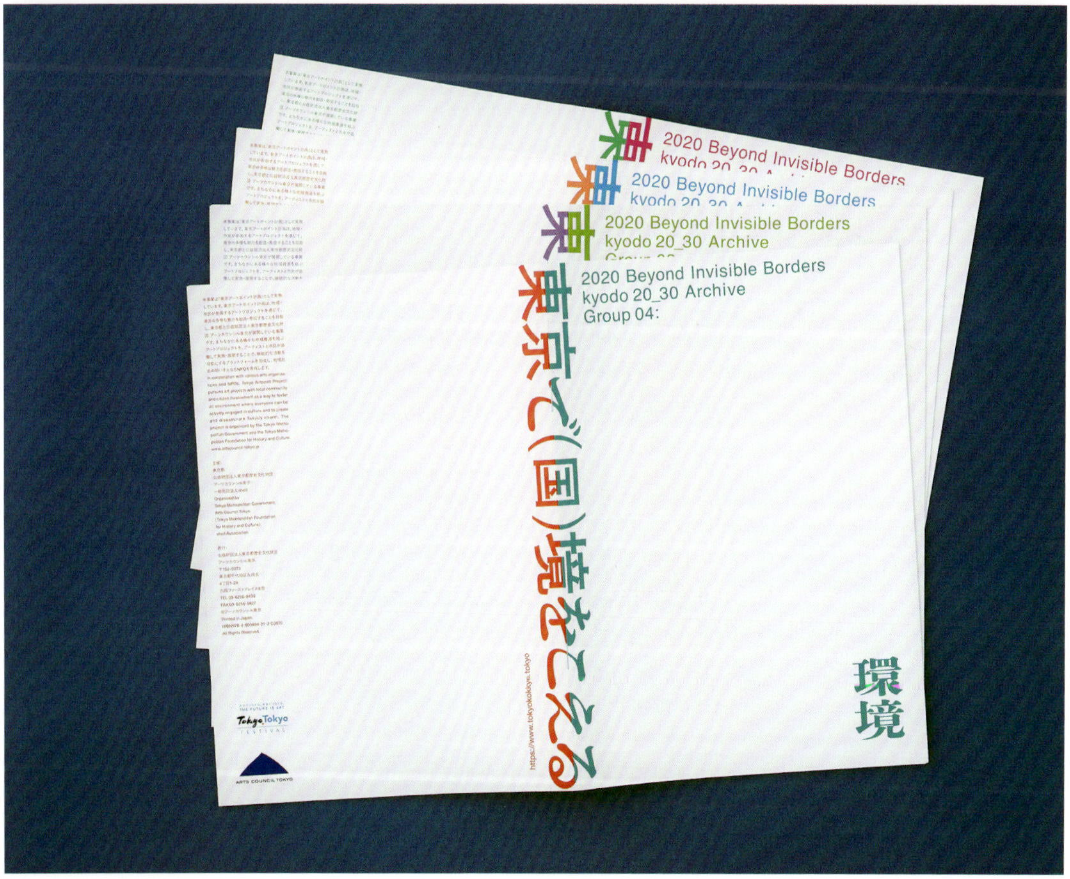

2020 Beyond Invisible Borders
kyodo 20_30 Archive

2020 Beyond Invisible Borders
kyodo 20_30 Archive

2020 Beyond Invisible Borders
kyodo 20_30 Archive

2020 Beyond Invisible Borders
kyodo 20_30 Archive
Group 04:

環境

Package Design

This is a candy for the artist Peter Doig's first solo exhibition in Japan. Peter Doig is known as a creator who relentlessly repeats the same motifs and compositions. Fascinated by one of the motifs, the canoe, Moe Furuya used a canoe as a container for sweets and put Bonbon a la Liqueur, a kind of sugar confectionery containing syrup of sake inside. The liquor uses craft gin made from seaweed called bladderwrack, which is made at a distillery in the northernmost part of Scotland, where Doig was born. This is the candy to set sail into the world of Peter Doig.

D	Moe Furuya
CA	Mio Tsuchiya
CL	The National Museum of Modern Art, Tokyo

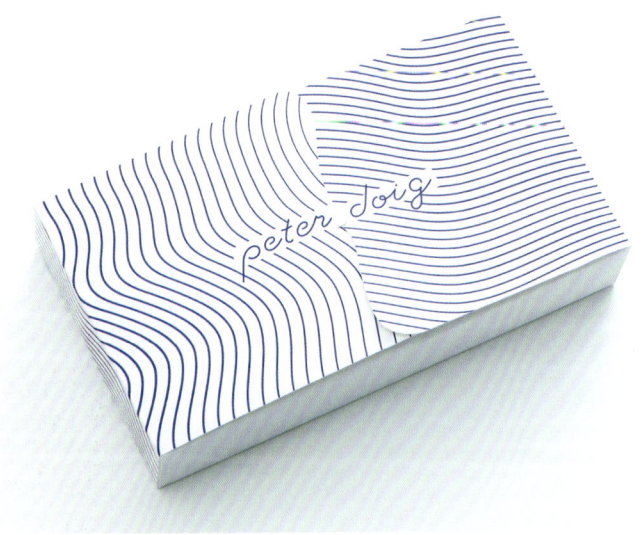

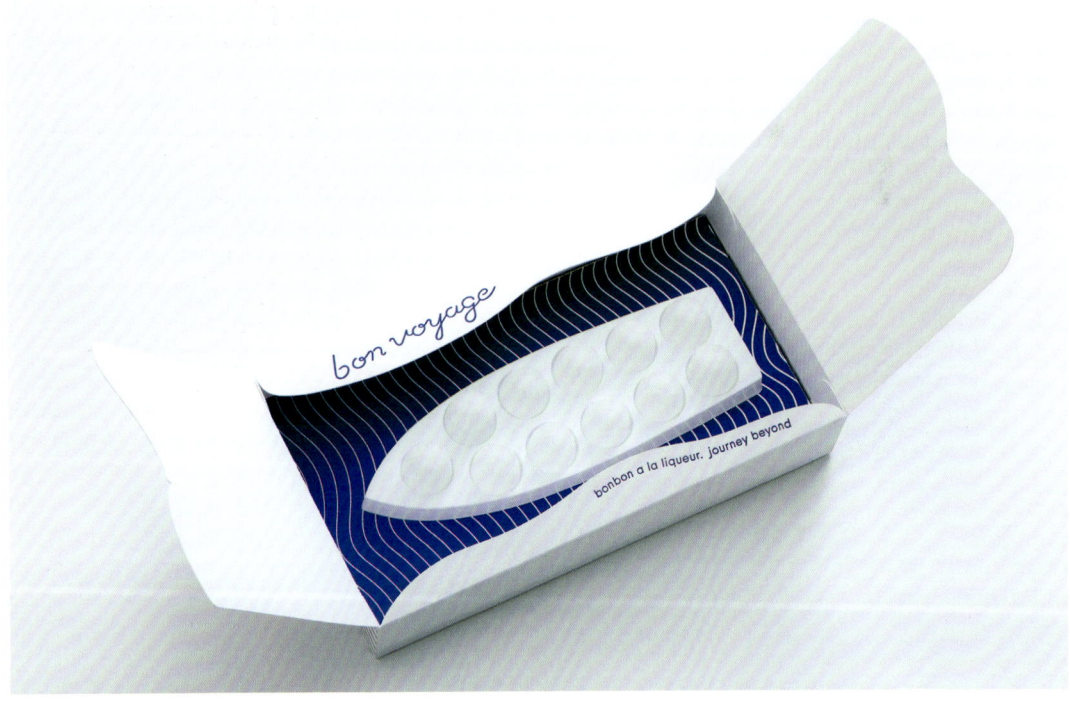

Bon Voyage

This is a package design for a long-established Kyoto-based traditional Japanese confectionery brand. To convey that the sweets are carefully hand-made, Akiko Sekimoto used handwritten brush strokes as the base of the packaging. In addition, to help people remember that the shop is located in a place called Shichijo in Kyoto, the Chinese character "七 (seven)" was designed as a symbol and laid out on the packages because "shichi" in "shichijo" means "seven" in Japanese. When the packages are lined up on the store shelves, the symbol will stand out.

AD   Akiko Sekimoto
D   Akiko Sekimoto
CW   Atsuko Fujishiro
PH   Mikiya Takimoto
CL   Shichijokanshundo Co., Ltd.

Shichijokansyundo

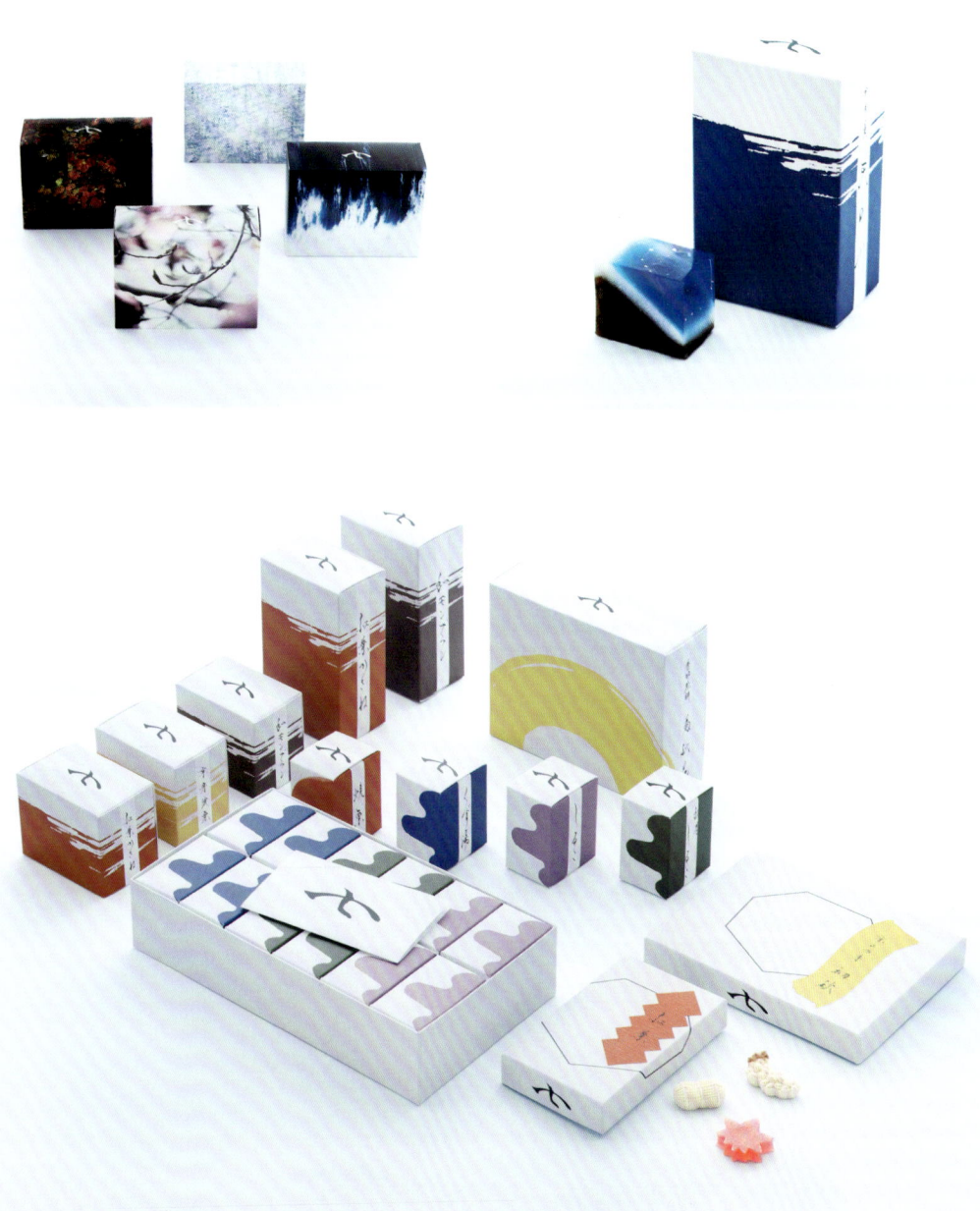

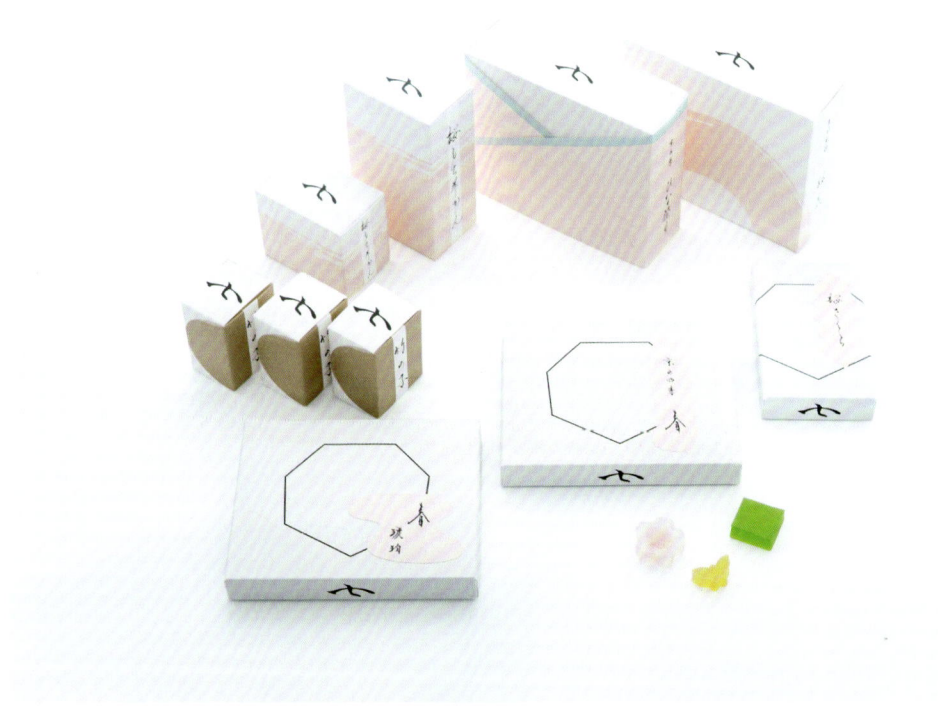

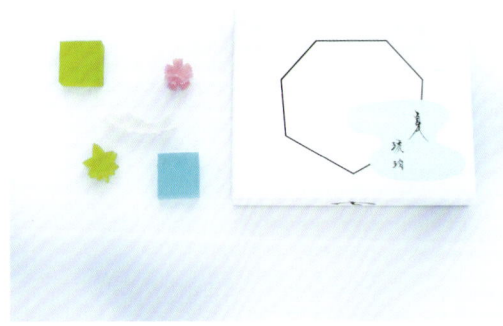

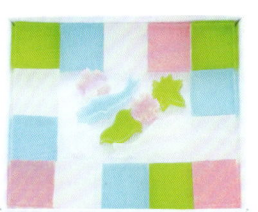

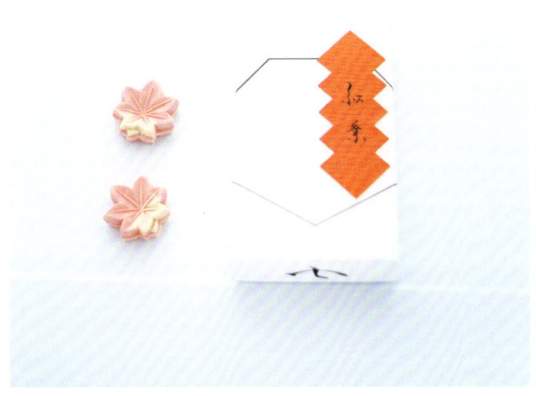

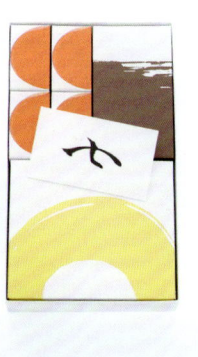

The design is a story about kitsune or fox. paragram made
the package and other items and they became a series
of picture books, illustrating the whole story of how the
kitsune encounters lemons. Every package represents a
scene of the story.

DA   paragram
AD   Yusuke Akai
D   Yusuke Akai, Miho Aoyagi
IL   Nishi Syuku
CL   Morozoff

Kitsune to Lemon

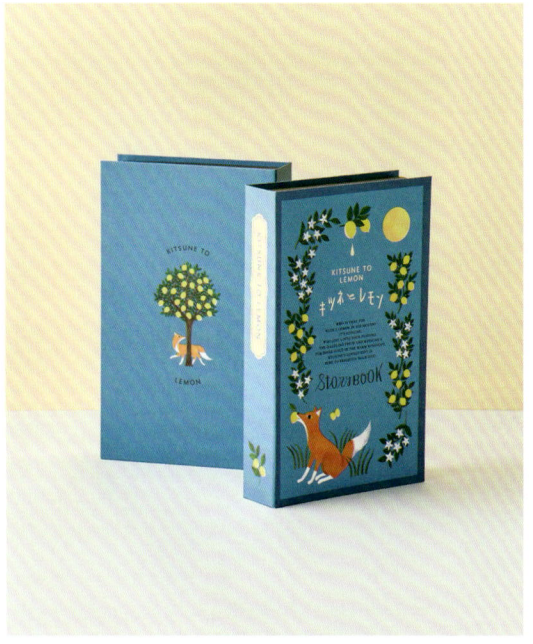

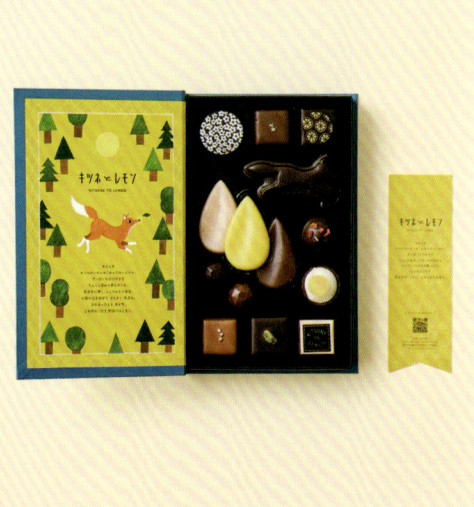

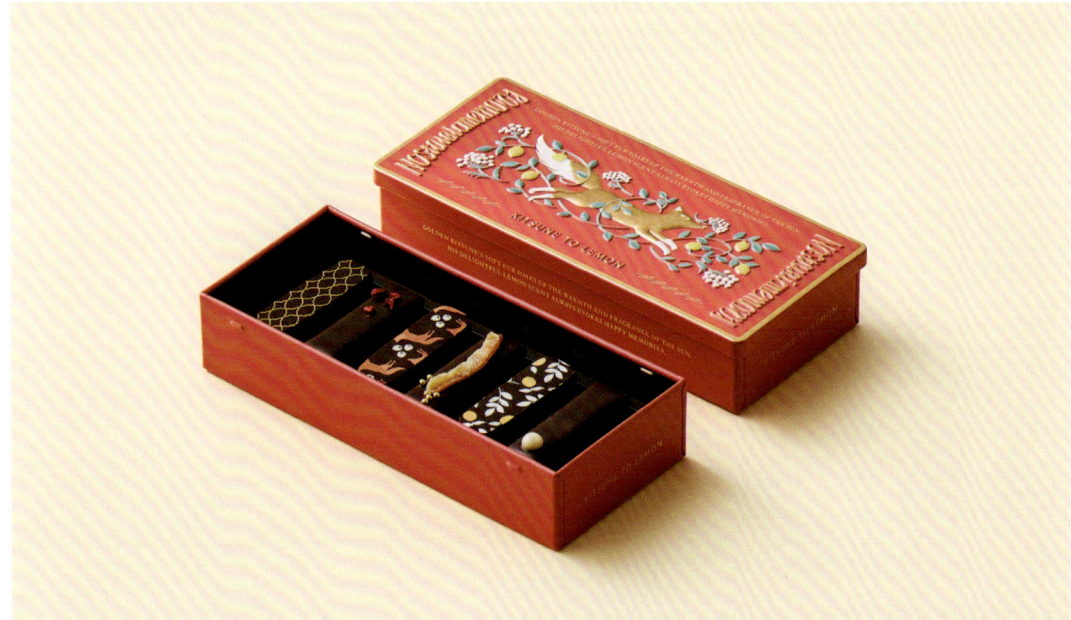

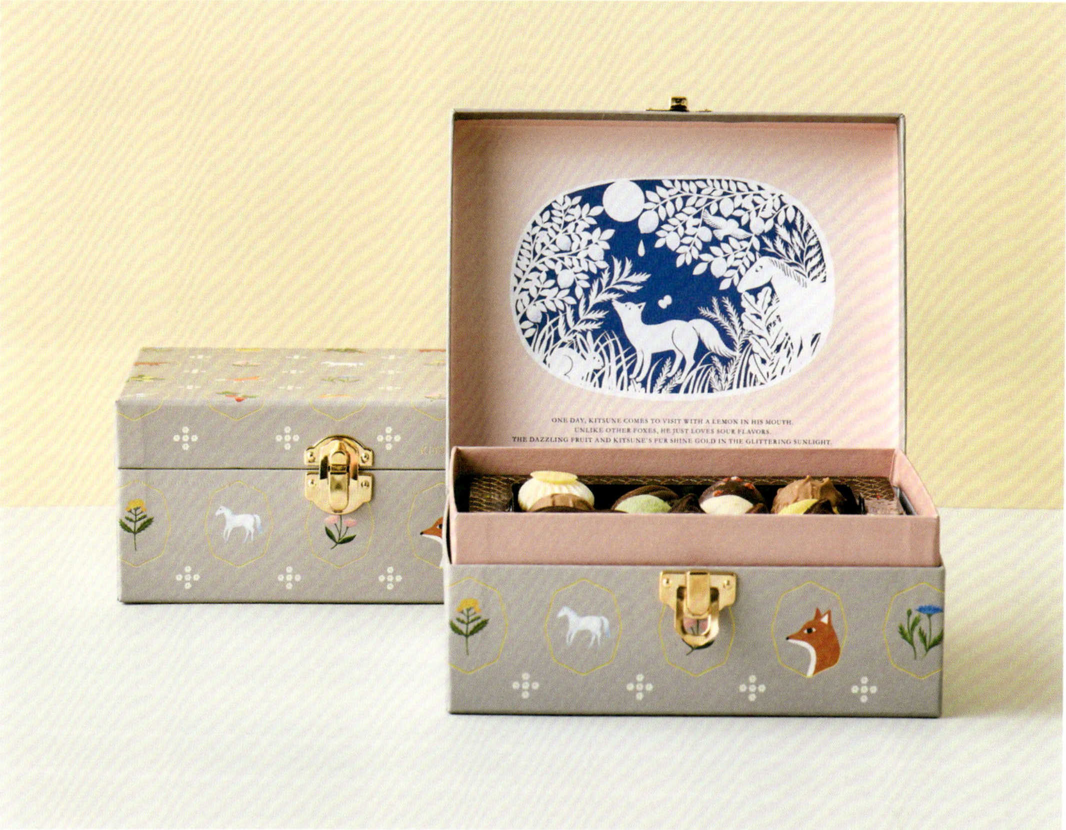

ONE DAY, KITSUNE COMES TO VISIT WITH A LEMON IN HIS MOUTH.
UNLIKE OTHER FOXES, HE JUST LOVES SOUR FLAVORS.
THE DAZZLING FRUIT AND KITSUNE'S FUR SHINE GOLD IN THE GLITTERING SUNLIGHT.

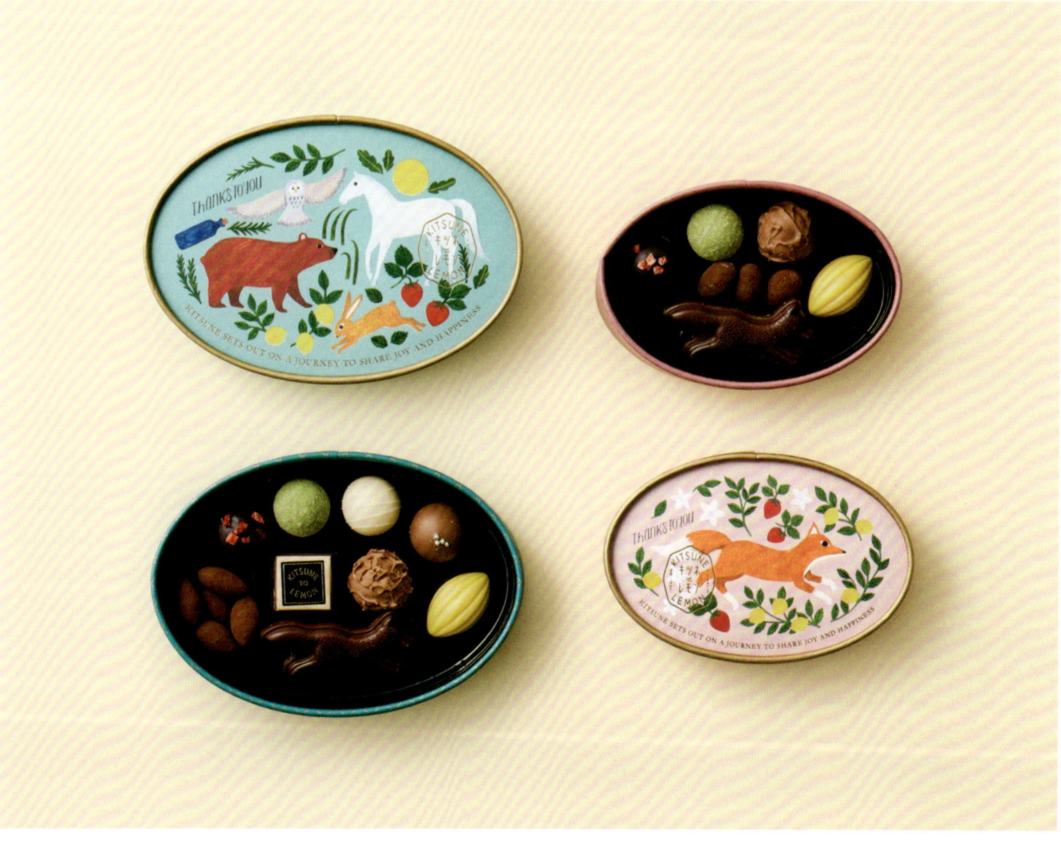

This is a limited edition chocolate for Valentine's Day made by Morozoff, which is a leading luxury confectionery maker in Japan. With the concept of "decorating package," paragram cooperated with various writers and illustrators to transform the package of chocolate into a decorative art.

DA paragram
AD Yusuke Akai
D   Mona Kiyono
IL Yuka Hiiragi, unpis, Peko Asano,
    Ayumi Hanamatsu, ZUCK,
    Haruka Yamakawa, Konatsu Tani,
    tupera tupera, Mao Horihata,
    Miroco Machiko, Nishi Syuku,
    Toshiyuki Fukuda, CHALKBOY
CL Morozoff

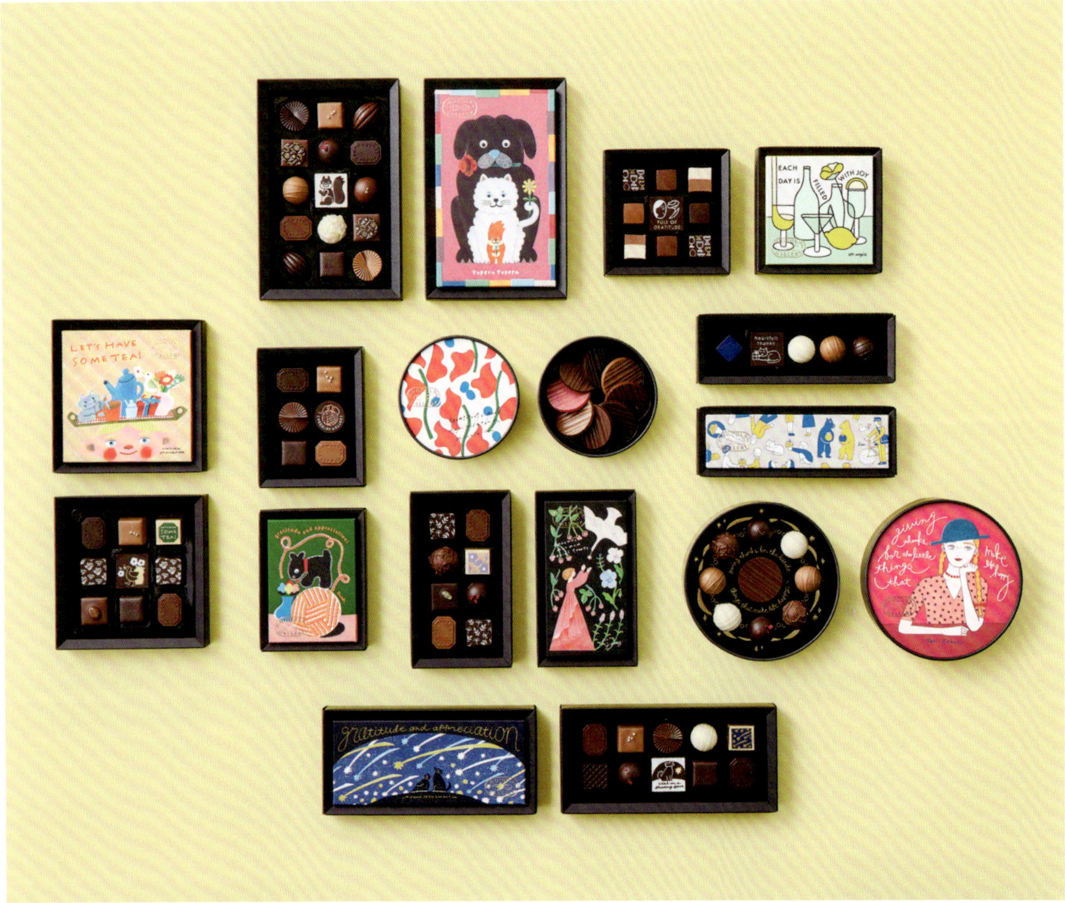

Chocolat Gallery

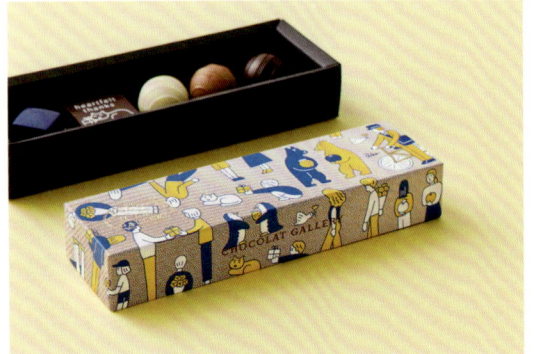

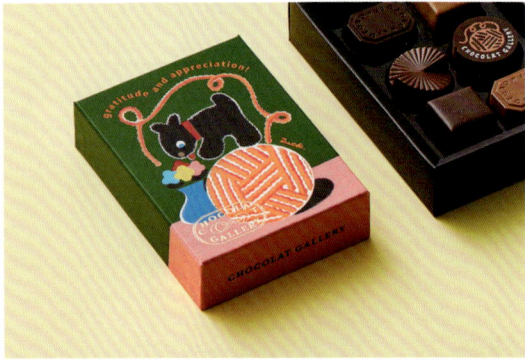

270

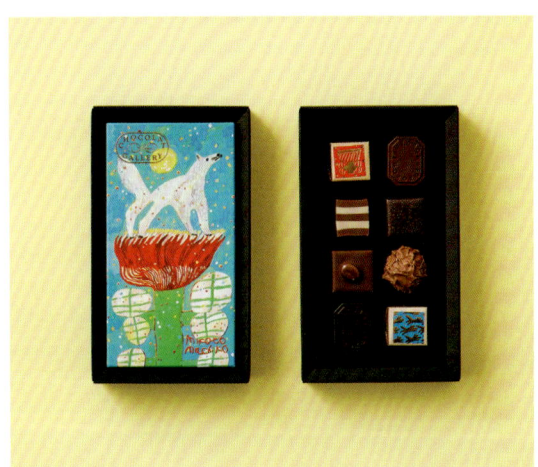

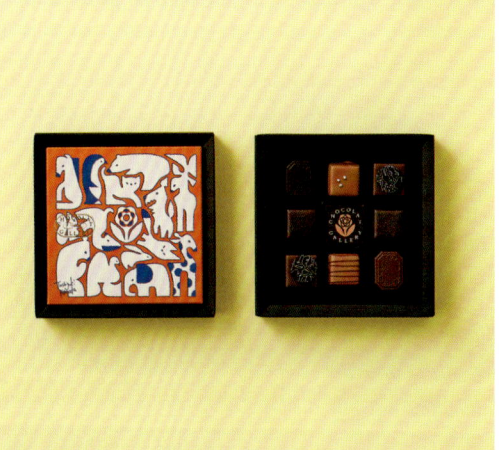

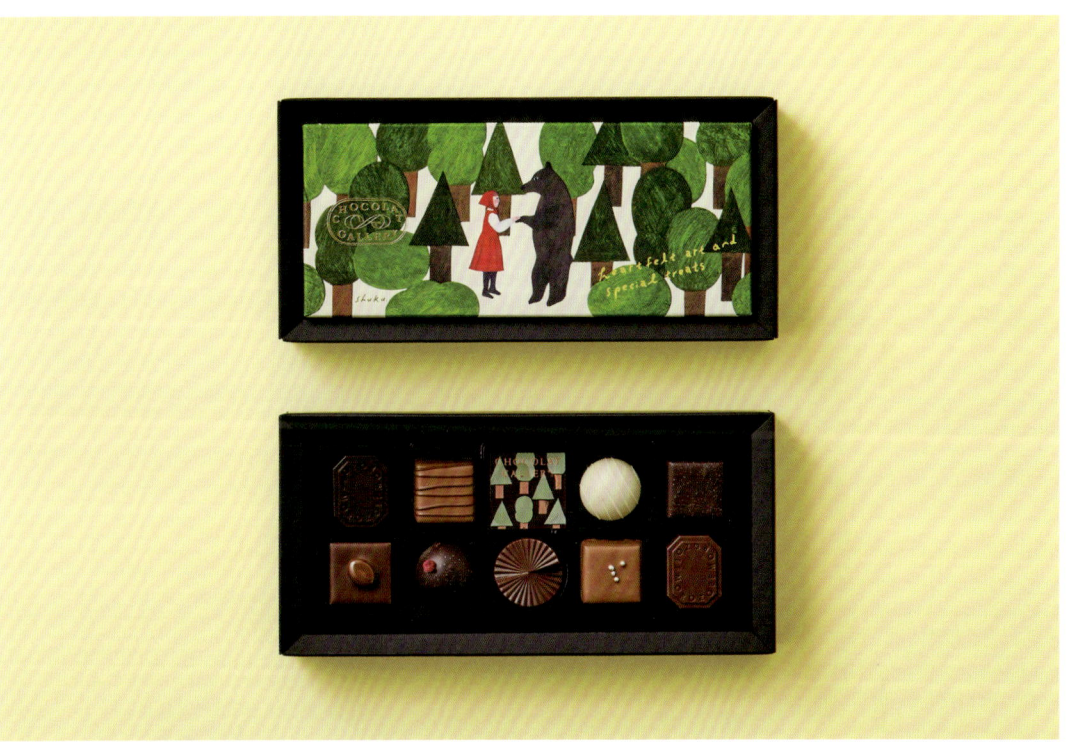

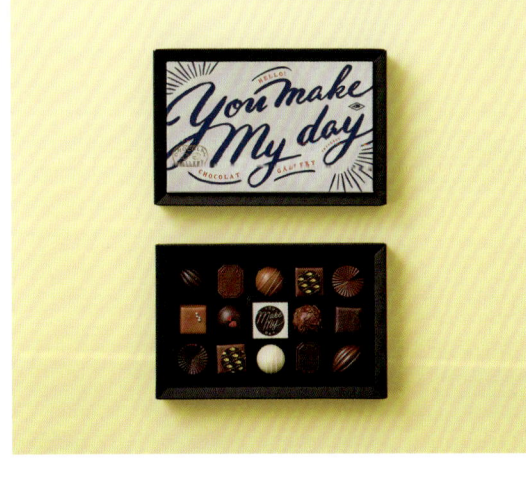

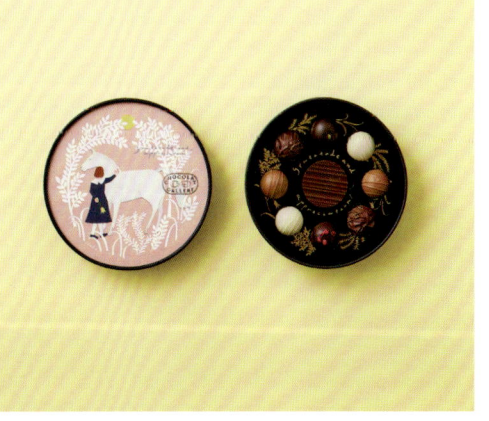

LIGHTS DESIGN created an environmentally-friendly package for kukka, an essential oil mist for insomnia. The illustrations on the package mimic the flowers with the combination of geometric shapes and colors, giving out a sense of playfulness.

DA	LIGHTS DESIGN
CD	Koichi Tamamura
AD	Satoru Nakaichi
D	Satoru Nakaichi
PD	Fumiyasu Kawamura (VYONE)
CL	Hinatabi Co., Ltd.

kukka

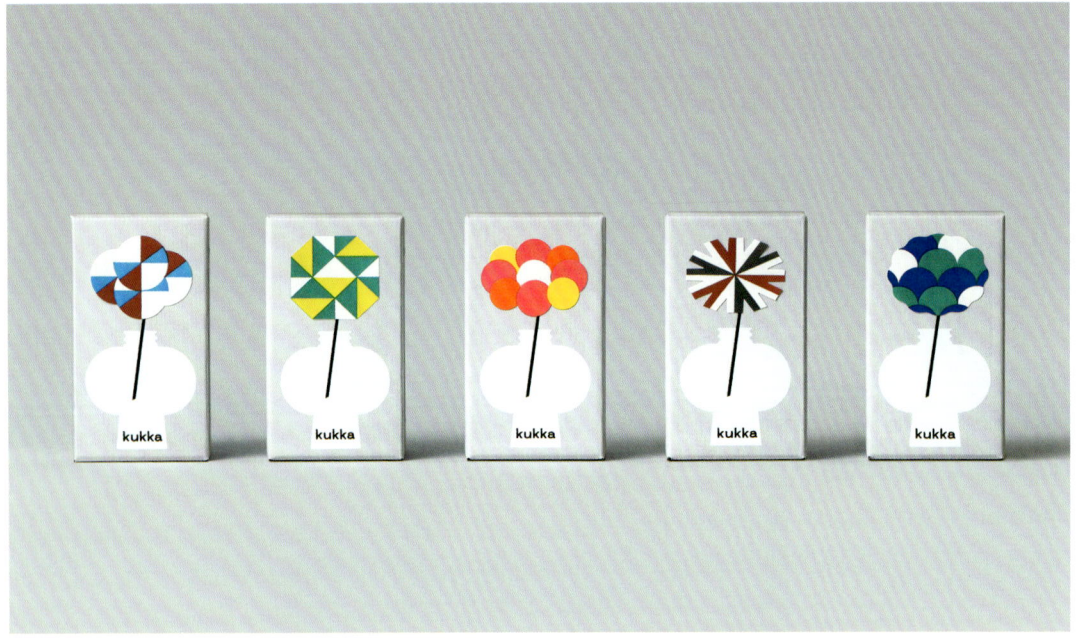

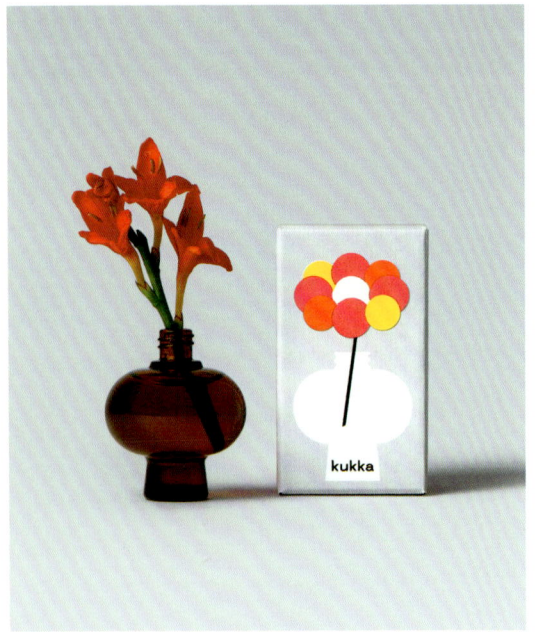

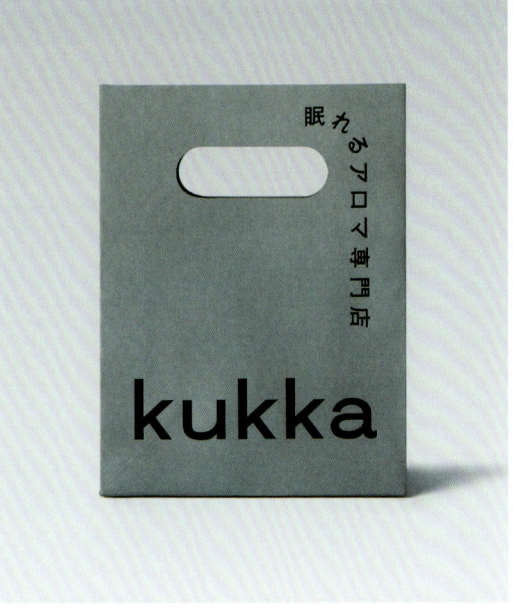

This is the design of cardboard boxes for Lumine Agri
Marche, an agricultural project run by Lumine. The project
is environmentally-friendly by aiming for a design that
serves as both a box for gifts and a box for mailing.

DA   MOTOMOTO inc.
AD   Kenichi Matsumoto
D   Kenichi Matsumoto,
        Naomi Sakamoto, Chihiro Sato
CL   Lumine Co., Ltd.

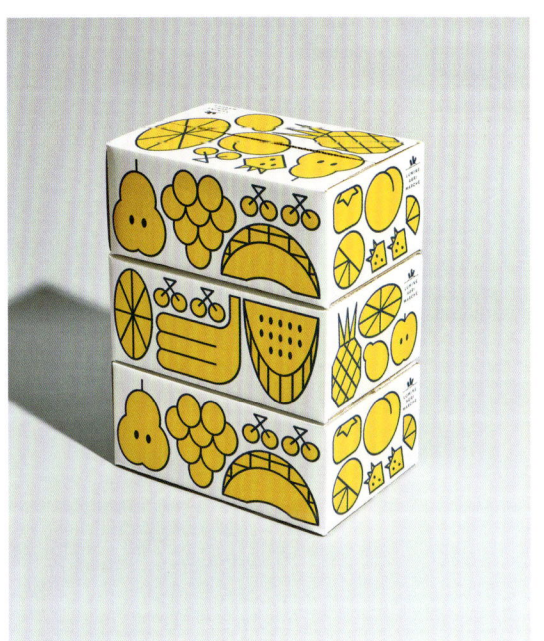

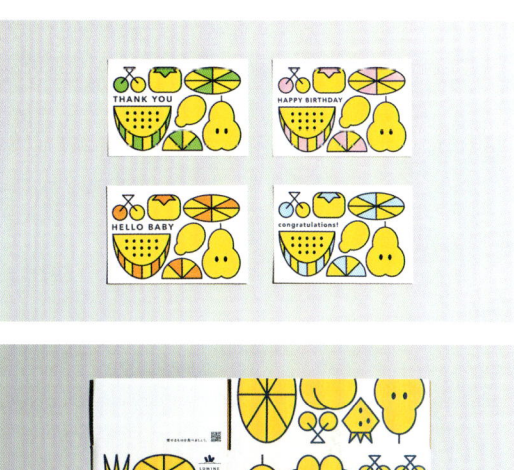

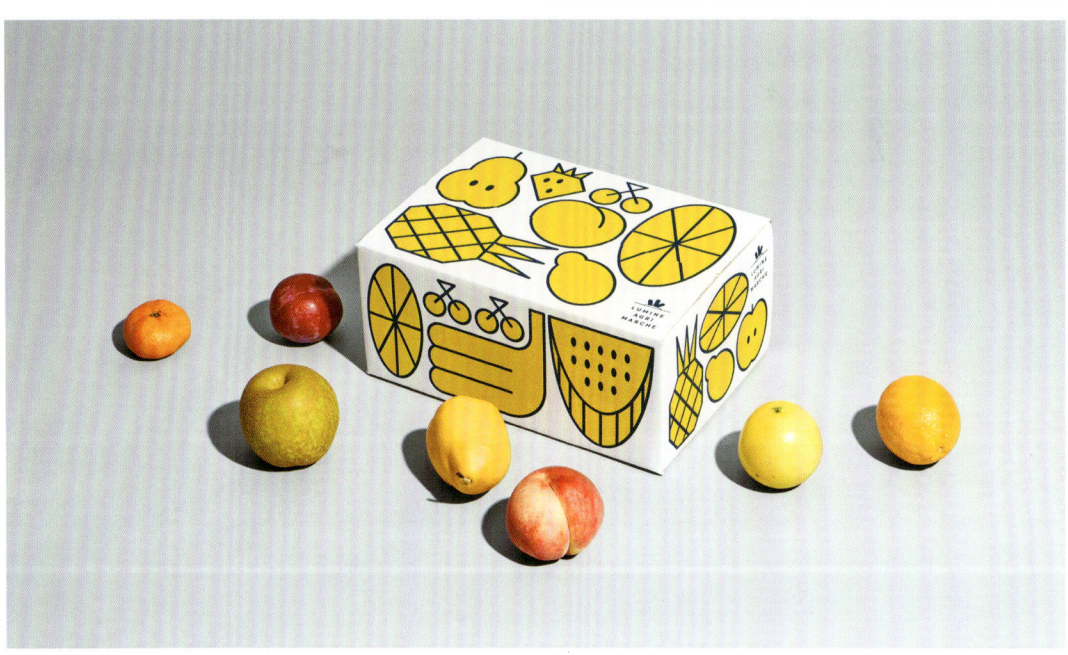

This is a branding project for a floral artist. The packaging was designed to be simple and colorless to show through the colors of the flowers, so that they will not detract from the artist's work. The logo is based on the Japanese kanji "花 (flower)" and all the materials were created around this logo. The logo also states Sakura Shimizu's position as a Japanese floral artist.

CD   Hitoshi Kobayashi
AD   Nobuya Hayasaka
D   Nobuya Hayasaka
CL   Sakura Shimizu

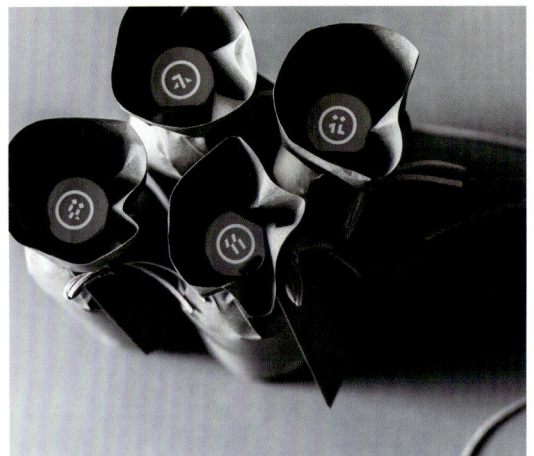
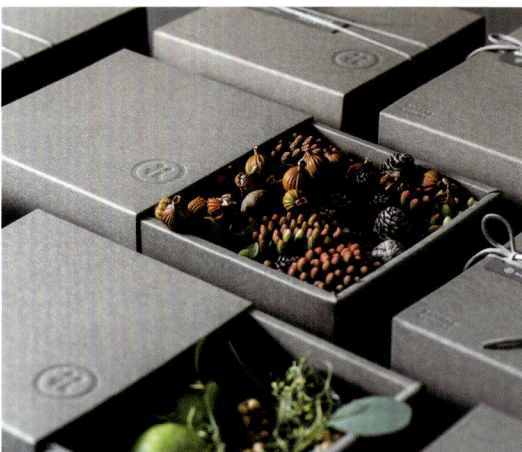

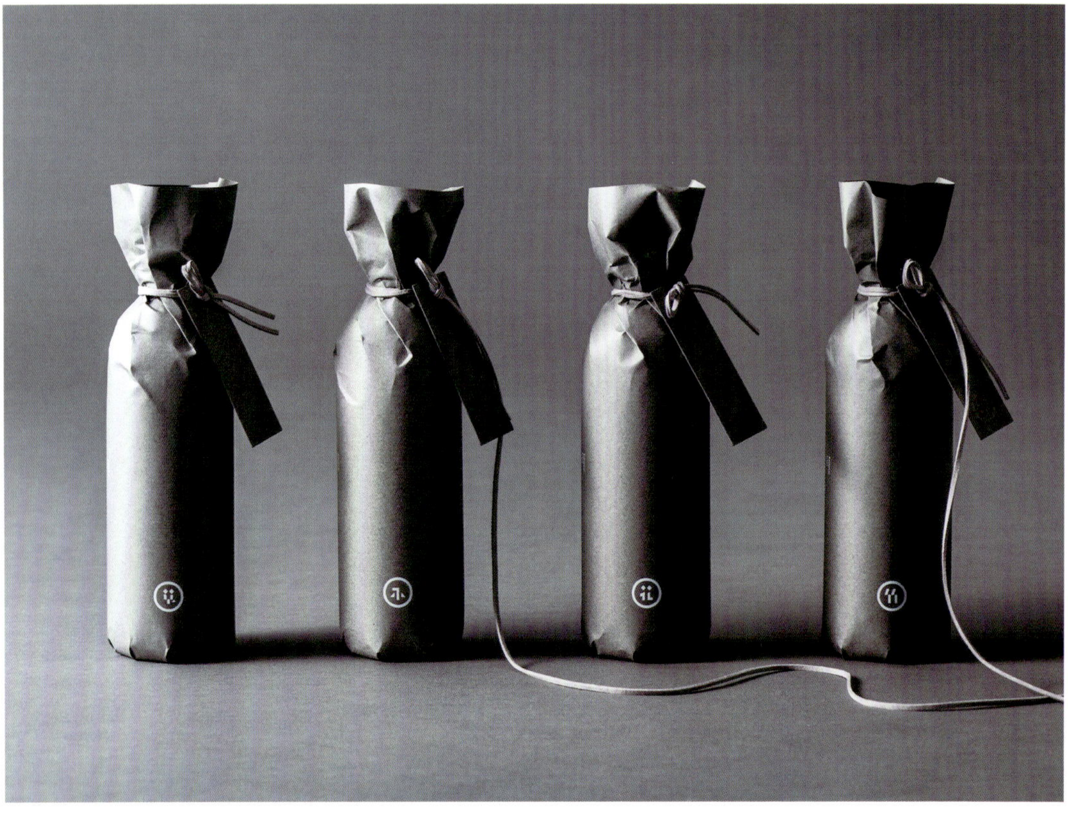

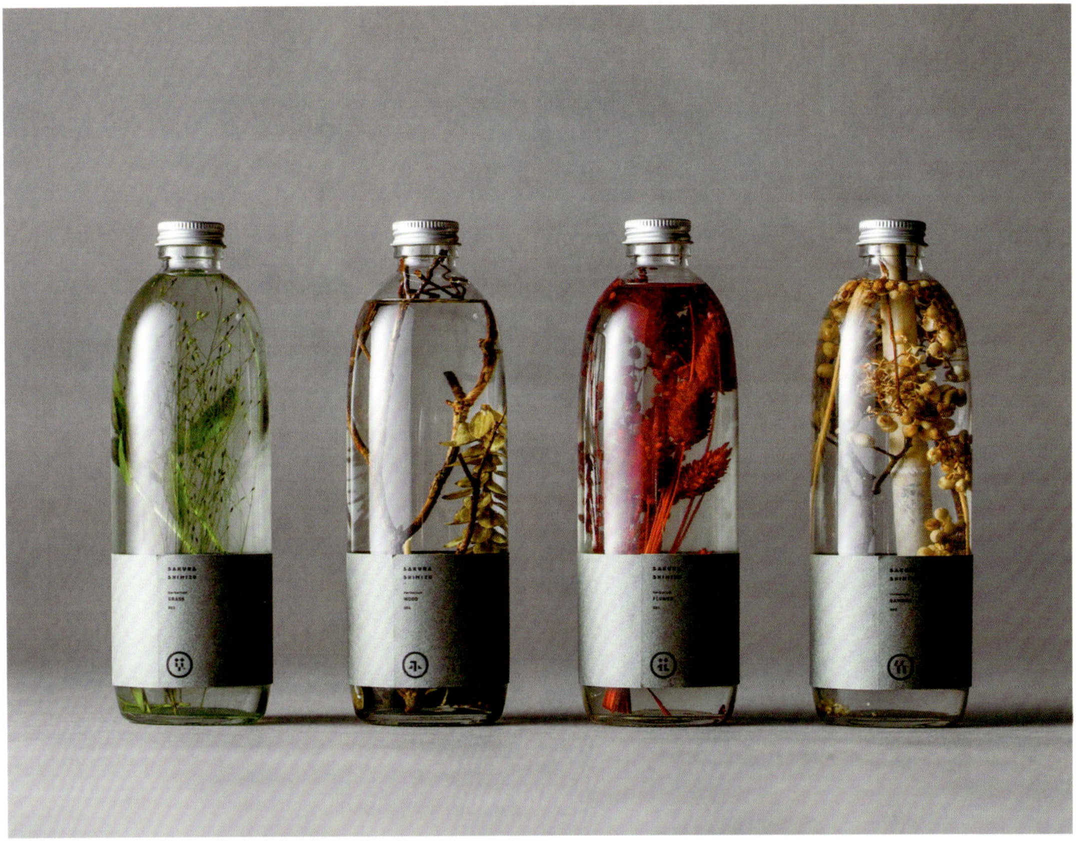
SAKURA
SHIMIZU
GRASS
SAKURA
SHIMIZU
WOOD
FLOWER

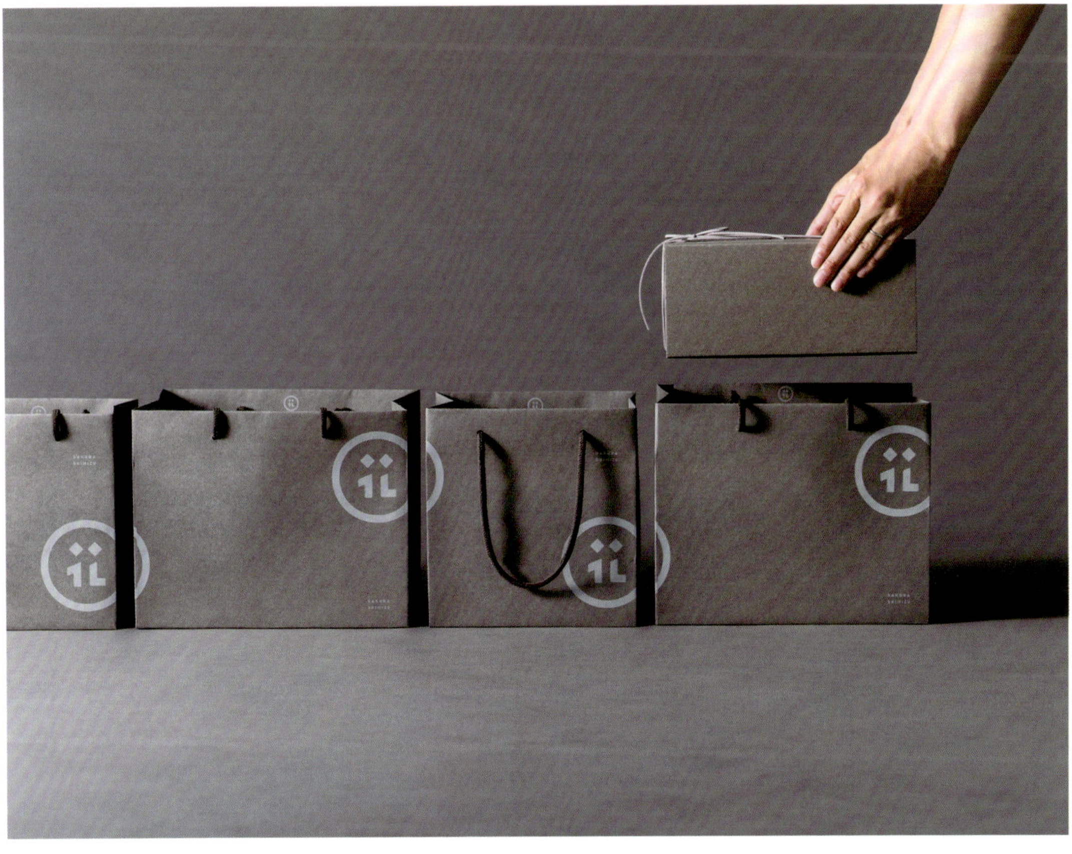

This is the gift package design for ISHIDA Coffee Shop, a coffee shop and roasting facility in a quiet, residential area of Sapporo. The package design expresses ISHIDA Coffee Shop's commitment to coffee and its people, coffee and space, coffee and music, and other coffee-based elements, with coffee brown, milk-white, and a color scheme inspired by the coffee beans. The soft gift package can be used for both 100g and 200g quantities by buckling buttons at different positions.

DA   Sitoh inc.
D   Motoi Shito
CL   ISHIDA Coffee

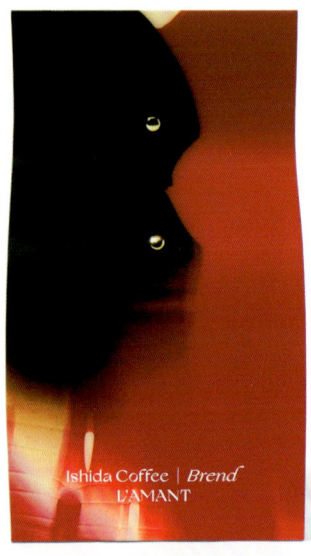

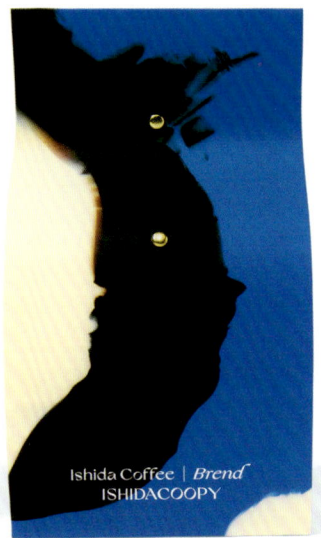

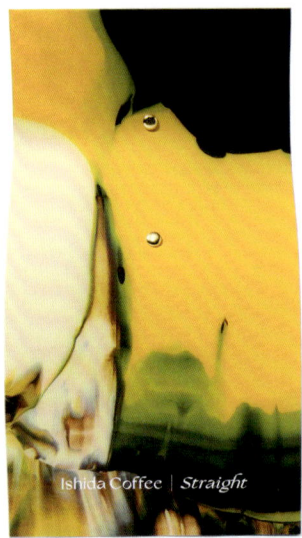

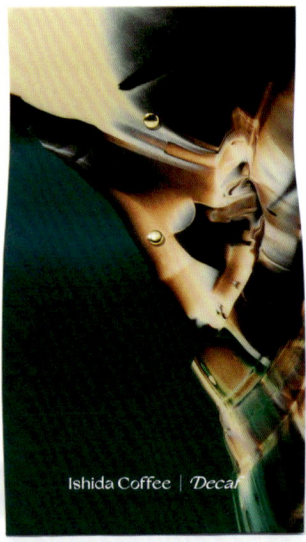

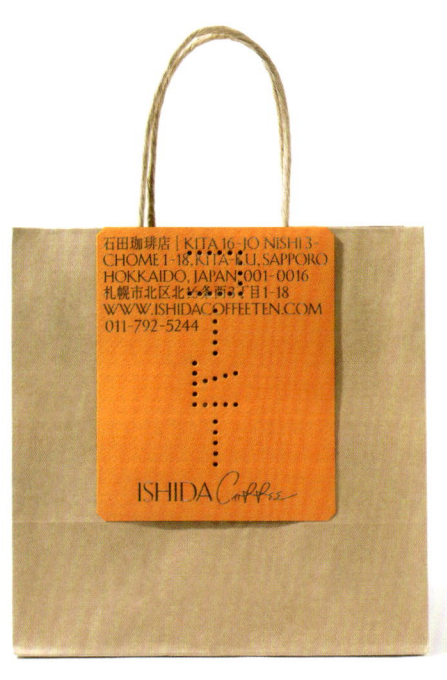

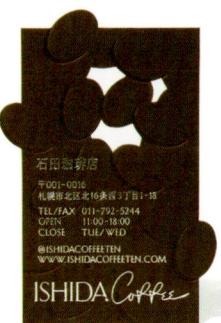

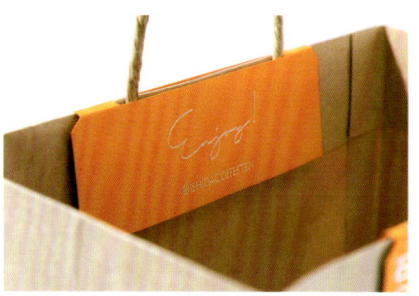

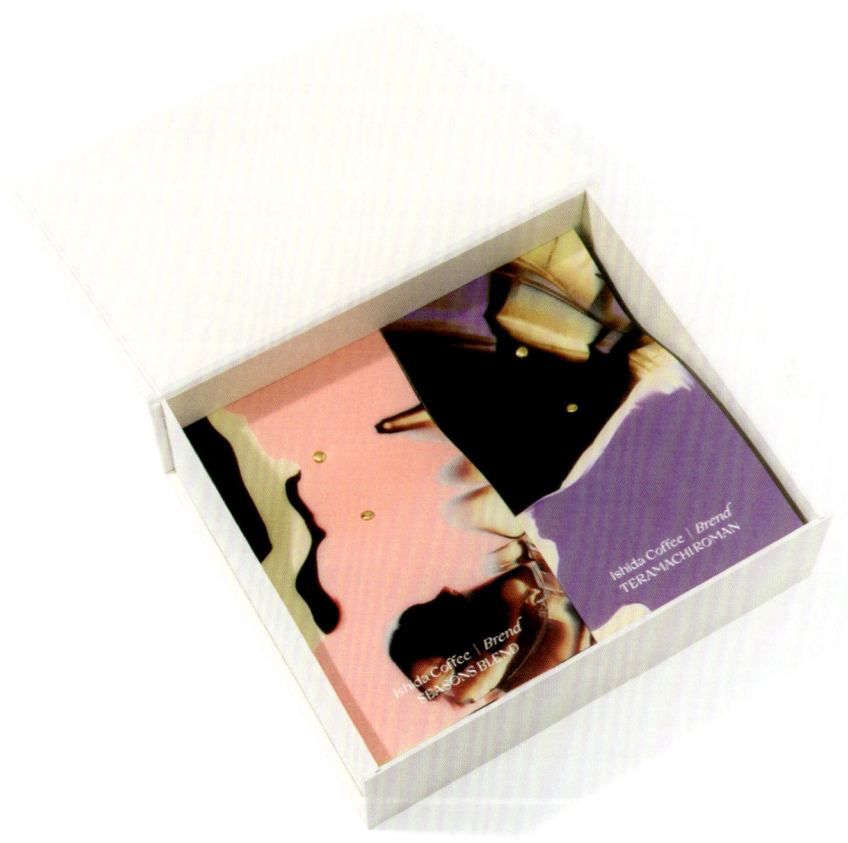

A full-page advertisement for sake made with brewer's rice that was grown using ingredients made from food and agricultural waste. The product is designed to minimize waste and the day the sake went on sale and was advertised in the newspaper, the extras were used to create the packaging labels. This product is Japan's first sake created with sustainable development goals using minimum waste. The company is planning on using returnable bottles in the future.

DA   OUWN
CD   Subaru Matsukura
AD   Atsushi Ishiguro
D   Atsushi Ishiguro
CL   KOBE SHINBUN

SDGs Sake MEGURU

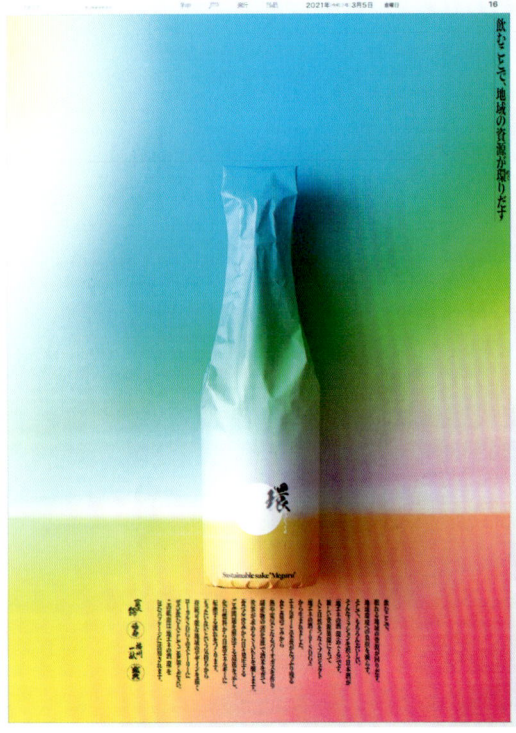

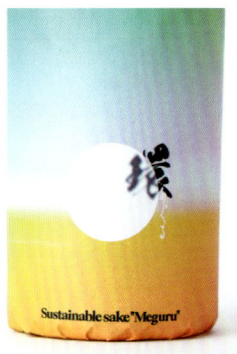

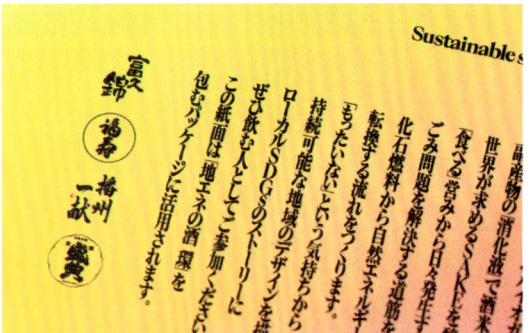

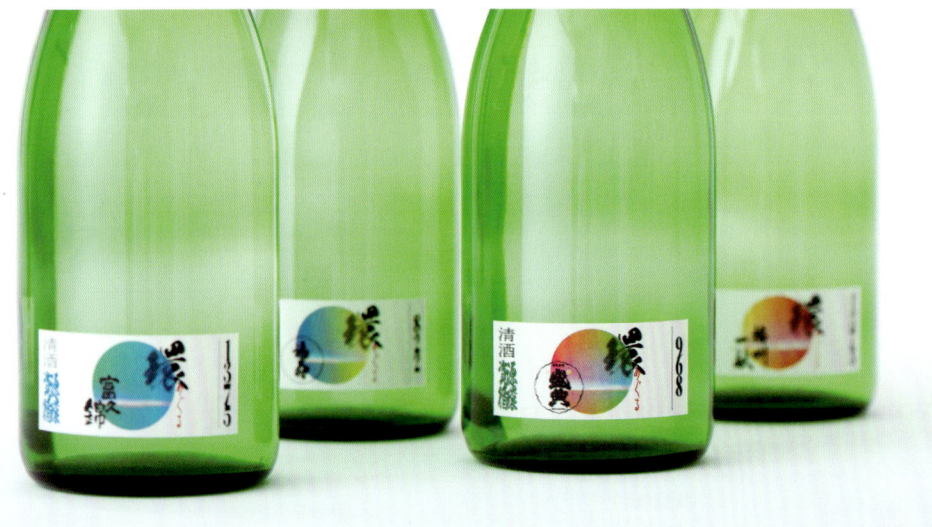

The taste of ginger syrup Peligro changes along with seasonal weather and the producer takes it as a uniqueness, not an error in production. The waving typography represents the flow of nature and the letter "i" expresses the spicy ginger. The background artworks were designed by Akari Uragami, interpreting the contrast of the danger and the prettiness.

CD   Maico Nishikoji (saicorom Inc.)
AD   Mayuko Kanazawa (KOKON Inc.)
D   Mayuko Kanazawa (KOKON Inc.)
IL   Akari Uragami
CL   Ginger&Company Inc.

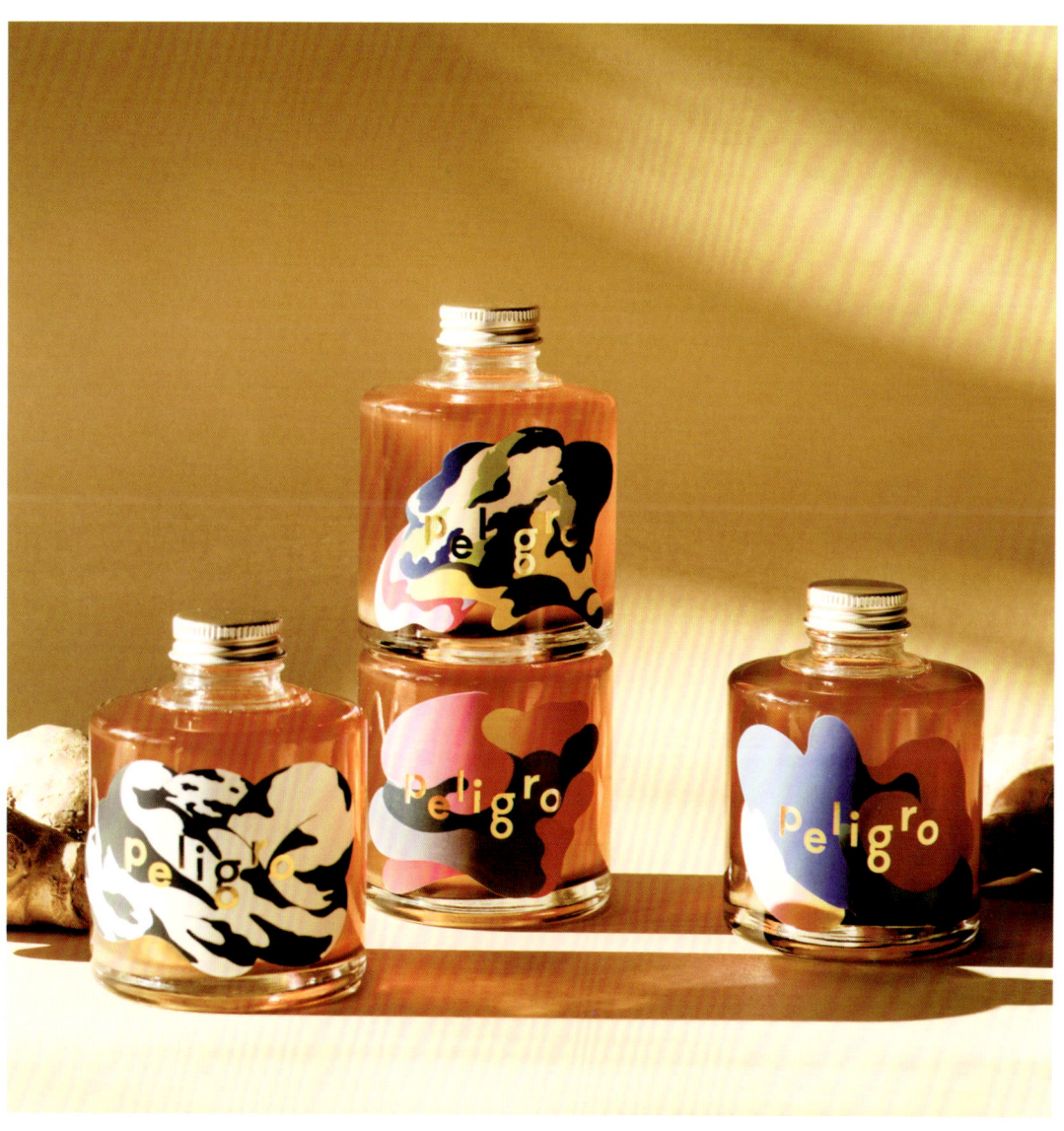

Peligro

279

This is the design for a honey brand from Vietnam sold in the Japanese market. The product is created to deliver a casual and friendly feeling for its target female audience who are in their 20s to 40s.

DA   SOAR NY
D   Masaki Hanahara
IL   Dona
CL   Mekon Megumi

Vietnam Honey

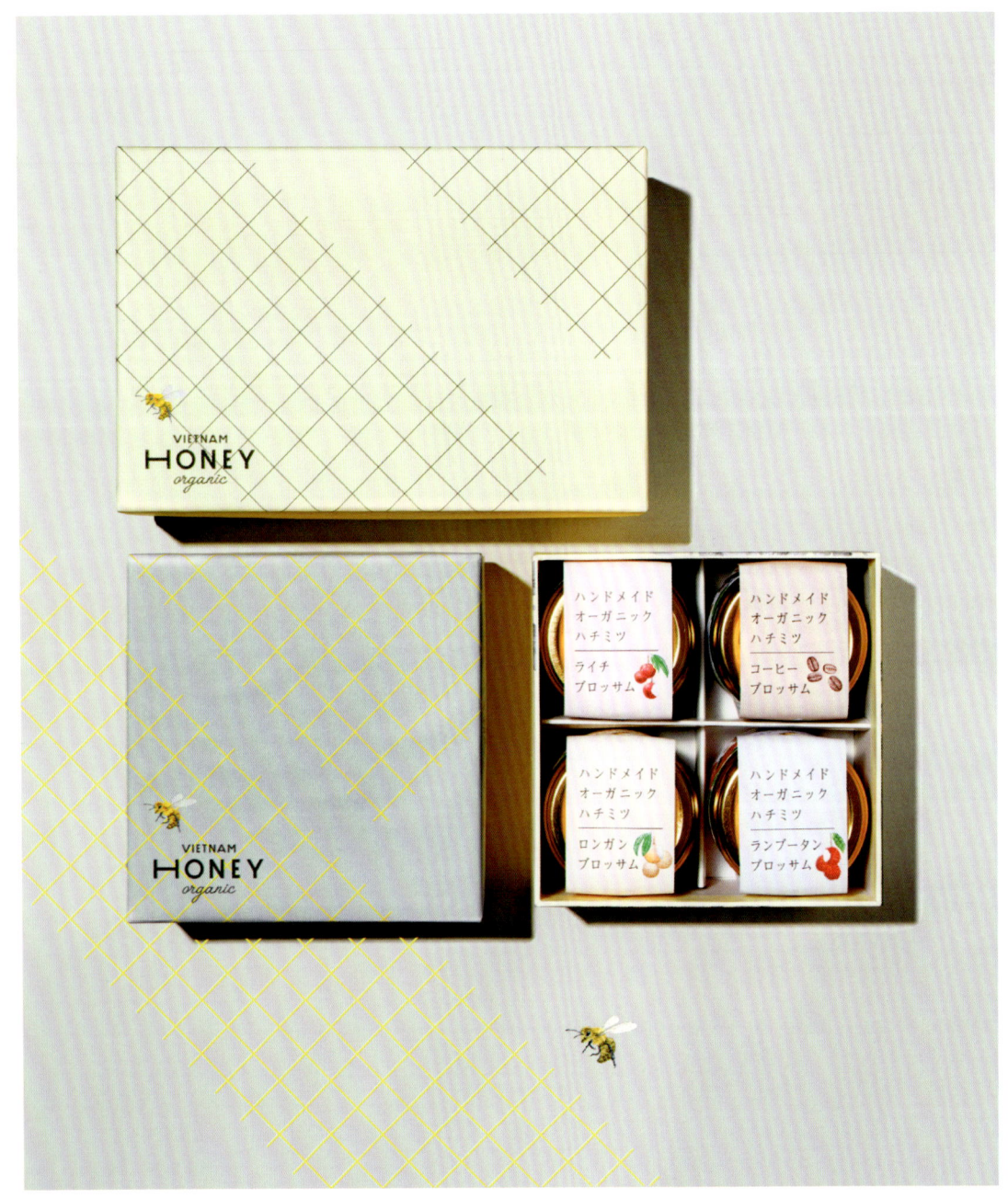

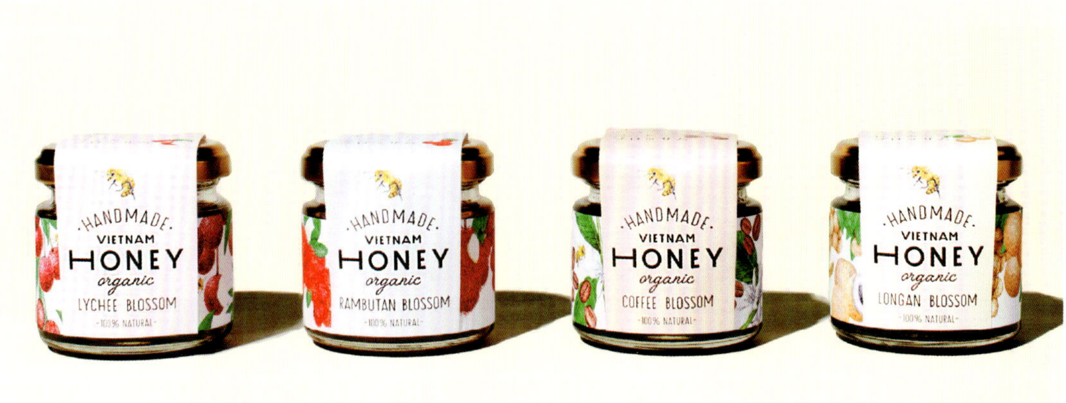
HANDMADE
VIETNAM
HONEY
organic
LYCHEE BLOSSOM
-100% NATURAL-
HANDMADE
VIETNAM
HONEY
organic
RAMBUTAN BLOSSOM
-100% NATURAL-
HANDMADE
VIETNAM
HONEY
organic
COFFEE BLOSSOM
-100% NATURAL-
HANDMADE
VIETNAM
HONEY
organic
LONGAN BLOSSOM
-100% NATURAL-

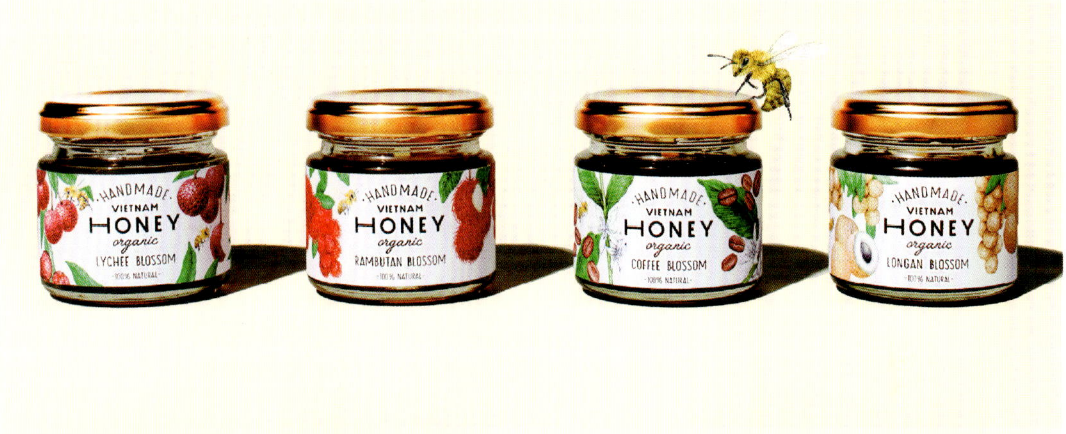
HANDMADE
VIETNAM
HONEY
organic
LYCHEE BLOSSOM
-100% NATURAL-
HANDMADE
VIETNAM
HONEY
organic
RAMBUTAN BLOSSOM
-100% NATURAL-
HANDMADE
VIETNAM
HONEY
organic
COFFEE BLOSSOM
-100% NATURAL-
HANDMADE
VIETNAM
HONEY
organic
LONGAN BLOSSOM
-100% NATURAL-

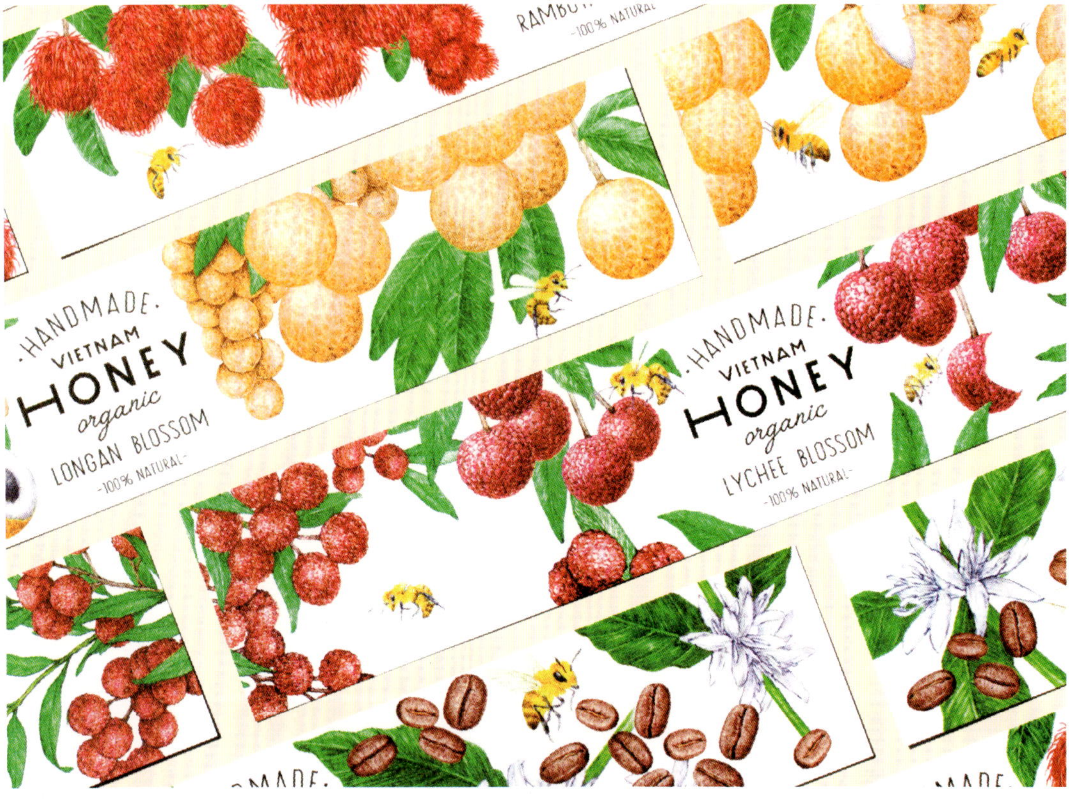
-100% NATURAL-
HANDMADE
VIETNAM
HONEY
organic
LONGAN BLOSSOM
-100% NATURAL-
HANDMADE
VIETNAM
HONEY
organic
LYCHEE BLOSSOM
-100% NATURAL-

Index

Akiko Sekimoto
akikosekimoto.com

Akiko Sekimoto is an art director and graphic designer. She finished her master's degree in design at the Tokyo University of the Arts. After working at DRAFT Co., Ltd., she established her studio, Hidamari Ltd. She utilizes graphic design and directs and develops renewals as well as start-ups of a variety of brands, shops, and products. Her works extend to brand logo creation, product development, package design, store design, etc. She is acclaimed for her timeless designs that will be loved for years.

Arata Kubota
aratakubota.net

Arata Kubota was born in Yamanashi Prefecture in 1981. He studied graphic design at Tama Art University and graduated in 2006 and joined Dentsu. He is also the recipient of the NY ADC Gold Award, the D&AD Yellow Pencil, and the Cannes Lions Gold Award.

Arata Takemoto Design Office
takemotodesign.com

Arata Takemoto Design Office is a design firm based in Tokyo. They focus on environmental graphics and are also active in other various fields of design.

Atsushi Hirano
affordance.tokyo

Atsushi Hirano is the founder of AFFORDANCE inc. AFFORDANCE inc. offers branding, VI, CI planning, signage planning, and space design with graphic design at the core of their work. They aim to create designs with depth that encompass humor and coincidence, born from careful study, ranging from digital to analog expression.

Aya Codama
bullet-inc.jp

BULLET Inc. is a design firm headed by Aya Codama. Aya graduated from Tokyo Zokei University and she established BULLET Inc. in 2013. Fascinated by design that can be touched and felt by hand that makes full use of the texture of materials and printing processes, she creates works that transcend the boundaries of graphics.

Ayari Nakamura
ayarinakamura.com

Ayari Nakamura is an art director and graphic designer from Dentsu.

collé
colle.co.jp

collé is a graphic design studio based in Tokyo. "Collé" means "glue" in French, and collé aspires to become the glue that connects its customers to their products.

Daigo Daikoku
daikoku.ndc.co.jp

Daigo Daikoku entered the Nippon Design Center, Inc. after graduating from the Kanazawa College of Art in 2003 and started Daikoku Design Institute in 2011. He moved to Los Angeles in 2018. His interests are art, lifestyle, and technology and he works closely in the above fields to create new value. His major awards include the D&AD, the NY ADC, the Clio Award, the One Show Design, the FRAME Award, the Tokyo ADC Hiromu Hara Award, the JAGDA New Designer Award, the JAGDA Award, the SDA Award, and many more.

インデックス

Index

インデックス

Motoi Shito is an art director born in Hokkaido, Japan in 1981. He established Sitoh inc. in 2016. Sitoh inc. is a design firm that designs communication from a design consulting perspective, connecting people, companies, societies, and cultures with a focus on graphic design. They build worldviews and contexts with clear ideas and strong design and provide a wide range of art direction from identity design to various types of design with a focus on branding.

Nobuya Hayasaka was born in 1987 in Sapporo, Japan and studied with a focus on media design at university. Currently, he is a director of Arica Design inc. He uses his experience in a wide range of fields to work on branding and art direction for stores, inns, and other companies. He has won national and international awards not only in graphic design, but also in the fields of illustration, video, advertising, and package design.

Norito Shinmura was born in 1960. He established Shinmura Design Office in 1995 and changed its name to Garden Inc. in 2021. He is a member of JAGDA and Tokyo ADC. He has won the JAGDA New Designer Award, the NY ADC Silver Award, the International Biennial of Graphic Design in Brno Gold Prize, and others.

OK design Inc. is a graphic design studio based in Tokyo, Japan. They provide graphic design services and design-related branding, such as CI/VI/logo design, environmental graphics, package design, and editorial design.

OUWN was established in 2013. The name OUWN is based on the wish for dialogue, empathy, and sharing between "U (you)" and "OWN (us)." Their activities range from direction to graphic, web, fashion, video, and sign design, with the hope of using various methods to bring people as many smiles as possible.

Founded in 2014, paragram is a design studio based in Osaka, with work available in Japanese, Chinese, and English. They provide a wide range of designs, such as logos, prints, packages, signage, and so on. They care about research and conversation, aiming to create the thing that stays close to everyone's life.

Shun Sasaki is a graphic designer and art director. He was born in Sendai, Japan in 1985. studied graphic design at the Tama Art University, graduated in 2010, and founded the graphic design office AYOND in 2016. In 2020, he was selected for the JAGDA New Designer Award.

Studio Wonder carefully considers and creates original brand design with a strong concept that will be differentiated from others and loved for a long time. One of Studio Wonder's strengths is the ability to develop a wide range of graphic tools, package design, sign design, and motion graphics.

Takahiro Eto
studyllc.tokyo

P169-171, 176-179

Takahiro Eto was born in Shizuoka in 1981. He received a doctoral degree from Tama Art University in 2010. In 2016, he established Study LLC. in Tokyo. He is experimenting to develop specific graphic design expressions in various fields. He has been an associate professor at Tokyo Polytechnic University since 2021 and a member of Tokyo TDC and JAGDA.

Taku Sasaki
kanaisasaki.com

P102-111

Taku Sasaki is an art director and product designer based in Tokyo. Born in 1985, he studied product design at Tama Art University and graduated in 2008 and then joined KOKUYO Co., Ltd. His works focus on design that crosses the plane and the solid, such as planning and design of product brands, spatial signage planning, and corporate branding.

UMA/design farm
umamu.jp

P146-147, 152-153, 156-157, 198-205

UMA/design farm was founded in 2007 by Yuma Harada. Based in Osaka, Japan, the company focuses on projects related to culture, welfare, and community, and aims to visualize ideas and create new experiences through graphics, spaces, exhibitions, and project development. With an emphasis on thinking and creating together, they practice design through repeated dialogue and experimentation.

Yoshiaki Irobe
irobe.ndc.co.jp/en/

P54-65

Yoshiaki Irobe was born in Chiba. He completed a master's course at the Tokyo University of the Arts. As the head of Irobe Design Institute, he works as a graphic designer and art director. He has won numerous domestic and international design awards, including the Yusaku Kamekura Award, the Tokyo ADC Award, the SDA Award, the JAGDA New Designer Award, and the One Show Design Gold Pencil. He is also a member of AGI, Japan Design Committee, Tokyo ADC, and JAGDA.

Yu Inoue
yuinoue.jp

P226-227, 232-235

Yu Inoue was born in Tokyo in 1992 and graduated from Tokyo Metropolitan University in 2014. He worked at C.C. Leman and canaria before going freelance in 2022. Yu Inoue specializes in branding design and graphic design. He is good at creating a worldview that organizes and then communicates the values and characteristics of a brand to people, and creating formative expressions that leave a lasting impression on people.

Yuuri Mikami
yuurimikami.com

P261-263

Yuuri Mikami is a graphic designer based in Tokyo. She studied visual communication design at Musashino Art University, graduated in 2008, and worked at Dentsu Tec from 2008 to 2014 and at Taku Satoh Design Office Inc. from 2014 to 2016. In 2017, she established the Yuuri Mikami Design Office in Tokyo.

インデックス

We would like to express our gratitude to all of the designers and agencies for their generous contribution of images, ideas and concepts. We are also very grateful to many other people whose names do not appear in the credits, but who have made specific contributions and provided support. Without them, the successful compilation of this book would not have been possible. Special thanks to all of the contributors for sharing their innovation and creativity with all of our readers around the world.

Acknowledgments